THE CORRESPONDENCE OF
EDMUND BURKE

EDMUND BURKE BY T. R. POOLE

THE CORRESPONDENCE OF
EDMUND BURKE

VOLUME IX

PART ONE
MAY 1796–JULY 1797

EDITED BY
R. B. McDOWELL

PART TWO
ADDITIONAL AND UNDATED
LETTERS

EDITED BY
JOHN A. WOODS

CAMBRIDGE
AT THE UNIVERSITY PRESS

THE UNIVERSITY OF CHICAGO PRESS
CHICAGO, ILLINOIS
1970

Published by the Syndics of the Cambridge University Press
Bentley House, 200 Euston Road, London N.W.1
and
The University of Chicago Press
Chicago 60637

Agents
For Canada: The University of Toronto Press
For Australia: Cambridge University Press Pty Ltd

Library of Congress Catalog Number: 58–5615

International Standard Book Numbers:
0 521 07600 5 Cambridge edition
0–226–11561–5 Chicago edition

Printed in Great Britain
at the University Printing House, Cambridge
(Brooke Crutchley, University Printer)

CONTENTS

The portrait of Burke facing the title page is from the wax medallion by T. R. Poole. The medallion was made in 1791, and is reproduced here by permission of the Trustees of the National Portrait Gallery

PREFACE

The first part of volume IX of the Burke *Correspondence*, covering a period of fourteen months, contains 162 letters by Burke. Of these eighty-three have not previously appeared in print. The *Correspondence* of 1844 printed only fourteen letters by Burke for the same period.

The second part of the volume contains fifty-six letters wholly new, eleven extracts not previously printed in this *Correspondence* and fuller or better texts of twenty-one letters previously included in some form. It concludes with a brief list of Burke letters the existence of which is known to us only from Autograph Dealers' Catalogues.

The volume begins with a number of letters relating to the school for the sons of French *émigrés* which had been started at Penn in Buckinghamshire and which was to involve Burke in a series of tiresome if trivial complications. The bulk of the correspondence, however, is concerned with the great political issues of the time, and though Burke during these months was at Beaconsfield or Bath, he was in continuous correspondence with his old friends and political pupils, with Lord Fitzwilliam and William Windham and with French Laurence, an able lawyer, who, as a result of Burke's intervention, secured a seat in Parliament in October 1796. Burke continued to be intensely concerned over the fate of Europe and he was greatly perturbed by the prospect of peace—being convinced that a peace negotiated with revolutionary France was bound to be unsatisfactory as well as morally dubious. He was also deeply distressed by the growing crisis in Ireland, and he writes on Irish conditions with power and pathos. In the letters which cover the last year of Burke's life there are frequent references to weakness and pain but his intellectual vigour is remarkable and he counsels and exhorts his friends with determination and force.

RULES OF TRANSCRIPTION

The rules of transcription for this volume continue to be those explained in volume I. The method of dating from franks which is explained in volume V (p. viii) has been continued. Where transcription from French letters occurs, the principles laid down in volume VI have been followed. The editor of the *Epistolary Correspondence of Edmund Burke and French Laurence*, Richard Laurence, discreetly omitted from his text the names of many persons mentioned in the letters. There is, however, a copy of the work containing manuscript notes by John Wilson Croker. On the fly-leaf Croker writes: 'By the Kindness of Archdeacon Cotton of

Lismore, who possesses the original letters, I have been enabled to fill the blanks, and to correct two or three not unimportant errors of the Press'. Where we have not been able to inspect the original letters we have accepted Croker's readings, which we have enclosed in angle brackets.

ACKNOWLEDGEMENTS

The editors continue to be grateful to the owners and custodians of manuscripts for permission to print material in their possession. Our thanks are especially due to Earl Fitzwilliam and to Mr James M. Osborn. Transcripts of Crown Copyright records in the Public Record Office appear by permission of the Controller of H.M. Stationery Office. The staff of the Sheffield City Libraries has continued with efficiency and friendliness to answer our demands on their services. We are particularly grateful to Miss Rosamund Meredith, the City Archivist, for her continued helpful cooperation, and to Miss Enid Gilberthorpe, the Librarian-in-charge of the General Reference Library, whose precise scholarship has been of the greatest value to us when dealing with the letters relating to the French school at Penn. The staff of the Northamptonshire Record Office has given us ready cooperation. Professor Donald Wormell of Trinity College, Dublin, has continued to be of the greatest help to us in identifying Latin quotations. Mr Gilmore Warner of Lock Haven, Pennsylvania, has kindly made available for our use his copy of the *Epistolary Correspondence of Edmund Burke and French Laurence*. We owe a great debt to Professor William B. Todd for his bibliographical knowledge and to Professor Frederick W. Hilles for readily providing us with information. Mr Basil O'Connell has assisted us in dealing with genealogical problems. We are again grateful to Miss E. M. Wilkinson for letting us read her thesis on the 'French Émigrés in England' and to Mr Graham Baggaley for his work as research assistant. Our thanks are also due to Mr Carl Newton for compiling the index and to Miss Margaret Oversby for again helping us with the proofs. We are indebted to Mrs Brinsley Ford, Mr Bolton King and Mr Roger Venables for much valuable information on family history. We also wish to thank Sister Angela Bolster, Father Benedict Cullen, Mr Michel Fuchs, of the University of Nice, Mrs Olive C. Goodbody, Curator of the Friends' Historical Library, Dublin, Dr Brendan O'Brien, Miss Peyser of the Westminster Diocesan Archives, Mr Francis W. Steer, Archivist at Arundel Castle, Miss M. V. Stokes, Archivist of Coutts Bank, and Dr J. A. Wallace, for affording us assistance on particular points.

Dr P. J. Marshall has once more provided us with authoritative advice on questions relating to India. The General Editor, Professor Thomas W. Copeland, has watched over the shaping of the volume continuously and his erudite and penetrating but always tolerant criticism has been of inestimable value. We continue to be greatly indebted to Mrs Valerie Jobling, the energetic secretary of the Edition, for performing for us with unfailing and ready competence a wide range of services.

R. B. McD.
J. A. W.

LIST OF SHORT TITLES

The following manuscript collections are cited in this volume by short titles:

Affaires Étrangères
  Ministère des Affaires Étrangères, quai d'Orsay, Paris VIIe.

Archives Nationales
  Archives Nationales, Hôtel Soubise, 30 rue des Francs-Bourgeois, Paris, IIIe.

Arundel Castle Archives
  Manuscripts belonging to the Duke of Norfolk, Arundel Castle, Sussex.

Bath Public Library
  City of Bath Municipal Libraries and Victoria Art Gallery, Bridge Street, Bath.

Blair-Adam MSS
  Manuscripts belonging to Captain C. K. Adam, Blair-Adam, by Kelty, Fife.

Bodleian Library
  The Bodleian Library, Oxford.

Boston Public Library
  The Boston Public Library, Copley Square, Boston 17, Massachusetts.

British Museum
  The British Museum, Great Russell Street, London, W.C.1.

California University Library (Santa Barbara)
  University of California Library, Santa Barbara, California.

Canning MSS
  Manuscripts belonging to the Earl of Harewood; now on deposit with the Central Library, Leeds 1.

Cecil MSS
  Manuscripts belonging to the Marquess of Salisbury, Hatfield House, Hertfordshire.

Clifton College (Bristol)
  Clifton College, Bristol 8.

Columbia University Library
  The letter of Burke to Garrett Nagle dated 2 August 1776 is in the Berol Collection, Department of Special Collections, Columbia University Libraries, New York 27, New York.

Crawford MSS
  Manuscripts belonging to the Earl of Crawford and Balcarres; preserved at Balcarres House, Colinsburgh, Fife.

Devonshire MSS
  Manuscripts belonging to the Duke of Devonshire, Chatsworth, Bakewell, Derbyshire.

Donoughmore MSS
Manuscripts belonging to the Earl of Donoughmore, Knocklofty, Tipperary.

Lord Dunsany
Lord Dunsany, Dunsany Castle, Meath.

Fitzwilliam MSS (Milton)
Manuscripts in the possession of the Earl Fitzwilliam, Milton, Peterborough, Northamptonshire.

Fitzwilliam MSS (Northampton)
Manuscripts belonging to the Earl Fitzwilliam; now on deposit with the Northamptonshire Record Office, Delapré Abbey, Northampton. These were formerly at the Fitzwilliam family seat at Milton, near Peterborough, and hence are sometimes cited by scholars under the name 'Milton MSS'. They include a portion—roughly a fifth—of Burke's private papers.

Fitzwilliam MSS (Sheffield)
Manuscripts belonging to the Earl Fitzwilliam; now on deposit with the Sheffield City Libraries. These were formerly at the Fitzwilliam family seat of Wentworth Woodhouse in Yorkshire and hence are sometimes cited by scholars under the name 'Wentworth Woodhouse MSS'. They include the main body of Burke's private papers.

Fortescue MSS
Manuscripts belonging to G. G. Fortescue, Esq., Boconnoc, Lostwithiel, Cornwall.

Glynn MSS
Manuscripts of the Glynn family, belonging to Lt D. H. J. Glynn, R.N., Cannon Cottage, Upton Road, Chichester, Sussex.

Harvard Library
Harvard College Library, Cambridge 38, Massachusetts.

Hauptstaatsarchiv (Stuttgart)
Hauptstaatsarchiv, Stuttgart, 7000 Stuttgart W, Gutenbergstrasse 109.

Professor Frederick W. Hilles
Professor Frederick W. Hilles, Yale University, New Haven, Connecticut.

Huntington Library
The Henry E. Huntington Library and Art Gallery, San Marino 9, California.

Hyde Collection
Manuscripts belonging to Mrs Donald Hyde, Four Oaks Farm, Somerville, New Jersey.

Mrs Valerie Jobling
Mrs Valerie Jobling, Waterloo Cottage, Reading Road, Goring-on-Thames, Oxon.

Keele University Library
The Library, University of Keele, Keele, Staffordshire.

Wilmarth S. Lewis
Wilmarth Sheldon Lewis, Farmington, Connecticut.

Lille Municipal Library
   Bibliothèque Municipale de Lille, 1 place Georges Lyon, Lille.

Lonsdale MSS
   Manuscripts belonging to the Earl of Lonsdale; on deposit with the Joint
   Archives Committee for the Counties of Cumberland and Westmoreland,
   Record Office, The Castle, Carlisle.

Mrs Donald Mead
   Mrs Donald Mead, Pengreep, Ponsanooth, Cornwall.

Minto MSS
   The papers of Sir Gilbert Elliot, 1st Earl of Minto; preserved in the National
   Library of Scotland, Edinburgh, 1.

Morgan Library
   The Pierpont Morgan Library, 33 East 36th Street, New York 16, New York.

Sir John Murray
   Sir John Murray, 50 Albemarle Street, London, W.1.

Murray Papers
   A collection of transcripts of Burke's letters made by the late Canon Robert
   Murray in preparation for a new edition of the correspondence. After Canon
   Murray's death it was deposited with the Bodleian Library, and later trans-
   ferred to the Sheffield City Libraries.

National Library of Ireland
   The National Library of Ireland, Kildare Street, Dublin.

National Library of Scotland
   The Trustees of the National Library of Scotland, Edinburgh 1.

Lady Neville
   Lady Neville, Sloley Old Hall, Norwich, Norfolk.

New York Public Library
   New York Public Library, Fifth Avenue and 42nd Street, New York 18,
   New York.

Northumberland County Record Office
   County Record Office, Melton Park, North Gosforth, Newcastle upon Tyne.

Osborn Collection
   James M. Osborn, Yale University, New Haven, Connecticut.

Österreichisches Staatsarchiv
   Österreichisches Staatsarchiv, Wien, VII, Stiftgasse 2.

Pennsylvania Historical Society
   Historical Society of Pennsylvania, 1300 Locust Street, Philadelphia 7,
   Pennsylvania.

Portland MSS (Nottingham)
   Manuscripts from the collection of the Duke of Portland; now on deposit
   with the Library of the University of Nottingham.

Princeton Library
   The Library, Princeton University, Princeton, New Jersey.

Public Record Office
Public Record Office, Chancery Lane, London, W.C.2.

Ramsden MSS
Manuscripts owned by Sir William Pennington Ramsden; now on deposit with the Central Library, Leeds 1.

Rosse MSS
Manuscripts belonging to the Earl of Rosse; preserved at Birr Castle, Offaly, Eire.

Society of Merchant Venturers
Society of Merchant Venturers, Merchants Hall, Clifton Down, Bristol 8.

Spencer MSS
Manuscripts belonging to the Earl Spencer, Althorp, Northampton.

Professor William B. Todd
Professor William B. Todd, Department of English, University of Texas, Austin 12, Texas.

Trinity College, Dublin
Trinity College, Dublin.

Father P. J. Venables
Father P. J. Venables, St George's, Buckland, Faringdon, Berkshire.

Victoria and Albert Museum
The Victoria and Albert Museum, Cromwell Road, South Kensington, London, S.W.7.

Professor and Mrs Charles G. K. Warner
Professor and Mrs Charles G. K. Warner, 68 Francis Avenue, Cambridge, Massachusetts.

Westminster Diocesan Archives
Westminster Diocesan Archives, Archbishop's House, Westminster, London, S.W.1.

The following printed works are cited in this volume by short titles:

Adam Catalogue
The R.B. Adam Library relating to Dr Samuel Johnson and his Era, 3 vols, London, 1929; 4th vol., Buffalo, New York, 1930. Citations are from vol. I, the portion separately paged and entitled 'Letters of Edmund Burke'.

Almon, *Memoirs*
[John Almon,] *Memoirs of a Late Eminent Bookseller*, London, 1790.

Amateur d'autographes
L'Amateur d'autographes. Revue historique et biographique. Ed. Gabriel, Jacques et Noel Charavay, Paris, 1862–1914.

American Book Prices Current
American Book Prices Current. A Record of Books, Manuscripts and Autographs sold at Auction in New York, Boston and Philadelphia. New York, 1895–.

Bettany, *Life of Jerningham*
Lewis Bettany, *Edward Jerningham and his Friends*, London, 1919.

Bisset, *Life of Burke* (1st ed.)
Robert Bisset, *Life of Edmund Burke*, 1st ed., London, 1798.

Bruton, Knowles Catalogue
Catalogue of the Library, Engravings, and Autographs of Mrs L. A. Evans.
Sold by Messrs Bruton, Knowles and Co., 15 December 1904. Gloucester
[1904].

Buckingham, *Memoirs of the Court and Cabinets of George III*
[Richard Plantagenet Temple Nugent Brydges Chandos,] Duke of Buckingham and Chandos, *Memoirs of the Court and Cabinets of George the third,
from original family documents*, 2 vols, London, 1853.

Burke–Laurence Correspondence
The Epistolary Correspondence of Edmund Burke and French Laurence, London,
1827.

Burke–Windham Correspondence
Correspondence of Edmund Burke and William Windham, ed. J. P. Gilson,
London, 1910.

Campbell, *Lives of the Chancellors*
John Campbell, 1st Baron Campbell, *The Lives of the Lord Chancellors and
Keepers of the Great Seal*, 8 vols, London, 1845–69.

Clifford, *Application of Barruel's Memoirs of Jacobinism*
Robert Clifford, ...*Application of Barruel's Memoirs of Jacobinism to the
Secret Societies of Ireland and Great Britain.* By the translator of that work,
1798.

The Collector
Walter R. Benjamin Autographs, 655 Fifth Avenue, New York, N.Y.

Corr. (1844)
Edmund Burke, *Correspondence between 1744 and 1797*, ed. Charles William,
Earl Fitzwilliam, and Sir Richard Bourke, 4 vols, London, 1844.

Christie Catalogue
Christie, Manson, and Wood Ltd., 8 King Street, London, S.W.1.

Dobell Catalogue
Percy Dobell and Son, 24 Mount Ephraim Road, Tunbridge Wells, Kent
(formerly P. J. and A. E. Dobell, 77 Charing Cross Road, London, W.C.2.).

Edwards Catalogue
Francis Edwards, Ltd., 83 Marylebone High Street, London, W.1.

Evans Catalogue
M. Evans and Co., (formerly) 39 Pall Mall, London.

Gentleman's Magazine
Gentleman's Magazine, London, 1731–1907.

Henkels Catalogue
S. V. Henkels, (formerly) 1304 Walnut Street, Philadelphia, Pennsylvania.

Hist. MSS Comm. (*Bunbury MSS*)
Historical Manuscripts Commission, Third Report, Appendix, London, 1872.

Hist. MSS Comm. (*Fortescue MSS*)
Historical Manuscripts Commission, Fifteenth Report, Appendix, Part III, London, 1892.

Hist. MSS Comm. (*Morrison MSS*)
Ninth Report of the Royal Commission of Historical Manuscripts, Part II, Appendix, London, 1884.

Inventaire des autographes
Inventaire des autographes et documents historiques réunis par M. Benjamin Fillon, décrits par Étienne Charavay, 3 vols, Paris, 1878.

Journals of the Irish House of Commons
Journals of the House of Commons of the Kingdom of Ireland, 19 vols, Dublin, 1796–1800.

Leadbeater Papers
Mary Leadbeater, *Leadbeater Papers*, 2 vols, London, 1862.

Leslie and Taylor, *Life of Reynolds*
C. R. Leslie and T. Taylor, *Life and Times of Sir Joshua Reynolds*, 2 vols, London, 1862.

M'Cormick, *Memoirs of Burke*
Charles M'Cormick, *Memoirs of Edmund Burke*, London, 1797.

Mackintosh, *Memoirs*
Sir James Mackintosh, *Memoirs*, ed. Robert L. Mackintosh, 2 vols, London, 1835.

Maggs Catalogue
Maggs Brothers, Ltd, 50 Berkeley Square, London, W.1.

Malmesbury, *Diaries and Correspondence*
James Howard Harris, 3rd Earl of Malmesbury, *Diaries and Correspondence of James Harris, First Earl of Malmesbury*, 4 vols, London, 1844.

Michelmore Catalogue
G. Michelmore and Company, 5 Royal Opera Arcade, Pall Mall, London, S.W.1.

Minto, *Life of Elliot*
The Countess of Minto, *Life and Letters of Sir Gilbert Elliot*, 3 vols, London, 1874.

Myers Catalogue
Myers and Company, 80 New Bond Street, London, W.1.

Parke–Bernet Catalogue
Parke–Bernet Galleries, Inc., 980 Madison Avenue, New York.

Parkes and Merivale, *Memoirs of Francis*
Memoirs of Sir Philip Francis, ed. J. Parkes and H. Merivale, 2 vols, London, 1867.

INTRODUCTION

By the spring of 1796 Burke had little more than a year to live and his letters from then on are strewn with distressing references to physical weakness and pain. He saw himself as a broken, isolated, ageing and ailing man, reduced to enjoying 'the melancholy privileges of obscurity and sorrow'.[1] But he was preserved from sinking into listless self-absorption and depression by his affection for his friends, his profound concern for the public weal, and it may be added by his exuberant and often humorous enjoyment of life. Intellectually he remained extraordinarily vigorous, and conscious how often 'public calamity' had been 'arrested on the very brink of ruin by the seasonable energy of a single man',[2] he strove to impress on the Government and public at large the dangers inherent in French principles and in a premature peace.

Burke could scarcely have achieved all that he did during the last few years of his life if he had not possessed a number of devoted friends who kept him in continuous well-informed contact with affairs. Of these friends two were active in public life: Lord Fitzwilliam and William Windham. Fitzwilliam's title, acreage, public spirit and obvious integrity were bound to make him a man to be reckoned with in eighteenth-century politics. Unfortunately his influence was weakened by his impetuosity, excessive sensibility, and moral intensity. Furthermore the abrupt termination of his Irish Viceroyalty in 1795 had left him badly shaken and isolated from both the major political parties. Convinced he had been betrayed by his colleagues, he had become an embittered antagonist of Pitt, while remaining a strong opponent of revolutionary France. His hypercritical tone, occasional petulance and obtrusive sense of his own moral superiority might have annoyed some practising politicians, but his behaviour towards Burke was marked by kindness and consideration and their friendship formed a happy partnership between a great magnate, too generous and affectionate to be termed a patron, and a man of genius.

Windham, a man of high ideals and charm, shared Burke's opinions on the Revolution and the war. Expressing deeply-held convictions with candid eloquence, he was a Rupert of debate. But he was also a competent administrator, and as Secretary at War and a Cabinet Minister, he had considerable political influence. Two of his subordinates, Captain Emperor Woodford and Edward James Nagle—a distant

[1] 'Letter to William Elliot', *Works* (Bohn), v, 70; (Little, Brown), v, 113.
[2] Ibid. *Works* (Bohn), v, 78; (Little, Brown), v, 124.

kinsman of Burke who served him as 'a sort of friendly secretary'[1]—belonged to a small group the members of which performed innumerable commissions for Burke, meeting lawyers, tracking down references, correcting proofs, handling publishers and placating creditors. This group also included French Laurence, John King, the Under-Secretary of State at the Home Office, his brother Walker King, and his brother-in-law Thomas Venables, who helped 'poor old William Burke'[2] to secure a refuge from his creditors in the Isle of Man. Laurence, having graduated at Oxford where he was a contemporary of Burke's son Richard, became a member of Doctors' Commons and built up a very large practice as a civilian. He was one of the Counsel to the Managers during the Impeachment of Warren Hastings, and in 1796 Burke persuaded Lord Fitzwilliam to return him for Peterborough. Once Laurence was in Parliament Burke followed his career with keen solicitude. Laurence was both a family friend and a political disciple and seemed well equipped for public life. Clearly a man of great integrity, he was learned, had a lawyer's power of rapidly assimilating information, and was a fluent if ungainly speaker. He even had a reputation as a wit (though Brougham compares his wit to 'the gamboling of the elephant').[3] Once Laurence was in the House of Commons Burke corresponded with him eagerly on public affairs and his letters to Burke are intelligent and informative. Nevertheless they have a touch of pathos. Diffuse and often opinionated, they disclose qualities which were bound to handicap him when pursuing a parliamentary career, and he never attained office.[4]

Walker King, who was associated with Laurence in producing the first complete edition of Burke's *Works*, after leaving Oxford had been for a time a tutor in the household of the Duke of Richmond, where he showed himself to be a man of spirit. Later he became an active and useful Whig supporter, who, as he himself said, for many years dedicated 'almost the whole of my time under the direction of Mr Burke, to the Service of the Public Cause'.[5] It is clear from his correspondence that King could not have honestly subscribed to the formula *nolo episcopari*, and in 1809 he was at length, through the joint influence of Fitzwilliam and the Duke of Portland, placed on the bench as Bishop of Rochester. It should, however, be said that he was a good preacher and a conscientious and farsighted diocesan. To Burke he proved an assiduous friend with a firm grasp on practicalities.

[1] Laurence to Fitzwilliam, 21 February 1797 (MS at Northampton, Box 51).
[2] Mrs Crewe to Portland, 13 July 1795 (MS at Nottingham, PwF3175).
[3] Henry, Lord Brougham, *Historical Sketches of Statesmen who flourished in the time of George III*, London, 1839, II, 83.
[4] Hist. MSS Comm. (*Fortescue MSS*), VIII, 12, 171–6, 179–80, 186.
[5] Walker King to Fitzwilliam, 30 December 1807 (MS at Sheffield, F115).

In the spring and summer of 1796 Walker King was called on to help when Burke was harassed by a series of trivial but irksome problems arising out of an educational enterprise. A small group, including Burke, the Marquess of Buckingham and Burke's old friend Mrs Crewe, early in 1796 decided to found a school which would provide the sons of *émigrés* serving in the British forces with a decent education. Burke drafted an appeal to the Government for financial assistance and persuaded the War Office to hand over an empty house at Penn. The school was only two miles from Beaconsfield, and Burke, who had greatly enjoyed his own school days at Ballitore, and who was intensely eager both to help the victims of revolution and to preserve the best traditions of the French *noblesse*, threw himself with tremendous energy into the mixture of academic and domestic problems involved in founding and running a boarding school. He had to secure a capital grant and a promise of future financial support from the Government, and he had also to engage a housekeeper, buy beds, sheets and kitchen utensils, deal with admissions, find suitable masters and cope with the inevitable difficult parent. Burke writes about these humdrum institutional problems with an emotional power which may seem somewhat disproportionate to the issues in question. But it must be remembered he was in bad health, that for a time he had to subsidize the school out of his own pocket, and that it was largely through his willingness to take endless trouble over minor details that the enterprise was successfully launched. The school soon had about sixty pupils and a staff of four, and for twenty years it met a real need. After the Restoration it was taken over by the French Government, which in the interests of the boys then enrolled maintained it for a short period until it was closed in 1820.[1]

But though Burke was intensely interested in his school and in the fortunes of his friends and relations, his attention remained firmly fixed on the great struggle between the revolutionary spirit and social order. He fervently believed that the French revolutionary leaders in carrying through a ruthless reorganization of society were destroying liberty. By sweeping away old institutions and by displaying a contemptuous disregard of property rights they were destroying the guarantees of that individual independence which to Burke was an essential element in a civilized and just community. And from the beginning of the war he had been concerned to impress on his countrymen that the struggle was a conflict over fundamental issues. The Allies were at war,

[1] Affaires Étrangères, Correspondence politique, Angleterre, 1815–19, Supplément, XXIII, fols 88, 94, 99, 127, 133, 142, 149–50. For the French school at Penn see also Prior (2nd ed.), II, 352–9, and J. Gilbert Jenkins, *A History of the Parish of Penn*, London, 1935.

he argued, 'with a system which by its essence is inimical to all other governments and which makes peace and war as peace and war may best contribute to their subversion'.[1]

At the time Burke retired from Parliament in 1794 it seemed as if the great European coalition would be able to hold the forces of the Revolution in check. But a few days after he left the House of Commons Jourdan's victory at Fleurus marked a definite turn in the tide of war. From then on the revolutionary armies were going over to the offensive. By the end of the year Holland was overrun. In 1795 Prussia and Spain withdrew from the Coalition. In 1796 although the Austrians succeeded in checking the French advance in Germany their successes were overshadowed and more than balanced by Bonaparte's astounding series of victories in Italy. By the end of the year his forces were besieging Mantua, the last barrier to an advance into the Austrian lands, and the Italian States had hastened to make their peace with France. As a result the Italian ports were barred to British shipping, Spain was encouraged to re-enter the war, this time as an ally of France, Great Britain was compelled to evacuate Corsica, the British fleet was withdrawn from the Mediterranean, and Great Britain's power to influence the continental conflict was seriously weakened.

Since it was only too clear that France could not be decisively defeated, the British Government was bound to consider the possibility of peace negotiations. Pitt was determined to resist French aggression, and he had of course been shaken by the excesses of the Revolution. But he had always made it clear that once there appeared to be a stable government in France, prepared to make peace on reasonable terms, Great Britain would be ready to enter into negotiations. 'The unguarded and warm expressions' of 'that great man', Mr Burke, Pitt specifically stated in the spring of 1796, were not to be regarded as an exposition of the Government's policy.[2]

Thermidor and the enactment of the Constitution of 1795 seemed to indicate that France was returning to conventional ways. As a young and able follower of Pitt wrote at the close of 1795 there was 'no doubt that most of those mischievous principles of universal application to all Governments are entirely renounced by the new Constitution, which I have carefully compared with that of 1793; namely, Equality, Natural Rights of Men, Insurrection, Right of daily or rather hourly Revolution; the *duties* of men on the contrary are now declared to be founded in nature; the maintenance of *property* is a duty; no club government; no

---

[1] 'Letters on a Regicide Peace', *Works* (Bohn), v, 164; (Little, Brown), v, 250.
[2] *Parliamentary History*, XXXII, 1132.

exercise of political rights but by legal assemblies; no mobs'.[1] What this spirited analysis ignored was that the restoration of internal stability in France might be accompanied by a revival of the principles which had traditionally governed French foreign policy, and that the expansionist ideals of Richelieu and Louis XIV might replace the revolutionary crusade against established governments. Moreover, with France organized for war, an expansionist policy would be supported by far more powerful forces than the *ancien régime* could have mustered. Burke had early prophesied that the Revolution might end in military dictatorship. In the Letters on a Regicide Peace he endeavoured to show that the French system was bound up with aggression. 'It is military', he wrote, 'in its principle, in its maxims, in its spirit, and in all its movements'.[2] Though Burke may have over-emphasized the extent to which the French system was inspired by Jacobinism rather than nationalism, he showed a shrewd awareness of how it was developing.

But the characteristics which distinguished French policy in the Napoleonic era were not yet clearly discernible, and from the beginning of 1795 Pitt, with restrained optimism, was putting out peace feelers. Burke, acutely aware that Great Britain might give up the struggle against France less from a lack of resources than from a failure of will, had from the end of 1795 been preparing a grand remonstrance against a policy which he believed to be dishonourable and disastrous. For months he hesitated over publication, and as a result of his procrastination the appearance of the *Two Letters on a Regicide Peace* was singularly well timed. They were published in October, two days before Lord Malmesbury arrived in Paris with the object of opening negotiations with the Directory. The *Letters*, in which passion, pugnacity and profundity were fused, attracted intense interest. Obviously they could scarcely have had a significant influence on the immediate situation, because a few weeks after their publication, the negotiations collapsed for the simple reason that neither government was prepared to make concessions which would satisfy the other. The French were flushed with success, and Pitt, if in Burke's opinion a lukewarm opponent of the Revolution, had a hereditary determination to maintain British interests in Europe and overseas. But the influence of the *Two Letters* was bound to extend far beyond the moment of publication, and during the year or so immediately following their appearance, they must have contributed to strengthen the British will to resist in hazardous and testing times.

At the end of December 1796 a French expedition reached the south-

[1] Mornington to Grenville, Hist. MSS Comm. (*Fortescue MSS*), III, 149.
[2] 'Letters on a Regicide Peace', *Works* (Bohn), V, 255; (Little, Brown), V, 375.

west coast of Ireland. Storms scattered the ships and prevented a landing, but the British fleet was slow to intervene—inexcusably slow, its critics asserted—and public opinion was startled to see how near the French had come to landing a substantial force in Ireland and opening up a new theatre of operations on the western flank of Great Britain. Then, during the early months of 1797, Bonaparte drove into Austria itself, and at the beginning of April forced the imperial government to sign the Armistice of Leoben. In March the Bank of England suspended cash payments and almost before this shock could be absorbed, mutiny began to spread through the squadrons in home waters. The two great pillars of British power, finance and the Fleet, seemed to be crumbling.

In the face of multiplying difficulties Burke remained unshaken and defiant. When the naval mutinies began he was at Bath and Wilberforce who brought him news of the first outbreak at Spithead records how Burke was insistent that the Government should take the most drastic steps to assert its authority over the mutineers. 'Burke', Wilberforce wrote, 'was lying on a sofa much emaciated; and Windham, Laurence, and some other friends were round him. The attention shown to Burke by all that party was just like the treatment of Ahithophel of old. "It was as if one went to inquire of the oracle of the Lord"'.[1] And it was with Burke's emphatic demand for strong measures ringing in his ears that Windham left to attend a Cabinet meeting in London.

Even when the fortunes of war seemed to favour France Burke was thinking in terms of counter-attack, and this accounts for his vehement criticism of one important aspect of the Government's military policy: he thought it deplorable that large numbers of men were being recruited, who, by the terms of their enlistment, could be employed only on home service. Admittedly, when a number of regular units were being sent to die of fever in the West Indies, where 'it was not an enemy we had to vanquish, but a cemetery to conquer',[2] it was bound to prove more easy to raise recruits for home rather than general service. But Burke was convinced that recruiting on such lines implied that the country was allowing itself to be committed to a defensive policy instead of thinking resolutely in terms of when and where it could resume the offensive in Europe.

Military considerations as well as other factors compelled Burke during the last year of his life to devote sustained and saddened attention to Ireland, a subject which had so frequently engaged his mind in the past. Throughout his career Burke was concerned that Ireland should

[1] R. I. Wilberforce, *Life of Wilberforce*, London, 1838, II, 211.
[2] 'Letters on a Regicide Peace', *Works* (Bohn), v, 240; (Little, Brown), v, 354.

be a contented country, closely linked by political and social ties to Great Britain, and early in life he learned to sympathize with the Irish Catholics, oppressed by the Penal Laws. Their disabilities taught him that men with proud traditions and an acute sense of honour could be the victims of ruthless power, unimpeded by checks and balances. Burke's sense of justice (and injustice) which was to be so powerfully active on behalf of oppressed Indian rajahs and the despoiled clergy and *noblesse* of France, was first aroused by the sufferings of the Catholic squirearchy of Munster.

The situation in Ireland had steadily grown more serious since Fitzwilliam's departure (needless to say Fitzwilliam assumed *post hoc propter hoc*). Agrarian trouble, which had been endemic throughout the century, had intensified from the early nineties, and the Irish radicals from the close of 1794 had been engaged in building up a new organization, secret, widespread and on military lines, called by an already familiar name, 'The United Irishmen'. It aimed at Catholic emancipation and parliamentary reform, including manhood suffrage and equal electoral districts. And it embraced both middle-class radicals and large numbers of the peasantry. (Lord Clare characterized it as a conspiracy of 'a deluded peasantry aided by more intelligent treason'.)[1] The organization spread throughout the country and was especially strong in Ulster where the Irish Presbyterians were concentrated and formed a large section of the population. In some Ulster areas there was also sectarian factional fighting between Protestant and Catholic groups. In 1795 the Orange Society, a militant Protestant organization, was formed, and in County Armagh many Catholics were driven from their holdings.

The Irish Administration's reaction to growing disorder, widespread conspiracy and the threat of invasion, was simple and direct. It displayed a stern and unbending determination to defend the existing order, a policy embodied in two measures: an Insurrection Act passed in the session of 1796, and the Suspension of the Habeas Corpus Act passed at the beginning of the session of 1796–7. The Irish Whigs, led by Henry Grattan and the brothers William and George Ponsonby, opposed these measures. They argued that a bold attempt should be made by sweeping concessions to try to conciliate the discontented sections of Irish society. When the Whigs had been in power during Fitzwilliam's brief Vice-royalty, their policy had been Catholic emancipation, administrative reform and a whole-hearted support of the British war effort. The growth of discontent in Ireland and possibly their sudden loss of power had impelled them to reconsider and broaden their programme, and by

[1] *Dublin Evening Post*, 21 March 1797.

1797 their objectives included not only complete Catholic emancipation but a parliamentary reform bill which would have enfranchised large sections of the population and an absentee tax. Moreover, they drew attention to the economic causes of Irish distress, dwelling with considerable emphasis on the condition of the peasantry, especially in the south and west. John Philpot Curran, referring to 'the inhuman degradation of the lower orders', asked 'can you call the hovels habitation—the covering clothes, the sustenance food, or the instruction education?'[1] and Grattan bluntly said that 'when gentlemen talk of the idleness or ferocity of the common people, let them look to the causes of their own wealth'.[2] Eager to reduce the pressure of population on the land by encouraging industry, Grattan pressed the Irish House of Commons to ask Great Britain to lower the duties on Irish imports into the British market. And if persuasion failed, he was ready to start a tariff war. Finally, when the war with revolutionary France was being debated in the Irish House of Commons during the sessions of 1796 and 1796 to 1797, it was clear that the Whigs' attitude to the war had changed since 1795. Their new approach could be summed up in Grattan's words 'when by misconduct war is rendered hopeless, peace is rendered necessary'.[3] In short the Irish Whigs, who were Portland Whigs in 1794, had become Foxite Whigs.

Burke remained a convinced supporter of Catholic emancipation, and his vehement contempt for the narrow and rigid conservatives who dominated the Irish Administration was as strong as ever. But he was dismayed by the Irish Whigs, who seemed to him to be carrying concession to the point where it invited catastrophe. And his perplexities were not diminished by his two principal correspondents on Irish matters, Thomas Hussey and Lord Fitzwilliam. Hussey, a suave ecclesiastic when he started his career in Ireland as President of Maynooth, seemed destined to play an important part in developing good relations between the Irish Catholics and the Government. But having for years moved easily amongst people of influence in England and on the Continent, he was quick to resent the disabilities under which the Irish Catholics still laboured. He typified, not the Irish Catholic community which had borne the brunt of the Penal Laws, but rather the militant and aggressive Catholicism of the nineteenth century. And a year or so after his arrival in Ireland he became embroiled in disputes with the Government; disputes which he described to Burke in a series of emotional letters.

[1] *Dublin Evening Post*, 30 January 1797.
[2] *Ibid.* 2 February 1797.
[3] *Parliamentary Register of Ireland*, XVII, 4.

Fitzwilliam had been deeply shaken by his failure in Ireland. The episode obsessed him, and as late as 1798 when he was offered the Lord Lieutenancy of the West Riding, he hoped that the appointment would be 'considered, not as a decision in his favour against his then colleagues, but as connected with a change of opinion in them from more reflection and experience'.[1] It is not necessary here to discuss the reasons for the abrupt termination of Fitzwilliam's Viceroyalty. It is enough to say that Fitzwilliam was convinced that his policy was sound, both morally and politically, and that he could have implemented it if he had been supported by his colleagues in the Cabinet. The two members of the Cabinet principally concerned with Irish affairs were Pitt and Portland. In a charitable mood, Fitzwilliam might find excuses for Portland, his old political ally and friend—after all, the Duke's indecisiveness was proverbial. But towards Pitt, an old opponent, he was obdurate. Naturally he was intensely hostile to the Administration which Pitt and Portland supported in Ireland, and from early in 1797 he was engaged in efforts to remove the leading Irish office holders. In March he and French Laurence prepared a long 'Representation' to the King, requesting a change of men and measures in Ireland, which was to be signed by a group of peers possessing estates in Ireland. Nothing came of this, but a few months later in May, Fitzwilliam, his friend Carlisle—also a sometime Irish Viceroy—and possibly even Portland, were considering schemes for remodelling the Irish Administration. And according to Laurence, Windham was 'fully impressed with the necessity of dismissing the present men', though he believed that his colleagues were 'more afraid of Lord Clare and the Beresfords, than of a Rebellion in Ireland'.[2] Burke, who was informed about these moves and continually consulted, was greatly disturbed. He was acutely conscious that Ireland was in a grave condition, with revolt impending, but he did not allow his strong antagonism to the governing group in Ireland to render him oblivious to the fact that dangerous political heresies were being voiced by the Irish Whigs.

The letters on Ireland which Burke wrote during the last months of his life have many perceptive flashes, springing from knowledge and generous emotion. But they are profoundly pessimistic, and uncharacteristically he fails to indicate with confidence a line of action. He is deeply conscious of the fact that in Ireland he is forced to face only a choice of evils. None of the contending parties would accept his policy—the maintenance of the existing constitutional and social order with full

[1] Laurence to Pitt, 10 February 1798 (Public Record Office, P.R.O.30/8/150, fol. 162).
[2] Laurence to Fitzwilliam, 15 May 1797 (MS at Northampton, Box 51).

Catholic emancipation. Even Grattan and the Irish Whigs in whom he had enthusiastically put his trust were no longer politically reliable. In May 1797 they seceded from the House of Commons and some weeks later their political views were crystallized in a dramatic document. At the beginning of July Grattan issued a long address to his constituents, the citizens of Dublin. Ostensibly it was the manifesto of a moderate, who avowed that he was urging emancipation and reform, with the aim of checking the spread of 'the democratic principle'. But Grattan, whose political expositions were always infused with poetic fire, and who was very conscious that his efforts had been baulked by conservative obstinacy, directed almost all his arguments against the British and Irish Administrations. And Burke, when the letter was read to him on 7 July, though he applauded the brilliancy of some of the declamation, censured the false taste of the whole and deplored 'the bad politics of beginning, continuing and ending with what is called parliamentary Reform'.[1] These were his last comments on a political publication. He had barely two more days to live. By the beginning of July his long dragging illness was approaching its end, and very early on the morning of 9 July he died.

[1] Laurence to Fitzwilliam, 9 July 1797 (MS at Northampton, Box 51).

THE CORRESPONDENCE

To the ABBÉ MARAINE—*2 May* 1796

Source: Copy (in Jane Burke's hand) in Fitzwilliam MSS (Northampton).

By the end of April the boys had begun to arrive at the French school at Penn, and for the next two months Burke was to be embroiled in a series of disputes over finance, the appointment of masters, and the selection of candidates for admission. As he himself wrote, the school had 'no regular or formal Establishment whatever', and his own position and powers as 'The Solliciter and Undertaker' of the project were undefined (see below, p. 37). The Abbé Jean-Marin Maraine (*c.* 1746–1830), who had written to Burke on 1 May (MS at Northampton), had been chosen as headmaster by the Bishop of St Pol-de-Léon (see below, p. 8).

Beaconsfield Monday
May 2d 1796

Dear Sir,

I am just now far from well; and therefore as it is always painful to me to write anything in French, I take the liberty of using my own Language, which may probably be quite as intelligible, as the Jargon I must speak and write, when I attempt yours.

I assure you, Sir, it adds not a little to the other causes of my indisposition, that in suggesting any arrangement as matter of consultation between us, I have been the means of giving you the smallest degree of uneasiness. I did nothing more in wishing the Journey of the other Gentlemen to be suspended, than to give us an opportunity of an amicable conference, upon an affair, that appeared to me a matter of no slight importance: But you have shut the door effectually against all discussion of the subject. You appeal to a *contract*; and insist, that I shou'd stand to it.[1]

I am sure you will have the goodness to excuse the infirmity of my understanding, if I do not enter fully into your Ideas of this supposed covenant. The money to be paid for the diet of Children, or for the Salary of the Master, may become, and often does become, the Matter of a Contract: But their *education* neither can, nor ought to be so. Such a contract wou'd be, not only against the nature of things, and therefore null and void; but as between us, highly fraudulent; as none of the parties concerned in Interest, are parties to the contract. You will not

---

[1] Evidently Burke, on a visit to the school on 30 April, had suggested that the Abbé should postpone appointing new masters until there had been further discussions. The Abbé's letter of 1 May insisted that two of his candidates were already appointed, and '. . . après les propositions qu'on leur avoit faites ont quitté des avantages assés considerables qu'ils avoient à Londres, ont remis leurs logements et vendus leurs meubles. N'escepas une espece de contrait que l'on a fait avec eux et peut il être permis de le rompre'.

lean too hard upon my Errour, if I think that Guardians and preceptors are made for the pupils; and not the pupils for the preceptors and guardians. This rule extends to me, Who have undertaken to superintend the Education of these young Gentlemen, as well as to you, who have been appointed to teach them. When a Sketch of your plan was sent to me,[1] I understood it, not as a convention to be signed, but as a matter of arrangement for deliberation; perpetually open to such alterations, as a nearer view of the subject, shou'd suggest for the Benefit of the precious pledges committed by providence to my Care. Since I have seen some of those Children, my anxiety about them is infinitely encreased. They are, in all respects, a set of the finest Boys I have ever beheld. Their Talents are extremely promising; their dispositions sweet and tractable; and their character modest, and at the same time manly. Neither, to this point, have their Parents been wanting in their care of them. They are all very considerably advanced for their Age. It is certain, that there is not one in the House; from my Wife, to the humblest domestick who is not charmed with them; and who do not look upon them with a tender interest, as if they were of our proper family. Our Guests here, Ladies and Gentlemen, French and English, were affected in the same manner; and are witnesses to the mode in which we all received the honour of having such persons intrusted to our attentions.

When I had prevailed on his Majesties Ministers, (almost every one of whom, either by myself or by my friends I sollicited) to adopt the plan I had the boldness to propose to them,[2] I consider'd myself as incurring a double responsibility: a responsibility to those, who administer'd the Publick money, for a faithful and discreet application of the sums that should be intrusted to me; and another, and that by far the greatest, to the French Nation; to the Parents, where they have any; to the relations of these Children; and in a future time, to the Children themselves. As to what regards the necessities of the animal, I am quite sure, I have not been wanting—as to what goes to forming the Man, and the future Citizen, it is matter of greater difficulty; and upon this, it becomes me to be more diffident of my own Judgement; particularly, when it has not the good fortune to be confirmed by yours. But I am persuaded, that you will be generous enough to allow, that such as it is, I should ill acquit myself of the responsibility that lies upon me, if I should totally abandon it, and blindly give over the trust committed to my hands even to you, Sir, whom, so far as I can Speak from the short acquaintance I have with you, I do not in the least doubt to be a man of virtue and

---

[1] The Abbé's plan has not been found.
[2] The original proposals for the school at Penn had been drafted by Burke; see vol. VIII, 396–7.

integrity and one whom I am disposed in a very high degree to esteem and respect.

You will permit me to lay before you the difficulties I am under from your Letter, and from the principles (wiser than mine very probably) on which you seem to me, in every instance to act. These Young persons are in very peculiar circumstances. They are all born in an honourable Station. They are to be inspired with sentiments and with a Character not misbecoming that place. At the same time they are the most compleatly destitute of the human race, and the most helpless; and the more so, perhaps, from the Circumstances of their Birth. They have not only a fortune to Make; but even a Country to seek; As to the first, they do not possess one of the usual means of advancing themselves. Every thing must depend wholly upon their personal qualifications. To enable them to proceed in their very difficult and delicate Situation a meer French Education, according to the Routine of a French College, will never answer for them. They wou'd be ruin'd by it; and I never will make myself the Instrument of the ruin of those whom I have undertaken to Serve; I have Ideas relative to their future Establishment,[1] which I shall confide to safe and zealous hands, to execute after my Death[2]—and to those Ideas, the whole plan of their Education must of necessity conform, whilst it is in my hands. By your undertaking to exclude from the House whom you please, you have forced a question, (which I wished of all things to decline) concerning the ownership of that House.[3] It is a question, which, therefore must be decided. But as it ill fits me to be a Judge in any matter that relates to my own conduct, I shall, as to *the matter of local possession*, refer myself to Mr Pitt; and as to the question, whether I shall have any part in the direction of the Education, I shall refer myself *to the sole natural guardians and Judges without appeal*, in whatever regards the Education of the French Noblesse, the Chiefs of your own Nation, and eminently of Monsieur,[4] who has condescended to be the protector of this little Establishment. God forbid, that I should attempt to obtrude myself as a guardian to the Children of other people, or into the Management of the means of another Nation, without their consent. But when they do consent, (if consent they should) I must do my Duty; and I will of course expect, that the plans, which I pursue, in

---

[1] MS: Establisment,
[2] A codicil to Burke's will (see below, p. 379) made provision for the management of the school.
[3] The school was lodged in Tyler's Green House, the former home of Burke's friend General William Haviland (1718–84). The house had been rented for three years by the Government, and was administered through the War Office, which had turned it over to Burke on 29 March; see vol. VIII, 451.
[4] Charles-Philippe, Comte d'Artois (1757–1836), the younger of the surviving brothers of Louis XVI; later Charles X.

concert with the best informed of the French Nobility, shall be chearfully complied with by all those with whom I have the honour to
cooperate. What you say of an English Master[1] does not meet my Ideas.
In everything English, I pretend, and in that alone, to be the Judge. As
to the Gentlemen, if any of them shou'd be put to inconvenience, I shall
make it my Business, that they shall suffer as little as possible. They are
not the worse off for being new Cloathed, as you seem to think.[2] If they
wanted it, they shou'd chearfully have the Coat from my back. I really
had flattered myself, that Frenchmen would have considered me as their
friend—as a weaker one, without doubt; but as a friend, warm, zealous
well intentiond; and would have had that regard for the common
welfare of their Countrymen, as to be a little partial to the Ideas of those
English, who cordially and actively interest themselves in their welfare.
I was sorry to find none of this indulgence from you. I have the honour
to be with very Sincere respect and regard Dear Sir

Your Most faithful
and obedient Humble Servant
EDMD BURKE

To EARL SPENCER—5 May 1796

Source: MS California University Library (Santa Barbara).
Endorsed: Rt Honble Edmd Burke | No place—5th | Ansd 9th | Dr
Carmichael Smyth.

George John Spencer, 2nd Earl Spencer (1758–1834), was First Lord of the
Admiralty 1794–1801.

My Lord,

I know very well how little entitled I am to be troublesome to your
Lordship; and I am sure, they are very few and very extraordinary
occasions, in which I should find myself disposed to it; knowing, as I do,
how much and how successfully your Mind is employd, upon the most
essential of all our publick concerns. But, I confess, it is on that very
Title I venture to take the Liberty of intruding myself on your attention
at this time. It is on a Business, which, as affecting the Navy, peculiarly
belongs to your Lordship, and as affecting humanity, belongs to us all.

---

[1] The Abbé felt that 'la vie commune' of his school would be more harmonious if
the masters who were to teach English were (like the other masters) Frenchmen of his own
choice. At the least '...il faut avoir tous francois, ou tous anglois pour que les choses
puissent bien aller'.

[2] The Abbé, in defending the two masters who he maintained were already engaged,
argued that Burke himself had given orders for clothing them.

The Gentleman, I have the honour of now recommending to you, has done more towards the conservation of the health of both branches of the military service, particularly of the Naval, than any man I have yet heard of. It is Dr Carmichael Smith.[1] His great knowlege and his application, have given an effect to what his humanity and his publick Spirit have impelled him to undertake. I have known him for some years, and know more good of him than of any other of my acquaintance. He has but one fault that I know of, but it is one very usual with merit, and its greatest Enemy his modesty.

He thinks, and many think with him, that the Office of a general superintendent of health for the navy, to regulate and methodize the whole System of the proceeding with regard to it, would be of infinite advantage. If that point were once[2] determined, I suppose there would be but one Voice on the preference which ought to be given to Dr Smith. Nothing could probably do more honour to your[3] Lordships generous and paternal Care of the Navy, than such a plan; nor to your Judgment on the choice of a person to execute it, than your appointment of this Gentleman who has not only devoted the Talents of a great Genius and the professional acquirements of a very learned and experienced man to this very Object, but has more than once risqued his very Life and exposed it to that contagion, he has been so successful in his endeavours to prevent.[4] I am certain that your Lordships enlarged mind will see this in its true point of Light; and will not suffer what will so essentially relate to your own glory and the publick Benefit to be decided by the narrow[5] Ideas of subordinate Office.

I have the honour to be with the most perfect respect and attachment
My Lord
Your Lordships
Most Obedient
and faithful humble Servant

May 5. 1796.   EDM BURKE

[1] Dr James Carmichael Smyth (1741–1821), a physician specializing in contagious diseases. Burke had already recommended him to Lord Spencer; see vol. VIII, 205.
[2] MS: one
[3] MS: you
[4] Dr Smyth's method of fumigation below deck by pouring vitriol over powdered nitre is described in his work *An Account of the Experiment made on board the Union hospital ship to determine the effect of the nitrous acid in destroying contagion . . . In a letter to Earl Spencer*, London, 1796. It has been stated that the use of this method 'certainly removed the stench; but any effective concentration would have killed the men before it killed the lice' (C. Lloyd and J. L. S. Coulter, *Medicine and the Navy, 1200–1900*, London, 1957–63, III, 76).
[5] MS: narow

The BISHOP OF ST-POL-DE-LÉON *to* EDMUND BURKE— 11 *May* 1796

Source: Fitzwilliam MSS (Northampton).
Addressed: Right Hone Edd Burke | Beaconsfield.
Postmarked: MA|11|96|F.

Jean-François de La Marche (1729–1806), the Bishop of St-Pol-de-Léon in Brittany, had been an army officer for some years before taking orders. An active diocesan, he refused to accept the Civil Constitution of the Clergy, and early in 1791 emigrated to England. A man of profound piety, energetic and gifted with considerable administrative powers, he played a leading part in securing and managing relief for the *émigrés*, clerical and lay (see vols VII, 207–10; VIII, 445). He was keenly interested in the fortunes of the school at Penn, and in his relations with Burke on occasion displayed a dash of imperiousness, episcopal or military.

Mon tres cher Monsieur

J'ay Receu la lettre que vous aviez confié à M. Negle[1] et lui ai Remis le pamphlet de M. de Montlosier[2] que j'ay lu avec indignation sur plusieurs points sans applaudir à aucun. J'y ai joint la lettre a vous de M. Maraine[3]—et pas autre chose parce que je n'ai Point Receu ce que vous me marquez m'avoir envoié par la poste ni le papier de My lord Buckingham[4] ni de M. Barentin[5] ni de my lord arundell[6] il faut qu'il y ait eu quelque *Mistake* il Reste douze enfant de premiere ou seconde classe[7] qui partiroient avec M. Negle samedi prochain s'ils etoient icy. Mais il y en à un a bristol, cinq ou six à jersey il y en a cinq icy ou à Richemond qui pourront partir Samedi. Vous en aurez donc dans la semaine au moins 25 en tout peutetre 30 ou 32 et j'espere que la semaine suivante vous en aurez une vingtaine de plus. Ou je me trompe fort ou au moins un maitre de plus seroit necessaire pour l'instruction et surtout la surveillance. Point si essentiel aux yeux de tout homme qui

---

[1] Edward James Nagle, a distant kinsman of Burke (see below, p. 68).
[2] François-Dominique de Reynaud, Comte de Montlosier (1755–1838). Perhaps the pamphlet the Bishop read was his *Des effets de la violence et de la modération dans les affaires de France*, Londres, 1796.
[3] Presumably his letter of 1 May to Burke; see above, p. 3.
[4] The Marquess of Buckingham; see below, p. 16.
[5] Charles-Louis-François de Paule de Barentin (1738–1819). He wrote to Burke on 17 and 27 June (MSS at Northampton), but no earlier letter of his has been found.
[6] Henry Arundell, 8th Baron Arundell (1740–1808), wrote to Burke on 4 May (MS at Sheffield) presenting a petition 'in favour of a most distressed and worthy French Family, in which if you can render them any Service, I shall esteem it as a great favour'.
[7] The following classes of boys were eligible for admission to the school: (1) those who had lost fathers, uncles or brothers at Quiberon; (2) those who had lost relations serving in units in British pay; (3) those whose close relations were receiving British pay; (4) those whose fathers had retired from the services owing to ill health; (5) children of magistrates (*Modèle de demandes de places à l'école royale établie à Penn*, Affaires Étrangères, Mémoires et documents, France, 627, fols 189–189v.).

comme vous met les moeurs au premier Rang—je me persuade que vous sentirez le Besoin d'un troisieme ecclesiastique[1] et parmi les deux qui devoient aller d'icy à votre ecole il y en à un tres instruit des belles lettres geographie histoire &c[2] j'attenderai vos ordres ladessus et surtout autre chose que je pourrai faire.

Vous connoissez les sentiments de Votre ⟨ami⟩
† J Fr. Ev. de Leon

11 mai 96

To WALKER KING—[post 14 May 1796]

Source: Fitzwilliam MSS (Sheffield).

On 11 May the Bishop had told Burke to expect twelve boys of the 'premiere ou seconde classe qui partiroient avec M. Negle samedi prochain'. The next Saturday after 11 May was 14 May.

Walker King (1751–1827), later (1809) Bishop of Rochester, was a close friend and disciple of Burke and one of the editors of his *Works*. He was taking an active part in the launching of the school at Penn, and being in London was often an intermediary between Burke and the Bishop.

My dear Walker, Things I am afraid are again coming to an unpleasant issue between the Bishop of Leon and me. A division of twelve was to be here on Saturday. The account Nagle had at Mrs Silburns[3] was, that four only were ready—and that of them three had fallen ill: But you know, that the earnest applications are not less than fourscore and if that set of Boys was not in readiness nothing ought to hinder their places being filled up, reserving room for those in the first detachment. From the Bishop I had immediately on my coming down a Letter[4] insisting on more *Priests*—and those *French* as essential to the morals and religion of the Boys. In a short Letter[5] I conjured him not to throw any new difficulties in the way of this Business, the consequence of which could

[1] The Bishop himself had chosen two priests to be masters at the school: the Abbé Maraine, who had been Superior of the Seminary of St Nicolas at Rouen, and the Abbé Charles-Gabriel Le Chevalier, also from Rouen (J. Gilbert Jenkins, *A History of the Parish of Penn*, London, 1935, p. 151; E. M. Wilkinson, 'French émigrés in England 1789–1801', unpublished B. Litt. dissertation on deposit in the Bodleian Library, Oxford; François-Xavier Plasse, *Le clergé français réfugié en Angleterre*, 2 tom., Paris, 1886). A military master, the Baron du Pac Bellegarde, who arrived on 9 May and remained at Penn until 1802, seems to have been nominated by Burke (Du Pac Bellegarde to Windham, 17 May 1800, Add. MS 45,723, fol. 38).

[2] Burke told Thomas Hussey on 25 May that he had refused two of the Bishop's nominees for positions as masters (see below, p. 20). These were possibly the two mentioned here.

[3] Dorothy, *née* Robinson (d. 1823), widow of Thomas Silburn (d. 1788), was at this time residing at 10 Little Queen Street, Bloomsbury. She devoted herself to helping the French refugees, and actively co-operated with the Bishop.

[4] Presumably the previous letter.

[5] Missing.

only be my retreat and the business being put by Government into subaltern mercenary hands—to this no answer. I wrote another Short note,[1] letting him know that every thing went on with us very well at Penn. In Truth there is great appearance of harmony between the obstinate people whom he sent me, and the Gentleman I have chosen.[2] To this Note also no answer. The obstinacy of Abbé Marraine is softend down; and I have submitted for Peace;—

—cuncta terrarum subacta praeter atrocem animum Catonis.[3]

I strongly suspect he[4] keeps back the Boys—I wish, that without delay, you would see him to know, what keeps the Boys, without insinuating to him my suspicions—and let me know the result, as soon as ever you can. It confirms those suspicions, that Mrs Silburn, who used to be as true as the Clock, eager and zealous, has not answerd my Letters[5] desiring her to provide some necessaries for the School. Two French Gentlemen,[6] one of them from Jersey, who has a Boy here a relation of his came down (from the Bishop I am persuaded) and told me, with his Cross of St Louis hanging to his Button hole, and with the King of Great Britains military uniform on his Back, that this was not to be a military School, but a school for classic authors—as if I was resolved to exclude them—if the Bishop has sent me two men incapable of teaching them, I cannot help it. I certainly never will receive another at his hands, for teaching Latin, Greek, or any thing else. I treat those he has sent nobly; they are satisfied; the Boys are happy. That is enough.—But I beg pardon for troubling you with this, at the time of a melancholy event in your family—Poor Mrs Ned Kings Death[7]—It is a sore loss to him; and Mrs Burke and I sympathise with him and with you all, most truly. Remember our love to your Mrs King;[8] and amidst sorrow congratulate John[9] on his new comer[10]—things are thus mixed. And pray get me as soon as you can a couple of pair of common School compasses and a scale of wood or Brass which ever is cheapest. If you could get an whole case of the common Instruments—as they generally go together, for the purposes of practical Mathematicks it would be very useful; and pray

---

[1] Missing.   [2] Apparently the Baron du Pac Bellegarde.

[3] All the world was subdued, except the unyielding spirit of Cato; see Horace, Odes, II, i, 24.   [4] The Bishop.

[5] Missing. King told Burke (in his part of a joint letter with the Bishop dated 2 May, MS at Northampton): 'I have executed your commissions with Mrs Silburn and she will attend to them as you desire'.

[6] Not identified.

[7] Walker King's brother Edward (1748–1824), Vice Chancellor of the Duchy of Lancaster, married first Henrietta Lang (b. 1754) of Leyland, Lancashire. In 1798 he married Dorothy Myers (1767–1846).

[8] Sarah, née Dawson (c. 1772–1822), whom Walker King had married in 1794.

[9] Walker King's brother John (see below, p. 82).

[10] Marianne, who later (1814) married Walter Campbell of Sanderland.

let us have both, at least the compasses, as soon as possible if you can by tomorrows Coach—and if there be any short and easy introduction of Theoretical to the Practical, it would best suit our purposes. God bless you. My Anxiety and my pleasure about this Business—encreases hourly: But I shall lose this Object also. The Treasury mean to issue the money to me, but as I understand thro' the Committee,[1] that is the Bishop of Leon. Without assigning this as my Reason I have desired Woodford[2] to refuse it in that manner. I will throw up, if I am to be directed in this Education by any one whatever. Left at Liberty, I answer for it—I will, under even the present disadvantages, produce as fine and interesting a set of Lads as was ever Seen—Adieu! Adieu— every blessing to you and yours and pray for the few I can have to me and mine.

E B.

To WALKER KING—[post 14 May 1796]

Source: MS Osborn Collection.

Undated. In the previous letter Burke asked Walker King to send him 'an whole case of the common Instruments'. These are perhaps the 'Instruments' for which he thanks him in this letter.

My dear friend

I long impatiently for the result of your Committee conference.[3] If I have but a single responsibility and a single account, what secures me the most punctual payment is the best. I wish the stoppage[4] not to be on the single parents;[5] but on the whole for one 600; and that the whole 22 pound per head,[6] shoud make one monthly payment of £100.[7] This would be every way better—but best of all if there should be no stoppage. It is hardly worth while for six hundred pound. Our man, I am afraid, is no better than a Bankrupt.[8] I thank you for the Instruments— There are Books enough for the present.

Yours E B.

[1] Burke is probably referring to the Committee for the Relief of the Suffering Clergy and Laity of France which was under the chairmanship of John Wilmot (c. 1749–1815).

[2] Captain Emperor John Alexander Woodford was Inspector General of Foreign Forces and was a subordinate of William Windham (see below, p. 43). If Burke expressed his wishes in a letter, it is missing.

[3] The 'Wilmot Committee', of which Walker King was a member (Public Record Office, T93/1).   [4] Deduction.

[5] Burke probably means 'payments' rather than 'parents'.

[6] Burke seems to have arrived at this figure by adding together the twelve guineas a year paid by the Wilmot Committee for each boy, and the sum produced by dividing the Government grant of £600 per annum to the school, by sixty (the number of boys).

[7] A grant of £22 per annum each for sixty boys would amount to £110 monthly.

[8] This may refer to John Owen of 168 Piccadilly, bookseller and one of the publishers of Burke's *Letter to a Noble Lord* (see vol. VIII, 388). Burke evidently expected him to

To Unknown Lord—19 *May* 1796

Source: Extract printed in *Maggs Catalogue,* 317 (November–December 1913), no. 3305.

Maggs Catalogue described this letter as addressed to 'My Lord' and as '2 pp., 4to. Beaconsfield, 19 May, 1796'. The recipient has not been identified.

You will be surprised to receive a Letter from a man who is no longer in this world, and who has not seen you, nor scarce any one else since he was with you, in company with a person worth your notice. But though in every other respect I am dead, I am not wholly extinct as to my friendships. A person,[1] whom I value and regard exceedingly, because he had the good opinion and good wishes of what was the best and dearest part of me[2] has an object in view to which your Lordship's patronage is necessary.

The Bishop of St-Pol-de-Léon *to* Edmund Burke— 21 *May* 1796

Source: Fitzwilliam MSS (Northampton).
Addressed: Right Hone Edd Burke | Beaconsfield.
Postmarked: MA|21|96|D.

Tres cher Monsieur

J'ay votre lettre du 19.[3] Mde Silburn attend d avoir Rempli vos intentions avant de vous Repondre. Je n'ai qu'un moment pour vous dire qu'il doit partir demain à 10 heures cinq ou six jeunes gens avec M. Negle—j'apprens qu'il en arrive de jersey j'ay Receu la nomination du marquis Buckingham à qui j'ay transmis toutes les Recommendations lettres et memoires que vous m'avez envoié ne voulant influer sur aucune nomination et pouvoir toujours dire avec la plus exacte verité que je n'ai eté pour tout le monde qu'un fidele et simple commis. Dans le courant de la semaine prochaine je pense que vous aurez augmentation de famille et dans la suivante que vous serez complet adieu nos affaires vont bien mal selon moi quoiqu'on nous dise qu'il y à sous Mr de puisaye[4] trente mille hommes et qu'il me demande quatre vint pretres

account for his receipts from sales of that pamphlet. Owen later contended that he had been made a clear gift of whatever profits there were to be, and therefore need not account to Burke. He went bankrupt on 20 May 1797 (*The Times,* 22 May 1797).

[1] Not identified.

[2] Richard Burke, Jr.

[3] Burke's letter is missing.

[4] Joseph-Geneviève, Comte de Puisaye (1755–1827), had played a leading part in organizing the Quiberon expedition; see vol. VIII, 141, 268–9, 273–4, 299.

pour quatrevingt division[1] partagez avec votre Respectable et bien
aimée dame les Respectueux hommages de votre fidel ami

† J Fr Ev. de Leon

21 mai 96

This short letter reveals an awkward misunderstanding. Burke was extremely
anxious that the *émigrés* should participate in the management of the school by
selecting the pupils, and he seems to have hoped that this would be done by the
French Committee—a committee of *émigrés* set up in 1792 to advise the English
committees who were striving to relieve the French exiles. The rules for admission to the school, however, presumably drawn up by the French Committee
(see below, p. 34), laid down that the Treasurer of the French Committee in
London was to send applications for admission (distinguished by a number only)
to the 'Lords Commissioners' who would make a selection. According to the
Bishop the Lords Commissioners were the Trustees of the school, namely,
Buckingham, Lord Grenville and the Duke of Portland. The applications were,
in fact, sent by the Committee to Buckingham who made a selection (see below,
p. 31). Buckingham explained that he considered the final decision rested with
Burke. But since the Bishop and the French Committee acted promptly on the
Marquess's decision, Burke felt he was being left with merely the invidious
power of rejecting boys who, it was believed, had secured places (Wilkinson,
'French Émigrés in England'; Affaires Étrangéres, Mémoires et documents,
France, 627, fols. 189–189v.; see also below, pp. 34, 37–9).

To Unknown Duke—[21 *May* 1796]

Source: Fragment of a draft in Fitzwilliam MSS (Northampton), A. xix. 4.
The Bishop's description of himself as 'un fidele et simple commis' much
irritated Burke, whose next seven letters all refer to it. The first, a frag-
mentary letter to an unknown correspondent whom he describes as 'Monsieur Le duc', was probably written on 21 May. At least, Burke says he has
received the Bishop's letter 'A cet instant'; he later told Lord Buckingham
he had received it on Saturday, 21 May (see below, p. 18). It may be noted
that Burke sent copies of the *Two Letters on a Regicide Peace* to the Duc
d'Angoulême and the 'Duc de Serrenty' (see below, p. 98), and that Jean-
Laurent de Durfort-Civrac, Duc de Lorge (1746–1826), was a member of the
French Committee.

⟨commencats⟩ a Leur donner, je Les feroit preparé avec bon coeur a un
Etat si respectable et si doux. Mais cela n'etant pas, Nous, et tous nos
affaires, et tous nos desires, doivent se conformer a des circumstances,
qui sont vraiment imperieuses, et plus puissantes que tous Les Rois ou
tous Les Parlemens du monde. Voila mes principes. Sil Le goverment
(ce que je ne pense pas) veut que cela se fasse autrement, que cela se
fit—mais pas par moi. Je ne recevra jamais Le depot de deniers du
Roi, ni celui des enfans de votre patrie, Les seules restes de biens de

---

[1] In a letter to Windham dated 29 April Puisaye stated that he had 6000 men under
arms and if he had the money to pay them he could recruit 50,000 (Charles-Louis
Chassin, *Études documentaires sur la Révolution française*, Paris, 1892–1900, IX, 463).

13

malheureuse La noblesse Francoises pour abuser Lés unes au ruine des autres. S'il Le Goverment veut continuer La confiance que jusquici il avoit reposé en moi, je ferai direger L'education de cette ecole, pas selon mes fantaisies mais selon La nature des choses. Si on ne me permet pas cela je donnera ma demission.

Je suis responsable au Gouverment de ne tromper leurs esperances— je suis responsable a vous autres Les representants de La Noblesse Francoise de n'abuser de La Tutele de tous ce qui vous est tres precieux. Voila mes Idees. Je ne me plaigne de personne. Je ne me degoute. Je ne me ennuye point du soins du travail que cette Tutele m'impose, ni de depense quil L'entraine : toute au contraire. Cest La seul consolation qui me reste; mais jabandonnera cette plaisir plutot que d'agir contre ma conscience.

A cet instant je recois un Billet[1] de mon ami L'Evêque de Leon— Le meilleur homme du monde et a qui tous Les Francois sont plus redevable peutetre pour existence même qu'aucune autre. Il me faut avouer que Cette Lettre m'afflige beaucoup Monseigneur. Il m'a fait esperer apres Les cinque ou six Enfans[2] d'aujourdhui, que je dois attendre L'arrivée dans Le courant du semaine prochaine; d'un division plus considerable et dans la suivante mon nombre sera complet, en m'avertissant au même temps qui ne sont envoye par lui; et qui n'est plus qu'un commis, pour remettre Les recommandations au my Lord Buckingham sans quil veut influer sur aucune nomination. Que pensez vous Monsieur Le duc de mon position. Jai pensai jusquici que tous Les jeunes persons que jai recu etoit de mains de L'eveque de Leon avec L'approbation du Commite Francoise. A present je suis instruit par La memoire de Monsieur de La Tour[3] et de plusieurs autres—que La committe Francoise desavoue La recommandation

To the BISHOP OF ST-POL-DE-LÉON—[22 *May* 1796]

Source: Incomplete draft in Fitzwilliam MSS (Northampton), A. VII. 44.
Burke calls the Bishop's letter of 21 May 'Votre Billet d'hier'. It is unlikely that this draft was finished or sent; the drafts of [*circa* 25 May] and 25 May seem to be answering the same letter of the 21st.

Monseigneur

Votre Billet d'hier n'etoit pas bien grand; mais L'embarras qui me cause n'est point petit.

---

[1] The previous letter.   [2] MS: Enfa Enfans
[3] David-Sigismond, Marquis de La Tour du Pin-Montauban (1751–1807), Grand Bailly de Malte. William Windham (see below, p. 43) had met him at Beaconsfield on 27 April (Windham, *Diary*, p. 338).

C'est pour La premiere fois, que je viens d'apprendre, que je me trompois, en supposant que vous et la Comite Francoise[1] a qui selon votre desir expres jai envoyé toute Les applications, qui me sont venu au mains, pour en juger, n'avoient pas apporté aucun decision entre Le concurrens. Je ne parle pas plus de confiance qui est due a L amitie. Je ne serois pas fondee en reclamant Les droit qui en appartient.

Toutes Les applications pour Lecole qui me sont venus aux mains furent envoyes a vous pour que vous, et Messieurs de la Committé puissent faire un decision entre Les concurrens. Ce fut apres votre desir que je me conduisoit dans cette maniere. Vous sçavez Monseigneur que jai ecrit sur le même principe, a My Lord Arundel, a Monsr Barentin,[2] et a plusieurs autres. Vous n'avez jamais marqué La moindre dis-approbation d une telle procedé. Ce n'etoit que hier pour La premier fois, que vous daignates d'ouvrir mes yeux a mon erreur, et m'apprenant que Le nombre de soixante fut complete que vous n'avois entre pour rien dans Le choix. Par La même poste par laquelle j'apprends de vous que Lecole est remplis je reçois des Lettres[3] qui me font connoitre que[4] Vous avez repondu a un appliquant, que vous ne vous meloit en aucune Maniere de ces nominations; et quils seroient toutes faites par Le Lords Commissaires apres les extraits que La Comite feroient des memoires,[5] il ajoute en s'addressant a moi 'que plusieurs Membres de La Comite L'avoient assuré, que toute dependoit a vous'—cest a dire a moi. Sur cette Idée generalement repandu que jai reçu un Lettre de   [6] que vous devez sçavoir meiux que personne n'etois pas consulte du tout ni même avertir d'aucune procede de vous, ni de La Commite Francoise, Ni de ceux que vous appellez Le Lords Commissaires nommer pour juger entre Les concurens. Je ne parle pas d'autre chose que La politique La plus ordinaire dans un affaire qui me doit interesser Beaucoup, de me faire avertir de L'existence d'un telle commission, de ses droits,[7] de ses provisions, de ces regles de La Lieu et Le temps ou ils ont tenu leurs seances; afin que je serois en etat, de faire par requeste ou autrement, telles representations que je jugerois apropos aussi bien que Les Petitionaires auroient Le moiens pour faire valuer leur pretentions respectives. Cela tient non seulement a La Politesse mais a La justice. Mais tout cela m'etoit soigneusement Caché. Jen suis sur que plusieurs entre Les partis interesses eux mêmes n'etoient pas averti de cette

---

[1] See above, p. 13. The Committee wrote to Burke on 13 June thanking him for his benevolence to their countrymen in distress (MS at Northampton).
[2] See above, p. 8. Both letters are missing.
[3] Missing.   [4] MS: que que
[5] Applications for admission.
[6] There is a blank in the MS at this point.
[7] Burke has crossed out 'droits' by mistake.

Bureau de Lords Commissaires quapres tout fut arrangée—et Le nombre complet. Voila Monsieur un belle procede. Vous avez reservé a vous ou bien donnes aux autres tout ce qui est de doux et d'obligeant, dans cette affaire et tres gracieusement abandonné a moi, Le portion de La rejection et de refus. Des le commencement de cette affaire votre resolution pour m'en degouter de me forcer de L'abandonner etoit sans relache—suivi et systematique.

Apres une conduite innoui, si reflechie et au meme temps si insultante, Je n'ai que de L'oublier, et apres ça, de me guider après Les dictes de mon devoir. Il faut dont vous avertir pour La dernier[1] fois, quapres avoir connu Les noms de jeuns gens qui quand vous Le jugerez[2] apropos je ne ferois d'Objection a aucuns. A Deiu ne plaise que ferois changer L'etat de personne. Mais tandis que Le Bureau de Guerre m'auroit Laisser en possession du maison a Penn,[3] vous sçavez qui me seroit contre toutes les regles de mon devoir que de permettre que personne entre La dedans sans L'ordre de persons qui avoueront que ce qui sont envoye etoient choisis Je ne me tiendrai autorise de les recevoir par eux entre Les appliquans. Il m'est necessaire d'avoir un person responsable pour Le choix comme je suis responsable pour Education. Ceux que jai deja reçue jai reçu comme étant de votre choix. Cela etoit assez pour me satisfaire. Si La Comite Francoise veut Les nommer comme de Leur choix je tiendra cela pour un

To the MARQUESS OF BUCKINGHAM—[24 May 1796]

Source: Copy in Fitzwilliam MSS (Northampton), A. VI. 44. Printed Buckingham, *Memoirs of the Court and Cabinets of George III*, II, 342–7.
Endorsed: Copy of Mr Burkes | Letter to the Marquis | of Buckingham. | dated, 24 May 1796.

George Nugent Temple Grenville, 1st Marquess of Buckingham (1753–1813), who had presented Burke's plan for the school at Penn to Pitt in March (see vol. VIII, 444), was one of the most active of the Trustees.

My dear Lord

Having received no answer to my last Letter,[4] I persuade myself there was nothing in it to displease you; otherwise your general politeness and your kind partiality to me would have led you to give me such instruction as might prevent me from falling into Errors in the delicate Business, in

---

[1] Burke has written 'premier' above the line.
[2] MS: jugeions   [3] See above, p. 5.
[4] On 20 April Burke had sent to Buckingham an account of expenditures at Penn, to be submitted to the Treasury. Burke's expenditures totalled £271.8.9.1/2 (MS at Northampton, A. XXIV. 89).

which, under your Countenance, and with your Approbation, I have engaged myself.

We look forward with a pleasure, mixed with some degree of impatience, to the visit which your Lordship and Lady Buckingham[1] have flattered us with the Hope of, though I am afraid the Heat of the General Election[2] will be over before we can enjoy that satisfaction.

I think, however unfortunate I may find myself in all attempts to please the Bishop of Leon, that your Lordship and Lady Buckingham will feel the same pleasing and affecting Interest in what is done here, that all have been touched with, who see what is going on. You will be pleased with the celerity, if not with the perfection of our work. Five and forty Beds are ready. The rest will be so, in a very few Days. An old bad Stable is converted into an excellent School room. The Chappel is decent, in place, and in furniture. The Eating room is reasonably good. Twenty five Boys are received clad in a cleanly and not unpleasing manner, and they are fed in an orderly way with a wholesome and abundant Diet. The Masters are pleased with their pupils; and the Pupils are pleased with their Preceptors; and I am sure I have reason to be pleased with them all. I see them almost every day, and at almost all hours; as well at their Play, as at their Studies and exercise—I have never seen finer Boys, or more fit for the plan of Education, I mean to follow for them as long as it pleases Government to continue that charge in my hands— I am responsible, that if they are left to me for six months, a set of finer Lads, for their Age, and standing, will not be seen in Europe.

The only unfortunate part of the Business is, that some of them speak not a word of English and they who are the most forward in it, are very imperfect. There is but one of the Masters who can be said to know any thing of it; and he is far indeed from the ability to teach it. There must be a person who besides going with them into all their Latin readings and construing them into English, will daily converse with them, and Ground them in the principles and the Utterance of that Tongue, which belongs to the Nation, which alone, promises them an Asylum upon Earth. For many reasons, I should prefer a Clergyman of their own persuasion, and of our Country. But though I have always known that their number was small, I did not conceive it to be so inconsiderable as I now find it. But some English Subject must be found to be about those Boys at all hours. It would be a terrible thing to condemn these poor Creatures to an universal exile, and to be perpetual Vagrants without a possibility of being in a state of effectual communication with the natives

---

[1] Mary Elizabeth, *née* Nugent (*c.* 1776–1812).
[2] Buckingham was taking an active part in the political campaign in Buckinghamshire; see below, p. 30.

of any Country, or incorporating themselves with any People—God forbid that under the pretext of a Benefit I should be the cause of their utter ruin.

The Bishop of Leon has written me a Letter[1] which in my present state of health, by no means the best, gives me a good deal of uneasiness. Hitherto I have received the Boys without any Enquiry, as they were successively sent to me by the worthy Prelate, considering them as the objects of his Selection amongst the Candidates for this Situation. To my Astonishment, in a Letter which I received from him last Saturday[2] he tells me that all the Vacancies are filled; but that he has had nothing to do with the matter, and that he is no more than a simple Clerk. Your Lordship will see by the Letters[3] that I have the honour to enclose to your Perusal, that after filling up all the places, the pleasure of rejecting the rest of the Candidates is thrown upon me. He has contrived matters so, that others have all the Grace of obliging and all the pleasure of being useful, and that all which is harsh and odious is thrown upon me as a reward for all the trouble and expence I have been [at] in this Business. On this I shall make no further remark. By the Letters, Your Lordship will see, that the Bishop of Leon tells the Applicants, that the Selection is to be made by certain Lords Commissioners. I never have been apprized by the Bishop of the existence of any Commission, or of any Commissioners for the purpose of a choice. If such a thing at all exists, I should have flattered myself that I should have been apprized of[4] it; of its rules, of its proceedings and of the times of its sitting. I beleive I am the very first person, who having had the Honour of proposing a plan to Government and being permitted to have the Management of it have been wholly out of the secrets of the appointment of its objects. The name of every Boy sent to me, was unknown to me to the moment of his arrival; the names of those who are to come are equally unknown. Not one circumstance relative to any of them is come to my knowledge. The poorest Country School Master would have been favoured with some better account of his Pupils.

I must beg leave to remark to your Lordship that the account given by the Bishop of Leon to the Applicants is wholly different from that which he gives to me. In his two last Letters to me[5] (one, and the most explicit of which I received just now) he tells me the Selection and nomination is not in any Commissioners but solely in your Lordship, and that he is no more than a Clerk. If I had not received it from so good an authority I

[1] The letter of 21 May.
[2] 21 May; that is the day on which the letter was sent.
[3] Missing.   [4] MS: of of
[5] That of 21 May and another of 23 May (MS at Northampton), enclosing a list of sixty boys.

could hardly have beleived, that your Lordship upon a mere abstract of Petitions without further examination, or any consultation, even with the Bishop of Leon, should have decided upon sixty out of perhaps fourscore Applications. But as I am sure you always act with Equity and discretion I am perfectly satisfied in your having assumed this very delicate and critical of all trusts. I only wish that I had been apprized of your Lordships having taken on you that Office, as though I should not have ventured to recommend a Single person, I really think I might, with all humility, have made some useful suggestions, which your desire of every matter being before you, that might guide you to a sure decision, would make you willing to receive, even from a person so very inconsiderable as I am in every point of view.

I am sure your Lordship wishes that in the very responsible situation in which I stand, that I may be able to give some sort of account of my Trust, and when I have engaged with Government for the education of sixty Boys I ought to know at whose hands, on whose authority, and on whose recommendation I receive them. Certainly they are not recommended or chosen by me; and when I go to the Treasury and tell the Minister who issues the money to me (whenever it shall be issued) that I have employed it in the maintenance and the Education of those whom I do not myself know, nor can tell in any regular or authorized manner, from whom I received them, I should make a very despicable, not to say a very criminal figure. I cannot take your Lordships pleasure from the Bishop of Leon, though he tells me he is, not your Lordships friend or adviser, but your Clerk. As you have never informed me of this his relation to you, I therefore, for my Voucher and justification, request that you will be pleased (the Committee and the Bishop of Leon absolutely disclaiming all choice) to send me a List of the names circumstances and descriptions of the Boys whom you send to me, or have sent, together with a Certificate that having duly examined into the several claims and pretensions of the Candidates, you have found these the best entitled. When I have received this attestation, as my authority and Voucher, far from cavilling, at either the person naming, or the names I shall receive them most chearfully; happy that your Lordship having generously and nobly taken to yourself the Election, these objects have obtained Security for a powerful protection, to place them as they successively shall be qualified, in some way useful to themselves and the publick. I shall take care that they do no dishonour to your Patronage, at least to the moment in which, (having received them from your Hands) I deliver them back into the same benevolent and protecting safeguard.

My dear Lord, have the Goodness to excuse the length of this Letter—

on account of the weight of my responsibility and the very difficult situation in which I stand. Mrs Burke begs leave to join me in the most truly respectful Compliments to Lady Buckingham, and if we may [be] permitted on very little acquaintance to Lord and Lady Temple.[1] No persons can more sincerely wish than we do all kind of honor and happiness to you, and all that belong to you.

I have &c
EDMD BURKE

To the REV. THOMAS HUSSEY—25 May 1796

Source: Fitzwilliam MSS (Sheffield).

This letter may have been commenced somewhat earlier than its date of 'May 25'. At least it speaks of only twenty boys at the school. Burke told Buckingham on 24 May that there were twenty-five.

The Rev. Thomas Hussey (1741–1803) had been appointed President of the new Roman Catholic College at Maynooth in June 1795. From January 1795 he had been in continuous correspondence with Burke on Irish matters.

(secret)

My dear friend,

I have been lately under a great deal of embarrassment. I had made a proposal to Government to found a School for 60 Boys, under my Care and inspection, the Children of emigrants. I succeeded. But knowing, that if I waited till the Treasury issued money the thing never could take place, I was resolved to set the Business agoing at my own Charge— leaving Government afterwards to reimburse me at its leisure. So far I have succeeded, that I have actually twenty lodged, cloathd and fed to their satisfaction—Books and paper &c provided. There are three Tutors—two of them given me by the Bishop of Leon—What the second of the two[2] is as a Teacher I know not as yet—but he is good humourd and practicable—The Chief[3] is a poor obstinate ignorant Clown neither more nor less—but him partly by firmness, partly by conciliatory means [I have brought] into reasonable good humour. I refused two more of the same stuff offerd to me by the Bishop[4]—and have resolved never to have another of his recommendation. A very respectable Officer, a man of quality has condescended to become a Tutor there.[5] The B. of Leon

---

[1] Buckingham's son Richard Temple Nugent Brydges Chandos Grenville (1776–1839), *styled* Earl Temple, later (1813) 2nd Marquess of Buckingham, and his wife Lady Anna Elizabeth, *née* Brydges (1779–1836).
[2] The Abbé Le Chevalier; see above, p. 9.
[3] The Abbé Maraine; see above, pp. 3, 9.
[4] See above, p. 8.
[5] The Baron du Pac Bellegarde; see above, p. 9.

opposed it with all his might—resolving to conduct this School on the principles of a seminary of Monks—and those too of *French*—opposing the Introduction of any *Englishman* whatever, Ecclesiastick or Layman— I really consider, the Idea of forcing the miserable French Boys to be foreigners here, is little less than downright madness; and the educating them as ecclesiastics, when we have nothing for them, by any possibility, but *some* chance of their struggling in *some* part of these dominions, in a military line, is I think not less so. I intend salvâ Religione parentum,[1] to give them a good dash of English Education. But I find it difficult, not to say impossible to get an English Catholick Clergyman; their number is so very small in the gross, to say nothing of the qualified. If such a thing cannot be had in England—do you know any thing of a Scholar as to Latin &c—and who can read English, in Prose and Verse, in a firm, manly, natural manner—a triffle of our Country accent, provided it was not gross and enormous,[2] would be no serious Objection. A Clergyman of an excellent Character, if possible—if not a Layman equally unexceptionable. The Bishop is so set against us poor Laity, that to quiet him the person should be in orders if possible. Why, if you can get such a Subject, should he not be ordained to put an End at least to the Bishops clerical Objection? God forbid, I should take you from your infinitely important Objects on the other side of the Water—But I never wanted you so much. This affair for the French, may be a beginning of infinite advantage to them—I am likely, by the intrigues of my French friend, to be driven out of it. And all my embarrassments are come from my consulting him and confiding in him without necessity. Ever my dear Sir most Affectionately yours with the best and most respectful attentions of all here most

truly Yours

EDM BURKE

Dont absolutely engage any Gentleman, least I should be obliged to take one here before I receive further advice from you. Perhaps I have done ill in telling you of some of the faults of our superior here without Letting you know the good qualities, which, on a balance of things have inclined me to acquiesce in him. Though a narrow minded, I believe him to be a virtuous man, painful, Laborious, and resolved according to his Ideas to do his Duty conscientiously. Again adieu, and believe me as sensible as I ought to be to the merit of what you are doing in Ireland.

May 25. 1796.

[1] While respecting the religion of their relations.
[2] William Drennan (1754–1820) commented on the 'native broadness and vulgarity' of Hussey's brogue. Referring to him and another able and well-travelled

To the BISHOP OF ST-POL-DE-LÉON— [*circa* 25 May 1796]

Source: Incomplete draft in Fitzwilliam MSS (Northampton), A. XIX. 5.
This is another draft of an answer to the Bishop's letter of 21 May. Burke
speaks of his letter of [24 May] to Lord Buckingham (see above, pp. 16–20)
as already written and sent.

Monseigneur

Je n'aime pas trop Les discussions particulierment avec ceux qui je
dois respecter.

Avant d'etre averti que Le nombre de sujets fut complet, vous n'avez
pas daignés de me communiquer en auccune maniere que Le choix entre
Les concurrens n'etoit pas, ni de vous, ni de La Commite Francoise, mais
seulment, et exclusivement de my Lord Buckingham. De même, Lord
Buckingham n'avait pas communiqué a moi ses Idées La dessus. Ces
sont Les circonstances (combinés avec bien Des autres) qui marquent,
que j'ai Le malheur que d'etre exclus entierment de votre confiance.
Jugez en, Monseigneur, si cela ne me doit causer quelque chagrin.

Vous m'ecrites, comme si j'eusse changé mes intentions et que je
voulois avoir Les nominations.[1] Cest que je nai jamais dit ni jamais
pensé.

Mon exclusion, comme vous sçavez mieux que personne, etoit volontaire, fait pour donner de L'exemple a tous Les Anglois, de s'abstenir
entierment de toute nomination, et bien même de toute recommandation et de ne reserver rien a aucun de nous autres, que, dans un cas de
difference, interminable entre Les Francois, un decision Anglois—en Le
dernier resort.

Vous etez trop instruit de La distinction qui existe essentielment,
entre une exclusion volontaire, motivé, faite par des raisons de convenance, de prudence, de moderation, et d'un exclusion forcée, formelle
et de droit. La premiere nous peut honorer—Lautre est flettrisante au
dernier degré. Il etoit de votre choix Monseigneur mon refus dans la
seconde acceptation.

Si m'imaginois, que les enfans de France netoit pas entierement dans
La Tutêle de Francois, Je ne me refuserais pas au plaisir d'etre entre Les
recommandans, et de ne reserver pas a moi que Le triste devoir de

Irishman, Drennan said 'It is singular that such men, both of the most ancient strain
of Ireland, and both in foreign courts the whole of their lives, should smack so strongly
of the bog-trotter' (*The Drennan Letters*, ed. D. A. Chart, Belfast, 1931, p. 228).
   [1] Perhaps this could be inferred from the Bishop's saying that he had sent Lord
Buckingham 'toutes les recommandations lettres et memoires que vous m'aves
envoié', and his profession of being a 'simple commis'. Burke had told Mrs Crewe in
February 'I certainly, for one, shall not name a boy' (see vol. VIII, 395).

repondre negativement au dix sollicitations tant personels que par Des Lettres. Mais cela est passé, et tout a fait irremediable. Nous n'en parlons plus.

Je n'ai pas La moindre objection a faire a aucun sujet des les recommandations. Je dois supposer quils meritent tous, La preference que leur etoit accordé. Tous ceux qui j'ai jusq'ici reçu, etoient traités comme sils etoient Les enfans de mes meilleurs amis, a L'exception, quils etoient reçus avec beaucoup plus de distinction. Mais comme je me trompois a Legard de leur nomination, pour L'avenir je serois obligé de ne pas recevoir aucun enfant, sans quelqu'un veut bien de L'avouer, et de prendre sur lui même, dirèctement et personelment, Le choix entre Les concurrens. Cest que j'eus fait avec La plus grande satisfaction; Si La nomination etoit a moi. Je ne Les recevrai pas comme Les Enfans trouves, sans que personne veut les avouer. Ce seroit honteux pour eux, honteux pour moi. Je m'etonne, Monseigneur, que vous n'etes nullement sensible a La position ridicule et meprisable dans Laquelle vous me placée. Pour m'en tirer, et pour que Les enfans nommés neussent perdre du temps, Jai ecrit La poste apres avoir reçu votre desaveu a My Lord Buckingham pour avoir de lui un certificat de son choix. Je ne demande plus. Tout est pret pour Leur reception avec toute L'allegresse possible. Toujour avec L'attachement Le plus respectueux

Monseigneur
votre tres humble
et tres obeissant Serviteur
EDM BURKE

To the BISHOP OF ST-POL-DE-LÉON—25 May 1796

Source: Copy in Fitzwilliam MSS (Northampton), A. XIX. 31.
Endorsed: Copy of Mr Burkes | Letter to the Bishop | of Leon, dated, 25 May | 1796.
This is probably the final form of Burke's answer to the Bishop's letter of 21 May.

Monseigneur,

Votre Lettre de 21st m'annonce a la fin la Complement du Nombre de Sujets qui sont capable d'etre admis, a l'ecole, et les nouvelles de votre   [1] et de votre etonnante metamorphose d'eveque en 'Simple Commis'. C'est a dire, quand tout est fait, vous etes resolu de ne vous meler en aucun maniere. Quand tous les proces sont Jugez, vous n'etes plus Magistrat. Je vous entend MonSeigneur, vous avez reservé a

[1] There is a blank in the MS at this point.

vous mêmê ou bien donner aux autres, tout ce qui est d'agreeable dans cet affaire; Les appointemens actuels; et vous avez precisement abandonné a votre pauvre ami tous les douceurs de Rejection et de Refus.

De le commencement de cet petit affaire; tous les Applications, sans en exceptér aucune, etoient envoyes a vous Monseigneur; afin que vous, et les Messieurs la Committée Francoise, peuvent donner une decision sur les pretensions des Concurrens. Ce fut selon votre desir expres que J'ai agi selon cet principe. Sur le même principe J'ai repondu a Lord Arundel, au Monsieur Barentin, et aux plusieurs autres. Vous m'avez marqué d'en etre mecontent. Vous n'aviez pas la Bonté de me communiquer même comme Secret du Cabinet, votre Caractère   [1] d'un Commis. Jusq'ici J'ai recu tous les Enfans comme venans de vous, et comme les objets de votre selection en vraiment, c'est une chose sure, que j'eusdemandé par quelle autorité ils etoient envoyés a moi? Sans le savoir[2] presomé de votre choix je ne me trouverai justifié en recevant les jeunes Gens qui n'etoient pas, ni de mon propre choix, ni choisi par aucun person qui etoit en Etat de me constater leur election regulier. Ce fut assurement que de mettre en vous une tres grande Confiance. Ainsi, il est vrai, que J'ai reposé en vous une Confiance presque sans bornes. Confiance en vous, comme Eveque, comme personnage d'un sagesse[3] reconnus; comme mon ami le plus intime, et non pas comme commis subaltern, sans jugement ni Capacité pour faire un selection entre les Candidates pour un petit place. Sil vous etes devenu, Monseigneur le commis de quelqu'un vous n'avez pas aupres moi l'autorité de cette Charactere. Aucun person jusque a cet instant vous avoues ou vous accredites, comme son Commis. Pour cette[4] raison je suis absolument obligé de ne recevoir aucun enfant de vous, sans l'autorisation expres de votre principal. Responsable comme je suis au Gouverment, Je suis obligé d'avoir un personne qui est en etat d'etre responsable pour son choix—D'agir autrement, vous en etes sensible doit etre un procedé plein d'absurdité et de danger.

Pour la même Post Je viens de recevoir [une lettre][5] qui me fait connoitre que vous avez repondu a un Appliquant que vous ne vous meloit en aucune manniere de ces nominations, et qui seroient toutes faites par les Lords Commissaires apres les extraits que la Comittée feroient des memoires.[6] Le Monsieur qui m'ecrit ŷ ajoute en s'addressent a moi 'que plusieurs membres de la Committée l'avoient[8] assuré que tout dependoit a vous—Edmd Burke'.[7] Vous devez scavoir mieux que personne qui

---

[1] There is a blank in the MS at this point.   [2] MS: Sans le scave   [3] MS: sagasse
[4] MS: ctte   [5] Missing.   [6] See above, p. 15.
[7] Burke has inserted an additional quotation mark before 'Edmd'.
[8] MS: d'avoient

n'etoit plus question de la reception d'aucun Sujet par Lords Commissaires ni par aucun, quelqu'il soit. Que le nombre en etoit complet fixe et decide, et que vous avez fait les arrangemens pour m'envoyer le dernier detachement dans le courant du semaine prochaine. Comme expliquer toute cela.

Vous devez aussi scavoir, que, loin que d'etre consulté on ne daigna pas même communiquer Les noms de votre choix avant l'instant de leur arrivé ni aucun autre circonstance qui leur appartient. Un espece de crasse ignorance durement imposé a un homme qui doit avoir la tutele[1] de leurs persons et la   [2] de leur education, et qui pouvoit etre a moi a plusieurs egards extrement embarressente et nuisible. La même ignorance systematique de tous les procedes de ceux que vous appelles Les Lords Commissaires, nommé, Je ne sai pas par qui, si ce n'etoit par vous Monseigneur, pour faire les nominations. Je n'ai Jamais vu leur Commission. On ne m'avoit même constate l'existence d'un tel commission. Jegnore profondement, leur regles, leurs pouvoirs. Les Instructions qu'ils ont recu de Part de Gouvernement. On ne m'a donner aucun avis ni de le Lieu ni de le temps de leurs seances. Pas un Copie de leur procés verbal ou de leur Journeaux. Pas le nom de leur Secretaire a qui on peut addresser des requedes. Si J'etois instruit d'aucun de ces circonstances J'eus eté en Etat, de leur faire quelques Representations qui leur pouvent etre de quelque utilité. Les Concurrens   [3] dussent etre avertis de toutes[4] ces particularites[5] afin qui puissent faire valoir Leurs pretensions respectives devant leur Bureau. S'il n'y a pas un tel Bureau (ce que je soupconne) pourquoi toujours mocquer les Gens en parlent sans cesse des decisions et des nominations de Lords Commissaires. Mais quelque il soit que cet Bureau il n'y a plus place pour leur deliberations.

Tous les procedes formels, et la langage tenue, par vous, et par Messieurs de la Committé, suppose l'existence actuelle d'un tel Commission, et de telles Commissaires. Mais dans les Lettres avec lesquelles vous avez la Bonté de m'honnorér il n'y a question de Lords Commissaires. Vous ne me parles que de Marquis de Buckingham; et de lui seul; qui examine tout et decide de tout sans partager la deliberation avec personne.

Il n'y un homme qui fait mon homage plus sincere aux Talens et aux Lumieres du Lord Buckingham que je ne fais. Mais s'il vous n'avez pas m'en assuré J'aurois beaucoup de Difficultes en me persuadent que

---

[1] MS: tusele
[2] There is a blank in the MS at this point. The missing word is probably 'charge'.
[3] There is a blank in the MS at this point.
[4] MS: de toutes de toutes   [5] MS: particularitesies

lui seul[1] dans son Chateau de Stowe,[2] eloigné en   [3] de Soixante Miles de Londres decide, et fait son choix definitif, sur peutetre un centaine de memoires, sur le simple extraits de piece sans consulter personne, sans se profitant de lumieres d'aucun Anglois, d'aucun Francois, pas même Monseigneur de Votres? Si J'avois l'honneur d'etre dans sa place Je ne refusera pas de vous consulter et si J'aurois demandé cet marque de votre amitié Je serois peu content d'un refus de votre part.

S'il my Lord Buckingham vous a commandé de rapporter tous les Applications a lui et S'il eut reclamé le droit d'un Juge, et s'il vous a defendu de vous en meler en aucune maniere, il n'y a vous blamer. On est oblige tres souvent a de soumettre, et de faire place son propre Jugement a des gens puissants dont la protection   [4] de plus ordinaire de me faire avertir du cet arrangement fait dans une affaire en lequel Je suis assez interessé. Mais S'il au contraire il etoit de votre part tout a fait volontaire toutes les recommendations, toutes les rejections sont aussi   [5] a vous, si vous L'avois faites en votre propre person et sous votre propre nom. Dans quelle Page de quelle ecriture, dans quelle piece trouves vous ecrit que le choix des Objets de cette ecole devoit etre attribue exclusivement au My Lord Buckingham, homme a tous les egards digne de toute consideration mais non pas designié dans une aucune piece pour cette office. Ce ne fut que apres votre interpretation, mais comme vous devois vous rappeller, que J'ai protesté au commencement contre cette attribution exclusive a aucune Anglois, dans tous les questions qui pourroient s'elever a l'egard d'interpretation d'une ecriture on Doit avoir secours a celui qui en etoit l'auteur. Je pris plusieurs fois la Liberté de vous marquer que quand J'ai sollicite ces personages distingues de notre province de l'interresser dans mon interference— ce fut par deux causes et ce deux seuls 1° pour assurer une protection pour l'ecole et si par hazard, la nouveaute de la chose pourroit exite quelque fermentation dans l'esprit populaire 2° pour marquer la disposition que J'avois de me rendre responsable dans toutes les manieres possibles pour l'applications de denieres du Roi fidelement a ses objets. Pour les engager je leur faisois toutes les honnetes possibles. Et J'ai parlai de moi même avec toute la humilité qui me convient et sur le ton qui m'est d'usage, quand Je ne suis forcée prendre un autre. Cet facon de s'exprimer n'est jamais pris pour une disqualification complete. On ne fait pas des arrangemens pour l'execution de leurs propres projets, pour entierement aneantir le projetteurs. Aussi ces Messieurs n'en auroit pas

[1] MS: sont   [2] The Marquess's seat in Buckinghamshire.
[3] There is a blank in the MS at this point.
[4] A sentence seems to have been left out at this point.
[5] There is a blank in the MS at this point.

la moindre idée—avec la Bonte de le faire entrer dans leurs esprits[1] aussi
il n'ont pas fait a moi aucune suggestion de l'exclusion que vous avez
imaginé. Je serois disposé a ramper dans la poussiere et de me mettre
sous les pieds de tout le monde pour avoir le moiens de faire mon devoir.
Mais de se degrader, seulement pour se rendre inhabile de ses devoirs—
voila ce que je ne veux pas. J'ai renoncé a toute recommendation a
l'etablisement, dont J'avoir la fortune d'etre, en quelque sens, le
fondateur, pourquoi cette abnegation?[2] Ce ne fut pas pour la donner
exclusivement a un autre Anglois, quelque soit sa respectabilité mais
pour on donner l'exemple aux autres des mes compatriotes de S'abstenir
de la decision de donner sa soulagement aux Malheureux Francois (a
vous principalement) de les permettre de decider de leur propre sort et
de Jouer une role dans leur propres affaires. Voila, ce que vous ai
expliqué dans des termes les plus clairs, et les plus precises quoique
toujours dans le mauvais Jargon de qui je me sers[3] dans une Lettre que
J'eus l'honneur de vous ecrire.[4] L'anneantisement total de tous les
Francois, de tous les Anglois, sans excepter vous même, dans cette
affaire, est votre seul ouvrage.

Si vous etes Monseigneur, realement reduit a la situation d'un 'simple
Comis' a une situation si peu digne de vous, ce n'est par moi que vous
etes ainsi humilie. Vous n'etes pas un Commis de mon Bureau. Je n'ai
Jamais eu la presumption folle et ridicule que de vous traiter en homme
fait seulement pour aposteller des Lettres ou pour transmettre des
memoires. J'ai vous[5] voulu traiter en ami; en ami intime, et confidential.
J'ai parlé de vous (il est comme de tous ceux qui Je suis connu)[6] comme
un de premiere homme de notre siecle. Homme probe, ferme, eclaire,
d'une tete admirablement conformé digne non etre consulter pour des
chetifs etres comme moi, mais bien par plus puissans souverains de
monde. Je n'etois pas obligée par aucune devoir ni par aucune principe
de Politique de me concerter avec vous ni dans cette affaire ni dans
aucun autre. En vous toujours consultant Je n'etois pas guidé par devoir
ni par politique, mais par choix par inclination, par respect. Quand par
hazard quelque difference d'opinion s'eleva entre nous J'ai etois toujours
pret de le terminer amicable, par la voye d'accomadement, par des
concessions mutuels. Voila la Fazon de proceder les amis. Ce ne sont pas
les ordres données par un chef de Bureau a ces Comis. Mais de vous etre[7]
tellement degradé, que pensez vous de ma situation, a lequel Je suis
reduit par vos menées.[8] Je n'ai pas cet honneur la que d'etre Commis. On

---

[1] MS: exprit   [2] MS: abregation?   [3] MS: serre
[4] The letter is missing.   [5] MS: vou
[6] Perhaps Burke means 'as all those with whom I am acquainted know full well'.
[7] MS: etes   [8] MS: menies

ne se comporter pas envers moi comme a un domestique de tant soit peu de Confiance. Rien ne me communiqué—J'ai ecrit au Lord Buckingham[1] lui priant[2] de me donner un liste et une Certificate de son selection des Enfans—Adieu Monseigneur

&ca

25 May 1796   EDMD BURKE
    Monseigneur
        Eveque de Leon

To the BISHOP OF ST-POL-DE-LÉON— [post 25 May 1796]

Source: Copy in Fitzwilliam MSS (Northampton), A. XIX. 10.
Endorsed (by Burke): Copy of 2d Letter | to the Bishop of Leon.

Burke tells the Bishop in this letter: 'Jai ecrit au My lord Buckingham pour son autorisation. J'ai vous ecrite aussi en tres long detail...'. These are doubtless references to the letters of [24 May] and 25 May (see above, pp. 16–20, 23–8).

Monseigneur,

Il y'a longtemps, que j'ai été pret a recevoir le nombre pour lequel je me tiens, sur ma propre proposition, engagé au Gouvernement. Par le retard qui m'est devenu necessaire, je ne veux priver aucun de son etat, ni de L'avantage de sa fortune. Mais comme j ai été averti, pour la premiere fois, par votre lettre du vingt Courant,[3] que vous ne vous melez pas dans aucune maniere avec des appointmens; et que vous n'etes pas plus q'un simple commis, sans choix, sans volonté, sans capacité deliberative, je suis obligé d'etre un peu plus sur mes gardes. Apres la decouverte que vous m'avez fait que vous avez remis purement et simplement toutes les recommandations au le Marquis of Buckingham, vous devois etre bien sensible, a la mine ridicule, absurde, et pire encore, que je ferois aupres de la Tresorerie en leur demandant L'argent pour l'usage de gens qui n'etoient pas nommer ni par moi-même, ni par aucun autre, de qui j ai été autorisé, dans aucune maniere directe et reguliere, de les recevoir. Le Marquis de Buckingham n'a pas signifié a moi que les nominations doivent être de lui. Les jeuns persons que jusqu'ici j ai reçu, j ai pensé d'etre de vous et de la commité Francoise, Mais depuis que vous m'avez dit a mon tres grand ettonnement, le contraire, vous en conviendrois Monseigneur, qu'il est devenu absolument necessaire a ma sureté et ma reputation d'avoir ses ordres expresses et reguliers—et de ne pas prendre ses idees par des voyes indirectes ou intermediaires

[1] See above, pp. 16–20.   [2] MS: prent
[3] Burke certainly means the Bishop's letter of the 21st.

quoique elles soient, comme elles sont effectivement, les plus respectables. Il n'y'a pas il est vrai aucune mode prescrit par Gouvernement
pour ces recommendations. Toute cela, comme tout qui regarde le
detail de mon petit entreprise doit etre arranger, selon nos idees de la
convenance entre moi et les personages distingués qui ont bien voulus
apres ma solicitation de m'aider de leurs conseils et de leurs protection.
Mais dans toutes les affaires on doit suivre quelque Methode. On ne doit
pas recevoir les ordres de ceux qui ne veulent pas avouer leur deliberation
ou leur election; au moins, qui ne produisent quelque procuration,
ou quelque autorité equivalent, de tout de leur principal. Je suis bien
disposé sans chicanant a L'egard de leurs pouvoires, de recevoir les
appointmens de toutes personages respectables qu'il veulent avouer leur
capacité deliberative, comme assurant de la protection pour ses Malheureux Orphelins de La Noblesse Francoise. C'est la seule chose que
j'ai au coeur. Jai ecrit au My lord Buckingham pour son autorisation.
J'ai vous ecrite aussi en tres long detail mes sentimens la dessus. Pour
les autres questions que vous me faites vous scavez que mes arrangemens
avec le gouvernement n'etoient que pour Soixante. Ce que jai demandé,
jai grande peur sera insuffisant pour cet nombre et que la difference se
portera sur mes epaules. Nous parlerons plus a notre aise, d'un Augmentation du nombre, quand le gouvernement vouloit bien M'assigner
quelque fonds, suffisans ou insuffisans pour L'entretien du nombre
accordé, ce qui n'est pas encore fait dans aucune maniere claire ou
precise. Jusqu'ici, quoique je me nourisse des esperances on ne me pas
donné un Shilling. Jai soutenu L'enterprise par mon propre argent et
par mon proper credit seuls et je ne me trouve *pas* peu embrassé par de
depense qui est beaucoup au dessus de mes forces. Mais je ne suis pas
degouté ni par la depense, ni le travail, ni par d'autre choses bien plus
facheuse tandis que *je* pourrois demontrer mon zele pour la cause. Ces
enfans sont pour moi la plus douce de toute les consolations.

Avec L attachement la plus respectueuse
toujour votre pauvre ami
EDM BURKE

The MARQUESS OF BUCKINGHAM *to* EDMUND BURKE— 26, 29 *May* 1796

Source: Fitzwilliam MSS (Northampton).
Addressed: The Right Hble | Mr Burke | Beaconsfield.
Franked: London May thirtieth | 1796 | Grenville.
Postmarked: MA|30|96 FREE.

MS torn.

Stowe
May 26th 1796

My dear Sir

The very heavy illness of Mr J. Grenville[1] has thrown upon me such a load of correspondence relative to his re-election,[2] that I have had very little time on my hands; and have neglected longer than I ought to acknowledge the very cordial satisfaction which I derive from reading your very interesting narrative of all that is already done by your exertions, and of all that still occupies your mind of intended acts of benevolence to your unfortunate Protegés. I am persuaded that you know these sentiments of respect and admiration are very sincere, and that I am checked in the detail of them only by the consideration of offending a delicacy of mind which is inseparable from the feelings and principles under which you have formed this humane and excellent institution. The accounts which you are so good as to give me of the manners, the characters, and the conduct of *your* boys are highly interesting; and I am sorry that you should have met with the slightest disappointment in the character or opinions of the persons first recommended to you by the Bishop of St Pol. We both know his indefatigable zeal for every good work, and in his recommendation of preceptors he could have no other object, than that which you share with him. The *decision* however must remain with you, and I have no doubt whatsoever, but that it has been made much to the advantage of the institution: As to an assistant tutor who may instruct the boys in the English language and may be a sort of companion to them, you will I doubt not find many ecclesiasticks now sufficiently masters of our language to meet your wishes: I have frequently been much surprized by the progress which several who have fallen under my eye have made in this attainment: Your object in giving it to your boys is certainly well imagined, whether we view them as destined to return to France, or to be domiciliated as English; and this I always understood to be your original idea in forming this establishment. I need not say how impatiently my wife and I look forward to the moment in which we shall have so much to admire: The principles which have suggested to you this meritorious undertaking, the zeal which you have given to it, the emotions which such a scene in all its branches and bearings must create will certainly contribute essentially to our gratification, and (I trust) to our improvement.

My time has been so repeatedly broken in upon by the multitude of letters and visitors which have crouded upon me in consequence of

---

[1] Buckingham's cousin James Grenville (1742–1825), later (20 October 1797) 1st Baron Glastonbury; M.P. for Buckinghamshire from 1790 until 1797.
[2] At the General Election of 1796.

Mr Praeds advertisement,[1] that I have already lost two days[2] having written thus far at four different times: My apprehension lest[3] I may again be interrupted must be my excuse for answering more shortly the most important part of your letter which respects the choice of subjects: I must in the first place beg to assure you that so far from considering the list as *filled and settled*, the entire list always was directed to be submitted to your controul, direction, and choice; to admit and to reject entirely as you may think proper: and the Bishop of St Pol clearly understands that upon this subject, I only wished to suggest to you those names which appeared Primâ facie to have pretensions from the memorials digested and certified by the French committee, but whose pretensions as to appearance manner character and even comparative merit must be referred to your decision. I understood that from the purest motives you wished the selection might not *originate* with you; the Bishop of St Pol felt the same (if not stronger) difficulties, and has not directly or indirectly given an intimation of preference in favour of any one, save in two instances where Mr Windham upon publick grounds desired that particular circumstances might be stated in favour of Monr de Choiseuils children,[4] and of another whose Uncle (Mr de Frottage)[5] now at the head of the Norman insurgents claimed particular attention. The French committee sent me the list without names, and though I afterwards desired to see the names before I sent to the Bishop the list of boys upon whom I always imagined you would entirely decide, yet I did not see reasons for altering any opinion which I had formed upon the pretensions as stated in the memorials: They are all strangers to me; in the selection and the names for your consideration I could have no idea of patronage where I had no friendships to consult, and no thanks to expect. But I really meant to do that which I thought most correctly met your ideas and from which no possible inconvenience can arise; for if you reject the entire list, be assured my dear Sir that I shall not only be content, but even gratified, for I shall then be sure that the selection will be made upon grounds better considered and more accurately weighed than either my time or my means allow to me. I am again interrupted and I fear my letter will be strangely incoherent. I find

[1] William Praed (1747–1833) of Tyringham, Buckinghamshire, M.P. for St Ives, had inserted an advertisement in *The Times* of 24 May hinting that, after sounding the feelings of the freeholders, he might offer himself as a candidate for Buckinghamshire against the two sitting members.

[2] Presumably this means that the Marquess is writing this passage on 28 May.

[3] MS: least

[4] Charles-Antoine-Étienne, Marquis de Choiseul-Beaupré (b. 1739), had eight children. Two of them, Eugène and Xavier, were at the school in 1796. A third son, Octave, attended later (Add. MS 37,868, fols 161–2; 45,723, fols 63–4. See also vol. VIII, 460.).

[5] Buckingham probably meant Marie-Pierre-Louis, Comte de Frotté (1755–1800). In 1795 he led a Royalist rising in the Norman Bocage.

since my list was returned to the Bishop that I am supposed not to have
attended sufficiently to the claims of some very respectable individuals
from some of whom representations have been transmitted to me,
particularly the case of a most respectable magistrate[1] who stands first
in the Class of the Magistracy, and who appears to have indeed very
strong claims; but as the Committee have expressly stated in their
report that this gentleman receives ten guineas per month in lieu of the
small Committee allowance, I still imagined the pretensions of one of his
brethren at the bar[2] with *five* children were preferable. I mention this
that you may be satisfied of the principles on which I endeavoured to
form my judgement; and that no improper motives were ever suggested
to me from any quarter whatsoever (for I have uniformly put by every
private sollicitation) in the selection which is to be presented to you for
your examination and decision: As to the children of the first and second
classes they were all (and as I understood in consequence of your wishes)
sent down as soon as they could be collected; for with respect to them no
difficulty could arise, save as with respect to their characters or morals of
which you alone could be to judge. I trust that this explanation will
leave your mind fully at ease: I know all that the good Bishop feels
towards you of regards, of attention, and of respect; I know likewise my
dear Sir that I am incapable of doing anything that could fail towards
you in any of those points: In truth I can have no object in it, but to see
that plant flourish in the hands of him who has sowed, who has fostered,
and who I trust will live to raise it, and to shelter himself from his evening clouds under the branches of it: The duties which I prescribe to myself are *those only* in which you tell me that I can assist your views; and
be assured that the wishes which I entertain towards these unhappy
victims to their religious and civil duties, are warmly urged and
stimulated on this occasion by the sentiments which you have permitted
me to express towards you. Lady Buckingham joins me ⟨in⟩ anxious
wishes for Mrs Burke's health, and in thanking you for allowing us to
break in upon you for a day, as soon as I am set at liberty.

  I have the honour to be with the truest regards and esteem
    Dear Sir
      Your very faithful and Obedient Servant
        NUGENT BUCKINGHAM.

May 29th 1796

P.S. I shall take the liberty of sending you sixty wastecoats and breeches
of white ticking which will be very good summer wear for your boys;

---

[1] Not identified.
[2] Not identified.

they have the County button which you may change if you disapprove it.
I likewise send some light black stocks which always are clean and give
an air of neatness.

To WALKER KING—[28 *May* 1796]

Source: Fitzwilliam MSS (Sheffield).

Burke complains of having heard 'not a word yet from the Marquess' and
dates this 'Saturday morn!!'. Buckingham's letter of 26, 29 May was postmarked 30 May, a Monday. Burke is therefore writing to Walker King on the
28th.

My dear Walker   I know you are busy enough. But I remember a
play of a very rough Kind we had at school, The Boys heaping each other
on some unfortunate Lad, which they called 'more sacks on the Mill'.
I must therefore throw this one sack more on your patient shoulders.
The Treasury talk of giving me a Warrant next month. Good as to the
thousand pound for the outfit.[1] I shall charge them no Interest for the
money I have been out of Pocket. But for the current monthly payments,
they must not take their commencement from the *time of the warrant*,
for that would be, nor more nor less, than a plain downright Robbery.
For I have been, near two months, very considerably at expence for the
Current; The Servants were taken; and the Masters were down very
early—The mans wages begin from the 25th of March last. There are
now and have been for some time twenty six Boys who arrived in three
divisions—So there are now, at meat and drink, three Masters, Three
Maid Servants, besides persons occasionally taken in to wash; one Man
servant; and the Boys; making in all thirty three persons. Therefore you
must take care to have the monthly allowance take its date from the 25th
of March or the first of April at furthest. Be so good to remember that
the allowance is—deducted from the Committee one Guinea per
month per Child—being the allowance, when my proposal was given in;
and fifty pound a month superadded—and I believe, when you consider that for this I shall have to feed, cloathe, and provide Books and
every sort of necessaries for sixty Boys, four or five Masters and ushers,
and a superadded servant, when all is full, you will hardly think, that
with my oeconomy, which I flatter myself is of the very best consistent
with abundance, that if Government does not favour me as much as
possible I shall be ruined by my enterprise. Pray represent this strongly
at the Treasury. I will not consent to begin at June—refuse the money
rather. A Storm of applications is come upon me. The good Bishop

[1] That is, reimbursing the money Burke had advanced for furnishing the school
buildings; see below, p. 44.

without asking my leave has given the whole Cream to Lord Buckingham—and left me the sour Whey. He has filled up the whole Number. He writes me, that he is only a Clerk; has had no share in the appointments—but that Lord Buck[ingha]m has decided on them.—Who desired him to do this? The number is filled. He has sent me the List. I am ready to receive the Boys: But Since he disclaims the appointment I must have somebody to own it—The Letters Nagle takes with this will explain the difficulty[1]—not a word yet from the Marquess. Our best loves to Mrs King. Adieu.

Yours ever
EDM BURKE

Saturday morn!!

The BISHOP OF ST-POL-DE-LÉON *to* EDMUND BURKE— 28 *May* 1796

Source: Fitzwilliam MSS (Northampton).
Addressed: to the Right Hone Edd Burke | Beaconsfield.
Postmarked: MA|28|96|D.

Mon cher et tres cher monsieur

Chaque ligne de votre lettre[2] m'a sensiblement affligé. Il est bien triste pour moi avec le desir de ne faire que ce qui vous etoit agreable d'avoir fait sans le vouloir et sans le savoir tout ce qui vous déplait. Vous m'avez si souvent déclaré que vous ne vouliez vous mêler d'aucune nomination que je n'ai pas du en douter et je ne l'ai pas pu dés que vous m'avez Renvoié toutes les demandes et toutes les sollicitations qui vous etoient adressées.[3] Que vous ai je Répondu que je les ferois passer fidelement au marquis Buckingham c'etoit le moment de me dire que vous ne vouliez pas qu'il s'en mêlat et si vous me l'aviez dit certainement vous auriez fait toutes les nominations car le comité francois m'avoit bien declaré qu'il ne s'en chargeroit pas et je ne suis pas assez depourvu de jugement pour prendre sur moi la charge de tous les Reproches et de toute la haine de ceux que je n'aurois pas pu choisir. Comme personne ne m'a d'obligation de son admission personne n'a de Reproche à me faire de son exclusion, n'ayant fait comme je vous l'ai marqué que l'office d'un fidel comis en me conformant àu Reglement imprimé[4] dont

---

[1] They are missing.   [2] Presumably Burke's letter of 25 May; see above, pp. 23–8.
[3] MS: addresséss.
[4] *Modèle de demandes de places à l'école royale établie à Penn* stated that the names of applicants, together with the service records of their fathers or near relations, should be sent to the Treasurer of the French Committee in London. Applications were to be certified by three French gentlemen whose quality was to be certified by two members of the French Committee in London or Jersey. Boys were to be admitted between the ages of seven and fourteen, and those who were receiving aid from the Committee in London or Jersey should continue to do so. Sixty boys in all were to be admitted on the Government establishment and only children who had received 'la petite vérole' were eligible.

je joins icy le texte contre lequel vous n'aviez fait aucune declamation lorsqu'il vous a été communiqué. C'est bien meme qui m'avez dit que les duc de portland, lord grenville et le marquis Buckingham etoient les *trusty* de votre etablissement. Ce n'est qu'avec Beaucoup de difficulté, apres plusieurs Refus de leur part que j'ay determiné messieurs du comité francois à faire en commun avec moi l'extrait tres detaillé et tres fidele de tout ce qu'il y avoit de favorable aux candidats dans leurs demand et j'ay tout passé comme je vous l'ai marqué au marquis Buckingham je ne me suis pas permis la moindre Reflexions pas meme en faveur de mes parents qui se trouvent n'etre point admis. Je n'ai pas cru me degrader en Rien en ne faisant dans cette partie comme je la fais dans Beaucoup d'autres la fonction de simple Rapporteur, ne pouvant pas prendre sur moi seul la charge que le comité trouvoit[1] trop d'inconvenient à prendre sur lui meme. J'avoue de tres bonne foi que je n'ai vu que vous ou le marquis comme un des *trusty* qui put faire la nomination. Vous vous y etes constamment Refusé je n'ai pas cru que vous ne vouliez pas que je la lui emporté d'autant que si vous voulez bien vous le Rappeler lorsqu'il à eté question des enfants de la 1ere et 2de classe qui sont partis les premiers je vous dis dans le tems que le marquis Buckingham avoit ete d'avis qu'ils fussent tous Receu de preference en consequence ils vous ont ete envoiés et vous n'y avez Rien opposé. Il est fort malheureux pour moi d'avoir si mal interpreté vos intentions et avec des vues aussi simples et aussi droites d'avoir fait tout de travers. Par la conduite que j'avois tenu j'etois assuré qu'aucun de mes compatriotes n'auroit à se plaindre de moi et je ne m'attendois pas que toutes les peines que j'avois prises n'aboutiroient qu'a eprouver votre mécontentement qui m'est infiniment sensible de la part de quelqu'un que je suis si eloigné de vouloir désobligér et que j'honnorerai et aimerai toujours quoiqu'il maltraite Beaucoup son fidel ami

† L'Eveque de Leon

28. mai 96

To the Bishop of St-Pol-de-Léon—30 [*May*] 1796

Source: Copy (in Jane Burke's hand) in Fitzwilliam MSS (Northampton), A. XIX. 7.

The 'June' of Burke's date-line is an error. This letter was certainly written on receipt of Buckingham's letter of 26, 29 May, the contents of which Burke communicates to the Bishop.

Voici entre nous deux, Monseigneur, une bien etrange controverse! Je veux accepter, comme de vous, sans demander d'autre chose que de

---

[1] MS: touvoit

votre consentiment, soixante enfans a nourrir et a elever, dans la maniere la plus honorable, au depense du Roi. Vous niez fortement qu'ils sont, ou de vous, ou de votre choix. Cependant vous insistez, que je les reçusse. Vous dites qu'ils sont de My lord Buckingham; Qu'il les a choisis; et que, de droit, leur election doit etre en lui. J'ecris a My lord Buckingham pour nous tirer de cette difficulté. Lord Buckingham me repond, dans les termes les plus honnêtes, et Les plus polis, mais clairs et distincts que lui n'a pas fait aucune arrangement definitif; qu'il n'avoit pas agi, qu'apres une liste a lui envoyé; et que le choix dans le dernier resort dependoit toujours, et qu'il devoit en effet, toujours dependre, a moi, et a moi seul. Il dit qu'il est a moi de rayer tous les noms de les etablir ou de les changer a mon gré. Il a raison.

Il est tems Monseigneur, que cette discussion, prete a devenir un peu ridicule, finisse. Elle est donc fini. J'accepte, purement et simplement, votre liste[1] sans y ajouter, ni oter, ni changer un seul article. C'est, j'avoue, par pure necessité que j'agis dans cette maniere, pour qu'un[2] etablissement, que je crois utile ne soit pas arête par aucune chose qui me touche personnelment. Les enfans de la Noblesse Francoises, desavoués partout, seront reconnus par moi, Je les accepte. Comme on rejette le choix sur moi; Votre Liste sera de mon choix. Les parens de ces jeunes innocens, sont avertis que Le sort fortuné est tiré par eux. Ce ne seroit moi, que de Les renvoyer[3] a des nouveaux proces. Monsieur Nagle passera chez vous, pour les recevoir, mais Monseigneur, si vous craignez, qu'en les recevant chez vous, ils seroient reputés d'etre de votre choix il fera un arrangement pour les rassembler ailleurs.

Peu de paroles en reponse au dernier lettre dont vous m'avez honoré.[4] Vous M'ecrites, comme j'eus change mes intentions; et que je voulois avoir les nominations a moi. C'est ce que je n'avois jamais dit, ni jamais pensé.

Mon exclusion, comme vous scavez mieux que personne etoit volontaire, fait pour donner un exemple a tous nous autres *Anglois* de nous abstenir entierement de toute nomination, et bien meme de toute recommendation; et de ne reserver a aucun des Anglois interessés dans cette affaire, que, dans le cas de difference enterminable entre les *François*; une decision en dernier resort.

Vous etes bien instruit, Monseigneur, de la distinction qui existe essentielment entre une exclusion volontaire, motivé, etablis selon les raisons de convenance, de prudence, de Moderation, et d'un exclusion forcé, formel, et de droit. La primiere peut nous honorer, L'autre est

---

[1] Enclosed with the Bishop's letter of 23 May (MS at Northampton).
[2] MS: qu'n   [3] MS: ronvier
[4] The preceding letter.

flettrissante. Vous etes toujours MonSeigneur d'avis que mon abnegation[1] seroit pris dans le dernier Sens.

Si j'eus m imaginé que les enfans de la France n'etoient pas sous la Tutele des François, je ne me refuserois pas au plaisir d'etre entre les recommendans; et de ne reserver pas a moi que le triste devoir de donner le refus a une foule de sollicitations[2] les plus vives et les plus pressantes. Mais cela est passé; nous n'en parlons plus. Pour conserver votre esteem, qui je vous en assure, est a moi, d'un prix infini, fermons a jamais toute discussions toute consultations. Jai L'honneur D'etre avec la plus grande consideration, et avec L'attachement la plus respecteuse

Monseigneur
Votre tres Humble
et tres fidele Serviteur
EDMD BURKE

Beaconsfield
June 30th 1796

STATEMENT CONCERNING ADMISSIONS TO THE FRENCH SCHOOL AT PENN

Source: Fitzwilliam MSS (Sheffield), Bk10*d*.
MS in the hand of Edward James Nagle but corrected by Burke.

In view of the misunderstanding which had arisen over applications for admission to the school, Burke drew up the following statement.

The Person, who has sollicitted with Government an Allowance, to enable him to open and to support a School for the Education of a limited number of the Children of Gentlemen suffering by the present usurpation and Tyranny in France, has within a few days received many Applications, and from very respectable Quarters, for Places in that School.

To prevent any further trouble to the persons concerned, it is necessary, that the true nature of the Business should be understood, concerning which certain erroneous and exaggerated Ideas are gone abroad.

This School, (tho' there is abundant reason from the general and invariable generosity and goodness of Government to be assured, it will receive support) has no regular or formal Establishment whatever. It were to be wished indeed, that things were otherwise circumstanced.—

---

[1] MS: abregation   [2] MS: de sollicitations de solicitations

37

But, for the present We are not in the least authorized to call it a Royal School, or a permanent public Establishment of any description. It has no *charter* or *Letters Patent*. It has nothing resembling a Corporate Capacity. There is no Commission for its Administration; nor, of course, any *Lords Commissioners*, or any other *Commissioners*, with any Powers to act in any Part of its Affairs; nor has Government made *any distribution* of Authority nor given any orders or directions, or any written, or even verbal instruction whatever relative to its conduct from the first proposition to this Hour.

The whole is nothing more, or better, than the attempt of a private person, more full of Zeal, than of means, to serve the meritorious French. Some few persons of Distinction in the County, where the School is placed, have, (in *common conversation*, and wholly in their *private* capacity), been pleased to manifest kind and protecting intentions to the Undertaker and Undertaking. In *all* this there is nothing *Official*. There is no meeting; no common Deliberation whatever. The Undertaker, like every person who shall receive public money, is, and is alone, accountable to the Treasury for the Just Application of the money which he shall receive, according to his own engagement.

The Solliciter and Undertaker of this Business has abstained strictly from any recommendation of his own, or any decision upon the recommendation of others; in an expectation, that the Chiefs of the French Nation, as its natural Representatives, should settle the whole business amongst themselves; except, upon discussions not easily terminated; in which, the necessity of the case might demand an English decision, in that extremity, and in that last resort only. He has been long of Opinion, that the French have not had that importance in their own Affairs which he desired. He has always thought that a standing French Committee, of the weightiest people of that Nation alone communicating with Government would be of great use to them and to the public cause. But whether right or wrong in this Idea, his voluntary exclusion of himself was totally founded upon it: otherwise he would not have denied to himself, in his own undertaking, that satisfaction which was open to every other English Gentleman.

The whole number of the Children for which this Person had engaged himself to Government, has been filled up, without any communication with him, relative to the claims of any of the Candidates, and without any previous notice that it would be filled up at a given time.

He does not state this, to impute blame to anyone or to avert blame from himself, but merely to explain a Situation. It became[1] impossible

---

[1] MS: beccame

for him (whatever his Powers in strictness may be) to open the Business to further discussions and competitions, without hardship on those Parents, who had assurances given to them of their having been nominated, by what they *were taught* to consider as a regular *Official* Authority.

The Undertaker has therefore accepted them exactly as they stand on the List transmitted to him; in confidence, that the persons in that List had been selected with discretion. He has provided carriages for the children; and has prevailed on a friend of his[1] to take care of them to his House, where he has entertained them, according to his means, with all the respect which is so abundantly due to their Relations and Parents; and from thence has had them delivered to their Preceptor on whom he has had the honor to wait, in order to receive their commands, almost every day.

The undertaker has no sort of authority to declare or any hope held out to him by Government, that any new Support, or new accommodation will be given to him for a greater number than that, for which he had at first sollicited.

To the MARQUESS OF BUCKINGHAM—1 *June* 1796
Source: MS Morgan Library.

My dear Lord,

I am extremely happy, that I have an opportunity of congratulating your Lordship on the vanishing of the transient trouble, that you had from Mr Praeds inconsiderate attempt.[2] I confess, I was but little alarmed at it, as I found that it caused very little, if any, sensation, in this side of the County. But in all Cases of this kind, every sort of precautionary measure is wise and proper. I hope to hear that Mr Grenvilles indisposition is of as little moment, and that it has terminated, as to his general health with an equally prosperous Event.

As to the little Business of the School which broke in upon you so unseasonably, I hope in future it will be less troublesome. I did easily conceive the difficulty not to say the impossibility, that in your Lordships situation, and at a time like the present, you could sit as a judge upon an hundred or more petty claims. Many of the Children, except those in the very first class, may be found in circumstances exactly

---

[1] Burke is probably referring to Edward James Nagle.
[2] See above, p. 31. The sitting members for Buckinghamshire, William Henry Cavendish Bentinck (1768–1854), styled Marquess of Titchfield, eldest son of the Duke of Portland, and James Grenville (see above, p. 30), had been returned (*The Times*, 28 May).

similar, or nearly so; and the option between them must, of course, be discretionary. If your Lordship found the final choice not very easy whilst the deliberation was open, what must my situation be to be liable to all sorts of sollicitation, when the discussion is in effect closed. My choice is indeed easy; but my condition is not over pleasant. It is true, that your Lordship is so indulgent to my poor Judgment as to leave the rejection of each or all of them to me. But when the Parents and relations of these poor children, have without the smallest communication in any way whatever with me, been apprised, that a choice is already made in their favour, and that some of them have been actually called from abroad, I should consider myself as inflicting a cruel hardship on them to open their situation to a new Enquiry and to a new competition. From the necessity, arising from the Equity of the Case, I take the list exactly as it is—though I am afraid I shall incurably offend some persons whom I am very desirous of pleasing. I had rather submit to this inconvenience, as well as to every indignity with which my friend the Bishop may choose to treat me, than to suffer the march of this Business, which I consider, as far as it goes, to be usefull to be impeded. As far as my scanty means would allow, we are prepared for the comfortable reception of the whole number. My consolation is that no Choice can be very wrong; because none can be received whose parents in some way or other are not meritorious and indigent. However such as the matter is, of the whole sixty there is not one of my recommendation. I have received[1] them in my house as successively they came, as the Children of the people of the first distinction of the Kingdom, and my best friends; but with rather something of greater attention; and I shall do so—though all are unknown to me.

Laying it down as a maxim, that this education is [to] be, at least one good half, if not three parts, English, I think I was guilty of a great Errour in the beginning, by not putting an Englishman at the head of it: But as any material change would have its inconvenience too, I acquiesce in the first arrangement; and endeavour to supply it as well as I can. One of the Gentlemen given to me by the Bishop of Leon does speak English, (as by the Courtesy of England we call it) that is as well as almost any of them; which is next to nothing at all. The Comte de Serrent, (so unfortunately lost)[2] spoke it the best of any[3] of the late refugees. He wrote it too very unexceptionably: But I never saw one, no not one, who could

---

[1] MS: recived

[2] Armand-Sigismond-Félicité-Marie de Sérent, Maréchal de camp (b. 1762), and his brother Armand-Léon-Bernardin (b. 1764), the only sons of the Marquis de Sérent (see below, p. 98), were killed near Dol in Brittany on 16 March (A. Révérend, *Titres, anoblissements et pairies de la Restauration, 1814–30*, Paris, 1906). The elder brother visited Burke in 1793 (see vol. VII, 472).   [3] MS: of any of any

read it in Verse, or even in prose. The little infant[1] of between five and
six year old who is running about me, and entertaining me with her little
talk is more capable of teaching English, than any I have yet seen of
that Nation—and to be sure the thought of teaching English, in the
middle of England, by French is a thought I cannot entertain—nor do
I know any thing which would more displease the Parents and relations
of these interesting Creatures than the Idea of their not profiting by the
only circumstance in their Exile, which can be useful to them. To those
Parents to whom God and nature has given the disposal of all the
Possessions of value they have left, I must consider myself as primarily
responsible, even paramount to my responsibility to Government. Any
one who takes the guardianship of other peoples Children acts in Trust
for them. Those of them who understood English when they came here,
have already gone back terribly in that respect, though advancing
rapidly in all others. We hope to be able to open our Mathematical Class
next Monday[2] at farthest. The Gentleman at the head of the School,
with whom alone I have had any discussion, though certainly not the
one I should have chosen, if I had not delegated (contrary to a known
principle of Law) a Trust to another,[3] is, I must do him the Justice to
say, a conscientious, diligent, and intelligent Teacher, who omits
nothing to discharge his Duty in the very best manner. Now that he sees
the necessity of agreeing with me with whom he is to cooperate, we are
on the very best Terms possible. I could not endeavour to be better with
one of my own choice; and hitherto I think I have succeeded. Hitherto
all is well—very well—I see them almost every day; and in my dreadful
state, this is the only consolation I am capable of receiving.[4] I hope to
send your Lordship our weekly return in a post or two—I am infinitely
grateful for the protection you are pleased to give to this little undertaking, and for the partial goodness, with which you regard my feeble
endeavours.

[1] Not identified.   [2] 6 June.
[3] A trustee cannot transfer his trust: *delegatus non potest delegare.*
[4] Prior describes Burke's extraordinary devotion to the welfare of the school:
'Instances of his personal kindness and attention towards the members of the establishment and their friends, were shown in a variety of little ways, more particularly in
presents from his larder of any delicacy which it did not so much lie in their way to
procure. This very often occasioned an amusing scene to the friends of the family,
between him and his housekeeper, Mrs Webster. She, it seems, had more regard for
the credit of her master's table than for the appetites of the emigrants, and whenever
there was any thing nice in the larder, such as a haunch of venison, or game intended
for the second course, she was obliged to keep watch over the dainty, lest it should be
slily dispatched off to the "French people" by her improvident master, and her skill
and management in conducting the repast be thus called in question by his visitors.
Sometimes however he contrived to elude her vigilance, and sometimes he was caught
and disappointed. In attempting one day to send off a present of venison intended to be
dressed for company, the wary housekeeper, who was upon the alert, darted upon him
as upon a thief caught in the fact—"Sir, Sir," she cried out, fastening upon the article

41

The Wastecoats and Trowsers will be very acceptable. As yet we can make no great use of the Cravats. The Boys in all the Schools hereabouts, have their Necks open; and I thought it would be right to continue them in this way for the present year at least. All their Shirts are made in that fashion which, without considerable charge, cannot be alterd.

We shall claim Your Lordships and Lady Buckinghams promise as part of your Protection. I have the honour to be with the greatest consideration and the most entire Respect and regard

My dear Lord

Your Lordships

Most obedient

and faithful humble Servant

EDM BURKE

Beconsfield June 1. 1796.

Government has given me hopes of reimbursement and support early in this month. Otherwise truly I touch the bottom of my rescources.

To the MARQUESS OF BUCKINGHAM—2 June 1796

Source: Extract printed in *Sotheby Catalogue*, 5 July 1900, no. 132.

The impending visit of the Duc de Bourbon (see the next letter) was probably Burke's reason for writing again to the Marquess of Buckingham. A letter advertised for sale by Puttick and Simpson (20 August 1862, no. 228) is described as 'A.L.S. 2 pages 4th. June 2, 1796, begging Lord Buckingham to visit the school, referred to in the previous letter, on the same day as the Duke of Bourbon'. An extract from this letter, described as '1 1/2 pp. 4to (2 June 1796), to the Marquis of Buckingham', was later given by Sotheby's when they listed it for sale:

I congratulate you on the Event of the Election,[1] but was very sorry to hear that Mr Grenville was not able personally to attend. I cannot tell when we may be able to flatter ourselves with your and Lady Buckingham's visit to the school.

in question—"I cannot part with my haunch—I cannot indeed—I shall be ruined if I lose my haunch—we shall have nothing else fit to dress for dinner." "But my dear Mrs Webster, pray consider these poor people—" "I can consider nothing, Sir, but that we shall have no second course—give it away to French people indeed?" "But these poor people have been accustomed to such things in their own country, and for one day I think we can do without them." "Bless me, Sir, remember there are Lord and Lady—— and Mr and Mrs—— coming to dinner, and without something of this kind I shall get into shocking disgrace—No, no, Sir, I cannot part with my haunch;"— and adhering rigidly to this determination her master was at length obliged to retreat, foiled in his object' (2nd ed. II, 357-8).

[1] See above, p. 39.

Buckingham replied on 12 June (MS at Sheffield) proposing that he and Lady Buckingham should pay a visit to the school the following weekend. Their visit was paid on the weekend of 26 June; see below, p. 51.

To WILLIAM WINDHAM—2 June 1796

Source: British Museum (Add. MS 37,843, fols 105–6). Printed *Burke-Windham Correspondence*, pp. 194–5.
Addressed: Rt Honble | William Windham | &c &c &c | Westminster.
Postmarked: BEACONS|FIELD   JU|3|96|B   FREE|JU|3|96|C.

William Windham (1750–1810) had long been a friend and disciple of Burke.

My dear friend,

Thanks to the good part of Norwich.[1] I think it was the only election in which I felt a real Interest. It was at least the first and deepest Interest I felt. I have now only to tell you that the D. of Bourbon[2] has signified his pleasure, that he will come hither to see our School on Monday.[3] He dines here, and goes away that Night after his Jaunt to Penn—which will be in the morning. If you could come hither on Sunday night, and go with them in the morning to see Penn it would be best of all; I do not insist on your returning with them. Mrs Crewe[4] is here; and tells me she has engaged you for Monday. So you must not tell her of this sollicitation. They were to have been here tomorrow; but they have put it off till the day I mention. Perhaps Woodford[5] may come with you. With my best congratulations on a really important event

ever most truly Yours
EDM BURKE

Beconsfield June 2, 1796

What the Devil Fox and Horne joined! and Government without another to run at them! I should not wonder if they carried it.[6]

[1] Windham with 1159 votes and Henry Hobart (1738–99) with 1622 votes were returned for the new Parliament which met on 27 September. The other Norwich candidate, Richard Hanbury Gurney (c. 1784–1854), received 1076 votes.
[2] Louis-Henri-Joseph de Bourbon-Condé, Duc de Bourbon (1756–1830), emigrated to England in 1789.
[3] 6 June.   [4] Mrs John Crewe; see below, p. 76.
[5] See above, p. 11.
[6] At the General Election there were three candidates for the Westminster seats: Sir Alan Gardner, 1st Baronet (1742–1809), later (1800) 1st Baron Gardner, a supporter of the Administration; Charles James Fox; and John Horne Tooke (1736–1812), whom Burke always called by his former name of Horne. On 1 June the *True Briton* declared that Mr Fox had 'formed a junction with *Parson* Horne, the man who, all his life, has been lavish in his abuse of Mr Fox'. The previous day on the hustings Tooke had denied that he and Fox had entered into a coalition but advised that his friends should vote for Fox. Two days later, at a dinner given for Fox, John Thelwall (1764–1834), speaking of his friendship with both Fox and Tooke, lamented the 'little jealousies and obstacles between the parties'. Fox, however, emphasized that he had been advised by his

Windham answered this letter on Sunday 5 [June], saying, 'I would certainly have been with you to day, if I had not been restrained by an engagement, from which I endeavoured in vain to set myself free' (MS at Sheffield). He promised to come later for a longer stay, and did pay a visit on 11 June (see below, p. 47).

To WALKER KING—4 *June* 1796
Source: MS Osborn Collection.

My dearest Walker, I send you a Note to pay Lee[1] for the Interest of the Purchase[2] made by that being so dear to us both, and whom I lost as on this day of the Week[3]—a day of shame, sorrow, and confusion to me—and on which I feel more Grief, than on the fatal Day itself. Well! Well! I must go through.

Nagle[4] comes down to me this day with eighteen Boys. My expences on this head begin to overpower me. But really the thing itself is pleasant and consolatary. However for Gods sake represent to the Treasury the condition I am in. I say nothing of the things I have got on Credit which more than equal the ready money I have paid. Whatever is done here, is all for ready money for we are as poor as Rats, and cannot afford to give Credit—Dont forget to push for the Whole Thousand for the outfits for the three months for the last four hundred, as called for at first is nearly if not altogether expired[5]—and it would be extraordinary, if because they had delaid the *first* payment, *which was to have been by advance*, that the *second* is to be delaid three months longer. So push for the commencement of the monthly payments at least from the 25. March. Oh! my Estimate was very short. At least I fear so.

Yours ever affectionately,
EDM BURKE.

June 4. 1796.

Mrs Crewe takes this.

friends to 'stand independent' and could not join with Tooke. At the close of the poll Fox was at the head with 5160 votes, Gardner had 4814 and Tooke 2819 (*Gazetteer*, 1, 3, 14 June).

[1] John Lee, an attorney of Chancery Lane.
[2] Probably the purchase of land on the island of St John's; see below, pp. 51, 110.
[3] 4 June 1796 was a Saturday. Richard Burke, Jr, died on Saturday, 2 August 1794.
[4] Edward James Nagle.
[5] In Burke's Proposal for a school at Penn, accepted by the Government, it had been laid down that the £1000 grant from the Government for furnishing the house was to be made in two payments: £600 on the inauguration of the school, and £400 three months after the occupation of the house; see vol. VIII, 397.

To DR JOHN DOUGLASS—*5 June* 1796

Source: Westminster Diocesan Archives (MS A Series, vol. 46, no. 212).
Addressed: Rt Reverend| Dr Douglas—| R.C. Bishop of the Southern
District| No. 4| Castle Street| Holborn| London.

Dr John Douglass (1743–1812) was Vicar-apostolic of the London District
and Bishop *in partibus* from 1790 until 1812. At the end of 1793 he had installed
in Old Hall Green Academy, Hertfordshire, the exiles from the English Roman
Catholic College at Douay.

Right Reverend Sir,

The flattering partiality which you have been pleased some years ago
to shew to my poor opinions and endeavours encourages me to take the
Liberty of resorting to your assistance in a Business in which I find great
difficulties, but which I have very much at heart. It is possible you have
heard, that in confidence of assistance from Government, I have ventured
to have a Shool opend in a Village in my Neighbourhood for the children
of the French emigrants who have had their parents or other near
relations killed in the Kings Service. As it is highly probable, that they
may never return to their Native Country, the only hope of an establishment which remains to them is in the military line in some part of
the British dominions. Without a compleat knowlege of the English
Language, you are sensible, that, neither in that line, nor in any other, is
it possible for them to get forward. They must lie perpetually under the
disadvantage of being, in the most essential part, foreigners. An English
Master in the House is to them absolutely necessary. As these young
Gentlemen are of the religion of their Parents, and that formerly
establishd in their Country, it is equally necessary that this Master
should be a Catholick. If he is a Clergyman too it will have its advantages
and its inconveniencies. To act under a Clergyman of the same persuasion,
but of another nation, will not be pleasant—nor will it be easy to
preserve the harmony in the Institution which I wish. On the other
hand, if he is not he will want something of Authority—nor have we
quite the same security for exemplary regularity and strictness of
morals. The qualifications I look for are, a good knowlege of Latin, and
a tolerable knowlege of Greek; and, if some elemental knowlege of
Mathematicks is added it will be the better—but the main fundamental
part is a mastery of our Native Tongue with a power of reading it, in
prose and Verse, in a firm, just, and manly manner. I am ashamed to say,
that in looking for these qualifications, I cannot offer any thing very
deserving of them. The best apartments are occupied by the other
Masters. The Room for this Gentleman—(though not wholly unpleasant

in its prospect) is not the best. The Table both for Flesh, and days of Abstinence, is abundant; and such as he will have no reason to complain of—He will be compleatly clad; and kept so—and as to the salary, over and above Diet, Lodging, and cloathing, it shall be such as you think fit.[1] You will be so good as to permit my Kinsman Mr Nagle to wait upon you on this Subject—and to take your Commands.

I have the honour to be with the most perfect respect and regard

> Right Reverend Sir
> Your most obedient
> and faithful humble Servant
> EDM BURKE

Beconsfield June 5. 1796.

Dr Douglass replied on 21 June, proposing the Rev. William Henry Coombes (1767–1850), Professor of Rhetoric at Old Hall Green Academy, for the post at the Penn School: '. . . he is one of my ablest Professors; whose abilities and conduct and virtue I greatly esteem; and whom I would not part with on any other account than to oblige a Gentleman, to whom the Catholic cause, and myself personally, owe so many obligations' (MS at Northampton).

To WILLIAM WINDHAM—[7 June 1796]

Source: British Museum (Add. MS 37,843, fols 107–8). Printed Burke–Windham. Correspondence, p. 195.
Endorsed: Mr Burke| June 7 p8m 96.
Whoever endorsed this letter seems first to have written 'June 9th', then written a '7' over the '9'. 7 June 1796 was a Tuesday. Presumably the 'p8m' stands for '8 p.m.'.

My dear Sir

I thank you for your kind sollicitude about Mrs Burke.[2] Except in the power of much motion she is tolerably well. In that disability she continues much as she was. There is no perceptible amendment. For myself I have my old windy complaints, which are rather disagreeable than painful. I have too a spasmodick affection in my right leg which comes and goes I know not why or how.[3] The sore, for which there is no salve gives me only a bad quarter of an hour now and then. As to the publick, like our great King, and great Armies I seek my safety in Flight

---

[1] The other masters who were émigré priests were receiving small allowances, of about thirty-five shillings or two pounds per week, from the Relief Committee.

[2] In his letter of 5 [June]; see above, p. 44. Windham had said: 'I hope from your silence about Mrs B. that I may conclude that she is pretty well'.

[3] Fifty years earlier, in 1747, Burke's friend William Dennis (c. 1730–74) had written, 'Ned has not been well today and the old pain in his hip which you might have heard him complain of has been very uneasy to him all day' (see vol. I, 94).

and ignorance. I never read the Newspaper; and only hear now and then what I cannot well prevent. One of the worst things I hear about the future, is the present Prince of Wales.[1] There is a sort of rebellion by anticipation. The Rehearsal is tolerably perfect; Gods will be done. Every thing, bating the loss of your Presence, went off very well.[2] The Scene was really affecting. I like the Duke of Bourbon extremely—he has a modest Dignity and perfect good behaviour—*qualis esse decet quos ardens purpura Vestit*:[3] But his, poor man, is stripped off.

Mrs Burke is very happy to hear of your intended Visit, and the more, as she just now learns that you have prevaild on Miss Lukin[4] to come along with you[5]—Adieu—believe me ever sincerely yours,

EDM BURKE

Tuesday.

To FRENCH LAURENCE—[11 *June* 1796]

Source: MS Osborn Collection. Printed *Burke–Laurence Correspondence*, pp. 243–4.

In this letter Burke is probably congratulating his friend and disciple French Laurence (1757–1809) on his appointment to the Regius Professorship of Civil Law at Oxford. This was made on Saturday 11 June 1796 (Public Record Office, Warrant Book 1796–8, H.O. 38/7, p. 116).

My dear friend, I have not heard, since, the day of my calamity, any thing which has given me half the comfort, which I received from your Letter,[6] which I received on this fatal Saturday morning.[7] If your departed friend were with us his satisfaction would have been at least equal to mine. The Duke has acted well.[8] I do not know whether the Letter I wrote to him,[9] stating the intrigue he was to expect, and the consequences which would result from giving way to it, was of any use in fortifying him, or not. I had no answer; from which I augured nothing ill; as I was sure, that if he had given way he would have made some

[1] The strained relations between the Prince and Princess were attracting public attention, and considerable sympathy was being expressed for the Princess.
[2] During the visit of the Duc de Bourbon to the school; see above, pp. 42–3.
[3] Such as those ought to be who are clothed in glowing purple; see Juvenal, *Satires*, XI, 155.
[4] Either Mary (1770–1800), later Mrs Foy, or her sister Kitty (1775–1861), daughters of Windham's half-brother.
[5] Windham noted in his *Diary* on 11 June: 'To Beaconsfield by dinner with Mr Cazales [see below, p. 73]; in the evening to the school with a new party of boys . . .' (p. 339). He does not mention a Miss Lukin accompanying him.
[6] Missing.   [7] See above, p. 44.
[8] On 6 September Laurence wrote to Fitzwilliam: 'I have great and recent obligations to the Duke of Portland. He gave me the Professorship of Civil Law the other day in the most handsome manner' (MS at Sheffield, F32c). Portland was both a Cabinet Minister and Chancellor of Oxford University.
[9] The letter is missing.

awkard apology. He has indeed done perfectly well; and if any thing can give us a chance, for protecting the Laws of the old world against the arms of the New, this Step, I may fairly say has done more towards it, than any I could think of. May the God of law and order forward and protect you. You are far above the need of any Counsel of Mine. Follow where your own Genius leads and you will go right. The times are gloomy indeed. What good can be done by what I write?[1] I have not been very well; nor am I. I am full of the detail of this School; But, please God, I will set to the work since you desire it; though I shall be torn Limb from Limb by all parties.

The Masters the good Bishop has furnishd me with, are good and virtuous men, I really believe; But I am afraid utterly unfit for this employment. God almighty bless you. Mrs Burke mends sensibly—and is able to go up stairs. She is abed—but will be full of comfort when she comes down. Again and again all sort of felicitation. This is good indeed. Your ever ever

EDM BURKE

Saturday

My dear friend, I have not heard from Walker King—but he must Stop the coming of any more Tutors, till we know something of their Capacity. They or at least one of them must speak English—The Boys speak it as well as Natives—and they will be ruind if they are put back and made foreigners again. The Bishop has been intollerable in this respect.

Yours ever
E B.

To IGNATIUS GEOGHEGAN—20 June 1796

Source: MS Copy Keele University Library. Printed *Corr.* (1844), IV, 347–8.
Endorsed (in the copyist's hand, corrected by another hand): The Rt Honble|
Ed Burke| To John Geoghegan Esqr.

The 'John Geoghegan' of the endorsement is an error. It was Ignatius Geoghegan who was father-in-law of the Baron de Montesquieu.

Ignatius Geoghegan (c. 1711–97), an Irish Catholic, was born in Westmeath and resided in Ireland for about thirty-five years. Later he settled in London where he built up a large social circle. Widely read, he was an entertaining conversationalist, though 'his transitions from one topick to another were so frequent and so sudden as sometimes to bewilder his hearers; but the strokes of pleasantry which he incessantly introduced made ample amends for want of

---

[1] Laurence had been very anxious that Burke should finish and publish his 'Letters on a Regicide Peace', which had been advertised as in the process of composition as early as 7 January (see vol. VIII, 368).

connexion'. He was said to be 'fond of the acquaintance of public men, and had a particular partiality to rank; a foible which he was studious to conceal' (*Gentleman's Magazine*, LXVII (1797), pt II, 712–13).

Beconsfield June 20th 1796

My dear Sir,

I congratulate myself and all your friends on the vigour and spirit of your eighty four: and I heartily wish, and now indeed hope, that you will live to see a better century with better omens than those with which we seem so near closing the present. Alas! my dear Sir, my House has no hope: But I ought thankfully to accept such consolations as it pleases God to give me. I make no visits since the day of my calamity. But when my old friends condescend[1] to visit the remains of a family that has outstaid its time, and the order of nature, I do not choose to shut my door to them—I do not wish to see many at once, nor can I make my house convenient or agreeable to them: For which reason as I expect one or two in the course of this week I must deny myself the pleasure of seeing you and Monser de Montesquieu[2] till Monday;[3] when I hope to profit of your goodness to Mrs Burke and me.

I am, with most sincere respect and affection
My dear Sir,
Your faithful
and most obedient Humble
Servant
EDM BURKE

To IGNATIUS GEOGHEGAN—22 *June* 1796

Source: MS Osborn Collection. Printed *Corr.* (1844), IV, 348–50.
Only the signature is in Burke's hand.

My dear Sir,

You have been very good and charitable in wishing to visit this infirmary—where my Wife, my poor old Friend Will Burke;[4] and myself are all lame; Mrs Burke of the very same lameness which took her some Years ago without effect to Margate, where we had the pleasure of seeing

---

[1] MS: condescends

[2] Charles-Louis de Secondat, Baron de Montesquieu (*c.* 1750–1824), son-in-law of Ignatius Geoghegan and grandson of the great Montesquieu. 'Banished from his native country by the horrors of the French Revolution, he resided for 35 years in England, eminently distinguished for every virtue which can adorn human nature' (*Gentleman's Magazine*, XCIV (1824), pt II, 285).

[3] 27 June.

[4] (1728–98), Burke's distant kinsman and close friend. He had returned from India in 1793 and was living at Beaconsfield with Burke.

you[1]—The sight of such a Sympathizing Friend is a comfort to those who are no longer in Society—Since my calamity I have not dined out of my own house; nor am I fond of receiving any new acquaintance; my Business and my pleasure in this Life being, both of them, completely over.

When I mentioned Monsr de Montesquieu, it was not as a man I wished to see, on account of his own distinguished merit, or the fame of his family, which the world is so full of, and to whose labours the world owes so much:—It is as a part of an old friend that I who refuse all new acquaintance took the liberty of desiring him to accompany you: Our house has very little lodging Room and it is all we could do to lodge you two. Our settled family takes up four beds and my old friend Dr Walker King, whom I have not seen for a good while and whom I am not likely to see for this year again, we expect here with his wife and Child[2]—we have not a bed for a third person—so that I must deny myself for the present (and it is a real self denial) the worthy and most respectable gentleman[3] you proposed to accompany yourself and your Son the Baron.[4] Alas my dear Friend, I am not what I was two years ago—Society is too much for my nerves—I sleep ill at night; and am drowsy and sleep much in the day—Every Exertion of spirits, which I make for the Society I cannot refuse costs me much; and leaves me doubly heavy and dejected after it—Such is the person you come to see; or rather the wreck of what was never a very first rated vessel—Such as I am I feel infinitely for the kindness of those old friends who remember me with compassion—As to new, I never see one, but such French as come to visit the School which supplies to me the void in my own family and is my only comfort—for the sake of that I submit to see some, who are still more miserable than I am.

Adieu, my Dear Sir, till Monday. Mrs Burke and my Niece[5] salute you cordially.

Ever Yours,
EDM BURKE

June 22. 1796.

[1] The Burkes had visited Margate in the summer of 1791; see vol. VI, 282–337.
[2] Mrs King (see above, p. 10) and her daughter Mary, who was born on 28 June 1795.
[3] Not identified.
[4] Montesquieu; see the previous letter.
[5] Mrs Thomas Haviland (Mary Cecilia French), 1766–1816.

EDMUND *and* JANE BURKE *to* WALKER KING—
26 *June* 1796

Source: Fitzwilliam MSS (Northampton).
Addressed: Revd Dr Walker King.

My dear King,

Mrs Burke has had the enclosed Letter from Hennessy.[1] You have seen by his accounts that in effect he thinks proper to charge twelve hundred pound, having actually raised six, for his no services in St Johns;[2] the last Expedition to which he made, merely on his own private account, and on a Trading adventure. Be so good to look among the papers of our ever dear Departed friend, to see whether you can obtain any light in this Business.[3] Did you tell Hennessy you would pay him? I hope not.

As to Owen, I suppose by my hearing nothing about him—that as to me he is a Bankrupt.[4] Can any thing at all be got from him? how much—and when? As to other things, I say nothing now, because I trust I shall soon see you. Only as to the Committee[5] settle before you leave Town my regular payment. I wish Heartily we could get it off that Fund.[6] There is a sort of irregularity and injustice in the thing as it now stands. Some of the Boys given to me never receivd the succour. Either then I must fall short of my estimated allowance—or I must charge on those, who are the least able to pay, what is laid out on those whose parents have something of their own. This last would be monstrous. The failure of the first would be my ruin. Mrs Burkes best love to Mrs King. Windham came and went yesterday. Lord and Lady Buckingham slept here, and go to day to see the School.[7] The five hundred saves me from absolute and present ruin—thats all. It neither pays Debts, nor provides for current expences.[8] I write this early in the morning lest I should not have time afterwards. Adieu God preserve you. Your ever affectionate

EDM BURKE

June 26. 1796.

[1] The letter is missing. George Hennessy (*c.* 1760–99), a general merchant specializing in the wine trade, was a distant kinsman of Burke.

[2] Richard Burke, Jr, who owned some land on St John's (now Prince Edward) Island, Nova Scotia (see vol. II, 517), had employed Hennessy in making a survey of it. Hennessy had made two trips, but Burke insisted that only the first had been commissioned by Richard (see below, pp. 110–11).

[3] Although his parents probably never discovered it, Richard had been somewhat unguarded in his last letter to Hennessy (dated 28 July 1794; MS Lady Neville). After wishing Hennessy *bon voyage* as he set off on his second trip, Richard added: 'The various occupations and cares of this year have again prevented me from doing anything effective with regard to the settlement. Anything that can be done by you I shall be glad of and I leave the whole to your discretion'.

[4] See above, pp. 11–12; below, p. 244.   [5] See above, p. 11.

[6] Burke objected to the Government subsidizing the school at Penn out of the grant made for the relief of the *émigrés*; see vol. VIII, 445.   [7] See above, pp. 42–3.

[8] The Government had agreed to assist the school by making a capital grant of

[Jane Burke begins here]

I say God bless you both, when are we to see you? for much we long for it. Have you settled with J Bourke?[1] if not do it before you leave Town, consider his age thats all; when you return to Town it may be too late. As to Hennessy's Charge it is quite impudent for he spent six Months the first time he went to St John's building a ship, and fraiting it for his own benefit; and on his return to England, he traveled in a Chaise and four that he might keep pace with a nebob he met on the road; our dear Richard was then alive, why did he not settle with him. His last excursion and Ship, was on his own account, for our Richard then did not imploy him; all this Mr ⟨Nangle⟩[2] can tell you. So that about him my Mind is quite easy; he wants to lay hold of the land at St John's, in hopes of selling it for something, but I am resolved he never shall have any thing to do with it. Again God bless you both.   Sunday.

To the BISHOP OF ST-POL-DE-LÉON—[*June* 1796]

Source: Fitzwilliam MSS (Northampton), A. XIX. 4A.
Undated but probably written in June 1796. Obviously some time has elapsed since Burke's dispute with the Bishop in May over the selection of boys for the school.

Monseigneur, et mon tres cher ami, Il n'y a rien qui peut m'affliger autant, que d'avoir aucune opinion qu'il soit contraire a votre. Mais je me' flattois, apres avoir eu ensemble a Londres un si clair explication par des Lettres, par des conferences personels, et par L'entremise des amis, qui vous sont tendrement attachées,[3] il ne peut plus s'elever aucune discussion entre nous. Malheureusement je me trompois. Vous revenez toujours a La charge. Je suis presqu'au desespoir.

Ces sont Monseigneur Les enfans de La malheureuse noblesse de la France fidelement attachés a Leur Loix, a Leur religion, et a Leur Prince. Il sont par Le plus grande nombre Les ⟨fils⟩ de ceux quils ont versé leur sang,[4] et quils ont servis dans les armée du Roi d'angleterre.

£1000 and an annual grant of £600 paid monthly (see above, p. 44). Early in July the Joint Secretary to the Treasury, Charles Long (1761–1838), acknowledged that the Government was indebted to Burke for £650 'and that another £50 becomes due this month—in the course of it you may receive both these Sums and the last whenever you send for it—and if it puts you to any inconvenience to wait for as long as I have mentiond—you shall receive it by sending to me at any time' (Charles Long to Burke, 8 July [1796], MS at Northampton, A. VI. 50).
[1] John Bourke (1724–1806), a distant relation of Edmund.
[2] Possibly Edward James Nagle.
[3] These friends have not been identified; the letters are missing.
[4] In rewriting this sentence Burke has crossed through 'ceux quils ont versé leur sang'.

Ces sont Les fonds[1] supplées par La Bonté du Roi et des Les Ministres, par Lesquels ils doivent etre nourris et eleves. Ces sont Les persons et pas moi, ni si j'ose dire pas vous même, Monseigneur, quils doivent decider sur L'Education de Les jeuns persons quils me sont confiés aussi Longtemps.

Les peres, Les meres, Les parens pour leurs propres Enfans, La noblesse pour L'education de La noblesse, Les Ministres du Roi pour La destination du Revenus publiques. Ces sont les juges naturels, et sans appel, dans une telle affaire et il n'est pas nullement agreeable a mes Idees de morale ou de religion, d'oter Les Enfans de Tutele naturel de leur Parens; ni de faire appliquer des deniers du Roi dans un maniere contraires a son bon plaisir. Sous L'influence de telles Maximes Jai commencé par fair rechercher et rassembler La mieux qui m'etoit possible. Jai fait demander Ladessus les sentimens[2] de personages Les plus qualifies et les plus eclairés de La noblesse Francoise. J'en suis instruit. Ils sont entierement de mon avis. Ils ne veulent pas du tout que cette ecole soit conduite apres Le Principes ou sur les reglès d'un seminaire de Pretres. Ils sont entierment opposes a cet projet. Vous ne me trouvois pas d'etre bon, que pour etre fournisseur du Lait et de pommes de terre. Cela pourroit bien etre.

Il y a[3] quelque temps Monseigneur que j'eus[4] Le Malheur de perdre entierment[5] votre confiance. Particulierement depuis que je tachois dinterresser Les Ministres Dans mon projet d'ecole pour Les jeuns Francoises.

To the REV THOMAS HUSSEY—[5 *July* 1796]

Source: Fitzwilliam MSS (Sheffield).
Addressed: The| Revd Doctor Hussey| No 5 Georges Street| Manchester Square.
Postmarked: 7⟨O'⟩CLOCK|6JY|96 NIGHT CHARING CROSS|UNPAID|PENNY POST.
Dated by the postmark. 5 July 1796 was a Tuesday.

My dear Sir

Mr Campbell[6] will tell you the conversation I had with the Prince de Trimouille.[7] He had conceivd that I was a man in the world who could

[1] MS: fomds
[2] Burke first wrote 'Les opinions' and in changing to 'sentimens' has crossed out 'Les' by mistake.   [3] MS: a y
[4] In revising Burke deleted 'que j' by mistake.   [5] MS: entiement
[6] Possibly the Abbé Campbell, mentioned by Henry Swinburne as dining with himself and Hussey in January 1792 (H. Swinburne, *The Courts of Europe at the Close of the Last Century*, London, 1895, II, 108). The name 'Campbell' appears on two pension lists of *émigré* clergy (Archives Nationales, o³* 757; Affaires Étrangères, Mémoires et documents, France, 616, fol. 240).
[7] Charles-Bretagne-Marie-Joseph, Duc de La Trémoille, Prince de Tarente (1764–1839). Hussey had given him a (missing) letter of introduction to Burke.

do something by solliciting, intriguing, and trickery, here and there. I am sure that such is the fact and I hope I convinced him of it that my meddling might do harm, but can do no good.[1] I think he has had hard measure; which is bad enough; but that he has been illegally and un-faithfully dealt with is more than I dare to affirm. Mr Windham will never, I am afraid, concent to discredit the persons[2] to whom he has confided this Business; and though I am convinced, every emigrant Cause is tried under very strong prejudices, it will not be quite easy to fix any thing against the general Character of the persons who have reported the Business of the Prince de Trimouille, so strong as to persuade Mr Windham to admit an appeal from their judgment—and if he did admit the appeal, I do not know, who they are, that would be more free from prejudices than Windham is, or those whom he was likely to name. At any rate, I am quite certain, that it would materially hurt the Princes Cause, if it was supposed, that he carried about complaints against his proceedings to his friends and acquaintance. As to Mr W. he is a man who will do much by himself—but he flies off when any attempt is made to lead him. Such is his Temper. As to me Whatever service I may do to the French is in the mass. It is impossible for me to Negotiate the affairs of any individual. Alas! I am unfit enough for that or any Business.

Mr Combes[3] has been here. I think he will do very well and he seemd not indisposed to undertake his share in our School. He reads English (besides his other qualifications) uncommonly well, both in prose and in Verse. He was to let me know his final decision on Tuesday last, (this day sennight)[4] but I have not heard a word from him more or less. We are now fifty five Boys, and expect the rest shortly. We suffer from the delay not a little. I hope you go on as well in Ireland as can be without yourself. I have a few Hints still to submit to you on that Business. The very being of Ireland depends upon it. Adieu my dear freind and beleive me, with all here, cordially Yours

EDM BURKE

Tuesday evening.

Replying to this letter Hussey protested that if he had had 'the smallest idea... of the Prince de la Tremouille's business with you, I should not be so free in giving him an introducting line to you. The fact is, that these good Emigrants get me into difficulties that provoke me; but when I reflect on the cause for which they suffer, I am again reconciled to them, and ready to be duped again' (Hussey to Burke, 14 July, MS at Sheffield).

[1] The Prince was pressing against the British Government financial claims arising out of his abortive efforts to raise a regiment in Germany (Add. MS 37,872, fols 149–58).
[2] Christopher Clapham Bird (c. 1771–1861; see vol. VIII, 376), and Lieutenant-Colonel John Ramsay (d. 1845).   [3] See above, p. 46.   [4] That is, on 28 June.

EARL FITZWILLIAM *to* EDMUND BURKE—9 *July* [1796]

Source: Fitzwilliam MSS (Sheffield).

William Wentworth Fitzwilliam, 4th Earl Fitzwilliam (1748–1833), was the nephew and heir of Lord Rockingham. Burke had sat for his borough of Malton until his retirement from Parliament in June 1794.

My dear Burke

By a letter I have receiv'd from town, I am made apprehensive, that since I had the pleasure of seeing you, you have been by no means in good health: there must have been a cause for the pains and cramp in your legs; probably it was not a local one, or it would have been more fix'd, and besides it would have manifested its nature by some outward appearance: the pains you had earlier in the winter, which if I recollect right, were in the foot, are a further confirmation that there is something floating in the general habit, which ought to be attended to: an ignorant pretender, a quack, like myself, and indeed like every man I meet, would decide peremptorily, that it was Gout, and that Bath was the cure; but such ignorance is not to be attended to: consult, my dear Burke, those, whose practice and experience have taught them to discover the causes of illness: pay to your health that attention, which the publick has a right to expect from a publick man, (not yet retir'd into his shell, as sometimes you are pleas'd to fancy) but in the full enjoyment of all his powers, and as capable as ever to enlighten and direct them in their worst of exigencies: pay to it that attention which Mrs B's affection has a claim to, and which your numerous and attach'd friends solicit at your hands.

Since we met, England is become richer in an Island, and a Gazette:[1] which of the two will prove of most value, remains yet to be prov'd: in the mean while, France has been driven back in one quarter, and has made impression on another: She has been driven back from a quarter, which She had already plunder'd, and disorganiz'd, but She has made the valuable acquisition of Fort Khell,[2] giving the command of the passage of the Rhine, and opening a country more capable than any other of supplying her armies with cattle, horses, &c, articles of the first necessity for her enterprizes: it renders besides, the hopes of a communication between her armies of the Rhine, and of Italy, being

[1] The articles of capitulation of St Lucia were published in the *London Gazette* on 4 July.
[2] On 24 June the French under the command of Jean-Victor Moreau (1763–1813) captured the fortress of Kehl, but further north, Jean-Baptiste Jourdan (1762–1833) and Jean-Baptiste Kléber (1753–1800) were compelled to retreat.

readily open'd—upon these considerations, I fear, we have to strike
the balance of the late harvest of news.

Once more entreating an immediate attention to the object of my
letter, I remain most affectionately

and truly Yours
W.F.

Milton[1] july 9th

To EARL FITZWILLIAM—11 *July* 1796
Source: Fitzwilliam MSS (Sheffield).

My dear Lord,

You follow the last fragments of your poor friend with the same
persevering Kindness, you have ever shewn to him, when he was as
entire as it pleased Providence to make him. Indeed, in no way except in
sensibility to your goodness was he worthy of it. I have taken some very
respectable medical advice. I do not think, that the faculty can do me
any sort of service. The Truth is, the Vice is in my Stomach; and not in
any thing it contains, or that can be put into it.[2] So far as I am able to
judge, its greater fulness or emptiness makes no difference; neither the
quality of any thing I eat or drink. All turns alike to a sort of thick
mucus a little acid, but not very greatly so; but which disposes me to a
small gnawing pain, or rather uneasiness, (for it hardly merits the
Name of pain) producing bursts of flatulance of a kind very extraordinary, the explosion of which costs me no difficulty, and probably
it is this, which prevents the pain from becoming any way considerable.
I have no reason to think, that it fares with the Medicines, otherwise
than with the food; but that, the one, as well as the other, turns to the
very same substance; and irritates the disease. In compliance, my dear
Lord, with your advice I will subject myself to further medical counsel.
If it pleases God, that it should be so, nature, by its own operation, will
dissipate this malady—if not, I ought to bless the hand of God, that
proceeds to my End, in so very lenient and gentle a manner; and
inflicts no other malady on me than a small encrease of that, which,
more or less has attended me thro' life.

As to any use to which I may be turned, I cannot flatter myself on
that head. The Effect of opinions very different from those of your
Lordship and of mine have had their full and final Effect. This days
mail brings the account of further advantages obtain by the Enemy

---

[1] Lord Fitzwilliam's seat near Peterborough.
[2] Burke was suffering from pyloric stenosis, due to a carcinoma of the stomach.

in Brisgaw;[1] and that they advance continually. The Pope has put all the essential Ports in his dominions into their hands.[2] The Grand Duke[3] receives a Garrison ⟨at⟩ Leghorn.[4] The King of Naples has sent to sollicit peace.[5] They certainly intend an attack on some part of these dominions. In this situation—is it worth while to live. Adieu, my dear Lord, my ever dear friend—whilst any little thread of this life remains it is full of Veneration, affection and Gratitude to you. My best love to Lady Fitzwilliam.[6] I think to return to Beconsfield tomorrow. I am ever ever your faithful and most oblig'd friend

EDM BURKE

Dr Kings[7]—July 11. 1796.

WILLIAM THOMAS SWIFT *to* EDMUND BURKE— 11 *July* 1796

Source: Gentleman's Magazine, LXVII (1797), pt II, 635–6.

William Thomas Swift, who had been a stationer, had been employed by the Burkes as a secretary from about 1788 (Public Record Office, C33/497/578). When Richard, Jr, was Joint Receiver General of Land Revenues (see vol. v, 8), he placed Swift in his office, and it was said Swift 'pillaged' him (French Laurence to Fitzwilliam, 13 February 1797, MS at Northampton, Box 51; see below, p. 240).

London, 11th July, 1796.

Sir,

Driven by the most forcible of every stimulus, that of stern necessity, I venture once more, with an unwilling hand and breaking heart, to state to you my situation, fondly and firmly presuming, that the former very great goodness and benevolence which I and my family have enjoyed from your hands will lead you to pardon the apparent impertinence of this almost unjustifiable intrusion.

For upwards of a twelvemonth, Sir, I was without any employment, notwithstanding my repeated advertisements, and every other mode of

---

[1] On 11 July *The Times* reported that the Austrians had been forced to abandon Freiburg in Breisgau 'so that the Imperialists, as well as the army of the Prince of Condé [Louis-Joseph, Prince de Condé, 1736–1818], have no resource left, but to withdraw into the Black Forest'.

[2] By an armistice concluded with the French at the end of June.

[3] Ferdinand III (1769–1824), Grand Duke of Tuscany.

[4] French forces had entered Leghorn on 28 June (*The Times*, 19 July).

[5] Ferdinand (1751–1825), King of Naples and King of Sicily 1759–1816, King of the Two Sicilies 1816–25. It was reported in *The Times* on 11 July that 'The King of Naples and the Pope have agreed to an armistice with the enemy, and their Ministers have arrived at Paris to negociate a peace with the Directory'.

[6] Charlotte, *née* Ponsonby, Countess Fitzwilliam (1747–1822).

[7] Burke was staying with Walker King at 64 Great Marylebone Street.

application my mind could suggest, to obtain one. You will, therefore, readily conceive what difficulties I must, during that period, have been driven to in order to obtain a bit of bread for my wife, myself, and two lovely children. For these last seven months I have been with Mr — , of the — — in the — ; but that gentleman's affairs, which have always been unhappily deranged, are now, I am afraid, approaching to another unfortunate crisis. So situated, he was unable to pay me my weekly salary with that regularity which my peculiar circumstances required; and which, consequently, fell into arrear. He is now confined in the Fleet prison, with but little probability of liberation; so that he has no occasion for my future services; and my poor due, I fear, is totally gone—it is so at least for a time. I am, therefore, with my family, again turned adrift upon the world, without a guinea in my possession, or the smallest knowledge where or how to earn one. Added to this, I am indebted for half a year's rent; and my landlord has given me formal notice that he will on Wednesday morning seize our furniture. The effect of this proceeding will necessarily be, that I, my wife, and lovely children, shall be turned into the streets without a habitation or a bed.

The boon, therefore, which I most humbly implore at your benevolent hands, is to lend me five guineas to prevent this disgrace and distress from being put in execution. And be assured, Sir, I will most faithfully return it with the truest gratitude the very moment I can obtain employment to procure it; which I fervently pray to God may not be at a distance; for, I am regardless of the nature of the employ, or in what part of the globe, so that I could but be happy enough to procure the necessaries of life for my family. I sincerely hope the blessings of health attend you and Mrs Burke; and most humbly supplicate the consolation of a line directed to me at Mr — 's.

I have the honour to be, Sir, your ever obliged and truly grateful servant,

W. T. S---T.

To the Right Hon. Edmund Burke.

The anonymous contributor who communicated this letter to the *Gentleman's Magazine* in 1797, after Burke's death, also reported the sequel: 'The relief requested ... was granted with that unhesitating benevolence which those, who knew Mr Burke, well know him to have possessed'.

JOHN KEOGH *to* EDMUND BURKE— 20 *July* 1796

Source: Fitzwilliam MSS (Sheffield).

John Keogh (1740–1817) was a wealthy Dublin merchant and had been a leading member of the Catholic Committee (see vol. VII, 5).

New Hummum's Covent Garden
20th July 1796

Sir

On my arrival here from Ireland I called at Doctr Kings as I considered it my Duty to wait upon You, and as far as I was able to possess you of the real state of Ireland, since the recall of Lord Fitzwilliam—for I have had the honor of knowing well, the Interest you take in the fate of Your Country—Government appear to forget that the Inhabitants of Ireland are about One third of *all* his Majesty's Subjects in Europe—for we See Men Selected for Power and Confidence—not because they Unite and Conciliate—but rather in proportion as they terrify and Silence, the great Body of our People—we have our Robertspiers, tho inferior in Talents to their Prototype—may contend with him for preeminence in Cruelty—and in the management of Plots and petty Factions—a thousand instances might be produced, but the Cruelties at Armagh[1] cry aloud, these the unoffending People [they] are extirpating—'tis the la Vendee of Ireland, altho in One week these persecutions coud be stopped, and peace restored it was reserved for this Age to see Ministers of acknowledged Abilities, at a crisis like the present, and on mature deliberation, leave a brave People to despair—altho without cost or sacrifice—on the part of England they coud be reconciled and attacked, had Ministers been Intoxicated with success—it might account for, 'tho not Justify this treatment, being taught by experience that 'tis vain to seek redress—I have not opened my lips upon this subject since I came to England, nor attempted to see Ministers or any appendage of Ministers.

Yet I have been tempted to intrude thus, upon your time—let it plead my apology—that I know you are so uncourtly as to be a true Irishman—to Love Your Country—may You live long its Ornament and Pride, the defender of Virtue, and of Ireland, and yet See her rise from her persecutions and persecutor's.

[1] From the middle eighties there had been sporadic sectarian rioting and raiding in County Armagh. This became more widespread and serious in the early nineties, and after the 'Battle of the Diamond' on 21 September 1795, the Catholic peasantry suffered severely from organized Protestant attacks.

I purpose to depart for Dublin in five or Six days shoud you have any commands I will consider myself honored by being their bearer, I am with the sincerest respect and Gratitude

Sir

Your obliged and

faithful humble Servant

JOHN KEOGH

Burke did not reply to this letter. Keogh wrote again when he returned to London in November; see below, p. 112.

To the REV. THOMAS HUSSEY—26 *July* 1796

Source: Fitzwilliam MSS (Sheffield).
Addressed: Revd Dr Hussey| No 5.| Manchester Square|London.
Postmarked: BATH   JY|2⟨7⟩|96|A.
MS torn. This letter was readdressed to Ramsgate.

My dear Sir,

The Gentleman, whom Bishop Douglas recommended for the School[1] is unluckily not permitted by his superiour, Dr Walmsley of this Place, who is Bishop for the Western district, to engage.[2] This distresses me a little; and indeed not a little; because I am unwilling, on the one hand to take any more masters without a previous examination; and on the other, I see all the purposes of the Institution, worse if possible, than defeated, if I cannot get an English Teacher. The Boys have indeed, most of them, already lost the little English they brought with them. Mr Coombes, the Gentleman who first offerd, on his declining recommended a Mr Footehead[3] who has been, and is reputably employd in Academies about Town; and is now with Dr Burney at Greenwich,[4] who is one of the first Scholars of the Age, if he be, as I beleive he is, the Son of Doctor Burney the Musician.[5] I think he would

---

[1] Mr Coombes; see above, 46.

[2] Evidently either Mr Coombes or his ecclesiastical superiors had had second thoughts about the position at the school, and Dr Charles Walmesley (1722–97), Vicar-apostolic of the Western District 1763–97, 'was engaged to extricate Mr C from the engagement by alledging that he could not be spared from the College at O.H.G. &c &c. Mr B acknowledged his school was not deserving of a Professor of Mr C's merit &c. and Mr C. returned to Old Hall Green with only an engagement to provide him with a Master' (Dr John Douglass's Diary, June 1796, Westminster Diocesan Archives).   [3] Not identified.

[4] Charles Burney (1757–1817). He had opened a school at Hammersmith in 1786, which seven years later he moved to Greenwich (*Gentleman's Magazine*, LXXXIX (1819), pt I, 369).

[5] Charles Burney (1726–1814), member of the Literary Club and an old friend of Burke. He was the father of the Headmaster, and of Fanny Burney (1752–1840), now Madame d'Arblay.

not have one not perfectly qualified for his assistant. The thing I mainly insist on, is the power of reading English well, in Prose and Verse. This Mr Coombes could do. This is too a military Academy; and I think some (not a very profound) knowlege of Mathematicks essential. Our Masters have all to begin in that way. The second[1] formerly had some knowlege in that way, and he can recover it. Whether the first Master[2] understands them I know not; certainly he does not attempt to teach them, and he has enough to do in the way of the Classicks. In truth I am cruelly embarrassed—and I wish you to extricate me as well as you can. I wish you and Dr Lawrence[3] to see Mr Footehead; if you cannot find me another qualified up to my wish. Not that I doubt about him, as far he speaks of himself, which is with Sense and propriety—but he says nothing at all of Geometry. It may appear a triffle; but there is a ridiculous *equivoque* in the sound of his name, which will set all French, men, boys, and Girls alaughing at the first utterance of it; and will alone perhaps destroy the Effect of all he can teach. If we have him, I should almost wish him to be content with the last Syllable of it. I send you his Letter,[4] which I like very well. As to the Object of this Jou[rney][5] I have not much to say. Neither Mrs Burke nor I have as yet drank the Waters. I have been too ill for it. I apprehend my Stomach is irrecoverably ruind. However, tomorrow, I shall commence the regular operations. Adieu, my dear friend, excuse all this trouble, I thank you for your last Letter.[6] The Prospect is gloomy indeed, if not desperate. Mrs Burke's[7] affectionate Complements and beleive me My dear Sir

most truly yours
EDM BURKE

Bath July 26. 1796.

[1] The Abbé Le Chevalier.
[2] The Abbé Maraine.
[3] French Laurence; see above, p. 47.
[4] Missing. In fact Footehead was not engaged. Another member of the staff at Old Hall Green, the Rev. John Devereux (d. 1838), a refugee from Douay, was appointed in his stead. He remained at the school until December 1796. In his diary, Dr Douglass noted on 16 September: 'this morning Rev: Mr Devereux sett off for *Penn school* to be Professor of English' (Dr John Douglass's Diary, September 1796, Westminster Diocesan Archives).
[5] To Bath. Burke's arrival was noted in the *Bath Journal* for 25 July.
[6] Hussey wrote to Burke on 14 July; MS at Sheffield.
[7] MS: Mrs Burke

To FRENCH LAURENCE—*28 July* 1796

Source: MS Osborn Collection. Printed *Burke–Laurence Correspondence,*
pp. 53–6.

Bath July 28. 1796.

My dear Laurence

I thank you for employing the short moment you were able to snatch from being useful, in being kind and compassionate. Here I am in the last retreat of hunted infirmity. I am indeed aux abois: But, as thro the whole of a various and long Life I have been more indebted than thankful to Providence, so I am now. Singularly so, in being dismissed, as hitherto I appear to be so gently from Life and sent to follow, those who in Course ought to have followd me, whom, I trust, I shall yet, in some inconceivable manner, see and know; and by whom I shall be seen and known. But enough of this. However as it is possible that my stay on this side of the Grave, may be yet shorter, than I compute it, let me now beg to call to your Recollection, the solemn charge and trust I gave you on my Departure from the publick Stage.[1] I fancy I must make you the sole operator, in a work, in which, even if I were enabled to undertake it you must have been ever the assistance on which alone I could rely. Let not this cruel, daring, unexampled act of publick corruption, guilt, and meanness go down—to a posterity, perhaps as careless as the present race, without its due animadversion, which will be best found in its own acts and monuments. Let my endeavours to save the Nation from that Shame and guilt, be my monument; The only one I ever will have. Let every thing I have done, said, or written be forgotten but this. I have struggled with the great and the little on this point during the greater part of my active Life; and I wish after death, to have my Defiance of the Judgments of those, who consider the dominion of the glorious Empire given by an incomprehensible dispensation of the Divine providence into our hands as nothing more than an opportunity of gratifying for the lowest of their purposes, the lowest of their passions—and that for such poor rewards, and for the most part, indirect and silly Bribes, as indicate even more the folly than the corruption of these infamous and contemptible wretches. I blame myself exceedingly for not having employd the last year in this work[2]

---

[1] Burke was anxious that a history of the Impeachment of Warren Hastings should be prepared and published; see vol. VIII, 418, and below, p. 71.

[2] In March Burke had begun letters to Henry Dundas (1742–1811), later (1802) 1st Viscount Melville, President of the Board of Control, and to Lord Loughborough (see below, p. 322), the Lord Chancellor, protesting against granting Warren Hastings a pension. Several incomplete drafts of these letters are at Sheffield (see vol. VIII, 422–42). The replies to Loughborough were probably provoked by a letter of 8 March from him

and beg forgiveness of God for such a Neglect. I had strength enough for it, if I had not wasted some of it in compromising Grief with drowsiness and forgetfulness; and employing some of the moments in which *I* have been rouzed to mental exertion, in feeble endeavours to rescue this dull and thoughtless people from the punishments which their neglect and stupidity will bring upon them for their Systematick iniquity and oppression: But you are made to continue all that is good of me; and to augment it with the various rescources of a mind fertile in Virtues, and cultivated with every sort of Talent, and of knowlege. Above all make out the cruelty of this pretended acquittal, but in reality this barbarous and inhuman condemnation of whole Tribes and nations, and of all the abuses they contain. If ever Europe recovers its civilization that work will be useful. Remember! Remember! Remember!

It is not that I want you to sacrifice yourself blindly and unfruitfully, at this Instant. But there will be a Season for the appearance of such a Record; and it ought to be in Store for that Season. Get every thing that Troward[1] has.

Your kindness will make you wish to hear more particulars of me. To compare my State with that of the three first days after my arrival, I feel on the whole less uneasiness—But my flesh is wasted in a manner which in so short a time no one could imagine. My limbs look about to find the Rags that cover them. My strength is declined in the full proportion; and at my time of life new flesh is never supplied; and lost strength is never recoverd. If God has any thing to do for me here— here he will keep me. If not, I am tolerably resigned to his Divine pleasure. I have not been yet more than a day in condition to drink the Waters—but they seem rather to compose than to disorder my Stomach. My illness has not sufferd Mrs Burke to profit as she ought of this situation. But she will bathe to Night. Give Woodford[2] a thousand kind

in which he says: 'I lament that the Allowance made to Hastings by the E.I. Company should have struck your Eye in a different point of View from that in which It has met my Sight'. Loughborough went on to warn Burke that to commit himself prematurely upon the question 'would be a departure from that System of Moderation and Composure which you have adopted and I confess the occasion appears to me too particular upon the great Scale of the Interests which call for exertions from a mind like yours; the last of which has had and will continue to have an excellent Effect on the Publick Mind...I must in Candour allow that a Judgment of acquittall places His Case in a more favorable point of View, that many Men conscientiously beleive He has always behaved well and more perhaps that His Services outweigh any demerits...A Restraint upon the Bounty of a General Court, or perhaps their Compassion to releive from Indigence a very Old Servant in very high Station would appear to arise more from personal Animosity than any other Motive, and I should lament it as a publick Misfortune if that could by any possible representation be imputed either to you or to the Board of Controul' (MS Osborn Collection).

[1] Richard Troward (d. 1815), one of the prosecution solicitors.
[2] See above, p. 11.

remembrances. Please God, I shall write to him tomorrow. Adieu.
Your ever true friend

EDM BURKE

Mrs Burke never forgets you nor what remains of poor William.[1]

To WILLIAM WINDHAM—1 *August* 1796

Source: British Museum (Add. MS 37,843, fols 109–10). Printed *Burke–Windham Correspondence*, pp. 196–7.

My dear Sir,

I take the Pen out of Mrs Burkes hands to express our common and very warm sense of the Kindness of your Sollicitude about my health. It is of some value, since such as you appear to take an Interest in it. Its value in other respects is not so apparent: But, if it pleases God it should be established for some short time, I conclude it must be for some good purposes, great or small according to the proportion an individual bears to the whole, as a link in a chain infinite in extent, and in duration. Of my Death I ought to conclude the same. But I have said enough on this. Remaining only for me to add, that though all the Symptoms of my complaint went on with an accelerated aggravation, for the first days after my arrival here, for these last four the progress of the evil, I may say has been stopped and weakness and emaciation excepted, I am not at all worse than when you saw me. As to what you are so good to expect from me,[2] I can do nothing at present; being wholly incapable of all application—and for what?—*Non si meus afforet Hector*![3]—If even you, in the full force of a youthful manhood,[4] in an high situation, with such Virtues, Talents, and acquirements, as God has dispensed to very few living, (if to any) can do nothing—if from your meridian lustre the publick can reflect no light, what can be done, by the expiring snuff of my farthing Candle? No there is no one thing which we can propose, that to those, who shut their Eyes to the Evil, (and therefore cannot conceive, what remedies are *proportiond* to it) that would not be thought monstrous, wild, and extravagant? Are we of the Stuff of those, who with Hannibal in the Bowels of Italy, would think of transferring the gross of our Strength to Africk and to Spain?.[5] I go no further—All must depend on individuals, a very few

---

[1] William Burke (see above, p. 49).

[2] Windham had been strongly urging Burke to complete his 'Letters on a Regicide Peace' (see vol. VIII, 447).

[3] Non si ipse meus nunc adforet Hector; no, not though my own Hector were here himself (see Virgil, *Aeneid*, II, 522).   [4] Windham was forty-six.

[5] During the second Punic war (218 B.C.–201 B.C.) while Hannibal was still campaigning in Italy the Romans sent armies to Spain and North Africa.

individuals, now, as always it has done. If the Duumvirate who direct all[1] (you will pardon me, if I do not call you a minister)—have not the courage to look our situation in the face themselves, and to state it to Parliament too, if they do not cease to consider, what is to be said to their adversaries there, as an eloquent Bar defence, grounded on the principles of those adversaries, rather than what ought to be done against the grand adversary, then I say there is not for us a Ray of Hope. Their Talents are great indeed—but if they are thus directed, better half with a just direction, than the whole, than twice the whole, in the present course. You talk of coming hither. To be sure, if it can be done without detriment to the great concern it will be a great consolation to me. But, indeed my dear friend—the times admit to no secondary attentions. Mrs Burke herself very lame and rather worse at Ease in her Limbs—desires a thousand grateful remembrances to you and to the Ladies of your family.[2] Ever ever   Yours—the remains of

EDM BURKE

Bath Augst 1st 1796.

To EARL SPENCER—12 *August* 1796

Source: Spencer MSS.
The present Earl Spencer has kindly supplied our transcript of this letter.

Bath, Augt 12 1796.

My Lord,

No man can be more sensible than I am, of my want of all Title to be troublesome to your Lordship; But I am forced by an application, which I cannot refuse, to make myself the Channel of letting your Lordship know the wishes of Rear Admiral Keppel,[3] the son of Lord Keppel,[4] to be employed in some manner; in which he might be useful to his King and Country. The object of his ambition would be to succeed Sir James Wallace,[5] whose time will expire in April next, on the Newfoundland Station. In the mean time he would be happy in any other employment.

It is not for me to say, how fit, a person so related to the first Marine Commander this Country ever bred,[6] and who has much of the spirit,

---

[1] Presumably Pitt and Dundas.
[2] The Misses Lukin; see above, p. 47.
[3] Rear-Admiral George Keppel (d. 1804), was the natural son of George Keppel, 3rd Earl of Albermarle (1724–72).
[4] Augustus Keppel, 1st Viscount Keppel (1725–86), the famous Admiral.
[5] (1731–1803), later (1801) Admiral; at this time Vice-Admiral and Commander-in-Chief at Newfoundland.
[6] Viscount Keppel. He had been a close friend and party associate of Burke.

and (as I am credibly told) of the Abilities of his father, is for any naval service. I really hope with much earnestness, that the gratification of the wishes of Rear Admiral Keppel may be found comfortable to your Lordship's arrangements for the publick service.

I have the honour to be with the most perfect respect

My Lord

your Lordship's most obedient and faithful

humble servant

EDM BURKE

Lord Spencer replied on 16 August (MS at Sheffield), explaining that he had 'unfortunately given expectations to an Officer much senior to Rear Admiral Keppel'. He added that Rear Admiral Keppel was not the son of 'our late and most excellent friend' but of Lord Albemarle, his brother.

The DUKE OF PORTLAND to EDMUND BURKE— 22 *August* 1796

Source: Fitzwilliam MSS (Sheffield).

William Henry Cavendish Bentinck, 3rd Duke of Portland (1738–1809), who had been a friend and correspondent of Burke's for thirty years, was Home Secretary from 1794 to 1801.

London Monday 22 August 1796

My dearest Burke

I have too long and too uniformly experienced Your affection and friendship not to give You the earliest notice of the Event which of all others contributes the most to my domestick Happiness. Lady Titch-field[1] was brought to bed very early yesterday morning of a Son;[2] and putting all the supposed partiality and vanity of a Grandfather out of the question, I sincerely think I never saw a finer child—I have besides the pleasure of knowing that at one this afternoon She was as well as could be wished and that the little infant was equally so and ravenous for food.

Pray assure Mrs Burke of my best wishes and beleive me always most truly and cordially

Your's &ca

PORTLAND

I was much obliged by Mr Hussey for the Report he made of You which I shall be happy to have confirmed.

[1] Henrietta, *née* Scott (d. 1844), Portland's daughter-in-law.
[2] William Henry Cavendish Scott Bentinck, was born on 21 August. He died in 1824.

To Earl Fitzwilliam—23 *August* 1796

Source: Fitzwilliam MSS (Sheffield), F32c.
Endorsed (by Fitzwilliam): Burke| augt 27th 96.

Bath Augt. 23. 1796.

My dear Lord

The first and best use I can make of the dawning of a recovery from my illness is, sincerely (after God) to thank your Lordship for the Kind Interest you are so good to take in the Ease and health of my poor remains. It seems, as if Providence had intended me some short reprieve,—I am bound to believe, and do believe, for some good and gracious Ends, relative to myself, or to those who are dear to me—though, in Truth, there is no one thing in the aspect of affairs round us, in any quarter, or in any matter, that may render life gay or cheerful, or lead us to forget private misfortunes in publick prosperity. My original complaint can hardly be said to be removed, though I think it mitigated not inconsiderably; and the consequences that usually attended it are without comparison less than for the first fortnight after my arrival here, when I went back very fast, and wasted exceedingly, both in strength and flesh. The last is a matter of little consequence; but, though I have not recoverd even the little Stock of Strength with which I left home, for the last fortnight, I have lost nothing. But this is enough upon this poor Subject.

It gave me great concern to learn this morning the afflicting news of poor Mr Benions Death at this place;[1] at the moment when every one thought his perfect recovery was a thing beyond all Doubt. But such are our affairs here. He was a most worthy man and most deserving of your friendship; a man of a soft heart, and of great integrity, without any obliquity or windings or turnings whatever. You cannot easily replace such a friend: But at this Crisis for your Seat, for Gods sake look for some man of a manly decided Character, who will belong to you, and to your principles, and who has some stock of real principles of his own. This needs not be much recommended to you—But you are used to great freedom in me; and I do not think you have ever liked me the worse for it, whether you fell in with my opinions or not.[2]

Mrs Burke gives a thousand thanks to your Lordship and Lady Fitzwilliam for your kind Sollicitude about us. It is time for me to

[1] Richard Benyon (1746–96), who had sat for Fitzwilliam's borough of Peterborough since 1774, died at Bath on 22 August.

[2] In January when a (mistaken) newspaper report had made him think that there was going to be a vacant seat at Fitzwilliam's borough of Malton, Burke wrote to Fitzwilliam urging strongly that it should be offered to French Laurence (see vol. VIII, 367–8).

think a little of her complaints for which I hope this place is not unfit. I suppose Lord Milton[1] is with you and well. I direct this to Wentworth,[2] as I must presume you are there by this time. Walker King and his Wife very kindly came hither and spent two days with us.

I am ever, my dear Lord, with the strongest Sentiments of a weak Gratitude

Your truly affectionate
and attachd friend and humble
Servant
EDM BURKE

To EDWARD JAMES NAGLE—23 *August* 1796

Source: MS Mrs Donald Mead.
Addressed: Edmund Nagle Esqr| War Office| White Hall| London.
MS mutilated. The full text was on the two sides of a single sheet, of which the upper half is now cut away.

Edward James Nagle (d. 1802), known as 'Edmund' by his relations, was a clerk in the War Office and probably the elder son of Walter Nagle (d. 1779); see vol. IV, 93. At this period he acted as 'a sort of friendly secretary' to Burke (Laurence to Fitzwilliam, 21 February 1797, MS at Northampton, Box 51).

deal in the total, I was obliged to send to Mrs Silburn who employ'd this man[3]—and in this very situation I must be again, (supposing me to live) if Government and the Committee are not both of them punctual. I really thought that the Baker[4] had been paid up to the 20th of July and that his months Bill, would not, of Course, be due until the twenty ⟨...⟩ thank God, ⟨...⟩ Burke, Mrs Nugent[5] and all here ⟨...⟩ their sincere love to you and to Newington[6]

faithfully and affectionately
Yours
EDM BURKE

Augst 23. 1796.

[1] Charles William Fitzwilliam (1786–1857), styled Viscount Milton, the Earl's son and heir.
[2] Wentworth Woodhouse, the Earl's Yorkshire seat.
[3] Not identified.
[4] Not identified.
[5] Lucinda, *née* Nagle (1762–1826), the second wife of John Nugent (1737–1813), Jane Burke's brother.
[6] The Nugents lived at Newington.

To the KING OF FRANCE—25 *August* 1796

Source: Copy (in Jane Burke's hand) in Fitzwilliam MSS (Sheffield).

After the death of Louis XVII, Louis-Stanislas-Xavier de Bourbon, Comte de Provence (1755–1824), was acknowledged by royalists as the King of France. In April, as a result of the French victories in North Italy, the Venetian Senate expelled him from Venice, where he had been living since June 1794. He took refuge in Germany and on 19 July an attempt was made to assassinate him at Dillingen, where he was staying (R. W. Phipps, *The Armies of the First French Republic*..., London, 1926–39, IV, 44–5; H. H. Robbins, *Our First Ambassador to China*, London, 1908, pp. 414–40; *The Times*, 4 August).

Sire

I cannot make my acknowledgements to your Majesty for the inestimable honour you have been pleased to confer upon me,[1] in a better manner than in returning My unfeigned thanks to the superintending Majesty of the world for the last of your deliverances from the Malice and Madness of Mankind.

Amidst the gloom which from every quarter Looms upon us all, I will indulge an hope, that this signal deliverance, which has given to your Majesty a new occasion for a display of your habitual presence of mind of your Magnanimity, and of your tender Sollicitude for others joined with but too much indifference for your own Sacred person may be an earnest to us that the time is not far off, when Knowledge, ability and Virtue in a King will not become; on the part of his Subjects, reasons for excluding him from his lawful Throne, or motives on the part of his fellow Sovereigns, his kindred and his Allies, for an active persecution of a Brother Monarch whom they ought to be proud to resemble in everything but his fortunes; nothing it is true can wear a more unfavourable aspect than the present temper of the Times, and the actual condition of affairs. But perhaps we ought not to despair. Prodigies were necessary to overturn the Monarchy of France—There may be miracles to restore it.

It is plain how your Majesties goodness and care will extend even to the minutest part of your great charge, (if heaven should listen to our Supplications) when you condescend so graciously to regard the efforts of an obscure, broken and insignificant individual Stranger. What I have attempted is, according to my measure, little indeed; But it would be unnatural, if we who mean to live and to die true to the dictates of honour and Party, should make no effort at all in favour of those who have persevered in a Noble fidelity, even when Sovereigns have proved unfaithful to their Dignity, to their trust, and to the protection of those

---

[1] If this was a letter, it is missing.

69

principles which support their Thrones? To receive so poor an homage as mine to those principles is in the usual tenour of your Majesties comprehensive goodness. It is a great reward the value of which I feel as I ought. I do not Know in what retreat this humble acknowledgement may find him, who by every Title is the first Monarch of the world—but I faithfully assure your Majesty, that your Royal approbation is more flattering to my pride and more consolatory to My heart, than if living at that time I had received the same tokens of acceptance from your Ancestor Louis the 14th dated from Versailles in the Meridian of his prosperity and glory.

As to me I am old, helpless, and consumed with grief and indignation at the sight of what providence has reserved me to behold. As to you Sire—you are in the vigour of your life, and I trust you will live to see, and largely to contribute to the happiness of a truly regenerated world.

With the Sentiments of the most perfect respect, gratitude, and attachment and the most sincere Veneration

Sire

Your Majesties

Most Obedient

and Most Obliged humble Servant

EDM BURKE

Bath August 25 1796

To FRENCH LAURENCE—26 *August* 1796

Source: MS Osborn Collection. Printed *Burke–Laurence Correspondence*, pp. 56–8.
Addressed: Doctor Laurence| Doctors Commons| London.
Postmarked: BATH   AU|27|96|A.

My dear friend,

When I receivd your last kind Letter,[1] I was in a way at best very doubtful, to my feelings, desperate. I make one of the earliest uses of a small returning degree of Strength, to thank you for that and for all other tokens of your friendship. It looks, as if Providence, for some wise Ends, relative to my own better preparation for Death, or for some services to those who are near and dear to me, was resolved to continue me here something longer than I lookd for. Your regard for me will justifye some detail of my Case. I find myself slowly, but with a nearly uniform progress, recovering. The mere complaint itself is very nearly

[1] Missing.

as it has been: But the consequences are not in the same in any painful or debilitating Circumstances. I am still indeed emaciated and comparatively weak: But not at all, as for the first fortnight after my arrival here, going perceptibly backward. I beleive the Bath waters cannot do much more for me than they have done: But for a long time, Mrs Burke, from her sedulous and unremitting anxiety for me, has not profited of the Bathing, which I believe good for her Case—so that on that account, I shall continue here some time longer.

The troublesome Legacy which I left to you,[1] was with the modifications, if I do not mistake, that your Letter mentions. God forbid, that I should lay that Load on the Shoulders of a friend to his Ruin. I am happy in the nature of the Causes that prevent your accession to this sad inheritance; Particularly, that you are got near to that Object, which I have by many ways endeavourd to compass, for you, or rather for the Country—and which my dear Son almost in his dying hours had strongly at heart.[2] Long may you serve the Nation, professionally, professorially, Parliament⟨aril⟩y; and long may you have a Nation existing to serve: Mrs Burke joins cordially in these Wishes.

I am ever with great affection and attachment
My dear Sir
most sincerely Yours
EDMUND BURKE

Bath Aug. 26.1796.

Poor Will is rather more feeble in his Limbs—in other respects in the way you saw him—What there is of him is very much yours.

WILLIAM WINDHAM *to* EDMUND BURKE—26 *August* 1796
Source: Fitzwilliam MSS (Sheffield).

Park str. Westr
Augt 26. 1796.

My Dear Sir

You will wish to know the issue of the business, that carried me to London.—The measure proposed for the reduction of the Regiments, will not be persisted in:[3] and the reduction of the Cadres will be

---

[1] See above, p. 62.

[2] Burke himself immediately after his son's death had dictated a letter to Fitzwilliam requesting that Laurence be returned for Richard's vacant seat; see vol. VII, 574.

[3] Five French units—Castries's and Montemart's corps, Loyal Emigrant, MacLean's Chasseurs and Rotalier's Artillery Corps—were maintained in the British service and at the end of the year sent to Portugal (see below, pp. 135, 206). But in November four

conducted in a way, consistent with the attention due to the situation and merits of the persons, composing them.—To preserve these latter entirely could perhaps not be contended for; At least would have been contended for in vain.

The D. of Y.,[1] who is absent at Weymouth, has been, I fear, the principal mover in this.—The time may come, when the treatment received by those who have sacrificed every thing to royalty, may be returned to the authors of that treatment, with a dreadful justice.

Of my consultations in Town some have had you for their subject, the state of your complaints, and the benefit to be hoped from Bath, or from other means. One of my Counsellors, you will allow to be a good one, Dr Carm. Smith;[2] and both He and Dr Blane,[3] of whom I cannot but have a high opinion, agree in thinking, that a Slight Chalybeate[4] promises to be the most serviceable; and the former of these, Dr Smith, insists strongly upon the advantages of Buxton:[5] the powers of which He states to have been strongly exemplified in the case of ⟨Sir⟩ Adam Ferguson.[6]—A letter, by the way, is just brought me from Dr Blane, for the purpose of being franked; which I hope may be from himself, and relative to the subject, that I have been speaking of.

They both likely agree in thinking, that a small tour, with the amusement, that it would bring, would not be less efficacious than medicine.— I wish, therefore, that your stay at Bath may be prolonged for a little while; when I hope it may be in my power to join you, and to offer such temptation, as I can contrive, to lead you in some small excursion, ending either at Beaconsfield, or what I should like better, at some place of the description abovementioned.

I wish I had any cordials for you from the state of Publick events. There is nothing good enough to be told: though the prospect

French cadre corps in the British service—Allonville's, Léon's, Du Trésor's and Williamson's—were disbanded. Windham seems to have opposed the reduction of the French corps, and on 11 September wrote to Grenville (William Wyndham Grenville, 1st Baron Grenville, 1759–1834) suggesting that 'such corps of French officers as may be furnished by the cadres' might be employed in Portugal. He thought that a 'body of six or seven thousand men, headed by good French officers, would go a great way in the defence of Portugal' and it would thus avoid 'the dreadful example of casting out, without the slightest means of subsistence, the remains of that body of people who have sacrificed everything to their attachment to royalty' (Hist. MSS Comm., *Fortescue MSS*, III, 249–50).

[1] Frederick Augustus, Duke of York (1763–1827), was Commander-in-Chief.
[2] Dr Carmichael Smyth (see above, p. 7).
[3] Dr Gilbert Blane (1749–1834), later (1812) 1st Baronet.
[4] A mineral water impregnated or flavoured with iron.
[5] The Bishop of St-Pol-de-Léon had already given Burke this advice: 'mon voisin m. carmichael Smith pense que les eaux de Buxton seroient celles que conviendroient le mieux à votre état' (letter of 11 August, MS at Northampton).
[6] Sir Adam Fergusson, 3rd Baronet (1733–1813).

in Italy seems to be some trifle less black,[1] than it appeared, when I left you.

With best respects to Mrs B. and the party on the Parade,[2] including M. Cazales,[3]

I am, My Dear Sir,
Your most faithful
Humble Servant
W WINDHAM

To WILLIAM WINDHAM—[27 August 1796]

Source: British Museum (Add. MS 37,843, fols 111-12). Printed *Burke-Windham Correspondence*, p. 201.
Endorsed: Mr Burke| Augst ⟨cir⟩ 27.1796.

Your Letter[4] has had the effect of powerful faith, and has removed a Mountain that lay upon my Breast. I am happy that the Regiments have been saved from slaughter—and that the Cadres will receive a tolerable Capitulation—Tho'! merciful God! is this a time to get rid of Officers or even of Soldiers? But really The consolation nearest to me is that you have got out of the most difficult of all situations with honour. As things go it to prevent the worst is a great good. I really think it would be proper for you to have a very conciliatory but at the same time a very serious conversation with the D. of Y.[5] that he may be made sensible that these are not merely military or merely official arrangements, but indissolubly connected with political considerations of the highest importance.

As to my health, in which you take so kind an Interest—I believe I am quite as well as my Age and foregone infirmities will ever permit me to be. The Physicians you mention[6] are both of an ability and one of a kindness not to be disputed. Chalybeates have hitherto been as poisons to me. As to parties of amusement they seem unnatural—and the thoughts of them are odious to me. I shall stay here at least a Week longer if not more. That depends upon Mrs Burkes finding Benefit to her limbs from the Pump. She had been advised to it from the beginning but she could not be persuaded[7] to it from her eagerness to attend to me, beyond the necessity of the Case. To be sure to have you of the Party would be to me the strongest of all inducements to the Scheme you recommend. Cazales has been a good deal out of Order,

[1] It was reported that Mantua had been relieved and that the French had left behind a considerable train of artillery (*The Times*, 26 August).
[2] Burke was staying at 11 North Parade, Bath.
[3] Jacques-Antoine-Marie de Cazalès (1758–1805).
[4] The previous letter.
[5] The Duke of York.
[6] Doctors Smyth and Blane.
[7] MS: persuade

but he gets better and is infinitely flatterd by your remembrance. No 11[1] presents its grateful compliments to you and yours. Salute Woodford for me and beleive me with affectionate and grateful attachment ever Yours

EDM BURKE

EARL FITZWILLIAM *to* EDMUND BURKE—30 *August* 1796

Source: Fitzwilliam MSS (Sheffield).

There is a copy of this letter in Fitzwilliam's hand at Sheffield (F 32c).

My dear Burke

Your letter[2] found me in the bustle of York races, and though it had reference to the loss of a very old and affectionate friend,[3] which is a cause of great regret, it brought me great comfort on the other hand, by your own account of your improving health. Have patience and perseverance to give the Waters a fair chance of doing all the good they are capable of. I have reliance on your doing so, as I collect from your letter, that Mrs B: has likewise receiv'd benefit from the use of them— for her sake then, and at the request of all your friends, persevere.

The opening made by the death of my poor friend affords me the opportunity of attending to a wish you formerly express'd with respect to Dr Lawrence:[4] I seize it with great satisfaction, as well on account of the high esteem I entertain for his character, as for the pleasure it gives me to do anything acceptable to you.

But on occasions of this nature it is for the future ease and comfort of each party, that there should exist such a coincidence in their opinions, both with regard to things and persons, that in all human probability they will not hereafter differ when they ought to agree. I rely upon having such justice done me both by you and him, that you will give me credit, when I express this sentiment, for not meaning a narrow, rigid conformity of conduct through all the inferior detail of business, but only a coincidence of opinion and principle upon the great outlines of the matters under publick consideration. It is but very lately, only since recent events, that I should have thought the least detail on such a subject necessary for *me*:[5] till this unfortunate epoch in my life, I should have obviated all the difficulty of explanation by pointing out some well known standard, as the establish'd point of resort on all occasions; but unfortunately it is now otherwise; Things

---

[1] No. 11 North Parade.   [2] Of 23 August; see above, pp. 67–8.
[3] Richard Benyon; see above, p. 67.   [4] See above, p. 67.
[5] After his short Irish Viceroyalty which had ended in a serious misunderstanding with his colleagues, Fitzwilliam was very conscious of the need for caution and precision in political negotiations.

and Persons no longer go together; Agreement on the Subject, is not agreement with the Person; and it is therefore that I feel the necessity of entring into a degree of detail with respect to my sentiments, both on things and persons: for being those of an Individual, detach'd from all Party, and arising out of circumstances in a great degree peculiar to himself, they can be collected through no other means, and from no other Quarter.

First then, with respect to Things, to[1] external considerations: here I may be short; because I can refer to my past conduct for what my sentiments have been, and I pronounce, That they remain *unalter'd*— They are become desperate, I grant, because they have never been *fairly* pursued, and more so, because they are now professedly abandon'd by *all*.[2]

Next, with respect to Internal considerations—I am the inveterate enemy of all Innovation, and hold it necessary to face and resist every attempt to introduce any—Though a friend to popular priviledges on ordinary occasions, and having no dislike to the check on publick men by popular discussion, I disapprove in the greatest degree of the abuse of these priviledges, and had rather see the good curtail'd, than the evil extended—I had rather see a bad Minister go uncorrected, than a good constitution stabb'd in its vitals.

Now to Persons—I hesitate not to say, that under no circumstances whatever, will I be in connection with Mr Pitt—it is sufficient for a man's life to have been duped once.

I hesitate no less to say that I will never hold communication with the Duke of Portland untill He has made the Amende honorable to those honorable men, those faithfull friends, steady adherents and followers of his,[3] whose character and Interests, whose weight and consideration in Ireland, he had made subservient to his own purposes and views in this country for such a length of time: but all of which He sacrific'd, (together with the tranquillity, the Liberties and security of that country,) to his new Connections.[4]

I avow, that my inclinations, my private attachments, the habits of my life, all combine to make me anxious to see the moment, when I may be able to give to the members of Opposition an honorable assistance: not incompatable[5] in my own opinion with general good—but

[1] MS: to to
[2] Fitzwilliam prided himself on being a consistent supporter of the war against France.
[3] Henry Grattan (1746–1820) and the Ponsonbys (see below, p. 351).
[4] Portland had agreed with Pitt and not with Fitzwilliam in the crisis over Fitzwilliam's Irish policy.
[5] MS: incompaable

in stating this, it certainly is not in my contemplation to become again an active member of an Opposition—Those days are over—circumstances have happen'd, that make me think, that I can be no more, usefully so; usefully, I mean, to those, whom I should wish to serve—I look therefore upon a regular, methodical Opposition on my part, as over—But in one word, should circumstances ever present to me the opportunity of doing essential injury to Mr Pitt's power, or of rendring effectual service to Mr Fox, I will not fail to seize it.

I have wish'd not to be too prolix, nevertheless not to be so short, as to leave my views and intentions doubtfull—I think I am explicit—If, my dear Burke, you, who know Dr Lawrence, think the offer of a Seat in Parliament from a man entertaining such sentiments, likely to be acceptable, do me the favor to propose Peterbro' to him—it will add to my satisfaction that the offer is made through you.

Believe me ever affectionately and truely Yours
W. F.

Wentworth
aug: 30th 96

MRS JOHN CREWE *to* EARL FITZWILLIAM— 1 *September* [1796]

Source: Fitzwilliam MSS (Sheffield), F 127a.
Addressed: Earl of Fitzwilliam| Grosvenor Square| London.
Postmarked: NAMPTWICH SE|2|96|D FREE|SE|2|96|⟨ ⟩.
This letter was forwarded to Wentworth| Rotherham.

Mrs John Crewe (Frances Anne Greville, d. 1818), the well-known Whig hostess, was unremitting in her attentions to Edmund and Jane Burke. Hearing a favourable report of Burke's health, she wrote to Lord Fitzwilliam.

1st Sept Crewe Hall

Dear Lord Fitzwilliam

I really cannot resist sending you the enclosed letter[1] which I received 2 days ago, tho' I hope by this time you have received such accounts as have set your mind at rest as much as mine is at present—our poor Friend Mrs Burke *too*, writes me word that her health mends,[2]

---

[1] A letter from Dr Caleb Hillier Parry (see below, p. 234) of Bath to Mrs Crewe reported that Burke had 'continued in a state of progressive amendment. His nights have been with very few exceptions tranquil and refreshing. His appetite is good, his strength decidedly increased; and those dreadful eructations under which you so constantly saw him labour are reduced almost to nothing. His spirits too are extremely good; and he acknowledges, without hesitation, that for at least a fortnight he has lost no flesh, and his complaints have been otherwise much less oppressive' (MS at Sheffield, F 127a, dated 26 August).

[2] Jane Burke's letter is missing.

and indeed it is impossible to say how much all those who have known this Family as you and I have done, must rejoice at this return of health to it. For my own part, I have no scruple to assert that they are the best Friends I ever had out of my own Family for above three and thirty years! and to *You* I will confess that alass! he is ever *more* to me than a *real* Parent!—Forgive all this, but indeed after the very melancholy Scenes I witnessed at Bath, and after so much despondency on this Cruel Subject, it is reviving to my heart to get such a letter as the enclosed and as I took the liberty of communicating my *fears* at *first* to *You*, it may perhaps be but Justice to myself to let you see that there are times when I *can rejoice!*—we are pretty *good* and *quiet* just now *here*, and the *fine Harvest* gives great pleasure to *all loyal Persons*. I hope Lady Fitzwilliam and Lord Milton are in perfect health and shall be obliged to You if You will present my kind and respectful Compliments to the former. Adieu my dear Lord

Your grateful and Obedient
Servant
F. A. CREWE

To EARL FITZWILLIAM—2 *September* 1796

Source: Fitzwilliam MSS (Sheffield), F 32c.
Endorsed (by Fitzwilliam): Mr Burke Sept 5| 1796.

Bath Septr 2.1796.

My dearest Lord,

I feel as I ought, but I never can express as I ought to do, my Sense of your astonishing, unexampled friendship to me; I was going to say unmerited too—but as friendship is merited rather by sentiments than services, I will not lower the value of what, I beleive, you are persuaded I feel for you.

I was, and am, clearly and uniformly of opinion, that you never ought to recommend a Member for any place in which you have an influence, who will not take your general Line, both as to persons and things—and mark a decided attachment to yourself—and this, not from honour and gratitude only, but from a Strong opinion, of the Wisdom of your Views, and the rectitude of your principles. I am so strongly of that opinion, that if I were myself in the vigour of my Life, and had as much desire, or indeed ten times more desire than I have ever had, of employing myself in the Service of the publick I should not hesitate to say, that you ought not to bring me into Parliament with an Obligation

to Mr Pitt hanging about my Neck. It would never indeed induce me
to go along with him in the Paths, in which, unguided by all moral
and all political principle, he has lately walked—But I never could with
decorum, join in that personal Hostility, in which you are so well
justified in bearing to him, in every thing which does not wound those
opinions and feelings, which have joined you to him, and seperated
you from him. Thank you for Laurence. I should never have thought of
him—God, God forbid! if I thought that he was capable of making
use of your Patronage, as the means of his own private advancement;
or that he could, for a moment, prevaricate and shuffle where your
honour was concerned. No! I am well convinced, that if he finds, but
an iota, in what you propose, to be such as he cannot promise absolutely
to comply with, he would rather keep out of Parliament for ever than
accept it. Such is my opinion of him; on which opinion (subject to
human errour) I have ever recommended him; full as much at least for
your sake as for his own. I love him and trust him—but I owe much
more to your Lordship, and I love you much more.

I go with your Lordship in every word almost that you have said. I
really do not know how I can directly dissent from *any* part of it: But
it is exceedingly to be lamented, that the course of Events, and the proceedings of all descriptions of persons have brought things to that pass,
that really there are but *two men in the Country*;[1] and that there appears
a sort of necessity, of adopting the one or the other of them, without
regard to any publick principle whatsoever. This extinguishes party, as
party; and even the Nation as a Nation. Every thing is forced into the
shape of a mere faction, and a contest for nothing[2] short, in substance
and effect, than the sovereign authority, for one or the other of the
chieftains: I was in serious hopes that the party[3] which was at last
rallied under its proper standards, a little time before I left Parliament,
might, either in Ministry or out of Ministry, as the publick necessities
required, become some sort of Asylum for principles moral and political,
and might control that disposition to factious servitude, which could
see nothing, in the constitution or the country, but the power of one or
two individuals: But by some mistakes in the manner of your coming
into Ministry, but much more, and more decisively, by the conduct
pursued towards your Lordship, not one Stone is left upon the other,
in that party—nor do I see the least possible chance for its reconstruction
either from the same materials or from any other. I am of opinion that
these two Leaders have done irreperable mischiefs to the Country,

[1] Pitt and Fox.   [2] MS: nothing for nothing
[3] The Portland Whigs, or 'Old Whigs'.

one in one way, the other in another, and very often both of them in the
same way. I think I am the furthest in the world from a personal
animosity to Mr Fox: but it appears to me evident beyond all doubt and
discussion, that if he is not quite out of his senses, and has any drift or
determined pursuit at all, that he founds his hopes upon something that
is neither in his Native Country nor in its antient constitution. His
Politicks are astray, and absurd; and he cultivates and studies nothing
at all at home but whatever is most wicked, unprincipled, dark, dangerous, and traiterous. His Enthusiasm in favour of Regicide France,
declared over and over again during the last Session, in defiance of all
the Maxims of Prudence, his evident Triumph in seeing their Arms
victorious over all nations—The part he had taken with every sort of
conspirators, and assassins of every description in this Kingdom—His
avowed adoption of one of the worst of their Leaders, publickly on the
Hustings at the late Westminster election,[1] if there was nothing else
would make all pretence of doubt concerning his principles, politicks,
and connexions perfectly ridiculous. It is for this reason, that I should
be far from recommending to your Lordship to make his establishment
in power one of the Objects of your Life. Pitt takes the part he does in
this French Business, thro' shabbiness, selfishness and a mean desire
to linger for some time, under the sufferance of France, in name a
British Minister; but Mr Fox has that connexion abroad, and all
belonging to it at home, as an Object of preference, desire, and predilection. Between them we are undone—but with this last much more
certainly, much more rapidly, and in a way beyond all cure. Whoever
takes up Mr Pitt only enlists with a set of low Wretches who follow him
backward and forward thro' all the windings and turnings of his unhappy politicks—They who inlist with Mr Fox, know the Terms of the
service, their Cause, and their Company. The Cause is avowed; and the
Band, both in the Officers in the first stage of subordination, and thro'
all the degrees, is regular, Systematick, firm, and consistent. God
almighty direct you! This is the only point of the Condition which, I
wish you not to make with any Member You bring in but to leave that
matter open. Indeed I would do so as to *both* the leaders—making it a
point to connect with no leader but thro' you. I beg you to recollect
that all the Evils which have befallen you have been owing to your
distrust of yourself, and your putting too much confidence in some
Leader. You have every capacity to be a Leader yourself, which Nature
and experience can give, except the disposition to it. Mr Fox would
never give you up, and sacrifice you thro' weakness. There is no danger

[1] See above, pp. 43–4.

of that; But under his Guidance you may be led, with sufficient fidelity and firmness to your person, into ways foreign both to your nature and your principles.

What I say on this head is merely as to yourself. To Laurence, I shall do nothing more than to lay your generous and noble offer before him for his consideration—which, whether he thinks it safe and honourable to accept, with the only thing which he may imagine a drawback on it,—(the Case of entering into Mr Foxes party. To his person he rather leans.) I am sure he will receive the honour intended for him with becoming, that is to say, with the greatest gratitude. If he should not, I wish you to have your Eye on some person on whom you may depend as wholly and exclusively yours. Except the man we talk of—I cannot point out one to you my acquaintance in the world is so poor and limited.

As to me, whose existence, nothing but your extreme partiality could make important, The bottom of my complaint always remains the same—but with far less of pain—with no dejection and with rather a recovery than any loss of strength. But as yet I am incapable of any application. Mrs Burke, thank God, is a little better—and joins in a thousand thanks and salutations to Lady Fitzwilliam. Ever My dear Lord the most Obliged of men. Yours truly

EDM BURKE

To FRENCH LAURENCE—2 *September* 1796

Source: MS Osborn Collection. Printed *Burke–Laurence Correspondence*, pp. 58–60.

My dear Laurence,

I am not a little surprised, that so long a time should pass without my hearing from you; and especially that you have not noticed my last Letter.[1] What I enclose[2] will save me the trouble of saying much; and indeed the letters coming in rather late, and the necessity of an immediate and very full acknowlegement of Lord F's kindness to us both, give me but very little time to explain myself—at large as I could wish to do. I certainly wish, above most things, to have an hours conversation with you—but that, before your answer to Lord Fitzwilliam, which cannot be long delayd, is a thing impossible. I do not know what the Nature and circumstances of the Seat are to which you alluded in your Letter to me.[3] If it be that which Woodford had in his Eye; and

[1] Of 26 August; see above, pp. 70–1.
[2] Fitzwilliam's letter of 30 August; see above, pp. 74–6.
[3] The letter is missing.

which, in the most profound secrecy, he entrusted to me,[1] I do not well know, what solid foundation, that Business stands on. This which is now Offerd to you, if not very favourable to your first Views of interest,[2] is, from the connexion, by far the most honourable that this Kingdom affords. Most of the Principles laid down in that Letter are such as we hold in common, as firmly as our incomparable friend maintains them; and as to personal attachment from Gratitude and Esteem, there is no doubt you will think of it in a different Veiw from that in which it is regarded by Serjeant Adair[3] and Mr Baldwin.[4]

As to the rest, I recommend nothing. Your Judgment is better than mine. I certainly wish to see you afloat in the Parliamentary Channel; and the Tide in the affairs of men[5] is not safely neglected. God direct you. If you cannot accept (which I dont think) from prior engagement or on the Veiw of things—I am sure your refusal will be such as will shew the sense you have of the highest honour we can receive, to be distinguishd by one of the most able and Virtuous men, if not eminently the most so, in the Country and age we live in. In or out of Parliament—Mrs Burke and I say, God bless you. Adieu faithfully yours

EDM BURKE

Septr 2.1796.

Say not a word of Lord Fitzwilliams Letter[6] to any human creature. Thinking it possible you may not be in Town, I enclose this to Woodford.

Laurence received Burke's letter, enclosing Fitzwilliam's, on 3 September, and wrote at length to Fitzwilliam on the 6th. He explained that though he agreed with Fitzwilliam politically he owed his professorship to Portland (see above, p. 47). He asked Fitzwilliam's permission to 'acquaint his Grace with the affair as arranged', and, subject only to Portland's 'negative', accepted Fitzwilliam's offer. Fitzwilliam replied on the 10th that he had 'no objection to any previous communication' Laurence might wish to have with the Duke. On receiving this letter Laurence must have written Portland immediately because on 13 September Portland wrote: 'I this moment receive Your very friendly and confidential letter for which I am duly thankful to You. If you like to be in Parliament, there are many circumstances in the mode by which this Seat will be obtained which give it upon the whole a preference in my mind to any

[1] Nothing has been discovered about Woodford's efforts to secure a seat for Laurence.
[2] The Duke of Portland had told Laurence two years earlier that if Laurence wished it he would 'make it his study' to provide him with a seat (Laurence to Fitzwilliam, 6 September 1796, MS at Sheffield, F 32c). Burke realized that Laurence might prefer to be connected with Portland, who was in office, rather than with Fitzwilliam, who was not.
[3] James Adair (c. 1743–98) sat for Fitzwilliam's borough of Higham Ferrers.
[4] William Baldwin (c. 1737–1813) was Richard, Jr's successor in his seat at Malton.
[5] See *Julius Caesar*, IV, iii, 218; also below, p. 93.
[6] MS: the Letter of Lord Fitzwilliam of Lord Fitzwilliam's Letter

other, although I must protest against *that* to which You refer as making any part of them. Everyone has a right to indulge what suppositions he likes, but He is not to infer that they are admitted if they happen to be let pass uncontradicted—However with respect to the War, my opinion is, that had it been other conducted by us it would have been given up long before this time'. On the same day Laurence informed Fitzwilliam: 'My communication was well received, and I am at liberty to obey my own inclinations and the wishes of Mr Burke' (MS at Sheffield, F 32*c*; Portland MSS, Nottingham).

To JOHN KING—3 *September* 1796

Source: Public Records Office (H.O. 100/64, fol. 206).
Addressed: John King Esqr| Under Secretary of State| &c &c &c| Whitehall.
Postmarked: BATH   FREE|SE|5|96⟨C⟩.

John King (1759–1830) was an Under-Secretary of State in the Home Department.

My dear King,

I hear with much satisfaction, that Mr Hussey, my old and good freind, is appointed Chaplain General to the Catholick Regiments serving in Ireland.[1] When I asked him concerning the appointments, he told me that he had required none, and that none had been offerd. This does great Credit to his unparralleld disinterestedness—but it makes Government look scandalous, that can confer Offices of Labour, Trust, and attendance, and take a man from his House and residence to transfer him to another Country, and leave him loaded with Duty without compensation. I am sure that the Duke of Portland[2] would be the man in the world the most averse to Governments taking an advantage of the nobleness of mind in any person; and that he does intend to annex a proper Salary, and fit for such a Duty and such a man; with a proper security for half pay on a reduction. I assure you these are my suggestions not his—But they are proper just and reasonable and I trust, my dear King, that you will, as such, put the Duke in mind of the matter; which, if it has escaped him, has escaped him thro' inadvertence. My affectionate and humble Duty to him, if you think it at all necessary to mention my Name, in a matter which will come more properly from yourself. I am a good deal better, I thank God;

[1] In August Dr Douglass noted in his diary 'Rev: Mr Hussey has informed me that Monsignor Erskine [Charles Erskine, 1739–1811, later, 1801, Cardinal] has obtained for him from Rome a Vicarial Authority over all the Military in the King's service' (Dr John Douglass's Diary, August 1796, Westminster Diocesan Archives). On 9 August Hussey's appointment as Chaplain to the Irish Brigade was officially announced. At the same time the appointments of Roman Catholic chaplains to each regiment in the Brigade were gazetted (Hussey to Portland, 10 July, Public Record Office, H.O. 100/64, fols 143–4; *Dublin Gazette*, 6–9 August).
[2] As Home Secretary the Duke of Portland was the British minister responsible for Ireland.

and I think Mrs Burke mends. Both our loves to Mrs King.[1] You have heard of the ugly accident which has happend to your Brother.

Ever truly Yours
EDM BURKE

Bath Sept. 3. 1796.

This letter bears two endorsements. The first is in John King's hand: 'Sepr 12.|96| Revd Mr Hussey| who has been| with me, dines| with Mr Burke| at Beaconsfield| on Wednesday—| He asked for| £100 to which| I added 50'. The second endorsement is by the Duke of Portland: 'I thought it was Your intention to have| placed £200 to Mr Husseys credit| at His Bankers—| Our friend Burke seems to have| misapprehended this appointment| from the beginning to the end, but| it does not signify'. Portland later explained what he conceived Hussey's position to be and why he did not consider him to be the holder of a paid appointment under the Crown. Hussey, Portland had been given to understand, had been empowered by the Pope to supervise the chaplains appointed to the Irish Brigade and to authorize their performance of ecclesiastical functions. That being so, the Government was prepared to appoint him Chaplain General, placing him in such a position as 'would qualify him or authorise him to dispense or distribute the Powers he had received from Rome' (Portland to Pelham, 1 November, Public Record Office, H.O. 100/62, fols 310–11).

To FRENCH LAURENCE—6 September 1796

Source: MS Osborn Collection. Printed *Burke–Laurence Correspondence*, p. 66.

Bath Tuesday Sept.6.1796

My dear Laurence,

We shall remain here till this day sennight:[2] But I do not know that it is absolutely necessary for you to come hither. It can hardly be without a great hindrance to your Business. If, on the whole, you should resolve to accept, I know of no Obligations that lie on you except to the D. of Portland—and none of them have been connected with any politicks of this time that I know of. Of course you will say nothing of this to him, until your resolution is in general taken—You will then communicate it to him without seeming to entertain any Sense of its being in any Event likely to be unpleasant to him. I take it for granted you will explain this matter distinctly to Lord Fitzwilliam. I need not again recommend to you, to let not a breath of air on this Business until it is necessary, by your election, if you should take upon [you] the explanation which I think it quite right Should be made. Ever Yours,

EDM BURKE

[1] Harriot Margaret, *née* Moss (*c.* 1768–1841).   [2] That is, until 13 September.

To WILLIAM WINDHAM—11 *September* 1796

Source: British Museum (Add. MS. 37,843, fols 113–14). Printed *Burke-Windham Correspondence*, p. 202.
Endorsed: Mr Burke| Sepr 11.1796. R̄ 14th.

My dear Sir,

I am beyond measure mortified at not being able to meet you at Oxford.[1] But it will do, I hope, to see you at Beconsfield on your return. There I *must* be, on Wednesday, at dinner;[2] and as I cannot leave this very early on Tuesday; and as Oxford, besides a worse Road is, I am told, twenty mile about, on that Road, I cannot, compass my Object on Wednesday. I bless God for it, I am much better; and this may be some satisfaction to the goodnature of friends, on a private account—but as for the publick, a fear of Enemies has multiplied them on all sides; and a desire of concealing appearances has aggravated the reality; and we seem to me to be descending to the Center of ruin with so accelerated a motion, thro' the thin medium of pusillanimity,[3] disgrace, and humilation, that it seems to be an attempt to fight with the establishd Laws of Nature, to stop the course which things are taking: But on this we shall talk more when we meet. We think national shame and degradation a sort of rescourse. God almighty bless you, and preserve you from your share in the Embassy of Mr Grenville.[4] Adieu. Adieu.

Your unhappy but ever
attachd friend
EDM BURKE

Bath Septr 11. 1796.

To UNKNOWN DOCTOR—[*circa* 14 *September* 1796]

Source: MS fragment Mrs Valerie Jobling.
MS torn. If Burke reached Beaconsfield by 14 September, as he intended to do, this letter was probably written on, or very close to, that date.

Dear Sir,

I am returned hither, on the whole much the better for the Bath expedition. Mrs Burke is also not the worse for it. So that it is not on our own account I now take the Liberty of troubling you; But one of

[1] Probably Windham in a (missing) letter had proposed meeting Burke on his way from Bath to Beaconsfield.
[2] Wednesday the 14th of September. Burke was to meet Hussey at Beaconsfield; see the previous page.   [3] MS: pusillanity,
[4] It had been reported that Thomas Grenville (1755–1846) was to go to Paris for the purpose of making 'fair, equitable, and moderate Proposals of Peace' (*True Briton*, 9 September).

the Boys at Penn School for the French Royalists has been for these nine days or thereabouts ill of a Fever of a bad appearance.[1] He is one of those who I find to interest me the most, on account of the Character of his father, a man of eminent Virtue and military Talents, and who was unfortunately massacred at the fatal Business of Quiberon. His mother also an excellent Woman[2] has him for her ⟨...⟩ so good to

To FRENCH LAURENCE—[15 *September* 1796]

Source: Burke–Laurence Correspondence, pp. 253-4.

Burke's 'Thursday' would appear to be the first Thursday after his return to Beaconsfield.

Thursday.

My dear Laurence,

I am truly happy with the turn this business has taken.[3] I suppose nothing, as yet, is to be said about it. Very few of the objects which my dear Richard had on his mind in dying, are, thank God, left wholly unaccomplished—the deliverance of Ireland from the hands of the Job ascendancy excepted—that was nearly done too—but Providence, for reasons above our wisdom, has suffered that great affair to be snatched out of the hands that alone seemed made for it.[4] However he was saved that pang, worse than any he could have felt in the parting of that fairest of all souls from a frail human body. Here we are, and with thankfulness we acknowledge it, returned to that house, in which we had many such moments as we never can see more. Our thankfulness, very sincere, I hope, did not hinder us from feeling that we were come to a place in which there was none to rejoice in receiving us; none in whom we could rejoice by being received! But that is over—all over, all our domestick comforts, the only comforts, are all at an end; and if we look abroad—what a dreadful horizon!

What you say of Jack Nugent's family[5] is worthy of your goodness of heart. Great advantages to it will be derived from your generous protection, I have no doubt; and we receive your intentions most thankfully, knowing as we do that the very line, in which we wished you to come in, must for a long time at least, be a barrier against all your hopes for

---

[1] Burke told Lady Buckingham on 23 November that one boy—presumably this same one—was 'ill in bed of a malignant low fever for forty five days' (see below, p. 128).

[2] Neither parent has been identified.

[3] See above, pp. 81–2.

[4] Burke believed that a 'junto' of Irish office-holders had been very largely responsible for the failure of Fitzwilliam's Lord Lieutenancy; see vol. VIII, 173–5.

[5] See above, p. 68.

yourself or for any body else: and we trust that you do not think that when your late friend, and myself, his unworthy and misplaced representative, wished you that seat, that any thing of the sort ever entered into our heads, much or little. Adieu till Saturday. Our cordial love to Woodford and Nagle, and to our friends on the south-side of Thames.[1]

Ever most affectionately yours,
EDMUND BURKE.

To DR RICHARD BROCKLESBY—19 *September* 1796
Source: Fitzwilliam MSS (Milton).

Dr Richard Brocklesby (1722–97), one of Burke's physicians, was also one of his oldest friends, having attended Ballitore School.

My dear friend,

My pilgrimage of health is over; and I bless God for it, with an effect as good, as in my broken state of body and mind, and in my advanced time of Life, with a distemper in some degree constitutional and habitual, could in any reason be expected. I am therefore to wait a little longer, in all appearance, the further disposition of Providence on this side of the Grave.

Mrs Burke has likewise[2] had some Benefit by the use of the same Waters, though the weakness and occasional stiffness in her Limbs is not removed. In other respects I think she is better, and even in the old complaint, some triffle mended. When will you come down; and enjoy, with the stock of health, I trust you have laid in by your marine excursions, the sight of the good you have done by your skill and friendship to this family.[3]

I am my dear Doctor whilst one part of me hangs to another most affectionately and faithfully

Your ever obligd humble Servant
EDM BURKE

Beconsfield Sept. 19. 1796.

---

[1] Perhaps Burke is referring to Major William Cuppage (1759–1832), a first cousin once removed of William Burke. He and his family lived at Charlton in Kent.

[2] MS: has likewise has

[3] Nagle, however, did not share Burke's opinion of the doctor. Writing from Beaconsfield four months later, he told Windham: 'Doctor Brocklesby is here—the more affected with his own infirmities, than attention to those of Mr Burke, seems utterly incapable of administering releif or comfort' (Add. MS 37, 843, fols 131–2).

To THOMAS VENABLES—20 *September* 1796

Source: MS The Rev. P. A. Venables.
Addressed: To | —Venables Esqr | &c &c.
This letter is in Jane Burke's hand, but signed by Burke.

Thomas Venables (1727–1803), having served as an Army officer, was appointed a Barrack Master in May 1794 and was probably serving at Chester (Public Record Office, W.O. 4/344). He was married to Anne (1745–1817), sister of Walker King.

(Duplicate)

Beaconsfield
Sept 20th 1796

My Dear Sir,

In the confidence of the friendship I have uniformly experienced from the family of the Kings, I take the liberty [of giving you] some trouble, when I tell you it is in favor of a friend in great distress, and in fear of greater—broken in Mind, Body, and fortune, it will be an additional recommendation to your humanity. To save more words.

My old friend Will. Burke has returned from India, the Country in which all other Men have made their fortune over-whelmed with debt. He can no longer Stand his ground here;[1] and *of himself*, in his feeble State cannot provide a retreat for himself. We trust to your active benevolence therefore to get him a comfortable private Lodging at Chester to be from thence by way of Liverpoole, if it cannot be directly from Chester to the Isle of Man[2] and that you would procure Some Safe and confidential person to convey him, who will have some reasonable compensation for his trouble; and that you will give him such recommendations as you think best to somebody there, who will Lodge and Board him and his Man[3] comfortably and reasonably. For any expense you may be at whilst he remains in England you will draw on me at any Sight you please; and you may depend upon it a full provision will be made for any Credits you may think it proper for him to have there (with as little use of his Name as possible) in any way you wish it to be settled—thro' Major Cuppage I believe will be the best. You will have the goodness to

[1] Evidently one of William Burke's creditors—probably Josias Dupré Porcher (see vol. VIII, 360)—was refusing to be pacified.

[2] An act of Tynwald of 1737 exempted a debtor from arrest in the Isle of Man for his 'foreign debts'. This made the island a haven of refuge for English debtors.

[3] On his return from India in 1793 William had been accompanied by a servant named Tombee. In his will William left £350 to pay Tombee's passage back to India and to restore his caste. When William died in 1798, Tombee set off for Beaconsfield. The Bishop of Sodor and Man (see below, p. 92) wrote to Mrs Burke: 'Poor Tombees respectful Love for his late Master seems to increase since his loss of Him, he tells me he is grown indifferent to India, and wishes to lay his bones as near his Good Masters as he can, and anxiously begs that a cast-Iron railing shoud be allowd to inclose the Stone' (letter of 25 April 1798, MS at Sheffield, Bk28).

write to me fully on the Subject. I need not say, that no time is to be lost; and that all secresy is to be used.—I am ever with Mrs Burkes and my best Compliments to Mrs Venables

> My Dear Sir,
>> Your faithful and
>>> affectionate Humble
>>>> Servant EDM BURKE

P:S: I am grown much better for my Bath expedition—and left Dr Walker[1] on our departure on his flight to London; his wife being again in a thriving way, tho' much better,[2] I employ a confidential friend to make a Copy of this Letter, which I send by Post,[3] in order that Mr Burke may take a duplicate with him.

>>> Yours ever
>>>> EDM BURKE

To EARL FITZWILLIAM—23 September 1796

Source: Fitzwilliam MSS (Sheffield), F32c.
Endorsed (by Fitzwilliam): Mr Burke| septr 26.96.

My Dear Lord,

Since my return I have seen Dr Laurence, who, I believe, is now at Peterborough.[4] I greatly deceive myself, if he does not feel in its full extent his obligation to your Lordship, as well as a comfortable interiour satisfaction in owing his seat rather to you than to any other person whatever. I do not think indeed, that at this time, that he, or even that your Lordship yourself, can do any good—but it is never amiss, (with the disposition) to be in a Situation of serving the publick; or at least of falling in good Company, in a good Cause, and in an honourable Struggle.

It must be of the greatest inconvenience to you to come up at this time: But I think your resolution is well taken. Your protest ought certainly to be made[5] and made, not only in fugitive words, but on the

---

[1] Walker King.　　　　　　　　　　[2] See above, p. 10, and below, p. 148.
[3] The copy sent by post is missing.
[4] Laurence wrote to Fitzwilliam from Peterborough on the 23rd: 'I have just time to inform your Lordship that my canvass is now finished' (MS at Sheffield, F 32c).
[5] Fitzwilliam had written to Burke on 17 September: 'For my part, however inconvenient it may be (and it certainly is exceedingly so) I shall go up for the Kings speech, to give my support if it holds out but the semblance of vigor or common sense: if on the other hand, it promises nothing but compromise with danger, I must enter my last protest against the system, as an excess of folly, and take my leave—the Parliament is a new one, and therefore it may be fit to take my line once more: otherwise I should have thought I had done enough already—do you approve' (MS at Sheffield). Parliament was to meet on 27 September.

records of the House.[1] I suspect you will be alone—but the protest will not be the less, but, I conceive the more proper on that account. I was thinking of a Sketch of something of the Kind,[2] which you will find at Grovenor Square when you come to Town, and myself along with it, if you think I can be of any use.[3] I am well enough for that excursion. I am certainly not quite recoverd from my complaint, neither shall I be, for my short time—but on the whole, I find my strength rather encreased than otherwise since I left Bath.

You see in what manner, the fourth humiliation of this Country has been received by the Regicide directory[4]—But nothing can quell the manliness, or fatigue the perseverance of our determined poltroonery. We have a sort of eagerness for disgrace, a sort of alacrity in sinking.[5] We have an opposition with principles false and dangerous, and a Ministry without any principle at all, both of them considering their Country as nothing, the one eager to get, and the other to keep the ruins of a degraded, precarious,[6] and submissive Government. In their Struggle of ambition there is not the least relish or smack of glory. The advantages obtain by the Archduke[7] will be used as motives to have our submissions admitted and our homage accepted—and I should not be at all surprised if the Tone of the Speech should be, that notwithstanding all these brilliant advantages, his Majesties disposition to a peace with the assassin republick. As to the people, they only want a word from above to be quite right. Our most respectful and most cordial remembrances to Lady Fitzwilliam. I trust your Gift from

---

[1] Fitzwilliam's Protest, dated 6 October, against the Rejection of his Amendment to the Address of Thanks, is printed in the *Journals of the House of Lords*, XLI, 15–17. It is a strongly expressed and reasoned attack on the 'Reiteration of Solicitations for Peace to a Species of Power, with whose very Existence all fair and equitable Accommodation is incompatible'.

[2] Burke's 'Sketch' is missing.

[3] Fitzwilliam replied on 28 September: 'I thank you for your intention of sending a protest to Grosvenor sq, but as you offer to come up to town, I shall not refuse that opportunity of seeing you' (MS at Sheffield).

[4] In the 'First Letter on a Regicide Peace' Burke lists four examples of what he calls England's 'diplomacy of humiliation': the mission of Christopher Clapham Bird (see above, p. 54) in 1795 (see vol. VIII, 376); the Speech from the Throne, 29 October 1795; the note addressed by William Wickham (1761–1840) to François, Marquis de Barthélemy (1747–1830) early in 1796; the request, made through the Danish Minister in Paris, in September, for a passport for an English plenipotentiary (see *Works*, Bohn, V, 167–87; Little, Brown, V, 253–80). From 19 September the press was commenting on the fact that no passport had been received (*The Times*, 19, 22, 23 September). In fact on 23 September the Danish Minister in London informed Grenville that the Directory would not receive 'Overtures transmitted through any intermediate Channel from the Enemies of the Republick' (*Journals of the House of Commons*, LII, 245).

[5] *Merry Wives of Windsor*, III, v, 13.   [6] MS: preccarious,

[7] At the end of August and the beginning of September, the Archduke Charles vigorously attacked Jourdan's army near Würzburg and compelled it to retreat to the Rhine. As a result the army of the Rhine and Moselle, commanded by Moreau (see above, p. 55), which was advancing into southern Bavaria, was forced to fall back.

God[1] will live to see better times. I am with the deepest Sense of gratitude and with unalterable Affection

My Dear Lord
ever faithfully Yours
EDM BURKE

Beconsfield Sept 23.1796.

To EARL FITZWILLIAM—26 September 1796

Source: Fitzwilliam MSS (Sheffield), F 32c.
Endorsed (by Fitzwilliam): Burke| septr 29th 96.

My very dear Lord,

I do not know whether my answer to your Lordships Letter from Wentworth[2] met you at that place or not. I have only to repeat, if it should not my Sense, (and I beleive his) of what you have done for Laurence—which, now it is done I trust and hope will be at least as much for your Lordships honour and for the publicks Benefit, as for the Credit of his Reputation. I told your Lordship of my great satisfaction in your resolution of coming to Town at the opening—and my Joy in your resolving on a protest, and that, not in fugitive words, but on the records of the House; at least it was thus I wish it understood. I informed you that I would prepare a sketch and with this I send it. You will improve it as you think proper—but I really wish as the ministers and the opposition have between them deadend the Spirit of the Nation and thrown false colours on the whole merits of this struggle I think a very full explanation, as full, *at least*, as I have sketched it, should be given. Reason is not easily run down. If you wish me to come to Town—thank God, I am able to do it—and every rag of this poor Body and mind, to the last thread, is, and ought to be, at your service.[3] May God direct and preserve you. I am with the most cordial attachment

My dear Lord
ever yours
EDM BURKE

Sept.26.1796.

I send this by my Servant[4] who will wait in Town for your Lordships directions.

---

[1] Fitzwilliam's son; see above, p. 68.
[2] The previous letter, answering Fitzwilliam's of 17 September.
[3] See below, p. 92.   [4] Not identified.

To THOMAS VENABLES—29 *September* 1796

Source: MS Osborn Collection.
Addressed: Thomas Venables Esqr| The Castle| Chester.
Postmarked: BEACONS|FIELD   PAID|OC|1|96.
Burke has written above the address: '(Post paid)'.

My dear Sir,

I do not know how I can sufficiently thank you for your most cordial and humane attention to my friend.[1] I am sure he ought to have taken your advice with regard to every thing proper for his safety; and I really thought he had actually taken the precautions about his Name that you recommended.[2] It ought however to be an English not a French name, because there may be difficulties be Started about passports which might embarrass our March, and call for explanations which would excite suspicion, which, as much as possible, we ought to avoid. The sooner he sets off on his Voyage the better, especially as the Irish Sea becomes tempestuous about this Season. You will not forget to draw for the sums necessary, in the manner I hinted to you. As to his establishment there,[3] no reasonable expence, consistent with propriety and his unhappy Circumstances, ought to be Spared to make his situation comfortable, reputable, and decent—This must be by Lodging him, and paying for his Board, or indeed rather for a moderate seperate meal for him, in some goodnatured and orderly family—for he is so helpless, as you see, that I doubt whether, with the family itself, he could be so well arranged; though that would otherwise be the best method for him. His washing, and that of his Man, ought likewise to be agreed for at a certainty, if possible; and only a certain sum given for his pocket, ⟨four⟩ Guineas to set out with, and afterwards a Guinea a week—but, without giving you notice, he must not draw for any thing. His Tea, Sugar, Wine &ca (of which last he does not drink a bottle in a Week) must be provided for seperately I take it for granted. I do not know what sort of place, with regard to expence of Living, the Isle of Man is. This must be confided to your Judgment—I shall chearfully acquiesce in whatever you do—We must not stand for a little more or less charge where real comfort is the question—but you know, how helpless he is; and as little as possible is to be left to his own discretion. The substance of this Letter, except The large powers I give you, is of Course not to be communicated to him; as it expresses a doubt of

[1] William Burke; see above, p. 87.
[2] Evidently Venables agreed with a suggestion Jane Burke had made in a letter of 23 September (MS Osborn Collection), that William would be safer under an assumed name.
[3] In the Isle of Man.

his sufficiency to manage his own affairs. Since the Bishop is so very humane, as at your request to have an Eye to him, I wish if there be equal convenience in his Neighbourhood as in Douglas, that he Should be near his Lordship.[1] Pray draw as I desired on Mr Cuppage,[2] the draft enclosed to me. I wish a Letter of Attorney to enable Major Cuppage to receive the part of The Salary[3] reserved for him by his Trustees properly attested by you and by another Witness should be made out and executed either before he leaves Chester, or as soon as he gets to Liverpole. The Letter of Attorney is sold stamped and it is to be filled up with the common words of a Letter of Attorney, but *not general*, but only to receive and give receipts in his name, for the portion of the Salary abovementiond. I do not know what to say for all this Trouble—but our poor friend has had two paralytick strokes and is infirm in body and mind and requires a general Nursing. Our best love to Mrs Venables. Ever

Yours most truly
EDM BURKE

Beconsfield
> Sept 29. 1796.
> Give our friend the enclosed.[4]

To FRENCH LAURENCE—[6 *October* 1796]

Source: MS Osborn Collection. Printed *Burke–Laurence Correspondence*, p. 67.
Addressed: Doctor Laurence| Doctors Commons.

This letter presents difficulty in dating. It seems to have been written after Laurence had accepted Fitzwilliam's offer of a parliamentary seat (see above, pp. 81–2). In an undated letter (MS at Sheffield) written from Doncaster Races on 'wednesday' (28 September?), Fitzwilliam suggested meeting Burke in London on Monday evening or Tuesday morning (the 3rd or 4th of October?). The ensuing 'Thursday evening' would be 6 October. It was probably during this visit to London that Burke wrote the following letter.

My dear friend,

May your days be many! may they be important! may they [be] happy! This will make full amends to me, for the fewness, insignificance, and unhappiness of mine. I do not know that I shall stay over tomorrow. I shall go that day if I can; if not on Saturday.[5] I should be

---

[1] Claudius Crigan (*c.* 1741–1813), Bishop of Sodor and Man 1784–1813, a graduate of Trinity College, Dublin, was chief mourner at William's funeral in 1798. The Bishop's Palace was at Bishopscourt, Kirk Michael, in the Isle of Man.

[2] See above, p. 86.

[3] William's official salary in 1797 was £1825 (*Reports from Committees of the House of Commons*, XII, 408).

[4] If this was a letter, it is missing.

[5] Burke did not leave London on Friday. Windham notes in his *Diary* on Friday 7 October: 'Dinner at Woodford's with Mr Burke. Reading "Regicide Peace"' (p. 343).

very unhappy if I disturbed you, or impeded the Course of Business, when I know you are at the (I hope fortunate) Crisis of your Life, and of every thing which can give you an honourable and independent Situation. 'There is a Tide &c'[1]—follow it. I have either lost or left behind me two Sheets at the beginning; They followed those I had sent last and led into the others. This at first mortified me; and in a manner made me despair of the Business: But I have recoverd it from my Memory pretty much to my Satisfaction; so far as I have gone; and I think I shall finish it before I leave Town. At present I dont want you at all—So stick to your affairs. I am sorry I know nothing at all of Bishop Hurd.[2] Yours most truly

EDM BURKE

Thursday evening.

To FRENCH LAURENCE—10 *October* 1796

Source: Burke–Laurence Correspondence, pp. 68–9.

October 10th, 1796.

My dear Laurence,

I have thought over and over again, and with much coolness, though not wholly without anxiety, on the subject of our last conversation.[3] The more I reflect on the matter, the more I am convinced, that the application you were desired to make is ill timed, and the channel through which it was to be made, ill chosen. If I know any thing of the person who holds the *feuille de Bénéfices*,[4] he would refuse the request; and not wholly without reason, because it was not made to himself directly—and next, your setting out in your new situation, and even before you were in it, with an obligation, which would make you appear dependent or ungrateful, would leave an awkwardness, that I do not wish to see in the gait of your proceeding—therefore, my dear friend, if you have spoken to the Duke,[5] (if my opinion could prevail) you would withdraw your application. If it was a matter in his Grace's own *private* patronage, (for ecclesiastical patronage of his own property I believe he has) I see no objection at all to your doing this; but in an application to a Minister for *Crown* favours through another Minister, it neither can, nor in reason ought to, be put to a private account. I must

---

[1] See above, p. 81.
[2] Richard Hurd (1720–1808), Bishop of Worcester. It is not known why Laurence was making inquiries concerning him.
[3] It would seem that Laurence had been requested to help in securing a piece of ecclesiastical preferment, probably in the gift of the Lord Chancellor, by approaching the Duke of Portland.
[4] Probably the Lord Chancellor, Loughborough (see below, p. 322).
[5] The Duke of Portland.

fairly say, that if I myself held the Crown patronage in trust, I should think it some degree of breach of that trust, if I gave away its means of influence without any assurance of a return. Forgive my freedom; it arises from the solicitude of my affection. Adieu. Mrs B. and all here salute you. A thousand thanks for the pains you take about the forlorn hope.[1] I am afraid I have been guilty of a great folly, in extreme age, infirmity and debility, in the jaws almost of death, to encounter the whole power of the world both at home and abroad! Once more farewell.

Yours ever most truly,
EDMUND BURKE.

FRENCH LAURENCE *to* EDMUND BURKE— 13, 14 *October* 1796

Source: MS Osborn Collection. Printed *Burke–Laurence Correspondence*, pp. 69–72.
Addressed: To| The Right Honble E. Burke| Beaconsfield.
Postmarked: OC|14|96|D   OC|14|96|D   FREE|⟨ ⟩|⟨ ⟩|⟨ ⟩.

This letter is mainly concerned with the printing of the *Two Letters on a Regicide Peace*. At its close Laurence refers to the peace mission of James Harris, 1st Earl of Malmesbury (1746–1820), to Paris. The *Two Letters on a Regicide Peace* appeared two days after Malmesbury sailed for France.

Doctors Commons
Octr 13, 1796.

My dear Sir,

The *three first* (or the *first three*) half-sheets are worked off. Two more I have now sent, but one intermediate half-sheet I have kept back, for your approbation of a Slight addition which I have made. In p. 30 (half-sheet E) you have interpolated a short passage. You say 'Let me add, that if our Government perseveres in its as uniform course of acting under instruments with such preambles, it pleads guilty &c &c'. I have ventured to soften it a little by introducing a parenthesis: 'Let me add—and it is with unfeigned anxiety for the credit and character of the Ministry that I do add—if our Government &c &c'. If you do not like these, insert any other words of personal civility to something of the same effect and let me have them.[2] By having kept that half-sheet back, I do not delay the press at all; only no words must be added or taken away so as to disturb the whole setting of the half-sheet. In the same half-sheet p. 31 are the words '*oglings* and *glances* of *Fraternity*.

---

[1] Burke was about to publish his *Two Letters on a Regicide Peace*.

[2] Laurence's wording (with minor exceptions) is that which appears in the first Rivington edition (p. 30).

Lest this *coquetting* &c &c.'. I am afraid here was something of an *incestuous* passion imputed to Britannia; I have put a feebler word, 'tenderness' instead of 'Fraternity'. If you can think of a better word, let me have it.[1]

Octr the 14th

A case for opinion interrupted and prevented my finishing yesterday. This morning I have dispatched 5 more half-sheets. In one or two places a word had slipt out so as to leave the sentence imperfect, which I have ventured to supply. If not quite as you would wish it, when you see it, correct it for the second edition. Some words I have changed, to remove an accidental jingle that offended my ear. I have taken these liberties, in execution of my full powers, with all possible moderation, but the saving of time was every thing. There is, as I understand a great expectation of your pamphlet, and Lord Fitzwilliams speech and protest are preparing your way with admirable effect.[2] I heard to-day, that his reasons had made many converts at Batson's[3] among the monied men. They say there are some things unanswerable in what his Lordship has advanced. The Speaker[4] (who by the way was very earnestly kind in his enquiries after your *health*, not your *book*) yesterday told me that he thought Lord Fitzwilliam, a man of high integrity; no person could say that his Lordship had abandoned his principles. As he laid himself so open; I did not think it generous to press him with a question which I longed to put, 'who then must have abandoned their principles?'.

I enclose you a half-sheet of the original copy which the Printer[5] says he never had back from you and knows not how or where it is to be introduced. I have looked as far as p. 120 in the last new copy and find no place for it; though from the contents of it, it seems as if it ought to come in before, but of that I am not sure. At any rate correct it and send it up, as soon as possible, and possibly the printer may be able to arrange it from the clue at beginning and ending.

I shall if possible come to you on Sunday[6] for a day, but I think you

---

[1] Burke accepted 'tenderness'.

[2] See above, pp. 88–90.

[3] Batson's Coffee House, 17 Cornhill, 'reckoned the seat of solemn stupidity' (Bryant Lillywhite, *London Coffee Houses*, London, 1963, p. 507).

[4] Henry Addington (1757–1844), later (1805) 1st Viscount Sidmouth.

[5] Not identified. Burke's letter to 'Nash' (see vol. VIII, 399) may be to a printer. In the preface to his unauthorized *Thoughts on . . . a Regicide Peace* (see below, p. 97), John Owen says he had taken the trouble of 'dancing backwards and forwards alternatively between Author and Printer, three or four times a day for almost three months, to attend to such a variety of alterations as can be conceived only by those who are acquainted with the whims, the caprice and the eternal versatility of genius'.

[6] 16 October.

had best send this back by the coach to-morrow to Mr Rivington[1] directly.

George Ellis,[2] I hear, goes or is gone with Lord Malmesbury. I scrawl in great haste. Adieu.

Ever most sincerely
Your grateful and devoted,
F. LAURENCE.

To MRS THOMAS VENABLES—24 *October* 1796

Source: MS Wilmarth S. Lewis.
Addressed: Mrs Venables| The Castle| Chester.
Postmarked: BEACONS | FIELD   OC | 25 | 96 | C.

My dear Madam,

Mrs Burke and I are infinitely obliged to you for yours and Mr Venables's Care of our poor friend.[3] The Power of Attorney will be sent as you desire. I have been in Town where I have seen the Dr and Mrs King, well, the latter ready to lie in.[4] Mr Venables or you will draw for the Charges as they occur—I first thought of your drawing on Dr King—but as he is not known in the way of Business, I think it better to draw on Boldero Adey & Co Bankers on Cornhill London[5]— That is, that Mr Venables should draw, and no mention be made of our friends name; and that, if possible, the drafts should be from Chester or Liverpoole and not the Isle of Man.

Mrs Burkes thousand and thousand compliments and goodwishes

Ever
My dear Madam
Yours affectionately
EDM BURKE

Oct. 24. 1796.

[1] Burke's major works for nearly forty years had been published by Robert Dodsley (1703–64) and James Dodsley (1724–97). Perhaps because of James Dodsley's ill health, which ended with his death in 1797, Burke changed his publisher at about this time. Charles Rivington (1754–1831) and his brother Francis Rivington (1745–1822) were joint publishers with John Owen of the *Letter to a Noble Lord* (see above, p. 11), and sole authorized publishers of the *Two Letters on a Regicide Peace*. French Laurence his brother the Rev. Richard Laurence (1760–1838), Walker King, and Thomas English (*c.* 1725–98), a friend of Burke's, all of whom had been taking a part in the management of the *Annual Register* for the Dodsleys, also shifted their allegiance at about this time and edited that periodical for the Rivingtons.

[2] George Ellis (1753–1815), Malmesbury's '*confidential friend*' who had accompanied him in the past on similar occasions (Malmesbury, *Diaries and Correspondence*, III, 264).

[3] William Burke.   [4] See below, p. 148.
[5] Burke's bankers.

We have great reason to hope that Mr Venables will shortly be freed from his Care and sollicitude and that the Business will be settled. You will be so good to charge the Postage of Letters.

To WALKER KING—24 *October* 1796

Source: MS Osborn Collection.
Addressed: Dr King.

Burke's *Two Letters on a Regicide Peace* were published by Rivington on 20 October. On the previous day John Owen brought out an unauthorized edition under the title *Thoughts on the Prospect of a Regicide Peace, in a Series of Letters.* He defended this publication in a long preface, in which he declared that Burke had given him both the *Letter to a Noble Lord* and the *Two Letters.* It is quite likely that Burke had not yet learned of Owen's piracy when he wrote this letter to Walker King.

My dear King,

I beg you to send to Mr Rivington. By some accident the addition which I intended and sent at p. 156. has been lost. If another Edition should come out, it must be inserted—and in a little advertisement at the beginning, this fact ought to be very shortly stated and the part printed on a seperate half sheet which should be advertised, as ready to be deliverd to the purchasers of the first Editions.[1] It is a very important part. The half Sheet for old purchasers should be marked at the page of the insertion. I send this Commission to you not to Laurence, who, I suppose, is gone to his Election.[2] Look over the proof. Adieu. Remember my Letter of last Night.[3] Ever Yours E B.

Oct.24.1796

To WALKER KING—[*post* 24 *October* 1796]

Source: MS Osborn Collection.
Addressed: Dr Walker King.

Burke thanks Walker King for his 'diligence about the insertion'—perhaps the insertion requested in the previous letter.

My dear Walker

I am not quite well and am lying at my length so Miss Hickey writes for me.[4]

Thank you for your care and diligence about the insertion. I have

[1] Rivingtons in their advertisement, dated 11 November, of 'the 10th edition' of the *Two Letters* stated that 'The addition made at page 156 of this Edition, and continued on the five following pages, is printed on a separate half sheet, and may be had, gratis, by the purchasers of the former Editions' (*The Sun*, 12 November). The addition beginning with the words 'As to the West Indies' and ending with 'regarded as folly and romance' is printed in *Works* (Bohn, v, 239–43; Little, Brown, v, 353–8).

[2] See below, p. 101.   [3] This letter has not been identified.

[4] Ann Hickey (*c.* 1757–1826) sometimes acted as Burke's secretary.

corrected it and wish it may pretty accurately follow the Correction. As to the Preface I thank Lawrence for it.[1] I cannot well judge of its necessity so I must again submit it to your joint consideration, as better able on the Spot and hearing the Opinions of people to know how far it may be useful. I am glad to hear that the piece is liked but much more so [that] it[2] seems to promise some good effect on the public mind which has been so woefully cowed and led astray by a shameful combination of the leaders of the two parties, who have never agreed in any thing but, in betraying the honor of their Country to an insolent enemy. I long to hear that the other matters are brought to a proper termination for which I know I can trust to your quiet activity.[3] God almighty bless you and Mrs King. I wish John extremely well as well as his own heart can desire but I am very angry with him about speaking to Lord Inchiquin before he had settled with me how to do it or indeed before he or I could be certain that it was in our power to do any thing at all in the business. But we must repair this indiscretion as well as we can[4] adieu I send this by the mail Coach. On recollection I may send it by post as I doubt whether it will cost more. You shall be repaid out of what may come from Rivington who I have no doubt will behave more honestly than Mr Owen though I am far from sure that this will prove so advantageous a job to him and me as the other has done to that Rogue—for after all the seasoning of personality recommended the Bedford dish;[5] and a part of the sale of this last work is in that Rascals pocket—on the Maturest thoughts I send it by the Mail Coach. Oh! pray send one to Dr Smith,[6] and another for the Comte de la Tour du Pin[7]—One to Lord Lucan[8]—one to Mr Barnard,[9] another to Lady Anne Barnard[10] and Lady Margaret Fordyce[11]—One very fine to Monsieur[12]—another Do to the Duc d'Angouleme[13] another to the Duc de Serrent[14]—One to the Abbé Edgworth[15]—He may transmit the three last to Edin-

---

[1] No preface appeared in the authorized version of the *Two Letters*.
[2] MS: its   [3] Burke is possibly referring to Owen's piracy.
[4] This may relate to a transaction in connexion with Sir Joshua Reynold's estate, of which Lady Inchiquin (see below, p. 218) was the chief beneficiary. Burke and John King acted jointly for her.
[5] Burke's *Letter to a Noble Lord*.   [6] Dr James Carmichael Smyth; see above, p. 7.
[7] See above, p. 14.   [8] Charles Bingham, 1st Earl of Lucan (1735–99).
[9] Andrew Barnard (d. 1807).   [10] (1750–1825), the wife of Andrew Barnard.
[11] Lady Margaret, |née Lindsay (d. 1814), the widow of Alexander Fordyce (d. 1789), the banker, lived with her sister Lady Anne Barnard.
[12] The Comte d'Artois; see above, p. 5.
[13] Louis-Antoine de Bourbon, Duc d'Angoulême (1775–1844), son of the Comte d'Artois; later (1799) married to 'Madame Royale' (Marie-Thérèse-Charlotte, 1778–1851), daughter of Louis XVI.
[14] Armand-Louis, Marquis (later Duc) de Sérent (1736–1822), gouverneur of the Duc d'Angoulême.
[15] Abbé Henry Essex Edgeworth de Firmont (1745–1807); he arrived in London on 27 August (Dr John Douglass's Diary, August 1796, Westminster Diocesan Archives) and wrote to Burke on 25 September (MS at Sheffield).

burgh. I think the Duc D'Harcourt[1] ought to have one, and to be requested to send one (very fine) to the King of France.[2] All the fine to be on the best Paper.

To WILLIAM LUSHINGTON—26 October 1796

Source: Fitzwilliam MSS (Sheffield).

After Burke's death William Lushington (1747–1823), M.P. for London, sent to Walker King 'a Letter from the late Mr Burke to me in wichh he strongly supports his original opinions on the present War and...a Copy/of the Speech to which he refers in his Letter—which was never published but privately printed at the Desire of the India Directors' (letter of 26 February 1798 at Sheffield, Bk 34). The letter is endorsed: 'Mr W. Lushington | with a letter from | Mr E. Burke to him | 1796 | and his printed Speech | at E.I. House— 1794'. The speech was almost certainly the one delivered at a General Court of the East India Company on 9 October 1794, pledging the Company's support for the Government (reported in W. Woodfall, *A Sketch of the Debate that took place at the India-House in Leadenhall-Street, on Wednesday, the 9th of October inst.*, London, 1794, pp. 1–14).

Sir,

It is a great Satisfaction to me that a Gentleman, of your abilities, and your powers of reflexion, has fallen into the same train of thinking into which I have been led by my poor unassisted meditations.

I find however, that tho I have the honour of coinciding with you in principle, I have the misfortune of differing as widely from you in the practical conclusion, as I can from those whose general principles are the most opposite. What the Effect of Peace with that sort of republick is likely to be forms the Subject of my future correspondence with the Gentleman thro whom I have ventured to address myself to the publick.[3] I cannot say that any Speculation on such a subject is infallible, though passing thro' a better head than mine. I see you are of the same opinion with the Jacobins, that the Faction in France has been irritated into the proceedings, which you reprobate, (and no man can set his face to defend) by the Hostility of the civilized powers. This I cannot think; nor that, of course, by their abandoning their Cause, the Faction would abandon those manners, those Maxims, and those Politicks, which have made them so dreadful to the world. However this is a matter of mere Speculation on the future. You yourself express an apprehension, that though the Fanatical Spirit may subside, the Spirit of Ambition may continue, in that Country, so powerful and so close to ours. If it now exists, (there is no doubt of it) what reason have you or I to imagine, that they will surrender all the present Advantages of that

---

[1] François-Henri, Duc d'Harcourt (1726–1802), writer, politician; formerly précepteur to the Dauphin.   [2] Louis XVIII; see above, p. 69.

[3] Burke was at work upon a 'Third Letter'; see below, p. 105. The 'Member of the Present Parliament' to whom the first three Letters were addressed has not been identified.

ambition and all the means of giving it an Effect in future, because *we* have a Speculation, on the Effect of a peace in improving the morals of the set of murderers and robbers now at the head of the new Republick? If it will not, where is the advantage of our preaching peace? Whatever others may do, you Sir, I am sure, do not think it right to leave them in possession of the actual conquests and universal preponderancy they have acquired. If they cannot be wheedled out of them, I know no mode of reducing them to reason, but by continuing the War. If, as you say, the conquest over the Faction is impracticable, in the present State of things to talk of wresting their acquisitions out of their hands (merely as an ambitious power) by any other means than war does not seem to be less so. If *every* resistance to them is impracticable, the System of humiliating ourselves before them I admit is reasonable. I cannot say what is practicable or not, 'till I know what the disposition is to give a proper direction to the publick force. This I know, that hitherto the smallest Effort has not been used to render the destruction of the Regicide System practicable. This I hope to explain very fully, if God continues to me Life with any tolerable degree of Strength. As to peace in *general* there is no End of a discussion extended to *Generals*. To speak properly of peace, we must know, or at least be able to guess, what the Terms of peace are to be. For my part, I candidly confess, that I do not see how the establishment of this Faction of murderers in France by our submission to them is likely to shake their power. If their *armies* revolt, now or then, it is over with them. As to what you talk of the *people* of France, I know of no such *people*. That community, as it now stands, is composed [of] an handful of Tyrants and some Millions of the most Abject Slaves ever heard of in the world. The opinion of these millions is not so much as dust in the balance. I always except the Royalists, a good many of whom still exist, and have not at all abandond their old principles; but having been themselves treacherously abandond, and even persecuted, by the Allies— they are for the present confounded in the general Mass.

I beg a thousand pardons for adhering to my old opinions when I find them no longer yours. It does not arise from a want of respect to your uncommon Talents, or from want of a Sense of my obligation to you in communicating to me your very able, eloquent, and impressive Speech.   I have the honour to be with great respect

Sir

Your most obedient

and humble Servant

Beconsfield Oct 26. 1796.   EDM BURKE

To EARL FITZWILLIAM—30 *October* 1796

Source: Fitzwilliam MSS (Sheffield).
Endorsed (by Fitzwilliam): Burke| novr 2.96.

My dear Lord,

I received a Letter from Laurence, Letting me know that your Lordships generous protection to him has had its effect, and that he is chosen for Peterborough.[1] I trust you have not chosen ill either for Peterborough or for yourself. I am sure he is a man of universal knowlege and great ability; but even those I should think poor recommendations, if I did not think him capable of gratitude, friendship, fidelity and honour things at all times preferable to the most brilliant parts, but without which at this time brilliant parts are, as we see both at home and abroad are dreadful things.

When I was in town for a couple of days,[2] I found that your Lordship had no reason to repent of the solo you played in the grand Orchestra.[3] I do assure you, that I found on all hands, that this piece of yours has made a greater and more general impression than all the harmony of the united Band, that chose to play in concert the *ça ira* and the *Marseillois Hymn*. Your Reasons were felt whilst you spoke in the House. They were relishd by the publick afterwards; and I think you will feel, as I did with satisfaction, that your personal weight and Character did as much as your arguments. There is sometimes an advantage in standing alone, provided the ground on which one stands is solid. As to the rest the people will, with more or less goodwill follow their leaders the way of Shame. It is a down hill road, and they travel at their Ease till they come to the Bog at the bottom. Our good friends the Regicides, in answer to our Embassy, treat us with a spanish War;[4] and whilst the emissary of our humiliation is opening his Budget[5] they shut, with greater strictness than ever, all the Ports of France.[6] However we comfort ourselves with the good reception we have had from the Ladies of the Nation:[7] and so the world goes on. I was at first in doubt, whether

---

[1] Laurence wrote to Fitzwilliam on 26 October from Peterborough, saying 'I am now Member for this city' (MS at Sheffield, F 32c). His letter to Burke is missing.

[2] In the first week of October; see above, p. 92.

[3] Fitzwilliam's speech on 6 October.

[4] Spain declared war on Great Britain at the beginning of October. On 27 October *The Times* reported that 'the Court of Spain has commenced *offensive operations* against this Country'.

[5] Malmesbury arrived in Paris on 22 October. He began discussions with Charles Delacroix de Contaut (1741–1805), the Foreign Minister, on 24 October (Malmesbury, *Diaries and Correspondence*, III, 268, 276; see below, p. 202).

[6] From the non-arrival of news from France towards the end of October the English newspapers had concluded that an embargo had been imposed on neutral vessels sailing from French ports to England (*The Times*, 20, 26, 28 October).

[7] *The Times* of 28 October described Lord Malmesbury's reception: 'On ap-

Your staying a Little in Town might not be useful—but in this as in all things you have judged best. Your going as you did was quite as proper as your coming. I have sent you my poor attempt to second what you had done:[1] The circulation of it is considerable—The effect of it I cannot divine. I shall go on with the rest or not, as I find any good done by what has come out, and as my health, which is very indifferent, will permit.

Some days ago Mr Eustace professor of Rhetherick in your College of Maynooth[2] called here. He left with me at my pressing desire a copy of Verses[3] which he made on declining[4] a complement of Form and office of the same kind which was desired by him 'who came in Triumph over Pompeys blood'.[5] I think the Verses full of Spirit; and far from ill finishd, though almost extemporaneous. They shew, that bad as things are in Ireland, principle is not quite dead amongst them. They who made sacrifices to decorum on that occasion were not I believe remote from the same feeling. Adieu! my dear Lord—may the God you are serving bless you, and long preserve you to your family, your friends and your Country. Ever most

                                          devotedly Yours
Oct. 30.—1796.   EDM BURKE

To WILLIAM WINDHAM—[1 November 1796]

Source: British Museum (Add. MS. 37,843, fols 115–16). Printed *Burke–Windham Correspondence*, p. 204.
Addressed: Rt Honble| William Windham| &c &c.
Endorsed: Mr Burke| Novr 1. 1796.

1 November 1796 was a Tuesday. Burke later refers to having been in London 'for a day'; see below, p. 106, and Douce and Rivington's account, under date 1 November (MS at Sheffield, Bk 32).

My dear Sir,

I was most unfortunately detaind when you waited here two hours for

proaching Paris, about 300 persons, mostly *Poissardes*, went out to *St Briez* [St Brice], two posts distance, in order to meet him, and congratulate his arrival. These ladies... insisted on taking the horses from his Lordship's carriage. Some of them went so far as to claim the privilege of giving him a fraternal embrace, to do which they opened the doors of his coach. The Noble Lord not having any predilection for such salutes, took a ready way of getting rid of their importunities, by throwing about 20 Louis d'ors among the mob, who, eager to scramble for the money, allowed his Lordship an opportunity to proceed on his journey without further importunities'.
[1] Presumably the *Two Letters*.
[2] The Rev. John Chetwode Eustace (c. 1762–1815), a Catholic priest educated at Douay, was Professor of Rhetoric at Maynooth 1795–7.
[3] A manuscript headed 'A person being required to draw up a compliment in verse for Lord C. . . . upon a late public occasion composed the following lines', endorsed by Burke 'Copy of Verses| at | Maynooth', is at Sheffield (Bk 27b). 'Lord C.' refers to John Jeffreys Pratt, 2nd Earl Camden (1759–1840), Fitzwilliam's successor as Irish Viceroy.
[4] MS: decling   [5] See *Julius Caesar*, I, i, 51.

me. I proposed to go to the Country directly; But when you have staid so long for me, it is fit, that I should wait your leisure. So here I continue this day—and am at your Service to go to you or to receive you here, when you please. The more I think of it the more I feel astonishd that the Ministry can think of putting the whole affairs of Europe blindfold into the hands of Lord Malmesbury:[1] and is [it] at this time they are mad enough to evacuate Corsica:[2] and is it now that they are to look for a fleet to confront that of Spain.[3] My head and heart are ready to split at once. Adieu.

Yours truly

Tuesday.   EDM BURKE

To WALKER KING—4 November 1796

Source: MS Osborn Collection.
Addressed: Revd| Dr Walker King.

My dearest Walker, I cannot tell you how much I am aflicted with two Strange Letters I have received, but could not read, from our unhappy friend in his place of retreat.[4] By the few words I can make out he has, madly and provokingly, rejected all the assistance he could receive. You will seal the enclosed,[5] and get your Brother to send it with a Letter from yourself to Mrs Venables, (for her husband,) franked by his Office frank.[6] She will send it to him, or give it to him, if returned. He need not seal it till he sends it—By it Mr Venables will see, that our poor friend is not to have what he desires, either a power of drawing, or a Credit, in any way whatever; and this Mr Venables is to signifye to the people he lodges with[7]—and if he can get the Bishop[8] to warn them in the same manner, it will be worthy of his Lordships humanity and Beneficence. I believe you know that respectable Prelate—If you write to him, you will beg of him not to abandon this unhappy man in his State of imbecillity, or, to his power, permit him to have any Credit—as he is wholly in Mr Venables's hands; and that we are moving heaven and earth, to bring him back.—It is odd, I have not heard a Word from Mr

---

[1] See above, p. 101.
[2] Towards the close of 1796 the British Government, influenced by the entry of Spain into the war and by Austrian defeats in Germany and Italy, ordered the withdrawal of British naval forces from the Mediterranean. Corsica was evacuated in October and Admiral John Jervis (1735–1823), later (1797) 1st Earl of Saint Vincent, reached Gibraltar with the Mediterranean Fleet in December.
[3] See above, p. 101.
[4] William Burke in the Isle of Man. The letters are missing.   [5] Missing.
[6] John King as Under-Secretary to the Home Office had the right to frank letters.
[7] When William died on 5 March 1798 he was 'at the house of Lieutenant Flemming of the Royal Navy' (Public Record Office, P.M.G. 1/57, p. 40).
[8] Of Sodor and Man; see above, p. 92.

Venables; nor from Cuppage. Perhaps you had better know from Parker[1] or Adey[2] what they are doing; or what hopes we have.

I trust the Bill is filed against Owen. Every hour it is delayd we suffer.[3]

I do not know What excuse we can make for troubling you in your present Circumstances. But we trust that abundant recompense will be made by our dear friend Mrs Kings presenting you with a fine Boy. Mrs Burkes pains have obliged her to put on a blister from which I hope to God, she will derive some ease, though thro' smart. Adieu and God bless you ever Yours

E BURKE

Nov.4.1796.

To EDWARD JAMES NAGLE—*7 November* [1796]

Source: MS Osborn Collection.

Jean-Gabriel Peltier (1760–1825), an *émigré* journalist, edited a periodical entitled *Paris pendant l'année...par M. Peltier.* On 5 November in volume nine of this periodical he had stated that 'Un travail long et pénible qui a occupé tout mon tems cette semaine (la traduction du dernier ouvrage de *M. Burke*), me force de renvoyer au Numéro prochain, qui sera le premier du Volume X, l'analyse raisonnée des événemens extraordinaires de ce mois'. His translation, entitled *Lettre d'Edmond Burke à un membre de la Chambre de Communes du Parlement d'Angleterre, sur les négociations de paix ouvertes avec le Directoire,* was published on 7 November. Two months later it seems that Burke paid him compensation for withdrawing his edition, and Peltier explained that the 'observations in the advertizement inserted in his journal...were never meant to give any uneasiness to Mr Burke but were directed to another person'. He went on to say that he would 'not now any more attempt the translation of Mr Burke's writings without that gentleman's approbation' (William B. Todd, *A Bibliography of Edmund Burke*, London, 1964; T. Gillet to Unknown, 12 January 1797, MS Morgan Library, V.8.A).

My dear Nagle—We are never to get rid of these Rogues the Publishers. Have you given my Notice to Peltier. He has advertised a Translation, in his last Number. I send you a sketch of an Advertisement which I desire you will be so good to transcribe and to get the Abbé de La Bintinnaye

[1] John Parker of Chancery Lane.
[2] Stephen Thurston Adey (d. 1801), Burke's banker.
[3] On 1 November a bill was filed in Chancery by Burke stating that he had employed Owen 'from a good opinion of him at that time' to print for Burke's own use parts of the *Two Letters*, but he had never given Owen 'any Right or Title to the said Work'. On 19 January 1797 Owen filed a defence in which he stated that in November 1795 Windham had expressed to him approbation of his conduct when he was examined by the committee of the House of Commons appointed to inquire into the publication of *Thoughts on the English Government* (see vol. VIII, 355), and that shortly afterwards Woodford had given him the MS of *A Letter to a Noble Lord* as a present. He went on to claim that in December 1795 he had also been given sheets of the *Two Letters* as a further gift (Public Record Office, C12/2180/6).

to translate it instantly;[1] and unless Laurence and Dr King are against it
to have the French Advertisement publishd in the Newspapers, that is
in the Times without delay[2]—I dont hear one word of the progress of my
suit against Owen.[3] Tell Dr King or Dr Laurence that if the Bill is not
yet filed it would be proper to charge what I had forgotten his offer to me
of a £1000 for these very Letters with security and that I refused him.
Now, tho' he may perjuriously deny it—the charge ought to be made—
unluckily I conversed with him without a Witness.

I send you the directions about the Stockings which Mrs Silburn[4] will
be so good to see to be furnishd agreeably to the Patterns. I do not think
the small sizes particularly the two last ought to be of the price of the
first. We want them directly—and they ought not to go to Credit but to
be paid for immediately.

We have not got the times. Is the Sale of the Letters over?[5] For if it
be, supposing that my health should Get better than it is, I ought perhaps to think of another.[6]

As to the translation Query to Counsel—Is not a translation of a work
against the express orders of the Author substantially a publication of
that work and a violation of the Authors property.[7]

I thank you for Monsieurs Note.[8] It is kind and Polite. Adieu my Love
to Woodford—ever Yours truly

EDM BURKE

Nov. 7.

[1] The Abbé François-Marie de La Bintinaye had himself been largely responsible
for Peltier's making an unauthorized translation. Burke had lent the proofsheets of
his *Two Letters* to the Abbé, who without Burke's permission had shown them to
Peltier; see vol. VIII, 409. The Abbé was making a translation of his own; see below,
p. 131.
[2] An advertisement warning the public against Peltier's unauthorized French
translation first appeared in *The Times* on 19 November; see also below, p. 131.
[3] On 9 November an affidavit was filed in Chancery stating that Burke's solicitors
had on 8 November served Owen with notice that they intended to move for an
injunction. On 10 November the Lord Chancellor granted an injunction restraining
Owen from selling *Thoughts on the Prospects of a Regicide Peace* (Public Record Office,
C31/282/16; C33/496/9; see also below, p. 243). [4] See above, p. 9.
[5] An 'eighth edition' of the *Two Letters on a Regicide Peace* was published on 31
October; copies of a 'twelfth edition' published on 24 October 1797 were still available
in 1800 (Todd, *Bibliography*, pp. 201, 204).
[6] The *Third Letter on the Proposals for Peace with the Regicide Directory of France* was
not published until 13 November 1797, that is, four months after Burke's death. It was
not a finished work, but a piecing together by its editors (French Laurence and Walker
King) of passages Burke had left in various stages of completion. On 3 January 1797
Laurence told Fitzwilliam that one of Burke's reasons for delaying his visit to Bath was
that 'he is eager to finish his third Letter, which is now in the press' (MS at Northampton,
Box 51; see also below, p. 217).
[7] The point Burke raises seems to have remained uncertain until the Copyright
Act of 1911 made it clear that a copyright could be infringed by the reproduction of
the whole or part of a work under the form of a translation (*Copinger and Skone
James on Copyright* . . ., 10th ed., London, 1965, p. 172).
[8] Missing. The last known letter from the Comte d'Artois to Burke is that dated
18 July 1796 (MS at Sheffield).

To MRS JOHN CREWE—7, 8 *November* 1796
Source: *Corr.* (1844), IV, 350–4.

November 7, 1796.

My dear Mrs Crewe,

We have been here but indifferently for some time past. Mrs Burke
has had a blister for the pain in her limbs, which had grown to be very
distressing. As to myself, I cannot say that I am, as I have been, at my
worst; but in truth, I am not very far from it. But these things will mend,
I trust, some way or other. This is enough on that unpleasant subject,
which I only mention, as the cause of our not having thanked you for
those wonderful letters of yours,[1] which no thanks can pay for, and for
which no person living can make you a return in kind. Well, since you
like my publication, I have not laboured in vain. I forgot to bring down
to Mrs Burke your letter to Windham, which he showed me when I was
in town for a day,[2] to swear at my little great rogue of a publisher. I
really think I have not seen anything so originally conceived or so well
expressed. It beats, as I think, even what you said to her on the subject;
which, however, is enough to satisfy the most voracious vanity. I wish
the error of your good-nature had not led you to take for your subject
anything of mine; for it makes (and it is the only thing that could make)
the impartiality of my judgment suspected even by myself. I am told that
it has put people in a mood a little unusual to them, which is all that, in
my reason, I could expect. It has set them on thinking. One might imagine
that the train of events, as they passed before their eyes, might have done
that. Well, since it must be so, 'let them think now who never thought
before.'[3] However, things go on just as if they did not think at all. The
ministers, with their own allies, the opposition, like Mr Baye's two kings
'smelling at the same nosegay'[4] of nettles, go on lovingly, hatingly, the
same Jacobin roads. They make no sort of preparation for war, in case
the Malmesbury peace[5] should not succeed, nor think of anything to
guard against the hostilities of the peace if it should be made. They are
afraid of an invasion of Ireland, and they prepare for the lame defence
of England. We shall certainly be safe in the hands of those who have
so well laboured for the preservation of the game.[6] It was a lucky thought.

[1] They are missing.   [2] On 1 November; see above, p. 102.
[3] The source of this quotation has not been found.
[4] As in 'The Rehearsal' a farcical comedy attributed to George Villiers, 2nd Duke of
Buckingham (1628–87).   [5] See above, pp. 94, 101–2.
[6] On 24 April John Christian Curwen (1756–1828), M.P. for Carlisle, proposed the
second reading of his bill for the repeal of the game laws. It was strongly opposed by Pitt
and defeated. John Crewe (see below, p. 208) was a teller for the minority (*Parliamentary History*, XXXII, 846–54).

I have no *manners*;[1] I have a few *garrans*[2] indeed, and they are welcome to them.

You cannot think how delighted we were with your moral and political map of Cheshire, and the counties that border on it. What you say of all the squires, especially those of the second and third class of fortunes, is fatally but too true. They are inferior to the merchant and manufacturing castes. It is a pity. This in itself is a woful revolution; for that class of men were formerly the hope, the pride, and the strength of the country. They are infinitely reduced in their numbers; and if those who remain are reduced too in other respects, it is a bad story. What shall I say about all the idle talk about the emigrants? What answer can be given to vague general charges? As to the animals who, by their poisoned slaver, hope to kill the little virtue that exists in the world, I think it no want of charity to wish that they had been placed between the fire of the regicides and the rear of the Austrian army, in the late engagement; in which, out of 650 killed, there were four hundred French gentlemen of family and condition;[3] most of them officers of twenty years' service, covered with the decorations of service or merit, and there employed and sacrificed as common soldiers; there, with unheard-of firmness, they bore the brunt of the engagement, and saved the army of that sovereign who had so inhumanly treated them and their king. Had your miserable slanderers been there, to make an intrenchment of their worthless carcasses, to save honour and virtue from so horrid a carnage, for the first time they would have been of some use. This is all I have to say of them, and of their low malignity. They who are licking the dust before the republicans, naturally slander those who face them in the field. I was nearly ending in indignation. Your friends here ought to begin and end in other sentiments when they turn to you. God Almighty bless you, and give to those who rule us better minds. Windham just this instant come in:—nine o'clock.

Nov. 8th. Windham is still here, and with great satisfaction we gave him your packets to read. We are sorry for the fidelity of your portraits; however, we were pleased with the colouring and drawing, and wish they were devoid of likeness.

[1] Burke is punning on the words manners and manors.
[2] Or garrons. 'A small and inferior kind of horse bred and used chiefly in Ireland and Scotland' (*Oxford English Dictionary*).
[3] In a dispatch dated 16 September, Robert Crauford (1764–1812) describes 'an affair' near Mindelheim which 'though not of sufficient importance to have any material influence on the general operations of the army . . . reflects so much honour on the Prince of Condé and his corps'. The Prince's losses were about 700 men; a Battalion of *Infanterie Noble* losing between four and five hundred men (*The Times*, 31 October).

I forgot, very blameably, to say anything of Lady J. Douglas's[1] wishes with regard to the presentation of a boy to Penn school. Her commands ought to be, as far as anything is in our power, a law to all who have any taste for goodness and humanity. The fact is, that the number for which government has made any provision had been full long before her ladyship's application. Besides, the young person for whom she has been so good as to interest herself, is not within the rules of reception.[2] The preference is to be given to those whose parents or near relations (a melancholy title) have been killed in this war; and others according to the double title of rank and indigence. However, in no class have we room; inform Lady Jane of this, with every mark of my respect. Mrs Burke again and again salutes you. No news, except such as makes one grieve and blush,—an evacuation of the Mediterranean, as a preliminary to a war with Spain. But I suppose this is to show how much in earnest we are for peace, by exposing our inability to make war.

To WILLIAM WINDHAM—11 *November* 1796

Source: British Museum (Add. MS 37,843, fols 117–18). Printed *Burke–Windham Correspondence*, pp. 205–6.

My dear Sir,

It is worth being ill to become the subject of so much indulgent and affectionate Sympathy as I have experienced from you. I think I get better. Though I threw up something from my Stomach today, and that with some difficulty, there was no blood—What came from me a day or two ago was very bloody, though without any effort at all. Dr Brocklesby,[3] who came kindly to visit me thinks nothing of that Circumstance nor does Dr Smith, from whom I had a letter today.[4] So it will pass off[5] I trust, and leave me where it found me, which though it was in no very good State is as[6] much as I can expect. I have not been out today—and at present change of place is not very fit for me.

The City Business is curious enough.[7] It is but a fortetaste of what Mr Pitt is to expect from his mistaken Politicks at home and abroad. His

---

[1] Possibly Lady Jane Douglas, daughter of William Douglas, 2nd Earl of March (1696–1730). Lady Jane Douglas may however be a mistake for Lady Jean (known as Jane) Dundas (1766–1829), wife of Henry Dundas (see above, p. 62).
[2] See above, p. 8.   [3] See above, p. 86.
[4] Dr Carmichael Smyth; the letter is missing.
[5] MS: of
[6] MS: is as as
[7] On Lord Mayor's Day, 9 November, on his way to the Guildhall, Pitt was hissed by the crowd and Fox's carriage was drawn in triumph (*Morning Chronicle*, 11 November).

favourite Commissary,[1] who left us for Lord North, and Lord North for him, contrives a Triumph for Mr Fox over him, when he is led before the Triumphal Cars of his Enemy, coverd over with obloquy and mud! Oh! but the Newspaper says these Mobs, that drew the one, and threw stones and dirt at the other, were hired Mobs. Possibly it may be so—but I am sure such hirelings would have fared but ill, if a general Sentiment, more mitigated indeed and decent, did not go with those who committed outrages.—The whole democratick Corps was there. Why was that? Ought wooden head[2] to have been left to his own indiscretion?

Indeed Mr Pitt will daily feel the effect of his leaving himself without a Cause, and without any independent and honorable support. He cannot hinder the world from Feeling that when he assumes Mr Foxes principles, that Mr Fox had the advantage of an earlier possession and proposed peace, when peace might clearly be made with more advantage than it can be made at present. The people, God knows, reason but little —But surely our shameful Flight from the Mediterranean must be felt as the most disgraceful Event, and possibly the most fatal that has ever occurrd in our History.[3] He would not suffer a spirit to be raised in favour of himself and his Measures. He will find a spirit raised against him and them, which he will endeavour in vain to resist. He will, by and by, be as ill treated in his person in London as he is by his substitute at Paris.[4] Well—God send you all well out of this ugly scrape.

Believe me, My dear Sir, with sincere Gratitude and affection ever most truly and faithfully yours

EDM BURKE

Friday Nov. 11. 1796

To JOHN JOSEPH THERRY—16 *November* 1796

Source: Copy in Fitzwilliam MSS (Northampton).

John Joseph Therry (1766–1803), a distant relation to whom Burke had been a guardian (see vol. II, 180, 244), wrote him from Cork on 3 November (MS at Northampton).

[1] Brook Watson (1735–1807), the Lord Mayor, had been a commissary in North America. In 1784 he entered the House of Commons as a supporter of Pitt.
[2] The Lord Mayor had a wooden leg, having been attacked by a shark in the West Indies; see also below, p. 130.
[3] Nelson agreed with Burke's opinion. Referring to the evacuation of the Mediterranean he wrote on 13 October: 'I lament in sackcloth and ashes our present orders, so dishonourable to the dignity of England, whose fleets are equal to meet the world in arms' ('Nelson's Letters to his wife', ed. G. P. B. Naish, *Publications of the Navy Records Society*, London, 1958, p. 305).
[4] Lord Malmesbury; see above, pp. 101–2.

My dear Therry

I have received your Letter this morning—I have been for some time, and I am still so infirm, that I find stooping down is[1] a very distressing[2] thing to me. I therefore make use of the hand of a young Lady whom you know,[3] to acknowledge the[4] receipt of your Letter.

I find that Mr Hennessy has thought proper to make a groundless and colourless demand upon his late Benefactor, his and your friend,[5] and to deliver it in as part of his Estate to his Creditors.[6] This is not the only example, which has been furnished to prove the danger of attempting to be of service to people in a distressed condition without the most certain knowledge that their Principles are of force enough to support their integrity against their difficulties—Your late friend had taken a liking to Mr Hennessy, or had a real desire of being of use to him. When he employed that Gentleman to take a view and to make a report of the State of the Grounds in the Island of St Johns, as he was without employment, he thought that the little resource might be beneficial to him, In no other view, for the purpose and for once only, did he employ Mr Hennessy. On this Commission of little or no importance, your late friend according to what you know of his Nature and disposition paid Mr Hennessy most liberally, and perhaps beyond what the object which he went to report on was then worth. For this service he is pleased to make an astonishing demand, even beyond the annual Allowance made by His Majesty to his Governor of the whole Island.

As to any undertaking in which Mr Hennessy may have been engaged upon a Speculation to his own advantage he put himself to extravagant expences, or had undertaken inconsiderate or unfortunate projects, it was no fault of the person who attempted to serve him even beyond his power, and certainly beyond the rules of discretion—To the best of my information Mr Hennessy had no direction from him for any one step in those proceedings.

It is very extraordinary that whilst your poor friend lived nothing of this pretended debt should have appeared, nor was any account made out, or stated before that time that I could hear of.

I have no concern nor never had in that property. I had known in general that my late Son had made two purchases there in addition to some

---

[1] MS: to   [2] MS: distress in
[3] Probably Ann Hickey (see above, p. 97).
[4] MS: to   [5] Richard Burke, Jr.
[6] Therry had explained in his letter that George Hennessy ' . . . in consequence of losses in trade and the critical state of the times has stopt payment and in the statement of his affairs which he made out for his creditors he mentions that a Sum of £650 remaind due to him from Mr Richard Burke in consequence of their connexions in the Island of St John's' (see above, p. 51).

lands which had been devised to him. It was all dead expence, without one Shilling of profit to the proprietor, whether of the Land purchased, or devised; but heavy as the expence has been, Mr Hennessy has thought proper to charge for looking on the Lands more than the whole ever cost.

Mr Hennessys Creditors, whoever they are, must know that such claims require not only to be made but to be proved—Mr Hennessy's Authority, and his orders ought to be produced—As I have said it is an affair in which I have no direct concern whatever; and in which no one living has any thing that deserves[1] the name of an interest, but I think I am authorized to say that not one shilling of that Demand which has nothing to support it, but boldness and ingratitude, ever will be paid—If any one is wild enough to consider such a demand as a transferable property to him he will take such measures as he thinks fit to pursue it, but certainly there shall be no further discussion with me on the Subject.

I am but very poorly—All your other friends here are tolerably well, thank God and desire to be remembered to Sir Patrick oConor[2] and his family. I am glad to hear that so worthy and honorable a person and of such ability both military and civil, as Mr Hutchinson is likely to succeed in an Object which He has at heart,[3] His interest ought to be as dear to every rational Protestant, as to every grateful Catholic—No man can be a friend to his Country who wishes to separate them in inclination or interest; or to set them up as factions against each other. The World will long feel the ill effects of those measures, which have been formed upon a principle of supporting the Greatness and ascendancy of one of those parties by the depression of the other.

Mr Hutchinson has not been guilty of this criminal folly; and I cannot sufficiently regret that Government has not been prevailed upon to understand the full value of the Talents, the spirit of Enterprise, and the steady Wisdom of such Men—But my Opinions are of no value. If there is any body in Cork who estimates them at any rate, you will be so good to let him know that He cannot gratify me more [or] in any way so much as by a Zealous Support of General Hutchinson—You may Copy this part of my Letter and shew it to any such friend, if any such friend I have—I am &c.

Signed EDM BURKE

Butlers Court
16th Novr 1796
John Therry Esqr

[1] MS: deseves
[2] (d. 1812), a prominent merchant in the city of Cork, married to a sister of Therry. He was knighted by Fitzwilliam on 9 February 1795.
[3] Major-General John Hely Hutchinson (1757–1832), later (1801) 1st Baron Hutchinson, son of Burke's old friend John Hely Hutchinson (1724–94). He was seeking

To JOHN KEOGH—17 *November* [1796]

Source: Copy in Fitzwilliam MSS (Sheffield). Printed *Burke–Laurence Correspondence*, pp. 278–84.

The copyist's 'Thoms Keogh' is clearly a mistake, although the editor of the *Burke–Laurence Correspondence* also identifies him as 'Thomas Keogh, Esq. Gray's-Inn Coffee-House'. There is a second copy of this letter in the Osborn Collection.

John Keogh (see above, p. 59) returned to London and again wrote to Burke. He apologized for his former intrusion but renewed his offer to give Burke 'any information' in his power about Ireland: 'It is a duty due to you and to your afflicted Country, that you should be *truly* informed of her present state, torn as she is by merciless factions, contriving to heap new miseries on those which Ireland hath so long and so patiently endured...' (letter of 16 November; MS at Shffield).

Beaconsfield 17 Novr

Sir

I am so much out of the world, that I am not surprized, every one should be as ignorant of, as he is uninterested in, the state of my Health, my habits of Life, or any thing else that belong to me.

Your obliging Letter of the 20 of July[1] was delivered to me at Bath, to which place I was driven by urgent necessity, as my only chance of preserving a Life, which did not then promise a months duration. I was directed to suspend all application to business even to the writing of a common Letter; as it was thought that I had suffered by some such application, and by the attendant anxiety before and about that time. I returned from Bath not well, but much recovered from the state in which I had been; and I continued in the same condition of convalescence for a month or six weeks longer. Soon after I began gradually to decline, and at this moment do not find myself materially better or stronger than when I was sent to Bath.

I am obliged to you for the Offer which you made in that Letter, of conveying any thing from me to Ireland; but I really thought you had known that I have no kind of correspondence or communication with that Country, and that for a good while I had not taken any part whatsoever in its affairs. I beleive you must have observed when last I had the honor of seeing you in London[2] how little any Opinions of mine are likely to prevail with persons in power here, even with those with whom I had formerly a long and intimate connexion. I never see any of His Majestys [Ministers], except one Gentleman,[3] who, from mere com-

re-election as M.P. for Cork City. Therry had told Burke, 'The Catholics have made some exertions for General Hutchinson who is pretty sure of his election'. He was returned at the subsequent General Election.   [1] See above, p. 59.

[2] Probably when Keogh was a member of the Catholic delegation which visited London in March 1795; see vol. VIII, 168.   [3] Windham.

passion has paid me some visits in this my retreat, and has endeavoured by his generous simpathy to sooth my pains and my sorrows; but that Gentleman has no concern in Irish Affairs, nor is, I beleive, consulted about them. I cannot conceive how you or any body can think that any Sentiments of mine are called for, or even admitted, when it is notorious, that there is nothing at home or abroad, in War, or in Peace, that I have the good fortune to be at all pleased with. I ought to presume that they who have a great public trust, who are of distinguished abilities and who are in the vigour of their Life behold those things in a Juster point of view than I am able to see them however self partiality may make me too tenacious of my Own Opinions. I am in no degree of confidence with the great Leader either of Ministry or of Opposition.[1]

In a general way I am but too well acquainted with the distracted state of Ireland and with the designs of the public Enemy pointed to that Kingdom. I have my own thoughts upon the causes of those Evils. You do me Justice in saying in your Letter of July, that I am a 'true Irishman'.[2] Considering as I do England as my Country, of long habit, of long obligation and of establishment, and that my primary duties are here. I cannot conceive how a Man can be a genuine Englishman without being at the same time a true Irishman, tho' fortune should have made his birth on this side the Water. I think the same Sentiments ought to be reciprocal on the part of Ireland, and if possible with much stronger reason. Ireland cannot be seperated one moment from England without losing[3] every source of her present prosperity, and even every hope of her future. I am very much afflicted deeply and bitterly afflicted to see that a very small faction in Ireland should arrogate it to itself to be the whole of that great Kingdom. I am the more afflicted in seeing that a very minute part of that small faction should be able to persuade any persons here, that on the support of their power the connexion of the two Kingdoms, essentially depends. This strange Error if persevered, (as I am afraid it will) must accomplish the ruin of both Countries—At the same time I must as bitterly regret, that any persons who suffer by the predominance of that corrupt fragment of a faction should totally mistake the cause of their evils, as well as their Remedy;—if any Remedy can be at all looked for, which I confess I am not sanguine enough to expect in any event, or from the exertions of any person; and least of all from exertions of mine, if I had either health or prospect of Life commensurate to so difficult an Undertaking. I say, I do regret, that the conduct of those who suffer should give any advantage to those who are resolved

---

[1] With Pitt or Fox.
[2] Keogh had said 'I know you are so uncourtly as to be a true Irishman...'.
[3] MS: loosing

to tyrannize. I do believe that this conduct has served only as pretext for aggravating the calamities of that party, which tho' superior in number, is from many circumstances much inferior in force.

I believe there are very few cases which will justify a Revolt against the established Government of a Country, let its constitution be what it will, and even tho' its abuses should be great and provoking; but I am sure that there is no case in which it is justifiable, either to conscience or to prudence, to menace resistance where there is no means of effecting it, nor, perhaps, in the Major part any disposition.—You know the state of that Country better than I can pretend to do, but I could wish, if there was any use in retrospect that those menaces had been forborn; because they have caused a real alarm in some weak tho' well intentioned minds; and because they furnish the bold and crafty with pretences for exciting a persecution of a much more fierce and terrible nature than I ever remember even when the Country was under a System of Laws apparently less favorable to its tranquility and good Government; at the same time that sober exertion has lessened in the exact proportion in which flashy menace had encreased. Pusilanimity (as often it does) succeeded to rage and fury. Contrary to all reason; experience and observation, many persons in Ireland have taken it into their heads, that the influence of the Government here has been the cause of the misdemeanors of persons in Power in that Country, and that they are suffering under the Yoke of a British Dominion—I must speak the truth—I must say, that all the evils of Ireland originate within itself; and that it is the boundless credit which is given to an Irish Cabal that produces whatever mischiefs both Countries may feel in their relation. England has hardly any thing to do with Irish Government. I heartily wish it were otherwise; but the body of the people of England, even the most active Politicians take little or no concern in the Affairs of Ireland. They are therefore by the Minister of this Country, who fears, upon that account, no responsibility here, and who shuns all responsibility in Ireland, Abandoned to the discretion of those who are actually in possession of its internal Government—This has been the case more eminently for these five or six last Years; and it is a System, if it deserves that name, not likely to be altered.

I conceive, that the last disturbances, and those the most important, and which have the deepest root, do not originate, nor have they their greatest strength amongst the Catholicks; but there is, and ever has been, a strong Republican, Protestant Faction in Ireland, which has persecuted the Catholicks as long as persecution would answer their purpose; and now the same faction would dupe them to become accomplices in effectuating the same purposes; and thus either by Tyranny or seduction would accomplish their ruin.

It was with grief I saw last year with the Catholic Delegates a Gentleman who was not of their Religion or united to them in any avowable Bond of a public Interest,—acting as their Secretary, in their most confidential concerns.[1] I afterwards found that this Gentlemans Name was implicated in a Correspondence with certain Protestant Conspirators and Traitors, who were acting in direct connexion with the Enemies of all Government and all Religion.[2]—He might be innocent and I am very sure, that those who employed and trusted him, were perfectly ignorant of his treasonable correspondences and designs if such He had in dangerous connexion—But as he has thought proper to quit the Kings Dominions about the time of the investigation of that Conspiracy, unpleasant inferences may have been drawn from it.[3]

I never saw him but once, which was in your Company, and at that time knew nothing of his Connexions character, or dispositions.[4]

I am never likely to be called upon for my advice in this or in any business; and after having once almost forcibly obtruded myself into it,[5] and having found no sort of good effect from my uncalled for interference I shall certainly, tho' I should have better health than I can flatter myself with, [not] again thrust myself into those intricate Affairs.

Persons of much greater Abilities, rank and consequence than I am and who had been called by their situation to those Affairs have been totally overwhelmed by the Domineering party in Ireland; and have been disgraced and ruined, as far as Independance, honor, and Virtue can be ruined and disgraced.—However if your leisure permits you to pay a visit to this melancholly Infirmary I shall certainly receive any

[1] Theobald Wolfe Tone (1763–98) accompanied as secretary the Catholic delegations to London in 1795; see vol. VIII, 256. He was a member of the Church of Ireland.

[2] At the trial of the Rev. William Jackson (c. 1737–95), a French agent who had been sent to Ireland, it was disclosed that Jackson had been in contact with Tone; see vol. VIII, 41, 256.

[3] Tone left Ireland for the United States in June 1795. At the beginning of 1796 he set sail from New York for France, landing at Havre de Grace on 2 February. In November he was on the staff of General Hoche (see below, p. 164).

[4] Tone later discussed Burke with Tom Paine in Paris: 'I mentioned to him', Tone wrote, 'that I had known Burke in England, and spoke of the shattered state of his mind, in consequence of the death of his only son Richard. Paine immediately said that it was the Rights of Man which had broken his heart, and that the death of his son gave him occasion to develop the chagrin which had preyed upon him ever since the appearance of that work. I am sure the Rights of Man have tormented Burke exceedingly, but I have seen myself the workings of a father's grief upon his spirit, and I could not be deceived. Paine has no children!' (Life of Theobald Wolfe Tone, ed. W. T. Wolfe Tone, Washington, 1826, II, 348).

[5] During Fitzwilliam's Viceroyalty.

Information with which you are pleased to furnish me with; but merely as news, and what may serve to feed the little interest I take in this world.

You will excuse my having used the hand of a confidential friend[1] in this Letter, for indeed I suffer much by stooping to write

I have the Honor &c

signed EDMD BURKE

Thoms Keogh Esqr

To FRENCH LAURENCE—18 *November* 1796

Source: MS Osborn Collection. Printed *Burke–Laurence Correspondence*, pp. 72–8.
Addressed: Postmarked: Doctor Laurence M:P |Doctor Commons| London.
FREE |⟨ ⟩|⟨19⟩|9⟨ ⟩.

My dear Lawrence

I have been out of sorts for several Days past, but have not been so much weakened by that circumstance as I might have feared. I dont desire long Letters from you, but, I confess, I wish a line now and then, I mean very near literally, *a Line*. The present state of things both here, and in Ireland, as well as abroad, seems to me to grow every moment more critical. In Ireland it is plain they have thrown off all sort of Political management and even the decorous appearance of it. They had for their Commander in Chief Cunningham,[2] A person utterly un-acquainted with military Affairs beyond what was necessary for a Quarter Master General in a peaceable Country—He had never seen War, hardly in any image,[3] but he was a Man of a moderate and humane dis-position and one, from whom no acts of Atrocity were to be apprehended —In order to remove him from the Command of the Army they have made him a Peer—[4] This was a step to the appointment of Luttrell, Lord Carhampton[5] to the full as little experienced in any real military Service as Cunningham but younger and of far different dispositions. In case of

---

[1] The Sheffield copy is in the hand of Edward James Nagle.
[2] Robert Cunninghame (d. 1801) was Commander-in-Chief in Ireland 1793–6. The Lord Lieutenant (see above, p. 102) complained that Cunninghame 'depends so much on information he receives from others, that it is almost impossible to transact business with him unless he is accompanied by his *advisers*' (Camden to Pelham, 13 August, Add. MS 33,102, fols 101-2).
[3] It was said that as a young man Cunninghame had served at Culloden (see *Complete Peerage*).
[4] Cunninghame was created 1st Baron Rossmore on 19 October.
[5] Henry Lawes Luttrell, 2nd Earl of Carhampton (*c.* 1737–1821), replaced Cun-ninghame on 10 October. Comparatively early in his career he had been Wilkes's opponent in the Middlesex election of 1769. Though defeated at the polls, he was declared elected by the House of Commons. In consequence, his conduct and character were subjected to severe criticism, Burke being one of his critics (see vol. II, 22-4, 97, 306). He was not the Irish Government's first choice for the office of Commander-in-Chief. The Lord-Lieutenant felt that though Carhampton's activity and zeal

an actual Invasion they could not expect any thing whatsoever from his military Skill or Talents. The only proof they had of either has been in his desperate promptitude, without either civil, criminal or martial Law to seize upon poor Ploughmen in their Cottages, and to send them bound where He thought fit.[1] By what he is capable of and by what he is incapable they shew in what manner it is they mean to provide for the Military defence and for the civil tranquility and happiness of Ireland. They have fomented a Spirit of discord upon principle in that unhappy Country—They have set the Protestants in the only part of the Country in which the Protestants have any degree of Strength to massacre the Catholicks. The consequence will be this, if it is not the case already that instead of dividing these two factions the Catholicks finding themselves outlawed by their Government which has not only employed the Arm of abused Authority against them, but the violence of lawless insurrection will use the only means that is left for their protection in a league with those persons who have been encouraged to fall [upon] them and who are as well disposed to rebel against all Government, as to persecute their unoffending fellow Citizens. The Parliament encouraged by the Lord Lieutenants Secretary[2] has refused so much as to enquire into these troubles. The only appearance of any enquiry which has been is that put into the hands of a person, I mean the Attorney General,[3] one of the avowed Enemies and persecutors of the Suffering people, and in the closest connexion with them. I see that the Affections of the people are not so much as looked to, as any one of the Resources for the Defence of Ireland against the Invasion which the Enemy will make Upon that Country, if they have force enough to do it consistently with their other views; but, I confess, that from the best reflexion I am able to make in the Intervals of pain and sorrow I do not think that the Invasion of either of these Countries is a primary Object in their present plan of Policy—Their views seem to me to be directed elsewhere, and their object is, to

'cannot be too much commended' he was certainly not of the calibre to be Commander-in-Chief, and hoped that General Sir Charles Grey (1729–1807), later (1806) 1st Earl Grey, might be persuaded to accept the post. But Grey 'positively declined' (Camden to Portland, 22 September, 3 September; Portland to Camden, 8 September, Public Record Office, H.O. 100/62, fols 235, 208, 224).

[1] In 1795 'Lord Carhampton was charged with the pacification of Connaught, and under his direction the magistrates took a great number of those whom they suspected of being Defenders, and without sentence, without trial, without even a colour of legality, they sent them to serve in the King's fleet—a tender sailing along the coast to receive them' (W. E. H. Lecky, History of Ireland in the Eighteenth Century, London, 1898, III, 419). The 'Defenders' were Catholic agrarian conspirators; see vol. VIII, 194.

[2] Thomas Pelham (1756–1826), later (1805) 2nd Earl of Chichester.

[3] Arthur Wolfe (1739–1803), later (1800) 1st Viscount Kilwarden, Attorney General 1789–98. At the Armagh Assizes on 1 April he stated that 'by order of the government who were determined to exert their powers to the utmost in order to restore and preserve the peace of the country he was come down to prosecute' (Dublin Evening Post, 2 April 1796).

disable this Country from any effectual resistance to them by alarming us with fears for our domestic safety. They have gained their ends compleatly. The Arrangements which We have and are making in both Kingdoms for that safety provide for it in the worst possible manner, whilst they effectually disable us from Opposing the Enemy upon his larger and real plan of Attack—We oppose to his *false* attack the whole of our *real* strength. I have long doubted of the use of a Militia, constituted as our Militia is; because I do not like in time of War any permanent body of regular Troops in so considerable a number as perhaps to equal the whole of our other Force, when it is only applicable to one and that but a very uncertain part of the Demands of general Service. Whether I am right or wrong may be a Question with persons better informed than I am, but it has been my Opinion at least these twenty Years. If I did not declare it in Parliament it was because, the prejudice was too strong to be prudently resisted; but when danger comes strong prejudices will be found weak resources.

Whatever the Merits of Militia may be I am sure that no prudent persons with whom I have ever conversed have been of Opinion that it ought to be extended beyond the old number. Other ideas however have prevailed. The infant resources of Ireland have been exhausted by establishing a Militia there upon the feeble plan of the Militia *Here*, and with consequences much more justly to be apprehended from an abuse of that institution. Whether with regard to the Œconomical and civil effects on the Military, they have now in both Kingdoms added immensely to that erroneous establishment, if erroneous it is, and have thereby doubled the weakness instead of augmenting the Strength of these Kingdoms. I beleive it will be found, that in both Countries there is by personal service or by public charge the burthen of an Army forming or formed of at least fourscore thousand Men utterly unapplicable to the general Service of the Country or to the conservation of what I shall ever think as much for its being as self defence itself, I mean the safety and liberty of Europe. The very idea of active Defence the only sure Defence which consists in Offensive Operations against your Enemy seems wholly to be abandonned.

I know it will be said that these Corps do not bring upon the Nation the burthen of Half Pay—This is true but in part, and in my Opinion, if War should continue it will become less and less of an object. At any rate it will be found as Œconomy a very poor resource to make out such a saving by the limitation of effect and service.[1]

[1] In 1793 the English and Welsh Militia, a force which could be called upon only for service in Great Britain, numbered 30,700. In November 1796 Parliament authorized the formation of a supplementary militia of 68,800 men, together with a 'pro-

I do not mean to say that such little aids to the Police as by an occasional use of a Yeoman Cavalry, which is in the Nature [of a] Marachausée is much to be condemned. If the service is not much, the charge is not ruinous, and our military Arm is not crippled. In my Opinion, the expence of these Arrangements would furnish such a Subsidy to Russia, as would enable that power to act with such a Body of Troops against the Common Enemy as to do more for our real defence than from any Home arrangements that we can make. I have said enough upon this subject, tho' by no means all that is in my mind, but if you agree with me in principle your own thoughts will more than supply my omissions.

I have suffered great uneasiness from another Scheme, the tendency of which evidently is (tho' I am of Opinion nothing is less intended) totally to disgust the people with the Continuance of this War—I mean that part of the people upon whose soundness and Spirit the very being of civil society at this time depends, that is that part of the people who live with a degree of decency upon an income not likely to improve.[1] They are the part of the Community which are naturally attached to Stability and to the resistance of Innovation, but are not qualified to afford pecuniary resources to the State. They may serve to furnish a Contingent in the way of Taxes which is to be supplied as their Income accrues, or as their Œconomy finds supply but they have no hords, and if you apply to them for a forced Loan, you drive them into the Toils of the Usurers, who will disable them from paying what they are already charged to the Support of the State—Sure it were better to borrow directly at a high interest, that is at the Interest of the public necessities and to lay upon those Men their Share of it than to take this perplexed circuitous course, which, in the end will weaken public credit by destroying most of the private credit of the Kingdom.

visional' cavalry force which, with volunteer cavalry units, seems to have numbered about 16,000. From 1795 onwards, Fencible Regiments were also being raised for the defence of the British Isles. The Irish Militia, which had been established in 1793, was augmented in 1795 to a force of 21,000 strong. From the standpoint of recruitment, there were obvious advantages in raising units with limited terms of service, but Burke, who was eager that Great Britain should engage in an offensive war, deplored a policy which committed a large number of men who were permanently under arms to home defence. His view prevailed during the Napoleonic war when 'the essential feature of the general militia as a purely defensive force was broken in upon' (J. W. Fortescue, *The History of the British Army*, London, 1899–1930, IV, 888–95; C. M. Clode, *The Military Forces of the Crown...*, London, 1869, I, 283–92; J. R. Western, *The English Militia in the Eighteenth Century*, London, 1965).

[1] On 11 November *The Times* published what it believed to be the general outline of a plan which Pitt intended to propose to Parliament. It was to be 'a public subscription from all the wealthy Corporate Bodies and private Individuals, who are to advance by installments to Government a certain sum in proportion to their wealth, for which they are to receive Exchequer Warrants, payable at the end of four years, with such an interest as to make it a fair and rather advantageous Bargain to the

I was going further when my friendly Emanuensis reminded me that it is near 10 oClock. I am afraid I have tired you tho' I tire myself somewhat less by dictating a Sheet than by writing 20 Lines—However, one is more wordy[1] when One dictates. I intended if I had time to tell you that Keogh is come to London and to wish to have yours and Lord FitzWilliams, as well as Mr Windhams thoughts upon the Subject of his Journey, when I know better of what Nature it may be. He shews a very great desire of seeing me and conversing with me upon the Subject of Ireland. I have fought it off by giving him very true reasons, that is to say my feeble state of health, and the *contempt* that is entertained for my Opinions, especially in what relates to Ireland—He tells me he has not been with any Minister. He is a man that on the whole I think ought not to be slighted, tho' he is but too much disposed to Jacobin principles and connexions in his own nature and is a Catholic only in Name—Not but that whole Body contrary to its Nature has been driven by Art and Policy into Jacobinism, in order to form a pretext to multiply the Jobs and to encrease the power of that foolish and profligate Junto to which Ireland is delivered over as a Farm. I shall let you know further about Keogh when I hear from him, and I shall send to Lord FitzWilliam his Letters to me as well as a Copy of my Answer to him[2]—I shall send you Another Copy—Good Night.

Yours ever
EDM BURKE

Friday Night 10 oClock
  18 Novr 1796
Doctor Laurence M:P

To EARL FITZWILLIAM—20 *November* 1796

Source: Fitzwilliam MSS (Sheffield).

My dear Lord,

A thousand thanks for your kind sollicitude about the little that remains of a friend, the constant Object both when entire and when in ruins, of your indulgent partiality and your generous protection. I find myself, I bless God for it, much better this morning, after having passed a Night, which for me, was a very good one. I wake to those thoughts

Lender. A second Plan is attached to the first, which will go to compel all those to contribute who, either from disaffection or from avarice, may refuse to come forward, without those advantages which will be attached to the voluntary lender'.
  [1] MS: worthy
  [2] Keogh's letters of 20 July and 16 November and a copy of Burke's reply; see above, pp. 59–60, 112, 112–16.

which I cannot put by through any discipline of my Mind; tho' they are far from pleasant with regard to the State of their Object, and far from clear with regard to any plan that might place it in a more chearful point of Veiw.

In a great measure I agree with your Lordship. I am satisfied that the politicks of Ireland were a main ingredient in the scandalous and mischievous sollicitation for Peace at Paris:[1] But I do not think they were the sole motives to that contemptible measure. Mr Pitt, except for the direct Objects of his own power, is not a bold Politician. Even for them I do not think that Great Courage is his Character. If he seems to hazard a stray measure, as in your Case he did, it is from his not seeing the danger that may attend it. The same is the Case of all those he acts with.

As to what has been done, and is now doing in Ireland, it is above all observation, as the Event is beyond all conjecture. It is plain that they are less sollicitous about preserving that Country from the Invasion with which it is threatned, than for the support of the miserable and corrupt faction which is the Cause of all its Evils. They venture all upon the bottom of that Faction. Instead of raising the Spirit of the people and giving it a proper direction, they wish wholly to break it, and to shatter and disunite the whole Kingdom. They are endeavoring by a course of new vexations to irritate the Catholicks—and to put them into a dilemma betwixt the Submission to a disgraceful Yoke or to seek for redress from that Jacobinism which must bring on universal confusion. The Catholicks unprotected, disowned and persecuted by their Government will take refuge in an Alliance with the protestant republicans who have been made by Government one of the Instruments of their persecution. The defence of the Country will then rest upon the narrow faction of Tyrants and peculators, and of those, whom fear, and fear alone, of greater Evils will arm for their support.

That Government means to bring things to that Issue there can be no Doubt. They have removed Cuningham a man no soldier indeed, but of a calm mind and moderate Temper; and they have placed at the head of the army a man universally odious without any pretence of greater military capacity, knowlege skill or experience, but only known in every stage of his Life, for a desperate defiance of publick opinion and the good will of mankind—and lately for the most

---

[1] In a letter of 10 November to Burke (MS at Sheffield; printed *Corr.* (1844), IV, 355–9) Fitzwilliam had suggested that one reason for Pitt's 'present precipitancy' in seeking peace with France might be 'the dread of an expedition slipping over to Ireland and erecting there the standard of revolt, which makes him drive Eng[land] headlong into peace—He is determin'd not to make friends with the Irish, and he doubts dragooning them into submission during a War'.

outrageous acts against poor people in open violation of all pretence and colour of Law. This leaves no doubt of their intentions. Of the dilemma betwixt their Scheme and Jacobinism. Look at Luttrels appointment to the Command of the Army and Mr Pelhams adjournment,[1] on the one hand, and to Mr O'Connors address to the County of Antrim[2] on the other.

In this State of things, what part are you, and are those who think with you to act? In the first place I am persuaded that your Lordship in those affairs can take no one rational Step but in concert with your friends in Ireland.[3] What Course they mean to pursue, I cannot in the least divine. On the Question of the Indemnity and the thanks to Luttrel most of them (not to say more of it) were so shy, that Grattan was obliged to give way for fear of being openly deserted and disavowed by the few that shewed any disposition to adhere to him.[4] On Currans motion, I do not find, that even he, thought it expedient to stand forward.[5] I am afraid that you cannot lead, but must attend their movements.

I never liked, as it is well known, that total independence of Ireland[6] which, without, in my opinion adding any security to its Liberty, took it out of the common constitutional protection of the Empire. Besides an Host of other inconveniences, it tends to put their chief Governour either under a subordinate responsibility, or to free him from any res-

[1] On 7 November Pelham proposed that the Irish House of Commons should adjourn for a fortnight. Though John Philpot Curran (1750–1817), speaking on the adjournment, declared that he had intended to move for an inquiry into the disturbances in County Armagh, the House adjourned (*Dublin Journal*, 8 November).

[2] Arthur O'Connor (1763–1852), until 1795 M.P. for Phillipstown in the Irish Parliament, was now standing as a candidate for County Antrim. In a rhetorical address to 'the free electors of County Antrim' he vigorously denounced the war, which had 'been undertaken for the destruction of liberty abroad, and for the preservation of a system of corruption at home', and declared that his aims were to promote a union of Irishmen and to place 'the Liberties of my Country on its True Republican Basis' (*Dublin Evening Post*, 25 October; *Morning Chronicle*, 31 October). In January 1797 he published another longer address equally radical in tone and was shortly afterwards arrested.   [3] See above, p. 75.

[4] On the second reading of the Indemnity Bill of 1796, Grattan moved an amendment to the effect that the reading should be postponed until the House had heard evidence concerning the condition of the disturbed counties. But he did not press his amendment to a division and the Bill secured an unopposed second reading. According to the Lord Lieutenant 'a very considerable proportion of the Country Gentlemen, of every description and connexion, supported the Bill, and opposed Mr Grattan's Motion for an inquiry' (*Irish Parliamentary Register*, XVI, 42–53; *Journals of the Irish House of Commons*, XVI, 177; Camden to Portland, 9 February, Public Record Office, H.O. 100/63, fol. 142 v.). In Burke's opinion the Indemnity Bill constituted an approval of Luttrell's conduct.

[5] On 26 October when Pelham moved that the House should adjourn to 7 November, Curran asked him to withdraw his motion, as he himself intended to move that the House should go into committee on 27 October to inquire into the disturbances in County Armagh. In the ensuing discussion Grattan recommended Curran to withdraw his motion (*Dublin Evening Post*, 27 October).

[6] In June 1782 with the repeal of the Declaratory Act (6 Geo. I) Ireland obtained legislative independence.

ponsibility at all. I remember, that before this business of total and absolute independence was wholly accomplishd in Lord Norths time, when a part of the Irish establishment was thrown on England on the Idea that Ireland was not able to maintain it, I proposed that an Enquiry should be made into that inability, real or supposed, and into the Causes of it, if real; particularly as it was brought before the House on the express authority of the Lord Lieutenant.[1] A Cry was raised against me particularly by Lord Nugent, as irritating the jealous independence of Ireland.[2] Several friends came round me and privately held the same Language. Grattan was under the Gallery (I am pretty sure it was he)[3] with some other of the leading Irish members. I went from my place to ask whether it would give offence in Ireland to enquire into a proceeding which touchd ourselves in a tender part, and which if Let pass, upon the Ideas on which the Enquiry was opposed would clearly put an End to the parliamentary Capacity for Enquiry of an English House of Commons. He told me, and so did the rest of them, in direct terms that such an Enquiry would give offence and wishd me to desist from it. I am therefore of opinion, that this is a question of great nicety in the handling, and on which you ought well to fortifye yourself (if you take any part in it,) with the sanction of your friends in Ireland. As to Mr Fox, all these things can make no part of his consideration. He acts so far as he does any thing in these matters in concert with and on the principles of the Jacobins in England and Ireland, and has no managements whatever. I know that O'Connor lived in very close connexion with him and his friends whilst he staid in England;[4] I am far from sure, that Keogh is not at this instant in the same Cabal. I enclose to you two Letters, one of them dated very lately, which I had from him.[5] I have reason to beleive, that he is no more a Catholick than Buonaparte[6] is—further than it serves his purposes. He is a man of very great natural parts; but a franc Jacobin, crafty, ambitious, full of

[1] Simon Harcourt, 1st Earl Harcourt (1714–77).
[2] On 15 February 1776 Thomas Townshend (1733–1800) drew the attention of the House to the fact that the Irish House of Commons had been informed that units on the Irish Military Establishment were to be sent abroad and replaced 'by an equal number of foreign Protestant troops', the cost of these troops being met by Great Britain. A vigorous debate ensued in which Robert Nugent, 1st Viscount Clare (1709–88), spoke. Burke is not mentioned as taking part in this debate (*Parliamentary History*, XVIII, 1128–43; *Parliamentary Register*, III, 313–28). There are however notes (in Burke's hand) at Sheffield (Bk 8i) for a speech in this debate.
[3] Since the Irish Parliament was meeting, Grattan was probably in Dublin. Thomas Conolly (c. 1737–1803), George Brodrick, 4th Viscount Midleton (1754–1836), and Welbore Ellis (1713–1802), all of whom had connexions with Ireland, are recorded as speaking in the 1776 debate.
[4] At O'Connor's trial for treason in May 1798, Fox, Sheridan, Samuel Whitbread (1764–1815), M.P. for Bedford borough, and the Duke of Norfolk (Charles Howard, 11th Duke of Norfolk, 1746–1815) were among the witnesses for the defence.
[5] Keogh's letters of 20 July and 16 November.   [6] MS: Buanoparte

dark and perlexed intrigue, and of very suspicious connexions. I send you the answer I made to him,[1] which, by my having nothing in reply, I suppose was not much to his liking.[2] I do not know whether he is here merely on his own account or in consequence of some delegation.

I think it not necessary to say any thing to the absurd plan of armament in both Kingdoms—by which it is plain the War is abandond, and that we propose nothing more than a passive defence at home, without the least attempt at annoying two such powerful Enemies as France and Spain. God bless you! my dear Lord—The times are difficult in the extream. May you see an happy End of our Troubles. Our best and most cordial respects to Lady Fitzwilliam. Ever my dear Lord your

drooping friend
EDM BURKE

Sunday Nov.20.1796.

To FRENCH LAURENCE—[23] *November* 1796

Source: MS Osborn Collection. Printed *Burke–Laurence Correspondence*, pp. 84–8.

Addressed: Doctor Laurence M P| &c &c| Doctors Commons| London.

Burke is replying to a letter from Laurence of 22 November (MS Osborn Collection; printed *Burke–Laurence Correspondence*, pp. 79–81). 23 November 1796 was a Wednesday.

Beaconsfield
Wednesday Mo—11 oClock
Novr 1796

My dear Laurence

I have had a bad night and am very faint and feeble. I do not know where the abstract you mention is in the Chaos of my Papers,[3] but if I get a little stronger this Day I shall look for it, but I send you the printed Paper which Nagle has just found.[4] You know that the far greater and the most oppressive part of those Laws has been repealed. The only remaining grievance which the Catholicks suffer from the

---

[1] i.e. a copy of Burke's letter of 17 November (see above, pp. 112–16).

[2] Keogh did reply to Burke on 24 November; see below, p. 133.

[3] In his letter of 22 November, Laurence had asked Burke to send him 'the fragments of the review, which you once made, of the laws against the Irish Catholicks' and also 'a bundle of printed papers on the question lately agitated, which I tied up myself and left on one of the shelves in my room at Beaconsfield. Will you desire Mr Nagle to look for it'. The review Laurence refers to was probably Burke's 'Tracts relative to the Laws against Popery in Ireland' which was published in his *Works* (Bohn, VI, 5–48; Little, Brown, VI, 299–360). There is a fair copy of part of it at Sheffield (R 103).

[4] Possibly *The Report of a Committee appointed by the Society of the United Irishmen of Dublin 'to inquire and report the popery laws enacted in this realm'* (2nd ed.), Dublin, 1792.

Law consists in certain incapacities relative to *Franchises*. The ill will of the governing Powers is their great Grievance who do not suffer them to have the Benefit of those capacities to which they are restored, nominally, by the Law. The Franchises which they desire are to remove the Stigma from them which is not branded on any description whatever of Dissenters in Ireland, who take no test and are subject to no incapacity; tho' they [are] of the old long established religion of the Country and who cannot be accused of perverseness or any factious purpose in their Opinions since they remain only where they have always been, and are, the far greater Majority of the Inhabitants. They give as good proofs of their loyalty and affection to Government, at least as any other people. Tests have been contrived for them to purge them from any suspicious political principles, supposed to have some connexion with their religion. These Tests they take, whereas the Persons, called Protestants; which Protestantism as things stand, is no description of a religion at all, or of any principle, religious, moral or political but is a mere negation, take no tests at all: so that here is a persecution, as far as it goes, of the only people in Ireland, who make any positive profession of the Christian faith; for even the Clergy of the established Church do not sign the thirty nine Articles.[1] The heavy load that lies upon them is, that they are treated like Enemies, and as long as they are under any incapacities their persecutors are furnished with a legal pretence of scourging them upon all occasions and they never fail to make use of it. If this Stigma were taken off and that like their other fellow citizens, they were to be judged by their conduct, it would go a great way in giving quiet to the Country—The fear that if they had capacities to sit in Parliament they might become the Majority and persecute in their turn is a most impudent and flagitious pretence, which those, who make use of it, know to be false—they could not at this Day get three members out of the *300*, and never can have the least probability from circumstances of becoming the tenth part of the Representatives, even, tho' the Boroughs made in the time of James Ist for the destruction of the then natural interests of the Country should be reformed, upon any plan which has as yet been proposed, because the natural Interests have been varied and the Property changed since the time of King James the Ist.[2] At present the chief Oppression

---

[1] On ordination a clergyman of the Church of Ireland was obliged to 'by subscription declare his consent' to a canon made by the Irish convocation of 1634 in which it declared its approval of the thirty-nine articles (E. Bullingbrooke, *Ecclesiastical Law . . . of the Church of Ireland*, Dublin, 1770, I, 210).

[2] Forty parliamentary boroughs were incorporated shortly before James I's Irish Parliament met in 1613 (T. W. Moody, 'The Irish Parliament under Elizabeth and James I', *Proceedings of the Royal Irish Academy*, XLV, 41–81).

consists in the abuse which is made by the powers of Executive Government, which may more effectually harrass an obnoxious people, than even adverse Laws themselves. I do not know Whether you are apprized of all the proceedings in the County of Armagh particularly of the Massacres that have been perpetrated on the Catholic inhabitants of that County with no punishment and hardly any discountenance of Government.[1] All this however is a matter of very nice handling in a British Parliament on account of the Jealous independance of that County. Neither the Court nor the Opposition party I am afraid would relish it, especially, as they pretend or may pretend that the Subject is to become a matter of their own enquiry. I have written my mind fully upon that subject to Lord Fitzwilliam,[2] but I have had yet no answer, nor, indeed, hardly could. The Jacobin Opposition take this up to promote sedition in Ireland; and the Jacobin Ministry will make use of it to countenance Tyranny in the same Place.

As to George Ellis, and Lord Malmesbury the Jupiter and his Mercury I dont care whether they are in the Clouds or in the Dung;[3] but one thing I see very clearly that nothing above or below will prevent the ministers from going thro' their dirty work. What has been written as argument or observation has had no answer, but it makes no impression unless perhaps to confirm some people in the obstinacy of their meanness.[4] Do you know that Mr Crewe[5] has wrote that D: of Pd, perfectly approves of every thing in the Pamphlet[6] and yet he has done every thing or concurred in every thing in diometrical opposition to his principles—He will do so, in every thing that can be proposed of the same nature. What think you of their finding no one but General Luttrell to whom the safety of Ireland could be committed at this crisis. All this must have passed thro the D: of Pd: who thinks one way, and who acts or is acted upon in the direct contrary way. I am very sick of all these things. As you know Keogh, I think there is no objection to your seeing him if you can contrive it. I do not know how you approve my answer to him, but I am sure he does not, by making no sort of reply to me.[7]

[1] See above, pp. 59, 117.

[2] In his letter of 20 November; the previous letter.

[3] See above, p. 96. Laurence had told Burke in his letter of 22 November: '. . . one of the French papers, after describing the severe and impressive look—not the flickering smiles which you were pleased to suppose—of our dignified sollicitor of disgrace, actually compares him to the *Jupiter tonans*? He seems to me rather in the weeping character of the *Jupiter Pluvius*; or perhaps there is another Jupiter whom you adore, and whom you may think his Lordship still more resembles, the *Jupiter stercoreus*, according to the epithet which the pretended fragments of Orpheus give him, of the "*dung-dweller*"'.

[4] MS: meaness.   [5] John Crewe; see below, p. 208.

[6] No comments by Portland on the *Two Letters* have been found.

[7] See above, p. 124; below, p. 133.

You will write to Mr Wilde[1] and let him know that I have been very ill from time to time, and that you have informed me of his Enquiry, and that I am much obliged to him for his sollicitude about me. The terms prescribed by the thieves of the Directory to the Pope are what might be expected.[2] He cannot help it being intrinsically weak in himself and we have refused to put him in a better condition for fear of the Statute of Preminire[3] and our fleet has thought proper to fly out of the Meditterenean and to evacuate all the Strong holds we had in that part of the World—I think a more sh—n figure than the Pope. In proportion to the Strength of Body which is enervated by meanness[4] of Spirit— 'Oh impotence of mind in body Strong'[5]—The Parcel waits—God bless you. If you can [get] Bollingbrookes abridgement of the Irish Statutes[6] which is extremely well done, you will see the materials upon which I went in the abstract of the old Popery Laws which I gave to the D— of P— on his going Lord Lieutenant to Ireland.[7] My poor Richard had[8] a compleat copy which he put into the hands of the Committee, with such alterations and additions as they thought proper.

Adieu—Mrs Burke has had a bad night as well as myself. Doctor Brocklesby has been here and is gone—Parochial news we have none. Yours ever

EDM BURKE

To the MARCHIONESS OF BUCKINGHAM— 23 November 1796

Source: MS Osborn Collection.

Madam,

I hope your Ladyship will add it to the other instances of your goodness, (which I feel in common with all others who stand in need

---

[1] John Wilde (*c.* 1764–1840), Professor of Civil Law at Edinburgh; see vol. VIII, 98. Laurence had sent Burke a letter he had received from him. The letter is missing.

[2] The terms were published in *The Times* on 19 November. By these the Pope withdrew from the coalition against France and promised to close the ports of the Papal States to France's opponents. He conceded Avignon, permitted the French to occupy Ferrara and Bologna, and promised to pay a large sum monthly to France until the ratification of peace with the Emperor.

[3] Burke seems to be referring to the opinion that the British Government was implicitly forbidden to have diplomatic relations with the Court of Rome by legislation passed in the reigns of Henry VIII and Elizabeth (24 Henry VIII, c. 12, 25 Henry VIII, c. 21; 5 Eliz. c. 1, 13 Eliz. c. 2). Offenders against these statutes incurred the penalty of *praemunire*—forfeiture of property and imprisonment during the royal pleasure.

[4] MS: meaness

[5] See *Samson Agonistes*, line 52.

[6] Edward Bullingbrooke, *An Abridgement of the Public Statutes of Ireland . . .*, 2 vols, Dublin, 1768.

[7] Portland went to Ireland as Lord Lieutenant during the Rockingham Administration of 1782.   [8] MS: has

of it) to beleive, that nothing but ill health could have prevented an earlier acknowledgement of the pleasing honour you have done me in sending me the Will of Louis the 16th.[1] It is the best Pourtrait of that most unfortunate of Princes and best of men. I shall place it between two worse Pourtraits, (which however came to me in a very flattering manner from Monsieur) of his unhappy Brother, and his still more unhappy Sister.[2] At this time the epithet of unhappy must always be tacked to every thing virtuous. Yours and Lord Buckinghams Sympathy has however done a great deal to soften the lot of persecuted merit. I suppose it is to your Ladyship, that we owe the ornament of the field days of our military school.[3] I trust that you and Lord Buckingham will come to see the Object of your Protection—when you may compare it, in its more adult State, with the infancy, in which you both first encouraged it. It will be no hard task on your goodnature, to allow, that every thing has been done, that the time could possibly afford room for. This is due to the Skill and indefatigable pains of the four excellent persons, one of whom is English, that have that institution in charge.[4] There is no praise that they do not merit; nor reward indeed, if it lay with us to reward them. The piece of ordance has been received; but the artillery exercise is not yet begun. There is much to do. I send Lord Buckingham the last return of the School. After the ill health of a few of the Boys, (one of them ill in bed of a malignant low fever for forty five days)[5] they are all now perfectly well. I hope in a few days to make up my half years accounts. I shall have exceeded the Estimate but very little—They wear out their Cloaths fast, and the first Cloth I bought was not of a good quality, having aimed at too low a price. They are now to be compleatly new-clad for the Winter. I took the Liberty some time ago of presenting one of my Pamphlets to Lord Buckingham. Will your Ladyship be pleased to permit me to send another as a poor mark of my homage to Pall Mall for you.

Mrs Burke and the Ladies here present their most respectful and

[1] There were numerous printings of the will of Louis XVI. Accompanying this letter in the Osborn Collection is a broadside printed by the Minerva Press, with an engraved portrait of Louis XVI and the printed text of his will, in French and English.

[2] Probably portraits of Louis XVI and Marie Antoinette, or possibly of 'Madame Élisabeth' (Élisabeth-Philippine-Marie-Hélène de Bourbon, 1764–94), Louis XVI's sister.

[3] According to Prior (2nd ed. II, 356), 'The Marquess of Buckingham made them a present of a small brass cannon, and a pair of colours, which were displayed on public days, and seemed a source of no little pride and gratification to those future defenders of loyalty'.

[4] The four were presumably the Abbé Maraine, the Abbé Le Chevalier, the Baron du Pac Bellegarde, and the Rev. John Devereux.

[5] See above, p. 85.

grateful compliments to your Ladyship and Lord Buckingham. I have the honour to be with the most perfect respect

> Madam
>> Your Ladyships
>>> ever obliged and obedient humble servant
>>> EDM BURKE

Beconsfield Nov.23.1796.

To MRS JOHN CREWE—23 *November* 1796
Source: Corr. (1844), IV, 360–3.

Beconsfield, November 23, 1796

My dear Madam,

Your letters[1] are a great consolation to us. Your sympathy makes our ill-health a great deal more tolerable. As to me, I shall determine nothing about Bath, until I know how a course recommended to me turns out:—it begins not amiss. I have many accommodations here, and many comforts which I cannot enjoy at Bath. Good air, principally; more room; my books more about me; a power of taking exercise whenever the weather permits it. If these will not do, I am off for Bath. My friends wish I should live; as to myself, I do not know what I ought to wish; but if I am to die, I had rather die here, of the two, than at Bath, if it is fit in those sort of things I should have any choice. Tell Mr Canning[2] that I am very much flattered in finding that a man of his genius and his virtue finds anything to tolerate in my feeble and belated endeavours to be useful, at a crisis of the world which calls for all the efforts of a rich mind like his, in the full vigour of all his mental and of all his bodily powers; but I am soothed in seeing that I continue the object of his early partiality. If I have written with any personal asperity towards Mr Pitt, it was very unwise and very unbecoming, and, I am sure, very contrary to my intentions; but having the misfortune of not being able to bring my mind up to the value of the measures that have been pursued, it was impossible that I should speak of them without the most marked concern, and without a strong feeling of the ill effects which have resulted from the system which had been adopted and is persevered in. Perhaps it were better I had never written at all; but I had this to say or nothing.[3]

---

[1] Missing.　　　　　　　　　　　　[2] George Canning (see below, p. 267).
[3] According to the editors of the 1844 *Correspondence*, who saw the manuscript of this letter, there was 'a mark of Mr Burke's' at this point. Burke refers to it at the end of the next paragraph.

Indeed, my dear madam, it grieves me to find, not that what I had written, (which is of no importance,) but that no experience will teach ministers to alter that woeful plan which has brought us into our present condition; on the contrary, 'tis persevered in with more firmness, and carried to a greater extent than ever. Under pretence of providing for our home defence, we are, in reality, disarming the kingdom, and rendering it absolutely impossible to make any effort which can tend to a happy termination of the war. I do not suppose that there is any gentleman or any lady, who can seriously believe that we can conquer the united powers of France and Spain by keeping a good home guard upon Cheshire cheeses and on Kentish hops. We employ the strength of the poorer sort, and all that can be squeezed from the more opulent, for that purpose, and for that purpose only. You speak of cockades and feathers from the ladies to encourage this new show. I have no objection, since we can amuse ourselves with these things, that we should play with them in any manner we like, till we, 'like smiling infants, sport ourselves to sleep.'[1] I hope it may not be a very long sleep. That's all I have to say on this business. My thoughts are wholly out of fashion, and my hand, I fear, altogether out of tune. I hear that the forced loan[2] is to be given up. If there was a strong spirit excited in the nation, I should have an opinion of a merely voluntary contribution; but how any thing voluntary can go on to any effect or extent without that spirit, totally passes my comprehension. I am sure that so far from endeavouring to excite this spirit, nothing has been omitted to flatten and lower it. In that situation of affairs, or, at least, my opinion of them, what sort of *bulletin* is it that I can write, and that would be fit for you to show? I have no objection to your communicating to Mr Canning, if you please, word for word, what I say of him, but not beyond the end of the last paragraph, marked with a little star.

I could not help smiling at the list of the persons that you mentioned in your last letter as fit to act together. It puts me in mind of the companies that my old acquaintance with the wooden leg, George Faulkener,[3] used to invite to dinner, in order to make out an harmonious society, or the assortment which his full brother with the wooden leg, the present Lord Mayor of London,[4] invites to his city entertainments. Alas! these people don't speak to one another; and I do not know any thing in the ministry, that is like a council in this kingdom. I hope you will pass your time pleasantly at Chester; I believe that place has more

[1] The source of this quotation has not been found.
[2] See above, pp. 119–20.
[3] (*c.* 1699–1775), the Dublin publisher. His leg was lost as a result of an accident, sustained, according to himself, when escaping from a jealous husband.
[4] Brook Watson (see above, p. 109).

of the stuff of a good provincial capital, than any town in England. God bless you! I employ the hand of my friend Mr Nagle,[1] as I find it more easy to dictate than to write. He is so good as to comply with my weakness, and you will be so good as to bear it. Mrs Burke is still lame, and rather more so than when you saw her; but otherwise she is well, and salutes you cordially.

To WALKER KING—23 *November* [1796]

Source: MS Osborn Collection.
Endorsed: Mr Burke to the Revd Dr| King.| Novr 23d.
This letter is not in Burke's hand.

Beaconsfield
23 Novr

My dear Walker

We partake I assure you some share of that nervous affection which your long protracted anxiety and reciprocation of hope and fear have given you for this Month past.[2] You are in no situation to attend to your friends concerns and yet your friends here have no other resource but in you. I do not [know] what to say to this undertaking of the Abbé de la Bintinnaye,[3]—in some particulars the Translation is very well and beyond what I expected. In others I do not at all wonder that He has wholly missed the Gist and particular point of the Metaphorical allusions sometimes used—It is no great matter. I have marked a few of them—If He cannot bring them into His French He must let the thing stand as it is, changing only a few words in which he has wholly mistaken the sense—Such as Illusion for Allusion—the great question is for what end he is to purchase it at all. The Foreign sale is already preoccupied by that Villain *Peltier*, who has thought proper not only to make a property of me but to insult me both in Letters to myself[4] and in his publick advertizement, which he has inserted in one of his Numero's[5]—It seems there is no law in the Country that can secure that Property, nor will the discretionary Power left over Aliens free the Country from an Audacious Mercenary Scoundrel who dares in this manner to rob me of the means of being useful to his Countrymen. I

---

[1] Edward James Nagle.
[2] Walker King's second child was not born until 1 December; see below, p. 148.
[3] The Abbé's translation of Burke's *Two Letters*; see above, p. 105.
[4] The letters are missing.
[5] See above, p. 104. Peltier also referred with scorn to a 'pauvre anonime' (obviously the Abbé de La Bintinaye) who had published in the press a statement to the effect that Peltier's translation was unauthorized and had anticipated the appearance of an authorized translation (*Paris...par M. Peltier*, X, 20; see also vol. VIII, 408–9).

am told that He has sent abroad, which is the great Mart of sale a great many thousands of them, and at a higher price than the Original is sold for.[1] I am in great doubt whether the English Sale of a 2d translation will even defray the expence. I do not know whether the difference of Merit between One translation and another of an English temporary Pamphlet in the French will sell an Edition supposing that this is better than Peltiers which I do not know as I have never seen his production. I'll leave it to you and to Laurence to judge whether I had not better pay the Abbé de la Bintinnaye for the trouble he has been at and prevent his having more trouble than to charge myself with the expence of the Impression of the Work which will lie much heavier upon me, if it should not sell which I am almost certain it will not. The charge cannot be suffered to lie upon that helpless poor creature, who, by the way, will not have finished his work untill all curiosity about it is at an end and untill some new subject has engaged the publick attention. I have enclosed your Letter about ⟨Hovenden⟩[2] With the strongest recommendation I could use to Woodford. I have no one to apply to but Windham, and by new applications I fear I shall only disgust him both with the new and the old; but however these things must go their train. Mrs Burke and I wish most cordially for your release by a happy increase in your family, in the mean time we sincerely partake in Mrs Kings and your sollicitude—adieu and beleive me,

Most truly Yours
E B

P.S.: As to myself I am pretty much as I was—have many hours of ease in 24 and some of uneasiness. Mrs Burke is I think rather worse in her limbs, and has passed a bad night from pain in them: She is more crippled than ever, but otherwise pretty well.

Shortly after Burke's death, when French Laurence was engaged in preparing *Three Memorials on French Affairs* for the press, the Abbé de La Bintinaye was employed to make a French translation (Laurence to Fitzwilliam, 28 July 1797, MS at Northampton, Box 52). In September 1797 *Trois Mémoires* was published in London (Todd, *Bibliography*, p. 216). At the beginning of 1798 the Abbé informed Walker King that it was selling slowly, and two months later, when asking King for financial assistance, he told him that 'Monsieur Burke a plusieurs fois formellement declaré qu'il n'entendoit pas que je Souffrisse aucun dommage doma traduction' (letter postmarked 19 March 1798, MS at Sheffield, Bk 33).

[1] The British edition was advertised for sale at '4 sh.'.
[2] Perhaps Richard Hovenden, a Captain in Tarleton's Light Dragoons, who had been on half-pay since 1783. In November 1797 he was restored to full pay as a captain in the 21st Dragoons and promoted Lieutenant Colonel in January 1798.

To FRENCH LAURENCE—25 *November* 1796

Source: MS Osborn Collection. Printed *Burke–Laurence Correspondence*,
pp. 81–3.
Addressed: Doctor Laurence M:P | Doctors Commons | London.
Only the signature is in Burke's hand.

My dear Laurence

I have heard at last from Mr Keogh, by his Letter which I enclose you see the cause of his delay.[1] He is not offended, but He says not one word of Tone his Secretary,[2] but probably reserves an explanation of this for conversation. As it will be of much more importance that you should hear what He has to say, than that I should, I think to write to him by this nights Post to call upon you, or if his Health should not permit it that you would call upon him at your first time of leisure.[3] I intend to tell him, that weak as I am I shall see him if he pleases. Not a word from Lord FitzWm which I am rather surpized at, knowing that in general He is punctual, and that these Affairs are very near his Heart. What you say about the Pope is very striking,[4] but He and his Troy will be burned to Ashes, and I assure all good Protestants that whatever they may think of it the thread of their Life is close twisted into that of their great Enemy. It is perfectly ridiculous in the midst of our melancholly situation, to see us forswearing this same Pope, lustily in every part of these Dominions and making absolute War upon him in Ireland at the hazard of every thing that is dear to us, whilst the Enemy from whom we have most to fear, is doing the same thing with more effect and less hazard to themselves. For we are cutting our own throats in order to be revenged of this said old Pope. It is very singular that the power which menaces the world should produce in us no other

[1] In his letter of 24 November (MS at Northampton) Keogh explained that he had been prevented by ill health from writing to Burke; 'I shall not fail', he said, 'to make enquiries as to your State of Health and if I have the pleasure to hear a favorable account in that case I will avail myself of your permission to pay my personal respects at Beaconsfield—provided my Health permits me to have that honor'.

[2] See above, p. 115. In a letter to Fitzwilliam on 7 December Laurence remarked that in 'two conversations' which he had had with Keogh he 'said not a syllable to me... on a subject which required explanation, and on which Mr Burke intimated, that it did so—I mean the appointment of Mr Tone, a dissenter of the Republican stamp . . . to be secretary to the Catholick Delegates . . .' (MS at Northampton, Box 50).

[3] On 28 November Laurence had remarked to Fitzwilliam 'I shall shortly call on Mr Keogh by Burke's desire and if any thing important passes, I will communicate it to your Lordship' (loc. cit.).

[4] Laurence had praised the Pope (Pius VI) for resisting the French: 'He is playing Priam

      arma diu senior desueta trementibus aevo
      circumdat nequicquam humeris.

I wish we had half his spirit; Europe might yet be safe' (letter to Burke, 24 November, MS at Sheffield; printed *Corr.* (1844), IV, 364–9). Laurence is quoting Virgil, *Aeneid*, II, 509–10: 'he vainly throws his long-disused armour, old as he is, about his shoulders, trembling with age'.

marks of terror than by a display of meanness and that this poor old bugbear who frightens no body else, and who is affrighted by every body and every thing is to us the great object of terror, of precaution and of vigorous attack—You remember the Fable of the Hare and the Frogs.[1] On this point, I verily begin to believe that Mr Pitt is stark mad; and[2] that he is in the *cold* fit of this Phrenetick Fever. I agree with you, and it was long the opinion of our dear departed friend;[3] that Mr Pitt keeping an underhand and direct influence in Ireland to screen himself from all responsibility does resolve on the actual dissolution of the Empire, and having settled for himself, as he thinks, a faction there, puts every thing into the hands of that Faction, and leaves the monarchy and the superintendancy of Great Britain to shift for themselves as they may.

Mrs Burke passed but a bad Day yesterday, with much bilious vomiting and a headache, but the latter is gone and she has had a very quiet Night tho' not much sleep; and tho' not up is light and easy—As to my self I have had four fits in the Night and several yesterday—Between the fits both in the afternoon and at Night I had rest enough—I send you this by the Coach and am affectionately

Yours
EDM BURKE

Beaconsfield
25th Novr

To WILLIAM WINDHAM—25 *November* 1796

Source: British Museum (Add. MS 37,843, fols 119–20). Printed *Burke–Windham Correspondence*, pp. 209–10.

My dear Sir,

I have not been very well—for which reason I have written most of my Letters by Nagles hand. But the little I shall say now, though from a very full heart, full near to bursting, shall be with my own—not because I distrust Nagles prudence, nor care a farthing whether my own Sentiments are known or not but when one tells ones private thoughts to a friend, that friend, by being the mere object of communication and passive in it, does become in some sort involved in the fault of the matter that is communicated. You know, what I think of the surrender of the Kingdom of Ireland to Luttrel. Portugal is now given as publick

---

[1] Aesop's fable of the 'Hares and Frogs in a Storm'.
[2] MS: but and
[3] Richard Burke, Jr.

report will have it to General Stuart.[1] What his military Capacity may be, whether equal to that of the General we formerly gave to that Kingdom, the Count of Lippe,[2] I know not. It may be so—but whilst I lived in the world I had never heard of the military abilities of Genl Stuart. Of his civil dispositions his late proceedings in our quondam Kingdom of Corsica afford a Sufficient indication.[3] This I am quite certain of that there is something strongly redolent[4] of madness in that family,[5] which marks (in a general) a mischievous and malignant turn. There is great pride, great impracticability, a propensity to obscure, dark, and puzzled Politicks. I look on Portugal as lost by this appointment. He certainly will not be long well with that Court and that Nation. He will despise and will quarrel with the emigrant Corps,[6] and in their discussions, it is not difficult to foresee on which side the decision of all controversies will be. We have abandond Italy, politically, commercially, morally; Spain is become our Enemy. Our Negotiation at Paris will serve no purpose, but to discover the limits of What it is we propose for the Emperor,—for the accommodation of the Regicides (much abler politicians than we are) in their scheme of opening a seperate Treaty with him; and now—our last hold of the Continent—Genl Stuart is to secure to us.—It is all over—no experience of the fatal Effects of Jobbs—will hinder Jobbers from Jobbing to the last. I say there is manifest recognized ability in the world and in our power, both at home and abroad—if we were not resolved to throw it away. I know how delicate an affair this must be to you; Both as to the person doing the Jobb, and the person for whom it is done. They will say truly that all this is personal. So it is. Every question of fitness for employment is personal; But then the use and effect of that employment depend wholly on the aptitude or unfitness of the Person. I commit this delicate Business to your thoughts. But I say both nations are betrayd if this man is sent. I fear you can do nothing. God direct

[1] Major-General Charles Stuart (1753–1801) was sent to Portugal at the end of 1796 at the head of a small British force to cooperate with the Portuguese in the event of a French invasion.

[2] Friedrich Ernst Wilhelm, Graf zu Schaumburg-Lippe (1724–77). In 1762, when in command of the British and Portuguese forces in Portugal, he successfully repulsed a Spanish invasion.

[3] When Commander of the British Forces in Corsica 1794 to 1795, Stuart had clashed with Burke's friend the Viceroy, Sir Gilbert Elliot (4th Baronet, 1751–1814, later (1813) 1st Earl of Minto; see the *Diary of Sir John Moore*, ed. Sir J. F. Maurice, London, 1904, I, 125–6, 131–2).

[4] MS: reddolent

[5] The General was the son of John Stuart, 3rd Earl of Bute (1713–92), the former Prime Minister.

[6] Stuart had a poor opinion of the foreign regiments placed under his command and strictly disciplined their French officers (Fortescue, *History of the British Army*, IV, 602–3).

you. I can write no more. I am a good deal worse this day or two past.
Yours with entire and affectionate attachment

EDM BURKE

Nov. 25. 1796.

Wherefore write? One days Jobb—defeats the Labours of a year.

EARL FITZWILLIAM *to* EDMUND BURKE— *27 November* [1796]

Source: Fitzwilliam MSS (Sheffield).
In answer to Burke's letter of 20 November; see above, pp. 120–4.

My dear Burke

I agree perfectly with your opinion, that with respect to Irish politicks, I must endeavour to make my conduct here, square with the
sentiments of my friends there, and indeed that if any thing arises here
in our house (unless it should prove personal to myself) I ought to take
just as much or as little part as they think most advantageous for our
general cause. I have delay'd doing this from a little difficulty I am
under, about the person, to whom I should make the reference: but it
shall be done without further delay. Not a day, hardly an hour passes,
that does not seem to bring the affairs of that country nearer to a crisis:
—What may be the treasonable intentions of the diggers of potatoes[1]
(en masse) I will not pretend to know: it is possible, that it may be
done to form magazines for an Invading enemy, and therefore Government may be justified in checking the practice: but of this I am sure;
Government never can be justified in surrounding a field by the
military, making the whole mob prisoners, picking out the stout and the
strong, and without trial, without pretence of Law, without even an
enquiry on the Drum's head, sending these last on board a tender; of
course to be dispos'd of, as any naval Bashaw may think fit.—These
were the practices of summer 95 under Lord Carhampton,[2] and they
are now recommencing—probably they will meet with the same sort of
reception among the different orders of people, at this time, as they did
at that: the execration and horror of the lower orders: the thanks and
approbation of the Higher, with acts of Indemnity from the Parliament—It is a state of things that cannot last, if the means of escaping

[1] During the autumn of 1796 crowds had collected at farms in the north of Ireland
and as a gesture of sympathy had dug the potatoes for the owners, some of whom had
been imprisoned. A proclamation issued by the Irish Government on 6 November
stated that in the disturbed areas in Ulster large bodies of men had 'arrayed themselves and marched in military order . . . under the pretence of saving corn and digging
potatoes' (*Dublin Evening Post*; *Dublin Gazette*, 8–10 November).
[2] See above, p. 117.

from it, should arise—We may have in our mouth, Liberty and free constitution, but in the practice in Ireland, it is a state of most odious oppression and abject slavery for the great body of the people—there are there, two Laws and two constitutions, one for the rich, and one for the poor.—Can it be a matter of surprize, or a cause of complaint, that there is no attachment, no seal for the safety of such a country—I saw in the papers, that when Charles Fox had mention'd Ireland (which he did, by the bye, in consequence of Mr Pitts allusion to it) he was abus'd and mob'd for what he said, by Mr Wilberforce and Mr Rider, in terms and insinuations rather unusual;[1] but if the grievances of the lower orders of Irishmen, are not agitated, either here or in Ireland; if their miserable cause is not taken up, in some acknowledg'd, constituted place of authority, they will seek redress at the hands of some *unconstituted* authority, some self-created establishment, some Usurpation. For reasons in your letter, I certainly should prefer their cause being taken in its proper place, their own Parliament—In that sentiment before the opening of the Parliament of autumn 95, I wrote to some of our friends, that though for the Magistrates, who had acted *subordinately, under the immediate direction of Government*, a bill of Indemnity could not be refus'd, yet that the vengeance of the Parliament should be levell'd against *those who gave those directions*, and that they should move an *enquiry*—Such was the Tide at the time, indeed such the fears and alarms of the higher orders, that our friends were dispirited, and did not find themselves in strength to do so—there were speeches, but no motions. In my opinion, it was a great misfortune, because it render'd the case of the oppress'd, desperate: They had no hopes left of redress from their own country: They found the parliamentary seal stamp'd on this principle—That, for *them*, every protecting Law was suspended, every penal one, doubled in its rigor—in short, that there was no Law, but to scourge and punish—It is disheartening to be protected but by a small minority in Parliament, but still in a practical point of view, it is most desirable that the cause of the oppress'd should be agitated: that the people may see they are not wholly abandon'd: that their rights and interests are not completely relinquish'd—It invites them, still to keep their eyes *at home*: it is still a glimmering ray of Hope, that may keep some at least, from

[1] On 2 November during the Debate on the Cavalry Bill Fox said that if the ministers were seriously afraid of an invasion of Ireland they should take steps to restore harmony there by adopting Fitzwilliam's Irish policy. Dudley Ryder (1762–1847), later (1809) 1st Earl of Harrowby, said Fox's speech 'might serve as a manifesto for a French general after having invaded Ireland', and William Wilberforce (1759–1833) declared that he never felt more surprise and regret than he did on hearing Fox's speech at a time when all party controversy should cease (*Parliamentary History*, XXXII, 1245–53).

looking abroad for protection—I must therefore try to fortify G. and the Ps[1] in making a shew of exertion: but then if possible to keep it in the proper line: in the House of Commons, not in popular societies— this is indeed difficult: finding ourselves weak within, we are too apt to look for strength, without.

I am almost sorry, you did not see Keogh: not that your letter[2] was a refusal, but it certainly was not a warm invitation. You would have heard from him some details though probably He would have been on his guard as to the quantity, and indeed nature of what he let out—but still there was a possibility of something being collected, that might lead to a guess of what is the actual state of things in Ireland—at present it is all surmize, at least, for us.

I see Curran has again said a few words upon the necessity of en-quiry: but the order of the day was, Silence—Pelham was mute, and adjourn'd for a fortnight.[3]

The papers of today hold out a hope of Italy being reliev'd: I know of no event, I should derive more pleasure from—Perhaps from an expectation of this event, the Sans-culottes have been at work, and have form'd the *Cis-padane* Republick[4]—They are determin'd to leave traces of their footsteps wherever they go—my dear Burke, here is our old friend return'd from Corsica: has he brought back his constitution, or is that left to vie with the Cis-padane,[5] and mark our progress.

I have the satisfaction to tell you, that there are many, many adherents to the principles of the Pamphlet—but there is one grand opponent,[6] more authoritative than all the rest, who weighs down every other opinion.

I hope I am soon to direct to Bath: recollect the use it was of to Mrs B. as well as to yourself.

Believe me affectionately and truely Yours
W. F

Milton
　　novr 27th

[1] Grattan and the Ponsonbys.

[2] Burke's letter of 17 November to Keogh (see above, pp. 112–16), of which he had sent Fitzwilliam a copy.

[3] When the Irish House of Commons met on 21st November, after an adjournment, Curran (see above, p. 122) again urged the need for an inquiry into the disturbances in the north (*Dublin Evening Post*, 22 November).

[4] The Cispadane Republic (Modena and Reggio and the Legations of Bologna and Ferrara) was set up under French auspices in October.

[5] Sir Gilbert Elliot, Viceroy since 1794, had withdrawn from Corsica; he returned to England in March 1797 (*The Times*, 10 March 1797). Sir Gilbert visited Burke at Beaconsfield on 1 and 2 June 1797 and found there 'the kindest and most affectionate reception it is possible to imagine' (letters to his wife, 1 and 3 June 1797, Minto MSS, M24).　　　　　[6] Presumably Pitt.

To EARL FITZWILLIAM—30 *November* 1796

Source: Fitzwilliam MSS (Sheffield).
Endorsed (by Fitzwilliam): Burke| decr 1st 96.

My dear Lord

Your Letter[1] on the melancholy subject of Ireland is just what must come from an heart and understanding like yours, the lives and Liberties of an whole Nation to be committed to the wild and savage discretion of Luttrel—Its safety to his ignorance, inexperience, and presumption!—I scarcely know where I am. But this System, and all other Evil Systems, will not only continue, but encrease and strengthen. We can do little more than lament. We are in a perpetual dilemma between Tyranny and Jacobinism; the Jacobinism too tasting of Tyranny, and the Tyranny rankly savouring of Jacobinism. I think with you, that my Letter[2] was too repulsive: But I wrote in bad health and in ill humour. I have however heard from him since;[3] and as he has expressed a desire to see me, notwithstanding the forbidding manner in which I wrote, my answer to him was in another Strain.[4] I invited him hither; and desired, that if his health were such as to make it inconvenient to him to come so far from Town as this, that he would meet Dr Laurence (with whom he is acquainted) as one connected with your Lordship and in your Sentiments; and that he might open himself to him with the same freedom he might use to myself. I have not yet heard from him; tho' I lost no time in writing my answer. I send your Lordship his Letter.[5] I suppose, that by this he has seen Laurence.

I am truly sensible about your Lordships indulgent sollicitude about my health. It has been various—at one time I was much out of order. I have my good days and my bad—but lately on the whole I have lost no strength. There is a pro and a con about Bath. It is a terrible place in Winter—no air—no exercise; Colds perpetually caught. Here I have air—every convenience and accommodation—My old habits—and the consolation such as it is of not being far from what was dearest to me, and which I wish (if one ought to have a wish on those matters) to be my place of rest. Our best and most respectful regards to Lady Fitzwilliam and believe me ever most devotedly

Your most affectionate friend
and obliged humble Servant
EDM BURKE

Beaconsfield Nov.30.1796.

[1] The previous letter.   [2] Burke's letter to Keogh.   [3] See above, p. 133.
[4] Burke's second answer to Keogh is missing.   [5] Of 24 November.

The REV. THOMAS HUSSEY *to* EDMUND BURKE— 30 *November* 1796

Source: Fitzwilliam MSS (Sheffield). Printed *Corr.* (1844), IV, 369–73.
There is a copy of this letter at Sheffield.

In 1795 Hussey had drawn Burke's attention to the case of James Hyland, a Roman Catholic soldier who had been punished for refusing to attend, under orders, a Protestant religious service (see vol. VIII, 124). The problem raised by the case was one which stirred Burke deeply, and which had been becoming more acute ever since the formation of the Irish Militia in 1793, the rank and file of this force being largely Catholic. In the autumn of 1796 the Irish Government was informed that the men of the militia regiments stationed at Ardfinnan in County Tipperary were being compelled to attend Protestant services. Their colonels repudiated this 'unfounded imputation', explaining that the 'Regiments are regularly paraded every Sunday with their arms, and as part of the Parade of that day, attend Divine Worship at the Drum Head—as soon as the Parade is dismissed, The Men are at Liberty to attend the Priest at an Altar erected for that Purpose in the Centre of the Camp Ground, and which they regularly do'. Pelham made it quite clear that the Irish Government considered it desirable that it should be arranged that after the Sunday parade there should be Protestant and Catholic services at the same time. The commanding officers protested that to make an alteration in the existing arrangements would be bad for discipline. However, early in October, General Sir James Duff (1752–1839), commanding the Limerick district, told Pelham that the 'weather at this season of the year will not admit of our *Service* being performed in Camp in the usual way; Therefore every possible difficulty is done away;—It shall be my duty to take care, that in future you are not troubled on such a subject' (Memorandum of the Commanding Officers to Camden, 2 October; Sir James Duff to Pelham, 11 October; Add. MS 33,102, fols 220–1, 257–8).

My dear Sir

In the midst of all your cares, and anxieties, for the public good, will you permit an old friend, and a very sincere one, to break in for a moment upon you, and to give you some account of myself, and hint a little at what passes around me. The first I owe to your friendship—the second to your Patriotism. The thoughts, as they arise in my mind, shall descend upon this paper, which I shall neither transcribe, nor correct.

You are acquainted with all the particulars relative to my journey to this Country[1]—I gave you my own ideas upon it, with that frankness, and candor, natural to me. Tho' conscious of my own loyal, and *Royal* principles, I dreaded the journey, from the knowledge I already had of this Country. Upon my arrival I was treated with great civility, by the Viceroy,[2] and his Secretary,[3] at least with as much Civility, as a Gentleman is entitled to. In my conversations with each, in private, I spoke

---

[1] See below, pp. 147, 180–1.   [2] Lord Camden; see above, p. 102.
[3] Thomas Pelham; see above, p. 117.

my Sentiments without any reserve. The following week I hastened down to this favorite Spot, this 'punctun saliens'[1] of the salvation of Ireland from Jacobinism, and anarchy—I found it advancing, in every respect, even beyond my expectations. But alass, I was soon assailed by letters from various parts of the Kingdom complaining of the violence made use of in compelling the Catholic Military, who had enlisted with the explicit promise, or at least with the expectation, that nothing would be required of them contrary to their religious tenets. I returned immediately to Dublin—endeavored to obtain a conversation with the Viceroy, or with his Secretary—but they were too busy in settling their bargains with the orators of College green, about the affairs of this world, to hear a man, who came to speak to them about affairs, which they imagine, can only regard the world to come. The Violence to the Military became in the mean time, not only a matter of notoriety, but of public Complaint, from some Catholic Noblemen, and Gentlemen, who hold Commissions here in the Army.[2] When the matter was spoken of in my presence, I expressed my Strong abhorrence; and this, forsooth, gave offence at the Castle, and even our Gentle friend, the Secretary of war,[3] told me, that Mr Pelham *felt himself much hurt at the opinions I uttered upon this subject!* Only consider, my dear Sir, the abject wretchedness of a Country, where a man is blamed for expressing his indignation, at the view of the worst of all oppressions! In the mean time, applications were made to me from several Military Corps, to know what advice I would give them. I felt myself between the two evils of oppression, or Jacobinism. You Know my principles too well to be ignorant of the choice which I would make—I exhorted the Soldiers to Patience, and promised that Steps would be taken to remove the grievance. I then drew up a Sketch of a Pastoral letter,[4] in Strong terms, but before I would publish it I sent

[1] The *punctum saliens* is the 'first trace of the heart in an embryo, appearing as a pulsating point or speck' (*Oxford English Dictionary*). Hussey is speaking of the College at Maynooth.

[2] Sir Edward Bellew, 4th Baronet (*c.* 1760–1827), a captain in the Louth Militia, informed his father-in-law that Catholic soldiers at Ardfinnan camp were discontented because they had to attend Protestant services and his father-in-law passed on his representation to the Government. Sir Edward's Colonel was most annoyed and Sir Edward was 'much alarmed in consequence of the Steps He has taken—all in camp, *poor wretch*, are against him' (Sir Eyre Coote to Pelham, 10 October, Add. MS 33,102, fols 253–4).

[3] William Elliot (d. 1818), Under-Secretary for the Military Department in Ireland 1796–1802. He was called the '" Spectre of the Castle" owing to his peculiar physique—he was almost a living skeleton' (W. Elliot, *The Elliots of Brugh and Wells*, London, 1925, p. 67). When Elliot was being pressed to accept the position of Under-Secretary he wrote: 'I still retain a great horror of the situation, and nothing but Burke's advice and *authority* could prevent me from rejecting it at once' (letter to Sir Gilbert Elliot, 13 July 1795, Minto MSS).

[4] Probably later incorporated into the Pastoral Letter Hussey published in the following year; see below, pp. 302–3.

it in to Mr Pelham by his Secretary,[1] for Mr P: was surrounded by the College green bargain-makers, and I could not see him. The Sketch however was Kept, nor did I hear a word from the Castle, neither did I go near it since that day, now more than two months ago. But this ungentleman like treatment, is not what grieves me most, but the Soldiers finding no general redress, have, I am given to understand, form'd associations even in the Camps, to redress themselves; and in a Country, not remarkable for military discipline, where this evil will end, heaven only knows. Even if France had not given warning, how dangerous it is for any state, to make religion a matter of indifference; surely no man would conclude, that in proportion to a Soldier's want of religion, he will be faithful and loyal to his King. Or that in proportion as the Soldier is compelled to act the hypocrite, in frequenting a place of worship contrary to his conscience, he will be proportionately brave in the King's Service. Hypocricy and cowardice are natural Companions. Who can see without indignation a man in a military garb—the garb of manly courage, and candor, with down cast head, and arms, whipped like a quadruped to a hostile Church, by a little Tyrranizing Officer, who neither fears god himself, nor perhaps believes in him, and this is the return he makes to the King—for his Uniform, his Commission, and his pay! How little does his majesty suspect, that those upon whom he heaps honors, and power here, are his greatest enemies, and the very men who are Jacobinizing this Country! They are urging these cursed Sentiments thro'out the Country; and under the name of United Irishmen, this evil is extending beyond imagination. Many thousands, I am assured, are weekly sworn, thro' the Country in such a secret manner, and form, as to evade all the law in those cases. When I recollect what I repeatedly foretold you, relative to several of the Powers of Europe, these two years past, all which was litterally verified; I am terrified at what I foresee regarding my own unfortunate native Country. To *pass by Parliament,* and *break the connexion with Great Britain,* is, I am informed, the plan of the United Irishmen. The wretches never consider that their grievances are not from England but from a junto of their own Countrymen; and that Camden—Pelham, and Elliot (whom notwithstanding my difference with them, I think the three most honest men in office here) are as compleatly junto-ridden; as my former Patron the King of Spain is convention-ridden. At any rate I am shut out from all conversation with the Castle. Persuaded as I am, that I have acted pro modulo,[2] as the most faithful, and

---

[1] Probably William Busby (1757–1807). *The Times* of 2 April 1795 reported that the 'Rev. Mr Busby is the Private Secretary of the Right Hon. Mr Pelham'.
[2] According to my measure.

loyal of his Majesty's subjects could, I cannot think of offering my Sentiments or opinions, where in all probability they would be unnoticed. I have so long found you ready to give me advice in the hour of need, that I flatter myself you may find a moment, to continue the same friendship and protection, especially at this moment, when I may be an instrument in your hands of National Utility. Let me at all events, request, you will direct some of your familly, to send a line to me, acknowledging the receipt of this tedious scraul from your faithful and affectionate

friend
T. HUSSEY

Royal College Maynooth 30 Nov: 1796

The Irish Government had its own opinion of Hussey's activities. On 26 October Pelham wrote to Portland that Hussey, 'who has conducted himself in such a manner as entirely to forfeit my confidence; he thought proper to speak of Government in shops and the publick places concerning a supposed restraint imposed upon the Catholic Soldiers at Arfinnan (in which he was totally mistaken) that he shocked those of his own persuasion as much as those who were friendly [to] Government. The supposition was that the Catholic Soldiers had been compelled to attend Protestant Service and prevented attending their own, upon enquiry it proved to be false: however Dr Hussey was absurd enough to endeavour to frighten me by alarming my private Secretary and first produced a letter which he pretended to be a copy of one he intended to send to a priest in the Neighbourhood instructing him to warn the Artillery Soldiers against the Sin of attending Protestant Service and directing them to resist by *force* any orders they might receive from their Officers upon that Subject; he was however too prudent to let this Paper go out of his hands, he then wrote a long exhortation to the Catholick Soldiers of Ireland in general, and as it is certainly written with ability, his vanity got the better of his Prudence and that Paper I have in my possession: I shall only say that it is the most inflammatory and dangerous Paper that Bigotry could suggest' (Pelham to Portland, 26 October, Public Record Office, H.O. 100/62, fols 298–303).

To EDWARD JENKINS—1 *December* 1796

Source: Fitzwilliam MSS (Northampton), Box 50.
Addressed: Edw. Jenkins Esqr| Eton.

Edward Jenkins (*c.* 1769–1839) was private tutor to Lord Milton (see above, p. 68), Fitzwilliam's son, who had entered Eton on 30 May, aged ten.

My dear Sir,

I have been so ill, that hitherto I have not ventured to indulge myself in the hope of seeing you and Lord Milton here. I cannot say that even now I can very surely count on two days health. Every thing is fluctuating and precaerious with me: But I feel at the present moment so much better, that I venture to request that you and Lord Milton will favour us with your company, as soon as conveniently you can, and to stay whilst the same convenience admits your stay. I have the honour to be with great Truth and regard

My dear Sir
very sincerely Yours
EDM BURKE

Decr 1. 1796.

EARL FITZWILLIAM *to* EDMUND BURKE— 5 *December* 1796

Source: Fitzwilliam MSS (Sheffield). Printed *Corr.* (1844), IV, 374–7.

My dear Burke

I return the inclos'd,[1] because I think it the original and not a copy—I am happy that you have invited him to Beaconsfield, (if not inconvenient to yourself in a private consideration). No harm can come of your seeing him, but possibly much good. The desire he has of communicating with you, goes a long way towards establishing a belief, that your opinions have weight with him; and if not that; then it is a proof that they have with his connexions, and that it is necessary that he should appear to them, as being on fair terms with you—it would be a pity that he should have to say, that you declin'd even the comunication of matters that concern'd them—Whilst they continue to look up to you, your opinions may not be the Law to them; but certainly they must have great weight with them, and may from time to time check mischievous projects.

I lament exceedingly that Grattan and the Ponsonbys are taking up the consideration of the Representation of Ireland, and I lament it still the more, because they are doing it at the *Whig Club*[2]—It is not, that the present Representation in I[reland] is not a grievance: it certainly is a most crying one, and is in a great degree the cause of the

---

[1] John Keogh's letter of 24 November to Burke; see above, p. 139.
[2] On 4 November the Irish Whig Club, with Grattan in the chair, agreed to resolve itself into a committee 'to enquire into the state of the representation of the People in Parliament; and to report their opinion touching the necessity of a Reform thereof'. On 2 December the committee reported that 'a Reform in parliament' was necessary—and that Catholic emancipation should be 'a fundamental and essential part of the same'. The Club believed that these measures were 'likely to establish public satisfaction and tranquility, and to promote a Union in support of the King and Constitution' (*Dublin Evening Post*, 5 November, 3 December).

misery of the lower Orders: its being so completely aristocratical, leaves the lower Orders *without protection*; and In that example we may learn, what Tyrants We Aristocrates can be, when there is no check whatever on the selfish bent of the human mind—Happy the Country, where there is such an Alloy of Democracy, as brings the overbearing inclinations of the great to a fellow-feeling for the Low: as makes it necessary that the one should court the other: This alone will secure to the lowest an equitable share of Protection from their superiors, and renders the latter the most usefull part of Society, even to the former—but still I tremble when I see antient arrangements meddled with: there is no ascertaining when once the Dyke is cut, how far the waters will flow—and I dislike it the more, when I see the consideration takes its rise, not in a *constituted*, but in a *self-created* authority—it savours of Jacobinism—I have lately thrown out a loose hint upon the subject, by strongly recommending to our Friends there, to stand firm in their *proper situation, the House of Commons*—to stick to *that*—but I fear the reason which above all others, would weigh with me, against agitating any *constitutional* question anywhere, but in Parliament, will not act in the same direction with everyone else—the fear of O'Connor[1] would above all things deter me from bringing a constitutional question before a club—The fear of that person may, I fear, induce[2] others to do the contrary, with a view, as it will be consider'd, of pre-occupying the ground—should it prove so, all I can say is, that, I fear, it will not prove in the event to have been well consider'd—this is however all surmize—may my alarms prove ill-founded—I know the good intentions and will rely upon the prudence of our friends: They are upon the spot to see the ground, and I trust, are assur'd of making the most advantageous dispositions.

The vast Scheme of Finance is at last out[3]—and it ends in the greatest job for the monied men—when was such a bonus given?—I have heard of vast premiums by the rise of Stock, but never of such a direct Bonus—Two points Mr Pitt has gain'd by his manouvring—the first is, He has gain'd the hearts of the monied men, (whom he had lost,) by the advantage he has given them: and the next is, He has terrified all the Landed Interest, into a support of his Jacobinical

---

[1] See above, p. 122.
[2] MS: induces
[3] On 1 December Pitt informed the Bank of England that the Government was considering introducing legislation to compel all persons whose means exceeded a certain level to contribute a fixed proportion, say a quarter, to the State. Subscribers to this forced loan would receive a five per cent stock, issued at a premium to the investor of twelve and a half per cent. Pitt went on to express the hope that many gentlemen would, without waiting to be compelled, voluntarily contribute on the same terms (*The Times*, 2 December).

Peace—by the Scourge he held up[1] against them—War He has render'd impossible—the terror of the Threat is still alive—As for myself, he has put me in an awkward situation, and has left me in a great doubt, what is fit for me to do—To subscribe, or not—I have left it in the discretion of my friend, Baldwin,[2] who will see what *others of my description* do—I am, in my own case, an instance of the folly of his threaten'd plan—I am in possession of a large Income arising from a settled estate: an admirable subject for regular taxation; but a person incapable of advancing a sum of money, without considerable embarrassment—yet had He not relinquish'd his plan, He would have extorted from me, that which I could not give, without distress, whilst he refus'd it from those, who, on proof, are very capable of supplying him and who wish it—But circumstanc'd as I am—the single, mark'd Opponent of Peace; if Men of landed property run down to put their names to the subscription, and to gain patriotism and plunder with one dash of the Pen, mine must not be the only one not to be found[3]—I have therefore left my conduct to B's judgement—let me hear that you continue to mend—more acceptable news can never reach your affectionate friend

W.F.

milton decr 5th 96

To EARL FITZWILLIAM—6 *December* 1796

Source: Fitzwilliam MSS (Sheffield).

My dear Lord,

The affairs of Ireland become more and more complicated every hour; and the difficulty of suggesting any thing to remedy the distracted State of that Country grows with the necessity of providing something of the Kind. I send you a Letter which I received from Dr Hussey this morning.[4] I know what I feel, but I swear I do not know what to advise. I have not yet finishd my answer; for it costs me a good

---

[1] MS: upon

[2] William Baldwin (see above, p. 81).

[3] Writing to Laurence, Fitzwilliam declared: 'As you desire my opinion upon the subject of *voluntary contributions*, by *return of post*, being one upon which my mind is most completely made up, and upon which I have already been as loud as I could in private, by declaring to all my neighbours, 'that let those who pleas'd contribute, I *never* would contribute one Guinea—I would not be the assessor of my own quota, nor desire any body else to fulfill so ticklish a task, being well assur'd, that no one would do it to the satisfaction of his neighbour—that it would prove the ground of universal calumny, every man against his neighbour, and nine times out of ten, the occasion of real dishonor—a situation I will never put any other man, and desire never to be plac'd in myself' (undated letter at Northampton, Box X515/140).

[4] Hussey's letter of 30 November; see above, pp. 140–3.

deal to fix my attention to any kind of Business: But I shall be able to finish, possibly, this night, if not time enough for tomorrows post. I shall keep a Copy of my answer,[1] and send it to you. I shall express my Sentiments on the measures of the people in power very freely; that is with contempt and indignation: But my advice, at least till I hear from your Lordship, will be, that he keeps as shy as his Duty will at all permit him to do—and confining himself to the College, forget for a while, that it was at the express desire of Government he went to Ireland.[2] I intended at first to send the Letter with my answer to the Duke of Portland—but on recollection I thought it would displease and make him unhappy without any good effect: But I am not sure that Hussey does not owe it to himself, to send to his Grace an account of the Success of his Mission. Lord Milton past a Night here.[3] He is a wonderfully fine Boy—and I think, Eton, besides other advantages, has got him considerably better of the Shyness, which was his only fault— but which, in persons of his rank, if it continues, is a fault indeed. I like Jenkins better every time I see him. I am myself pretty much as I have been. We are all, as we ought to be much devoted to Lady Fitzwilliam. I am ever

> My dear Lord
>> most faithfully and affectionately
>> Yours

Decr 6. 1796.   EDM BURKE

Your Lordship will send me the Letter[4] when you have read it.

To THOMAS VENABLES—6 *December* 1796

Source: MS Boston Public Library.
Addressed: Tho: Venables Esqr| Chester Castle| Chester.
This letter is in the hand of Jane Burke, but signed by Burke.

My Dear Sir,

Before I give you any new trouble let me renew my acknowledgements for those you have already taken, you will be so good as to give directions to the gentleman whom you entrust with the care of our

[1] See below, pp. 161–72.
[2] On 1 September Camden wrote to Portland, 'I am of opinion under the present circumstances it might be expedient that Dr Hussey should come to Ireland. It will be desirable to communicate with the principal Catholic's both Clergy and Laity and I do not know, so proper a Person, through whom to communicate with the former as Dr Hussey' (Public Record Office, H.O. 100/62, fol. 204).
[3] The night of 4 December. Edward Jenkins wrote to Fitzwilliam on 5 December: 'We have seen Mr Burke yesterday. He was rather better and seemed in pretty good spirits, but is by no means recover'd from his illness. Lord Milton walked this morning to the French-school and seem'd much pleased with the appearance and manoeuvres of the boys' (MS at Northampton, Box 50).   [4] Hussey's letter.

friend,[1] to supply him with Money for his smaller expenses, but with very little at a time, and that he will look very particularly to his not falling into Debt for any Sums great or Small and that he will particularly look to his falling into the Hands of designing People who under pretence of Supplying his wants, will get paper security from him to any Amount and without any reflexion on his part. You will be so good as to Draw for his quarters Board, as it becomes due and for such other moderate allowance—as is necessary for his extra expenses. You will be so good as to desire some friend in Liverpool, to send him four pounds of Tea, green and of the best Sort, for he is not content with the Tea he finds in that Island—and I wish this done as soon as your Correspondent can send it. I give you joy of the Safe delivery of our friend Mrs Doctor Walker King for whom we were under some alarms.[2]— Our very best Compliments to Mrs Venables.

I am My Dear Sir
Your very affectionate
and obliged Humble Servant

Beaconsfield   EDM BURKE
6th Decbr 1796

I shall be obliged to you to give me notice.

To EARL FITZWILLIAM—7 December 1796

Source: Fitzwilliam MSS (Sheffield).
Endorsed (by Fitzwilliam): Burke| decr 10. 96.

My dear Lord,

Keogh has seen Laurence[3] and he shews a great disposition to pay a Visit here. I do not however think his influence among the Catholicks to be very great, and I am quite sure, that he is here without any deputation, real or understood, from that body. I do not just now expect him. He is Asthmatick; and the weather and roads are unfavourable to his coming.

The question about your Subscription is decided by the closing of that subscription.[4] Nothing could be more absurd than the Idea of

---

[1] William Burke.   [2] Ann King was born on 1 December.
[3] In the letter of 7 December to Fitzwilliam (see above, p. 133), Laurence remarked that Keogh 'was all the time playing the orator, but some things escaped, which did not perfectly please me'. According to Laurence, Keogh blamed the Irish Administration for the growing discontent in Ireland and declared that the Catholics had 'no longer their hereditary terror of a republic'.
[4] On 7 December Fitzwilliam wrote to Burke, 'I find there was no occasion for Mr Baldwin to exercise his judgement about subscribing for me to the loan: before he got my letter, the loan was fill'd and the subscription clos'd' (MS at Sheffield, printed Corr. (1844), IV, 378–9).

calling on the Landed Interest, as such, for a Loan. That Interest in all
the Masses that are considerable, is half at least under Settlement, and
the other half perhaps in Mortgage—whilst the very enormity of the
Quantity and the high Terms of the publick Loan, of course cripples
the private Credit from whence such a rescource was expected. As to
the Terms of The Loan, considering the State of Stock, I do not think
them very exorbitant; and I doubt much whether the Subscription will
bear any considerable premium. If it were to be laid out to any good
purpose: but most assuredly nothing less is meant. I suppose it is the
first time that an army of near 100,000 men (no fewer there are here
and in Ireland, under various denominations of old and new Militia
and fencibles)[1] who are under an absolute legal disability of being
employd against the Enemy except in one case only and that absolutely
in his Choice. This is sad work.

As to the part Grattan and Ponsonby take about a reform,[2] I am
perfectly sensible of the mischief that must arise from the success of the
Scheme, or even from the Struggle: But what can be done? With what
face can any person say to men of rank and Talents in their Country
who have run every risk and made every sacrifice to serve not only
English Government which they approved, but that which they de-
tested and abhorred, and in recompense have not only been dis-
countenanced and suppressed but even persecuted that they are to be
content to be annihilated and disgraced in their Country, when neither
you, nor any man living can assure them, that the Grievances they complain of can be redressed in any other way?

Another consideration would make me shy of interfering. It is, that
Ministry keep this very door to popularity, which is to be shut to these
Gentlemen, open to themselves. Mr Pitt is a declared Zealot (whether
in earnest[3] or not does not signifye sixpence) for these Parliamentary
reforms; and those too to be carried on by Clubbs and associations. It is
not the first time, that this kind of Trick has been playd on Grattan. He
had proposed a set of œconomical propositions for reform partly of
saving, partly constitutional. For a whole Session he was run down in
both Kingdoms, as a person who wanted to strike at the Crown and
destroy the Connection of the two Countries. Having got the advantage
of that popularity, and made good thereby their party on this side of the
Water, The very next Session, on the Irish side, the Castle agents took up
the same plan, (only with a more strong operation against Government

---

[1] The English and Irish Militia and the Fencible Regiments, amounting in all to
about 80,000 men, and the Volunteer Corps, were enlisted only for home defence; see
above, pp. 118–19.
[2] See next page.   [3] MS: eanest

and with fewer Temperaments) and having taken to themselves this popular ground, without any shame, ran down Grattan the original proposer.[1] This method (their constant method) of playing fast and loose, makes it a very arduous thing for any honest men to advise in so delicate a Case.—What will come of it all God only knows—but the only man I know, who could preserve the Rights and Interests of Government[2] with the Good will of the people of all descriptions, without compliment I mean yourself—is fairly, or rather foully, abandon by all men and all parties. The Providence of God can only bring into order this Chaos of confusion.

Ever My dear Lord
Yours most truly
EDM BURKE

Decr 7.1796.

I return the Letter which you sent me by mistake.

To FRENCH LAURENCE—[8 December 1796]

Source: Burke–Laurence Correspondence, pp. 257–60.
Burke refers in this letter to Pitt's difficulties over the Imperial Subsidy. This question was first raised by Fox in the debate of 7 December (see below, p. 160) and reported in the press on the 8th.

My dear Laurence,

We are obliged to *Woodford* for what he has attempted; he could do no more; and considering how well I know that Windham cannot bear to be solicited, he did more than I should have ventured to do.[3] He has a way of his own of walking, and if we hope to do any thing with him, we must follow him, and not cross him in his walk. I am sure he is my only resource for being useful to any human creature. I have nothing to say against the rule which Mr Windham has laid down. He has adhered to it in all other cases, I take it for granted. As to any hope in the Commissariat of Musters, it is on the face of it, except in the case of a

---

[1] From 1790 Grattan was advocating a programme of administrative reform which included a place bill, a pension bill and a responsibility bill, designating the persons 'who should be responsible to Parliament for the issues of public money'. This programme was adopted by the Government in 1793, the Chancellor of the Exchequer, Sir John Parnell, 2nd Baronet (c. 1746–1801), pointing out that though the Government's bills (33 Geo. III, c. 34 and c. 41) were 'not exactly the same with the measures annually offered by the other side of the house, yet being on the same principle, will render them unnecessary' (*Proceedings of the Parliament of Ireland 1793*, Dublin, 1793, III, 57).

[2] MS: Goverment

[3] On 2 December Laurence asked Burke to inform Nagle that on 28 November he had had 'a conversation with Woodford, and another in the evening with Mr Windham, both of which will I hope give him pleasure' (MS Osborn Collection; printed *Burke–Laurence Correspondence*, p. 90).

vacancy by death, wild, chimerical, and utterly hopeless. The office[1] is
the only resource, though I am utterly incapable of conceiving how a
corps of foreign troops can be kept here in time of peace, especially,
when I consider how little the disposition was to keep them up even in
time of war, and that we shifted them upon Portugal as the only resource for saving them. However, this official chance, which I look
upon to be nearly desperate, from the reasons I have given you, is the
only thing that remains to us, and therefore it would be intolerable for
me to preclude Nagle from attendance on the office in which alone he
can have any hope to rise, by my keeping him here for my conveniency,
at the expence of his almost certain ruin. I therefore propose to send
him off on Monday or Tuesday morning[2]—and tell Woodford so, and
my reasons for it, with my best love and thanks. Nagle himself has
nothing to do in this business, for he is too willing to stay; but it has
never been my mode, I hope, to sacrifice other peoples existence to my
accommodation.[3] I confess to you I grow quite out of heart about any
hope from what I may hereafter attempt in the way of writing. It must
more and more offend the people in power, and it will teach nothing
either to them or to the Opposition. The former wish to make a *plausible*
peace with France; the latter are resolved that it shall be a bad one, not
only in substance but in appearance. A Ministry wanting to conciliate
with the Regicides—an Opposition desirous to be incorporated with
them. A pretty kettle of fish Mr Pitt has cooked up about the Imperial
Subsidy. All his trouble is from a want of direct and manly proceeding.
I cannot think that his application of the vote of credit is, in strictness,
illegal, or even unconstitutional, but sure I am that it is not direct, nor
at all according to Parliamentary course, nor in its deviation warranted
by any publick necessity. Had the subsidy been avowed as it ought to
have been done, it would have given strength and credit to the alliance—
And as to the remittance, it would have been open to him to consult
convenience on that subject, as well as if the whole transaction had been
concealed. In fact it was not such a secret as they thought; for it was
publickly talked of at Bath last summer, to my knowledge, or at least to
the end of autumn. I am afraid the whole of this business, in its not
being done in the last Parliament, arose from the resolution of making
peace, even separately from the Emperor.—I have had a letter from
Hussey,[4] giving me a woful account of the pranks that are playing by the
Lilliputian Directory in Ireland. Instead of preparing to resist the
French, they are making war with all might upon Popery; 'ex stultis

---

[1] The Foreign Department of the War Office.
[2] 12 or 13 December.   [3] *Burke–Laurence Correspondence:* accommomodation.
[4] Presumably the letter of 30 November.

insanos'¹ some dæmon makes them. Adieu. God grant a submission to his will. I have had two or three bad days and nights, and though my flesh is further reduced, I do not find my strength impaired nor my spirits in any degree. God bless you.

E.B.

To FRENCH LAURENCE—9 *December* 1796

Source: MS Osborn Collection. Printed *Burke–Laurence Correspondence*,
pp. 91–2.
Addressed: Doctor Laurence M.P.| Doctors Commons| London.
Postmarked: FREE|DE⟨10⟩|96|S.
Only the conclusion of this letter is in Burke's hand; see note below.

My dear Laurence,

The Budget Day² was a matter of great Speculation. Pitt rather less insolent—Fox as furious as I expected.³ Grey has come forward and taken a sort of Lead.⁴ Sheridan heads I suppose a Corps de Reserve.⁵ Tell me in three Lines your remarks upon the general temper of the House on that Night and on this. A fine business this of La Fayette.⁶ Good God—among all the imprisonments confiscations, murders and exiles to find no one object for a British House of Commons to take up but Citizen de la Fayette. I see Fox proposes the repeal of the two anti Jacobin Acts⁷—What do you think of making your Debut upon them. Lord Fitzwilliam concurred in them. Unless perhaps you think that that Ground is a little worn out. I think the taxes on the whole, if likely to be productive, are unexceptionable—The House tax is the worst.⁸ Why did not Pitt tax the lower Teas⁹—a small Duty would not have been felt and surely Tea Drinking, tho' it would be idle to

---

¹ Fools into madmen; see Terence, *Eunuchus*, II, 257.
² 7 December.
³ Fox summed up Pitt's Budget Speech as 'the most false account that could have been given of the state of the finances' (*The Times*, 8 December).
⁴ Charles Grey (1764–1845), later (1807) 2nd Earl Grey, argued that Pitt over-estimated the yield from taxation.
⁵ Richard Brinsley Sheridan (1751–1816) is not reported as speaking in the debate.
⁶ Since August 1792 Marie-Joseph-Paul-Yves-Roch-Gilbert du Motier, Marquis de La Fayette (1758–1834), had been detained in Austrian prisons. On 7 December Richard Fitzpatrick (1747–1813) gave notice in the House of Commons that he would raise the question of La Fayette's treatment. On 16 December he moved that an address should be presented to the King requesting him to represent to the Court of Vienna that the detention of La Fayette was highly injurious to the allied cause. His motion was rejected by 132 to 50 (*The Times*, 8 December; *Parliamentary History*, XXXII, 1348–86).
⁷ On 7 December Fox gave notice that after the recess he would move the repeal of the treason and seditious meetings bills which had been passed in the previous session.
⁸ The Budget changed the principles on which the house tax was assessed.
⁹ Pitt proposed an increase of ten per cent on the tea duty. But as an increased tax on tea 'might bear hard upon the poor' he exempted tea priced at less than two shillings a pound from the additional duty (*The Times*, 8 December).

restrain it is not an object of direct encouragement amongst the lower orders of the people. Good night My Storms have raged all yesterday, all last Night and a great part of this Day with ten fold fury, but a vomitting came on me and I am a good deal easier this evening. Once more adieu. Mrs Burke's affectionate Compliments.[1] I wrote to you by the Coach yesterday[2]—Yours ever   EDM BURKE

Decr 9.1796.

To CAPTAIN EMPEROR JOHN ALEXANDER WOODFORD— 9 *December* 1796

Source: British Museum (Add. MS 37,843, fols 121-2). Printed *Burke–Windham Correspondence*, pp. 211–13.
Only the conclusion of this letter is in Burke's hand; see note below.

My dear Sir

The Renewal of your hopes gives us great and sincere Joy, and we trust that is only a beginning to a Satisfaction most solid and permanent. The Weather is sadly against you, as it is to all who must submit to any Operation. I have read the Debate on the Budget.[3] I think Pitt was less lofty and loud in his Triumph than I expected. As to Fox he seemed in a perfect paroxism of Rage and fury. However I cannot help remarking that the business of la Fayette is not at this moment brought up for nothing. I take it for granted the Ministers will negative so bold and absurd a proposition; but I think the tone in which they take up the matter is very material, and I wish you would let Mr Windham know that I think so. Mr Fox has all along professed, that we ought to have nothing to do with the interior affairs of another Nation, however oppressive they may [be]. Citizen la Fayette is not our fellow Subject, nor do we [know] of any merit he has towards this Country. If we forget his going from the Kings Levee where he was received with distinction to kindle up a War against His Majesty in America[4] We may have occasion for that act of oblivion, and it may be right for us to grant it;—But when we forget this we forget all that we, as Englishmen, know about him. We well know what sort of Subject He was to his own Sovereign whom He three times imprisoned[5]—We

---

[1] The remainder of the letter is in Burke's hand.
[2] The previous letter.   [3] See the previous letter.
[4] Shortly before he left for America early in 1777, La Fayette was presented at the Court of St James's by his uncle (Emmanuel-Marie-Louis, Marquis de Noailles, 1743-1822), the French Ambassador in London.
[5] Burke probably refers to three occasions—in October 1789, at Easter 1791, and after the flight to Varennes—on which the King was publicly subjected to humiliating pressure while La Fayette was in command of the National Guard.

know his cruel and insolent treatment to the French Noblesse at Paris, when on the 28 of February 91 they attempted with their side Arms to defend the King against one of the most atrocious attempts that was made against his Life[1]—Are we to forget that this Man in whose favor we want to break open the Emperors prison, himself imprison'd the unhappy Foulon and delivered him over to a wicked gang of his Brother conspirators who put him to Death with all circumstances of the most unparallelled[2] cruelty[3]—Are we to trouble ourselves about his prison who has been the cause of the imprisonment of more than a Million of innocent victims, multitudes of whom have been dragged out of those Jails only to be massacred in a manner inferior only to the cruelty exercized upon *Foulon*. Are we to prescribe to the Emperor what degree of resentment He should shew to any of the persons who so cruelly insulted and imprison'd one of his nearest Relations[4] who locked her up in a Jail at Paris out of which she never went but to another Jail and thence to a cruel execution. What are his merits then towards us, towards his Master and towards the Emperor. I should rather have thought that if Mr Fox was touched with the Fate of a person cruelly and against the Laws of War imprison'd He would rather think of moving an Address for an instruction to Lord Malmsbury in favor of his meritorious Countryman Sir Sidney Smith;[5] or if he was influenced by general motives of Humanity that He would move that something might be stipulated in the treaty of Peace for the 20,000 Priests that are at this Hour, kept in Prison in France, and support the proposition of la Crettelle Junr for their enlargement[6] whom he knows, or may know if he pleases are in prison and ready to perish for famine—Why does he not move that Provision may be made in the treaty for the return to their Country and their property of the innumerable victims of La Fayettes rebellion, of which this Country is full and who are scattered all over Europe a heavy tax upon the Humanity of Mankind—But no, there is no person worthy the attention of a British Parliament but Citizen la Fayette—With what face can Mr Fox

[1] On the so-called *journée des poignards*; see vol. VI, 264.

[2] MS: unparralled

[3] La Fayette attempted to remove Joseph-François Foullon (1717–89) to prison when he was already in the hands of an angry mob. The attempt failed and Foullon was hanged and beheaded; see vol. VI, 107.

[4] Marie Antoinette was Francis II's aunt.

[5] Sir William Sidney Smith (1764–1840) was captured off Le Havre in April by the French, who resenting the part he had played in burning the ships at Toulon in 1793 held him a prisoner in the Temple. In 1798 he managed to escape.

[6] In November Jean-Gabriel Peltier (see above, p. 104) printed in his magazine *Paris...par M. Peltier* (vol. X) an article by Jean-Charles-Dominique de Lacretelle (1766–1855)—a right-wing Parisian journalist known as 'Lacretelle le jeune'—entitled *Sur les prêtres détenus*, calling for the release of the 20,000 priests who, though accused of no crime, were detained in prison.

desire a national interference with the Emperor for this man, at the very moment when He is opposing as all along he has opposed, the grant of any Loan or Subsidy or assistance whatsoever to this Our Ally[1] and who, in the moment of his proposition instead of an attempt to sooth or soften him speaks an insulting language, such as was never heard before in this time and before this time never would have been tolerated in relation to an Ally of this Country.[2] I think the *manner* in which this Business is to be opposed is of very high importance, as I take it for granted there is no idea of yielding to it publickly or privately. In the name of God what is the meaning of this project of Mr Pitt concerning the further releif of the Poor.[3] What releif do they want except that which it will be difficult indeed to give to make them more frugal or more industrious. I see he's running for popular plates with Mr Fox. Adieu—Forgive all this trouble. Mrs Burke cordially salutes you.[4] I am one day better another worse. Michaelmas with all its Riggs is not more tempestuous than the Aeolian Cave of my Stomach. I find it difficult to apply to any thing—Lord Malmsbury fills me with despair, or rather those who have sent him. Are they quite mad to found their Treaty on a Basis of Exchanges and mutual Cessions?— Why did Mr Pitt conceal the succours he gave the Emperour. Policy required they should be as publick as possible; Why not state that he intends to give him a further subsidy? Faithfully and affectionately Yours

EDM BURKE

Beconsfield Decr 9. 1796.

EARL FITZWILLIAM *to* EDMUND BURKE— ## 9 *December* 1796

Source: Fitzwilliam MSS (Sheffield).
This letter was finished on Friday 9 December, but evidently begun earlier. There is a copy of it at Sheffield.

[1] The Emperor.
[2] On 8 December during the debate on the Budget, Fox criticized the Government for advancing money to the Emperor without the consent of Parliament. In the course of his speech he implied that the Emperor was a despotic ruler (*Parliamentary History*, XXXII, 1273–7).
[3] On 12 February 1796, during the debate on a bill to regulate the wages of agricultural labourers introduced by Samuel Whitbread (see above, p. 123), Pitt threw out a number of suggestions for the amendment and improvement of the Poor Law. In November he introduced a bill which provided advances to poor persons for the purchase of a cow, for children's allowances, and for the establishment of parochial industrial schools and parochial funds which would insure subscribers against sickness and old age. The bill never reached the statute book. On 7 December he gave notice that he intended shortly to bring forward again the scheme for the relief of the poor which he had outlined in the previous session (*Parliamentary History*, XXXII, 705–12; J. H. Rose, *Pitt and Napoleon*, London, 1912, pp. 79–92; *The Times*, 8 December).
[4] The remainder of the letter is in Burke's hand.

My dear Burke

Many thanks for the comunication of Dr Husseys letter:[1] it is of a most interesting, and I am sorry to add of a most alarming nature—to have described an army as discontented, and as associating hostilely, against its Government, one should have thought as alarming a picture, as could well be fancied: but what must be the danger, when added to this, one knows, that this discontented, associating army, is the staff, and the only Staff, upon which Government rests and depends for keeping in subjection, an aggriev'd, disaffected people—so full as the measure of danger is, can it be a question, whether the D: of Portland is to be appriz'd of the crisis to which the affairs of that country are rapidly drawing, the salvation of which he profess'd to be one great motive for his taking Office[2]—can it be a question, whether he is to be submitted to the pain of hearing the truth, when he holds a situation which renders him personally responsible for every event that may happen in Ireland—can it be a question whether in this encreasing state of danger, a person, who has at a former period foreseen the dangers likely to arise from the abominable system of the Government, shall be appriz'd, that we are at the very eve of the day, when his foresight will be brought to pass, and all his predictions fully verified— my dear Burke, Dr Hussey may despair of any good arising from the comunication to that quarter—sent over in the manner in which he himself was, from that quarter, and treated in the manner in which he has been by the Castle, it is natural that he should consider the person who sent him, incompetent to do either good or harm: that the comunication made to *him* would be vain and fruitless—but in-significant as certainly the D of P is, in the state in which he suffers himself to be;[3] Let him be rouz'd to decision and energy, it still may be in his power to avert the greatest evils—circumstanc'd as he is with respect to Office, He has the means of *forcing* a total change of System: Half measures will not be the cure, nor even a palliative for the rancour of the disease—the people of Ireland must have, not only their grievances redress'd, but the assurance of the fair intentions and goodwill of the Government and a total change in its complexion—Promises and Concessions They have had enough of, from the present Government, but they have also the experience how easily they are evaded by trick and chicane—Nothing can recover their affection and confidence but a total

---

[1] Of 30 November, which Burke had enclosed to Fitzwilliam; see above, p. 146.

[2] With Pitt in the Coalition of 1794.

[3] A year earlier, Sir Gilbert Elliot, Viceroy of Corsica, complained that 'the Duke of Portland will look at his nails and raise his spectacles from his nose to his forehead for a fortnight or so before he answers me' (letter to his wife, 17 August 1795, printed Minto, *Life of Elliot*, II, 325–6).

change of *men*, as the only bond to be relied on, for a total change of principles—It would be bold to say that, brought to the crisis things now are, this would do: but it is a certainty that nothing short of this will—It is still in the D: of P's power to attempt to force this: if he fails in the attempt, He may preserve his character from the disgrace of being found the responsible personage for evils, he took office specially to prevent; and his mind from the remorse of never having made one vigorous effort to ward them off, and in the cause in which he engaged.

Here Milton[1] arriv'd from Eton: the occurrence has delay'd this, till this, friday, morning: and I am not sorry that it has, as the post of this morning has brought me a letter from Laurence with an account of his interviews with Keogh.—The details of the horrors comitted in the North by the Protestants against the Catholicks are what I already knew; the encouragement given to the perpetrators of these horrors by Government, had also reach'd me through other channels, as unquestionable as any, that come from K:—his fair conception of the case, stating this encouragement not to come within the reach of legal proof, but the effect the manner of treating the case by the Castle virtually produc'd, is just as it has been represented to me by others.— Though the particular instances reported by K are new, the sum of the whole, is what I already knew,—as to the fact of the Horrors comitted, and the system pursued by the Castle—But there is a part of his Representation, which wounds me to the quick; of which I was apprehensive; and foresaw from the nature of things, that it would happen sooner or later—it is this, that the lower Orders of Catholicks have lost all confidence, not only in the Government, but in *all publick men*, and in the Gentry of their own persuasion, and even in their own Clergy—Whoever recommends *moderation*, is a false friend, or rather an undoubted enemy They conceive—a mischief, as I said before, to have been foreseen, as necessarily arising out of the duplicity of the Government, but it is a state of mischief, that really drives one to despair—But whatever credit is due to K's representation, (and I am sure I cannot withhold my belief) still that country cannot be saved without the most complete change of *Men*—it may produce no effect, but still it is the last, and the *only* chance left—foreseeing and fearing this worst of all evils, I have been lately urging the only men in the country, who deserve its confidence, to shew themselves in their *proper place*, still the friends and protectors of the oppress'd—to try by so doing, to keep the eyes of the people still fix'd on the true constitutional source[2] of redress, and from wandring to something new, to

---

[1] Fitzwilliam's son.   [2] MS: sourse

Usurpers for protection—the D of P may possibly yet save Ireland—to attain one of the objects of his junction with the present Administration would be a great point gain'd for the benefit of civil Society and the Empire; for his own character, and the comfort of his own mind—as for the other, that is already abandon'd—We have fraterniz'd with Jacobinism, and establish'd it—Upon these considerations I cannot help urging you to communicate to the D: of P. the information you have receiv'd—is it certain that he receives from any other, the real state of facts—I doubt it—Has he represented it to the King—does H M know how that crown totters on his brow—What advice you may give to that loyal and honorable man Dr Hussey, under the difficulties he now finds himself, I do not pretend to know, but I suspect it will be moderation, but not submission—I could not refrain from opening to you my own feelings of what is necessary to be done *here*—they are for the consideration of your sober judgement.

Ever affectionately Yours
W F.

Milton
decr 9th 96

To EARL FITZWILLIAM—[*post* 9 *December* 1796]

Source: Fitzwilliam MSS (Sheffield).
In answer to the preceding letter.

My dear Lord,

I agree with you perfectly, that nothing but a very complete change of men in Ireland promises any sort of quiet or security to that distracted Kingdom: But that cannot be, without as complete a change of men, of principles, and of opinions here. The consequences, either of the continuance of the present System in both Countries, or of a total change in both, I cannot bear to contemplate. But as long as this Ministry continues, I am as sure as I am of my existence, that the sinking of that Island to the bottom of the Sea would be sooner risqued, than the change, not only of the whole of that Knot of low Jobbers, but even of one of the very meanest amongst them. We do not hold them up for the sake of the Government of Ireland; but we keep the Government of Ireland to accommodate them. The Rats are not tolerated, because it is hard to keep rats out of Ships, but the Ship is kept up for the Benefit of the Rats. I confess, I am astonishd on what it is your Lordship grounds any the least hope from a communication made of

Dr Husseys sentiments thro' me.[1] To enter into these Views, and to recur to the old Ideas, and politicks, which he has so entirely, not only abandond but reprobated, (and in those who entertained them persecuted too,) would be such a confession of Error as I do not expect from the common force of human nature. I am sure he thinks himself too far embarked in the present System to leave it within his power to recede.[2] You made to him the very same representations: you were his equal in Rank—you were a Member of the same faction in the State—you looked to him as your Leader—You were in an official Situation to which (except for very grave reasons to the contrary) Credit must always be given; you concurred in opinion with all those in whom he had recommended you to have confidence; you concurred with all those to whom he was partial; with his oldest friends, his nearest relations, and his closest Habitudes whilst he was in the very same place in Ireland himself: Yet you have felt the consequence. The grievance was not removed, but you, the complainant and the reformer, was—and by whom? by Himself, who stepd forward, and taking off the responsibility from the first movers, voluntarily and zealously made the act his own. I think as well of my friend Hussey, as I do of any man—but I cannot put him in comparison, for weight and authority, with the whole aggregate of what you are, and much less of what you then were—to say nothing of your having been the closest, and I verily believe, the nearest to his heart, of all his friends. If he sent Hussey to Ireland—did he not send you? and send you, not as a private man of some influence, but as a representative of the King himself? There, my dear Lord—you mistake his Graces situation. When you first came in he was a man (though even then somewhat fallen from the irresolution and uncertainty of his Conduct) high in reputation, strong in connexions, a man much looked up to, much trusted, and even in some degree feard. How is he now? without connexions, without power, without any thing more than a mere private reputation, without official, personal, or Court authority. What is, if possible worse, I am persuaded he has thoroughly made up his mind to that situation. Of this I am certain, that he has not one man about him, no not one about him, subordinately in Office, or connected by confidence, that is better than a rag on a Dunghill. I have also good reason to think that he never in a Case of difficulty consults any person whatever—and trusting very little to himself, he trusts full as little, in any other person. So that those who are masters in the first digestion of measures necessarily become his Masters. He takes all his statement of Facts, implicitly from Pelham;[3] officially as

---

[1] To the Duke of Portland.   [2] MS: reccede.   [3] See above, p. 117.

secretary, confidentially as a friend—and how can he form a reasoning, or state a remonstrance in the Cabinet directly in the Teeth of all his information both official and private? Unluckily too, we cannot conceal from ourselves, his well known nullity in that Cabinet—that he rarely opens his Mouth in it—and that from some natural impediments, or rather from evil habits, he cannot get out three perfect sentences in a regular sequel. This defect, of which he is abundantly sensible, disables him from making any sort of struggle with those who take the lead—at the same time, that a feeling of pride rather inclines him to adopt Measures as his own, which he finds himself unable to resist, than to confess himself in that odd situation, of not yielding to the reasons of others, and not being able to enforce his own. I do not mention all this as laying Load on one that I have always loved and valued and always shall,—but to give you my Reasons, why I think all my interference with him, directly or indirectly, to be a thing quite improper and quite desperate—but I have no Objection at all that Hussey should do it himself, though I am far from sure, it will not rather bring him into some scrape than be of use to the Business he was sent on: But I know that personal risques are as nothing to his Courage.

As to what is doing here, I see nothing short of insanity. Pitt and Fox are not contending for the Government of an independent Country, but who should be the Viceroys deputy under a French Lord Paramount. Fox offering to yield his Country bound hand and foot, without a Struggle, Pitt mingling something of the Bully with his submission. As to Fox His french Fanaticism is such, that on the Budget day his eagerness to let loose Citizen La Fayette,[1] and to unite him in Paris with Montesquiou,[2] Autun,[3] D'Aiguillon,[4] and the rest of that Gang,[5] to make something of a plausible system of connexion for the Jacobins here, made him miss that blot, so easy for him to hit, about the Imperial Supply—but in his railing at the Emperor about La Fayette, he entirely forgot that wound to the constitution on whose cure he supposed the existence of Parliament to depend, when he came to consider, that there

---

[1] Speaking in the debate on the Budget on 7 December, Fox remarked that 'he would maintain that his Imperial Majesty by no means possessed all the concomitants of valour or heroism while he lay under the foul disgrace of still keeping M. de La Fayette in cruel captivity' (*The Times*, 8 December; see also below, p. 185).

[2] Anne-Pierre, Marquis de Montesquiou-Fézensac (1739–98), Deputy of the *noblesse* of Paris. He joined the Third Estate and became a general in the Revolutionary Army.

[3] Charles-Maurice de Talleyrand-Périgord (1754–1838), Bishop of Autun 1788–91.

[4] Armand-Désiré-Vignerot du Plessis-Richelieu d'Agenois, Duc d'Aiguillon (1761–1800). A Deputy from the *noblesse* of the *sénéchaussée* of Agen, he voted with the Constitutionals.

[5] The Duc d'Aiguillon and a Marquis de Montesquiou are included in a list (in Burke's hand) endorsed: 'Noblesse | who have betrayd | their Trust' (MS at Sheffield, Bk 29).

was something else than this poor puppy de La Fayette in the world. As to the way of proceeding, It certainly was not in strictness illegal—no nor against the Spirit of the constitution—but it was indecent, unparliamentary, impolitick, and I am afraid arose from a desire of keeping the Emperour from hour to hour in a State of dependance, in order that he might be driven (as he is driven) to humiliate himself, along with our Court at Paris. This cursed Peace is at the bottom of all the mad things done both by Ministry and opposition. I feel so uneasy, that though far from well, and tho' the weather is far from improved, I think I shall go to Town tomorrow—and see a little more nearly how the land lies. I have written to Hussey;[1] but shall not send off my Letter until I know how you like it. Ever my dear Lord most devotedly Yours

EDM BURKE

P.S. On looking over this, some part of it is so improper to get into other hands that I wish it burnt.

To the REV. THOMAS HUSSEY—[post 9 December 1796]

Source: Draft (corrected by Burke) in Fitzwilliam MSS (Sheffield). Printed Corr. (1844), IV, 379–401.

MS torn. This is in answer to Hussey's letter of 30 November (see above, pp. 140–3). Although Burke told Fitzwilliam on 6 December that he might finish it 'possibly, this night', he had not yet dispatched it when he wrote again to Fitzwilliam [post 9 December]; see previous letter. There is a copy of the last part of this draft at Sheffield (see note below).

My dear Sir

This morning I received your Letter of the 30th of November from Maynooth. I dictate my answer from my Couch, on which I am obliged to lie for a good part of the Day. I cannot conceal from you, much less can I conceal from myself, that, in all probability I am not long for this world. Indeed things are in such a Situation independantly of the Domestic wound that I never could have less reason for regret in quitting the world than at this moment; and my End will be, by several, as little regretted.

I have no difficulty at all in communicating to you or, if it were of any use to mankind at large, my sentiments and feelings on the dismal state of things in Ireland; but I find it difficult indeed to give you the advice you are pleased to ask, as to your own conduct in your very critical Situation.

[1] The next letter.

You state, what has long been but too obvious, that it seems the unfortunate policy of the Hour, to put to the far largest portion of the Kings Subjects in Ireland, the desperate alternative, between a thankless acquiescence under grievous Oppression, or a refuge in Jacobinism with all its horrors and all its crimes. You prefer the former dismal part of the choice. There is no doubt but that you would have reasons if the election of one of these Evils was at all a security against the other. But they are things very alliable and as closely connected as cause and effect. That Jacobinism, which is Speculative in its Origin, and which arises from Wantonness and fullness of bread, may possibly be kept under by firmness and prudence. The very levity of character which produces it may extinguish it; but the Jacobinism which arises from Penury and irritation, from scorned loyalty, and rejected Allegiance, has much deeper roots. They take their nourishment from the bottom of human Nature and the unalterable constitution of things, and not from humour and caprice or the opinions of the Day about privileges and Liberties. These roots will be shot into the Depths of Hell, and will at last raise up their proud Tops to Heaven itself. This radical evil may baffle the attempts of Heads much wiser than those are, who in the petulance and riot of their drunken power are neither ashamed nor afraid to insult and provoke those whom it is their duty and ought to be their glory to cherish and protect.

So then the little wise men of the West, with every hazard of this Evil, are resolved to persevere in their manly and well timed resolution of a War, against Popery. In the principle and in all the proceedings it is perfectly suitable to their character. They begin this last series of their Offensive Operations by laying traps for the consciences of poor Foot-Soldiers. They call these wretches to their Church (empty of a Volonteer congregation) not by the Bell, but by the whip. This Ecclesiastic military discipline is happily taken up, in order to form an Army of well scourged Papists into a firm Phalanx for the support of the Protestant Religion. I wish them Joy of this their valuable discovery in Theology, Politicks and the Art military. Fashion governs the World;[1] and it is the fashion in the great French Empire of Pure and perfect Protestantism, as well as in the little busy medling Province of servile imitators that apes, at an humble distance, the Tone of its Capital, to make a Crusade against you poor Catholicks. But whatever may be thought in Ireland of its share of a War against the Pope in that outlying part of Europe, the Zealous Protestant Buonoparté has given his late Holiness far more deadly blows in the center of his own power and

[1] MS: Wold;

in the nearest seats of his influence,[1] than the Irish Directory can arrogate to itself within its own Jurisdiction from the utmost efforts of its political and military skill. I have my doubts, (they may perhaps arise from my ignorance) whether the Glories of the Night expeditions in surprizing the Cabin fortresses in Louth and Meathe[2] or whether the Slaughter and expulsion of the Catholic Weavers by another set of Zealots in Armagh,[3] or even the proud trophies of the late potatoe Field in that County,[4] are quite to be compared to the Protestant Victories on the Plains of Lombardy; or to the possession of the Fiat of Bologna,[5] or to the approaching Sack of Rome where even now the Protestant Commissaries give the Law. In all this Business great Britain, to us merely Secular politicians, makes no great figure; but let the glory of great Britain shift for itself as it may. All is well, provided Popery is crushed.

This War against Popery furnishes me with a Clue that leads me out of a *Maze* of perplexed politicks, which without it I could not in the least understand. I now can account for the whole. Lord Malmsbury is sent to prostrate the dignity of the English Monarchy at Paris, that an Irish Popish common Soldier may be whipt in to give an appearance of habitation to a deserted protestant Church in Ireland. Thus we balance the account. Defeat and dishonor abroad; Oppression at Home—We sneak to the Regicides, but we boldly trample upon our poor fellow Citizens. But all is for the Protestant Cause.

The same ruling principle explains the Rest. We have abdicated the Crown of Corsica,[6] which had been newly soldered to the Crown of Great Britain and to the Crown of Ireland, lest the British Diadem should look too like the Popes triple Crown. We have ran away from the People of Corsica, and abandonned them without Capitulation of any kind; in favour of those of them who might be our friends. But then, it was for their having capitulated with us, for Popery, as a part of their Constitution. We make amends for our Sins by our Repentance, and for our Apostacy from Protestantism by a breach of faith with popery. We have fled, overspread with dirt and ashes but with hardly enough of Sack Cloath to cover our nakedness. We recollected that this Island, (together with its Yews and its other salubrious productions) had

---

[1] See above, p. 127.
[2] Burke is probably referring to the methods used in repressing Defenderism.
[3] See above, p. 117.
[4] See above, p. 136.
[5] 'The Senate of Bologna has issued a proclamation by which it announces to the inhabitants of that new Republic, that the Constitution is completed, and that it has been sent to General *Buonoparte*, and the Commissioners of the Executive Directory, for their approbation' (*The Times*, 9 December).
[6] See above, p. 138.

given birth to the illustrious Champion of the Protestant World Buonoparté—It was therefore not fit (to use the favorite French expression) that the Cradle of this religious Hero should be polluted by the feet of the British Renegade Slaves, who had stipulated to support Popery in that Island whilst his friends and fellow Missionaries are so gloriously employed in extirpating it in another—Our policy is growing every day into more and more consistency. We have shewed our broad back to the Meditterrenian. We have abandoned too[1] the very hope of an alliance in Italy. We have relinquished the Levant to the Jacobins. We have considered our Trade as nothing—Our policy and our honor went along with it; but all these objects were well sacrificed to remove the very suspicion of giving any assistance to that Abomination, the Pope, in his insolent attempts to resist a truly protestant power resolved to humble the Papal Tiara, and to prevent his pardons and his dispensations from being any longer the standing terror of the wise and virtuous Directory of Ireland; who cannot sit down with any tolerable comfort to an innocent little Job, whilst his Bulls are thundering thro' the world. I ought to suppose that the arrival of General Hoche is eagerly expected in Ireland;[2] for He, too, is a most zealous Protestant; and he has given proof of it by the studied cruelties and insults by which He put to death the old Bishop of Dol;[3] whom, (but from the mortal fear I am in lest the suspicion of Popery should attach upon me) I should call a glorious martyr and should class him among the most venerable prelates that have appeared in this Century. It is to be feared however, that the Zealots will be disappointed in their pious hopes by the Season of the Year, and the bad condition of the Jacobin Navy, which may hinder him this Winter from giving his Brother Protestants in Ireland his kind assistance in accomplishing with you what the other friend of the cause, Buonoparté, is doing in Italy; and what the Masters of these two pious Men the Protestant Directory of France, have so thoroughly accomplished in that the most Popish, but unluckily whilst popish the [most] cultivated, the most populous and the most flourishing of all Countries the austrian Netherlands.

When I consider the narrowness of the views and the total want of human wisdom displayed in our Western Crusade against Popery, it is impossible to speak of it but with every mark of contempt and scorn— yet one cannot help shuddering with horror when one contemplates

---

[1] MS: abandonned to

[2] General Louis-Lazare Hoche (1768–97) was in charge of the French forces which had been assembled at Brest (see below, p. 221).

[3] Urbain-René de Hercé (1726–95), the Bishop of Dol, had been executed on 28 July 1795 after Hoche's defeat of the royalists at Quiberon; see vol. VIII, 301.

the terrible consequences that are frequently the results of craft united with Folly—placed in an unnatural elevation. Such ever will be the issue of things, when the mean vices attempt to mimick the grand passions.—Great men will never do great mischief but for some great End. For this they must be in a state of inflammation and in a manner out of themselves—Among the nobler Animals whose blood is hot, the bite is never poisonous, except when the Creature is mad; but in the cold blooded reptile race, whose poison is exalted by the Chemistry of their icy complexion, their venom is the result of their health, and of the perfection of their Nature—Woe to the Country in which such snakes, whose primum Mobile is their Belly, obtain wings and from Serpents become dragons. It is not that these people want natural Talents and even a good cultivation; on the contrary, they are the sharpest and most sagacious of mankind in the things to which they apply—But having wasted their faculties upon base and unworthy objects, in any thing of a higher order, they are far below the common rate of two legged animals.

I have nothing more to say, just now, upon the Directory in Ireland which indeed is alone worth any mention at all. As to the Half Dozen, (or half score as it may be) of Gentlemen, who, under various names of authority, are sent from hence to be the subordinate agents of that low order of beings, I consider them as wholly out of the question—Their virtues or their vices; their ability or their Weakness, are matters of no sort of consideration. You feel the thing very rightly—all the evils of Ireland originate within itself. That unwise body, the United Irishmen, have had the folly to represent those Evils as owing to this Country, when in truth its chief guilt is in its total neglect, its utter oblivion, its shameful indifference and its entire ignorance, of Ireland and of every thing that relates to it, and not in any oppressive disposition towards that unknown region. No such disposition exists. English Government has farmed out Ireland, without the reservation of a pepper Corn rent in Power or influence, publick or individual, to the little narrow Faction that Domineers there. Thro' that alone they see, feel, hear, or understand, any thing relative to that Kingdom; nor do they any way interfere that I know of, except in giving their countenance and the sanction of their Names to whatever is done by that *Junto*.[1]

Ireland has derived some advantage from its independance on the Parliament of this Kingdom; or rather it did derive advantage from the arrangements that were made at the time of the establishment of that Independance. But human blessings are mixed; and I cannot but

---

[1] The copy at Sheffield begins at this point.

think, that even these great blessings were bought dearly enough, when along with the weight of the authority, they have totally lost all Benefit from the superintendancy of the British Parliament. Our Pride is succeded by fear. It is little less than a breach of Order, even to mention Ireland in the House of Commons of Great Britain. If the people of Ireland were to be flayed alive by the predominant faction it would be the most critical of all attempts so much as to discuss the Subject in any public Assembly upon this side of the Water. If such a faction should by its folly or iniquity or both, provoke disturbances in Ireland, the force paid by this Kingdom would infallibly be employed to repress them. This would be right enough, if our public Councils here at the same time possessed and employed the means of enquiry into the merits of that cause in which their blood and treasure were so laid out. By a strange inversion of the order of things not only the largest part of the Natives of Ireland are thus annihilated; but the Parliament of Great Britain itself is rendered no better than an instrument in the hands of an Irish faction—This is ascendancy with a Witness! In what all this will end it is not impossible to conjecture; tho' the exact time of the accomplishment cannot be ⟨fixed⟩ with the same certainty as you may calculate an Eclipse.

As to your particular conduct it has undoubtedly been that of a good and faithful Subject, and of a man of integrity and honor—You went to Ireland this last time,[1] as you did the first time,[2] at the express desire of the English Minister of that Department, and at the request of the Lord Lieutenant himself.[3] You were fully aware of the Difficulties that would attend your Mission; and I was equally sensible of them—Yet you consented, and I advised, that you should obey the voice of what we considered as indispensible duty. We regarded as the great Evil of the time the growth of Jacobinism, and we were very well assured that from a variety of causes no part of these Countries were more favorable to the growth and progress of that Evil than our unfortunate Country. I considered it as a tolerably good omen, that Government would do nothing further to foment and provoke the Jacobin malady, that they[4] called upon you, a strenuous and steady Royalist, and an enlightened and exemplary[5] Clergyman; A man of birth and respectable connexions in the Country; a man well informed and[6] conversant in State Affairs, and in the general Politicks of the several Courts of Europe, and intimately and personnally habituated in some of those Courts. I regretted indeed that the Ministry which had my most earnest good wishes de-

---

[1] Hussey had spent the summer of 1796 in England.
[2] See vol. VIII, 124.
[3] See above, p. 147.
[4] MS: they they
[5] MS: exemplarary
[6] MS: and and

clined to make any sort of use of the reiterated information you had
given them of the designs of their Enemies, and had taken no notice
of the noble and disinterested Offers, which thro' me, were made for
employing you to save Italy and Spain to the British Alliance.[1] But
this being past and Spain and Italy lost I was in hopes, that they were
resolved to put themselves in the right at home by calling upon you that
they would leave on their part no cause or pretext for Jacobinism except
in the seditious disposition of Individuals; but I now see that instead
of profiting by your advice and services, they will not so much as take
the least notice of your written representations or permit you to have
access to them on the part of those whom it was your Business to reconcile to Government as well as to conciliate Government towards
them. Having rejected your services as a friend of Government, and in
some sort in its employment, they will not even permit to you the
natural expression of those sentiments which every man of sense and
honesty must feel, and which every plain and sincere man must speak
upon this vile plan of abusing Military discipline and perverting it into
an instrument of religious persecution. You remember with what indignation I heard of the scourging of the Soldier at Carrick[1] for adhering
to his religious Opinions[2]—It was at the time when Lord FitzWilliam
went to take possession of a short lived Government in Ireland—Breves
et infaustos populi Hiberni amores.[3] He could not live long in power
because he was a true Patriot, a true friend of both Countries a steady
resister of Jacobinism in every part of the World. On this occasion he
was not of my Opinion. He thought, indeed that the Sufferer ought to
be relieved and discharged and I think he was so:[4] But as to[5] punishments to be inflicted on the Offender, he thought more lenient measures
comprehended in a general plan to prevent such Evils in future, would
be the better course. My Judgement, such as it was, had been, that
punishment ought to attach so far as the Laws permitted, upon every
evil action of subordinate power as it arose. That such acts ought at least
to be marked with the displeasure of Government because general
remedies are uncertain in their Operation when obtained, and[6] that it
is a matter of great uncertainty whether they can be obtained at all.
For a time *his* appeared to be the better Opinion. Even after He was
cruelly torn from the embraces of the people of Ireland, when the
Militia and other Troops were encamped, (if I recollect rightly, at

[1] James Hyland.
[2] See vol. VIII, 124, 136, 200.
[3] Brief and unblest the loves of the Irish people; see Tacitus, *Annals*, II, 41.
[4] It is not known what finally happened to Hyland.
[5] MS: to to
[6] MS: and but

Loughlinstown) you yourself with the knowledge and acquiescence of the suceeding Government publickly performed your function to the Catholicks then in Service.[1] I believe too that all the Irish who had composed the foreign Corps taken into[2] British pay had their regular Chaplains.[3] But we see that things are returning fast to their old corrupted Channels. There they will continue to flow.

If any material Evil had been stated to have arisen from this Liberty that is, if Sedition Mutiny, or disobedience of any kind to Command, had been taught in their Chappels, there might have been a reason for not only forcing the Soldiers into Churches where better doctrines were taught, but for punishing the Teachers of disobedience and Sedition,— But I have never heard of any such Complaint. It is a part therefore of the Systematic illtreatment of Catholicks—This System never will be abandonned as long as it brings advantage to those who adopt it—If the Country enjoys a momentary quiet it is pleaded as an argument in favour of the good effect of wholesome rigours—If, on the Contrary, the Country ⟨grows⟩ more discontented; and if riots and disorders multiply, new Arguments are furnished for giving a vigorous support to the[4] authority of the Directory on account of the rebellious disposition of the people. So long therefore as disorders in the Country become pretexts for adding to the power and emolument of an odious Junto, means will be found to keep one part of it or other in a perpetual state of confusion and disorder. This is the old traditionary policy of that sort of men. The discontents which under them break out among the people become tenure by which they hold their situation.

I do not deny, that in these Contests the people however oppressed are frequently much to blame, whether provoked to their excesses or not, undoubtedly the Law ought to look to nothing but the Offence and to punish it. The redress of grievances is not less necessary than the punishment of disorders; but it is of another resort. In punishing however, the Law ought to be the only rule—If it is not of sufficient force, a force, consistent with its general principles, ought to be added to it. The first duty of a State is to provide for its own conservation. Until that point is secured it can preserve and protect nothing else; but, if possible, it has a greater interest in acting according to strict Law, than even the Subject himself. For if the people see, that the Law is violated to crush them they

---

[1] During the summer of 1795 a number of regiments were encamped at Loughlinstown, north-west of Dublin. It was reported that 'at the earnest solicitation of the Rev. Mr Hussey Roman Catholic chaplaincies [*sic*] have been appointed...for all the regiments of militia now encamped at Lehawnstown' (*Hibernian Journal*, 6 July 1795).

[2] MS: into in

[3] In August 1796 Roman Catholic chaplains were appointed to each of the regiments in the Irish Brigade (*Dublin Gazette*, 6–9 August).

[4] MS: their

will certainly despise the Law, They on their part will be easily Led to violate it whenever they can, by all the means in their power. Except in cases of direct War, whenever Government abandons Law, it proclaims Anarchy.

I am well aware, (if I cared one farthing for the few Days I have to live, whether the vain breath of men blow hot or cold about me) that they who censure any Oppressive proceeding of Government are exciting the people to Sedition and revolt. If there be no oppression it is very true or if there be nothing[1] more than the lapses, which will happen to human infirmity at all times and in the exercise of all power, such complaints would be wicked indeed—These lapses are exceptions implied: an allowance for which is a part of the understood covenant by which Power is delegated by fallible men to other men that are not infallible; but whenever a hostile spirit on the part of Government is shewn the Question assumes another form.—This is no casual Errour, no lapse, no sudden surprise. Nor [is] it a question of civil or political Liberty. What contemptible stuff it is to say, that a Man who is lashed to Church against his conscience would not discover that the whip is painful, or that He had a conscience to be violated, unless I told him so? Would not a penitent Offender confessing his Offence, lamenting it, and expiating it by his blood, when denied the consolation of Religion at his last moments, feel it as no injury to himself or that the rest of the world would feel so horrible and impious an oppression with no indignation, unless I happened to say it ought to be reckoned amongst the most barbarous acts of our barbarous time. Would the people consider their being taken out of their beds and transported from their family and friends to be an equitable and legal and charitable proceeding, unless I should say that it was a violation of Justice, and a dissolution, 'pro tanto,' of the very compact of human Society? If a House of Parliament whose Essence it is to be the Guardian of the Laws, and a Simpathetic protector of the rights of the people (and eminently so of the most defenceless) should not only countenance but applaud this very violation of all Law, and refuse even to examine into the Grounds of the necessity upon the allegation of which Law was so violated, would this be taken for a tender Solicitude for the welfare of the poor, and a true proof of the representative Capacity of the House of Commons, unless I should happen to say (what I do say) that the House had not done its duty either in preserving the sacred rules of Law or in justifying the woeful and humiliating privilege of necessity.[2] They may

[1] MS torn at this point; the words 'or if there be nothing' have been taken from the copy.   [2] See above, p. 122.

indemnify and reward others. They might contrive, if I was within their grasp, to punish me, or if they thought it worth while to stigmatize me by their censures; but who will indemnify them for the disgrace of such an Act? Who will save them from the censures of Posterity? What act of Oblivion will cover them from the wakeful memory, from the Notices and issues of the[1] Grand remembrancer, the God *within?* Would it pass with the people, who suffer[2] from the abuse of lawful power when at the same time they suffer from the use of lawless violence of Jacobins amongst themselves that Government had done its duty and acted leniently in not animadverting on one of those Acts of violence? If I did not tell them, that the lenity with which Government passes by the Crimes and oppressions of a favourite faction, was itself guilty of the most atrocious of all Cruelties. If a Parliament should hear a declamation, attributing the Sufferings of those who are destroyed by these riotous proceedings to their misconduct and then to make them self-felonious, and should en effet refuse an enquiry into the fact, is no inference to be drawn from thence, unless I tell men in high places, that these proceedings taken together form not only an encouragement to the abuse of Power, but to riot, sedition, and a rebellious Spirit which sooner or later will turn upon those that encourage it?

I say little of the business of the Potatoe field,[3] because I am not yet acquainted with the particulars. If any persons were found in arms against the King, whether in a field of Potatoes, or of Flax, or of Turnips, they ought to be attacked by a military Power, and brought to condign Punishment by course of Law—If the County in which the Rebellion was raised, was not in a temper fit for the execution of Justice, a Law ought to be made, such as was made with regard to Scotland[4] on the Suppression of the rebellion of 45 to hang the Delinquents. There could be no difficulty in convicting men who were found 'flagrante delicto'. But I hear nothing of all this. No Law, no tryal, no punishment commensurate to Rebellion; nor of a known proportion to any lesser delinquency, nor any discrimination of the more or the less guilty. Shall you and I find fault with the proceedings of France, and be totally indifferent to the proceedings of Directories at home. You and I hate Jacobinism as we hate the Gates of Hell—Why? Because it is a System of oppression. What can make us in love with oppression because the Syllables Jacobin are not put before the *ism.* When the very same things are done under the *ism* preceded by any other Name in the Directory of Ireland.

---

[1] MS: the the   [2] MS: suffering   [3] See above, p. 136.
[4] 'An Act for the more easy and speedy Trial of such Persons as have levied, or shall levy War against His Majesty...' (19 Geo. II, c. 9), which was passed in 1746.

I have told you, at a great length for a Letter, very shortly for the Subject and for my feelings on it, my sentiments of the scene in which you have been called to act,—on being consulted you advized Sufferers to quiet and submission; and giving Government full credit for an attention to its duties you held out, as an inducement to that submission, some sort of hope of redress. You tryed what your reasons and your credit could do to effect it. In consequence of this piece of Service to Government you have been excluded from all communication with the Castle; and perhaps you may thank[1] yourself that you are not in Newgate. You have done a little more than in your circumstances I should have done. You are indeed very excusable from your motive; but it is very dangerous to hold out to an irritated people Any hopes that we are not pretty sure of being able to realize. The Doctrine of Passive obedience, as a Doctrine, it is unquestionably right to teach; but to go beyond that, is a sort of deceit; and the people who are provoked by their Oppressors do not readily forgive their friends, if whilst the first persecutes and the others appear to deceive them. These friends lose all power of being serviceable to that Government in whose favor they have taken an illconsidered Step. Therefore my Opinion is, that untill the Castle shall shew a greater disposition to listen to its true friends than hitherto it has done, it would not be right in you any further to obtrude your services. In the mean time upon any new Application from the Catholics you ought to let them know simply and candidly how you stand.

The Duke of P——d[2] sent you to Ireland from a situation in this Country of advantage, and comfort to yourself and of no small utility to others. You explained to him in the clearest manner the conduct you were resolved to hold. I do not know that your writing to him will be of the least advantage—I rather think not; yet I am far from sure, that you do not Owe it to him, and to yourself to represent to his Grace the matters which, in substance, you have stated to me.

If any thing else should occur to me I shall, as you wish it, communicate my thoughts to you. In the mean time, I shall be happy to hear from you as often as you find it convenient. You never can neglect the great object of which you are so justly fond; and let me beg of you not to let slip out of your mind the Idea of the auxiliary studies and acquirements, which I recommended to you to add to the merely professional pursuits of your young Clergy; and above all, I hope that you will use the whole of your influence among the Catholics to persuade them to a greater indifference about the Political Objects which at

---

[1] MS: think   [2] The Duke of Portland.

present they have in view. It is not but that I am aware of their importance; or wish them to be abandond. But that they would follow opportunities and not to attempt to force any thing. I doubt whether the priveleges they now seek or have lately sought are compassable. The Struggle would, I am afraid only lead to[1] some of Those very disorders which are made pretexts for further Oppression of the oppressed. I wish the leading people amongst them would give the most Systematic attention to prevent a frequent communication with their adversaries. There are a part of them proud, insulting, capricious, and tyrannical. These of Course will keep them at a distance. There are others of a seditious Temper who would make them at first the instruments and in the End the[2] Victims of their factious Temper and purposes. Those that steer a middle course are truly respectable but they are very few. Your friends ought to avoid all imitation of the Vices of their proud Lords. To many of these they are themselves sufficiently disposed. I should therefore recommend to the middle ranks of that description in which I include not only all merchants but all farmers and tradesmen, that they would change as much as possible those expensive modes of living and that dissipation to which our Countrymen in general are so much addicted. It does not at all become men in a State of persecution. They ought to conform themselves to the circumstances of a people whom Government is resolved not to consider as upon a par with their fellow Subjects. Favour they will have none. They must aim at other rescources to make themselves independent in fact before they aim at a nominal independence. Depend upon it, that with half the privileges of the others, joined to a different System of manners they would grow to a degree of importance to which, without it, no privileges could raise them; much less any intrigues or factious practices. I know very well, that such a discipline among so numerous a people is not easily introduced; but I am sure it is not impossible—If I had youth and strength, I would go myself over to Ireland to work on that plan, so certain I am, that the well being of all descriptions in the Kingdom, as well as of themselves depends upon a reformation among the Catholicks. The work will be very slow in its operation but it is certain in its effect. There is nothing which will not yield to perseverance and method. Adieu! My dear Sir—you have full liberty to shew this Letter to all those (and they are but very few) who may be disposed to think well of my Opinions. I did not care, so far as regards myself, whether it was read on the change; but with regard to you more reserve may be proper—But that you will best judge.

[1] MS: to to   [2] MS: End of the

To FRENCH LAURENCE—[13 *December* 1796]

Source: Burke–Laurence Correspondence, pp. 256–7.

This letter seems to have been written before the debate of 14 December on Fox's vote of censure on the Government for advancing money to the Emperor without the consent of Parliament. Burke is writing on a Tuesday from Nerot's Hotel, King Street, St James's Square, where he sometimes stayed after he had ceased to rent a house in London. 13 December 1796 was a Tuesday. The names in angle brackets are John Wilson Croker's readings (see above, pp. vii–viii).

Nerot's, Tuesday.

My dear Laurence,

I have passed a night without a wink of sleep. This sleeplessness has rather given me employment in thinking, than that thought has interrupted my sleep. I have turned over the affair of the Subsidy in my mind, together with ⟨Lord Fitzwilliam⟩'s letter.[1] On the coolest and maturest consideration, I am perfectly convinced of three things—1st, That the Subsidy proceeding is *not* illegal—2d, That *it is* unconstitutional, that is, against the spirit, use, and fundamental duties of the House of Commons—3d, That in the then state of things (whether induced by Mr Pitt's want of a previous manly course of action, or not) it was necessary for the preservation of publick credit, and not to run across and traverse the Loan. The paper I enclose[2] proves, I think, the last point. So that if you agree with me, I do not see but that your falling in with ⟨Lord Fitzwilliam⟩, doing the thing with political modesty and management as you proposed, may be very right.[3] I see it will be difficult to disentangle the political consequences of this proceeding from the constitutional. To come to a direct censure would damn the war and all our alliances. The first act of my opposition— was in conjunction with others to force Pitt's father and Lord Camden[4] to take an act of indemnity.[5] But there, though the not sitting of Parliament, was a better excuse than here is had,—yet the act itself was

---

[1] Fitzwilliam had written Laurence on 11 December strongly criticizing the Government's method of subsidizing the Emperor. 'An opinion of the Wisdom and fitness of the measure of granting the loan or subsidy to the Emperor, is not the question', he wrote, '(had five times the sum been demanded, and it had depended upon my vote, I would have given it at every risk of censure and punishment)—but the question is, whether *Parliament sitting,* sixpence shall be given without its consent' (MS at Northampton, Box X 515/128). For Great Britain's subsidy policy between 1793 and 1797 see John M. Sherwig, *Guineas and Gunpowder...* (Cambridge, Mass., 1969), pp. 1–96.

[2] It is missing.

[3] Burke seems to be agreeing to a proposal that Laurence should make his maiden speech on the question of the subsidy.

[4] Charles Pratt (1714–94), 1st Earl Camden.

[5] In November 1766 the Government introduced a bill into the House of Commons indemnifying those who, acting under a recent proclamation, had enforced an embargo on the export of wheat. The Opposition argued that 'though this bill provided for the indemnity of the inferior officers, who had acted under the proclamation, yet it passed by the council who advised it' and insisted successfully that the bill should be

directly *illegal*. But as to the unconstitutional tendency, there was none in it. They resisted for awhile the indemnity—but they were beat out of it. There was no censure, but on the contrary, the necessity was admitted—the obstinacy of adhering to prerogative, only blamed and scouted. The ministry[1] did not suffer by it—nor will Mr Pitt, if he will be well advised. But this we shall talk over. Woodford may not be well. I wish to see you, if possible, before you go to the House. I dine at home. God bless you.

Yours ever,
E.B.

To FRENCH LAURENCE—[14 *December* 1796]

Source: MS Hyde Collection. Printed *Burke–Laurence Correspondence*, pp. 254–5.
Addressed: Dr Laurence| Doctors Commons.
Burke's date-line is blotted. It might be read as 'Tuesday' but he seems to be writing on Wednesday. His 'this days Business', refers to the debate of Wednesday, 14 December, on Fox's motion of censure.

My dear Lawrence,

The Gentleman, whom you left with me[2] is easy and confident about the result of this days Business. He enterd into a full detail of the whole money part of the transaction. With that I had indeed been before fully satisfied. The thing itself is he says not at all new, either in the Practice or the attack made upon it, nor in the approbation of Parliament; of which he gave an instance in the affair of the Hannover Troops during Lord Granvilles short administration,[3] and another in the Reign of G. the 2d also which I dont recollect.—His precedents went back to the war of Queen Anne.[4] They are not present to me. I suppose the matters will be found in the Parliamentary Debates. I find Mr Pitt has a large meeting of the Members, who are his friends, to whom he has explaind the whole matter at large. He will attempt to turn the adversary and to have a Strong Vote of approbation—but this I am not authorised to talk of. On the whole since it is so ardently wishd, that

made one for indemnifying 'such persons as have acted for the Service of the Public, in advising or carrying into Execution the order of Council' (7 Geo. III, c. 7). The discussion of the question is summarized at some length in the *Annual Register* for 1767, p. 45; see also vol. I, 277–80.

[1] *Burke–Laurence Correspondence*: minority   [2] Possibly Windham.
[3] When John Carteret, 2nd Earl Granville (1690–1763), was Secretary of State between 1742 and 1744, the employment of Hanoverian troops by the British Government was vigorously attacked in both Houses of Parliament.
[4] In the debate on 14 December Pitt quoted precedents from the reigns of Queen Anne and George II for paying subsidies to foreign powers without previous parliamentary sanction (*The Times*, 15 December; see also *Diary and Correspondence of Charles Abbott, Lord Colchester*, London, 1861, i, 77–9).

you should give a minority Vote,[1] I cannot think you could have a better occasion—it will open a way the better and plainer to the resistance of the other projects. Ever and ever Yours

EDM BURKE

⟨Tu⟩esday morn.

EARL FITZWILLIAM *to* EDMUND BURKE— [14 *December* 1796]

Source: Fitzwilliam MSS (Sheffield).
In answer to Burke's letter of [*post* 9 December]; see above, pp. 158–61.
14 December 1796 was a Wednesday.

My dear Burke

My hopes of any good arising, from a comunication of the intelligence convey'd in Dr Husseys letter, and of his sentiments upon the alarming state of Ireland, to the D: of P,[2] were not very sanguine: but trembling as I do about the critical state of that ill-fated country, I am ready to snatch at every twig—the accounts I have receiv'd of late so very frequently, from such different, and from such unsuspected quarters, leave me allmost in despair upon the subject—can I hear from Lord Rossmore (Genl Cuningham) 'That as soon as it is authenticated that a foreign enemy is landed (tho' not in great force) on any part of the Island, Rebellion, Assassination and Rapine would soon follow'[3]— can I read in the newspapers, that a ship is taken—going to Ireland, with 37,000 Stand of Arms, and 25 pieces of Ordnance,[4] and be told every day of Traitors arrested, who were carrying on treasonable correspondencies with your Enemies, and not feel anxious that the slenderest of all possible chances should be tried, in hopes of averting the evil—Bad, almost desperate I confess myself to think the chances of any good arising from exertions of the D: of P—I know pretty well the degree of weight he has in the cabinet, I dont much doubt of the

[1] See the previous letter. On 15 December Laurence explained to Burke that he had voted with the minority on Fox's motion but found it impossible 'to get an opportunity of saying some few words as I wished' (MS Osborn Collection; printed *Burke–Laurence Correspondence*, pp. 95–7). In a letter to Fitzwilliam referring to his vote, Laurence declared that his connexion with Fitzwilliam forced him 'to the true impartiality of a judge' (letter of 15 December, MS at Northampton, Box 50).
[2] The Duke of Portland.
[3] Cunninghame (see above, p. 116) used these words in his letter of 5 December to Fitzwilliam (MS at Sheffield, F 30c).
[4] 'The Olive Branch (American vessel) which was taken and carried into Portsmouth, a few days ago, by the Audacious man of war, on examination, appears to have 37,000 stand of arms, instead of 20,000 as first stated, and about 25 pieces of artillery, mostly brass ' (*The Times*, 14 December). In subsequent Prize Court proceedings it was contended that the arms were for the use of the Vermont Militia (Public Record Office, H.C.A. 32/794).

degree of submission he has made his mind up to in a general way, but I look to the fact of his sending Dr Hussey to Ir[eland]—as a shadow of hope—That was an effort of *his own*, arising from the impression the state of that country had just then made upon his mind: at that instant He thought for himself, and feeling that the present system was driving fast to certain ruin, he determin'd to try something else, or at least to get at a knowledge of the state of facts by an *instrument of his own*—the reception Dr H. met with from the Castle,[1] is an ample proof, that there he was not consider'd as coming from real Authority here: and of course, though he was treated with *Gentlemanly civility*, he was laid upon the shelf immediately:—But Dr H. being sent, is a proof of another thing, and that is that the D of P himself, had no confidence in Pelham, and that he meant to ascertain from *other* information than his, the real state of facts—Whatever therefore may have been the conduct of the Castle to Dr H., the D of P is entitled to hear *his* representation, be it what it will, and the conduct of the Castle to the Dr should not preclude him from it—Whether you may chuse to make yourself the channel through which that information may reach him, is a point for your own consideration, but if it does not pass through you, it ought to go directly from Dr H—I must again repeat the very slender expectation I have of the D. of P acting consistently, and pursuing the late dictates of his own feelings, when it comes to the point, and when he is to act upon them in the face of his Master[2]—Nothing less than the most vehement incitement of persons about him, never quitting him, and unceasingly urging, and goading him on, could induce him to assert his own opinions and act upon them, against the authority of Mr Pitt— where are those persons, those friends to him, and to his country, to be found—I fear, not in Burlington house[3]—but he should have fair play, and Ireland the miserable chance of his firmness, for wretched as it is, it is its only chance of salvation.

I find the business of the Imperial advance taken up in the House of Commons—your letter[4] has suggested the most probable ground for this very extraordinary proceeding, the determination to keep the Emperor in a state of dependence: but no motive (not even a good one) can justify the proceeding—If we mean to establish Jacobinism in the country, there is no more certain way, than to begin a squabble about Rights, between the different members of the Government: and to insure its success let the first attack be made by the Crown—let the Ministers pass by the House of Commons in matters of money and

---

[1] See above, pp. 140–1.   [2] Pitt.
[3] Portland's London house.   [4] See above, pp. 158–61.

assume to themselves the disposal of the purse, without the participation of Parliament and then let them send down their Dragoons to superintend the execution of the Law, as I see they have done on the other side of this county,[1] and the business will presently be done— These are the subjects of a single week's conversation—These things must be put a stop [to], or we shall be lost.

Ever truely and affectionately Yours
W.F.

wednesday night

To EARL FITZWILLIAM—[15] *December* 1796

Source: Fitzwilliam MSS (Sheffield).
Endorsed (by Fitzwilliam): Burke| decr 16.96.

In this letter Burke refers to the debate of Wednesday, 14 December, as having 'lasted till after three this morning'.

My dear Lord, I am just come from London to which place I went tho' far enough from well, finding myself more ill at Ease in mind than in body. I was resolved to be at hand, in Case any Event should make it tolerably hopeful to make an application to the D. of P.[2] finding how much your Lordship seemd to wish that something of the kind should be done—but the first thing I heard on my arrival was that Sir John Parnell,[3] with some Irish nearly of the same Calibre, together with Sir Hugh Massie,[4] and others *minorum gentium*[5] were come to Town, who reported, that the five troubled Counties[6] (which by the way made two Counties more than I had any Notion of being troubled) were perfectly composed and pacified. This news was communicated to the Assizes, and gave great satisfaction. I thought it would be blowing against the North Wind to employ a puny Breeze in opposition to this Storm: However, as Lord John Cavendish[7] was kind enough to call upon me this morning, I shewed him Dr Husseys Letter[8] and yours, in

---

[1] According to a letter printed in the *Morning Post* of 12 December, during the first meeting for the Brackley division held by the magistrates under the new Militia Act, a troop of cavalry paraded and obstructed the door of the Inn where the magistrates were meeting. They had not asked for military assistance but the officer commanding the detachment produced orders from the War Office signed by one of Windham's clerks.

[2] The Duke of Portland.   [3] See above, p. 150.

[4] Probably Sir Hugh Dillon Massey, 1st Baronet (d. 1807).

[5] Of the lesser tribes.

[6] The proclamation issued on 6 November (see above, p. 136) stated that 'divers ill-affected persons have entered into illegal and treasonable associations in several parts of the counties of Antrim, Down, Tyrone, Londonderry and Armagh'.

[7] (1732–96), a leading member of the Rockingham party. It is very probable that it was on his recommendation in 1765 that Rockingham made Burke his secretary; see vol. I, 207.

[8] Of 30 November; see above, pp. 140–3.

conse[quence] of it,[1] and asked his opinion. He was quite convinced, that the communication would not only be fruitless but possibly in some degree mischievous. I saw no soul to give me an account of the grand debate, which lasted till after three this morning, except his Lordship, who came away without voting. He seemd to think the precedents for the conduct many and strong; and indeed that the proceeding must, more or less take place in all wars—but still that it was of a dangerous nature, and such as precedents how much soever they might excuse could never authorize. Perhaps his did not differ much from my own opinion. It is a sort of discretion little short of absolute necessity; but discretionary powers are the natural soil of abuses. Had Mr Fox made the affair rather a matter of *censure* rather of crimination he would have done more good. Pitts speech, which I hear was of his best, (as I learn from the Lobby reports—to which place I sent a person[2] to enquire about eleven last night) turned the minds of many Members;—for at first the Torrent ran Strongly against him: Foxes first speech was not very impressive; his Last in his very best manner. I confess I am quite sick of the political atmosphere. In all attempts of a constitutional domestick Nature, there is, undisguisedly, so much French principles and wishes, that it is not easy to foresee success in the former, without a certainty of its playing the Game of the common Enemy. Adieu! my dearest Lord! The storms of my stomach worse by far today than ever hinder me from saying more and perhaps I have said more than enough. God long preserve you and yours. Yours most faithfully

EDM BURKE

Thursday night—Decr—1796.

To FRENCH LAURENCE—16 *December* 1796

Source: MS Clifton College (Bristol). Printed *Burke–Laurence Correspondence*, pp. 98–100.
Addressed: Doctor Laurence M : P : | Doctors Commons| London.
Postmarked: BEACONS|FIELD   FREE|DE|⟨17⟩|96|⟨ ⟩.

16 Decr. 1796.

My dear Laurence

Since you were so well able to reconcile it to your own mind I am exceedingly glad of the part you took and of the manner in which you have taken it.[3] I am sure that in a Debate in which two Speakers[4] occupied more than 7 hours it was impracticable for you to come out with any effect. You will have I am afraid but too many opportunities of

---

[1] See above, pp. 155–8.   [2] Not identified.
[3] See above, p. 175.   [4] Pitt and Fox.

explaining yourself upon this question whenever such opportunities occur, I hope you will distinctly mark the difference you make between the Political application of the money and the mode of proceeding which has a tendency to affect the authorities and duties of your House. I think it is visible as the meridian Sun that Fox takes up the Œconomical and constitutional part of the Question in order to embarrass the Political. I therefore submit to you whether what you shall hereafter say should not be rather an explanation of your former vote and in support of a renovation of a further proceeding in the same spirit and for answering the same bad purposes. The House, whether right or wrong has decided, and the continual reiteration of this question under new shapes can answer no other purpose than to render all assistance to our allies impracticable and odious.—If I were in Mr Pitts place this Error or necessity or whatever it may be called, or may be would only animate me in my cause and give me an Opportunity of putting the whole matter to issue by an early proposition of giving vigorous assistance to the Emperor and to Russia specifying the Sum not to be exceeded and leaving the mode of the application to the discretion of the Crown. For I think that Mr Pitt was in the right in securing an application of this money to its immediate and proper object; But I am afraid with you that He would rather be defeated on the Rhine or *Po* than suffer a Badgerring every Day in the House of Commons. How did that great Lawyer your worthy colleague Baldwin vote on this occasion.[1] I suppose that the learned chief justice[2] did not wish to precipitate his re-election. I take it for granted that you have written to Lord Fitzwilliam. A shortish Letter might probably be best, as I see that his mind grows to be ulcerated and inflamed and that little is wanting to make him again precipitate himself into the Fox connexion[3] —Therefore the business is a little critical. To do any thing which might greatly encourage or seem earnestly to lead to a dissuasion from such a Step would equally tho' in different ways tend to goad him to it. At the time while I am now lying on the Couch you are in the middle of your Fayette debate. The Chancellor[4] was of Opinion that this Fayettism ought to be driven out of the House with indignation and scorn; and He

[1] William Baldwin (see above, p. 81) is not listed as voting with the minority.
[2] Burke is probably referring to James Adair (see above, p. 81), Chief Justice of Chester from 1796 until his death in 1798. He is not listed as voting with the minority.
[3] In fact, a few days earlier, on 10 December [1796], Fox had written to his old school friend: 'Dear Fitz Not withstanding our difference of opinion on the subject of the war and as I fear upon many other points respecting the internal state of the country yet I cannot help hoping that you must think as I do upon Pitt's audacious defiance of the constitution in regard to the money sent to the emperor' (MS at Northampton, Box X 516/32/1).
[4] Lord Loughborough; see above, p. 322.

agreed with me in thinking that it never was brought thither but for the purpose of bringing his favorite original Authors of Rebellion into Play again, as forming such a link as would best unite the Jacobin factions in the two Countries. Good Night, God direct and guide you. I passed a very bad Day yesterday. The very worst I have ever had. To Day I bless God for it I am a good deal better and Mrs Burke is certainly not worse. I find Mr Sheridan has made an attack on Mr Pitt about the Pensioner.[1] It is poor stuf and if I were to judge of his Speech by what appears in the News Paper it had a great deal more of smoak than fire in it.

　　　　　　　　　Ever affectionately yours
　　　　　　　　　　　　EDM BURKE

I take it for granted that Sheridan will Let fly one of his forty eight pounder Philippics at Windham and that the Fort of the Latter[2] will be defended by no outworks.

To EARL FITZWILLIAM—18 December 1796

Source: Fitzwilliam MSS (Sheffield).

In answer to Fitzwilliam's letter of [14 December].

　　　　　　　　　　　　　　　18. Decr 1796

My dear Lord,

　　The foundation of all your hopes from the Duke of Portland is in his having sent Dr Hussey to Ireland; from whence you very naturally infer that he doubted of the information he receivd; and wishd to receive a State of that Country thro' less interested Channels. I am afraid this affair has never been properly explained to you. Dr H. had not seen the D. of P. for a very long time, and though he had been sometimes at his Graces door, was not fortunate enough to obtain admittance. It was Lord Camden who wrote to the D. of P. to send over Dr Hussey;[3] and to send him over without a moments *delay*. The D. of P. seems to have been but passive, and merely official in the Business. Hussey, knowing the then situation of things in Ireland, was apprehensive (and it turned

---

[1] In the debate of 14 December Sheridan had complained that under Pitt's régime 'one of the most illustrious pensioners of the crown had not even been rebuked for saying, that courts of justice were become nothing more than schools for sedition' (*Parliamentary History*, XXXII, 1339). In the 'First Letter on a Regicide Peace' Burke had said that 'Public prosecutions are become little better than schools for treason; of no use but to improve the dexterity of criminals in the mystery of evasion; or to show with what complete impunity men may conspire against the commonwealth; with what safety assassins may attempt its awful head' (*Works*, Bohn, V, 163; Little, Brown, V, 247–8).

[2] MS: Later 　　　　　　　　　　　[3] See above, pp. 140, 147.

out that he was not mistaken) that Lord Camden had sent to claim him from the D. of P. only to make him an instrument in quieting the Catholicks under the cruel Treatment which they had received, and the further oppressions they were to look for—and even to make him active in obtaining addresses of satisfaction in that Government, from whence they had experienced the most bitter hostility. He told the D. of P. his resolution, not to be concerned in the execution of any such design, with the utmost Freedom. His Grace heard him as usual with great Patience; and with what is near as usual to him without any observation one way or the other, at least that I can recollect to have heard. He then waited on Mr Pelham who at the time was in London. He found that Lord Camden had taken this Step without any previous communication with that Gentleman. In rather a cold manner, he told him he was much pleased with the measure of my Lord Lieutenant though he had not been consulted, and hoped he would lose no time in complying with his Excellencys Request. Hussey plainly perceived by his manner, that the thing gave him no great Satisfaction. However he explaind himself as clearly and as fully to the Irish Secretary,[1] as he had done to the Secretary of State.[2] In fact I consider his Business as completely done before his arrival in Ireland; and that it was his declaration in London, and nothing that happened in Dublin, that has produced the consequences to him that we have seen.[3] I asked him in what Character he was to be employd in Ireland? He said as Chaplain General to the Irish Brigade, as a sort of superintendant to the Regimental Chaplains. What Salary? He had asked none and none had been mentionnd. I told him I thought all this very wrong—That his Expences, under any management would be considerable—and that I would certainly write to John King one of the D. of P's under-Secretaries to represent this to his Grace. I did write accordingly.[4] Kings answer[5] was, that no salary was or had been intended; That the employment under the Warrant was intended to do him honour, and that this was thought sufficient. I confess I was somewhat provoked at this Kind of answer from my friend King. I saw our friend his Brother[6] not long after, and could not help remonstrating on this Kind of Policy in taking advantage of a mans disinterestedness to defraud him of that fair recompense, which every man is intitled to who serves the publick in any situation under its authority—does Mr King, does the D. of Portland, do the Lord Lieutenant or his Secretary content themselves with the honour (though much higher honour), of their several Situations. I have

[1] Pelham.   [2] Portland.   [3] See above, pp. 140–2.
[4] On 3 September; see above, pp. 82–3.   [5] Missing.
[6] Presumably Walker King.

no Doubt; that this second remonstrance was made to John King; and probably (tho' I am [not] quite sure) to the D. of P. But of this I am certain, that nothing was done in it—and Hussey remains with the two honours of two Offices. One, President of the Maynouth College—the other, his General Chaplaincy; and no Salary or appointment to either.[1] I cannot find by any Enquiry that his Grace is in the smallest degree dissatisfied with the proceedings of Government in Ireland—or with his own situation here. What can be done? for what was Luttrel named to suceed to Cunningham? This arrangement if it did not actually pass thro' the D. of Portlands Office must have been with his full knowlege. I never heard of the slightest opposition to it. For what qualities and for what previous services was the whole military defence, and whole military police, put into the hands of this General? I go no farther.

Has your Lordship read the capitulation of Genoa.[2] The uniformity of all their proceedings is very striking. As to the Parliamentary Business here I am in despair about it. The proceeding about the Emperor was irregular at best. But the proceedings on the other side will prevent our ever giving any succour to that our sole Ally, and the sole hope of Europe, regular, or irregular. That I am afraid is all over. As to the opposition I confess I cannot think of them without Horrour, who can see *all* Europe thus either actually, or in imminent danger of being subdued, whilst the same Enemy menaces the internal safety of these dominions, without *even the decorum of pretending*, either dislike, or indignation, or fear at this Portentous State of things—If they supported us in a fair and open connexion with our allies—they could not be too Zealous for Privelege and open account—but they discover on all occasions, not only no attachment to those allies; but they never fail to vilifye, insult, and degrade them. But let them like Prussia or Spain pass over to France or like the latter become direct and avowed Enemies to their Country not a word more of dislike or blame. God knows we are in a terrible way between our diseases and our Physicians. Ever devotedly your Lordships obliged friend

EDM BURKE

[1] At a meeting of the Maynooth Trustees on 25 June 1795, Hussey was appointed President at a salary of 100 guineas a year. He does not seem to have accepted the salary (J. Healy, *Maynooth College: its Centenary History*, Dublin, 1895, pp. 110, 169). Portland did not consider Hussey should receive a salary as Chaplain to the Irish Brigade; see above, p. 83.

[2] It was reported on 16 December that 'a convention has been signed at Paris between the French and Genoese, by which the English are excluded from the Ports of Genoa' (*The Times*, 16 December).

To EDWARD JERNINGHAM—18 *December* 1796

Source: MS Huntington Library. Printed Bettany, *Life of Jerningham*, pp.39–40.
Addressed: Edwd Jerningham Esqr | Green Street | Grosvenor Square |
London.
Postmarked: BEACONS|FIELD ⟨ ⟩|19|96.
Only the signature is in Burke's hand.

Edward Jerningham (1727–1812) was a fashionable poet and dramatist. He
ended his poem *Peace, Ignominy, and Destruction* (London, 1796) with the lines

Oh, Sage of *Beaconsfield!* indulge the muse
Who the same track (thou hast adorn'd) pursues;
Who gleans thy scatt'rings, grasps the falling grain
From the full harvest of thy loaded wane!

My dear Sir

You will have the goodness to excuse me in using the hand of a
Friend[1] in making the acknowledgements which are so justly due to you
on my part for the valuable present of your fine poem. The publick is
much concerned in this exertion of your genius, and my Fame, if Fame
could or ought [to] be an object to me gives me a concern in it. The best
use I could make of my hand would be to make it express the dictates
of my heart on this occasion; but the truth is, I have been, and am, extremely ill, and there are few hours in the four and twenty which I am
not obliged to pass in my bed[2] or on my Couch. 'Infirmity', (as one of
you Poets says,) 'doth still neglect all office';[3] I assure you I read your
piece with great pleasure. The conceptions are just; the sentiments
Affecting, and the pictures forcible and true. I can say; that I am not
particular in this opinion, nor am I bribed to it by your indulgence to
me your weak fellow Labourer in the same cause. Mr Windham, I
understand, and he has a Judgement not to be deceived or corrupted by
praise thinks of your Poem as I do. There are some lines in it less
finished than the thoughts conveyed in them deserve. The Poets of
this time fall short of their immediate Predecessors, rather by[4] not
labouring their compositions to the perfection of the Art than in any
want of natural capacity. After the elaborate things that we have seen
at the end of the last Age and nearly to the middle of this, we are become more fastidious[5] than perhaps we ought to be with regard to the
last hand that is given to Verses—You are yet happily young and
strong enough to be able to give to the work of your genius all the
advantages of art and discipline with regard to the more mechanical,

[1] The letter is in the hand of Edward James Nagle.
[2] MS: bead
[3] See *King Lear*, II, iv, 106.
[4] MS: rather than
[5] MS: festidious

183

but not least essential part of poetical composition; and I have the satisfaction of observing that your last piece is far less deficient in these more minute excellencies than any of your former, whilst it exceeds them in vigour and spirit.

> I have the honor to be, with more sincere
> respect and regard, Dear Sir
> Your most obedient, most obliged
> and most faithful humble Servant
> EDM BURKE

Beaconsfield
18 Decr 96

To FRENCH LAURENCE—18 December 1796

Source: Burke–Laurence Correspondence, pp. 100–1.

18 Dec. 1796.

My dear Laurence,

I see that it was perfectly impossible for you to come in with your Fayettic on the last debate,[1] though I am really vexed that you had not the opportunity. There was no room for you, but in answer to Fox; and Dundas was not to be stopped,[2] as it was very essential that some person in ministry should take a more direct and manly line than Mr Pitt thought proper to do. After that, the thing was impossible. I think, however, that they are so eager in their Fayettism that they may furnish you with another occasion, because they will be incessant in their attacks upon the Emperor, and will take up the cause of the alliance with rigour and decision. Mr Windham came out with great manliness and his usual ability;[3] and I am very glad to find by you that the House felt on that occasion as it ought.—I had but an indifferent evening yesterday, and this day has been one of my *worst*. Mrs Burke is, I think, rather a trifle better to-day. You talk of our poor Woodford as better, and I trust in God he is so; but I did not at all like the way in which I left him. The operations which are performing upon him seem to me to be in the highest degree critical and dangerous. Pray let me hear from some one or other how he goes on. God bless you.

> Ever yours,
> E.B.

[1] The debate of 16 December.
[2] Henry Dundas (see above, p. 62) spoke at the close of the debate.
[3] See the next letter.

To WILLIAM WINDHAM—18 *December* 1796

Source: British Museum (Add. MS 37,843, fols 123–4). Printed *Burke–Windham Correspondence*, pp. 213–15.

Sunday Dcr. 18. 1796

Though writing, my dear Sir, is not to me the pleasantest of all operations, I should deny myself a very great pleasure, well purchased by more pain than I have in writing a few Lines, if I faild to thank you, in the name of *true* humanity, for what you have done to expose the *false and spurious*. The whole drift of this motion[1] is subservient to the general plan of making every power in alliance with this Country odious. If Mr Fox were a cheerful supporter of this alliance, and a person earnest in voting to the Emperour the amplest supplies for the assertion of the Common Cause, then it might possibly be supposed, that this interposition arose from an earnest Zeal for the Emperours honour, and the Interests of humanity: Nothing less. This alliance is, and has been from the beginning, the Object of his execration. As I should have expected, even from the report of your Speech in the Sun,[2] the impression it made on the house was great and decisive. Laurence told me, that this impression did honour both to the Speaker and to the feelings of the House, which he states to have been on both sides, just what they ought to have been. Nothing can exceed the Ability of that Speech; and it was necessary it should be so; as no overabundant Zeal was shewn for the general Cause of sovereign powers by those who had spoken before you. I do not think it was necessary to be over earnest in disclaiming any part that our Court was guessed to have had in that Transaction. For the sake of Truth it might be disclaimed; but not as an imputation which would have reflected disgrace on our Court if it had been true. Some Philosopher (not of modern Paris) on hearing a Hymn of some Poet to Diana, wished that the Poet should be rewarded with a Daughter, resembling the Diana he had described. I am sure, that any Prince, taking an Interest in Citizen La Fayette, well deserves[3] that he should find so loyal a subject and so faithful a Commander of his Guards, and such an Active protector of himself and his family, as

---

[1] Fitzpatrick's motion on the imprisonment of La Fayette; see above, p. 152.

[2] Windham's speech filled four columns of the *Sun*. Having begun by saying he had not intended to speak he argued at some length that La Fayette's imprisonment was not contrary to the law of nations. La Fayette had been actuated by guilty ambition and had betrayed his country and his King. Windham, who said he felt very little consideration for the beginners of revolutions—'could not separate the idea of M. La Fayette from the millions who were suffering from his crimes' (*The Sun*, 17 December).

[3] MS: deseves

Citizen La Fayette! What a Folly was the Precedent of Asgil?[1] Was Asgil a person who had rebelled against any Sovereign? Had Asgil imprisond, and deliverd over to Hangmen, any of the Queen of Frances relations? He was an innocent Gentleman, without a pretence of Crime, taken out by Ballot from some English Prisoners by General Washington to be made a subject of retaliation. Compare the Cases. Nothing but Mr Foxes wild Enthusiasm for the Revolution in France could make him think of the Case as a precedent. As to the pair of Wretches taken with this La Fayette[2] they are (if possible) more detestable Ruffians than he.

The Fact is, that the minority here must consider the *mere fact of Rebellion* to be the most transcendent of all merit. Be it so, with them, if they please: But is that a plea that is likely to be prevalent with sovereigns? However I shall always take it as an infallible criterion of the principles and dispositions of any men of our time, that they think a rebellion against such a prince as Louis the 16th, and at the moment too when he was making immense sacrifices of his power to the establishment of order and Liberty, to be the most meritorious of all actions, or an action of any merit at all. God save me from falling into the merciful hands of those who think the Business of Foulon and Bertier—no act of cruelty.[3] God save you from their humanity and compassion.—This has been a very bad day with me. But I have begun to work—I see I must fortifye myself on the point of the Nations ability to prosecute the War. I would not wish, however, to call much attention to the collection of materials I wish you [to] procure for me. I think they may easily be had at the Excise and Customs.[4]—I dont at all like the way in which I left poor Woodford. I confess I feel alarmed for him. His Cure seems more dangerous even than the distemper; again and again I congratulate you on your manliness. Ever truly yours

EDM BURKE

[1] Sir Charles Asgill (*c.* 1763–1823), after being chosen by lot from among the British prisoners taken after the capitulation of Yorktown in 1781, was condemned to death by the Americans in retaliation for the murder of an American officer by the loyalists. He was reprieved. In the course of the debate on 16 December his case was referred to by Pitt, Sheridan and Hawkesbury (Robert Banks Jenkinson, 1770–1828, styled Lord Hawkesbury).

[2] Marie-Charles-César de Fay, Comte de Latour-Maubourg (1757–1831), and Jean-Xavier Bureaux de Pusy (1750–1805) were taken prisoner by the Austrians along with La Fayette.

[3] Joseph-François Foullon (see above, p. 154) and Louis-Bénigne-François de Bertier de Sauvigny (1737–89), his son-in-law, were murdered by the Paris mob in 1789; see vol. VI, 263.

[4] These were materials for the 'Third Letter'; Burke was still without them in January (see below, p. 222).

WILLIAM WINDHAM *to* EDMUND BURKE—
20 *December* 1796

Source: Fitzwilliam MSS (Sheffield). Printed *Corr.* (1844), IV, 401–4.

Park str. West
Decr 20th 1796.

My Dear Sir

I hope in future, and so long as writing shall continue painful, you will never abate my satisfaction in the receipt of your letters by the reflexion of their being written in your own hand. Expressions so kind, and approbation so flattering can never fail to be wellcome, in whatever hand, they may be conveyed.

The speech, that you so obligingly commend, is a source to me of satisfaction, from better considerations, than any opinion, that I entertain of its merit: In that respect, it is of as little consequence, as need be: But its effect has been beyond, both its merit, and any expectation that I could have formed from it; and is a strong proof of what may be done with the publick mind, and how easily men may be made to think and feel rightly, in innumerable cases, where at present they do not, were reason fairly applied to them. You cannot conceive, how many people, I have had, who have thanked me for speaking *their* sentiments: and what a quantity of right disposition there has Appeared upon this question, which would absolutely have languished and died, and been lost both now and for ever, if it had not been revived, and animated, and sustained in life by this seasonable encouragement and protection.

All that I have to regret is, that out of respect to other's cold caution, and from fear of meddling with a subject not absolutely my own, I abstained from saying anything on the situation of Sir Sydney Smith,[1] Whose case seemed created for the purpose of confounding those, who, being Wholly indifferent about him, were thus anxious for the fate of a stranger,[2] known only by his treason to his own Sovereign.

Wilberforce, as you will perceive, appeared in his full lustre.[3] What a state is a country in, whose measures are to be guided by such Counsellors! There was a part, that I meant against him, and such 'Simulars of Virtue'[4] that I am afraid did not receive its proper application, and was

[1] See above, p. 154.   [2] La Fayette.
[3] William Wilberforce spoke in the debate on 16 December, suggesting an amendment to the motion.
[4] See *King Lear*, III, ii, 54. In the course of his speech Windham declared: 'Gentlemen boasted pretty largely of humanity and feeling, at the expense of others. Nothing was more mean or dishonest, than to endeavour to catch at reputation by a display of

very probably not repeated in the papers. It might indeed be understood of some higher personages, than He. Upon [the] whole this speech, though nothing in itself, has done Knights service, by counteracting that chapter of a Sentimental Novel;—for such Fitzpatricks speech[1] was: to which the House was about to sacrifice its character, its policy, and its justice.

By accounts received to day, that Tyrant Ally,[2] against whom every presumption is to be admitted, is going on rendering nearly as much service to Mankind, as Wilberforce would do by his humanity, and is pushing the war with all possible vigour and success, both in Italy, and on the side of Kelh.[3] I inclose you the Official report—There is at least the hope, that if Peace must be made, it will be upon [terms] so disadvantageous to France, as besides diminishing their means, and their authority, will put people so much out of conceit of the Government, as to facilitate any endeavours, that may be made, to put things into a better state.

I will do the best, I can, about your Queries, and am ever, My Dear Sir,

most faithfully Yours
W WINDHAM

To EARL FITZWILLIAM—20 *December* 1796

Source: Fitzwilliam MSS (Sheffield).
Endorsed (by Fitzwilliam): Burke decr 22.96.

My dear Lord,

Laurence has communicated to me, by your Lordships desire, the Letter you had from Mr Grattan.[4] I think it better to send it to you directly, rather than let it take further Circuits. The account he gives of the Sum total of things is truly melancholy. It is plainly in Ireland little less than a war declared between property and no property—between the high and the Low, the rich and the poor, brought on, partly by the Circumstances of the Country; but, I may say, much more by the fault of Government, which has fomented the Evil, and widend the

virtue at other persons cost; to be courageous with other men's valour; to be generous with other men's money; to be charitable and magnanimous at the expense of the feelings of others' (*Parliamentary History*, XXXII, 1381).
  [1] On introducing his motion; it opened the debate.   [2] The Emperor.
  [2] On 20 December Grenville received dispatches from Robert Craufurd (see above, p. 107) dated 23 and 28 November, in which he described the progress of the siege of Kehl by the Austrians. These dispatches were published in *The Times* of 21 December; see also below, p. 200.
  [4] Grattan's letter of 11 December (MS at Sheffield, F 30c). Laurence had enclosed it to Burke in a letter of 19 December (MS Osborn Collection; printed *Burke–Laurence Correspondence*, p. 102).

Breach between the parties. The nature of this War, now being made between Wealth and want, renders it almost above human Wisdom, to tell what Course ought to be taken. As long as Government Stands, and sides with that property (which it must do or it will not long be Government) it must be victorious; being possessed of all the Revenues and all the forces of the State. The other party can do nothing at all but aggravate the Tyranny by provoking it, unless by the aid of a foreign Jacobin force and in that Case their Victory would be the utter subversion of human Society itself, of all religion, all Law, all order, all humanity, as well as of all property. What mediatorial power is there. I know of none. This Parliament never will be that power; because it never will be made to believe that the Case of such a War exists in Ireland. How many Peers could you draw to you in an attempt to make such an Enquiry? If you call on the Secretary of State[1] to Lay his correspondence before you, he will probably refuse to grant it: But if the correspondence should be given, I do not know any thing more likely to be fatal, not only to the effect, but to the very Credit of the motion. It will be the representation (and nothing else) of the party you accuse, trumpd up to cover their own Conduct, to vilifye you, and to load those you protect. If you resort to the Testimony of the Irish here, it is clear it will be all as adverse as possible to all your honest purposes. The same difficulties will occur in the House of Commons where besides we are very certain that the Business will be taken up on principles, and pursued for purposes very different from yours. The English interference, if defended by Grattan, will lose him a very great part of the Influence he yet possesses; and the Idea on which he defends it is such, that I do not see how you can adopt[2]—or if you could do it with regard to Strict Truth, how can [you] do it without the utmost peril to things the most dear to you; that is, 'that all the Evils of Ireland have originated from this Country'—a proposition, at best, of a mixed Nature; the part of which that is true, is certainly not the largest part. However in my present perplexity I do not know how to form any thing like a clear opinion, until I see the plan. One thing I greatly fear that under the present Circumstances, every thing being against you a cry will be raised, as if you wished to inflame the people of Ireland at the moment when an Hostile invasion is certainly meditated.[3] The way is full of

---

[1] Portland.

[2] In his letter of 11 December Grattan heartily welcomed Fitzwilliam's 'Idea of introducing the irish subject into the British Parliament'. He thought Fitzwilliam was justified in doing so on the grounds that 'the subject is english as well as Irish' because of 'the revival of the legislative power of England contrary to her own renunciation by the domination of her cabinet in the Irish Parliament'.

[3] See below, pp. 221-2.

Trous de Loups, and Chevaux de Frises. God direct you. The extreme difficulty of the Case hinders me from giving an answer to Husseys Letter.[1] Adieu! my dear Lord, and believe me to the last Rag of this poor Frame Yours devotedly Yours

EDM BURKE

Decr 20.1796.

To FRENCH LAURENCE—20 *December* 1796

Source: MS Trinity College, Dublin. Printed *Burke–Laurence Correspondence*, pp. 103–5.
Addressed: Doctor Laurence M:P: | Doctors Commons | London.
Postmarked: BEACONS|FIELD.

My dear Laurence

I begin to have very little hopes of poor Woodford and I shall feel his Loss very deeply—even at a time when I can have very few objects in Life and very little of Life for my objects. I expect every moment to hear that all is over with him.

As you Lawyers pretend not to love circuity and as you were desired to communicate Mr Grattans Letter to me I transmitted it directly to Lord FitzWilliam with my first thoughts upon it. I do not in the least see what can be done. It is directly contrary to my Opinion both with regard to the truth of the Fact, and to the impression that it will make in Ireland and here to charge English Government with being the cause of all the evils of Ireland. This you see is the ground upon which Grattan Justifies English Interference. Lord Fitzwilliam's failure will serve only to give new Credit to the assertions of the United Irishmen upon that Subject, and will lead further and further to an Alienation of the minds of that people from this Country. What documents are they ⟨Lord FitzWm⟩ can[2] call for which will justify his Motion, or what papers can He call[3] for from the D— of P——ds office,[4] which, if granted would not militate against it. I stated this and somewhat more at large just now to ⟨Lord FitzWm⟩.[5] I believe the common people and the most active of the orders next to them, have lost (as ⟨Lord F.⟩ in a former Letter [said] they have) all confidence in the leading men.[6] I can readily believe the fact without imputing blame at least to Grattan. It is impossible for a man to keep the good opinion of the Castle without running all the lengths of absurd tyranny or to preserve the affection of the discontented without going the full Lengths of the most frank

---

[1] No letter of Hussey's since that of 30 November (see above, pp. 140–3) has survived.
[2] MS: can ⟨Lord FitzWm⟩ can   [3] MS: can He can call
[4] The Duke of Portland's office.   [5] In the previous letter.
[6] Fitzwilliam had said this in his letter of 9 December; see above, pp. 155–8.

Jacobinism. It is the alternative, *exactly* on that side of the Water and in a degree, tho' a much smaller degree in this Country. When you come to speak on *Pitts* Message—But I recollect the Business is over,[1] I was going to say that you would do well to make on a contracted scale a pretty political Map of Europe if you have not yet done it—occasions enough will be open to you. What do people think of the disposition of the new *Czar*.[2] It is common in that Country still more than in any other to make a change in the Political System in every new reign. I doubt He will never make himself so well obeyed as His Mother has been. Mrs Burke, I thank God for it, is better of her usual Complaints, and I am not worse. I walked to Day tho' in the midst of a very bad fit to the amount of about two miles. I find young Elliott[3] is come over on the occasion of His Mothers Death.[4] I suppose you have not yet seen him—Adieu God Bless you ever

                                                                    E B

Beaconsfield
    20 Decr 96

To WALKER KING—21 *December* [1796]

Source: MS Osborn Collection.
This letter is not in Burke's hand.

My dear Walker

I forgot to mention to you in my Letter of last Night[5] the Affair of Madame *Tiballier*,[6] who, you know, has had several months to deliberate upon what she means to do with relation to her child, who certainly is here in a place the least fit for him that is possible. First, she must resolve in what religion he shall be bred; She must tell you whether she is a Catholic or Protestant, for I will not breed the child of any Protestant in the Roman Catholic Religion. I know that she has a

---

[1] A message from the King recommending the House of Commons to make provision for continuing to pay subsidies to the Emperor was considered on 17 and 19 December (*Journals of the House of Commons*, LII, 213, 215). On 26 December, the King, in a message to Parliament, stated that 'with the utmost Concern' he found 'His earnest Endeavours to effect the Restoration of Peace' had been frustrated (*ibid.* LII, 237).

[2] Paul I (1754–1801) had succeeded on the death of his mother, Catherine II, on 17 November.

[3] William Elliot; see above, p. 141.

[4] 'At Reigate, aged seventy-one, Mrs Elliot, relict of William Nassau Elliot, Esq' (*The Sun*, 24 December).

[5] The letter is missing.

[6] The mother of one of the boys at the Penn School. He left in January (see below, p. 232), but may have returned; a Hubert de Tiballier appears on the list of prize winners at the school in January 1803.

Notion that I have the means of establishing all these children in the world as soon as their education is finished. I saw it was in vain to tell her the contrary or to persuade her that at the advanced Age in which she saw me, and with my infirmities I should not live to provide for a child of 6 years old when He should be 17 or 18. You will be pleased to read this to the Lady and to let her know that she is not to be at a greater expence for her Son at Mr Adisson's School[1] than she is at the French School. These Children are bred Catholicks because their parents or other near relation in whom alone the choice is, will have it so— But if this Gentlewoman is herself a protestant of any of the descriptions so called she is to know that I shall do as much ten or twelve Years hence for her Son as I should do for any of the others—That is to say I have no distinct hopes Of making any provision at all for any of them, but you are sensible enough that with regard to the younger Boys it would be ridiculous in me to have any thoughts upon the Subject. Tell Madame Tiballier that she must make her option.

All here give their Love to Mrs King. We are about as we were yesterday, or if there be any difference, rather better

ever yours—
E B

Beaconsfield
21 Decr.

JAMES MACKINTOSH *to* EDMUND BURKE—
 22 *December* 1796

Source: Fitzwilliam MSS (Sheffield). Extract printed in Mackintosh, *Memoirs*, I, 87–8.
Addressed: Right Honble Edmund Burke | Gregories | Beaconsfield | Bucks.
Postmarked: DE|22|96|E.
There is a copy of this letter in the British Museum (Add. MS 52,451, fols 28–9).

James Mackintosh (1765–1832), later (1803) Sir James Mackintosh, published in 1791 his *Vindiciae Gallicae*, an able reply to Burke's *Reflections* from the standpoint of a moderate liberal. In November and December 1796 he published in the *Monthly Review* two unsigned articles on the *Two Letters on a Regicide Peace* in which he argued that the war with France was unjust and unnecessary, though he expressed his admiration for Burke's intellectual powers and literary style.

Sir

The liberty which I take in addressing you is so great and the nature of the address so peculiar that I certainly should not have hazarded such

---

[1] 'Mr Adisson' has not been identified.

an address to a mind of a different Cast from yours.—From you however I venture to hope that a Simple and ingenuous Statement of my feelings will at least procure me pardon if I should fail in obtaining the success to which I presume to aspire.

From the earliest moments of reflexion your writings were my chief study and delight. The instruction which they contain is endeared to me by being entwined and interwoven in my mind with the recollection of those fresh and lively feelings of youth which are too pure and exquisite a pleasure to be twice tasted by the human heart.

The enthusiasm with which I then embraced them is now ripened into solid Conviction by the experience and meditation of more mature age. For a time indeed seduced by the love of what I thought liberty I ventured to oppose your Opinions without ever ceasing to venerate your character. I speak to state facts—not to flatter—You are above flattery. I am too proud to flatter even you.—Since that time a melancholy experience has undeceived me on many subjects on which I was the dupe of my enthusiasm.—I cannot say (and you would despise me if I dissembled) that I can even now assent to all your opinions on the present politics of Europe. But I can with truth affirm that I subscribe to your general Principles; that I consider them as the only solid foundation both of political Science and of political prudence; that I differ solely as to some applications of them which appear to my poor understanding not entirely accordant to the scheme and Spirit of your System; and that above all if the fatal necessity should arise (which God forbid) there is no Man in England more resolutely determined to Spill the last drop of his blood in defense of the Laws and Constitution of our Forefathers.

Even this much Sir I should not have said to you if you had been possessed of power.—I should for ever have imposed silence on my feelings if the act by which I now gratify them could be ascribed even by calumny herself to any base or unworthy motive.

But I hope that the pure desire of expressing my gratitude and veneration is at least a venial impropriety though it should overstep a little the bounds of Strict decorum. Suffer me then to express my Solicitude to be admitted to the honour of a few minutes conversation with you on some of your visits to town.—There are few boons in any man's Power to grant which will be a greater gratification to the Suitor.

Whatever may be the fate of this request I can only safely entrust the Construction of so Singular a Step as that which I now hazard to such a mind as yours; and I am perfectly confident that you will not so far punish my presumption as to expose me to the sneers of those who are less generous by disclosing any Circumstance of this address.

I have the honour to be
Sir

with the most unfeigned and (suffer me
to add) the most affectionate veneration
Your faithful humble Servant,
JAMES MACKINTOSH

No 14 Serle Street Lincolns Inn
22nd December 1796

To JAMES MACKINTOSH—23 December 1796

Source: British Museum (Add. MS 52,451, fols 30–1). Printed Mackintosh, *Memoirs*, I, 88–9.
Addressed: James Mackintosh Esqr | No 14 Serle Street | Lincolns Inn | London.
Postmarked: BEACONS|FIELD   DE|2⟨3⟩|⟨97⟩|A.
In Nagle's hand, but signed by Burke. There is a draft of this letter (corrected by Burke) in Trinity College, Dublin.

Sir

The very obliging Letter with which you have honoured me, is well calculated to stir up those remains of vanity, that I hoped had been nearly extinguished in a frame approaching to the dissolution of every thing that can feed that passion. But, in truth, it afforded me a more solid and a more sensible consolation. The view of a vigorous mind sub-duing by its own constitutional force the maladies which that very force of constitution had produced, is, in itself, a Spectacle very pleasing and very instructive. It is not proper to say any more about myself, who have been, but rather to turn to you who *are*, and who probably *will* be, and from whom the world is yet to expect a great deal of instruction and a great deal of service. You have begun your Opposition by obtaining a great victory over yourself, and it shews how much your own Sagacity operating on your own experience is capable of adding to[1] your very extraordinary natural Talents, and to your early errudition. It was the shew of virtue and the semblance of publick happiness that could alone mislead a mind like yours; and it is a better knowledge of their substance which alone has put you again in the way that leads the most securely[2] and most certainly to your End. As it is on all hands allowed that you were the most able advocate for the cause which you supported, your sacrifice to truth and mature reflexion, adds much to your glory.

For my own part (if that were any thing) I am infinitely more pleased

[1] MS: to to   [2] MS: securety

to find that you agree with me in several capital points than surprized that I have the misfortune to differ with you in some. When I myself differ with persons I so much respect of all Names and parties, it is but just (and, indeed, it costs me nothing to do it) that I should bear in others that disagreement in Sentiment and Opinions, which at any rate is so natural, and which perhaps arizes from a better view of things.[1]

Tho' I see but very few persons, and have, since my misfortune[2] studiously declined all new acquaintances and never dine out of my own family, nor live at all in any of my usual societies, not even in those with which I was most closely connected, I shall certainly be as happy as I shall feel myself honoured by a visit from a distinguished person like you, whom I shall consider as an exception to my rule. I have no habitation in London, nor never go to that place but with great reluctance, and without suffering a great deal. Nothing but necessity calls me thither; but tho' I hardly dare to ask you to come so far, whenever it may suit you to visit this abode of sickness and infirmity, I shall be glad to see you. I dont know whether my friend Doctor Laurence and you have the happiness of being acquainted with each other; if not, I could wish it to be brought about. You might come together, and this might secure to you some entertainment which, my infirmity, that leaves me but a few easy hours in my best Days, will not afford me the means of giving you by those attentions that are your due.

You will have the goodness to excuse my making use of another hand to answer your Letter, but of late I have found it very irksome and inconvenient to me to stoop to my Desk. I therefore dictate from my Couch whatever I wish to say to my friends at a distance. I have the honour to be Sir, with great respect and regard

> Your most obedient and very
> much obliged humble servant,
> EDM BURKE.

Beaconsfield
23d Decr 1796

Mackintosh accepted Burke's invitation and spent a few days at Beaconsfield. A friend with whom he later discussed his impressions of Burke preserved them in a rough summary. Mackintosh, the friend reported, '... described, in glowing terms, the astonishing effusions of his mind in conversation: perfectly free from all taint of affectation; would enter, with cordial glee, into the sports of children, rolling about with them on the carpet, and pouring out, in his gambols, the sublimest images, mingled with the most wretched puns.—

[1] From 'For my own part ... of things' is omitted in the draft.
[2] The printed text's note at this point is: 'The loss of his son'.

Anticipated his approaching dissolution with due solemnity but perfect composure;—minutely and accurately informed, to a wonderful exactness, with
respect to every fact relative to the French Revolution. Burke said of Fox, with
a deep sigh, "He is made to be loved"' (Mackintosh, *Memoirs*, 1, 91–2).

To FRENCH LAURENCE—23 *December* 1796

Source: Fitzwilliam MSS (Sheffield).
Addressed: Doctor Laurence M: P: | Doctors Commons | London.
Postmarked: BEACONS|FIELD ⟨   ⟩|DE|24|96|⟨C⟩.
This letter is not in Burke's hand.

My dear Laurence

It is as you Judge a real comfort to me that I had seen Lord John
Cavendish before his Death[1] and that He died in Charity with me. I
never ceased for one moment to love and honor him nor to consider
him as such a man deserved to be considered; and I never regarded some
peevishness of his towards me, for I never observed or heard of any
thing more than as what was very natural and might be well justified by
the idea of the Services which, in pursuit of other objects I had done to
those, whom, with the best reason, he looked on, not only as Enemies
to the cause we had espoused in common, but to himself personally.
The Duke of Portland took him too readily at his word when He resolved
to discontinue those Services for which he had met so ill a return from
the Publick.[2] Retired from the world he latterly saw things only in the
posture in which he had left them, and the sore feelings which he had
at that time influenced his temper with regard to all the subsequent
events. Undoubtedly the manner in which the D: of Portland conducted the late Coalition[3] was the cause of the utter dissipation of the
Party, and Lord John imagined that I had a large share in giving that
form to things; but tho' the Coalition itself in its principle was what I
earnestly desired and long laboured to bring it about, yet, as you know,
with regard to the execution there was no consultation with me, nor
even the least communication—else, I flatter myself that things would
have been put upon a more solid bottom; and what would have secured
something else than two Heads of personal factions in a distracted
Country. Tho' habituated to the fall of every thing about me I was
much struck with the Death of Lord John Cavendish. It was but a very

[1] Lord John Cavendish (see above, p. 177) died at his brother's house at Twickenham on Saturday, 17 December (*St James's Chronicle*, 17–20 December).
[2] Lord John lost his parliamentary seat at York—which he had held for sixteen
years—in the election of 1784 which followed the Fox–North Coalition. He did not
sit in Parliament again until 1794.
[3] The Coalition between the Portland Whigs and Pitt in 1794.

few days before that I had seen him in as good health, as, to all appearance, a Man of his Age could be. We talked with much good humour and confidence and we did not differ very much except in one point which was that He did not beleive there were any Jacobins in England. Well God has disposed of him for the best, and I beleive few purer souls have ever come into his presence, or less polluted by the World. I beleive he is taken in a good time before He could see the ravages of that Jacobinism which his benevolent and unsuspecting mind could not have thought to have existed in this Country.

The Letter which I received to Day and which I enclose to you[1] will rather surprize you as it [did] me. It is as civil as possible and what he says of his antient partiality to me is I believe strictly true. I wrote him such an answer[2] as so very civil a Letter deserved and such as the encouragement which ought to be given to all converts of Talents justly demands from those who wish seriously well to the Success of their own principles. I told him that I could never reckon upon any time of being in Town, but wished of all things that He should be acquainted with you and that you should come to this place together. I wish you by degrees to become a central point to which Men of talents might be aggregated. It would prevent them from wandering without a guide according to their several wild imaginations. I rejoice at your intending to give us your Christmas Day.[3] I fancied that you had only thoughts of going to Lord FitzWilliam but that He had not positively engaged you.

Woodford wrote a Letter with his own hand to Mrs Burke to Day. He writes in spirits and with Hopes—but I am not very sanguine about him. I suppose you'll see him to morrow Evening and bring us word How he goes on.[4] Mrs Burke continues as she was, and if I am not better certainly I am not at all worse—Adieu. Adieu, and may you live for many a Christmas, and may that festival of Glory to God on High and peace and good Will to man be long continued for your happiness and Edification. Say every thing for us to Woodford.

Ever Yours
E B

Beaconsfield
  23d Decr 96

[1] The letter from Mackintosh.
[2] The previous letter.
[3] Laurence did not spend Christmas day with Burke; see below, p. 204.
[4] For Woodford's illness, see above, p. 190. His letter to Mrs Burke is missing.

To WILLIAM WINDHAM—23 *December* 1796
Source: Corr. (1844), IV, 404–11.

Beconsfield, December 23, 1796.

My Dear Friend,

I make use of the saturnalian liberty with which you have indulged your Davus[1] at the close of this December. I write with the hand of my friend and kinsman, Nagle,[2] who has indeed been very helpful to me. His brother,[3] a captain-lieutenant in Mahony's chasseurs,[4] whom you had seen at the Duke of York's head-quarters, and who, we conceived, had been killed, is now reported to be somewhere alive, and a prisoner. I give no great credit to the report, because, had he been alive, I think he must have found some way of letting his friends (though he might be afraid of making known his connexion with me) have some intelligence of his situation. The report arises from a letter, written by Count Mahony himself to his brother in Ireland,[5] the very day before the Count was killed. I never heard before this time of Colonel Mahony having been killed, and therefore the date of the letter (of which I have not been informed) might go something towards clearing the way for further inquiry into the fate of this young man. Perhaps they may know something of the time at the Duke of York's office,[6] or at my Lord Grenville's,[7] or from the secretary of Count Starembergh.[8] If no intelligence can be had here (which I think the most likely), could you prevail upon Mr Canning to write to Colonel Crawford,[9] or his brother,[10] to set on foot an inquiry on this subject; for I shall be very well pleased to find this worthy creature, in whom I took a very great interest, alive.

I have been looking in vain for a curious print which I had in my hand yesterday. It is concerning the imprisonment of La Fayette. It is far from ill-executed. It was torn from a small pocket-book, called the

---

[1] A standard name for a slave in Roman comedy.
[2] Edward James Nagle.
[3] James Nagle (d. 1801); see vols IV, 93; VII, 376, 378, 382.
[4] William Mahony (1760–96), who was born in Ireland, had entered the Imperial service. At the outbreak of the war with France he formed the Chasseurs corps of Dandini, later known as Mahony's Chasseurs. (Österreichisches Staatsarchiv, Kriegsarchiv).
[5] Mahony had three brothers: Daniel (d. 1832), Denis and Dermitius.
[6] The Duke of York was Commander-in-Chief.
[7] The Foreign Office.
[8] Ludwig Josef Maria Georg, Graf von Starhemberg (1762–1833), Austrian Ambassador in London. His secretary has not been identified.
[9] Charles Gregan Craufurd (1761–1821), British representative with the Austrian Army. George Canning (see below, p. 267) was Under-Secretary of State for Foreign Affairs.
[10] Robert Craufurd; see above, p. 107.

Minor's Pocket-book[1] for the year 1797, to which it served as a frontispiece. It is printed for Darton and Harvey, Gracechurch-street; it fronts a narrative, said to be taken from a monthly magazine. It is, as you will see, a neat abstract of General Fitzpatrick's speech,[2] and finds nothing about Monsieur de la Fayette worth relating, except the sufferings of his family under Robespierre;[3] and his exile, in consequence of an attempt to save the life of Louis the Sixteenth.[4] I mention this, to let you see with what art and system this business is worked up, and that the sentimental novel is, in reality, a political contrivance that has some more meaning than the display of a hypocritical humanity. Why should it not be a pretty subject for a series of prints like the 'Rake's Progress,' or the 'Harlot's Progress,' to give the *Rebel's* Progress, in which the heroic exploits and various fortunes of citizen La Fayette might make an useful moral lesson to all English generals who might be inclined to imitate at home what they so greatly admire in their friend abroad? By the way, I totally forgot from whom it was I heard a very accurate detail of the attempt made, with great regularity and well-combined contrivance, by Mr Church,[5] and others of the Fox party here, to effect the escape of that suffering hero from Olmutz.[6] I heard the name of the physician, who was sent to Vienna for the purpose,[7] though I do not recollect it. He was a young physician of London, and insinuated himself so well into the good graces of some persons of importance in the imperial court, that when Mons. de la Fayette, having had his cue, sent to Vienna to request, if possible, the assistance of an English physician, in whose skill alone he pretended to have any confidence, this emissary was sent to him without any difficulty. The governor of the castle had the humanity to permit La Fayette, upon the doctor's representation of the necessity of air and exercise for his cure, to go out in an open chaise with him for several days together; until, all things being settled for the escape, two horses were provided, upon one of which the doctor mounted, and gave the other, with cash for his journey, to the prisoner. The doctor got clear off; but the other, falling into confusion, and tumbling from blunder into blunder, was discovered, and carried before a magistrate, who delivered him over to the

---

[1] This magazine has not been found.
[2] See above, p. 152.
[3] Marie-Adrienne-Françoise, *née* de Noailles, Marquise de La Fayette (1759–1807), was imprisoned from September 1793 until January 1795.
[4] In June 1792 just before the overthrow of the Monarchy, La Fayette hastened from the frontier to Paris and tried to stiffen the resolution of the moderates.
[5] John Barker Church (*c.* 1746–1818); M.P. for Wendover.
[6] La Fayette was imprisoned in the fortress at Olmutz.
[7] Justus Erich Bollman (1769–1821), a young German who studied medicine at Göttingen. He spent about a year (1792–3) in England.

governor. This was the date of any unusual closeness and rigour in his confinement; and was the cause, as I take it, of the precautions that are taken with regard to the entry and exit of all persons who may visit him in his prison. It is right, of course, that persons who have attempted to make their escape, should be guarded with double vigilance. I wish you would ask Laurence whether he recollects from whom I had this detailed account, and the name of the physician who was the principal actor in the business. Nagle seems to think he has read some short account of it in a newspaper; but it is rather extraordinary, if it had been thus published, that Fitzpatrick should have taken no notice of it, either to refute the story, if it were public and not true, or to repel the inferences which would arise, in order to diminish the effect of his tragical tale.

I think that the substance of what you have said relative to the humanity of politicians of the first or second order, is touched in the account given of your speech in the *Sun*;[1] and to me, the application was very intelligible. As to Mr Pitt's speech, there was nothing at all in it, but a dry point of law.[2] Nothing was said but what might have been urged, if the case had been that of the most innocent, virtuous, and meritorious sufferer that had ever experienced the severity of fortune. I am sure that the faction will not let the matter rest here. I thank you for the *bulletin*; but, on considering the whole matter, I think things still in a very trembling balance, and the final result of the campaign still very doubtful. It is plain that the Austrians were surprised at Kehl;[3] and that it was rather an escape than a victory. For God's sake, why is the subsidy (or whatever it is) to the Emperor reduced to £500,000, when the King of Prussia, who had much less need of it, and did much less for it, had fourteen hundred thousand a year, not as a loan, but as a subsidy?[4] I am afraid we have too much in view a little fallacious economy, which is, in war, little less than madness. I am afraid, too, that we conduct war upon the principles of favouritism, and that we feed the objects of our affections at the expense of our interests. I see nothing said of a provision for the army of Condé,[5] which has stood

---

[1] See above, p. 185.

[2] Pitt argued that since it could not be shown that the British Government was in any way responsible for La Fayette's imprisonment, the matter did not come under the cognizance of the House of Commons (*The Sun*, 17 December).

[3] On 22 November the French made a vigorous attack on the siege works at Kehl (*The Times*, 21 December, but the fortress capitulated in January 1797).

[4] By the Convention of April 1794 Great Britain and Holland agreed to grant Prussia a subsidy of £1,800,000 a year, Great Britain paying £1,400,000.

[5] A force recruited in 1791 from the French *émigrés*. It was taken into British pay in 1795 and served with the Austrians. In 1797 it entered the Russian service, was paid by Great Britain in 1800 and disbanded in 1801 (T. Muret, *Histoire de l'armée de Condé*, 2 tom., Paris, 1844; R. Bittard des Portes, *Histoire de l'armée de Condé*, Paris, 1896).

the brunt of the war upon that side. The death of the Empress of Russia[1] seems to be a sad *contretemps*. What will become of the French enterprise against Portugal, is now the first object of anxiety. One sees that an active use of the smallest force may keep in check, and possibly baffle, the greatest which chooses to act upon the mere defensive,—a part always unsuitable to great force. Oh! how open to us was the French and Spanish force at Cadiz!—which place, at the beginning of this century, was an object of what, in the beginning of this century, we knew the value—active enterprize directed against an enemy in his weak points. That expedition failed from causes so evident, that a knowledge of them might have assured against a second failure. The defeat of that expedition not abating the vigour of enterprize, gave us the glorious success at this very Vigo.[2] In itself this event was great, and might have been improved into anything; but as long as the war is conducted on its present principles, our proceedings, at their best, can only baffle some particular design of an enemy. They can never be followed up so as vitally to affect him. I pray to God for the success of Admiral Colpoys;[3] but I do not like, after having expended more on the navy (perhaps twice as much as in any former war), that in the two most essential naval ports of Europe,[4] we should be fairly out-numbered by them. I believe that this Brest fleet is contemptibly equipped and manned, and hardly able to stand an engagement, or even the sea and sky; but as to this latter, they have the advantage of the finest and most opportune ports in the world to run into; so that, if they should miss Vigo, they may get into Ferrol or Corunna, where they may join the Spanish force intended against Portugal,[5] with nearly the same effect as from Vigo itself. Alas! Europe, for us, hardly opens one hospitable port. Adieu!

Things at St Domingo seem to have something of a pleasanter aspect,[6] but they are owing rather to the dissensions of the barbarians themselves, than to any efforts of ours, which amount to no more than a poor and uncertain defence of a line too long, too poorly manned, to be of

[1] See above, p. 191.
[2] In 1702 an expedition commanded by the 2nd Duke of Ormonde was directed against Cadiz. It failed to capture Cadiz but a landing was effected at Vigo and the Spanish treasure ships anchored there were captured and destroyed.
[3] Admiral John Colpoys (*c.* 1742–1821) commanded the Advance Squadron of the Channel Fleet; see below, pp. 221–2.
[4] Presumably Brest and Cadiz.
[5] After Spain declared war on Great Britain in October, France and Spain pressed Portugal to break the Anglo–Portuguese alliance and make peace with France. A Spanish invasion of Portugal was expected and a British force was sent to assist the Portuguese in resisting the attack (see above, p. 135). In fact Spain did not attack Portugal until 1801.
[6] Dispatches which were published in the *London Gazette* on 20 December referred to some gains made by the British forces in St Domingo. These were partly attributed to divisions amongst the enemy.

any real strength. I should have great satisfaction, however, in this glimmering, if I did not know, with all the rest of the world, that the final effect of our success or defeat will be nearly the same; and that we are spilling the blood of those planters whom we had refused to protect, until they had become our subjects, as well as the best blood of our own, and of the royalists of Europe, to make this a more savoury morsel for the regicides. You will have the goodness to excuse this letter, made up of the wanderings of an anxious mind, inhabiting a feeble body; which dictates its dreams, whilst it is stretched all its low length upon the couch of inaction.

I am glad to find that poor Woodford seems, to himself at least, to mend. Poor Lord John Cavendish, who very kindly came to see me a day or two before his death, is gone a little before me. The world never produced a more upright and honourable mind; with very considerable talents, and a still more considerable improvement of them. He retired from the world exceedingly irritated at the triumph of his enemies, which was carried pretty high against him personally; and somewhat disgusted with the coldness of his friends, who, at that time, showed little energy of mind, and considered his retreat with too much indifference. No more last words of Mr Baxter,[1] but that I am most zealously and most affectionately,

Yours, &c. &c.

EDM. BURKE.

P.S.—I have found the print, and send it to you enclosed.[2]

WILLIAM WINDHAM *to* EDMUND BURKE—
24 December 1796

Source: Fitzwilliam MSS (Sheffield). Printed *Corr.* (1844), IV, 412–13.

In October 1796 the British Government sent Lord Malmesbury (see above, p. 94) to Paris to open peace negotiations on the basis that Great Britain would compensate France for the restitution of its continental conquests by restoring the French colonies. As the negotiations proceeded it became clear that France was determined not to cede an area which Great Britain was most reluctant to see under French control: the Austrian Netherlands, annexed by France in 1795. It also became apparent that Great Britain intended to retain two of the Dutch colonies, the Cape of Good Hope and Ceylon. Towards the end of December the Directory broke off negotiations and ordered Malmesbury to leave Paris in forty-eight hours. Windham interrupted his dinner to convey this news of Malmesbury's dismissal to Burke (see his *Diary*, p. 349).

[1] Neither Mr Baxter nor the allusion has been identified.
[2] It is missing.

Decr 24th 1796.

My Dear Sir

I cannot refuse myself the satisfaction of informing you, that the news, that you will see in the papers is true, and that Lord Malmesbury is about to spend a happy Christmas with his friends in London, having received *pour toute reponse* to his terms, a declaration, that the Republick could enter into no treaty for countries, attached by the Constitution to France, and an order to quit Paris in eight and forty hours— His exit will be as splendid as his entry.[1]—He affords a brilliant example of the manner in which the Embassadors of suppliant Kings should be treated by a high-minded Republick.

'So should desert in Arms be crowned'.[2]

I fear, however, this new humiliation will only animate us[3] with new expedients and contrivances of meanness.[4]—At present to be sure every avenue seems to be shut.—We must go on with the war, perforce: But I much doubt, whether even this necessity, and the privation of all other means, will put us upon making any use of the good dispositions of the Interior—I have much to say to you upon that:— But I have already perhaps said more than I ought, considering how ardently I ought to be supposed to wish for Peace, even with the power, with which we thought it necessary that every country ought to be at War.

Yours Dear Sir
In great haste
W W.

To FRENCH LAURENCE—25 *December* 1796

Source: MS Trinity College, Dublin. Printed *Burke–Laurence Correspondence*, pp. 105–7.
Addressed: Doctor Laurence M:P. | Doctors Commons | London.
Postmarked: BEACONS|FIELD   FREE|DE|26|96|C.

My dear Laurence

I agree with you that the footing upon which the Ministers had put their negotiation involves them in difficulties with the regard not only to the Opposition, but to themselves, and their sole Ally,[5] and to the sole Ally which they had hopes of acquiring,[6] as well as to the miserable

---

[1] See above, pp. 101–2.   [2] See Dryden, 'Alexander's Feast'.
[3] MS: us to   [4] MS: meaness.
[5] The Emperor.   [6] Holland.

Inhabitants of the Islands[1] who had incorporated themselves upon our faith into the British Empire; and who never henceforward, can strike a blow with heart either in their own favor, or that of our feeble or perfidious Government. Surely, this business will give you a fair Opportunity of coming forward; You cannot appear with more lustre or at a better season for explaining[2] the silent vote you have given as well as in asserting the principles which might seem to be rendered doubtful by that vote. I suppose Lord FitzWilliam will come up[3] in consequence of the Duke of Bedfords motion,[4] if not upon the Message.[5] Pray send me word by the Coach whether it went down yesterday, and if it did not when it is to be looked for. It is a very extraordinary thing, that merely because Lord Malmsbury, in execution of his wretched and contemptible Office proposed to keep two places[6] that We had taken and not from France, that He should be turned off at eight and forty hours notice. Good God, what were the humiliations which the President de la Rouillie and the Marquis de Torcy suffered in Holland[7] in comparison of this. They never were sent away at all; on the contrary tho' their Offers were not received they were invited in the most pressing manner to stay. I fear the Nation is not equal to this tryal, and that having been once kicked they may think they may as well be kicked on to the end of the Chapter. 'Rome thou hast lost the breed of Noble Bloods'[8] and Lord Malmsbury will be found, at least I greatly fear it a true representative of the people of England. Adieu, and many happy returns of the Season. We are sorry not to have had you at our Turkey and roast beef. Alas! the times have been when you would have found a more full and chearful family, but I was unworthy of it and have lost it by my own fault. Learn from me never to trifle with such blessings as God may give you. I forgot to speak to you about Mackintosh's supposed conversion. I suspect by his Letter that it does not extend beyond the interior politicks of this Island, but that, with regard to France and many other Countries He remains as franc a Jacobin as ever. This conversion is none at all, but we must nurse up these nothings and think these

[1] In the West Indies.   [2] MS: its plain
[3] Fitzwilliam took part in the debate on the Message on 30 December.
[4] 'The Duke of Bedford gave notice, that he should take an early opportunity after the recess, to bring forward a motion relative to the *idea* of the Minister's advancing money to any foreign power, without the consent of Parliament' (*St James's Chronicle*, 20–22 December).
[5] Of 26 December, respecting the failure of the negotiations with France.
[6] The Cape of Good Hope and Trincomalee, the great port of Ceylon (Malmesbury, *Diaries and Correspondence*, III, 358).
[7] Pierre Rouillé (1657–1712) and Jean-Baptiste Colbert, Marquis de Torcy (1665–1746), the French representatives at the abortive peace negotiations at The Hague in 1709.
[8] See *Julius Caesar*, I, ii, 151.

negative advantages as we can have them. Such as He is I shall not be displeased if you bring him down:[1] bad as he may be He has not yet declared war along with his poor friend *Wild*[2] against the Pope.

Ever, ever yours

E B.

Beaconsfield 25 Decr 96

The accounts from poor Woodford seem to be a little better. This Weather is sadly against a case and cure like His.

To WILLIAM WINDHAM—*25 December* 1796

Source: British Museum (Add. MS 37,843, fols 125–6). Printed *Burke–Windham Correspondence*, pp. 223–4.

Only the last four words, signature and date-line are in Burke's hand.

My dear Friend

I received your kind Letter.[3] The return of Lord Malmsbury is just in all its circumstances what it ought to be, and indeed, just what might be expected. This Mongrel has been whipped back to the Kennel yelping and with his Tail between his Legs.[4] This will be a great triumph of Ministry of Opposition, and of the Nation at large. The Opposition only will be true to its principles. Woeful fidelity and consistency when such are the principles. The rest will certainly fail on the tryal. Indeed they have so much relyed on the certainty of Peace, and have provided if for any War, only a War at Home, that I do not see how they can carry on any other with energy and effect. However, any thing is better than a Jacobin Peace. In every other posture of things there are at least chances. I am quite sure that notwithstanding all that Lord Malmsbury has suffered, both as a Negotiator and as a Gentleman, that in order to Justify himself in his first step, kicked in as he has been and kicked out, He will still in the House of Lords, hold out some sort of Hopes. He will endeavour to keep open to himself a road[5] to some such infamous employment in future. You know better than I do, who know nothing of the subject, what is to be done with the *Interiour* of France, but of

---

[1] For Mackintosh's visit to Burke, see above, pp. 195–6.

[2] See above, p. 127. In a letter to Burke written on 30 March, Wilde had explained that though he did not wish to speak of the Pope or any Catholic 'but in terms of the highest respect', he believed that 'the whole Roman Catholic system is that perversion of christianity which the Bible denominates Antichrist' (MS at Sheffield).

[3] Of 24 December; see above, pp. 202–3.

[4] 'Some one observing to Burke that, as the weather was bad and the roads broken up, Lord Malmesbury's journey must be slow, Burke rejoined: "It must indeed be slow, as he must go the whole way on his hands and knees!"' (Earl Russell, *The Life and Times of Charles James Fox*, London, 1859–66, III, 89).

[5] MS: rode

this I am sure if nothing can be done there, nothing can be done with effect any where. Unfortunately we have disabled ourselves of our best means by sending the French Royalists to Portugal,[1] but that is no fault of yours who advized that measure in order to save these unhappy Corps from being broke as Criminals with every sort of disgrace, or sent with equal disgrace and with every sort of other ill consequence to the West Indies. God Almighty bless you and support you in the endeavours which yet you will make use of for the Salvation of your Country and of betrayed Europe. For two Days I had recovered (except in my flesh, which continues under a uniform decay,) to my astonishment, so that I hoped to resume my task with vigour, but last Night my disorder returned on me with violence and to Day I am as ill as ever.

By the way is it quite sure that the French Squadron and force are going at all to Portugal, and may not the Brazils be their object; or something in America or the West Indies.[2] I hope your Intelligence is good. Once more, adieu—The cordial wishes of this Season from all this House to you and the accomplished Ladies of your Family,[3] of whose partiality to us we are more proud than that of a whole Academy of Letters.[4] Ever most devotedly yours

EDM BURKE

Beaconsfield
25 Decr 1796

To MRS JOHN CREWE—*27 December* 1796

Source: Corr. (1844), IV, 413–18.

Beconsfield, December 27, 1796.

If infirmity had not the trick of assuring to itself strange privileges, and having them allowed by the good-nature of others, the old man and woman of this house might well be ashamed in receiving so many of your letters,[5] and sending so little in return. We import things of great value, and, in return, export little or nothing. The truth is, we have had various health, but never any that deserved to be called good. As to news, or speculation upon news, this place affords very little. We see fewer and fewer people every day; and every day, almost, death

---

[1] See above, p. 201.
[2] It was reported on 22 December that the Brest Fleet was at sea. According to the Paris papers its objective was Portugal (*The Times*, 22 December). In fact on 25 December it was off the west coast of Ireland, a number of ships being in Bantry Bay; see below, pp. 221–2.
[3] See above, p. 47.   [4] The remainder of the letter is in Burke's hand.
[5] Missing.

thins the stock of our friends, as it has done our family. It is long since I ceased to write anything with my own hand; and our friend Ann Hickey[1] is a good-natured and able secretary, both for Mrs Burke and myself. She is, indeed, very patient, like a good Christian as she is, of a great many disagreeable circumstances of my particular complaint.

You write to the Duke of Portland and Mr Windham, through Mrs Burke and myself, about the military and civil, or uncivil politics, of the county of Chester. As to your letters, we do very frequently communicate them to Mr Windham, or did so through poor Woodford, as long as he was in a condition to communicate anything to any person. I do not know that he has anything to do in militia matters, or very little. The management of the army is with the Duke of York; the conduct of the war is with Mr Dundas. As far as I know anything of Mr Dundas's office, it is merely executory. Of what nature the Duke of Portland's office is, I know nothing; for, comparatively, it is but of a new creation, and nobody can tell better than yourself, that retired as I am, from the world, and not willing to intrude myself on any one, therefore I never see his Grace, nor have any correspondence with him. Though we have so little to do in these matters, we love to read your letters, because you are a good painter, and because you put us in the middle of all the hurry and bustle of your politics. I have told you, I think, two or three times over, that I hate and despise all this militia business;[2] if it is not good to divert the ladies, I am sure it is not good for anything else. We cannot make peace, and we will not make war. The enemy despises and laughs at us, threatens us with invasions, keeps us at home to watch our hen-roosts, and does as he pleases about the rest of the world. If he keeps clear of the sea, he has nothing to fear from little Britain and doating old England with the young head upon his old shoulders. How came you to tell me that I said Mr Pitt was the man to save us from his Jacobin peace? I said, indeed, what I thought; that he was more likely to do it than another; because, however shaken, he has more of the confidence of the king and the nation, than any of the rest. But, if what I say was worth remembering, you might recollect that I added, that, if he succeeded in his regicide peace, we should not long

---

[1] See above, p. 97.

[2] See above, p. 130. Writing about this time to Caroline Fox, Mrs Crewe gives a lively account of the Militia: 'The humour at Chester was to talk on nothing but recruits. Mr Crewe I suppose you have heard, is going to *head this Vale Royal*—He is now a much greater *Alarmist* than some of our other Friends *ever* were, and is for ever saying now that he is determined *coute qui Coute* to defend his own property.—All the *Nobility* and *Gentry* are preparing like Old Pistol to 'trail the Puisant Pike' and so we were for some Days all *military mad* and the Prince (as Earl of Chester) presents the Colours, and so you will hear of nothing new from this part of England but our *red Coated Squires* our Militia Balls &ca &ca' (Add. MS 51,960, fol. 50 v.).

have a king or a king's minister. Well, since it is your pleasure in Cheshire, on the stage and off the stage, to drink success to Lord Malmesbury, you had better invite him to eat Christmas pies with you at the Deanery, or at the town-hall at Chester, and there to drink success to his future negotiations; for his 'eight-and-forty hours' is finished some time since, and the next news we expect to hear from him is from London. 'Oh! London is a fine town! It is a glorious city; for all the ladies there are fair, and all the men are witty!'[1] There is a great deal in the old song said of their beauty and their wit, and a couplet or two might be added about their riches; but, as to their wisdom, little is sung, and less is to be said. Don't you long to see that hero, after his achievements? I know you love chivalry, and he is a Knight of the Bath;[2] and as how he vanquished the directory with the odds of five to one against him; besides the little dwarf, Charles La Croix.[3] He is now returned to repose upon his laurels; and Lady Lavington[4] and Mrs Crewe will weave a garland for his head, which will make him look very spruce after he has struck his national three-coloured cockade, which I am credibly informed he and his trusty squire-arrant, the lean long Sancho Panza,[5] have worn whilst they were performing their enchanted adventure. Don't you long to be in town to hear from their own mouths all the delightful things about Paris; and how much you and we were mistaken in our opinion about those worthy thieves and murderers? Really, they are not so bad as people would take them to be at a distance. What a pity it is he did not leave his promising white-headed pupil[6] to learn a little longer in their academy! Well! my dear Madam, the shame and misfortune of our country would make one almost mad, if these punchinello statesmen did not sometimes come out to make us laugh, though through a sad countenance and aching heart.

I suppose that a call of the House will shortly bring Mr Crewe[7] to town, and that you will not stay very long after him. I suppose the opposition will contend that we ought to have taken peace in a dirty clout, and not have struggled for anything; but it is hard to say what

[1]
> O London is a dainty place,
> A great and gallant city!
> For all the Streets are pav'd with gold,
> And all the folks are witty.
>> *The Common Muse: an Anthology of popular*
>> *British Ballad Poetry*, ed. by V. de S. Pinto
>> and A. E. Rodway, London, 1957, p. 145.

[2] Malmesbury was created Knight of the Bath on 24 February 1779.
[3] Charles Delacroix de Contaut; see above, p. 101.
[4] Frances Lambertina Christiana Charlotte Harriet Theresa, *née* Kolbel (d. 1830), wife of Ralph Payne, 1st Baron Lavington (1739–1807).
[5] George Ellis: see above, p. 96.   [6] Ellis.
[7] John Crewe (1742–1829), later (1806) 1st Baron Crewe; M.P. for Cheshire.

submission or surrender of court Jacobins, or opposition Jacobins, would satisfy their regicide majesties. I suppose Lord Auckland[1] will be next to try his hand. The talk of the town is of a marriage between a daughter of his[2] and Mr Pitt; and that our statesman, our *premier des hommes*, will take his *Eve* in the garden of *Eden*. It is lucky there is no serpent there, though plenty of excellent fruit. Adieu! Forgive all this trifling, and believe that there are no persons who wish you better in this season, or in all seasons, than your old friends of this house.

We have lost poor Lord John Cavendish; he has not left a better man behind him, nor, if the world had known his value, one more capable of being of use to it than he was in his day.

His mother's death has brought young Elliot to England.[3] He is much affected with his loss, as I am told, for I have not yet seen him. No more last words of Mr Baxter;[4] and so, Adieu!

To LORD FREDERICK CAVENDISH—27 *December* 1796

Source: Devonshire MSS.

Lord Frederick Cavendish (1729–1803) was Lord John's elder brother.

My dear Lord,

I do not well know how I can be justified in my intrusion on your Lordship, at such a distressing moment as this, with any expressions of sympathy in your sorrows. You have lost a person not more near to you in blood, than resembling in Character and disposition: The same rectitude, the same honour, the same publick Spirit; the same generosity; the same noble frankness; the same steadiness in friendship and in principle—the same body of intrinsick Virtue, without the smallest ostentation or oblique design of any kind. His parts were of great natural force, and of much and various cultivation. There has been scarce any act of great and allowd utility in his time, in which he had not a distinguishd share; nor any evil attempted, to which he was not as distinguishd in his opposition. If he did not do more, it was because the Country was not patient of more good; nor of the sharpest sagacity in distinguishing the best actions and the best men. He was indeed the ornament and the reproach of the Age he lived in. May your Lordship remain long in the world to cherish his Memory, to continue his example, and to console your friends for their great Loss.

[1] William Eden, 1st Baron Auckland (1744–1814), who had been Ambassador to France, Spain and the United Provinces.
[2] Eleanor Agnes Eden (1777–1851). She married Robert Hobart, 4th Earl of Buckinghamshire (1760–1816), in 1799.
[3] See above, p. 191.   [4] See above, p. 202.

Every sort of consolation at this time has something of melancholy in it: but it was a comfort to me beyond my power of describing, declining fast as I am in Life, and faster in health that having been accidentally in London I received a Visit full of kindness from Lord John a few days before his final departure, that I saw him in as apparent good health as he had enjoyd for many years, with all his faculties in their full perfection, and with a cheerful Vigour of mind fresh and youthful in him. So that, since it was the pleasure of God to call to himself a Soul, that had as little to repent of as, I believe, the Lot of humanity will allow, he did not go thro' all those tedious preliminaries to our departure, which make the most trying part of it; but ended in a manner, which, on his account, cannot be deplored, a Life filled with every Virtue, and free from every moral stain. If, in the state I am in, I were to think of any thing on this side of the Grave, I should consider it as the great honour of my Life, that with, and under Lord John Cavendish, I began my publick Course, that though we now and then differd in opinion, we agreed in the substance of our principle; that he was always so indulgent to me as to consider my Errours, as mistakes, that he did full justice to my intentions, and that preserving his good-will to me unimpaird to his last hour in his last Visit he manifested to me full as much kindness, affection, and confidence as he had done in any period since I had the happiness of being known to him.

Excuse, my dear Lord, once more, this intrusion. I pay a very poor Tribute of justice and Gratitude to Lord Johns Memory—In the State in which I am, if I cannot indulge myself in those Gratifications, I have nothing that can give me pleasure. I am almost certain that I apply for pardon to the best natured man alive—especially as what I write does not call upon any the least exertion of yours, and in reality requires only to be allowd, not answerd.

I am with the Sentiments of the sincerest respect and most cordial affection

> My dear Lord
> Your most faithful
> and most obliged humble Servant
> EDM BURKE

Beconsfield Decr 27. 1796.

Fitzwilliam wrote to his wife, 'I am happy in the thoughts, that poor Lord John's life was not terminated before that friendly, cordial interview with Burke—He differ'd with B. most completely on the subject in question, but then, I think it was more as to the measures to be pursued by us, than as to the mischief of the thing itself—He always contended, that had they been left alone,

They would have cut each others throats . . . The recollection of the interview
will always be pleasing to Burke . . . Those, who differ the widest from him,
still esteem him, and do justice to his sincerity' (letter dated 'sunday', MS at
Northampton, Box X515/135).

To EARL FITZWILLIAM—28 *December* 1796

Source: Fitzwilliam MSS (Sheffield).
Endorsed (by Fitzwilliam): Burke | decr. 29.96.

My dear Lord—Oh! what a dreadful, shameful, scandalous act of incurable Phrensy the declaration is![1] Nothing can convince our statesmen
of the impolicy of meanness. They are resolved not to profit of their own
experience; nor to grow ashamed of their degenerate patience, nor to be
roused on the brink of ruin to any thing resembling Spirit, nor to suffer
any thing that savours of that Spirit to arise amongst the People. I had
been at work, before Lord Malmsbury was kicked out of Paris, on this
scandalous negotiation[2]—But the sad Event of Lord John Cavendishes
most unexpected fate threw me back for some time. The health, even
equal to what I thought his very best, in which he appeard a very [few]
days before, made this stroke, as the more unexpected, the more distressing to me. Our Interview was however a true cordial to me. I saw
him with Joy; and at no time did he, who was no man of shew or profession, give me greater proofs of his regard and confidence. Alas! he
has left few men of the same integrity, honour, and sense behind him.
I direct this to Grovenor Square on a supposition that Fridays business[3]
may bring you to Town. I do not think this Negotiation founded on
Trick. No not at all. It was the direct result of pure Cowardice and want
of resources in the mind for a great and arduous Course of action. That
he was disposed to try some bungling Trick in the progress of the
Business, is undoubted—and to piece up the very great scantiness of his
Lions skin with the abundance he possesses of the Foxes Tail. The
Regicides, I beleive, did not break off, and kick his Morrice Dancer off
the Stage, on account of his wishing to keep Ceylon and the Cape
(though that to him was scandalous enough) but from their resolution
to get rid of him and his; and to prosecute the War, as they always intended to our destruction, or until they could make a peace more
destructive than any War. This he knew; and ought not to have

[1] The Message from the King relating to the failure of the Peace Negotiations;
see above, p. 204.
[2] Burke is presumably referring to the 'Third Letter on a Regicide Peace' which is
largely devoted to showing the futility of Malmesbury's attempt to open negotiations
with France; see below, p. 217.
[3] The Lords debate on the King's Message was to take place on Friday, 30 December.

triffled with his situation. God direct the Virtue he has given you by his Wisdom; and may he support it with his power! You are alone in your struggle. If the Effect is the less; the Glory will be the more ever my dearest Lord with unalterable Gratitude and affection

most truly Yours

Decr 28. 1796. EDM BURKE

To FRENCH LAURENCE—28 December 1796

Source: MS Trinity College, Dublin. Printed *Burke–Laurence Correspondence,* pp. 107–8.
This letter is in Nagle's hand.

My dear Laurence

The declaration,[1] tho' it has not astonished me has not given me great dejection of spirits. There is a sort of staggering and irresolution in the cowardice of others, but there is a sort of unconquerable firmness and a kind of boldness in the pusilanimity of Mr Pitt. His madness is of the moping kind, but it is not the less Phrenzy for being fixed in lowness and dejection. He is actually taking every means to divest this Country of any alliance or possibility of alliance, and he is determined that no spirit shall arize within this Country, not knowing what course that spirit might take. I do not know whether I ought to be glad or not, of Lord FitzWilliams coming to Town. I think it is impossible to attack Pitt for want of sincerity in this Negotiation; tho' for wisdom it cannot be defended, I do not wonder that they endeavour to struggle for a port in the East Indies[2] and for a halfway House at the Cape, for unless they had made Holland truly independent and fixed her in attachment to us, these places would be virtually given to the French, and we could not maintain ourselves in the West Indies, out of which at some time or other they mean to drive us. When I say I do not wonder at it I am so far from approving it that my soul abhors it, but I much more abhor their fatal System out of the perplexities of which nothing can disengage them but their totally abandoning it.

I am glad that the business is put off to friday,[3] because your cold may then become better: This thaw favours your recovery. A Cough is not to be trifled with, especially in a full habit like yours, unless a Physician had dissuaded it I wished you had been blooded. I wish you to take advice that bleeding may yet be useful.

Mrs Burke and myself, tho' neither of us passed a good night are not

[1] See the previous letter.   [2] Trincomalee.
[3] The Commons debate on the King's Message took place on Friday 30 December.

worse to Day. God bless you. The times are bad when experience does nothing towards the correction of error.   Yours ever   E B

Beaconsfield
   28 Decr 96

To DUDLEY LONG NORTH—28 *December* 1796

Source: Copy in Devonshire MSS. Printed in *Corr.* (1844), IV, 549–52.
There are copies of this letter in the Osborn Collection and at Sheffield.

Dudley Long North (1748–1829), a Foxite Whig M.P. who had been one of the Managers of the Impeachment of Warren Hastings, was an old friend of Burke.

My dear Sir,

The late melancholy event of Lord John Cavendish's death, as soon as it came to my knowledge, made the trifling strain in which I wrote to you,[1] appear to me as a sort of impiety, at the moment when one of the oldest and best friends I ever had, or that our common Country ever possess'd was perhaps in his last Agony—I was then totally ignorant of that Circumstance, and without the least apprehension of any thing like it: The truth is, that it affected me more than I thought I could be affected with any thing, long as I have been familiar with Death at home, and having reason daily to expect my own dissolution. Lord John appear'd so very well, and so very strong, far beyond what could be look'd to from his age, that his Departure came on me like a Thunderstroke; I am told, that it was to your goodnatur'd Visit to me, and to your having let him know, that I was in Town for a day or two, and broken and afflicted as I was, I should be happy to see my old friends, I owe the solid comfort I feel in having embrac'd him for the last time, and of finding in him, so near our last hours, marks of sympathy, of cordiality, and of confidence, at least equal to any I had receiv'd from him at any period since I first had the happiness of being acquainted with him.

There is lost to the world, in every thing but the example of his life the fairest mind that perhaps ever inform'd a human body. A mind totally free from every Vice, and fill'd with Virtues of all kinds, and in each kind of no common rank or form; benevolent, friendly, generous, disinterested, unambitious almost to a fault; Tho' cold in his exterior, he was inwardly quick and full of feeling, and tho' reserv'd from modesty, from dignity, from family temperament and not from design, he was an entire stranger to every thing false and counterfiet: so great

---

[1] Burke's letter to North is missing.

an Enemy to all dissimulation active or passive, and indeed even to a fair and just ostentation, that some of his Virtues, obscur'd by his other Virtues, wanted something of that burnish and lustre which those who know how to assay the solidity and fineness of the metal wish'd them to have. It were to be wish'd that he had had more of that Vanity of which we who acted on the same stage had enough and to spare. I have known very few men of better natural Parts, and none more perfected by every species of elegant and usefull erudition. He served the publick often out of Office, sometimes in it, with Fidelity, and diligence, and when the occasion call'd for it, with a manly resolution. At length when he was overborne by the Torrent, he retir'd from a world that certainly was not worthy of him. He was of a character that seems as if it were peculiar to this Country. He was exactly what we conceive an English Nobleman of the old Stamp, and one born in better times, or what in our fond fancies we imagine such men to have been and in such times.

As to my connexion with him, I began my weak career of publick Business under his Auspices.[1] I was of too free a spirit not to have opinions of my own; and He was too generous to think the worse of me on that account. Differing with him sometimes about measures, I think we never had any material difference in principle, no not upon one point. As with him I began my Course, so with him most certainly I would have retir'd, If the Business in which you and I were so long engag'd had not appear'd to me to be a solemn and indispensible engagement[2] from which no human consideration could discharge me untill redress was obtain'd for a suffering people, or that in the judgement of all kinds nothing further could be done. When the latter happened I lost not one moment to execute my purpose. As to the Nation, God of his mercy grant they may not suffer the penalties of the greatest and most shamefull Crime, that ever was committed, by any people: Excuse me! talking of our departed friend, my Pen has run on—I now seldom write but dictate what I have to say to any absent friend. Be assur'd that the consolation you have procured me in the last interview with Lord John Cavendish is an obligation very near my heart, I owe you many; but this is the greatest. I am with very cordial regard

My dear Sir
your most faithfull
and obedient humble Servant

December 28 1796   E. BURKE

[1] See vol. I, 207.
[2] Burke seriously considered retirement in 1782–3 (see vol. V, 20), but once he had begun his pursuit of 'Indian delinquency' felt obliged to remain in the House of Commons until the conclusion of his work on the Hastings Trial.

To LORD FREDERICK CAVENDISH—29 *December* 1796
Source: Devonshire MSS.

My dear Lord

Your Letter,[1] which I receivd this day, is a new proof added to the many, which for a long Course of years I have received of your condescension and indulgent friendship to me. I did not know of the loss of your invaluable Brother for two or three days after this great calamity had happend. As soon as I was ascertaind of that melancholy Event, I took the Liberty of writing to your Lordship[2] before I had known of the kind and generous manner in which he was pleased to distinguish me in the last settlement of his affairs.[3] I directed the Letter to your house at Twickenham Park, not knowing that you were in Town. I hope, that by this it has been fortunate enough to find its way to you. My having been so happy as to have a last interview with Lord John but three or four days before his Death is an inexpressible consolation to me. His friendly, kind, affectionate, and confidential manner in that conversation, gave me ten thousand times more pleasure than even the noble Testimony he had given me of his good opinion, in the solemn act which your Lordship has been pleased to communicate. I honourd and loved him whilst he lived; and perhaps knew his value more than most men. If I were to talk of such a Life as mine, I should say I shall ever gratefully and respectfully regard his Memory. I began my Life of Business with him and under his auspices—and with him should certainly have quitted the active Scene, if engagements, of which he knew the force, had not made me linger far beyond my inclination.

Accept, my dear Lord, once more my thanks for all I owe to Lord John, to yourself, and to the whole of a Family, to whom it is a matter of pride to be obliged, and believe me with sincerity, affection, and unfeigned Respect

> My dear Lord
> Your Lordships
> most faithful humble Servant
> EDM BURKE

Decr 29.1796.

[1] Missing.
[2] On 27 December; see above, pp. 209–10.
[3] In the codicil to Lord John Cavendish's will, dated 28 May 1794 from Billing, he left 'to the Mr Burkes the money they are indebted to me and I give to Mr Edmund Burke the further sum of one thousand pounds'. Lord Frederick was sole executor of the will. The amounts of Edmund's and William's debts to Lord John are not known.

To EARL FITZWILLIAM—29 *December* 1796

Source: Fitzwilliam MSS (Sheffield).
Endorsed (by Fitzwilliam): Burke on Ld John's Legacy | decr 30. 96 | Codicil
dated may 28 94.

My dear Lord,

A pretty sharp pain in my Bowels, mitigated I thank God, this afternoon made me sensible that my going to Town, though the not going was to me an act of real self denial, would not have been very safe for me in this sudden change of weather. You know by this what a kind and generous Testimony Lord John Cavendish had given me of his friendship in his Will. Lord Frederick, (there lives not a worthier man) announced to me the honour he had done me in that handsome remembrance. I was, and am gratefully and sensibly affected with it— But I do not set half the value on it, that I do on the Style and manner of the last conversation I had with that great and good man. This is a real balm to my wounded mind.

I have read this morning some of the last papers in the Negotiation. On reflecting on them, I agree with your Lordship that Holland was virtually to be given up, since conditions were proposed, which indicated at least, that it was probable she might not remain in a State of real independence after the Treaty. I suppose you will have Lord Malmsbury in the House of Peers tomorrow.[1] I should not be surprised, if he were yet to hold out hopes from some further Treaty. May God bless your endeavours; You can do nothing but preserve your honour—but that is very safe in the hands of your Spirit and your discretion. I am with more affection and attachment than I am able to express—ever My dear Lord

most truly Yours

EDM BURKE

Decr 29.1796.

I am sorry to find that Laurence has got a bad cough.

[1] Malmesbury apparently did not take part in the Lords debate on the failure of the Peace Negotiations.

To WALKER KING—30 *December* 1796
Source: MS Osborn Collection.
This letter is not in Burke's hand.

My dear Walker

We have received your Letter upon the enclosures.[1] I shall speak tomorrow, tho' I doubt whether it is necessary as Mrs Burke has already written upon the subject to Mrs Venables.[2]

I send you a packet with which I rather trouble you, tho' at a vast distance from its destination, than Doctor Laurence, as I imagine that He may be gone with Lord FitzWilliam to Milton. You will be so good as to send to Mr Rivington and to desire him to advertize as in the Press a third Letter on the *prospect* of a Peace &c— &c—[3] and desire him to send me two proofs as soon as possible, (but not till he has printed off what I now send) printed on a Paper with a very broad Margin and of a quality when it is dried to be wrote on. Stitched and *inter*leaved. I wish him to strike off two more for you and Laurence. I want the opinion of you both upon the plan I pursue. You see, it is to make out one of the points, promised in my first Letter of the ability and willingness of the Nation to carry on the War.[4] By the nature of this part it cannot be so entertaining as either of the first Letters, even tho' it were in better hands than mine 'ornari res ipsa negat'.[5] You will both therefore tell me very candidly, whether you think that the publick which loves much better to be entertained than instructed will relish this for it will be eazey to me to rest upon my *oars* keep myself safe and to trust to the impression of whatever it is, that is[6] made by the first Pamphlet: but judge on the printed proofs and not the manuscript. I am sorry to find that Mrs King does not recover more quickly. You dont say whether you have received the plan of the Cottage—Your Brother John has not

[1] The letter and its enclosures are missing.

[2] Jane Burke's letter is missing.

[3] On 3 January 1797 the *True Briton* announced that Burke's 'Third Letter' was in the press. The next day the Rivingtons inserted the following advertisement in *The Times*: 'In the Press and speedily will be published A Third Letter to a Member of the Present Parliament, on the Proposals for Peace with the Regicide Directory of France. By the Right Hon. Edmund Burke. Printed for F. and C. Rivington, No. 62, St Paul's Churchyard; sold also by R. White, Piccadilly. Of whom be had, the 11th Edition, of the Two Letters, price 3s. 6d.'. The 'Third Letter' did not appear in Burke's lifetime; see above, p. 105.

[4] When the *Two Letters* were published, Laurence wrote: 'Mr Pitt professes to subscribe to the reasoning, only he says that he does not see the means of execution, which part of the subject he complains that Mr Burke has rather unfairly reserved for future discussion' (Laurence to Fitzwilliam, 5 November, MS at Northampton, Box 50).

[5] The thing itself refuses to be ornamented; see Manilius, III, 39.

[6] MS: it

thought fit to let me know whether he has received my letter to Lady Inchiquin[1] and transmitted it.

I am ever truly
Yours

Beaconsfield   E B
30 Decr 96

EARL FITZWILLIAM *to* EDMUND BURKE—
[1 *January* 1797]

Source: Fitzwilliam MSS (Sheffield). Printed (incomplete) in
Corr. (1844), IV, 418–20.

1 January 1797 was a Sunday: the first after Fitzwilliam spoke in the Lords debate on 30 December.

My dear Burke

I made my feeble effort to recall the House of Lords to their principles and their senses;[2] but of course, in vain—it is not the fashion of the day —the boast on the one side was, how far they had gone in humiliation: on the other, you have not gone far enough: neither party willing to give up this post of fame.

Stating as I did, that the destruction of the system in France was the principle of action three years ago, was treated as visionary, and misconception: it was positively denied by Lord Spencer to have been the basis of coalition,[3] and by Lord Grenville ever to have been studiously avoided by Administration: holding himself out, as the person best able to explain the intent of the Declaration of October 93,[4] he asserted that it would be found to guard against such a misconception—the basis of my amendment, which was founded upon the principles of that declaration, and extracted from the sentiments of our Address of January 94,[5] which professes to arise out of that declaration communicated to the House, was therefore set at nought, as founded upon garbled parts

[1] Mary *née* Palmer, Countess of Inchiquin (1751–1820); Sir Joshua Reynolds's niece. The letter is missing.

[2] In the debate in the House of Lords on 30 December Fitzwilliam had emphasized that the French had not retracted 'the offensive decree of 1792, encouraging the people of other countries to rise up against their established governments' and that 'there could be no safety in fraternizing with such people'. He also proposed an amendment to Grenville's motion thanking the King for his Message (*Parliamentary History*, XXXII, 1503, 1507). The amendment, which was rejected, is printed in the *Journals* of the House.

[3] Lord Spencer (see above, p. 6) declared that 'From the commencement of his acting with Ministers' he considered that the objects of the war were 'to secure the important interests of this country, to restore tranquility to Europe, and to provide for the maintenance of that tranquility' (*The Times*, 31 December 1796).

[4] The Declaration, setting out Great Britain's war aims, published 29 October 1793 (*Parliamentary History*, XXX, 1057; see also vol. VII, 463, 465–6).

[5] The Address of Thanks voted by the House of Lords on 21 January 1794.

of the address, and upon the misconceiv'd principles of the declaration—
I trust you will like the amendment; it must be left for the publick to
judge between the parties, which of the two gives the truest account of
past principles and facts—that is, in the plain acceptation of words, and in
the obvious construction of conduct—but I have done—my conscience
is satisfied by the feeble efforts I have made, and by the unequivocal
declarations of adherence to what I, *in my misconception,* understood
to be principles of action.

By a letter received from Laurence this morning, I find he could not
get an opening for the delivery of his sentiments on friday:[1] having
fail'd, he has given notice that after the holidays he shall take up the
subject[2]—it is very consoling to me, that this is his intention—I shall be
happy that the same sentiments which I have recorded on the journals
of our house, are likewise recorded on those of the House of Commons—
It is heartbreaking to think that they are first abandon'd by those,
whose greatest interest it is, longest to maintain them—the country
still adhere to them: but the country will be beaten off, when all the
higher powers are combin'd to suppress them—perhaps it is still the
more vexatious, considering the tendency of the present state of France:
everything there seems running to an end: Jacobinism cannot exist
without the system of terror: jealousy between the Councils and the
Directory prevent that system being carried to the length necessary for
their own preservation: and I believe,[3] Delacroix truely says, the powers
of the Republick are on the decline[4]—relâche from exertion alone can
hold it together—it must crumble to pieces, or the true revolutionary
system be regenerated: the attempting which, offers always a chance of
the complete breaking up of the whole—but we interpose for the

[1] That is, in the Commons debate of 30 December.
[2] On 31 December 1796 in the House of Commons 'Doctor Laurence gave notice,
that he would shortly after the recess call the attention of the House to the adoption
of a measure concerning the present war, in which should be considered the situation
the country has been in since the commencement of the war; the present situation of
the country; and the basis on which any future Negociation might be carried on; and
the object of this motion should be to reconcile the different opinions that existed
amongst those who thought the present a just and necessary war; and to prevent the
frequent discussions that have hitherto taken place on the subject, in consequence of
motions brought forward by Gentlemen on the Opposition side of the House' (*The
Times*, 2 January). On 3 January Laurence informed Fitzwilliam that he had told the
House that it was 'my object to put fairly to issue, once for all, some themes of declamation, which were perpetually recurring on the other side, and to unite, as far as
was possible, all who might still think that the war was and is just and necessary'. He
said that 'It will take about 4 Resolutions as I have at present schemed it' and that he
had opened his design at length to Burke and 'he highly approves my purpose' (MS at
Northampton, Box 51). See also below, p. 250.
[3] MS: belive,
[4] Fitzwilliam seems to be referring to Delacroix's remark to Malmesbury that
during the war 'England, by its conquests, and by the activity and judgment with
which it governed its colonies, had doubled its strength' (*Parliamentary History*,
XXXII, 1427).

preservation of Jacobinism—it was for this, I am now told, I became a member of the present administration—good God—adieu ever affectionately yours

W.F.

Milton
Sunday.

The happiness I feel in being here again, is more than I can express— the Atmosphere I have left, has no salubrious qualities for my poor frame.

To EARL FITZWILLIAM—4 [*January*] 1797

Source: Fitzwilliam MSS (Sheffield).
Endorsed (by Fitzwilliam): Burke | janry 6.97.
Burke's 'Decr' is clearly an error.

Decr 4, 1797.

My dear Lord,

I do not in the least wonder, that you were so soon, and so compleatly sick of London. The emulation between parties, which of them should bid highest for the destruction of their Country, and who should be the most forward in betraying it, is a spectacle never before presented in any publick Council. As to our old friends, they are so many individuals, not a jot more seperated from your Lordship, than they are from one another. There is no mutual affection, communication or concert between them; and in this way they are sensible, each of his own seperate weakness, without the will, or even the wish of putting himself in a better condition, either out of Office or in it. I verily believe, they totally forget on what Terms, or with what Views they came into their present places. They find themselves where they are, and that is all they know of the matter. They find themselves in a sort of subjection, by, what appears to them as if it were, the order of Nature, and they think nothing more of it. I am not surprised at what you tell me of Lord Spencers Speech. He knows best for what purposes *he* came in. It is no matter. He has good parts, with a narrow mind; with a coarse vulgar conception of things, without retrospect, without foresight, without a power of combining the Circumstances which are about him. He only judges on the point of Business directly before him, without taking in any of its relations; and on that, which comparatively is a poor matter, he judges not amiss. It is remarkable, that not one word of the Debate, as your Lordship States it, is to be found in the Sun,[1] the Court

---

[1] *The Sun* of 31 December reported that 'Earl Fitzwilliam spoke at considerable length—he censured part of the conduct of Members—deprecated the Negotiation, as

220

Newspaper which I take in. If I dont forget, your Lordship shewed me a Copy of the Letter, you wrote to the D. of P. about the time of your coming in.[1] You promised me a copy of that Letter as well of his Graces to you.[2] I wish much to have them.

I send you in separate Pacquets three Letters which I received this morning from Cork.[3] You see what provision was made for the defence of Ireland, in point of intelligence, in point of Force, in point of distribution, and in the Choice of Generals. Every thing was exposed and open; and at length, all their defences entrusted to those descriptions of people in the Country and in the army, which they had done every thing to irritate, and to alienate in every possible way. I am sure I do not know, whether the Conduct of that unfortunate people has more of good or of evil example. But let these things go as they will—God almighty preserve you and yours to better times. Ever my dear Lord faithfully and gratefully yours

EDM BURKE

To WILLIAM WINDHAM—*5 January* 1797

Source: British Museum (Add. MS 37,843, fols 127–30). Printed *Burke–Windham Correspondence*, pp. 225–7.
This letter is in Jane Burke's hand.

A French expedition, composed of eighteen ships of the line and twenty-seven other vessels, under Justin-Bonaventure, Comte Morard de Galle (1741–1808), carrying a military force of about 14,000 men commanded by Hoche (see above, p. 164), sailed from Brest on 15 December, bound for the south-west coast of Ireland. The Channel Fleet which was responsible for the blockade of

being as disgraceful as it was impolitic.—He took a copious view of the French system and their proceedings, and reprobated both in the strongest language.—He argued, that no safe or permanent peace could be made with France under its present system, and said, that, after the present question was disposed of, he would propose an Amendment to their Lordships, the object of which was (as we understood the Noble Earl), to support His Majesty in the vigorous prosecution of the War, until such a form of Government was established in France as was capable fully of maintaining the relations of peace and amity, and such as was consistent with the safety of this Country, and the tranquility and liberties of Europe'.

[1] Probably a letter of Fitzwilliam to Portland endorsed 'June 15. 94'. In it Fitzwilliam states that he 'entertained little doubt, that the sentiments of Administration coincided very generally with ours upon the great political questions, that agitate not only this country but all Europe'. But that it seemed to him that 'in the management of the business, from the outset to this day, there has been one great, important failure: the cause has not been made either by declaration or by conduct, the cause of the unfortunate oppressed classes of Frenchmen' (copies at Sheffield, F31*b*).

[2] Portland replied to Fitzwilliam on 19 June 1794 that he had seen Pitt who had assured him that 'the reestablishment of the Crown of France in such person of the Family of Bourbon as shall be naturally entitled to it was the first and determined Aim of the present Ministry' (MS at Sheffield, F31*b*).

[3] One of the three was probably a letter from Sir Patrick O'Conor (see above, p. 111) to Burke dated 29 December, referring to the French ships being off Bantry Bay and to the preparations being made to resist a landing (MS at Northampton).

221

Brest was commanded by Alexander Hood, 1st Baron Bridport (1727–1814), later (1801) 1st Viscount Bridport. In December 1796 Bridport, with part of his Fleet, was at Spithead; the advanced squadron commanded by Admiral Colpoys (see above, p. 201) being off Brest. Colpoys, who was about forty miles off Brest when the French expedition sailed, failed to intercept it, and, uncertain of its destination, hovered off the Lizard. Bridport sailed from Spithead on 25 December but was detained at St Helens by south-westerly gales until 3 January. He was off Bantry Bay on 8 January. Seventeen French ships which entered the Bay, after sustaining nearly a week of stormy weather, had left on 27 December, without putting their troops ashore. Nine others which had arrived on 1 January had left by 6 January. During January the expedition straggled back to France (E. H. Stuart Jones, *An Invasion that Failed*, Oxford, 1950).

My dear Sir

I have had two very bad days; this last the worst. So that I coud not work much; even if I had the materials. This difficulty at the Excise Office I wish I had forseen; because while Parliament was sitting, any Member might have moved for those Accounts.[1] I never knew them refused. I should have no difficulty of writing to Mr Long[2] myself upon the Subject, but I do not wish to have my Scheme blown upon, and I know, that there is such a connection between the Public Offices and the News Papers, that they woud have the accounts full as early as I should. It is a vile thing to see this communication constantly kept open, and as constantly disowned. The use that I intend to make of these accounts, if they come up to my Ideas, as I think they will, is to finish my demonstration;—That no Class of the People[3] hath as yet felt the War in any sort of Privation.[4] I am infinitely rejoiced to hear that poor Woodford goes on with good appearances.

If Ireland was the Object of the Brest Armament, (and it now looks not improbable) what handsome provision has been made for its defence! No Depot of Force in any Central point, no preconcerted arrangement. Agamemnon General in the South, with Cooks for his Aid de Camps; and so corpulent, that I am told he cannot go on Horseback.[5] Had Hoche landed in Bantry Bay, or in any Bay more commodious for his purposes, as many there are on that Coast, nothing coud have hindered him from making himself Master of Cork; of

---

[1] See above, p. 186.   [2] Charles Long; see above, p. 52.
[3] MS: Poeple
[4] In the *Third Letter*, when replying to the argument that the war was crippling England economically, Burke employed a number of taxation returns to demonstrate that there was in fact 'every indication of increased and increasing wealth'; see *Works* (Bohn, v, 328–54; Little, Brown, v, 475–508).
[5] General William Dalrymple (d. 1807), who was in command at Cork, was, according to Lord Clare (John Fitzgibbon, 1st Earl of Clare, 1749–1802), an efficient officer. The Lord Lieutenant, however, considered that owing to the state of his health 'or the *unweildiness*' of his person, much active service could not be expected from him (Camden to Pelham, 28 June 1796, Public Record Office, H.O. 100/64, fols 129–36).

putting that place under Contribution of Money, and provisions; and having routed the weak force in that part, from Marching forward and beating all the rest in detail. The apparent want of intelligence of the Enemy's design was truly deplorable. But if intelligence was received and credited, That the Enemys design pointed at Ireland, in the Name of God, how did it happen, that no Fleet was off Ireland to oppose the Enemy on his approach, or on failure to intercept him on his return? While the Jacobin Fleet was at Anchor in Bantry Bay, Lord Bridport was at Portsmouth, and Colpoys, after going God knows where, returns himself into harbour. The French leave Bantry on the 27th of December, and Lord Bridport Sails from Portsmouth to look for them on the 3d of this month, if he meets any of them it is a miracle; and it must be owing to the terrible condition which they are in. So much for Intelligence, Foresight, and Precaution.

For my own part I never believed, that the French could have thought of Ireland, equipped as they were, in such a Tempestuous Season; because I could have no intelligence, and only grounded myself upon conjecture of what it would have been rational for Them to do. I therefore concluded that They would get into the Ocean as soon and as deep as they could, and make their way for Nova Scotia, an Object infinitely important for them to possess. The Season of the Year is I know adverse also for this; but nothing coud be worse for them than the Coast of Ireland, where they coud not remain long without being a Prey to the English Naval force, let their successes on Land be what they woud. But the fate of that expedition[1] is, I trust, now decided by an Arm stronger than ours, and by a Wisdom capable of counteracting our Folly.—Yet, My Dear Friend, I do tremble, lest the boldness of these Men in risquing every thing, and our negligence or Misfortune in not providing for any thing, may not always find the Heavens so propitious. I confess I tremble at the danger whilst I am rejoicing in the escape. However I sincerely congratulate you upon it. I consider you so much as a Friend to whom I am used to disburthen myself, that I forget I am writing to a Minister with whom I ought to have managements when I discuss anything relative to the Conduct of his Colleagues. The want of a Steady intelligence both from Paris, and from Brest, is a thing I cannot comprehend; because I am sure it might have been obtained.[2] God bless you I am very faint, and perhaps peevish, but ever most truly Yours

E: B.

Jany 5th 1797

[1] MS: expidition   [2] See the next letter.

WILLIAM WINDHAM *to* EDMUND BURKE—
6 *January* 1797
Source: Fitzwilliam MSS (Sheffield).

Park str. Westr
Jany. 6th 1797.

My Dear Sir

I perfectly agree with you in every sentiment respecting the danger, to which Ireland has been exposed, and the total want of judgement and foresight, in providing anything like an adequate defence. I see no reason, why Bantry Bay may not have been their place of final destination. Though better may possibly be found, this was certainly sufficient: and my own firm persuasion is, that if the weather had not been such as to disperse their fleet, and prevent their landing, there was no force in that quarter, even with Gen. Dalrymple at its head, that would have prevented Gen. Hoche, with 15 or even 12 thousand men from getting to Cork. They would then have been in possession of Cork Harbour; and by a small work on Spike Island; which we have never thought fit to fortify; would have made it utterly impossible for our fleet to retake it.

If their fleet is now too much disabled, and they act in the spirit of their former counsels; which to be sure will be difficult, considering the opposition, that has already been made to this Enterprize; they will instantly renew the attempt, while we, reposing in the glories of our escape, may be still more off our guard, than we were before.—The destination of the fleet as far as information could go, was no secret. The Royalists have told me of it, months ago: and, for a long while back, every post from Jersey has brought more detailed information from those, who had been sent there, or rather who had gone on purpose.—They even told us, what has since turned out to be fact, but which, (because perhaps the information was French,) was not believed, that they had provisions only for three weeks. Still to be sure, it was doubtful; whether they might not mean Portugal: or whether there might not be an expedient for victualling at some other place.

The great Inference to be drawn from the proceeding is the inefficiency of a fleet, if employed merely for defence; and the consequences, that result from suffering the war in the Enemies own country to be extinguished. During the first three years of the war, when the Enemies Marine was entire, when their armies more numerous, and their supplies more ample, not a word was heard of Invasion—The

Royalists are suppressed, and the attempt commences instantly:—and, one may add,—does not succeed, simply from the operation of causes, wholly distinct from any exertion of ours.

The Queries, you sent me,[1] I see the Importance of for your purpose, and the little importance of them for any other:—Yet I am at a loss how to obtain them. However thoroughly I wish you to possess them, with a view to giving all the effect possible to the Argument, of which they are to form a part, I feel upon reflexion a little squeamish about becoming myself the means of procuring them; or at least about furnishing a handle to charge or suspicion, that would extend far beyond the fact itself—I am afraid it will not be possible for me to get the information without availing myself of that confidence, which, on the part of those, by whom it is given, would not be thought consistent with the purposes for which the information is wanted.—I have put the Queries into the hands of Woodford, who being under no restraint of the same sort, may get them by any means, by which they are to be had.

The most material circumstance, which made me take up my pen, remains. I wish if this weakness continues, that you would come for a day or two to London, to know, as far as Medical skill can tell, whether it is merely accidental, or whether it should be an occasion of trying some other methods, than those, which you are already practising.—A small party consisting of Lawrence, Sir William Scott,[2] Walker King and Bowles,[3] are to dine with me on Monday.[4] I have proposed dinner at 1/4 past 5; but we will have it five precisely, if you will give me hope, of seeing you.—We will take care also to provide you a comfortable Lodging, if you will give authority for that purpose—Yours ever

My Dear Sir, &c

W W.

To WILLIAM WINDHAM—9 *January* 1797

Source: *Corr.* (1844), IV, 420–3.

Beconsfield, January 9, 1797.

My dear Sir,

I cannot properly express my thanks for your friendly and generous solicitude about me and my health. That physicians can do nothing for me, I am perfectly convinced. I know what they have prescribed, and in which the first men in the profession had agreed, has been of no service

---

[1] See above, p. 186.   [2] (1745–1836), later (1821) 1st Baron Stowell.
[3] John Bowles (1751–1819), author and pamphleteer.   [4] 9 January.

to me, but has rather aggravated my complaints. I must wait the will of
God, and the natural course of things. Bath had been undoubtedly of
service to me; but I doubt very much, whether, at this season of the year,
it would be of equal utility; and I do not think that either Mrs Burke
or myself are in a condition to travel. My last London trip[1] did not at all
agree with me. I went there but for very little other reason than that my
thoughts on the present strange state of things did not leave me much
at my ease at home; but the very idea of going to Bath at a full season,
when I cannot take a glass of water but in a crowd, frightens me so
much, that I am sure the crowd would do me more *harm* than the
waters would do me *good*. Here I have appetite enough, better, I think,
than at Bath; but everything I eat and drink turns to tough phlegm
and storms of wind, which scarcely give me half an hour's interval the
whole day. I pass the greatest part of it on my couch; yet, notwithstanding this, I pass my time in bed with less uneasiness than anywhere else.[2] I hope you've passed this day agreeably. Your set would
have suited me very much. I was very uneasy that Laurence could find
no place into which he could come with propriety to declare his sentiments in the late debates.[3] Two men occupy the whole scene[4] till the
public attention is completely exhausted, and the auditors want to
refresh themselves between the acts; and it is not only that a *quarta
persona*, but even a *tertia* cannot speak without labouring for it; such
are the laws of your drama. Certainly, neither yourself, nor any other
person ever suspected of sentiments like yours, will be permitted to
utter them, if either side of the House can help it. I am glad to find
that Laurence has taken the only way that was open to him. I approve

[1] In the second week of December; see above, pp. 173–7.
[2] Burke's friends were fully aware of his condition and were trying to protect him
from unnecessary worry. On the very day Burke wrote this letter, 9 January, Mrs Crewe
wrote from Bath to Caroline Fox about an attack on the French school at Penn:
'I return you a thousand thanks' she says 'and so does poor Mrs Burke, for your goodness in so soon sending to Lord Lansdowne about the school. He was so good as to
write to us *immediately* and to put our minds quite at ease, so that she had no more fears
about her Husband's hearing what would affect and agitate him to a great degree if the
danger still continued! and in such times as these, there is no saying what mobs will
do! *I*—who have had *some experience* in these matters, and who know that not only
Towns, but *Magistrates* will *sometimes defend their Conduct*, am more inclined to fear
them than others perhaps, but the *threat* sent to Beckonsfield was certainly *not pleasing*
after the school had been *once insulted*, and that every window of it was broke, that the
wall had been partly pulled down and the good woman who acts as Housekeeper for
these unhappy Children, had been *once* wounded near her eye by a Stone!—nothing
could be more kind more obliging, nor more *polite* than Lord Lansdowne's letter, and
Mrs B. keeps it to shew to her husband when she shall think his spirits equal to such a
subject—he is certainly better than he has been for some Months past, but still in a very
precarious state, and of course his Friends are very anxious to keep every thing from
him which may create *new Griefs*, and these poor Boys have been almost his only
comfort since he lost his own Son' (Add. MS 51,960, fol. 52).
[3] See above, p. 219.
[4] Pitt and Fox.

his plan exceedingly, and I hear with pleasure that he gave notice of it in a very proper manner.[1] If the newspapers do not deceive us, the French fleet, by design or distress, still continues hovering over the Irish coast.[2] I do not know what instructions our naval force has received, but I agree with you most completely, that a naval force is a very unsure defence. I do not in the least apprehend that, in landing in any part, they would be suddenly joined by any considerable number; but, if they can nestle in the country for any time, especially in the northern parts, they cannot fail of profiting of the discontents which prevail so generally in all that part of the kingdom. My hope is, that, if they should be abandoned by their navy, they will find that part of the country overpeopled, as it is; and, hardly capable of maintaining itself, utterly incapable of subsisting an army; especially a French army, wholly unaccustomed to their mode of living. If a battle should be fought with them, and they should prove victorious, they would be more reinforced, and they would be better provided. I still go on with the work I have in hand,[3] but with terrible interruptions. God Almighty preserve you to a time, when your counsels will be more respected, and when it will not be too late to suffer them to be beneficial. Mrs Burke still suffers under her cold, which is the worst I ever knew her to be affected with. I hope that poor Woodford continues to mend. Unless you have something very particular to say, don't inconvenience yourself by answering my letters. You have enough to think of, 'enough for meditation, even to madness'.[4] Adieu! Once more I recommend you to God.

Yours ever truly,
EDM. BURKE.

EARL FITZWILLIAM *to* EDMUND BURKE— [9 *January* 1797]

Source: Fitzwilliam MSS (Sheffield).

In his letter of 4 [January] Burke mentioned forwarding three letters from Cork. Fitzwilliam appears to be acknowledging them on the next ensuing Monday.

My dear Burke

Many thanks for the letters from Cork: Mr Therry wrote to me at the same time,[5] and I receiv'd other letters from Dublin with all the

[1] See above, p. 219.   [2] This was stated in *The Times*, 9 January.
[3] The *Third Letter*.
[4] The source of this quotation has not been found.
[5] John Joseph Therry's letter of 29 December 1796 to Fitzwilliam is at Sheffield (F 30c).

accounts that came to Government—It is a providential escape—whatever may have been the zeal, alacrity and general temper shewn outwardly on the occasion, I am glad these appearances were not put to the severe test of an Invasion: other inclinations might have shewn themselves, had an enemy been fairly landed in force—a scatter'd, and shatter'd fleet upon the coast, and a Lieutenant and six men on shore (Prisoners too)[1] are not very tempting inducements to a rising; they are circumstances rather to keep under, than to give vent to a flame of disaffection—it is not, that I doubt the cordial attachment of the better orders of Roman Catholicks to the country itself, though I believe not to its actual Government, but I am very glad the inclinations of the lower Orders were not brought to the proof: for if Defenderism[2] was not a fabrication and mere trick of Government, there is a spirit, I hope no occasion will bring into action—if Defenderism is but a trick, Good God, what scores and hundreds have paid for it with their lives; and what thousands with their liberty—I understand, a sullen discontent manifested itself in the North on this occasion—no reliance could be place'd in their efforts, or even in a passive attachment on their parts—thus We find Government reduced to the necessity of courting the assistance of those, they are in the daily habit of vilifying and irritating, and what is more, whom they will treat just as ill as ever, as soon as the storm is fairly blown over—in the mean while, let us be thankfull for this providential escape; as such we must consider it—the facility with which the whole armament might have been landed, before their arrival in one of the best harbours was even known, should be a lesson to this country, that Ireland must be defended by itself, and to be so, there must be cordial affection, concord, and union amongst all the different descriptions of people—Cork, Limerick, the South might have been lost; before a man from Lehaunston camp[3] could have reach'd those parts to dispute the point: the defence must have rested with the Inhabitants.

I am glad you approve so thoroughly Laurence's intention after the adjournment:[4] the more I consider the subject, the more I feel the propriety of one effort in the House of Commons: though why should I call it an effort, when there is no prospect of success—it is but the

[1] William Brabazon Ponsonby (see below, p. 351) had written to Fitzwilliam from Dublin on 29 December: 'A Lieutenant of a French Frigate in endeavouring to make his way from his Ship which was dismasted, was forc'd on Shore at Bantry in a Boat with six men and immediately taken by the common people with pitchforks' (MS at Sheffield, F 30c). The incident was widely reported in the newspapers.
[2] See above, p. 117.
[3] The military camp at Laughlinstown; see above, p. 168.
[4] See above, p. 219.

gratification of private sentiment: but still it is fit to be done; it is a debt to the justice of the cause—the more I consider the subject, the more I am convinc'd that no compromise can be made without the most imminent danger, with the System in france—every ground of War, four years back (then only speculation, and reasoning upon principles) is now strengthen'd and confirm'd by experience—the hostility to all antient establishments proclaim'd by them, is now carried into effect from day to day; and were I to say, which of all their gross violations of the rights of independent Nations, I think the worst, the most outrageous and flagitious, it is the last—the Cis-padane Republick—four independent Nations, without connection, probably —with different laws, usages, and prejudices, are toss'd pellmell into one revolutionary cauldron to be stew'd into a mess of Democracy, without a plea of offence on their parts, to color this horrid act of outrage against the happiness of these unfortunate Victims[1]—The Rights of Sovereigns, I put quite out of the question, considering it only in the spirit of an Individual, as an act of savage oppression against Individual happiness—Surely if the Declaration of these Intentions was ground of War, the carrying them into effect is not a motive for Peace—I hope you can give a better [account] of Mrs B's cold, and when I hear from you, that you will give a more comfortable account of yourself, or that you will not defer the Bath expedition[2]—ever affection-ately yours

W F.

Milton monday

WILLIAM WINDHAM to EDMUND BURKE— 17 [January 1797]

Source: Fitzwilliam MSS (Sheffield). Printed Corr. (1844), IV, 424–7.
The 'July' of Windham's date-line is clearly an error. 'The Birth-day' which is to postpone his trip is the Queen's Birthday of Wednesday, 18 January. Windham's Diary also mentions under the date of 17 January his writing a 'strong and earnest letter to Mr Burke in consequence of accounts received' (p. 351).

Part str. Westr
July. 17th.
6 o'clock.

My Dear Sir

What I have understood of the state of your health for some time past, and still more, what I understand at this moment, must supersede all that unwillingness to obtrude[3] my advice upon you, that has often

---

[1] See above, p. 138.   [2] See below, p. 235.   [3] MS: obstrude

restrained and make me urge my entreaties and remonstrances, with a degree of earnestness, that I have never hitherto allowe'd myself, but which the importance and urgency of the case will no longer suffer me to forbear.

You must really, my Dear Sir, come fairly to the point of deciding in the first instance, whether you *wish* to recover.—If life is really become so Insipid or painful, that you are really impatient for the scene to close, and if you can reconcile that wish with the interest, you feel, in the happiness of some of those, whom you will leave behind, or with the conviction, which you cannot fail to entertain, that your life is at this moment of more consequence than that probably of any other man now living, or than it has been at any preceding period, (Suppositions which I merely make for the sake of form, and without a suspicion, that they can all of them be true) then indeed there is no room for further discussion.—It is in vain to urge a resort to such means as human precaution, and prudence may point out, if the end, which they are to obtain, is not wished.

But, if such is not the case, if duty, though not inclination, must enjoin to you the preservation of a life, which cannot cease but to the infinite affliction of those, whose happiness is most dear to you, and with a loss to the world, such as it could never have produced or been known at least to produce, at any other period, then surely you will not have acted up to your own ideas, or to the expectations, which others would have reason to form of you, if you persist in resisting those means, uncertain as they may be, which in the judgement of any persons tolerably skilled may afford you any means of relief.—Such means have certainly not been wanting, nor, should the first fail, were others to be despaired of, had there been a fair disposition to go in search of them.— But in fact the first had not failed: Bath, which every one had agree'd to recommend, Bath, the most simple, and ready, and easily resorted to, Bath had been tried, and succeeded on the trial, to the full extent, that had been hoped.[1]

Can you, my Dear Sir, Justify it to yourself, can you justify it to your friends, and those most dear to you, that you have sufferd yourself to be diverted by a repugnance, founded on nothing but a dislike of what you call going into Publick, to defer a repetition of that remedy, till your disorder has now gained such ground, that no one certainly can pretend to rely with equal confidence on the power of Bath water to stop it.

At all events let that, or whatever else may be thought preferable, be

---

[1] Burke himself had agreed to this in September; see above, pp. 84, 86.

tried without delay. I beg only, and claim in the name of myself, and of those, whose claim must necessarily be far stronger, that you will take without an instants delay the best advice, and follow implicitly, what that advice shall recommend.—For this purpose if you will not consent to come up to Town, I shall set off on Thursday[1] (The Birth-day must prevent my going to-morrow)[2] and, if you do not forbid it, endeavour to bring down Dr Blane,[3] in whom I feel a considerable confidence, with me. Should He be of opinion with the rest, that Bath is that which promises best, I shall be ready, putting off an excursion, that I had some slight thoughts of, into Norfolk, but to which however there were several objections, to accompany you thither as soon as you please, and to stay with you till the meeting of Parliament.[4]—I shall endeavour also before I come to see Dr Warren.[5]

My Dear Sir, though I hope and trust, that your last decay of flesh and strength is no more than that which you experienced, previously to your going to Bath first, and may be recovered by the same means, I should certainly never think it necessary in talking to you, to dissemble any part of my apprehensions.—It is on the contrary in consequence of those apprehensions, that I am thus urgent, and thus solemnly adjure you, that you would suffer no time to be lost.

My fear of being too late for the post, obliges me to close this, without saying more: nor do I know indeed, what more could be said.— The reason of the case lyes in a very small compass; That I have said so much is the result only of that earnest affection,

with which I am, my Dear Sir,
most Faithfully and Anxiously
Yours
W WINDHAM

To WALKER KING—*25 January* 1797

Source: MS Osborn Collection.
Addressed: Revd Doctor W: King Harley Street London.
Postmarked: BEACONS|FIELD I⟨A⟩|2⟨6⟩|9⟨ ⟩|B.

MS torn by the seal. Only the latter part of this letter is in Burke's hand. The cover bears a note in Edward James Nagle's hand: 'To be opened | by Mrs King | if the Doctor has | left Town'.

[1] Windham went down to Beaconsfield with Walker King on Thursday, 19 January. On 20 January he returned to London accompanied by Burke, who left for Beaconsfield again on 24 January (Windham, *Diary*, p. 351).

[2] On 18 January, to celebrate the Queen's birthday, a Grand Court was held and the Ode for the New Year was performed; Windham was present (*The Times*, 19 January).

[3] Dr Gilbert Blane; see above, p. 72.   [4] Parliament met again on 14 February.

[5] Dr Richard Warren (1731–97).

Beaconsfield
25 Jany 97

My dear Walker

Doctor Broclesby[1] is so good as to take Tiballier[2] to Town; His Mother's conduct has been abominable, from the beginning, for we find by the Boys chat, who is very loquacious and very violent, that His mother sent him to some Protestant church whilst He was in her hands —She then, without any application made to me, brought him to this School of Catholick Children and Masters, to be educated a Catholick. You remember, that early last Summer, soon after I discovered that she was an American, and therefore as I thought in all likelyhood a Protestant, of some kind or other, I prevailed on you to write to her and her friends to let her know that if she chose to educate her Child a Protestant, he should be maintained out of the fund at Mr Addissons School,[3] which you, as well as others of my friends, thought to be of the very best. You know that she could be got to give no answer or to come to any determination so that about two Months ago, when I went to Town and was kindly Lodged at your House,[4] you know I sent for her, and did positively insist that she should come to some determination. You cannot but remember the idle and shuffling discourse which she held, and that when I insisted upon her making her option she desired time to think on it, as well as I recollect a few Days. However when I grew very ill and thought I must again remove to Bath, I wrote to her directly myself,[5] declaring to her, that I never would have the least hand in educating a Child of Catholick Parents in the Protestant Religion; nor the Child of a Protestant Parent, in the Catholick; thinking that untill they came to the Years of discretion to choose a Religion for themselves, all Children ought, in that Respect, to be at the absolute disposal of their Parents, without the intermedly of any Stranger, tho' under the specious pretence of being a Benefactor. I let her know at the same time that there should be no biass on her mind either one way or the other—That she had the choice of Mr Adisson's School or of this without putting her to any expence for either; telling her at the same time, that she must let me know what religion she professed. I must send her Child back to her without giving her the former option or having any thing farther to do with her. You have the answer she wrote me,[6] in which she refused to let me know what religion she professed; but said, that her Husband[7] having been a Roman Catholick,

---

[1] See above, p. 86.   [2] See above, p. 191.   [3] See above, p. 192.
[4] Possibly during Burke's visit to London at the beginning of November; see above, pp. 102–3.
[5] Burke's letter is missing.   [6] It is missing.   [7] Not identified.

and that He would have educated his Son in that religion, she wished to have *him* educated in it also; and hoped, that I would not remove him from the School. The very next Day[1] (the day I think of my leaving Town) she sent Mr Campbell[2] to you to let you [know][3] that she had changed her mind; and would have him sent to ⟨Mr⟩ Addisons; and until he could be sent thither to be sent to her. I have accordingly had him removed hither—without a moments delay; and he will be at your house some time tomorrow. I dont know, whether this will arrive before your departure: but as Mrs King knows something of Mr Campbell, I must beg her to give directions, that he may be put into his hands by some safe person—The charge attending on it I will pay; and will write to Mrs King for that purpose. The inconvenience, that arises from the absurd conduct of this Woman is, that the Boy has taken a great liking to his companions—and finding by the conversation I had with the Masters, that it is on account of religion he is removed, he is highly dissatisfied with the Cause of his removal and has been unusually open to the impressions made on him not to submit to a change of the religion of his father, and his ancestors. He is a sharp Boy, and you cannot conceive how he talks on the subject; and with how much passion. Ever affectionately Yours

EDM BURKE

To MRS WALKER KING—[26 *January* 1797]

Source: MS Osborn Collection.
Addressed: Mrs. King.
Dated by the previous letter. 26 January 1797 was a Thursday.

Thursday morn

My dear Madam, Dr Brocklesby will deliver little Thiballier into your hands, as I imagine, that Dr W. King is on his Journey to us. May I beg, that you will get some careful person to take him to his mothers or to Mr Campbells's and I will be at the expence of it, and repay you with thanks. Mrs Burke is a triffle better, and I am sorry I can say no more on that matter; for she is weak, and her cough still distresses her not a little. I continue as I was since I left you; and if there be any difference, it is in my finding myself mended. I am not wholly free from Wind—but I have not had one of these fierce fits, no not any one very violent burst. Mrs Burke is still asleep—but is always most truly yours—as I

---

[1] From this point the letter is in Burke's hand.
[2] Not identified.
[3] The word is covered by the seal.

am with great gratitude and no little shame for having been so burthen-some a guest.[1] Ever my dear Mrs King

most affectionately Yours
EDM BURKE

To DR CALEB HILLIER PARRY—29 *January* 1797

Source: MS Hyde Collection. Printed *Adam Catalogue,* 1 (Letters of Burke), 23.
Addressed: Dr Parry | Bath.
Postmarked: ⟨ ⟩|⟨ ⟩|97.
The letter is not in Burke's hand.

Dr Caleb Hillier Parry (1755–1822) was a well-known Bath physician. In a letter to her friend Caroline Fox Mrs Crewe wrote: 'I cannot resist telling you, the accounts from Docr Parry are very comforting to all Mr and *Mrs* Burke's Friends and I should think myself (for *one*) *unjust* as well as *ungrateful* if I did not Speak in the highest praise of the Phisician who has paid so much attention to poor Mr Burke's case, and not only appeared to treat it with the common skill of a *Phisician*, but with the tenderness of a man who could *feel* for his Misfortunes' (Add. MS 51,960, fol. 40).

Dear Sir

They must be very great faults which are to be covered by a plea of procrastination, which is no small fault in itself. But the truth is, that I can not charge myself with ingratitude to you for your extraordinary and successful attention to me whilst I was at Bath.[2] I ought at least to have acknowledged it; but a very uncertain health, some occupation, much anxiety, a good deal of attempt at oblivion, all conspired together to feed that procrastinating humour which made me from day to day put off the account which I may fairly say I every day intended to give you of myself and my proceedings. At length despair induced me and perhaps some mixture of a better principle to submit quietly, and without further struggle to the common lot of Humanity. But some of my Friends in a manner forced me to be removed to London, and to take the advice of four Physicians there,[3] in addition to what I received from Dr Brocklesby then in my House. I followed their prescriptions which had all Bath in the tail of them; I have been relieved, and am still well from those wearing bursts of wind which had at last taken away my rest, wasted my flesh, and reduced my strength exceedingly. For some days I may say I was very much better; but the Complaint has ap-

[1] Burke appears to have been staying with the Kings on his visit to London 20–24 January.
[2] In the summer of 1796.
[3] On his visit of 20–24 January; see above, p. 231.

peared in some what of another shape, and accelerated still more the decay of my flesh and my strength, so that I am little more than a shadow, much thinner[1] than you have seen me at my worst. I mean to set out for Bath to morrow.[2] In which place, (if I should live to arrive at it,) I shall tell you more fully the history of the decline and fall not of The Roman Empire, but the Kingdom of Me. Till then Do me the honour to believe me

with great truth and gratitude,

Dear Sir your obliged, humble Servant
EDMUND BURKE

Beaconsfield
 Sunday Janry 29th 1797.

An undated letter advertised in Sotheby's *Catalogue* (19 March 1930, no. 567) is described as 'A.L.S. 1 p. 4to, Whitehart, Bath, n.d.' and summarized as 'to Dr Parry, saying he and Mrs Burke will receive the doctor in about an hour and a half'. A second letter, advertised in *Maggs Catalogue*, 215 (November 1905), no. 124, is described: 'A.L.S. to Mrs Bunbury, 1 page, 4to, "Feb.2, 1797" Sending thanks for enquiries after Mrs Burke and his own health by the Duchess of York'. Catherine, *née* Horneck (d. 1799), was the wife of Henry William Bunbury (1750–1811), a Groom of the Bedchamber to the Duke of York.

FRENCH LAURENCE *to* EDMUND BURKE—
9 *February* 1797

Source: MS Osborn Collection. Printed *Burke–Laurence Correspondence*, pp. 114–15.
Addressed: The Rt Honble Edmd Burke | Bath.
Franked: Free | F Laurence | London, February the ninth, 1797.

O Rem ridiculam, Cato, et jocosam,
Dignamque auribus, et tuo cachinno!
Ride, quicquid amas, Cato, Catullum.[3]

And yet I doubt whether I should so begin, for there is one tragical incident in my story. You may have heard that a great Dutch House in the City, that of Muilman, Nantes, & Co, has failed. The occasion is now the talk of the Exchange.[4] They had in their hands £44,000 received from Holland on account of *Mrs Hastings*.[5] This was

---

[1] MS: thiner
[2] Burke was in Bath on 3 February (*Bath Journal*, 3 February).
[3] O, Cato, what an absurdly funny thing, worthy for you to hear and laugh at! Laugh, as much as you love Catullus, Cato; see Catullus, *Poems*, LVI.
[4] The firm of Richard Muilman and Company had gone bankrupt following the suicide of Richard Muilman Trench Chiswell (1753–97), the chief partner.
[5] This is a remarkably well informed estimate. When payments were stopped, Richard Muilman held £60,000 in three per cent consols and £13,000 in four per cent

confidentally entrusted to them during the Trial. Now Mrs Hastings (I suppose wholly without the knowledge of that innocent and persecuted man her husband) began to enquire a little too pressingly, when it would be convenient for Messrs Muilman & Co, to transfer into her own name (I know not whether Imhoff or Hastings)[1] the stock which she supposed to have been purchased with her money. It was all gone. I am sorry to add, Mr Muilman finding an exposure of his affairs unavoidable shot himself, his partner[2] has disappeared and the House has broken to pieces. Very few annas in the Rupee are expected to be recovered.

Remember me to Mrs Burke. I am just returned from arguing on seven different sides, and have a noble Lord just come to me as a Client on another interest in the same cause. I scrawl in very great haste.

Believe me to be

My dear Sir
Ever most gratefully and affectionately Yours
FRENCH LAURENCE

EDMUND BURKE *and* EDWARD JAMES NAGLE *to* FRENCH LAURENCE—IO, I2 *February* 1797

Source: Burke–Laurence Correspondence, pp. 115–21.

Bath, Feb. 10th, 1797.

My dear Laurence,

I have been very weak for some days past, and so giddy that I am hardly able to walk across the room. At the first coming on of this bad symptom I was not able to do so much—so that I am not without hopes that it may go off, though, take me on the whole, I am without all comparison worse than when I came hither, but yet the violent flatus's have not been quite so troublesome to me since the complaint in my head is come on. They have taken the town, and are now attacking the citadel—But enough of this. The affair of Mrs Hastings has something in it that might move a third Cato to a horse-laugh, though the means, I am afraid, by which she and her paramour have made that and all the sums which they have got by their own dishonesty, or lost by the dishonesty of others or the confusion of the times, [might cause] the

consols on behalf of Warren Hastings's wife, Anna Maria, *née* Chapusetin (1747–1837); at current prices this stock was worth £42,275 (see P. J. Marshall, 'The Private Fortune of Marian Hastings', *Bulletin of the Institute of Historical Research*, XXXVII (1964), 245–53).
[1] Mrs Warren Hastings was first married to Baron Karl Imhoff (1750–1803).
[2] Henry Nantes.

laughing Democritus to weep as much as his opponent:[1] but let whoever laugh or weep, nothing plaintive will make Mr Pitt or Mr Dundas
blush for having rewarded the criminal whom they prosecuted, and sent
me and nineteen members of Parliament to prosecute, for every mode
of peculation and oppression, with a greater sum of money than ever
yet was paid to any one British subject,[2] except the Duke of Marlbro',
for the most acknowledged publick services, and not to him if you take
Blenheim, which was an expence and not a charge, out of the account.[3]
All this and ten times more will not hinder them from adding the
Peerage,[4] to make up the insufficiency of his pecuniary rewards. My
illness, which came the more heavily and suddenly upon me by this
flagitious act, whilst I was preparing a representation upon it, has
hindered me, as you know, from doing justice to that act, to Mr
Hastings, to myself, to the House of Lords, to the House of Commons,
and to the unhappy people of India, on that subject. It has made me
leave the letters that I was writing to my Lord Chancellor and Mr
Dundas, as well as my petition to the House of Commons, unfinished.[5]
But you remember, likewise, that when I came hither at the beginning
of last summer, I repeated to you that dying request which I now
reiterate,[6] That if at any time, without the danger of ruin to yourself, or
over-distracting you from your professional and parliamentary duties,
you can place in a short point of view, and support by the documents in
print and writing which exist with me, or with Mr Troward,[7] or yourself, the general merits of this transaction, you will erect a cenotaph
most grateful to my shade, and will clear my memory from that load,
which the East India Company, King, Lords, and Commons, and in a
manner the whole British Nation, (God forgive them) have been
pleased to lay as a monument upon my ashes. I am as conscious as any
person can be of the little value of the good or evil opinion of mankind
to the part of me that shall remain, but I believe it is of some moment
not to leave the fame of an evil example, of the expenditure of fourteen
years labour, and of not less (taking the expense of the suit, and the

---

[1] Democritus (c. 460–370) was known as the 'laughing philosopher'; Heraclitus
(c. 535–c. 475) as the 'weeping philosopher'.
[2] In 1796 the East India Company with the consent of the Government had awarded
Hastings an annuity of £4000, backdated to 1785, and had made him an interest-free
loan of £50,000 (see vol. VIII, 385).
[3] After the victory of Blenheim the House of Commons voted Marlborough a
pension of £5000 a year and Queen Anne declared that she would pay for the building
of Blenheim Palace. In the event, a considerable part of the expense of building
Blenheim had to be met by the Duke himself.
[4] On Hastings's return from India his supporters in Britain had pressed for a
peerage for him (see vol. V, 203). The suggestion was not renewed after the Impeachment.
[5] See vol. VIII, 422–42.   [6] See above, p. 62.   [7] See above, p. 63.

costs paid to Mr Hastings, and the parliamentary charges) than near
£.300,000.[1] This is a terrible example, and it is not acquittance at all to
a publick man, who, with all the means of undeceiving himself if he was
wrong, has thus with such incredible pains both of himself and others,
persevered in the persecution of innocence and merit. It is, I say, no
excuse at all to urge in his apology, that he has had enthusiastic good
intentions. In reality, you know that I am no enthusiast, but [according]
to the powers that God has given me, a sober and reflecting man. I
have not even the other very bad excuse, of acting from personal resentment, or from the sense of private injury—never having received any;
nor can I plead ignorance, no man ever having taken more pains to be
informed. Therefore *I* say, *Remember*.

Parliament is shortly to resume the broken thread of its business[2]—if
what it is doing deserves that name. I feel the same anxiety for your
success as if what has been the best part of me[3] was in your place, and
engaged as he would have been in the same work, and I presume to
take the same liberty with you that I would have done with him. The
plan you have formed,[4] like all the plans of such comprehensive minds
as yours, is vast, but it will require all the skill of a mind as judicious
and selecting as yours, to bring it within the compass of the apprehensions and dispositions of those upon whom it is to operate. There
would be difficulty in giving to it its just extent in the very opening, if
you could count even upon one person able and willing to support you;
but as you will be attacked by one side of the House with all its force,
reluctantly heard and totally abandoned by the other, if you are permitted any reply at all, a thing which under similar circumstances has
been refused to me, it will not be heard by the exhausted attention of
that House, which is hardly to be kept alive, except to what concerns the
factious interests of the two discordant chiefs, who with different
personal views, but on the same political principles, divide and distract
the nation. But all this I must leave to your judgement, which, with less
parliamentary experience, has infinitely more natural power than mine
ever had, when it was at the best. This, only, I shall beg leave to suggest,
that if it should be impossible (as perhaps it may be) to bring your
opening speech within any narrow compass, such as two hours, or
thereabouts, that you will make your reply as sharp, and pointed at the

---

[1] Burke is exaggerating. The cost of the prosecution after taxing amounted to
£39,887; Hastings's indemnification was calculated on a figure of £71,080 for his legal
expences; the costs of erecting the court, printing and clerks' fees, as listed in the
Journals of the House of Commons, amounted to £34,258.
[2] The House of Commons had adjourned on 31 December 1796 to 14 February
1797.
[3] Richard Burke, Jr.   [4] See above, p. 219.

personal attacks that I am sure will be made upon you, as you can; and that you will content yourself with reasserting the substance of the facts, declaring your readiness to enter into them if ever you are furnished with the means. I have no doubt that in the course of the debate, or in this session, you will find opportunities to bring forth what your discretion may reserve on the present occasion for a future one, when you may be at more liberty. Though I am sensible enough of the difficulty of finding a place in debate for any of those who are not arranged in the line of battle, abreast or ahead, in support of the one or the other of the great admirals. My dear friend, you will have the goodness to excuse the interposition of an exhausted and sickly judgement like mine, at its best, infirm, with a mind like yours, the most robust that ever was made, and in the vigour of its faculties; but allowance is made for the anxious solicitude of those, whom sex, age, or debility exclude from a share in those combats in which they take a deep concern.

Yours ever,
EDMUND BURKE.

12th February.

P.S. My health continues as it was when I began this letter.—I have read Erskine's pamphlet, which is better done than I expected to find it.[1] But it is little more than a digest of the old matter, and a proposal to remove all our evils by a universal popular representation at home, by giving to France at once all that we have thought proper to offer, on supposition of concession, and all that she has chosen to demand without any regard to our concession, together with a cordial connexion with her and a total alienation from other powers, as a pledge of future peace. This, together with bringing Mr Fox into power, forms the whole of the pamphlet. This would certainly make short work of the treaty.— This pamphlet does not make your motion the less necessary, and without a reference to it you may keep it in your eye.—Mrs Burke, thank God, is better of her cold: She salutes you.

[Edward James Nagle begins]

Dear Sir,

I have suppressed the newspapers—He knows nothing of this

---

[1] Thomas Erskine (1750–1823), later (1806) 1st Baron Erskine, the famous advocate, published on 11 February a pamphlet entitled *A View of the Causes and Consequences of the Present War with France*, which ran into thirty-seven editions. (*Studies in Bibliography*, XII (1959), 189–94.) In it he argued that an honourable peace with France could be obtained and that a peace should be followed by a parliamentary reform bill on moderate lines.

disagreeable business;[1] but I am in hopes, from Dr King's letter to me, that an injunction will be laid early to-morrow,[2] to prevent the sale, and that you all will pursue such rigorous measures against Swift and Owen, as the law will enable you to do.[3] I had a letter by the coach, informing me of it.—Will you beg of Doctor King to write to Mr Burke to-morrow, and tell him what he has done in Rivington's business.

Yours truly,

E. NAGLE.

To WILLIAM WINDHAM—12 February [1797]

Source: British Museum (Add. MS 37,843, fols 135–6). Printed Burke–Windham Correspondence, pp. 233–4.
Only the signature is in Burke's hand.

My dear Friend

How can I find thanks any way proportioned to your unwearied kindness. I must be silent and restrain my busts of Gratitude as you desire me to restrain the busts of my Stomach: In the latter I will do what I can. I received your Letter[4] when I was half the channel over in Mr Erskines Pamphlet, which would have landed me safely in a good harbour of the Republick one and indivisible and that too, as Mr Erskine says, upon my own principles.[5] The Pamphlet is better written and less full of Vanity than I expected to find it; but it is the old matter new hashed up—France would have been very good if she had not been provoked by the wickedness of Great Britain and other powers who

---

[1] At the beginning of 1797 John Owen, the publisher, who had already offended Burke by his unauthorized edition of the Letters on a Regicide Peace (see above, p. 97), embarked on a new enterprise. He secured from William Thomas Swift (see above, p. 57) an incomplete manuscript of the confidential letter Burke had sent to the Duke of Portland and Earl Fitzwilliam in September 1793 (see vol. VII, 436–8), setting forth in a kind of formal arraignment, Burke's criticisms of Fox's attitude. This work was advertised for sale on 11 February and published on 13 February, under the title A Letter from the Rt Honourable Edmund Burke to his Grace the Duke of Portland, on the Conduct of the Minority in Parliament. Containing Fifty-Four Articles of Impeachment against the Rt Hon. C. J. Fox. From the Original Copy, in the Possession of the Noble Duke, printed for the editor, and sold by J. Owen, No. 168 Piccadilly, 1797. On 13 February Laurence gave Fitzwilliam an account of Swift's 'villainy against poor Burke' and informed him that he had 'wrote to Bath to have all newspapers kept from him [Burke] and to prepare Mrs Burke'. In reply Fitzwilliam wrote that he heartily wished the 'Ruffian' 'may be skin'd alive' (MSS at Northampton, Box 51; Fitzwilliam to Laurence, n.d., Box x 512/133).
[2] See below, p. 243.   [3] See below, p. 244.
[4] Of 11 February (MS at Sheffield; printed Corr. (1844), IV, 427–8). The 1844 editors, understandably, omitted Windham's long passage on how Burke might restrain himself from belching.
[5] Erskine's pamphlet referred to 'the immense magazine of military and political wisdom' to be found in Burke's writings, and argued that what he had said of the need for conciliating America in the 1770s might be applied to France in the 1790s.

are confederates not against her ambition but against her Liberty—
That she was right in every point and at all times and with all Nations.—
That the cure for all disorders consists in your making your Representation at home as like hers as possible—In making Peace with her by
giving her all that you offer and all that she demands—That by excluding her from all the Continental powers she will become well disposed to you; and that you and she will become Guardians of liberty
throughout the world. And as to our safety, it will be perfect provided we
do nothing to provoke that irresistible[1] power—and lastly, in which
alone I think with him, that for making such a peace it is proper that
Mr Fox and his Friends should come into power. I think this is a just
Analysis of Mr Erskine's pamphlet which he says he has formed on my
Opinions, not with relation to France, but with relation to America.

I am to observe once for all, that these Gentlemen put the case of
France and America exactly upon a Par, and always have done so. I
leave them to rejoice in that discovery and in my inconsistency, and the
antidote they have found in one part of my writings against the poison
that exists in another. You will observe, that *their* Alliance with France,
and a change in this Constitution are things that always go hand in
hand, and I think, consistently enough. The only point upon which he is
strong, but on which I dont think he makes the most is Mr Pitts having
refused to make proffers of Peace whilst our affairs were in a prosperous
condition.[2] When He allows that any Peace at all can be made with the
Regicide powers that is likely to be safe and lasting. But Mr Pitt unfortunately is in the condition of 'Paulo purgante'.[3] He cannot make
peace and he will not make war 'Deus dabit his quoque finem'[4] which I
beleive I will not live to see. I wish [I] may live to make my final
protest against the proceedings of both factions. God bless you and
reserve you to better times, for which bettering of the times your preservation may be very essential. I continue just as I was, with the
difference of a bad Night—Doctor Parry has just given me a purgative
Medicine, and I assure you I implicitly obey his directions. I cannot yet
walk or stand firm, but I can read upon my back and dictate as I do
now, whilst all the great hunters are driving their Spears into a dead
Boar. Once more God bless you and for the few moments I have to
live, beleive me devotedly

Yours

Bath

EDM BURKE

12th Feby.

[1] MS: irrestible   [2] In 1793.
[3] In Matthew Prior's poem 'Paulo Purganti and his Wife'.
[4] To this, too, God will grant an end; see Virgil, *Aeneid*, I, 199.

FRENCH LAURENCE *to* EDMUND BURKE—
14 *February* 1797

Source: *Burke–Laurence Correspondence*, pp. 121–4.

London, Feb. 14th, 1797.

My dear Sir,

Many, many thanks for all your kind anxiety about me, and especially in your late long letter.[1] May I prove not unworthy of that sort of implied adoption, which is the honour of my life! Without any second intimation, *I should not have forgotten*: so reminded, in connexion with what followed, I feel it a filial duty to remember. I will not, however, yet receive this as a dying request. Though your account of yourself is very far from satisfactory, yet I will look to the good part of it, that your stomach is rather better: the new symptom in your head does not much alarm me, since it is not an uncommon effect, as I have been told, of the Bath-waters.

Your observations respecting my business perfectly accord with my own purposes.[2] I shall compress the first part as much as I can, so as to put strong and sweeping negatives, throwing the proof on the other side. I have gone through all the debates of the Convention leading to the war with the Emperor. They are decisive beyond my hopes, that the leaders did not pretend in truth to consider the concert of princes (whatever it was and whenever it began) but as *defensive*, and that they especially believed the Emperor to have *wished negociation and not war*. I have the debates abstracted and translated, and shall hold them in my hand, asserting the general result in few sentences, and challenging the proof in detail. I mean my reply to be as sharp as I can make it, avoiding details there also, and threatening, if the House approves, specific resolutions hereafter on all the facts. Novelty and curiosity will probably secure me some sort of hearing. Erskine's pamphlet, which I have, but have not yet read, will give a propriety and life to the first part of my motion.

I am afraid, I have done the public lately some mischief, in my zeal to consult your private delicacies. In your sleep you have done great and good service here without knowing it, but Dr W. King, Woodford, and myself, with a little stretching of Mr Rivington's conscience, have stopped your career of fame. Not to keep you in suspense, Owen, by the means of Swift, as I have been informed, has published a paper of yours, which is very much admired, wherever it has been seen. It is

---

[1] Of 10, 12 February; see above, pp. 236–40.   [2] See above, p. 238.

the paper, of which I got the original rough-copy from Swift, if I recollect right, about a year ago, and of which, on my giving him a lecture and a guinea, he assured me that he had kept no transcript.[1] In reality it was your justification to the Duke of Portland and Lord Fitzwilliam for pursuing your own line of conduct, when they chose to concur in the vote of *confidence* from the Whig Club to Mr Fox.[2] By Dr W. King's active exertion, on Mr Rivington's oath of his belief that the production was yours, we got an injunction yesterday, *the very day of publication*,[3] and gave public notice in the papers of this day.[4] Some copies (and I believe a considerable number) did however get abroad in spite of us.[5] Accidentally coming out at the very same time with Erskine's, it crossed him in many and indeed most of his principal topics, and it is thought, fairly laid him on his back.

The Duke of Portland (Dr King says) is perfectly at ease on the subject; and I wrote yesterday to explain it to Lord Fitzwilliam.

From the complaints, which I hear of the publication being stopped, I am almost willing to desire that a correct edition may be given, the consent of the Duke and of Lord Fitzwilliam, of course, being obtained.[6]

Besides the injunction against Owen, we are preparing a bill of discovery against Swift, to get from him all your papers, and an injunction against the publication of any of them.[7]

[1] Swift had in fact kept a copy, corrected by Burke. It is now in the Houghton Library at Harvard.

[2] See vol. VII, 353–5.

[3] On 13 February the Court of Chancery granted an injunction restraining Owen from publishing the pamphlet (Public Record Office, C33/496/128). The Attorney General (Sir John Scott, 1751–1838, later, 1821, 1st Earl of Eldon) who appeared for Burke, referring to Owen's behaviour said, 'my mind is hardly equal to the subject of framing observations sufficient to describe such a transaction' (*The Times*, 14 February).

[4] *The Times* for 14 February printed a formal notice—presumably supplied by Laurence and Walker King: 'Messrs Rivington have been authorized by the Friends of Mr Burke, to express their indignation and astonishment at finding a work under the above title, advertised for Sale during his absence, and in his present state of health. They think it their duty to assure the Public, that Such Publication is neither printed with Mr Burke's Knowledge or Consent, nor from any Copy as falsely asserted to be in the Possession of his Grace the Duke of Portland. An injunction has this day been obtained from the Court of Chancery, restraining John Owen and all other persons from printing and selling the above work. All Persons are therefore cautioned, not to incur a contempt of the Court of Chancery, by selling any Copies of it, or publishing extracts from it. Feb. 13th, 1797'.

[5] Writing to Lord Loughborough (see below, p. 322) after Burke's death, Laurence estimated the number: 'Notwithstanding your Lordship's friendly and equitable promptitude in granting your injunction against it, three thousand copies at least were sold, and exist in the three kingdoms' (letter of 27 September 1797, printed *Burke–Laurence Correspondence*, p. 293; see also Todd, *Bibliography*, pp. 209, 234).

[6] An authorized version, under the title 'Observations on the Conduct of the Minority', finally appeared in the fourth volume of the quarto edition of Burke's *Works* published by Laurence and Walker King in 1802.

[7] An account rendered by Douce and Rivington itemized: 'Febry 16—Mr Owen having given notice that Memoirs of Mr Burke with several of his original Letters

I write in great haste; having just returned from the Treasury, and now going down to the House. Remember me to Mrs Burke, and believe me to be,

My dear Sir,

Ever most gratefully and affectionately
Your faithful and devoted
FRENCH LAURENCE.

On 1 July, Owen having become bankrupt, Burke's solicitors attended his final examination and claimed £600 as a debt due to their client (MS at Sheffield, Bk 32). On 5 August 1797 Jane Burke filed a bill in Chancery requesting an injunction to restrain William Thomas Swift, Charles M'Cormick and Vincent Griffiths from printing or publishing letters and literary works of the late Edmund Burke. On 9 August an injunction was granted (Public Record Office, C12/2186/2; C33/497/578). Later in the year M'Cormick published *Memoirs of Burke* which contains a few fragments of original letters.

To FRENCH LAURENCE—15 *February* 1797

Source: Copy (incomplete) in Fitzwilliam MSS (Sheffield). Printed *Burke–Laurence Correspondence*, pp. 124–8.
Endorsed: Mr Burke to Dr | Lawrence—(copy) | febry 15.1797 | on Swifts base pub- | lication of a stolen | copy of Mr B.'s Lre | on the conduct of the | Minority in the Session | 1792–3.
Only the first half of this letter is preserved in the MS copy at Sheffield. This portion corresponds (with minor alterations) to what was printed in vol. IV (pp. vii–viii) of the 1802 quarto edition of Burke's *Works*. The remainder of the letter is here printed from the text in the *Burke–Laurence Correspondence*.

Bath February 15. 1797

My dear Laurence

On the appearance of the advertisement[1] all Newspapers and all Letters have been kept back from me till this time. Mrs Burke opened yours, and finding that all the measures in the power of Dr King, yourself and Mr Woodford had been taken to suppress the Publication, she ventur'd to deliver me the letters of today, which were read to me in my bed about two o'clock.

This affair does vex me, but I am not in a state of health at present to be deeply vexed at any thing. Whenever this matter comes into discussion, I authorize you to contradict the infamous reports, which (I am inform'd) have been given out, that this paper had been circulated through the Ministry and was intended gradually to slide into the

would be published attending Mr King and advising thereon', the usual charge 6/8d (MS at Sheffield, Bk 32). William Henry Douce and Henry Rivington were attorneys in Fenchurch Buildings. The 'Memoirs of Mr Burke' was presumably the biography by Charles M'Cormick (c. 1755–1807) which was to contain materials supplied by Swift.
[1] See the previous letter.

Press.[1] To the best of my recollection, I never had a clean copy of it but one, which is now in my possession; I never communicated that but to the D. of Portland from whom I had it back again. But the Duke will set this matter to rights, if in reality there were two copies and he has one.[2] I never shewed it, as they know, to any one of the Ministry. If the Duke has really a copy, I believe his and mine are the only ones that exist, except what was taken by fraud from loose and incorrect papers by S——[3] to whom I gave the letter to copy. As soon as I began to suspect him capable of any such scandalous breach of trust, you know with what anxiety I got the loose papers out of his hands, not having reason to think that he kept any other. Neither do I believe in fact (unless he meditated this villainy long ago) that he did or does now possess any clean Copy. I never communicated that paper to any out of the very small circle of those private friends, from whom I concealed nothing.

But I beg you and my friends to be cautious how you let it be understood, that I disclaim any thing but the mere act and intention of publication. I do not retract any one of the sentiments contain'd in that Memorial, which was and is my Justification, address'd to the friends, for whose use alone I intended it. Had I designed it for the Publick I should have been more exact and full. It is written in a tone of indignation against the resolutions of the Whig Club, which were directly pointed against myself and others, who in consequence seceded from that Club;[4] which is the last act of my life, that I shall under any circumstances repent. Many temperaments and explanations there would have been, if ever I had a notion that it should meet the publick Eye.[5] But no wonder that such villains as Owen should proceed as they do, when our courts of Justice seem by their proceedings to be in league with every kind of fraud and injustice. They proceed as if they had an intricate settlement of 10,000 a year to discuss in an affair that might as well be decided in three weeks as in three hundred years.[6] They let

[1] Burke's friend and physician Dr Richard Brocklesby wrote to him on 14 February: 'Your letter to the D. of P. in 1793, has got abroad and is much read and by most approved of, the Foxites pretend, that manuscript Copies of it had been from that time in circulation by all the Ministers from that time to this and that it was originally intended to slide into the press to manifest your Sentiments to the World at large' (MS at Sheffield).
[2] Burke's 'clean copy' has not been found. The Duke's copy is among the Portland papers at Nottingham.
[3] Swift.   [4] See vol. VII, 353–5.
[5] From this point, the text is taken from the *Burke–Laurence Correspondence*, pp. 126–8.
[6] Burke had already been warned about the delays that might be inherent in a Chancery suit. When Douce and Rivington informed him they had filed a bill containing interrogatories against Owen they explained: 'By the practise of the Court of Chancery he is allowed three orders for time to put in his Answer, the first (which he has obtained) will expire on the 14th of December, the second will be for three weeks, and

people die while they are looking for redress, and then all the proceedings are to begin over again by those who may think they have an
interest in them. While one suit is pending, they give knaves an opportunity of repeating their offences and of laughing at them and their
justice, as well they may. I wish heartily that, if the lawyers are of
opinion that they may spin out this mockery a year or two longer, I may
not vex my dying hours in fruitless chichane, but let the villany, which
their maxims countenance, take its course. As to any relief in the other
courts, I have been in them, and would not trust the fame and fortune
of any human creature to them if I could possibly help it. I have tried
their justice in two cases of my own,[1] and in one, in which I was concerned with others in a publick prosecution, where they suffered the
House of Commons in effect to have the tables turned on them, and
under colour of a defendant to be criminated for a malicious prosecution.[2]
I know them of old, and am only sorry at my present departure, that I
have not had an opportunity of painting them in their proper colours.
Why should not the Court of Chancery be able to know, whether an
author gives an imperfect copy to a printer to be published whether he
will or no, and has not left himself master of his own thoughts and reflexions? This is the very case made by the wretch himself, but a court
can't decide in years whether this thing ought to be done or not. In the
meantime he enjoys the profits of his villany, and defies them by
villanies of the same kind and to the same person. But I allow that it is
better that even this kind of justice should exist in the country, than
none at all.—Adieu. I am now in my third dose of physick which I have
taken in the course of thirty-six hours. The symptoms of my disease
are quite changed. I have hardly any excitation, but my strength,
rest, and flesh, are gone. Nothing goes through me. I cannot walk
alone from my couch to my bed. The giddiness is not the effect of the
Bath waters, for I do not drink them, nor have except for two days in the
beginning, and when I had no giddiness. The opiates I have totally
left off. Yet things remain where they were. I am perfectly satisfied with
my physician, both in point of skill and profession; but nature is too
strong for him, and I grow worse hourly.—What day is fixed for your

the third for a fortnight longer, and if he avails himself of all the delays which the
forms of Court allow, we cannot compel him to answer until the latter end of January.
He was served with the Injunction some time ago, and we shall take care to press him
on as fast as a practise so indulgent to Defendants will allow' (letter of 29 November
1796, MS at Sheffield).
[1] Burke had brought an action against a newspaper in 1781 for 'certain scandalous
paragraphs' published about him, and in 1784 he secured damages against Henry
Sampson Woodfall (1739–1805); see vols IV, 350–1, V, 159–60, 165.
[2] The prosecution of John Stockdale (c. 1749–1814), the publisher, by order of the
House of Commons; see vol. VI, 54.

motion?[1] I suppose the Opposition have not neglected this affair of Ireland, and the Ministers well deserve whatever may happen, from the insolent manner in which they received the warnings of Mr Fox, particularly as what he said was no more than a repetition of what they chose to forget.

Yours ever,

E. BURKE.

WILLIAM WINDHAM *to* EDMUND BURKE—
17 [*February* 1797]

Source: Fitzwilliam MSS (Sheffield). Printed Corr. (1844), IV, 429–30.

Friday. 6'oclock. 17th

My Dear Sir

You may imagine, what our anxiety is, when your fate almost may hang upon the report, which each day is to bring. Dr Parry's opinion has every air of being right. God Grant that your strength may hold out, so as to give a fair chance to the course, that He is pursuing.

In such a state of uncertainty about what is so infinitely precious, one has no heart to talk much about other things; I should otherwise like to tell you, that the paper, which Villainy has thus brought out, is received in a manner, which could leave you nothing to regret, but the havock it is making with the character and credit of Mr Fox. One hardly knows, what to wish upon that subject; but with respect to you, nothing can be more satisfactory. Mr Pitt, with whom I first saw it, when we met at the Speakers,[2] was not only highly gratified with it, (more perhaps than one wished him to be) but thought it a model of the sort of stile, in which it was written; and which by the way, when it suits the subject, is more forcible than any other; and always accords more with the general taste.

Another satisfactory circumstance which I would like to dilate to you, in the midst of an ocean of calamity, is the manner in which the fatal reverses in Italy, have been received at Vienna. No despondency, no change or relaxation of purpose, a determination to pursue the war to the last extremity.[3]

The Secretary of Sir Charles Whitworth, too, who is come over from

[1] See below, pp. 250–1. [2] See above, p. 95.
[3] It was reported on 17 February that the Emperor had refused to enter into an armistice with the French (*The Times*, 17 February), but on 18 April the preliminaries of peace between the Austrians and French were signed at Leoben.

Petersburgh,[1] gives hopes of the Emperor of Russia: But of that, when you hear, that He is an Illuminé,[2] your hopes any more than mine, notwithstanding many favourable circumstances, will not be sanguine.

> Ever My Dear Sir
>> most faithfully
>>> Yours &c &c
>>>> W WINDHAM

I have sent you some partridges, hoping that you will be able to eat them.

FRENCH LAURENCE *to* EDMUND BURKE—
20 *February* 1797

Source: MS Bodleian Library. Printed *Burke–Laurence Correspondence*,
pp. 130–3.
Addressed: The Rt Honble Edmd Burke | Bath.
Franked: Free | F Laurence | London, Feby the twentieth, 1797.
Postmarked: FREE|FE|2⟨ ⟩|⟨ ⟩.

London Feby 20th 1797

My dear Sir,

Your letter[3] and the subsequent account from Nagle which I received on Saturday, very sincerely and deeply afflicted me. Yet I will not lose my hope in the mercies of Providence, not to you, but to the remaining fragments of your family, to your friends, and to your Country. If the Supreme Disposer of all has yet employment for you in doing good, he will preserve you for his own season. Your symptoms do not to me seem desperate, but alarming they certainly are, as indeed I should think any new turn of your disorder, because it would bring a new danger, the extent of which it would be difficult immediately to estimate.—Nothing from Nagle to-day. It is the first time that he has given me the most distant reason to complain; but after the two last accounts, it would have been kind to have written had he any thing comfortable to say: it would have been some satisfaction even to have heard that you are not worse.

I have several times reproached myself for not having answered your letter for three days. But in truth it was morally and almost physically impossible. What you authorized me to say, I have circulated without

---

[1] Early in January William Eton had been sent by Sir Charles Whitworth (1752–1825), later (1800) 1st Baron Whitworth, Envoy Extraordinary at St Petersburgh with dispatches. He arrived at Yarmouth on 15 February (Whitworth to Grenville, 12 January; Grenville to Whitworth, draft dated February, Public Record Office, F.O. 65/36).
[2] A disciple of the *philosophes*.
[3] Of 15 February; see above, pp. 244–7.

appearing to be studious of doing it, as I have never met with the suggestion mentioned by Dr Brocklesby.[1]

Mr Adair[2] has written a foolish letter in some of the Papers,[3] generally denying the charge,[4] but the denial is very equivocal. The charge stated by himself is that he was guilty of a treasonable misdemeanor; by denying this, it has been observed by his own friends that he may only have denied the Law; he means therefore to justify himself more specifically.

You are very curiously defended—*by Mr Miles*! He had alluded in one of his pamphlets to the same charge against Fox and Adair. The latter has now spoken very contemptuously of him, and has roused a sleeping hornet.[5]

Erskine's pamphlet I have by different mighty efforts forced myself to read half-through. I never saw in the same space so many glaring errors and so many palpable misrepresentations of facts. My copy is pretty fully noted and I wish to put it into the hands of Nagle's friend, Mr Mccullen.[6] Will you be so good as to desire Nagle immediately to write to him and beg him to call upon me Wednesday about noon? I will also thank Nagle for his address.

Mr Whitbread has given notice for a motion for an enquiry into the late measures for the attempted invasion of Ireland. It stands for Friday.[7] I am afraid that I shall be wished to go a little beyond my own opinions. My line would be, according to my own feelings, to disapprove the neglect of the real defence of Ireland by neglecting to conciliate the affections of the People and to make them a very efficient member of the

---

[1] See above, p. 245.
[2] Robert Adair (1763–1815) was a close friend of Fox. In 'Observations on the Conduct of the Minority' Burke had attacked Fox for sending Adair to St Petersburg in 1791, at a time when Anglo–Russian relations were strained, 'to frustrate the objects for which the minister from the crown was authorized to treat' (*Works*, Bohn, III, 472; Little, Brown, v, 10).   [3] MS: Paper,
[4] Adair in his letter to the press, putting 'a large and liberal construction' on Rivington's statement that the 'Observations' had not been printed from a copy in the Duke of Portland's possession, declared he assumed the statement to mean that Burke never stated that his journey to St Petersburg was injurious to Fox. He ended by saying that 'if any better sentiment than curiosity can be gratified by my justification, I am ready to enter upon it without delay' (*Public Advertiser*, 16 February).
[5] In his letter Adair remarked that the charges made against him in the 'Observations' had been made before 'but always from quarters below my notice'. This remark was taken up by William Augustus Miles (*c.* 1753–1817), the radical pamphleteer. He had strongly criticized Fox and Adair for their relations with the Court of St Petersburg in his *Conduct of France towards Great Britain examined* (1793) and in his *Authentic Correspondence with M. Le Brun...* (1796); in a letter which filled two columns of *The Times* of 20 February he reiterated his criticisms.
[6] Not identified.
[7] On 17 February Samuel Whitbread (see above, p. 123) gave notice that on Friday, 24 February, he would 'move for an Enquiry into the Conduct of Administration with respect to the Measures pursued for defeating the Expedition planned by the French Republic against Ireland' (*The Times*, 18 February). When his motion was debated on 3 March it was defeated by 209 votes to 62.

confederacy against Jacobinism; to argue offensive measures to be the only safe defence; to doubt the vigilance of administration on the late occasion but to decline an enquiry, because if they should be found undeserving of confidence there is no party to whom the confidence of Parliament can be transferred. It cannot be bestowed on men who are always maintaining the Justice of France against England and thinking of peace only as affording an opportunity for changes in the Constitution. I think this ground might be made impressive. But I know not how it might please in a quarter,[1] where I should be sorry to give the least dissatisfaction. If I did, what I have sketched, I should do it with assertions of the general Constitutional doctrines about confidence and enquiry against my own determination in this instance, but I should rest my conduct on the strange disjointed condition of the Times; and I should throughout express myself with regret as considering the disqualification of opposition for the government of the Country, as one of the greatest evils.—I have a considerable doubt on the score of prudence, whether it may not a little take off from the effect of my own motion, by depriving me of the advantage of novelty.— Whatever I do, or do not, I shall feel myself a little the stronger, as I have this day paid my own election bills of nearly £500 at Peterborough.

As to my own motion, I purpose to bring it forward on Monday the 6th of March. It is the first leisure day which I have from professional business after our term, which does not end till the 2d and Friday the 3d is occupied by Mr Fox. The Admiralty Court will sit all March except on Mondays and Saturdays; so that if I cannot have the 6th it must go to the next Monday. The end of this week I hope to send you my Resolutions.[2] I shall a little enlarge the scheme of them, to include most if not all the Parliamentary declarations of principle, because many of them have been quoted in a most garbled and distorted manner by Erskine. I shall meet his falsifications, but without professedly particularizing them.

Adieu, my dear Sir! I must go to the House; where it is supposed a message may come relative to the intended invasion, and a loan; but I speak from common report not from any authority.

I am my dear Sir
Ever most gratefully and affectionately Yours
FRENCH LAURENCE

[1] Lord Fitzwilliam.

[2] A copy of 'Resolutions Dr Laurence | had thoughts of moving' is in manuscript at Sheffield (F 32g). There are twenty resolutions, nineteen summarizing the declared aims of British policy towards France from December 1792 to the close of 1796; the last affirming the determination of the House of Commons, 'not despairing of the public weal, but confident in the resources and spirit of the people of Great

To FRENCH LAURENCE—[*post* 20 *February* 1797]

Source: *Burke–Laurence Correspondence*, pp. 128–9.
Apparently an answer to the previous letter. The names in angle brackets are Croker's readings (see above, pp. vii–viii).

Bath, 5 o'clock. [1797.]

My dear Laurence,

I should be sorry that you and ⟨Lord Fitzwilliam⟩ differed. I hope you have wrote to him the state of your mind. The question is delicate and difficult, even though it were not complicated with collateral considerations of no small weight. The abstract merits of the question are with the Opposition—the political consequences of carrying it are not less certain; but I think there is little danger, especially after the declaration of the Irish Parliament,[1] that it should be carried. In my opinion you may vote as you feel, without injury to your honour, one way or the other: And therefore, perhaps ⟨Lord Fitzwilliam⟩'s opinion ought to turn the scale. But, on this point, I am no way confident. The neglect has indeed been shameful, and has been owing to Mr Pitt's absolute disbelief of any such intention on the part of the enemy, notwithstanding his having received very sufficient intelligence upon that head. I enclose to you in two other covers, a letter I have received from Sir Lawrence Parsons.[2] If I had had heart and strength enough, I should have answered it, and sent it to ⟨Lord Fitzwilliam⟩, but certainly not to be communicated for the purposes of Opposition, that would be a breach of trust. Assure him of my sentiments of gratitude in my extremity, and communicate the letter with these cautions (unless you feel some objection) to ⟨Lord Fitzwilliam⟩. I should think there was less difficulty in your case, if I did not think that the same question will infallibly be agitated in the House of Peers, and the part which ⟨Lord Fitzwilliam⟩ will take can be little doubted. I don't like that all his members should be found voting against him.[3] But again, God direct you—Adieu.

Yours ever,

EDMUND BURKE.

Britain', to support the Government in the prosecution of a war, begun to repel aggression 'founded on principles subversive of the whole political, civil and religious system of Europe'. Laurence did not move his Resolutions on 6 March (see below, pp. 293, 296, 305).

[1] On 16 January the Lord Lieutenant communicated a 'message' from the King to the Irish Parliament. On 17 January the House of Lords unanimously, and the House of Commons by 90 to 7, voted addresses thanking the King. These implied parliamentary approval of the way in which the Peace Negotiations had been handled and of the measures which had been taken for the defence of Ireland (*The Times*, 23, 24 January).   [2] See below, p. 277.

[3] None of the members for Fitzwilliam's seats were in the minority which supported Whitbread's motion.

FRENCH LAURENCE *to* EDMUND BURKE—
24 *February* 1797

Source: MS Bodleian Library. Printed *Burke–Laurence Correspondence,*
pp. 134–6.
Addressed: The Rt Honble E. Burke | Bath.
Franked: Free | Laurence | London, Feby the twenty-fourth, 1797.
Postmarked FREE|FE|24|97 FREE|⟨ ⟩|⟨ ⟩|97|D.

London Feby 24th 1797

My dear Sir,

Since the receipt of your last letter,[1] I have not had a moment's leisure: I now take advantage of a long reading of voluminous evidence in the Court of Admiralty to scrawl two or three lines.

The system, on which your physicians are now proceeding, approves itself very much to my reason. I remember also, that it is the system, which my youngest brother (who is a medical man)[2] suggested to me for your case, when I was talking to him on the subject some little time since. My principal fear was your want of Strength to bear the necessary discipline. But to my great surprise and satisfaction, if I can trust Nagle's accounts, you seem to receive strength from every fresh evacuation. I begin again to have strong hopes, which at one moment had nearly forsaken me, that Providence will yet spare you to us. I consider you (like the emigrant Clergy and Nobility of France) as a sort of pledge of mercy to us from the Divine disposer of all.

The enclosed letter[3] will speak for itself. There is one point, you will perceive, on which I have now for the first time extorted *a reluctant assent.* Yet the concluding reasoning almost starts away from it again. I cannot comprehend how a peace made by Fox would more save the national honour than a similar measure conducted by Mr Pitt. Would any State of Europe believe it a choice? Would it in fact be so, on the part of the nation? Certainly not. Neither do I see any thing dishonourable in laying down your arms, when resistance is impracticable, or success is desperate, if that be the case, which I deny, but which Mr Pitt will certainly declare to have been his reason for making

[1] The previous letter.
[2] John Laurence (1765–1826), having practised as a surgeon, in 1813 was appointed secretary of the London Assurance.
[3] Presumably an undated letter from Fitzwilliam in which he states that he agrees with Laurence 'much more than I wish I did, in that opinion that such is the state of Party in this country, that I know not how to wish for a change of Ministry, lest a change in the Ministry should lead to a change in the *constitution*'. But Fitzwilliam ends this letter by arguing that 'Peace would be made by him [Fox] more to advantage, because made by him, there would be virtually a saving of the Country's Honor—made by Mr Pitt, the Country is *beat* into it: made by Mr F. it is a measure of choice' (MS at Northampton, Box X515/4).

peace, whenever he shall have made a peace. On the other hand, Mr Fox's negotiation I think would begin by stamping an indelible brand on the national honour; for the preamble which he and his friends always tell[1] they mean to prefix is a humble confession of our injustice in the origin of the war, and of our participation in a plot against the liberty and territory of France, which (whatever we may chuse to do for ourselves) we have no right to confess for our past and present allies. When a negotiation had ever been attempted on *this principle,* how long after could he expect the Emperor to remain firm to his alliance with us against all the temptations, which The Republicans have thrown, and will throw out to him again?

The question announced by opposition is narrowed to an inquiry into the conduct of the war, in one particular instance. They have also threatened a general inquiry. If I vote for one, how can I in common consistency oppose the other, as I should be inclined to do on account of the certain political consequences? In reality it seems to me (if I do not refine too much) an ambuscade laid to take Lord Fitzwilliam prisoner, that his name and authority may be used on other occasions for higher objects. I shall write a managed reply to the enclosed a little on that notion. If there was not some such view, as I suppose, I cannot conceive, why opposition so circumscribed their own ground to the conduct of ministers, *while the French were off Ireland.* Remember me to Mrs Burke and believe me

> My dear Sir
> > Ever most gratefully, faithfully and affectionately Yours
> > FRENCH LAURENCE

P.S. I have been during the writing of this page listening to a speech which I am to answer.

To UNKNOWN—[*February* 1797]

Source: Fitzwilliam MSS (Northampton), A.XI.12. Printed *Works* (Bohn, VI, 80–90; Little, Brown, VI, 415–29).

In the preface (pp. xv–xvi) to the fifth volume of the quarto edition of the *Works* (1812) Walker King could only describe this letter as 'written in the Year 1797' and dictated, as Burke himself says, from his couch at Bath. Burke was in Bath on 3 February; see above, p. 235. The MS is in Nagle's hand but extensively corrected by Burke.

Dear Sir

In the reduced state of body, and in the dejected state of mind in which I find myself at this very advanced period of my Life, it is a

---

[1] MS: tells

great consolation to me to know, that a cause, I ever have had so very near my heart, is taken up by a man of your activity and Talents.

It is very true that your late friend, my ever dear and honored Son, was in the highest degree solicitous about the final event of a business which he also had pursued for a long time with infinite Zeal, and no small degree of success. It was not above half an hour before he left me for ever, that He spoke with considerable earnestness on this very subject. If I had needed any incentives to do my best for freeing the body of my Country from the grievances under which they labour, this alone would certainly call forth ⟨all⟩ my endeavours.

The Person[1] who succeeded to the Government ⟨of⟩ Ireland about the time of that afflicting event had been all along of my Sentiments and yours, upon this Subject; and far from needing to be stimulated by me, that incomparable person and those in whom he strictly confided, even went before me in their resolution to pursue the great end of Government, the satisfaction and concord of the people with whose welfare they were charged. I cannot bear to think on the causes by which this great plan of policy so manifestly beneficial to both kingdoms has been defeated.

Your mistake with regard to me lies in supposing that I did not, when his removal was in agitation, strongly and personally represent to several of his Majesty's Ministers, to whom I could have the most ready access, the true state of Ireland and the mischiefs which sooner or later must arise from subjecting the Mass of the people to the capricious and interested domination of an exceeding small faction and its dependencies.[2]

That representation was made the last time, or very nearly the last time, that I have ever had the honour of seeing these ministers. I am so far from having any credit with them on this, or any other public matter, that I have reason to be certain if it were known, that any person in office in Ireland from the highest to the lowest, were influenced by my Opinions and disposed to act upon them, such a one would be instantly turned out of his employment. You have formed, to my person a flattering, yet in truth a very erroneous Opinion of my power with those who direct the public measures. I never have been directly or indirectly consulted about any thing that is done. The Judgment of the eminent and able persons who conduct public Affairs is undoubtedly superior to mine; but self partiality induces almost every man to defer something to his own. Nothing is more notorious than

[1] Lord Fitzwilliam.
[2] For Burke's efforts to influence members of the Cabinet, see vol. VIII, 156–7, 167, 173, 177.

that I have the misfortune of thinking, that no one capital measure relative to political arrangements, and that no one military plan for the defence of either Kingdom in this arduous War has been taken upon any other principle, than such as must conduct us to inevitable ruin.

In the state of my mind, so discordant with the tone of ministers, and still more discordant with the tone of Opposition, you may judge what degree of weight I am likely to have with either of the parties who divide this Kingdom; even tho' I were endowed[1] with strength of body, or were possessed of any active situation in the Government which might give success to my endeavours. But the fact is, since the day of my unspeakable calamity,[2] except in the attentions of a very few old and compassionate friends, I am totally out of all social intercourse. My health has gone down very rapidly; and I have been brought hither with very faint hopes of Life, and enfeebled to such a degree, as those, who had known me some time ago, could scarcely think credible. Since I came hither my Sufferings have been greatly aggravated, and my little strength still further reduced; so, that though I am told the Symptoms of my disorder begin to carry a more favourable aspect, I pass the far larger part of the twenty four hours, indeed almost the whole, either in my Bed, or lying upon the Couch, from which I dictate this. Had you been apprized of this circumstance you could not have expected any thing, as you seem to do, from my active exertions. I could do nothing if I was still stronger, not even 'Si ⟨...⟩ meus adforet Hector'.[3]

There is no hope for the body of the people of Ireland, as long as those who are in power with you shall make it the great Object of their policy to propagate an Opinion on this side of the Water, that the mass of their Countrymen are not to be trusted by their Government; and that the only hold which England has upon Ireland, consists in preserving a certain very small Number of Gentlemen in full possession of a monopoly of that Kingdom. This System has disgusted many others besides Catholicks and dissenters.

As to those, who, on your side of the Channel are in the Opposition to *oppose* Government, they are composed of Persons several of whom I love and revere. They have been irritated by a treatment too much for the ordinary patience of mankind to bear, into the adoption of Schemes which, however *argumentatively* specious, would go *practically* to the inevitable ruin of the Kingdom. The Opposition always connects the emancipation of the Catholics with these Schemes of reformation: Indeed it makes the former only a member of the latter project. The

[1] MS: indered
[2] Burke is referring to the death of Richard, Jr.
[3] See above, p. 64.

Gentlemen who compose that opposition are in my opinion playing the game of their adversaries with all their might; and there is no third party in Ireland, (nor in England neither) to seperate things that are in themselves so distinct, I |mean the admitting people to the benefits of the constitution, and a change in the form of the Constitution itself.

As every one knows, that a great part of the Constitution of the Irish House of Commons was founded about the year 1614, expressly for bringing that House into a state of dependance; and that the new Representative was at that time seated and installed by force and violence,[1] nothing can be more impolitic than for those who wish the House to stand on its present basis, (as for one I most sincerely do) to make it appear to have kept too much the principle of its first institution, and to continue to be as little a virtual, as it is an actual representative of the Commons. It is the *degeneracy* of such an institution *so vicious in its principle*, that is to be wished for. If Men have the real Benefit of a *Sympathetic* Representation, none but those who are heated and intoxicated with Theory will look for any other. This sort of Representation, my dear Sir, must wholly depend not on the force with which it is upheld, but upon the *prudence* of those who have influence upon it. Indeed without some such prudence in the use of Authority, I do not know, at least in the present time, how any power can long continue.

If it be true that both parties are carrying things to extremities in different ways, the object which you and I have in common, that is to say the Union and concord of our Country *on the basis of the actual representative* without risquing those evils which any change in the form of our Legislature must inevitably bring on can never be obtaind. On the part of the Catholics (that is to say, of the body of the people of the Kingdom) it is a terrible alternative, either to submit to the Yoke of declared and insulting Enemies, or to seek a remedy in plunging themselves into the horrours and Crimes of that Jacobinism, which unfortunately is not disagreeable to the principles and inclinations of, I am afraid, the Majority of what we call the Protestants of Ireland. The protestant part of that Kingdom is represented by the Government itself to be, by whole Counties, in nothing less than open Rebellion. I am sure that it is everywhere teeming with dangerous conspiracy.

I beleive it will be found, that tho' the principles of the Catholics and the incessant endeavours of their Clergy have kept them from being generally infected with the Systems of this time, yet wherever their situation brings them nearer into contact with the Jacobin Protestants, they are more or less infected with their doctrines.

See above, p. 125.

It is a matter for melancholly reflexion; but I am fully convinced, that many persons in Ireland would be glad, that the Catholics should become more and more infected with the Jacobin madness in order to furnish new arguments for fortifying them in their monopoly. On any other ground, it is impossible to account for the late language of your Men in power. If Statesmen (let me suppose for Argument) upon the most solid political principles conceive themselves obliged to resist the wishes of the far more numerous, and as things stand, not the worse part of the Community, one would think, they would naturally put their refusal as much as possible upon temporary grounds, and that they would act towards them in the most conciliatory manner, and would talk to them in the most gentle and soothing language. For refusal, in itself, is not a very gracious thing; and, unfortunately, men are very quickly irritated out of their principles. Nothing is more discouraging to the loyalty of any description of men than to represent to them, that their humiliation and subjection make a principal part in the fundamental and invariable policy which regards the conjunction of these two Kingdoms. This is not the way to give them a warm interest in that conjunction.

My poor opinion is, that the closest connexion between Great Britain and Ireland, is essential to the well being, I had almost said, to the very being, of the two Kingdoms. For that purpose I humbly conceive that the whole of the Superiour, and, what I should call, *Imperial* politics, ought to have its residence here; and that Ireland, locally, civilly, and commercially independent, ought politically to look up to Great Britain in all matters of peace and of War, in all those points to be guided by her, and, in a word with her to live and to die. At Bottom Ireland has no other choice, I mean no other rational choice.

I think indeed that Great Britain would be ruined by the seperation of Ireland; but, as there are degrees even in ruin, it would fall the most heavily on Ireland. By such a seperation Ireland would be the most compleatly undone Country in the world; the most wretched, the most distracted and, in the end, the most desolate part of the habitable Globe. Little do many people in Ireland consider, how much of its prosperity has been owing to, and still depends upon, its intimate connexion with this Kingdom but more sensible of this great Truth than perhaps any other man, I have never conceivd, or can conceive, that the connexion is strengthened by making the major part of the Inhabitants of your Country beleive, that their ease, and their satisfaction, and their equalization with the rest of their fellow subjects of

Ireland, are things adverse to the principles of that connexion, or that their Subjection to a small monopolizing Junto, composed of one of the smallest of their own internal factions, is the very condition upon which the harmony of the two Kingdoms essentially depends. I was sorry to hear that this principle or something not unlike it was publickly and fully avowed by persons of great rank and authority in the House of Lords in Ireland.[1]

As to a participation on the part of the Catholics in the privileges and capacities which are with-held without meaning wholly to depreciate their importance, if I had the honour of being an Irish Catholic, I should be content to expect satisfaction upon that Subject with patience until the minds of my adversaries, (few but powerful,) were come to a proper temper: because, if, the Catholics, did enjoy without fraud, chicane, or partiality, some fair portion of those advantages which the Law, even as now the Law is, leaves open to them, and if the Rod were not shaken over them at every turn, their present condition would be tolerable as compared with their former condition, it would be happy, but the most favourable Laws can do very little towards the happiness of a people, when the disposition of the ruling power is adverse to them. Men do not live upon blotted paper. The favourable or the hostile mind of the ruling power is of far more importance to mankind; for Good or evil, than the black Letter of any Statute. Late acts of Parliament, whilst they fixed at least a temporary bar to the hopes and progress of the larger description of the Nation, opened to them certain subordinate objects of equality, but it is impossible that the people should imagine, that any fair measure of advantage is intended to them, when they hear the Laws, by which they were admitted[2] to this limited qualification, publickly reprobated, as excessive and inconsiderate. They must think that there is a hankering after the old penal and persecuting code—Their alarm must be great, when that declaration is made by a person in very high and important Office, in the House of Commons, and as the very first specimen and auspice of a new Government.[3]

All this is very unfortunate. I have the honour of an old acquaintance, and entertain, in common with you, a very high esteem for the few English persons who are concerned in the Government of Ireland; but

---

[1] Burke is probably referring to speeches made on 13 March 1793 in the debate on the Catholic Relief Bill by Fitzgibbon (see above, p. 222) and Charles Agar (1736–1809), Archbishop of Chasel.

[2] MS: admited

[3] Shortly after his arrival in Ireland, Pelham, in the debate of 4 May 1795 on Grattan's Catholic Relief Bill, stated that the Government were opposed to the admission of Catholics to Parliament (*Parliamentary Register of Ireland*, xv, 233–8).

I am not ignorant of the relation, these transitory ministers bear to the more settled Irish part of your Administration. It is a delicate topic, upon which I wish to say but little; tho' my reflexions upon it, are many, and serious. There is a great cry against English influence. I am quite sure that [it] is Irish influence that dreads the English Cabinet.

I cannot, however, avoid adverting to the course which justice has taken of late Years in cases of tumult, and disorder, where the body of the people are of the Catholic persuasion, or where the same or greater disorders have broken out in other descriptions. You must readily recollect many things in the nature of the prosecution, the character of evidence, the temper of the tryal; the mode and circumstance of the Executions; and many other points more capable of giving alarm than any thing of privileges and immunities with-held. Partiality, tho' not very laudable is tolerated in the grant of favours; but where it extends to the Courts of Justice no man can think himself safe.[1]

Great disorders have long prevailed in Ireland. It is not long since, that the Catholics were the suffering party from those disorders. I am sure they were not protected as the Case required. Not one person has been punished on that account; or, that I can find, so much as questioned.[2] Their sufferings became a matter of discussion in Parliament. It produced the most infuriated declaration against them that I have ever read. An enquiry was moved into the facts. The declamation was at least tolerated, if not approved. The enquiry was absolutely rejected.[3] Very soon after we find, that many if not most of that description so covered were represented by the Government which had covered those excesses as in Open rebellion, or conspirant against the State.[4] In that case, what is left for those who are abandoned by Government, but to join with the persons who are capable of injuring them or protecting them, as they oppose or concur in their designs. This will produce a very fatal kind of union amongst the people; but it is an union which an unequal administration of Justice tends necessarily to produce.

If any thing could astonish one at this time, it is the War that the rulers in Ireland think it proper to carry on against the person, whom they call the Pope, and against all his adherents, whenever they think they have the power of manifesting their hostility. Without in the least derrogating from the talents of your Theological politicians, or from the military abilities of your Commanders, (who act on the same principles,) in Ireland, and without derogating from the Zeal of either,

---

[1] The above paragraph has been crossed out in the MS.
[2] The last sentence has been crossed through in the MS.
[3] See above, p. 122.
[4] The last sentence has been crossed through in the MS.

it appears to me that the Protestant Directory of Paris, as Statesmen, and the Protestant Hero Buonaparté, as a General, have done more to destroy the said Pope, and all his adherents in all their capacities,[1] than the Junto in Ireland have been ever able to effect. You must submit your fasces to theirs; and at best be contented to follow, with Songs of gratulation, or invectives, according to your humour, the triumphal Car of those great Conquerors. Had that true Protestant *Hoche*, with an Army not infected with the slightest[2] tincture of Popery, made good his landing in Ireland, he would have saved you from a great deal of the trouble which is taken to keep under a description of your fellow Citizens obnoxious to you from their religion. It would not have a months existence supposing his Success. This is the Alliance, which, under the appearance of hostility, we act as if we wished to promote. All is well, provided we are safe from Popery.

It was not necessary for you, My dear Sir, to explain yourself to *me*, (in justification of your good wishes to your fellow Citizens) concerning your total alienation from the principles of the Catholics. I am more concerned in what we agree, than in what we differ. You know the impossibility of our forming any judgment upon the Opinions, religious, moral, or political, of those who in the largest sense are called Protestants; at least as these Opinions and tenets form a qualification for holding any civil, Judicial, Military, or even ecclesiastical[3] situation. I have no doubt of the Orthodox Opinion of many both of the Clergy, and Laity, professing the established religion in Ireland, and of many even amongst the Dissenters, relative to the great points of the Christian faith: But that Orthodoxy concerns them only as *individuals*. As a *Qualification* for employment, we all know that[4] in Ireland,[5] it is not necessary that they should profess any religion at all. So that the War that we make is upon certain Theological tenets, about which, scholastic disputes[6] are carried *aequó Marte*[7] by controvertists on their side as able and as learned and, perhaps, as well intentioned as those are who fight the Battle on the other part. To them I would leave those controversies—I would turn my mind to what is more within its competence and has been more my study, (tho' for a man of the world I have thought of those things) I mean the moral, civil, and political good of the Countries we belong to, and in which God has appointed

---

[1] See above, pp. 57, 127.   [2] MS: slighest
[3] MS: eclesiastical   [4] MS: that that
[5] Two lines (which are barely legible) have been crossed through in the MS. They may read: 'many even amongst the Dissenters relative to the great points of the Christian faith admit'.
[6] Burke has changed 'scholastic difficulties and controversies' to 'scholastic disputes'.   [7] In even battle.

your station and mine. Let every man be as pious as he pleases; and in the way that He pleases; but it is agreeable neither to piety nor to policy to give exclusively all manner of civil privileges and advantages to a *negative* Religion;—(such is the Protestant without a certain Creed) that is to say, to no religion at all; and at the same time, to deny those priveleges to men whom we who beleive according to the Establishment here, know to agree to an Iota in every one *positive* doctrine, which all of those who profess the religion authoritatively[1] taught in England, hold ourselves according to our faculties bound to beleive. The Catholics of Ireland (as I have said) have the whole of our *positive* religion; our difference is only a Negation of certain Tenets of theirs. If we strip ourselves of *that* part of Catholicity we injure Christianity. If we drive them from that holding without engaging them in some other positive religion, (which you know by our qualifying Laws we do not) what do we better than to hold out to them terrours on the one side and bounties on the other, in favour of that which, for any thing we know to the contrary, may be pure Atheism.

You are well aware that when a Man renounces the Roman Religion, there is no civil inconvenience or incapacity whatsoever which shall hinder him from joining any new or old sect of Dissenters, or of forming a sect of his own invention upon the most Antichristian principles. Let Mr Thomas Paine obtain a pardon (as on change of Ministry not improbable he may),[2] there is nothing to hinder him from starting up a church of his own in the very midst of you; He is a natural born British Subject. His French Citizenship does not disqualify him, at least upon a peace. This protestant Apostle is as much above all suspicion of Popery as the greatest and most Zealous of your Sanhedrim in Ireland can possibly be. On purchasing a qualification (which his friends of the Directory are not so poor as to be unable to effect) he may sit in Parliament, and there is no doubt that there is not one of your tests against Popery, that He will not take as fairly, and as much *ex animo* as the best of your zealot Statesmen. I push this point no further, and only adduce this example (a pretty strong one, and fully in point) to shew what I take to be the madness and folly, of driving men under the existing circumstances from any *positive* religion whatever into the irreligion of the times, and its sure concomitant principles of Anarchy.[3]

When Religion is brought into a question of civil and political

---

[1] MS: authoritavely

[2] Thomas Paine (1737–1809) had been tried for sedition in his absence from England in December 1792, and outlawed. His publication of the *Age of Reason* in 1794–6 had further damaged his reputation among the orthodox.

[3] The copyist has repeated from 'no civil inconvenience' to 'of Anarchy' on a separate sheet which is now crossed through.

arrangement, it must be considered more politically than Theologically; at least by us who are nothing more than meer Laymen. In that light the case of the Catholics of Ireland is peculiarly hard whether they be layity or Clergy. If any of them take part, like the Gentleman you mention, with some of the most accredited Protestants of the Country and with the far the most suspicious body of the Protestants[1] in projects (which cannot be more abhorrent to your nature and disposition than they are to mine) in that Case, however few these Catholic factions who are united with factious Protestants may be, (and very few they are now whatever shortly they may become) on their account the whole Body is considered as of suspected fidelity to the Crown; and as wholly undeserving of its favour. But if on the contrary in those districts of the Kingdom where their numbers are the greatest, where they make in a manner the whole body of the people (as out of Cities in 3/4ths of the Kingdom they do) these Catholicks shew every mark of loyalty and zeal in support of the Government which at best looks on them with an evil eye, then their very loyalty is turned against their claims. They [are] represented as a contented and happy people, and that it is unnecessary to do any thing more in their favour. Thus the factious disposition of a few among the Catholicks and the loyalty of the whole mass are equally assigned as reasons for not putting them on a par with those Protestants, who are asserted by the Government itself which frowns upon Papists, to be in a state of nothing short of actual rebellion, and in a strong disposition to make common cause with the worst foreign Enemy that these Countries have ever had to deal with. What in the End can come of all this?

As to the Irish Catholic Clergy, their condition is likewise most critical, if they endeavour by their influence to keep a dissatisfied layity in quiet, They are in danger of losing the little credit they possess, by being considered as the instruments of a Government adverse to the civil interest of their flock. If they Let things take their course, they will be represented as colluding with sedition or at least tacitly encouraging it.—If they remonstrate against persecution they propagate rebellion. Whilst Government publickly avows hostility to that people as a part of a regular System—there is no road they can take which does not lead to their ruin.

If nothing can be done on your side of the Water, I promise you that nothing will be done here. Whether in reality or only on appearances I cannot positively determine, but you will be left to yourselves by the ruling power here. It is thus ostensibly and above Board; and in

---

[1] The line 'and with the far . . . Protestants' has been crossed out in the MS.

part I believe the disposition is real. As to the people at large in this Country, I am sure they have no disposition to intermeddle in your affairs. They mean you no ill whatever; and they are too ignorant of the state of your affairs to be able to do you any good. Whatever Opinion they have on your Subject is very faint and indistinct; and if there is any thing like a formed Notion even that amounts to no more than a sort of humming, that remains on their ears of the burthen of the old Song about Popery. Poor souls they are to be pitied; who think of nothing but dangers long past by; and but little of the perils that actually surround them.

I have been long, but it is almost a necessary consequence of dictating and[1] that by snatches as a relief from pain gives me the means of expressing my sentiments. They can have little weight as coming from me and I have not power enough of mind or body to bring them out with their natural force, but I do not wish to have it concealed, that I am of the same opinion to my last breath, which I entertained when my faculties were at the best; and I have not held back from men in power in this Kingdom, to whom I have very good wishes any part of my sentiments on this melancholy subject, so long as I had means of access to persons of their consideration. I have the honor to be &c.

To FRENCH LAURENCE—1 *March* 1797

Source: Fitzwilliam MSS (Sheffield).
Addressed: Doctor Laurence M: P | Doctors Commons | London.
Postmarked: BATH   FREE|MR|2|97.
This letter is not in Burke's hand.

My dear friend,

In the hurry in which your business engages you I ought to be thankful to you rather that you write at all, than that you do not write fully.[2] The only thing that I have to blame is, that you have not sent me word whether you have received or not the Pacquets which contained Sir L: Parsons's Letter to me on the state of Ireland.[3] A word would have done this. There is but one Opinion, and there can be but one Opinion, on the manner on which the safety of Ireland was provided for. It was certainly the grossest of all abuses, of Parliamentary confidence,

[1] MS: and and
[2] Laurence had written to Burke on 20 and 24 February (see above, pp. 248–50, 252–3) and on 28 February (MS Bodleian Library, printed *Burke–Laurence Correspondence*, pp. 136–9).
[3] Which Burke had enclosed in his letter of [*post* 20 February] to Laurence; see above, p. 251.

for Government to take the opportunity of the general wish to support them in order to produce, not a silence upon their neglects, or a pretention of them in a general Compliment, but a direct Panegeric upon the vigilance of those, who, to the knowledge of every member who voted, had been sleeping in profound security. You see by Sir L: Parsons's Letter the reasons which influence the votes of several of those who consented on political motives against their Opinion, to subscribe to this shameful Panegeric.[1] I do admit that the members were in a dilema with regard to a general address of support and confidence; and here it was that the Castle was so infinitely culpable in pushing the matter further, for which, in my Opinion, no good political motive could be assigned.

If the Parliament of Ireland has not done its duty in the melancholly state in which the two Kingdoms stand related to one another, in which no degree of subordination is provided for, I am sure the Parliament of England cannot do much Good by an impotent interference, even if it should interfere at all. We must consider our condition. It is not the invasion of Ireland only that is threatened, but of this Kingdom also; and I am by no means apprized, or of Ability to resist this double attack, but this I know that the Partizans of France are not one Jot more likely to defend us from it than those who have hitherto (with whatever incapacity) been the Enemies of that power. You know better than any one what I think of the conduct of Mr Pitt in the whole of the War which has passed, and what is likely to come in the War which he is going rather to suffer than to pursue. I have no partiality at all to him or to his measures against which latter nothing but the accelerated motion of my illness[2] could have hindered me from publishing my Opinion before this time, but between my disapprobation of Mr Pitts measure and my horrour of those, of Mr Fox there is some difference. I have attended very carefully to all Mr Fox's declarations upon occasion of the Treaty Debate.[3] I have not forgot to compare them with the uniform tenour of his Speeches at the time of his Election, and between those two periods.[4] I find in all that tremendous consistency which makes me look on his power as one of the most dreadful evils which could fall upon the Country. I have compared those Speeches with those of the Peers and Commoners that adhered to him in Parliament; I find them all in exact unison with those of their Chief. I have looked at two of the Pamphlets which have been written under his inspection by

---

[1] See above, p. 251.   [2] MS: ilness
[3] Fox spoke at length in the debate of 30 December 1796 on the failure of the Peace Negotiations (*Parliamentary History*, XXXII, 1466–93).
[4] Between the General Election of 1796 and the close of the year.

his closest friends, and for the avowed purposes of his exaltation—I mean those of Mr O'Brien,[1] and Mr Erskine;[2] the one, in fewer and distincter words; the other with more Verbiage, avowing the principles of the French Revolution, condemning the councils of this Nation for our not taking an active part in favour of it, by overawing those Powers who might seem disposed to prevent its march and the consequences of that march. I see them disclaim all Alliance with the Powers of Europe, and, in effect, that placing ourselves in a state of Vassalage to France on pretence of a Communion with them and an alienation from all others, upon the supposed principles of Freedom. I find, as the result of all this Speculation that Mr Fox is to be forced upon the King, (and upon no small part I think the majority) of this Nation, as a person agreeable to the French Republick for his uniform friendship to her, and his disposition to abandon the publick faith given to our Allies and to seperate himself wholly from them. Accordingly, they propose, (as he had before proposed,) to deliver a Country belonging to our Allies, and indeed, a great deal more, which they who can speak no language but the new French, choose to call Belgium,[3] but which neither by that name, nor with any certain bounds or limits, is to be found in any Map. You, who are conversant in Science, know how near the adoption of a new Nomenclator, approaches to the adoption of a new System. These new Appellations have been adopted in order to support the new System of giving to modern France the limits of antient Gaul, the Northern part of which had been antiently called Gallia Belgica. I say nothing of their new Christening the United States of the Netherlands into the Batavian Republick,[4] in order to render it under the false name of a Confederate, and dependant on that Republick which they affect to form on the maxims of the Commonwealth of Rome. As to the rest of Europe they are profoundly silent. This is a Summary of their foreign Politicks—On this principle they propose to make their Peace: But, these Politics are not so foreign as to be supposed to have no influence on the domestic, for Mr Fox proposes and has reiteratedly pledged himself to make some undefined changes in the Constitution, the nature of which he has never discovered; but he has not been equally reserved as to the effects which he states to be to make the influence of what He

---

[1] Dennis O'Bryen (1755–1832) had recently published *Utrum Horum? The Government or the Country*, London, 1796. His aims were to show that the continuation of the war would lead to the ruin of the country but that the best peace which could be expected from the existing ministry would be an even greater calamity than the continuation of the war.   [2] See above, p. 239.

[3] The Austrian Netherlands, described by the revolutionaries as Belgium, were annexed by France in 1795.

[4] After being conquered by France in 1795, the United Provinces were termed the Batavian Republic.

calls the People *every thing*, and that of the Crown—*Nothing*, which I conceive to be the definition of a compleat Democracy, or I do not know what a Democracy is. It is for this grand end, he proposes that kind of Peace which he recommends and is one of the chief advantages which he expects and very rationally expects at some period or other from such an arrangement. A Peace with the Regicides may be made with more honour to himself personally by Mr Fox than by Mr Pitt. He would be consistent with himself first and last. He would dissociate[1] himself from Europe and Join in whatever unequal league and with whatever consequences to the Glory, and safety and the fundamental policy of this Country with the new Powers of France; but the Country must appear in the character of a Renegade confessing its violence and injustice, and must abandon all its maxims. Of the two, I think it very probable that the Regicides of France would prefer Mr Fox as Minister. It is very natural, and indeed, if we once place ourselves in a state of inferiority they will now, and at all times, in effect, name a minister to this Country. There never has been a superiour power who would suffer a dependant Province substantially to name its own Minister. From my part, if I were to count myself amongst the living I should make it one of my chief objections to have Mr Fox Minister, that He is, and that his conduct and opinions have been acceptable to this cruel, imperious, and oppressive Master. However, in reality, neither this declaimer and sophister, nor the declaimer and Sophister his rival, can make any Peace which will not carry shame and ruin on the very front of it. I call them Sophisters and declaimers because they have melted down all the faculties that God has given them into those characters; and in proportion to their perfection in those they sink in every other respect. Neither of them have even the shadow of a statesman. I shall say no more on this melancholly Subject being convinced that the evil is incurable and that the very abilities of the persons concerned tend to render all change impossible from the presumption which they excite in themselves and the admiration which they cause in their blind followers. I see, that unless Mr Pitt takes a much more decided tone, the Minority will every day encrease, and the depreciation of publick Credit will go on more rapidly. He must make up his mind so as to declare whether he means in good earnest and at whatever charge to support the only Ally we have, or he will see his cause, if any cause he has totally ruined, and even that Majority in which he vainly trusts and which he vainly hopes to keep by prevaricating compliances, melt away under his Eyes.

[1] MS: associate

Give my most sincere love to Lord Fitzwilliam and assure him that living or dying I am entirely his. That if I live for any little time longer, I shall live praying for him. If I die, the first among my dying vows, will be for his happiness and prosperity and that God will keep him in the same virtuous Course in which he has hitherto run, but, with better fortune. The state of my health is exactly this. I enjoy much longer intervals of ease, I thank God, than I did some time ago and my Nights are a good deal better, but the radical complaint remains, tho' with less noise in the Symptoms. My head is perfectly releived from that Giddiness which alarmed me more than any other Symptom—I am told by others that my Strength is increased—I am by no means equally sensible of it myself, tho the weakness does not seem to be any thing so considerable as when it was complicated in the Giddiness.

Such is my real state, or such it appears to myself without any exaggeration one way or the other. Mrs Burke's complaints still continue, tho' she holds up much better than could be expected.

Ever Affectionately yours

Bath 1st March
1797
E B

To George Canning—1 *March* 1797

Source: Canning MSS.
Only the signature is in Burke's hand.

George Canning (1770–1827), the future Prime Minister, as a school boy and undergraduate was a strong Whig. He was, however, alarmed by the French Revolution and radical agitation in England, and he entered Parliament at the beginning of 1794 as a strong supporter of Pitt. When he made his maiden speech on 27 January, Burke came across the House and said, 'I lament that the Debate upon this subject is at an end—I want to say *aloud* to tell the House what I think of you—I would get up on purpose to do so—but that I think that would look as if I thought you *wanted* help. It is more dignified to let you *go alone*' (Canning's Journal, quoted in D. Marshall, *The Rise of George Canning*, London, 1938, p. 59). On 11 March 1797 Canning wrote to the Rev. William Leigh, 'Tho it is not true, as you have heard—that I have been writing to Mr Burke my sentiments on the present state of politicks—though he has written his to me.—My letter to him, (to which I owe his answer), was simply five lines, inclosing a packet which had come for him, under my cover, from the Continent.—His answer is in truth, a very valuable piece of writing and full of good sense, and spirit, and truth.—Though I am not sure that it is wholly unmixed with speculations of a more gloomy cast than are justified by the actual situation and prospects of the Country.—I will send you the letter some day or other, (for it is one that I shall most assuredly preserve as long as I live—one of the last letters perhaps of one of the greatest men of his time)—but I cannot part with it just at present' (letter in the Canning MSS).

Dear Sir

I am infinitely obliged to you for the generous partiality which you have shewn in the vigour of your Life and abilities towards my declining person, and my worn out faculties which, at best, were very unequal to the favourable estimate you are pleased to make of them.

The Pamphlets, which you were so good to send to me,[1] are on the Subject of the general Revolution which has been finished in France, and is in the course of its accomplishment every where else. It is a subject which I cannot contemplate, even, at the moment of my probable departure, without a deeper interest than I ought perhaps to take in any human affairs, my Notions may be weak and Heterodox; but the confidence you are pleased to repose in my intentions induces me to expose them to you with more freedom perhaps than prudence. I think I see nothing short of the total and inevitable ruin of the Kingdom, even in the means that seem to be provided for its safety. When I see an Army, amounting, as I hear, in both Kingdoms to 150,000 Men, who, by the very terms and conditions of their Service, cannot strike a blow at an Enemy,[2] I see already a fatal termination of the War. What has an Enemy to fear from a Nation who confines herself to an inert, passive, domestic, defence? By continually threatening, tho' without ever striking a blow, and by the demonstration of the smallest forces, they can ruin you in your resources of Revenue and of Credit. This is a matter of demonstration, if not, of intuitive certainty. To say that this is more agreeable to the People, is to say nothing, when the question is concerning, not their humour, but their existence. When Ministers have failed in other sorts of attempts, this may be an excuse for the failure; but it can be none for having disarmed the Nation under a false appearance of putting it in a military posture. But I will say no more, because, either the hint will suffice, or a long and laboured detail will be necessary, which, tho' I have the matter present to my mind, in my present state, and with a Strong Paroxism of my disorder, tis impossible for me to enter upon; but the whole scheme, of, what is called defence, must be altered before the end of this Session, or nothing but the extraordinary Providence of God, can save us.

I do not altogether like the complexion of Monday's debate.[3] Mr

[1] The pamphlets and Canning's letter to Burke are missing.
[2] See above, p. 118.
[3] On 26 February the Privy Council had issued an order empowering the Bank of England to refuse cash payments. On Monday, 28 February, the House of Commons debated a message from the King informing it that this step had been taken. During the debate Sheridan argued that specie should not be exported for the use of the Emperor. The Order in Council suspending cash payments was confirmed by 37 Geo. III, c. 45, continued by 37 Geo. III, c. 91 and 38 Geo. III, c. 1.

Pitt must much more distinctly avow his cause, his principles, and his Allies, than He did in that Debate, or his Enemies will every day gain some new advantage over him; and all the Shabby part of his friends, which always form a very large part of those who belong to the Men in Power, will, by degrees, desert him. Some much more distinctive lines, than hitherto have been traced, must be drawn between him and his Adversaries, else he will find the publick favour towards him grow cooler every day untill there is a total indifference in whose hands Ministry shall be placed: For at the very hour in which I write, I have reason to be quite sure, that He owes the adherence of many People in Parliament and of more out of it [more] to a dread of certain chiefs of the Opposition, than to any zeal in his favour. As to the present flurry about publick Credit, there is no cause, I think, for alarm, unless the means that are taken to support it, should not undermine its foundations. There is the same Quantity of Gold and Silver in the Country, (or nearly the same quantity) that there was a month ago. The National income is the same, and the Stock of individuals, whether in Land or Goods, is not impaired. Credit has long been overstrained, a cause and consequence of National prosperity, and National exertion. If the last is a fruitless exertion, as I think it is, any solid and permanent remedy will be utterly impracticable. But, for the present, if the general interest is appealed to in support of Credit, Credit will be supported, and Cash will, by degrees, reappear, from the necessity of its reappearance but if a low Paper Currency is once admitted, the Market will be overloaded, Gold and silver will be more and more withheld and if Guinea Notes, or any thing resembling them, are once put into Currency, you will never see a Guinea; whereas if you keep the Currency where it is and support it with vigour, necessity will draw out the Gold and silver. Excuse, I beg you, these crude ideas. No man wishes more than I do, that all my ideas should be found vain and frivolous upon experience. Your usual goodness will induce you to pardon my freedom. Be assured my dear Sir, That no Man has a higher value than I have for your virtues and talents, or is more desirous of keeping a place in your kind estimation. I have the honour to be with the highest respect and regard,
Dear Sir,
                    Your most faithful
                        and obliged humble Servant
Bath   EDM BURKE
    1st March 97

P.S: You will excuse my using the hand of a confidential friend,[1] as I have not been able for a long time to do any thing more than dictate.

----

[1] The letter is in the hand of Nagle.

Almost thirty years later, in the debate on the Bank Charter and Promissory Notes Acts in February 1826, Canning quoted Burke's opinions and referred to this letter: 'I came, Sir, into parliament, two years before that great man retired from public life. I had the good fortune to enjoy, during the short remainder of his natural life, a small portion of his private friendship. A letter—the only letter which I ever received from him—and which I have treasured up as a memorial of departed genius, was on this very subject. It was written at Bath, on that bed of sickness from which he never afterwards rose. After discussing the arguments for and against the measure of the Bank restriction, the letter concluded with this remarkable sentence—"Tell Mr Pitt, that if he consents to the issue of one-pound notes, he will never see a guinea again" (hear, hear!). Mr Burke, like most prophets, was not believed at the time of uttering his predictions. One-pound notes were issued in abundance; they expelled, as had been foretold, guineas from circulation...' (*Parliamentary History*, 2nd series, XIV, 331).

To FRENCH LAURENCE—5 *March* 1797

Source: MS Osborn Collection. Printed *Burke–Laurence Correspondence*,
pp. 141–5.
This letter is not in Burke's hand.

My dear Laurence

I am extreamly pleased that under whatever disadvantages of time and preparation you have made your debut;[1] I am pleased likewise with the short reply you made, and it was sufficient to the miserable buffoonery which was the only answer that could be made to you.[2] I shall send you as a Postscript to this, a Copy of what Mr Windham has written to Mr Nagle on occasion of that commencement. You do not tell me how you voted on the Irish question. Since you could not be heard 'till 3 oClock, I am glad you did not attempt to speak, tho' I much

---

[1] Laurence made his maiden speech on 1 March against Fox's Motion for a Committee to Inquire into the Causes of the Order of Council respecting the Stoppage of Cash Payments at the Bank. Windham described it: 'Dr Laurence's first performance, you may tell Mr Burke succeeded perfectly well. He keeled a little in the launching, which gave me some minutes anxiety. But he soon righted, when he touched the water, and shewed, as he is, a grand first rate' (letter quoted *Burke–Laurence Correspondence*, p. xxvi). According to the editor of the *Burke–Laurence Correspondence* this passage is from a letter to Sir Edmund Nagle (1757–1830). Although the nautical metaphor makes this a possibility, it is more likely that the recipient was Edward James Nagle.

[2] Laurence had expressed regret at the attribution of corrupt motives to ministers, pointing out that 'If so gross a practice of vilifying the integrity and dignity of the House were Introduced and permitted, it would ultimately tend to annihilate them'. When he sat down John Courtenay (1738–1816), M.P. for Appleby, compared him 'to Tilburina in the Critic, when she exclaims, "Dear Mr Puff, spare my feelings!"'. He presumed 'the innate modesty of the doctor must have been greatly strengthened and improved in Doctors' commons in the nice examination of *crim-con.* transactions, and in the elucidations of subjects of divorce and separation *à mensa et thoro*'. Courtenay was nearly coughed down and Laurence in reply declared 'his feelings arose from the considerations of the present situation of his country' (*The Times*, 2 March; *Parliamentary History*, XXXII, 1557–61).

approve the line you proposed to take. The invasion of Ireland, as an unforseen event could not be better provided for, but it was an event that ought not to have been unforseen—Herein is placed the true *gist* of the question. As to the armed neutrality[1] who were coquetting with you some time since, 'tis, I conceive, composed principally of the Persons of which it was formed in the last Parliament. They are a Body without Sense and without principle, and are and can be true to nothing. They are utterly unfit to form that third Party of your Constituent and your Country, which you hinted at with so much propriety.[2] If any of them speak a word to you again upon any publick business, you ought to answer him with all the coldness and reserve that is possible. I look upon Tiers parties to be in themselves things very critical, sometimes very necessary, but that cannot, and perhaps ought not, to endure long. That division of party, which I loved and trusted[3] did for some time form that tertium quid, but, thro' the error of the *excellent* person who then led them, they were or rather He was, not neutral, but perplexed and inconsistent. When it joined Ministry, it neither could or ought to preserve its neutrality, but it ought to preserve its credit and coherence and to have given a new biass to the body to which it was aggregated. How that came to fail we all know but too well. I am far from being sure that time and events may not make up a new party but it can never be from altogether the same elements. I am exceedingly mortified at this scheme of issuing small Paper.[4] Still more so, at the repeal, or temporary suspension, which will lead to more suspensions, of two most salutary acts of Parliament made to prevent the abuse of private credit,[5] which abuse so strongly militates with the use of publick Credit, and perhaps, now at this time more than ever. It prevents all possible operation of the certain remedy which the evil

[1] Early in March it was reported that an attempt was being made to form a third party in the House of Commons which would 'act independant of either Mr Pitt or Mr Fox'. Sir John Sinclair, 1st Baronet (1754–1835), M.P. for Petersfield, and John Pollexfen Bastard (1756–1816), M.P. for Devon, were amongst its leaders and it issued 'a card' declaring that its aims were retrenchment and peace (*The Times*, 11, 13 March; the *Oracle*, 13 March; *London Chronicle*, 9–11 March). In his letter of 3 March Laurence had informed Burke that 'the whole sixteen of the armed neutrality voted against Mr Pitt' (MS Bodleian Library; printed *Burke–Laurence Correspondence*, pp. 140–1).

[2] In his speech Laurence had emphasized that it was undesirable when selecting a committee to follow a practice which 'would avowedly divide the House into two parties under two adverse chiefs'. He himself 'would never...repose a blind confidence; but he would repose a general confidence...' (*Parliamentary History*, XXXII, 1560).

[3] The Portland Whigs. For the Whig party during the period 1792–4 see F. O'Gorman, *The Whig Party and the French Revolution*, London, 1967.

[4] It had been suggested that the bank should issue notes of £2 and £3.

[5] An act to suspend for a limited time, the operation of two acts of the fifteenth and seventeenth years of his present Majesty for restraining the negotiation of promissory notes and inland bills of exchange under a limited sum (37 Geo. III, c. 32), was introduced on 2 March and received the Royal Assent on 10 March.

would have furnished to itself—Had I been in Parliament and in my strength I should most certainly have spoke and voted against these, I apprehend, fatal measures. All the circumstances of Sir John Jarvis's affair[1] render it a very brilliant piece of service, but still the Naval power of the common Enemy is not materially impaired. The French armament from Holland is a serious matter,[2] if we have no fleet in the Downs as I suspect we have not. At any rate it is sufficient to prove the utter insufficiency of a passive defence whether by Sea or Land for the protection of these Countries, or for sustaining their Credit. As I have now some moments of ease, tho' more reduced in my flesh than ever, and that I fall away every day, I have a mind to anticipate in part, the work I was preparing, and in a Letter to you or to some other friend, if you should think it not adviseable to address it to you, I might give rather results, and conclusions, than formal detailed discussions against the plans of Armament which can end in nothing but our ruin.[3] All these false and ill-understood[4] precautions against danger serve only to augment the public alarm to waste the resources of the Country, and to destroy the vital principles of publick Credit. How comes it, that we have no established course of intelligence, which I am sure, easily might have been had, in Holland; but I strongly suspect that amongst all our expenditures very little is laid out in this way. To say a word of myself, tho' falling away to a shadow, I find my little Strength rather increased, than impaired, and my Nights thank God are unusually good—Not having had a bad one for these last 4 past, and the two last quite as good as in my best health. I am taken once in about seven or eight days with a vomiting, which gives me great temporary relief, but contributes at the same time to emaciate me more than any thing else even more than the purging, which is the only means by which I can be kept open.—For I dont know what the medium is, in this respect. God bless you. Remember me affectionately to Lord FitzWilliam, and with all gratitude. Mrs Burke is better of the Rash which had broken out upon her and she does not seem thank God, to be in other respects, worse. I am ever

Most affectionately Yours

Ed B

Bath

5 March 97

[1] Admiral Jervis (see above, p. 103) had defeated the Spanish Fleet off Cape St Vincent on 14 February.
[2] The Dutch Fleet was lying in the Texel, watched by Admiral Adam Duncan (1731-1804), later (30 October 1797) 1st Viscount Duncan.
[3] See the next letter.
[4] MS: ilunderstood

To FRENCH LAURENCE—[*circa* 5 *March* 1797]

Source: Walker's Hibernian Magazine (August 1803), pp. 490–1.
There is an incomplete copy of this letter in the Osborn Collection. In the
previous letter Burke speaks of preparing a work on the insufficiency of a
passive defence. In this letter to Laurence he also mentions his wish to
undertake such a work. *Walker's Hibernian Magazine* supplies a heading:
'Mr Burke's Letter to Dr Lawrence. Written from Bath in the Spring of
1797', and an introductory paragraph states that this letter was quoted by
Laurence in the House of Commons on 23 June 1803. Laurence spoke on the
second reading of the Army of Reserve Bill concluding his speech 'with reading a letter, partly written and partly dictated, by the late Mr Burke in
his last moments. This letter severely censured the system of raising a Supplementary Militia for defensive, instead of a Standing Army, for offensive
operations' (*The Times*, 24 June 1803).

My dear Sir,

The very first relaxation of my complaint, which gave me leisure and
disposition to attend to what is going on, has filled my mind with many
uneasy sensations and many unpleasant reflections. The few who have
protracted life to the extreme limits of our short period, have been
condemned to see extraordinary things—new systems of policy—new
opinions—new principles—and not only new men, but what might
appear a new species of men. I believe that they who lived forty years
ago (if the intermediate space of time were expunged from their memory) could hardly credit their senses, when they heard from the highest
authority, that an army of 200,000 men was kept up in this island?
that in the neighbouring island there were at least fourscore thousand
more:[1] but when he should hear of this army, which has not its parallel,
what must be his astonishment to hear, that it was kept up for the mere
purpose of an inert and passive defence; that, in its far greater part, it
was disabled, by its constitution and very essence, from defending us
against an enemy by any one preventive stroke, or any operation of
active hostility?—What must his reflections be, on hearing that a fleet
of 500 men of war,[2] the best appointed, and to the full as ably commanded, as this country ever had upon the sea, was for the greater part
employed in acting upon the same system of unenterprising defence?
What must his sentiments be, who remembers the former energy of
England, when he is given to understand, that these two islands, with
their extensive and every where vulnerable sea-coast, should be con-

[1] In the debate on 3 March on Whitbread's motion (see above, p. 249) Dundas had
declared that there were upwards of 200,000 men under arms for the defence of Great
Britain and Ireland (*Parliamentary History*, XXXIII, 16). See also above, p. 119.
[2] The forces in Ireland, regulars, fencibles and militia, in 1797–8 amounted to about
50,000, together with a yeomanry force, the formation of which had been authorized in
1796, which by 1798 was 37,500 strong (*Journals of the Irish House of Commons*, XVII,
pp. lxxxvi, xciv, cccliii).
[3] In his speech Dundas referred to 'fifty sail of the line'.

sidered as a garrison sea-town?—What would he think if the garrison of so strange a fortress should be such as never to make a sally; and that, contrary to all that has been hitherto seen in war, an infinitely inferior army may with safety besiege this garrison, and, without hazarding the life of a man, ruin the garrison and the place, merely by the menaces and false appearances of an attack? What must his surprise be on finding, that with the increases of trade, and balances unknown before, and with less outgoing than at any former time, the public credit should labour, even to the edge of a bankruptcy; and that the confidence of the people in the security of their property should lessen in proportion as all apparent means of their safety are augmented? The last part of this dreadful paradox is to be solved but by one way; and that is by an obscure, undefined sense which the people entertain, that the apparent means of their safety are not real, nor well understood, and that they confide in their government more from their opinion that some sort of government should be supported, than from a conviction that the measures taken by the existing government for the public safety are rational or well adapted to their end. Had it pleased God to continue to me even the late weak remains of my strength, I purposed to make this the subject of a letter,[1] which I intended to address to a brother member of your's,[2] upon the present state of affairs; but as I may be never able to finish it, I regard this matter of defence as so much the more important of all considerations at this moment, that it supersedes all concern of my bodily and mental weakness, and urges me, by an impulse I cannot resist, to spend at least my last breath in laying before you some part of the anxious thoughts with which I have been oppressed, and which more than any bodily distemper, have sunk me to the condition in which you know I am. I have no hand to write, but I am able to dictate from the bed on which I pass my nights and days.

What I say may have no weight; but it is possible that it may tend to put other men of more ability, and who are in a situation where their abilities may be more useful, into a train of thinking. What I dictate may not be pleasing either to the great or to the multitude; but looking back on my past public life, though not without many faults and errors, I have never made many sacrifices to the favour of the great, or to the humour of the people. I never remember more than two instances in which I have given way to popularity;[3] and those two are the things

[1] The passage of about forty lines beginning 'The few...' until this point is printed (with variations) in the 'Third Letter on a Regicide Peace' (1st Rivington edition, pp. 114–16). [2] Not identified.

[3] Burke may be referring to his support of John Wilkes during the Middlesex election dispute (see vol. II) and to his support of the petitioning movement in 1780 (see vol. IV, 199–200).

of which, in the whole course of my life, now at the end of it, I have the most reason to repent. Such has been the habit of my public life, even when individual favour and popular countenance might be plausibly presented to me as the means of doing my duty the more effectually. But now, alas! of what value to me are all those helps or all those impediments. When the damp chill sweat of death already begins to glaze our visage, of what moment is it to us whether the vain breath of man blows hot or cold upon it? But our duties to men are not extinguished with our regard to their opinions.

A country, which has been dear to us from our birth, ought to be dear to us, as from our entrance, so to our final exit from the stage upon which we have been appointed to act; and in the career of the duties which must in part be enjoyments of our new existence, how can we better start, and from what more proper post, than the performance of those duties which have made occupations of the first part of the course allotted to us?[1]

French Laurence *to* Edmund Burke—*7 March* 1797

Source: MS Bodleian Library. Printed *Burke–Laurence Correspondence,*
pp. 145–8.
Addressed: The Rt Honble E. Burke | Bath.
Franked: Free | F Laurence | London March ⟨the⟩ seventh, 1797.
MS torn.

March 7th, 1797

My dear Sir

I perfectly agree with you as to the difficulty of making or of keeping together a third party. I agree also as to the persons, of whom only a third party is now to be made.[2] Strictly speaking, a third party is not what I should wish to see formed. My only view would be to hold out to Ministers and to opposition, that there are men who would support the Minister stoutly, if he would do his duty, or transfer that support to opposition, if they would be candidates for power on fair terms consistently with the honour and interests of their country. Such a third party as I would make, if I could, would be to be dissolved, the very moment that they had made themselves seen, heard, and felt. But there is not the most remote chance of such a party. Ten good men and true would be sufficient, but half the number cannot be found. There is a little troop collecting, perhaps thirty, forty, or fifty, of a very different description most mischievously weak. They are afraid of Fox and his friends: they wish to save Mr Pitt, and they are now angry with him

[1] This letter seems never to have been finished. Windham inquires about its progress on 25 April; see below, p. 312. [2] See above, p. 271.

because they think him obstinate in wanting really to continue the war and refusing to negotiate (as they say) with an Emissary of the French now here.[1] I have had a conversation with one of them. They are to have a meeting, and want me to attend it, and to give up my motion of course. The latter I decidedly refused to do; as to the former I neither agreed, or dissented.

The repeal of the two bills restraining the issue of small notes by Tradesmen[2] did not please me; but it passed without notice. I really did not know the fact that there was such a bill in the house, till I heard it read (short of course) a third time, and the ayes in the common form declared to have it.

Adey[3] wants to have bank-notes declared a legal tender, as many Jacobins demand gold and threaten to bring actions. The whole situation at present is full of difficulties; and I fear that though it is really in its nature and cause no more than temporary, the general tenor of the measures taken and to be taken looks to something like permanency, since they are such as will work themselves into the general system of our public and private credit too extensively to be again easily eradicated. But I really have not had leisure to think over the nature, magnitude and bearing both of the evil and the proper remedy for it, so accurately as I could wish. Will you favour me with your general view of it, as the great opportunity of talking upon it is yet to come.

What you intimate in your last of the honour, which you intend me, would be most dear to me, but I do not take too much to urge you to exertions which may affect your health.

Remember me to Mrs Burke. I hope her rash will be beneficial to her general health. It is not an infrequent consequence.

> I have the honour to be
> My dear Sir
> > Ever most gratefully and affectionately,
> > FRENCH LAURENCE.

P.S. I write in great haste, having stolen out of the Admiralty Court for that purpose while the evidence I am to speak upon is reading. The French papers say that the greatest efforts are making at Vienna to relieve Italy. *Vienna alone,* though so many of the nobility have to lament relations killed or taken ⟨in the⟩ late corps of volunteers, raises a new corps of 6000 Men. Yet the armed Neutrality here ⟨say⟩ we must not be too nice about *faith and honour* and such old notions.

---

[1] There is no other evidence the French Government had dispatched an emissary to London at this time.
[2] See above, p. 271.   [3] See above, p. 104.

To SIR LAWRENCE PARSONS—8 *March* 1797

Source: Rosse MSS.
Addressed: Sir Laurence Parsons Bt | M:P. | Dublin.
Postmarked: BATH MR|12|97.
Only the signature is in Burke's hand. There is a copy of this letter in the Osborn Collection.

On 31 January Sir Lawrence Parsons, 5th Baronet (1758–1841), later (1807) 2nd Earl of Rosse, an able and independent-minded Irish M.P. who was Colonel of the King's County Militia, wrote a long and powerful letter to Burke on 'Ireland's deficiency in military force' which had been revealed by the threat of a French landing in Munster (see above, pp. 221–2). Though theoretically there were 40,000 troops in the country, when the sick and untrained and the forces stationed in Ulster were deducted, only 16,000 men could be mustered for the defence of the south. Moreover the forces in Ireland were badly equipped, their artillery and medical services being seriously inadequate. Parsons advocated the adoption of a 'grand scale of defence' which would have involved raising more men and building extensive fortifications. He also was in favour of Catholic emancipation, both as 'a fair reward for approved loyalty' and as facilitating 'the great levies which the times require'. He urged Burke 'day after day to represent our danger until measures are taken to countervail it'. He also urged in the Irish House of Commons on 21 and 24 February that additional forces should be raised for the defence of Ireland (MS Osborn Collection; *Dublin Evening Post*, 23, 28 February).

Dear Sir

You cannot overrate my regard for Ireland, As it is the Country to which I am bound by my earliest instincts, and as it is a part, which I cannot seperate, even in thought, of this great Empire, to the head of which I am bound by my maturest habits, by duty and by gratitude: But you may easily overrate, (as you do,) my ability to serve it. I am sunk deep in age and still more sunk in Affliction and infirmity. I was brought to this place,[1] with very little hopes of recovery, as my last resource, and here I have lain a long time in a state of utter inability for any exertion of mind or body, having been reduced nearly to the last extremity. It was in that condition, and in this place, that I received the honour of your Letter,[2] full, as I might justly expect of public spirited anxiety for your Country and of many just views of what is proper in its present situation. I do not find any inconsistency, that is a moral or political inconsistency, between your publick Votes and your private sentiments.[3] Without condemning a different proceeding in

[1] Bath.
[2] According to the editor of the *Burke–Laurence Correspondence* (p. 129) Burke received Parsons's letter on 9 February.
[3] Parsons had apologized to Burke for the disparity between the tone of frank alarm in his letter and the rather different tone of his public utterances. You will not,

other Gentlemen, I know nothing more consistent with the character of a man of honour and virtue than to conceal the faults and errors of a Government, which circumstances oblige him to support from fear of worse evils and a full exposure of the same neglects and mismanagements in an amicable manner to those in whose power it is to correct them, and who having omitted[1] the performance of their duty in prevention, are but the more bound to the duty of furnishing a remedy. However, you have totally mistaken in your application to me, tho' I am infinitely sensible of the honour you have done me by that Application. When I was in a much better state of health, than I have long since enjoyed, I never had any communication whatsoever, with the men in power, except one Gentleman in Office,[2] who sometimes from compassion visits me, as an old and infirm friend, but with whom I do not talk on public business. His Majesty's principal Minister I have not so much as seen, to the best of my recollection, for nearly 3 years. All I can do is to give you merely a private Opinion, and you have every title, that it should be a fair one. I do not enter into the circumstances of the measures which have been taken for the defence of either kingdom. I am afraid that the descent of the Enemy in Ireland was not credited, and therefore could not be provided for. A Naval defence must be in its nature in the highest degree uncertain; but if it were better, than it is, it must be perfectly ruinous, to keep the most formidable Navy that Great Britain ever possessed, meerly as a Coast guard. It is wholly to mistake the nature and purpose of a Naval force.—It is also my poor opinion, but formed upon an attentive consideration of the subject, begun several years ago upon something of a similar occasion,[3] that it is impossible to secure the Coast of these kingdoms particularly the South west Coast of Ireland by any fortifications. That the very attempt would be mischievous, and possibly ruinous, if extended beyond a few Naval Stations. I am in the same errour, if it be an errour, with regard to all the other modes of passive defence, such as old and new Militias, for home service. Yeomen Cavalry, and Infantry, Volonteers &ca except in such small numbers as may be subservient to a vigilant Police: For by keeping up in the two Kingdoms the expence of an Army of *200,000* Men,[4] who, by the very terms of their service, cannot strike a blow at an enemy except at his pleasure—That Enemy may compleatly ruin our finances and destroy our public Credit, even by the menaces of his

he said, '. . . impute to me inconsistency if you shoud find in the Newspapers my language in Parliament different from what it is here; for there prudence must suppress, nay even deny our infirmities'.
[1] MS: omited   [2] Windham.
[3] Probably when a Franco–Spanish invasion was threatened in 1779.
[4] See above, pp. 119, 273.

hostility, without putting to the risk, or expence of a single hostile step. I wish we may not already have experienced the ill effects of this policy, so contrary to all the rules and principles hitherto observed in War. I am sure it is directly contrary to the Policy and proceeding of this Country in any period of its former Wars, where our best defence has been ever found in the offensive measures we have pursued against our Enemies. But now it has happened, that our apprehensions are increased as might have been expected in the exact proportion to the magnitude of the mistaken provision that is made for our safety. I am very well aware that the seed of this mistaken policy has not been sown at this time, but at this time it has been watered and manured to the growth in which we see it. Can that Nation expect even the shadow of an honourable and advantageous peace who is resolved not to strike one preventive blow at an Enemy, and which, with the burthen of an Army and a Navy, which well managed and jointly employed, might go a great way in giving Laws to the world, employs the Navy, meerly as an outwork, and the Army, meerly as a Garrison to cover the most extensive Coast, taking the two Islands together, which the same measurement of Land affords upon the habitable Globe. Nothing gives me greater grief than that I have not strength enough to protest at large and in the most publick manner against putting these Islands into a state of Siege, whilst almost all Europe is conquered before our Eyes, and every Port with which we can maintain a Commercial intercourse with the world, has fallen or is falling into the hands of those Enemies, whose own territory we consider as sacred.

I beg pardon for the freedom which your liberality of sentiment has encouraged me to take with you. I am an old Man, and have old Notions; and if you reject my Opinions, you will be so good at least, as to pardon my weakness. I have the honour to be, with the highest respect and regard

Dear Sir

Your most faithful humble

Servant

Bath 8th March   EDM BURKE

1797

P.S. You will be so good as to excuse my making use of another hand,[1] for tho' I am now able to dictate I have been long since unable to write.

Burke had sent Parsons's letter to Laurence (see above, p. 251), who forwarded it to Fitzwilliam, explaining it would be 'a breach of trust to use it, or to put it in the way of being used for the purposes of Opposition; especially after the

[1] The letter is in the hand of Nagle.

concluding explanation of Sir Lawrence himself, that prudence compells him to talk a different language in Parliament'. Laurence asked Fitzwilliam to return the letter 'as soon as may be convenient, in three covers. Burke put up one of the sheets in a single sheet of letter-paper and I had to pay between two and three shillings. If I had no privilege, it would have cost me a shilling. It is a trifling instance, but I think there is a sort of captious penalty in this regulation which is very much in the character of our present Ministry, whom it is a pain to feel yourself under a political and moral necessity of supporting with all their faults' (letter of 22 February, MS at Northampton, Box 51). Laurence seems to be complaining about the regulations laid down by the Act for further regulating the sending and receiving Letters free from the Duty of Postage (35 Geo. III, c. 53). This Act limited the number of letters which a member of Parliament was entitled to receive free of postage to not more than fifteen a day.

FRENCH LAURENCE *to* EDMUND BURKE—14 *March* 1797

Source: MS Bodleian Library. Printed *Burke–Laurence Correspondence*,
pp. 148–51.
Addressed: The Rt Honble E. Burke | Bath.
Franked: Free | F Laurence | London March the fourteenth.
Postmarked: FREE|MR|14|97.

March the 14th, 1797

My dear Sir

It is several days since I have directly heard from you, but thank God, Adey communicated to me the substance of a very comfortable letter from our dear Mrs Burke.[1] Lord F. who will remain here at least a week longer, is very anxious about you from time to time; and I will thank Nagle, especially for this week or so, to be kind enough to write to me a little more regularly. I wish you would scold Woodford for me— He promised me to write, but not a syllable yet have I received from him.

Last night I was dragged up again in debate;[2] at least I could not sit silent. It was on a motion of Mr Harrison for an enquiry into our Offices for the purpose of retrenchment. Mr Pitt moved the previous question, but—agreeing to instruct his Committee appointed to examine the finances, to enquire also into possible retrenchments of Offices. I did not intend to have Spoken, being very much dissatisfied with the shabby principle on both sides. But you were the Helen of the war. Fox quoted half a dozen of your works in different ways.[3] It was late and his speech

[1] The letter is missing.
[2] In the debate on Mr Harrison's Motion for the Reduction of Useless Places, Sinecure Offices, &c. John Harrison (1738–1811) was M.P. for Thetford.
[3] Pitt first brought Burke into the debate, by referring to his plan for Economical Reform (presented to the House of Commons in 1780). Sheridan quoted a passage from the *Letters on a Regicide Peace*, and Windham praised Burke, before Fox rose.

produced a long and warm squabble between him, Rose,[1] and Canning. These things were unfavourable but I resolved to notice the more prominent quotations from you.

I took the opportunity of premising my opinions very shortly—I said that I should vote for the previous question, but not the intended instruction which I thought equally objectionable with the motion. I declared against any of these enquiries, which begged the question of something generally wrong in the whole system, raised an expectation of some great relief to the people and then left [them] sore with disappointment, as any serious relief from such paltry savings is impossible. Real abuses I would ever assist in reforming; but the evil must be specifically pointed out, its nature shewn, and the safety, propriety, and expediency of the remedy made clear to my judgement.

I considered your œconomical Reform as the very reverse of Mr Harrison's proposition. It was on a principle of removing influence, not making little savings, it was undertaken in truth to prevent such crude proceedings; which had been started in another House;[2] you took a view of the whole system; gave your reasons for what you condemned and what you spared, and in your own language you heaved the lead every inch of way that you made. Let them proceed now in the same manner, if any new abuses had risen since your bill.

Mr Fox said the war had been supported by corruption and the influence of the Crown. I reminded him of the Associations signed by himself at the end of 1792;[3] his humble explanation of his own conduct in his printed letter to the Westminster Electors,[4] and the failure of the Whig club in procuring addresses for peace; asking him as to each of these instances, if the public opinion proceeded from the influence of the Crown. I then went to his false quotation of your two letters, as sanctioning the opinion that the minority in the late Parliament spoke the sense of the nation.[5] I told him you stated that as conversation, but the whole member on that subject ended with a declaration that you thought otherwise.

[1] George Rose (1744–1818), Secretary to the Treasury.
[2] Burke's motion of 1780 was announced in the Commons in December 1779 at nearly the same time as Lord Shelburne [William Petty, 2nd Earl of Shelburne, later (1784) 1st Marquess of Lansdowne] made a similar announcement in the Lords.
[3] Burke in 'Observations on the Conduct of the Minority' comments severely on Fox's reasons for advising his supporters in December 1792 to join the associations which had been formed to check the circulation of seditious writings (see *Works*, Bohn, III, 478–80; Little, Brown, v, 18–21).
[4] *A letter from...Charles James Fox to the worthy and independent Electors of the City and Liberty of Westminster* (1793).
[5] In the debate Fox 'appealed to the authority of Mr Burke, in that passage of his "Letters on a Regicide Peace" where he intimates a suspicion, that the minority in the House of Commons express the sense of the majority of the country' (*Parliamentary History*, XXXIII, 102; Burke's *Works*, Bohn, v, 188; Little, Brown, v, 282).

He had quoted against Windham a passage from one of your early works of men leaving their party and their principles, on specious motives and sinking into insignificancy.[1] I enquired, if in that passage he found that when two sets of men who had formed one party, thought differently, on such subjects as the character of the French Revolution, the French faction here, and the justice of a war with France (all put at length and rhetorically) they ought to continue together? Whether he any where found in your writings that such men acting together, were a *party* at all? Whether he did not find that you called them under such circumstances a faction? Each set of men I said ought in such cases to follow their principles, and if they acted from principle, neither had a right to accuse the other of desertion, but both were to be judged by their consciences, their god, their country the world and posterity. Fox was very civil to me; he came up to me and assured me that he thought your writings the best repository of principles, and he accordingly read them all with diligence.—A member near me (I did not know him) was very complimentary to me. Lord Hawkesbury[2] came up and said he quite agreed with me, as Anstruther[3] also said.— Windham told me he was at one time anxious. When I stated the question before them they expected a formal and long argument, but as I left it in three or four sentences they then attended very well.— Pitt was very gracious to me in the Lobby.

Yours ever most gratefully and affectionately
F. LAURENCE

P.S. I have drawn a long State Paper[4] of which I will inform you perhaps tomorrow.

To EARL FITZWILLIAM—15 *March* 1797

Source: Fitzwilliam MSS (Sheffield).
Endorsed (by Fitzwilliam): Burke | march 16.97.
Only the signature is in Burke's hand.

My dearest Lord

Your kind concern in me will add much to the satisfaction of whatever measure of recovery it may please Providence to allot to me, which cannot after what I have gone thro' and at my time of Life be any thing

---

[1] Presumably the passage in *Thoughts on the Cause of the Present Discontents* (*Works*, Bohn, I, 326–7; Little, Brown, I, 462–3).
[2] See above, p. 186.
[3] John Anstruther (1753–1811), later (1798) 1st Baronet; one of the Managers of the Hastings Impeachment.
[4] See below, p. 291.

considerable, or, of any long duration. If, what is most likely, the same Providence should chuse to call me away, your kind and persevering regards will be amongst my best consolations. Since you are desirous of knowing particulars about me, I am to tell you that if compared with the degree of apparent strength, which I had when I came hither, I am far worse than I was at my arrival. If I compare it with what I was at some of the intermediate times, I am much better; but I am still in an extream state of emaciation, and so feeble, that I cannot walk above a few steps without assistance; so, that if it were in my desire, it is not in my power to quit this place. I cannot say that I am much indebted to the use of the Bath Water, of which I have drank but little, and irregularly. What benefit I have had has arisen from other methods prescribed to me by my Physician Doctor Parry.[1] This is the true state of my case.

The condition of publick Affairs is far from conducing to my comfort. I shall say nothing of England, which by the efforts of two factions discordant in their affections and interests, but agreeing in their false principles, is going its own way to destruction. Ireland is not only emulous of these proceedings, but goes far beyond them. The Castle has used no one politic means of composing the minds or gaining the affections of the people. The Opposition, your Lordships friends and let me add, my friends, have gone the full length of Jacobinism, and are doing all they can to pull up the land-marks of private property and public safety, and to disunite the two Kingdoms;[2] and that upon the falsest grounds both of fact and principle, which, I might easily prove, if I had heart or strength for such a task. I confess whilst I blame the conduct of the minority in that Kingdom I know how to excuse it. They, who provoke the passions of Men beyond the limits of human prudence, are primarily and much the most heavily responsible for all the excesses into which men are led by these passions. But the effect on the publick is the same, whoever may be culpable. I am extreamly glad that your Lordship has resolved on the defence of those persons who residing in the seats of their ancestors, and living in the Country in which they are born, possess Property in Ireland.[3] I cannot enter into

[1] See above, p. 234.
[2] On 28 February Grattan supported a motion to the effect that 'a tax of 2s. in the pound should be levied on all rents belonging to persons who shall be absent from this country more than 6 months in each year, persons holding naval or military situations abroad being excepted' (*Dublin Evening Post*, 2, 4 March; *The Times*, 10 March). In the debate on 22 February an absentee tax of four shillings in the pound was mentioned (*Dublin Evening Post*, 25 February). When a similar tax had been proposed in 1773 Burke had strongly opposed it (see vol. II, 474–81).
[3] In a debate on the state of Ireland in the House of Lords on 21 March, Fitzwilliam stated that the House was entitled to express an opinion on conditions in Ireland, but he does not seem to have referred to the Absentee Tax (*Parliamentary History*, XXXIII, 132).

the case of every individual; but of this, I am sure, that several of you have been basely calumniated by the Opposition in Ireland, as you have, I dare say, upon this, as I know upon a former occasion you were, scandalously betrayed along with the interests of the two Kingdoms, to the union of which, you formed one of the principal links, by the ministry here. You are branded by the odious Name of Absentees, as if you were bound to be present in Ireland at every roll call as if you were Soldiers, and the very people, a great part of the power and consideration of whose families has arisen from English Matches, as their Estates have arisen from English grants, have endeavoured to make English intermarriages impracticable, and the inheritance of Irish property by Englishmen odious and precarious. I am glad that your Lordship intends to exert yourself upon this occasion.

God bless you, and forward you in this and all your undertakings; for they will be such, I trust, as will merit the divine protection, as I beleive they are undertaken in conformity to the divine reason. What your Lordship says of Laurence I beleive is true.[1] He will stand, I have no doubt alone, but I think it impossible he should have none to second him whilst your Lordship has any friend in that House that has not betrayed your principles; for if the ground of this War cannot be defended, it is impossible that you can be defended. Adieu my dear Lord! and beleive me ever, living or dying,

Most truly yours
EDM BURKE

Bath
15 March 1797

P.S: Many thanks from Mrs Burke and me to Lady FitzWilliam for her kind solicitude about us.

To FRENCH LAURENCE—16 *March* 1797

Source: *Burke–Laurence Correspondence*, pp. 152–7.

March 16, 1797.

My dear Laurence,

It is very unlucky that the reputation of a speaker in the House of Commons depends far less on what he says there, than on the account of it in the newspapers. Your speeches, which are made late in the night, supposing no foul play, (which however I suspect) are taken by the journeymen note makers, and when there is not room for them in the

---

[1] If this was in a letter it is missing.

paper, even if they were able to follow you. In the late instance, however, this was unavoidable, since you spoke to vindicate the reputation of
your friend, which no consideration of prudence with regard to
yourself could prevail on you to omit.[1] As you stated [it] in your letter,[2]
it must have been very impressive, and as honourable to your abilities,
as it was to the goodness of your heart. As to Mr Fox's speeches, he
seemed to have laid [aside] his abilities along with all decency, liberality, and fairness; and placed himself in the rank of the Adairs, the
Bastards,[3] and those gentlemen whose cause he supported, and to
whose understandings,[4] 'by an extraordinary alacrity in sinking,'[5] he
chose to level himself. What he said of me was nothing more than his
old song, frequently sung, though with a little more liberality in my own
presence, and always responded to without a possibility of reply. The
major part of his topics have been answered by me in print, and the
publick must judge between us; but there is one fact, which as it
passed fifteen years ago most people may not so well remember; though
that too, I discussed with him in the House of Commons without a reply, or the possibility of his making any. He has the impudence to say
the reduction of places that I made was not sufficient, and that more
would have been made in Lord Rockingham's and his administration, if
time had been given to them for that purpose.[6] Both are absolutely
false;—In the first place, any lessening of the reduction proposed in my
original plan and that which appeared in the Act, was not of my doing,
but of his own, and the cabinet to which he belonged; and I was no
way consulted about it, though I certainly acquiesced in it, and, on the
whole, thought it sufficient. In the next place, I do solemnly declare
that I never heard him, nor any body else of that cabinet, propose any
reduction of offices, but of the two, were of opinion that the matter had
been carried too far, rather than that it had fallen short of their mark.
They must have thought that it did not fall short, because they knew
very well that they never could have had an opportunity so favourable

[1] Laurence who 'rose principally to vindicate the name of a Right Hon. Gentleman
(Mr Burke) which had been long dear to him' asserted that Fox, without referring in
the debate to Burke's Economical Reform Bill, 'had misquoted Mr Burke, and mis-
construed his meaning' (*The Times*, 14 March).
[2] See above, pp. 280–2.
[3] In the debate of 13 March on Harrison's motion (see above, p. 280) John Pollexfen
Bastard (see above, p. 271) had strongly criticized Windham's arguments; James
Adair (see above, p. 81) had stated he was in favour of retrenchment but would vote
against the motion (*Parliamentary History*, XXXIII, 99, 100).
[4] *Burke–Laurence Correspondence*: undertsandings,
[5] See *Merry Wives of Windsor*, III, v, 13.
[6] Fox, having referred to Burke's Bill of 1782, had gone on to point out that 'it
was well known, that it never had its full effect, and that the plan, on account of the
short duration of what was commonly called the coalition administration, was only
partially executed' (*Parliamentary History*, XXXIII, 101).

for reduction as during the dependence of that bill, and in the flood tide of its popularity. Mr Fox now thinks that neither this, nor the Pay Office Bill, nor the Contractors' Bill, which, though moved by another, was left wholly to my management, as it was originally schemed by myself,[1] nor of Mr Dowdeswel's[2] and my plan, to his and our honour adopted by Mr Crewe,[3] were of the least significance, in lessening the influence of the Crown in that House, and in the other, or in the Scotch election for peers by the abrogation of the Scotch Lords of Police.[4] I know he told me, and that to the best of my recollection in the presence of others, that the Acts which he now finds to be so very frivolous, were the means of turning out Lord Lansdowne, and that he had lost his question in the same number of votes as the places that had been suppressed.[5] As to those that had been retained, he perfectly agreed with me both in the policy and the justice of retaining them, considering them as I did as right in themselves; and with regard to the holders in possession or reversion, as property, to all intents and purposes. I cannot say exactly in what form Mr Rose[6] put the recriminatory charge which he made on Mr Fox with regard to the places of that kind, which Mr Fox had held, and disposed of. Mr Fox's reply seems to indicate that he was charged with squandering away their income and value. If so, his reply was proper, because the charge was unparliamentary, and not at all to the purpose in argument.[7] But if it was urged, as it ought to have been, that Mr Fox had himself considered those places his property, as an argument ad hominem, it would have been conclusive against him. For if he sold that as property which was not such, by his own admission he was guilty of a fraud. But it were an endless task to go through all the nonsense and ribaldry which he chose to vent upon that occasion. As to his arguing for a change of his

[1] The bill was introduced by Sir Philip Jennings Clerke, 1st Baronet (1722–88), M.P. for Totnes; see vol. IV, 218, 447.

[2] William Dowdeswell (1721–75) was Chancellor of the Exchequer in the first Rockingham Administration.

[3] See above, p. 208. For his bill to disfranchise revenue offices see vol. IV, 219, 447.

[4] The Scottish Lords of Police were abolished by 22 Geo. III, c. 82 (Burke's Economical Reform Act).

[5] Shelburne's Ministry was decisively defeated in the House of Commons on 17 February 1783 by 224 votes to 208 after a debate on an Address Approving the Terms of Peace.

[6] See above, p. 281.

[7] In the course of his speech Fox attacked Rose for having secured the reversion of the office of Clerk of the Parliaments for his son. Rose retorted that 'he deemed it no more scandalous in him to obtain that reversion for his son, than it was in the father of Mr Fox to obtain the reversion of two patent places for him' and went on to refer to the way in which 'those reversions had been disposed of, by the right hon. gentleman'. Fox replied that his opponents did not feel 'the least displeasure at his having dissipated his fortune; they were only angry, that he had not been so mean as to resort to those measures to repair it, to which they themselves were so partial' (*Parliamentary History*, XXXIII, 105).

opinions from the greater burthens which now exist on the publick, 'tis perfectly absurd[1]—First, because injustice is not less injustice, though it may admit some palliation on account of the necessities of those who are guilty of it; and next, because those remnants of remnants of savings, which Mr Windham has so justly ridiculed, become more and more contemptible according to their disproportion to the weight of the charge which they are brought to counterpoise. He has used another argument which seems to have more weight, which is, that it may be necessary for maintaining the character and credit of the Opposition; but at a miserably low ebb is that character and credit which is obliged to have recourse to such frauds and impostures. Mr Pitt was very wrong in giving to them the countenance he had given, and which, after the able speech he had made, was no proper conclusion to be drawn from his arguments. Mr Windham, in my opinion, even from what I see in the papers, never made a more able and eloquent speech. I particularly admire the manly tone of scorn with which he treated the miserable imposture of the motion. I thank him heartily for his speech, and subscribe an unfeigned assent and consent to all the articles of his creed. I forgot to say a word about fees, which it seems is one of the articles of charge against Mr Windham's office. Whether they be exorbitant or not, is more than I can judge, but that they are profitable to the officer is no objection, provided they are not onerous to the publick, or oppressive to those that pay them. This was so much my principle upon the reform, that I carefully reserved the fees to the Pay Office; but in the progress of the bill I was absolutely forced by the frauds of Colonel Barré,[2] acting on the principles of Lord Shelburn, who attributed every sort of publick evil to fees, in a famous speech of his,[3] and by the unparalleled treachery of our own party I was beat out of my plan, and compelled, whether I would or not, to bring from that abolition a charge of £.6,000 a year, or rather more, upon the publick, for the official expences which before had cost nothing, except for the Paymaster's salary and some other salaries, which latter were insignificant.[4] Whether the office has been impaired in its

---

[1] Fox had said that if he were asked why he had changed his opinions on retrenchment since 1782 he would answer that circumstances had greatly increased the burden of taxation (*ibid.* XXXIII, 102–3).   [2] Colonel Isaac Barré (1726–1802).
[3] Possibly Shelburne's speech of 5 April 1786; see *Parliamentary History*, XXV, 1359–61.
[4] Burke's Act for the Regulation of the Paymaster's Office (22 Geo. III, c. 81) provided that the fees should be funded and used to augment salaries. In 1783 Burke introduced an amending bill. When it was in committee it was drastically altered, apparently 'on the motion' of Colonel Barré, by the insertion of new clauses which *inter alia* abolished fees (*Parliamentary Papers...1731–1800*, XIII, 446, 447; *Parliamentary Register*, X, 111–16; 23 Geo. III, c. 50; J. Norris, *Shelburne and Reform*, London, 1963, pp. 224–5).

diligence and its spirit of accommodation from that time, is more than I can positively say, but I believe that it has. I am sorry to have troubled you so much on these matters, but as they relate to facts which may not be so generally known, I wish you not to throw away this letter. I have no objection to your shewing it to any body, but do not desire it to be shewn to any one but Lord Fitzwilliam and Mr Windham. As to you, 'Macte esto virtute tua'[1]—don't be discouraged from taking the independent line, which makes you vote with different men, but always upon the same principle, and not like these vile and most abject wretches who compose the armed neutrality;[2] who, if they were not the most contemptible of the human race, would be the most odious.— Thank God, you have but one political friendship to attend to, and in that you will never find any clashing with publick principle.—As you are still solicitous about my health, I am to tell you that to-day has been one of my best days; and though I can't walk without an arm, I have moved about a good deal, at least a good deal for me. Flesh as before. Adieu.

Yours ever,   E.B.

P.S. Will the gentlemen do any thing in my affair with Owen—or have they given it up? If they have given it up, why is it so?[3]

To Lord Frederick Cavendish—21 *March* 1797

Source: Devonshire MSS.
Endorsed: Mr Burke March 1797 | abt his Legacy.
Only the signature is in Burke's hand.

My dear Lord

The extream good nature and kindness of your former letter[4] so perfectly consonant to your uniform goodness to me ought not to have remained unanswered, untill my receipt of that which came to my hands this day:[5] But I was in daily expectation for some time past of being able to perform that task without having recourse to the Assistance of a friend;[6] However, tho' much better than I have been, tho' I am well enough able to dictate, I cannot stoop down to write, without suffering a good deal. Nothing could be more kind or humane than your

---

[1] A blessing on thy well-doing; see Horace, *Satires*, I, II, 31.
[2] See above, p. 271.
[3] On 6 May Douce and Rivington itemized in their account: 'Attending Mr Nagle at the War Office with a copy of Mr Owen's answer and inquiring for evidence to prove the peticase' (MS at Sheffield, Bk 32).
[4] Of 8 February; MS at Sheffield.
[5] Lord Frederick's second letter is missing.
[6] The letter is in Nagle's hand.

Lordships communications of those methods which you yourself had found useful in a similar complaint. A little before the receipt of your Letter by advice I had made tryal of Opiates, the first effects of which proved favourable beyond expectation; but the continuance of them brought me almost to an extremity. It affected my head in such a manner as to disable me from walking or almost standing and left me, when that disorder was removed in a state of the greatest debility; so that I have been obliged wholly to give up the use of this medicine and to resort to other methods, which in a small degree and very slowly begin to produce rather good effects. So that whatever good effects Opiates may have had in other cases, and I know of much good done by them, they seem to be unsafe in my particular disease and constitution.

I did not expect that your Lordship would have been so prompt in the discharge of the melancholly, but to me most flattering duty imposed upon your Lordship, by your Brother my late invaluable friend;[1] But since your goodness anticipates the usual time allowed in such cases, I obey your Commands and Doctor King will receive what I ought ever gratefully to acknowledge, both to your Lordship and to the memory of Lord John. If therefore you are so good as to send to Doctor Walker King I shall write to him by this days post requesting him to deliver to your Lordship my receipt for the Legacy,[2] and he will also receive the Bonds which have been so generously cancelled in my behalf and that of my friend.[3]

I have the honor to be, with the highest possible gratitude, respect and Affection,

My dear Lord,
Your Lordships most faithful
and obliged humble Servant
EDM BURKE

Bath
21st March
1797

[1] Lord John Cavendish.
[2] See the next letter.
[3] William Burke; see above, p. 215.

To WALKER KING—21 *March* [1797]

Source: MS Osborn Collection.
Addressed: Revd Doctor W: King | Harley Street | London.
Postmarked: MR | 22 | 97 | ⟨B⟩.
Endorsed: Ed. B. Bath 21. March— | Ld J. Cavendish. and Beconsd Bills.
Only the signature is in Burke's hand.

My dear Walker

I received a very kind Letter from Lord Frederick Cavendish, desiring to know to whom the legacy from Lord J: Cavendish to me, should be paid. It was earlier than I expected. I therefore must trouble you to receive the money and to discharge the Legacy tax, which I beleive is pretty high;[1] but Doctor Laurence knows what it is and he will direct you. I do not know whether it is to be deducted from the money in the hands of the Executor[2] or to be paid by the Legatee. I would not have given you this trouble but would immediately have desired His Lordship to pay over the money to Adey,[3] if there had not been some Bonds which have been remitted by Lord John's will, which I rather wish to be delivered to you to be canceled, than to any other person. I send you a receipt for the Legacy. I desired Lord Frederick to send for you, and when you have received the money you will be so good as to give it in, on *my* account, to the House of *Boldero Adey and Co.* That is to Adey himself to be so put in.

Now I am to beg leave to ask you whether my Account with Rivington is finally settled, and whether he had paid the £300 which he intended,[4] for Adey has never written one word on the Subject. I must trouble you to remit to Joshua[5] thirty eight pounds to discharge a Bill of Mr Fellows the Mealman,[6] and also twenty five pounds to help Joshua himself in his payments on account of the Farm. Making in all Sixty three pounds. May I beg that you will not forget the application to John Bourke of the City.[7] He has not behaved properly, presuming I suppose upon the probability of my speedy death—But be that probability what it may, you ought as if it were without design and meerly as giving him a piece of good news to represent me as recovering very fast. You have said nothing to me about a french tenant for my Cottage at Penn. You know the qualifications I expect with such a tenant.

[1] It was six per cent if the legatee was a 'stranger in blood' (S. Dowell, *A History of Taxation and Taxes in England*, London, 1884, III, 149).
[2] Lord Frederick was his brother's sole executor.
[3] Burke's banker; see above, p. 104.
[4] According to a letter of Charles Rivington to Walker King dated 17 March 1798, £300 was paid to Burke (MS at Sheffield, Bk 32).
[5] Not identified. Probably a bailiff at Beaconsfield.   [6] Not identified.
[7] John Bourke of Tokenhouse Yard (see above, p. 52).

It has got late or I should write more. We hope Mrs King and the Children[1] go on well.

Ever affectionately yours

Bath

EDM BURKE

21 March

P:⟨S⟩.

Fill up the date in the Receipt.

To FRENCH LAURENCE—[*ante* 22 *March* 1797]

Source: MS Osborn Collection. Printed *Burke–Laurence Correspondence*, pp. 162–3.
Laurence replied to this letter on 22 March; see tailnote.

The situation in Ireland had been steadily growing more serious and in March Laurence and Fitzwilliam drew up 'A Memorial on the State of Ireland' to be presented to the King on behalf of a group of peers who were large landowners in both Great Britain and Ireland. The Memorial emphasized the importance of separating the Irish Catholics from the northern radicals and suggested that complete Catholic emancipation should be granted and that those members of the Irish Administration who had shown themselves to be strongly anti-Catholic should be dismissed. (There is an incomplete copy of the Memorial at Sheffield, F 30*f*, endorsed: 'Memorial on the state of | Ireland, prepar'd for H. | M. 1797 | not presented'; it is summarized in a letter of Laurence to Burke, undated but possibly [*circa* 18 March 1797], printed *Burke–Laurence Correspondence*, pp. 157–62.)

I take it for granted that you have not been authorized to communicate to me the substance of your Secret Letter: so that I am somewhat at a loss how to State my Ideas, such as they are to ⟨Lord F⟩. But you may throw them out as matters ⟨offered⟩ for consideration from yourself.

I had a Letter from Lord F. not long since, in which there was an obscure and unformed hint of this Business. In my answer I wholly mistook his plan.[2] I now see it distinctly. I make no question but, as to the execution, the work is perfect. With regard to the measure itself I have great doubts; first from the attendant circumstances, and then from the dispositions of some of the persons who are to be principally and most actively concernd. Had this remonstrance been an insulated measure I am convinced it might be very proper; but following immediately on the heels of a Parliamentary motion, The answer (if any) will be, that the King cannot act on the Sense of individuals, however respectable, the Parliament in both Kingdoms thinking differently. I confess I do not see what reply can legally and constitutionally be made

---

[1] Mary and Ann; see above, pp. 50, 148.
[2] Fitzwilliam's letter is missing. Burke's answer is probably his letter of 15 March; see above, pp. 282–4.

to this—and I am afraid it will be employd to make much ill blood on both sides of the Water. I do not like to have Lord F. much engaged with ⟨Lord Hertford[1] with Lord Moira[2]⟩ and above all with Lord Abercorn.[3] They are all men of ambition—the first is timid; and the two last very irregular in their Ideas; and, in their views full of ambition, and designs, of which self is in the Center. I think it certain, that if any Benefit is derived from this, they will take away all the Credit; and if it fails (or indeed whether it fails or not) Lord F. will be the Victim. I do not like these associates in any design. What turn opposition in Ireland will take on it I cannot divine. They are running the full length of Jacobinism—and meaning something little short of the disunion of the two Kingdoms—they may take this opportunity of making the absentees (as they are called) odious—and I assure you the Court will join with them in the End. Adieu. God direct our friends.

On 22 March Laurence replied to this letter as follows: 'I very much agree with the contents of your answer . . . It was not within my knowledge, as I told you in my last, whether any thing had been done, or was actually to be done with the paper of which I gave you the substance. I can now say, nothing will be done with it'. Laurence went on to explain that originally there had been no intention of raising the question in Parliament, but that later Lord Moira 'hinted his purpose of moving an address'. Laurence emphasized that Moira must 'not be led under any circumstances into details, which might be thought to give encouragement to the enemy'. To Laurence's disgust Moira remarked 'that by *appearing in his place on the side of the people of Ireland, he might save his estate in the event of a revolution*' (MS Osborn Collection; printed *Burke–Laurence Correspondence*, pp. 163–6).

FRENCH LAURENCE *to* EDMUND BURKE—28 *March* 1797

Source: MS Osborn Collection. Printed *Burke–Laurence Correspondence*,
pp. 169–72.
Addressed: (Secret) | Rt Honble E. Burke.

(Secret)
                               Admiralty Court
                               March 28th 1797

My Dear Sir,

Lord Fitzwilliam is gone down to Milton,[4] very melancholy as to the situation of things here. Yesterday I received a letter from him,

[1] Francis Seymour Conway, 2nd Marquess of Hertford (1743–1822).
[2] Francis Rawdon-Hastings, 2nd Earl of Moira (1754–1826). On 21 March he moved in the House of Lords that an address be presented to the King 'imploring his majesty's paternal and beneficent intervention, to remedy the discontents which unhappily prevailed in his majesty's kingdom of Ireland' (*Parliamentary History*, XXXIII, 127–30).
[3] John James Hamilton, 1st Marquess of Abercorn (1756–1818).
[4] His seat in Northamptonshire.

which I enclose.[1] It is kind and friendly in the extreme. He is more anxious for my personal success, than I am myself. I answered shortly, that I came into Parliament knowing that I could only do my public duty by making personal sacrifices. But under the circumstances (not having at present even my seconder, Lord Milton, in Town, who has been sent down by order of Government to his Corps in Dorsetshire)[2] I shall wait a little and watch opportunities, if any offer. What are the purposes of Ministers I know not; I believe, they know not themselves. They seem to value themselves, as I understand, on good conduct in suffering the most decisive resolutions to be carried against them without a struggle in the Common Hall of London, and since of Southwark.[3] It is said, they intend to get counter-petitions. But in my judgement, they will fail. If they seriously meant it, they should have made a battle, and then men would have warmly promoted a counter-address. Now all will be flat and languid. They hope, I fancy, to escape the storm by bending before it. Our friend W.[4] speculates that they will grow more shabby. Yet if they find that shabbiness will not do, it is possible, they may from necessity advance one step more towards honesty. Before I determine on my *time*, I shall endeavour to learn what they actually mean.

I have prepared two sets of Resolutions,[5] one larger and more detailed, going through all the Parliamentary documents and every where incorporating the words of Mr Pitt himself, if the State papers, to which I allude, be, as I suppose them, from his pen. There are *twenty* Resolutions in that set. The other consists of *twelve*, containing the marrow of the former set, and admitting just as much argument in speaking as the longer and fuller resolutions.—I hope to have copies enough to send you one of each to-morrow by the coach, as both sets would take up more than my legal number of franks. They will be with a half margin and I will thank you to make as many remarks as you please.

[1] Perhaps a letter dated 'Milton sunday' (MS at Northampton, Box X515/157) in which Fitzwilliam writes that he is afraid that Laurence, by introducing his Resolutions at this time will run the risk of incurring unpopularity by 'forcing upon the publick a topick it had no relish for' and by 'forcing upon the House a motion, which proves its own inconsistency, versatility, and weakness (a crime of the blackest die, never to be forgotten or forgiven)'.

[2] George Damer, styled Viscount Milton (1746–1808), later (1798) 2nd Earl of Dorchester; M.P. for Malton. He had been appointed Colonel of the Dorset Yeomanry in 1794.

[3] On 23 March at a Common Hall of the City of London held at the Guildhall it was resolved to petition the King to dismiss his ministers. On 27 March the electors of Southwark also decided to petition (*The Times*, 24, 28 March).

[4] Windham.

[5] For Laurence's first set of Resolutions see above, p. 250; his second set is printed in *Corr.* (1844), IV, 535–47; no MS copy has been found.

W. to whom of course I have communicated them, does not think that the Minister will like them. I shall however try to negociate through the Speaker.[1] I am sure I have left every thing open enough for Mr Pitt. While I shall have an opportunity of stating my sentiments, there will be nothing to tie him up from being to-morrow again as shabby as he pleases, except a little about the Netherlands.

Lord Lansdowne last night declared[2] that he thought 'Belgium' ought not to be insisted upon by us: and that is the creed and the object of the armed neutrality. ⟨The Prince of Wales⟩ with his friends seems now avowedly to have joined opposition,[3] and I believe that Lord ⟨M⟩[4] in truth was sent for on the late occasion, to be a mediator with Fox, but that scheme did not take. Fox has lowered his tone of late. He said in confidence to Lord ⟨M⟩ what must on no account be repeated;— that he thought this the worst time since the commencement of the war for making peace. Till lately he did not doubt the ability of the country to carry on the war for two or three years more. When he was talking with me the other night in the House and some member near me whose name I know not, I observed in reference to something from him,—that I had rather hear him blowing a war-point on his trumpet; he paused a little and then answered, that he doubted whether the country could carry on a war for two or three years—Alas!—if he were willing, he has put himself in a situation that he could not do it with effect.

Believe me to be my dear Sir

Ever most gratefully and affectionately Yours

F. LAURENCE.

To FRENCH LAURENCE—29 *March* 1797

Source: *Burke–Laurence Correspondence*, pp. 172–3.

Bath, 29th March 1797.

My dear Laurence,

In reading the Irish debates upon the state of the north of that kingdom,[5] I find that the Chancellor[6] had justified the proceedings of

---

[1] See above, p. 95.

[2] In the debate in the House of Lords on the Earl of Suffolk's Motion for the Dismission of Mr Pitt (*Parliamentary History*, XXXIII, 192).

[3] The Prince of Wales was in close touch with Lord Moira and on 8 February he had transmitted a memorandum on the Irish situation to the Prime Minister, stressing how dangerous it was, suggesting concessions might be made to the Catholics, and offering to accept the office of Lord Lieutenant (*The Correspondence of George, Prince of Wales, 1770–1812*, ed. A. Aspinal, London, 1963–, III, 313–16).   [4] Lord Moira.

[5] On 20 March both Houses of the Irish Parliament debated the measures taken by the Government to restore order in Ulster.   [6] Lord Clare; see above, p. 222.

Government, upon the precedent of proclamations issued in 1780;[1] and which he has said had been then approved by the then leader of Opposition. The then leader of Opposition was Lord Rockingham.[2] I did not much like that he or any of his friends should be quoted on the occasion, though I do not mean directly to condemn what has been done in Ulster, as I cannot speak to the necessity of it;[3] but if I recollect matters rightly, it has no other resemblance to what was done here in 80, except that in both cases a military force has been employed. But the manner of their employment, and the powers given to commanders, to the best of my recollection are altogether different. As the proclamations then issued in England are referred to, I wish to have a copy of them, as early as possible. You can speak to some friend who may put you in the way of finding them. They may be in the Annual Register,[4] or some other of the periodical works of the time. I myself took a very active part, but I do not like to speak upon memory to the tenour or purport of the proclamations; for tho' many of the Opposition who were then members of the Privy Council were summoned (at least towards the beginning of this business) I knew nothing of it personally, not being then a Privy Counsellor.[5] Lord Rockingham attended but once.[6] During the greater part of the disturbances, tho' there was a garrison in Lord Rockingham's house, he was ill and confined to his bed. I believe

[1] During the Gordon Riots proclamations were issued on 5, 7 and 9 June 1780. The proclamation of 7 June declared that 'as it is necessary...to employ the Military Force...We have therefore issued the most direct and effectual Orders to all Our Officers' (*London Gazette*, 6–10 June 1780).

[2] The Lord Chancellor pointed out in the debate, that during the Gordon Riots 'military law was resorted to'. He is not however reported as mentioning Lord Rockingham by name. Lord Glentworth (Edmond Henry Pery, 2nd Baron Glentworth, 1758–1844, later, 1803, 1st Earl of Limerick) however, who also spoke in the debate and referred to the Gordon Riots, said that a proclamation was issued putting London and Westminster under martial law, 'and a bill was immediately introduced into the House of Commons by the leading opposition member of the day justifying it' (*Dublin Evening Post*, 21 March).

[3] On 13 March General Gerard Lake (1744–1808), later (1804) 1st Baron and (1807) 1st Viscount Lake, had issued a proclamation ordering all persons in the district under his command to surrender their arms and ammunition.

[4] These do not appear in the *Annual Register* for 1780, but Laurence found them in the *Remembrancer* (letter of 1 April, MS Bodleian Library; printed *Burke–Laurence Correspondence*, pp. 177–8).

[5] Burke became a Privy Counsellor in 1782.

[6] Wraxall gives a vivid description of how Rockingham attended the Council meeting: '. . . in an undress, his hair disordered, and with testimonies of great consternation. Nor did he, when seated at the Table, where the King was present, spare the Ministers, for having, as he asserted, by their negligence, or want of timely energy, allowed the Assemblage of People to take place in St George's Fields' (N. W. Wraxall, *Historical Memoirs*, London, 1815, I, 337–8). Wraxall mistakenly states that this happened on the morning of 7 June. Rockingham did not attend the Council meetings on 5, 7 and 9 June which approved the proclamations directing the suppression of the disturbances. But he was present at a Council held on the evening of 9 June which discussed the measures which should be taken to restore order (Public Record Office, P.C. 2/125, fol. 138).

Mr Lee,[1] clerk assistant of the House of Commons, can better put you in the way of getting these proclamations than any other person.—I jog on here pretty much as usual. My last night was a very bad one. God bless you.

Yours ever,
E.B.

French Laurence *to* Edmund Burke—29 *March* 1797

Source: MS Osborn Collection. Printed *Burke–Laurence Correspondence,*
pp. 174–7.
Addressed: (Secret) | Rt Honble E. Burke.

Admiralty Court
March 29, 1797

My dear Sir,

The enclosed from Lord F. is on the same subject with the last, which I sent you yesterday.[2] Between this and Monday,[3] I shall look narrowly about me in the House, to see if I can find any fit man beside Lord M;[4] as Lord F.[5] and myself agreed before, that the measure would come better to the judgement of the country, if it did not apparently come from one and the same quarter. Sheridan's motion on Friday[6] may afford an opportunity of feeling my way a little by preluding to my greater design, if I shall find it expedient; or at least of learning by the general temper of the House, whether there be yet any spirit left in the Parliament. There has always been a cry, by no means unpromising, whenever the Ministers have, as incidentally they have, touched on the danger of French Principles. I am satisfied, that the Ministers alone are the real causes of the prostration of the public mind. But Friday will probably shew more. Sheridan's motion, you know, is to prevent any more money being advanced to the Emperor, even under the vote of credit actually passed for that very purpose by the House. This is in my opinion to propose a breach of implied faith. For in putting so much money in the discretion of Government as a Loan to the Emperor, I feel that we did in effect assure the Emperor of our assistance to such an amount. The question, if Government does not run away from it, seems to me therefore to be strong in their favour. Pray let me have your opinion by Friday morning. If I have any fair opportunity, I

---

[1] John Ley (1733–1814).
[2] See above, pp. 292–4.   [3] 3 April.
[4] Lord Milton.   [5] Lord Fitzwilliam.
[6] On Friday, 31 March, Sheridan announced that he would introduce a motion Respecting Loans to the Emperor on Tuesday, 4 April; see below, p. 305.

intend to speak; but detained as I am till 4 'o'clock in this Court, and then unable to go away immediately to an important debate without some refreshment, I never get down till the first speakers, who take the general ground, have done; and before I can collect from what follows, the tenor of the whole, it grows late, and the House, harrassed as it is by daily attendance, becomes impatient. This alone prevented my speaking on the late Irish question, for which I went prepared with my documents in my pocket.—In what a state is Ireland! If I get well through my first great business, I have a mind to move a specific address relative to the Irish Catholics, founding it on the words of Lord Westmoreland's Speech from the throne in 1793;[1] and arguing the dismission of the Castle-Cabal merely as a collateral point necessarily arising out of the conduct, which they before held, and which they have pledged themselves for ever to hold against the claims of their fellow-subjects of the Roman communion. At Woodford's the other day, I accidentally met Sir Walter James, brother-in-law of Lord Camden.[2] Woodford was alarmed at first at my coming which he did not expect, and prohibited politics. Sir Walter, however, began, and I did not actually avoid the subject; when to the surprize of our good host, we agreed very well on many points. The distinction made by the Irish between the personal character of the Vice-Roy, and the character of his government, Sir W. fully admitted on Lord Camden's own authority. He also concurred with me about the Catholics, as I put the case, and thought that if the Chancellor had so pledged himself against them, his continuance in power ought not to stand in the way of the peace of the Kingdom. This appears to me the best mode of putting the dismission of the Irish Cabal to the minds of our Ministers here, who are thus in truth, made parties against the Cabal, and find it difficult to answer in their defence.

I do not know whether I have yet ever told you the Continental news. In august last when the French were in the heart of Germany, the King of Prussia made a convention agreeing to guarantee what is called Belgium, and Holland on the left bank of the Rhine.[3] He has

---

[1] In his Speech from the Throne on 10 January 1793, Lord Westmorland (John Fane, 10th Earl of Westmorland, 1759–1841) declared, 'I have it in particular command from his Majesty to recommend it to you to apply yourselves to the consideration of such measures as may be most likely to strengthen and cement a general union of sentiment among all classes and descriptions of his Majesty's subjects in support of the established Constitution; with this view his Majesty trusts that the situation of his Majesty's Catholic subjects will engage your serious attention, and in the consideration of this subject he relies on the wisdom and liberality of his Parliament'.

[2] Walter James James, 1st Baronet (1759–1829), was married to Jane, *née* Pratt (1761–1825), a sister of Lord Camden.

[3] See *Annual Register* for 1796, p. 232.

lately expressed his approbation of our terms offered through Lord Malmesbury.[1] Both these very different acts of his were made known about the same time to the Emperor of Russia, who observed that he would not say of his brother of Prussia, what in a similar case he should say of a private person '*C'est infame*'. The French, you know, are very uneasy about the Prussian movements; which looks so far well, as at least his plans cannot be concerted with them in consequence of his convention.

I am My dear Sir,

Ever most gratefully and affectionately Yours

FRENCH LAURENCE.

To the BISHOP OF WATERFORD—[29 *March* 1797]

Source: Fragment in Fitzwilliam MSS (Sheffield).
Endorsed: Ed: Burke | to Dr Hussey | sent to Ireland in | 1795 or 6 | publish.
These few lines, in Edward James Nagle's hand, may be a portion of Burke's (missing) letter of 29 March, to which Hussey refers on 2 April (see below, p. 303). The endorsement by the editors of the 1844 *Correspondence* names Hussey as the person addressed, and Burke (if he was the composer, and had dictated the letter to Nagle) might be discussing the measures taken for restoring order in Ulster which had been debated in the Irish Parliament on 20 March.

The Rev. Thomas Hussey (see above, p. 20) had become Roman Catholic Bishop of Waterford and Lismore in January.

break such a prison and to dispose of the prisoners. He is bound to give to the King and to Parliament a clear and satisfactory account of this proceeding which prima fronte[2] is an act of Rebellion; and the Parliament is bound to demand such a detailed Account else it has not only betrayed the Laws of which it is the natural Guardian as well as the Maker, but it has betrayed the melancholly privileges of necessity itself which alone can cover a deviation from Law.

To FRENCH LAURENCE—30 *March* 1797

Source: MS Osborn Collection. Printed *Burke–Laurence Correspondence,*
pp. 230–1.
Addressed: Doctor Laurence M:P | Doctors Commons | London.
Postmarked: BATH FREE|MR|31|97|C.
This letter is not in Burke's hand.

[1] '. . . we understand that the Court of Berlin has *very recently* given an explicit approbation to the terms of pacification offered by this country through Lord Malmesbury' (*The Times*, 27 March).
[2] At first appearance. MS: prima fonté

My dear Lawrence

I have but time for a very few lines. I send you back Lord Fms note[1]—As to the inclosure you refer to as coming by yesterdays Post I received no Letter from you by that Post and consequently no inclosure.[2] How this has happened I know not. Nothing can be more unlucky than the contrariety between your times in your Court and in the House of Commons. I can think of no way of reconciling them, even tolerably, but by your taking the refreshment which you state to be necessary, in the Chop House of Commons. During such a period of the Debate as you think can best bear your absence. The whole proceeding of the Minority goes systematically and with unwearied application to the destruction of our credit at home, and of every connexion which we can have abroad. This is not one of my best Days; but tho' I have had much pain I do not find myself proportionably weakened; and I am at this minute very easy. Mrs Burke cordially salutes you and in all states I am faithfully and affectionately

Yours
E B.

Bath

    30 March 97

To WILLIAM WINDHAM—30 *March* 1797

Source: Corr. (1844), IV, 431–6.

Bath, March 30, 1797.

My dear Friend,

Though my mind is full indeed of all that is going on, in a strange kind of harmony of discord, between both sides of the House, I thought it unnecessary to trouble you with any of my melancholy reflections upon that sad subject. The opposition have never manifested, at least not in so great a degree, or so avowedly, their ill-intentions to their country, as to its credit, its finances, or its policy,—I may almost say, to its being. They have gone so far as to attempt to force the bank paper, which they had done every thing to depreciate, upon the soldiers and the sailors;[3]

---

[1] Lord Fitzwilliam's note which Laurence had enclosed in his letter of 28 March (see above, pp. 292–3).

[2] Laurence had promised on 28 March to send on 'two sets of Resolutions' in the next day's post. In his letter of 1 April (MS Bodleian Library; printed *Burke–Laurence Correspondence*, pp. 177–8) he explains why they had not been sent ('My copyist disappointed me'). On 3 April Burke acknowledges having received them; see below, p. 304.

[3] On 24 March when the Bank Indemnity Bill was in committee, the Opposition criticized a clause permitting the Bank to retain a sufficient quantity of specie to

and thus, by discontenting these descriptions, to leave it without an army or a navy, or, perhaps, what would be worse, an army and navy full of mutiny and sedition. To the plausible part of their objections an answer is made; but nothing is said, within or without the House, to expose the designs which have given rise to this sort of discussion. In debate, as in war, we confine ourselves to a poor, disgraceful, and ruinous defensive. What is the reason that Mr Pitt does not avow the principle of a firm and effective alliance with the Emperor? Why does he continually postpone a full declaration of his sentiments on that head? Why does he suffer an ally of Great Britain, who, while he is such, is an integrant part of the strength of Great Britain, and in a manner part of Great Britain itself, to be called a foreign power, and the assistance afforded him to be considered as money thrown away, as if we had no relation whatsoever to him? Since we are resolved to make no active use of our own forces, he is the only energetic portion of the British power; and the question is, whether, in such a war as this, we ought to disarm that portion of our strength which alone discovers any life. The consequence of all this must be as fatal to Mr Pitt as to the king and the nation. He cannot make peace, because he will not make war. He will be beaten out of all his entrenchments. The enemy is turning his flanks. I find he is left alone to make his defence, and perhaps he chooses to be so; but it has a very ill aspect to those who speculate on the duration of a ministry. These speculators multiply. They increase the confidence of the leaders of opposition, and they add to the number of their followers. All this arises, as I conceive, from Mr Pitt's considering the part he has taken in this war as the effect of a dire necessity, and not of a manly and deliberate choice. But when a man shows no zeal for his own cause, we are not to be surprised that no others will show any zeal for his person. He would not consider those who are attached to him *from principle*, to be his friends, and he will find that he has a very insecure hold of those whose attachment is wholly *without principle*. They who make a man an idol, when he is off his pedestal will treat him with all the contempt with which blind and angry worshippers treat an idol that is fallen.

You are the only person who has taken a manly part; and I can truly assure you, that your enemies are so far from being exasperated, that they are rather softened by this conduct. It is the only conduct that can mitigate the animosity of enemies like yours.

Ireland is in a truly unpleasant situation. The government is losing

enable the Government to pay the Army and Navy in cash. In the course of the discussion Pitt explained that most of the payments to the forces would be made in paper (*The Times*, 25 March).

the hearts of the people, if it has not quite lost them, by the falsehood
of its maxims, and their total ignorance in the art of governing. The
opposition in that country, as well as in this, is running the whole
course of Jacobinism, and losing credit amongst the sober people, as
the other loses credit with the people at large. It is a general bankruptcy of reputation in both parties. They must be singularly unfortunate who think to govern by dinners and bows, and who mistake
the oil which facilitates the motion, for the machine itself. It is a terrible
thing for government to put its confidence in a handful of people of
fortune, separate from all holdings and dependencies. A full levée is
not a complete army. I know very well that when they disarm a whole
province, they think that all is well; but to take away arms, is not to
destroy disaffection. It has cast deep roots in the principles and habits
of the majority amongst the lower and middle classes of the whole
Protestant part of Ireland. The Catholics, who are intermingled with
them, are more or less tainted. In the other parts of Ireland, (some in
Dublin only excepted,) the Catholics, who are in a manner the whole
people, are as yet sound: but they may be provoked, as all men easily
may be, out of their principles. I do not allude to the granting or with-
holding the matters of privilege, &c., which are in discussion between
them and the Castle.[1] In themselves, I consider them of very little
moment, the one way or the other. But the principle is what sticks with
me; which principle is the avowal of a direct, determined hostility to
those who compose the infinitely larger part of the people; and that
part, upon whose fidelity, let what will be the thought of it, the whole
strength of government ultimately rests. But I have done with this
topic, and perhaps for ever, though I receive letters from the fast friends
of the Catholics to solicit government here to consider their true interests.[2] Neglect, contumely, and insult, were never the ways of keeping
friends; and they had nothing to force against an enemy.

I suspect, though Woodford has said nothing of it, and perhaps the
more for his having said nothing of it, that the perfidious and cowardly
design of destroying the French corps in our service still goes on.[3] A
part of the aim, I suspect, is at yourself. It will undoubtedly require the
utmost diligence and firmness, as well as so much temper as can consist with those qualities, to carry you through. God Almighty direct
you, for this matter is almost above my hand.

It is evident that the opposition have directly, and without any
management at all, embraced the French interests, and mean to shake

[1] The Irish Administration.   [2] These letters seem to be missing.
[3] See above, pp. 71–2, 135, 206.

our credit and resources at home, and destroy all possibility of connexion abroad. It is equally plain that, except by yourself, they are not
met manfully upon either of these grounds. Their best fire is only to
cover a retreat. What is the reason that Gifford's book[1] is not strongly
recommended and circulated by them and theirs? There are but a very
few pages in that book to which I do not heartily subscribe; but *they*
ought to subscribe to the whole of it, unless they choose to be considered as criminals soliciting for a pardon, rather than as innocent men
making a defence. However, I have great satisfaction in telling you,
that your manly way of proceeding augments the number of your
favourers every day; and not only your nature, but your policy, will
induce you to proceed in the same course. I have attempted to resume
my work,[2] but the variable state of my health continually calls me from
it; otherwise, our scheme of defence, founded solely upon fear and
meanness, would not be persisted in. Adieu! and believe me ever with
the truest, most affectionate, and most grateful attachment,

My dear friend,
Yours, most sincerely,
EDM. BURKE.

Five o'clock.

My last night was pretty good, but I have not passed an equally good
day. My strength, however, improves. Otherwise, I make no great
progress. Mrs Burke, thank God, is, on the whole, rather better than
when we came here.

The BISHOP OF WATERFORD *to* EDMUND BURKE— 2 *April* 1797

Source: Fitzwilliam MSS (Sheffield). Printed *Corr.* (1844), IV, 437–9.
Addressed: Right Honourable | Edmund Burke | Bath.
Postmarked: WATERFORD.

In April Dr Hussey, the new Bishop of Waterford, issued *A Pastoral Letter to
the Catholic Clergy of the United Dioceses of Waterford and Lismore.* In this letter
he dwelt on the two centuries of persecution the Catholics of Ireland had endured and emphasized that 'as the Catholic Faith is a Religion preached to all
Nations and to all People so it is suitable to all Climes and all Forms of Govern-

[1] At the end of March John Gifford (1758–1818), an Anti-Jacobin writer, published *A Letter to the Hon. T. Erskine; containing some Strictures on his View of the
Causes and Consequences of the Present War with France.* Towards the end of April it
had reached a fifth edition (*St James's Chronicle*, 28–30 March; 18–20 April; see also
below, p. 320).
[2] Presumably on the 'Third Letter' or the letter to Laurence on the militia problem
see above, pp. 273–5.

ment—Monarchies or Republics, Aristocracies or Democracies. Despotic or Popular governments are not the Concerns of the Catholic Faith'. He expressed his disapproval of the practice of sending Catholic children to Protestant schools and he informed his clergy that 'if in any of your districts the Catholic military frequent protestant places of worship, it is your duty to expostulate with them'. 'Instruct them' he directed 'that in all matters regarding the service of the King, their officers are competent to command them, and that they are bound to obey; but in all Matters regarding the Service of the King of Kings, their officers have no Authority over them'. There were at least six editions of this Letter.

My ever dear Friend

Your letter of the 29th March,[1] which I rece[ive]d yesterday was a cordial to me, in this my honourable exile. Tho' your bodily infirmity forced you to employ another hand to write it, yet the sentiments were your own—'Spiritus intus latet'[2] and Providence still preserves you for some wise, and weighty purpose. You need not regret not having seen my letter to Mrs Burke, upon a late false report regarding you,[3] as it was written in the most cordial paroxism of grief, the sentiments it contained were probably unfit for any eye. I sent it to Mr King, who very properly returned it to me unopened. I have not had the smallest communication with the Castle, since my complaints of the compulsion employed to whip the Catholic military to Protestant worship. Scarce *a Sunday* passes without instances of this outrage occurring in some part of this Country. Our friend Dr Moylan[4] had an audience two months ago of the Lord Lieutenant[5] to shew him a letter from his Vicar General the Parish Priest of Kinsale,[6] complaining of two Privates of the Sligo Militia, who for refusing to assist at Protestant Worship, were tried the next day by a Court Martial, and sentenced to [7] lashes, and I am told that one of them is since dead of his wounds. His Excellency treated the affair with such coldness, and the reception was such, that Dr Moylan, whom you know to be the meekest, and most humble of mankind, came away quite disgusted. The instances are so frequent in this Diocess of this impolitic[8] Tyranny, that when I convened the Clergy of my Communion, it was one of the articles of my Pastoral Charge to them, to use all their *spiritual* power to resist it. The whole of my pastoral letter (which is a short one, and

[1] See above, p. 298.
[2] Spiritus intus alit; a spirit within sustains. See Virgil, *Aeneid*, VI, 726.
[3] On 20 January *The Times* had reported that 'yesterday evening we received information of the death of the Right Hon. Edmund Burke, at his house at Beaconsfield'. This was contradicted by them the next day. Hussey's letter to Jane Burke is missing.
[4] Dr Francis Moylan (c. 1735–1815), Roman Catholic Bishop of Cork.
[5] Lord Camden; see above, p. 140.
[6] The Rev. Timothy Hurley (c. 1759–1828) who had been transferred to Kinsale in 1792.
[7] There is a blank in the MS at this point.   [8] MS: impolotic

intended only as a preface to a longer one) will be printed in a week,[1] and a copy of it shall be sent for you, under Mr King's cover. I know that its' contents will not be acceptable to some, but I am come hither, not to flatter my enemies, but to do my duty. I have not, nor will I ever resign the Presidency of Maynooth.[2] As I receive neither Salary, nor emolument from it, I feel no dishonor, and I see the necessity of holding it, at least untill the plan be finally settled. As to the other Commission,[3] which you desire me not to give up, I still hold it, without ever having enquired whether any or what Salary is annexed to it. Enough for me that it contains his Majesty's signature, to whom I am attached, not only as every Subject ought to be, but also from personal consideration for the honourable mention, which he has graciously condescended to make of me at different times. I have not said any thing about these last circumstances to Mr Wyndham. Have the goodness to direct me. I am with unalterable respect and friendship

ever faithfully your's
THOMAS HUSSEY

Waterford 2d Apl 97

The military authorities reacted sharply to Hussey's criticisms. General William Fawcett (c. 1750–1826), writing from Waterford, required 'some explanation from Mr Hussey' of the unqualified assertion that 'Catholic Soldiers were *forced* into Protestant Churches'. Hussey replied saying that 'Two of the instances which happened during some months back, occurred a few days ago in the 5th Dragoons, and in the detachment of artillery quartered in Clonmel: and Mr Hussey is happy to embrace this opportunity, of doing justice to the Liberality, and humanity of their respective Commanders ... who gave orders to prevent any cause for similar complaints in future'. In Fawcett's opinion this reply 'entirely does away his whole assertion and further stamps his publication with the strongest marks of illiberality' (Fawcett to Pelham, 18 April; Hussey to Fawcett, 15 April, Add. MS 33, 103, fols 376–7, 378).

To FRENCH LAURENCE—3 *April* [1797]
Source: Burke–Laurence Correspondence, pp. 178–81.

Bath, 3d April, [1797.]

My dear Laurence,

I received your pacquets[4] by the evening coach. The first paper of *Resolutions* is undoubtedly the most full and satisfactory. The latter I fear is alone practicable, and what is deficient in it, may be supplied in

[1] The first edition appeared on 14 April (*Hibernian Journal*, 14 April).
[2] The Trustees, however, at their annual meeting on 29 January 1798 removed him from the presidency for 'non-residence' (*Journals of the Irish House of Commons*, XVII, p. dciv). [3] Hussey's chaplaincy of the Irish Brigade; see above, p. 82.
[4] See above, p. 299.

the opening or in debate. I think both of them skilfully and ably drawn. I have no serious objection to the wording in any part. If I could wish any thing changed it would be in the ninth resolution, where instead of the words 'This House has not yet received,' perhaps it might be better to say, 'That this House, on combining all the aforesaid circumstances, together with the proceedings of the French in Italy, has found by experience that His Majesty's and the public's hopes have been disappointed, and that this House,' &c. &c.—In resolution 12, page 19, to omit the words 'not despairing of the public weal, but.'—Resolution 11, instead of the word 'pleasure [satisfaction.]'. I am not very confident that the alteration which I have suggested is for the better, on considering the matter fully; I must leave it to your discretion.[1] I see the perilous position in which you stand, and could almost wish you never had engaged, (indeed I don't see how you can go on) without a living soul to second you—A *second* you must secure at any rate or you must drop the business entirely, and find, or make an opportunity on Mr Sheridan's motion[2] of delivering your sentiments upon our general policy, with regard to the Regicides and our alliance with regard to the Emperor.

I thank you for the Proclamations[3]—they turn out very much as I expected. They have no resemblance to the proceedings in Ireland, but they are perfectly legal. There is no proclamation at all on the part of any general officer. Lord Amherst's orders of the 7th of June are only orders to the military to act without a magistrate, in using force for dispersing the illegal and tumultuous assemblies of the people.[4] On the legality of this order, which is however no proclamation of martial law, there was a great doubt and there is still upon my mind, of the legality; but afterwards Lord Mansfield and the Judges of the King's Bench declared it to be law 'That in all cases wherein by law every man is made a Constable for the preservation of the publick peace, the military do not lose the civil character, nor the duty and obligation of acting as other men ought to act in like cases.'[5] Admitting this doctrine to be true, and

---

[1] Burke is commenting on the shorter set of Resolutions; see above, p. 293. In the text as printed in *Corr.* (1844), the words 'this House has not yet received' in the 9th Resolution still appear; the words to be deleted from the 12th do not appear; 'pleasure' is still in the 11th (IV, 544, 546–7). Laurence never moved the Resolutions.

[2] On 4 April Sheridan moved that the House of Commons should go into committee to inquire 'whether it is consistent with a due Regard to the essential Interests of this Country, that . . . any further Loans, or Advances should be made to his Imperial Majesty' (*Journals of the House of Commons*, LII, 453).

[3] Copies of the Proclamations issued during the Gordon Riots; see above, p. 295.

[4] Jeffrey Amherst, 1st Baron Amherst (1717–97), had issued orders on 7 June 1780: 'In obedience to an order of the king in council, the military to act without waiting for directions from the civil magistrates, and to use force for dispersing the illegal and tumultuous assembles of the people' (*Annual Register* for 1780, p. 266).

[5] In June 1780, immediately after the Gordon Riots, Lord Mansfield (William Murray, 1st Earl of Mansfield, 1705–93) in a powerful speech in the House of Lords

---

to this hour, I am sorry for it, it stands uncontradicted, there does not exist a *scintilla* of illegality, though in a time of such necessity much illegality might have been excused in the whole transaction. General Amherst's orders purport that they were issued under an order of the King's Council. The words 'King's Council' are equivocal, and may signify the King's learned Counsel: because the usual style of an order in council is by His Majesty in Council. Can Mr Faukener[1] procure for you a copy of that order? at least he can know, whether Lord Rockingham, the only Privy Counsellor then in *our* Opposition that attended any Privy Council—and that was on the 4th or 5th of June. All the time after he was extremely ill, and for some days kept his bed.—I send you executed the bond to Mr Wallis,[2] and you will be so good as to take care, that the bond to Garrick for which this is exchanged should be delivered up and cancelled. I have heard nothing about the suit against Owen,[3] nor why it is suspended; for if we do not proceed in it, all my former expence in it is absolutely thrown away.

God Almighty bless and direct you. The boyish spirit of Ministers makes one laugh in vexation. They are in war, and their whole trust is in the enemy, who, whilst they are thinking of the elections, are menacing them with an invasion.

Yours ever,
E.B.

The bond is in a separate cover.[4]

To FRENCH LAURENCE—II *April* 1797

Source: Burke–Laurence Correspondence, pp. 185–7.

Bath, 11th April 1797,
5 o'clock

My dear Laurence,

I am glad to have heard from you at last.[5] This terrible war on the continent has come to a crisis. Whether our pacific War is come to *its*

emphasized that 'every person acting in support of the law is justifiable respecting such acts as may arise in consequence of a faithful and proper discharge of the duties annexed to his office' and that the military had been called in 'not as soldiers, but as citizens: no matter whether their coats be red or brown, they have been called in aid of the laws' (*Parliamentary History*, XXI, 694–8).

[1] William Augustus Fawkener (1747–1811), Clerk in Ordinary to the Privy Council 1778–1811.

[2] Albany Wallis (1714–1800), one of David Garrick's executors; see vol. VIII, 115. Burke had borrowed £1000 from Garrick in 1769; see vol. II, 31.

[3] See above, p. 244.

[4] The bond is missing.

[5] Laurence had written to Burke on 3 and 10 April (MSS Bodleian Library; printed *Burke–Laurence Correspondence*, pp. 181–5).

terrible crisis, is a matter of great doubt; but unless God interposes in some signal way, it must terminate in a peace which, like Scylla, has a thousand barking monsters of a thousand wars in its womb.[1] God preserve us from such peace and such wars. As for himself, Windham is perfectly in the right to be governed by circumstances;[2] but as for you, who act with no party and are in no office, your own honour and your personal reputation are the sole circumstances by which you are to be guided.—Therefore profit of the first opening. If the Emperor's defection[3] is solely owing to the bad state of his own affairs, than which nothing I admit can appear worse, we have much to lament and nothing to blame; but if the spirit of the debates in the English Parliament have tended to bring on despair, or if our want of a supply to his necessities has crippled his armaments, then we have at once to lament and to blame. However, there is the hand of God in this business, and there is an end of the system of Europe, taking in laws, manners, religion and politics, in which I delighted so much. My poor Son was called off in time—'ne quid tale videret.'[4]

I understand that Ellis spoke handsomely of me,[5] for which I thank him; and do you so too, through yourself or any medium you can find. As to Windham he never fails, but of this there is not a word; by our paper I should have thought he had not spoken:[6] but it is no matter—all our plans are defeated by the settlement which the peace will make of the French system in the West Indies. Mr Huddlestone's letter is very obliging,[7] but I really wish him to keep all his sentiments concealed until he can get into the direction. Tell him that this is my opinion, and

---

[1] It is not Scylla in the *Odyssey* but Sin in *Paradise Lost* who has barking monsters in her womb.

[2] Laurence, commenting on a motion by George Augustus Pollen (*c.* 1775–1807) for Peace with France, told Burke in his letter of 10 April that Windham 'believed the purpose was to let it pass with very little debate, and wished me not to press forward, but be guided by circumstances'.

[3] It was becoming ominously clear that Austria, with its armies badly battered in Italy, might make peace.

[4] Lest he should see anything of the kind; see Virgil, *Aeneid*, XI, 417.

[5] In the debate of 6 April on the condition of the Negroes in the West Indies, Charles Rose Ellis (1771–1845), later (1826) 1st Baron Seaford, referred to Burke having many years ago applied his 'great abilities and extensive knowledge to the formation of a plan, for the regulation of the trade on the coast of Africa, and the civilization of the negroes in the West India islands' (*Parliamentary History*, XXXIII, 253). At some time around 1780 Burke had drawn up 'A Sketch of a Negro Code' (*Works*, Bohn, V, 521–44; Little, Brown, VI, 255–89; see also vol. VII, 122–5), the aim of which was the gradual abolition of the slave trade and the emancipation of the slaves.

[6] At the end of the debate Windham referred to the regulations which had been recommended by Burke (*Parliamentary History*, XXXIII, 294). Laurence told Burke in his letter of 10 April that Windham 'paid your name some very just and handsome compliments, very honourable both to the subject and the panegyrist'.

[7] John Hudleston (*c.* 1749–1835) became a member of 'the direction' of the East India Company in 1803. His letter, now missing, which was enclosed with Laurence's letter of 10 April, presumably dealt with some proposal for reform of the Company's government in India.

that then perhaps he may steal some little good; for we, who had for fourteen years struggled to do more, have been miserably defeated, if not with our own, yet with the national disgrace.

I wrote to Mr Troward,[1] and wonder you have not seen him. You had better call on him, as he lies directly in your way. Pray let me hear from you as often as you can, though it were but by a line. Your coming hither must be very inconvenient to you, and where is the use of your seeing me in the body of this death.[2] In truth, I suffer very little pain, but I gain no strength at all. If I find any difference it is that my little strength declines. Adieu. God bless you.

Yours ever,
E.B.

Mrs Burke is a trifle better of her cold—and Webster,[3] who has been dangerously ill, is also better.

EDMOND MALONE to EDMUND BURKE—14 *April* 1797
Source: Fitzwilliam MSS (Sheffield).

Edmond Malone (1741–1812), the famous Shakespearean scholar, was a fellow member of the Literary Club and an old friend of Burke.

Queen Anne St. East. Ap.14.1797.

My dear Sir,

I enclose a Letter intended to be sent to the Representatives of Prince Potemkin, which you will be so good as to sign, and to return to me by the post.[4]

I have at length got all the works of our late dear friend Sir Joshua Reynolds, through the press;[5] and have put together as well as I could a short account of his Life, to be prefixed, which I much regret I have not had an opportunity of shewing to you in MS; but indeed it has been all written within this month past, and must take[6] its fate in the world without the benefit of many hints which I am sure you could have suggested on the subject.—The title-page not being yet work'd off, I

---

[1] See above, p. 63. Burke's letter is missing. Laurence tells Burke on 25 April (MS Bodleian Library; printed *Burke–Laurence Correspondence*, pp. 188–9) 'Troward has just been with me to exchange the bonds. I have cancelled the former, which I enclose'.

[2] Romans, VII. 24.   [3] William Webster (d. 1810), Burke's servant.

[4] Burke, Malone and Philip Metcalfe (1733–1818), the executors of Sir Joshua Reynolds (1723–92), were about to send a letter to the heirs of Prince Gregory Aleksandrovich Potemkin (1736–91), the favourite of Catherine the Great, to obtain payment for a painting; see below, p. 311.

[5] Malone's edition of *The Works of Sir Joshua Reynolds*, 2 vols, London, 1797, was advertised in the *London Chronicle* for 28 April.

[6] MS: takes

beg your advice with respect to the Motto.—The original motto to the 8vo volume containing *seven* of the Discourses,[1] was taken from Junius, and has, I[2] think no great merit. It is as follows:

> Omnia fere quæ præceptis continentur, ab ingeniosis homini-
> bus fiunt; sed casû quodam magís quam scientia. Ideoque
> doctrina et animadversio adhibenda est, ut ea quæ interdum
> sine ratione nobis occurrount, semper in nostra potestate sint;
> et quoties res postulaverit, a nobis ex præparato adhibeantur.
> Aquila Roman. de figuris sententiarum apud Junium.[3]

Among his loose papers I have found the following motto, which he intended for a second volume, supposing a second volume had been published singly, to complete the first; (which is not the case now, for the whole works appear in two vols 4to and contain, beside the Discourses, his Journey[4] to the Netherlands, &c)

> —Quasi non ea praecipiam aliis, quæ
> mihi ipsi desunt. Cicero.[5]

This motto, and this alone, I think of using, but wish for your opinion and approbation. The modesty of it, I think, will do him credit, and with respect to *desunt* I suppose no one will apply it seriously to him, any more than they would to Cicero as an orator.—Do you recollect where in Cicero these words are, as I should wish to turn to the passage, lest he should have made any mistake in transcribing them. I thought I might find them in the beginning of his book de Oratore, but I have searched there in vain.

I was extremely concerned to hear that you were not so well last week as you had been for some time before; but Windham, whom I saw two days ago, gave me reason to hope that this relapse was but of short continuance, and that you were now nearly restored to your former

---

[1] Reynolds himself had brought out *Seven Discourses delivered in the Royal Academy by the President*, London, 1778.

[2] MS: I I

[3] Omnia enim fere quae praeceptis continentur, ab ingeniosis hominibus et in dicendo se exercentibus fiunt; sed casu quodam magis quam scientia. Ideoque doctrina et animadversio adhibenda est, ut ea quae interdum sine ratione nobis occurrunt semper in nostra potestate sint; et quoties res postulaverit, a nobis ex praeparato adhibeantur. For almost all the things which are preserved in precepts are done by clever men who practise speaking; but by chance, for the most part, rather than by knowledge. And therefore study and observation must be applied, so that those things which sometimes occur to us by accident may always be within our power; and as often as the matter may require can be used by us with preparation. (See Aquila Romanus, 17.)

[4] MS: Jouney

[5] Quasi vero, inquit, non ea praecipiam aliis, quae mihi ipsi desint. As though I could not teach others what I lack myself [though certainly I am credited with not even keeping accounts]. See Cicero, *De Oratore*, II, 97.

state—That you may soon be *perfectly* restored, and know no more relapses of any kind, is wished most sincerely and ardently by, my dear Sir,

Your most affectionate
and faithful Servant,
EDMOND MALONE

As the Sheet, containing the Motto must be worked off[1] on Monday,[2] I beg a line by Sunday's post.—I have introduced a long tirade against our *parliamentary Jacobins*, that I hope you will be pleased with.[3]

To EDMOND MALONE—*16 April* 1797

Source: MS Osborn Collection.
Addressed: Edd Malone Esqre | Queen Anne St East | London.
Franked: Free | F Laurence | Bath, April the sixteenth, 1797.

This letter is not in Burke's hand.

My dear Sir

I am very glad that after you have detected imposture and exposed dulness,[4] you are going to do justice to real merit and genuine genius. Nobody can pay this debt of friendship better than yourself. As to the motto, I dont think it of much consequence. It is only a little Sentence of modest disqualification and I am sure I dont know where it is to be found.

I sign and inclose to you the Letters to the Executors of Prince Potemkin. I really thought that this application had been made a good while ago;[5] but even [if] it had, it is right to renew it. I am certainly some Trifle better; but as yet not in a condition to write with my own hand, without the greatest inconvenience.

I am, my dear Sir,
With the most sincere respect and regard,
your most obedient and much obliged
humble Servant,

Bath

16 April 97

EDM BURKE

---

[1] MS: of   [2] 17 April.

[3] In his biographical introduction, Malone emphasized Reynolds's disapproval of 'those turbulent and unruly spirits among us, whom *no King could govern, nor no God could please*'; those '"Adam-wits", who set at nought the accumulated wisdom of ages, and on all occasions are desirous of beginning the world anew', and he explained the hope 'that we have *stamina* sufficiently strong to resist the pestilential contagion suspended in our atmosphere: and my confidence is founded on the good sense and firmness of my countrymen' (p. i, pp. lvii–lviii).

[4] By his book on the Ireland forgeries; see vol. VIII, 454.

[5] A letter was probably addressed to Potemkin's heirs at the time the executors wrote to Catherine the Great in January 1793; see vol. VII, 337.

310

EDMUND BURKE, EDMOND MALONE AND PHILIP METCALFE *to the* HEIRS OF PRINCE POTEMKIN—[*circa* 16 *April* 1797]

Source: Draft (in Malone's hand) in Bodleian Library (MS Malone 41).
Endorsed (by Malone): Letter from the | Executors of the | late Sir Joshua | Reynolds to the | Heirs of Prince | Potemkin— | to be put into | French.

This draft seems to have been composed in two stages: the earlier probably in 1793, when a letter asking for payment for a picture was sent to Catherine the Great; the later close to the time when Burke was asked to sign and enclose to Malone 'Letters to the Executors of Prince Potemkin' (see the previous page). There is also in MS Malone 41 a French version of this letter which was transmitted to Malone on 24 March 1797.

As Executors of the late Sir Joshua Reynolds, we beg leave to inform you, that a picture, the Subject of which is the Continence of Scipio, was painted about the year 1788,[1] by that celebrated Artist, for the late Prince Potemkin who commissioned Lord Carysfort,[2] when he was at St Petersburgh, to order a picture to be executed for him by Sir Joshua Reynolds, leaving the subject to his own choice. This order was given by Prince Potemkin at the same time that her late imperial Majesty was pleased in his presence to commission Lord Carysfort to get a picture painted for her majesty, which was accordingly executed on the subject of Hercules strangling the Serpents, for which her imperial Majesty remitted us fifteen hundred guineas.[3]

The piece above mentioned, ordered by Prince Potemkin was accordingly painted by Sir Joshua Reynolds, and transmitted some years since to St Petersburgh: and the price affixed to it was five hundred Guineas. The death of Prince Potemkin some time afterwards prevented this sum being remitted to England, as without doubt it would otherwise have been, on the receipt of the Picture. We therefore request, that as the heirs[4] of Prince Potemkin, you will be pleased to remit by the first opportunity the said sum to us, who alone are entitled to receive it; and we also beg leave to add that more than six years[5] have now elapsed since this piece was transmitted to St Petersburgh.—In all events, we trust, that if the heirs of the late Prince Potemkin, shall not hold themselves bound to pay for the said picture, they will immediately transmit it in its frame and case, to England, consigned to us, the Executors of the late Sir Joshua Reynolds. We have the honour to be &c.

[1] It was exhibited in 1789 (Leslie and Taylor, *Life of Reynolds*, II, 536). The words 'about the year 1788' are above the line and marked for insertion.
[2] John Joshua Proby, 1st Earl of Carysfort (1751–1828).
[3] This sentence—beginning at 'This order...'—is written at the top of the sheet, with a marginal note 'This paragraph to come in below at the mark x'. There is a mark 'x' after 'his own choice'.
[4] The first draft read 'as Executors'.   [5] The first draft read 'a few years'.

WILLIAM WINDHAM *to* EDMUND BURKE—25 *April* 1797

Source: Fitzwilliam MSS (Sheffield). Printed (incomplete) in
Corr. (1844), IV, 439–44.

Fulham.
April. 25th 1797.

My Dear Sir

I cannot help troubling you with a few lines, to enforce the purpose, which you appeared to have formed when I left you, of putting out a short letter, on the measures necessary to be taken for the immediate safety of the country,[1] or at least with a view to anything like a successful termination of the War.—The danger is coming thundering upon us; and, as far as I can perceive, will find us miserably unprepared, in means as well as in spirit, for such a crisis, as it is likely to bring with it. When the fund of submissions fails us, we have no other; and it seems, that liberally as we are disposed to draw upon that resource, there is not much more that it can yield us. Though the East Indies should follow the West, though Ceylon, and the Cape should go the same road,[2] as Martinico, St Domingo, and all the splendid possessions, that we have purchased at the expence of the force, by which they were to be retained, yet it is not clear, that the Enemy will vouchsafe us peace; and still less clear is it, that the Country could survive such a peace three years.

In this state, it seems impossible; at least it is not to be wished; that the country should go on long without some great struggle,—a struggle to throw off this load of peccant matter, that oppresses it, and to set the vital powers free; if they yet retain sufficient force and spring to recover us from the state of debility, to which we are reduced. The idea of a country perishing as we are doing, not by the course of nature; not by the decay of any vital part, hardly even by disease or sickness, but by the constraint of a situation, in which all our powers are rendered useless, and all our efforts serve only to exhaust ourselves, is more horrible, than any other mode of ruin; and recalls to ones thoughts, what I recollect to have read of, a year or two ago, of a man, who having wedged his hand in a rock on the sea-shore was held there till the tide flowed over, and drowned him.—We are fixt in a similar cleft: and here, I fear, we shall remain, struggling and beating ourselves to pieces, till the green Revolutionary tide pours over us, and whelms us never to be heard of more.

I cannot but think, therefore, that at such a moment, a letter, like that which you had in contemplation, would be of the most seasonable

---

[1] See above, pp. 273–5.   [2] Be surrendered in the course of peace negotiations.

use; by shewing to the country a way, in which its zeal and energy, if it has any, may find vent. I have but little doubt, that there is in the country a considerable deal of energy, at least in comparison of anything, that has yet appeared: But it is the want of knowing how to exert it, that has repelled and kept it down. It is the suppression of this wind, that has caused it to be absorbed: which otherwise might break out in loud explosions, louder than I wish to be used in other cases.

The common feeling of people is, and that which sinks them into inaction and despondency, that there is nothing to be done, that every means have been tried, or at least that none now remain.

The idea of Offensive war is so totally lost, the means of such a war appear so totally exhausted, the ignorance of people is so complete, or rather their ideas are so false, of the state of things in the Maritime Provinces, and of the effects to be produced there, if we are really to direct our efforts on that side, that they never will conceive of themselves the possibility of such a war, nor ever I fear be brought to it, except by being made to understand, that peace is absolutely unattainable, and that an attack upon the Coast of France is the only means of defence.

It must after all be confessed, that when the whole force of France and all its dependencies shall be transferred to this side, the dispositions of the Royalists, aided by all the efforts, that we can make, will find it sufficiently difficult to produce any effect.—Still it is the only chance, and that which affords you the benefit of other chances.—The commotions namely which may be expected in other parts of France, and which such a diversion is most likely to bring on, as well as turn to account.

I have not an idea, while I am stating this, that such a plan will ever be attempted by the present Cabinet; nor would the attempt of bringing the country to such ideas, be made with most advantage, in their persons.—But necessity may bring on something of the sort: attempts continually made on our coasts, may lead in the end to a return; commotions in France may again raise the Vendée and the Chouans; and thus a war be gradually formed, in which the Royalists of both countries may find themselves united, against that union, which has long taken place between the Jacobins of the two Countries.—The difficulty I fear will be, to find the Royalists here—It will hardly be in Mr Fox and his friends: and I do not think that among Mr Pitts friends, the spirit of Royalty burns with too bright a flame.

The business of the fleet is as well over as such a thing can be.[1] I am

---

[1] On 16 April the crews of the ships of the Channel Fleet at Spithead refused to obey orders and petitioned for an increase of pay. On 23 April they were informed that their grievances would be redressed and 'the men gave three cheers and declared they were ready to obey orders'; see also below, p. 347.

almost inclined to wish, that the Admiralty had refused to comply, and tried the bringing home Jarvis' fleet[1] to stop any attempt of the Mutineers to carry the fleet to the Enemy; depending upon the dissensions that would have arisen among them, and the dread of consequences, when they had time to contemplate them, for reducing them to submission in the mean-time.

What news may be in London at present, I don't know; as I write this from Fulham. The last gives the possibility of some turn, that may save the Emperor from immediate submission; but it is only a possibility. —One anecdote of the Emperor I cannot forbear mentioning—When his Courtiers were beseiging him with demands for peace, and urging that Vienna must fall.—He answered by saying—Eh bien! est ce que Vienne est L'Empire?

The Emperor and Thugut,[2] however, are the only persons, who stand upon that ground.—I believe, we also have an Emperor, here, to do the same; but where is the Thugut?

Farewell! My Dear Sir, To keep as distant as possible one of the Great calamities of the time, take care of yourself, conform to Dr Parry's directions, and, I should still be inclined to add, consent, now that you are going on to well, to let Dr Fraser[3] be prepared with a knowledge of your case. I do not see, what levity there could be in this: and I certainly see the chance at least of some advantage.

> I am, My Dear Sir,
> most truly and Affectionately
> Yours
> W WINDHAM

Let me beg you to add my best respects to Mrs Burke, and compliments to the rest of your family.

To WILLIAM WINDHAM—26 *April* 1797

Source: British Museum (Add. MS 37,843, fols 174–6). Printed *Burke–Windham Correspondence*, pp. 241–3.

My dear Sir

I have not been so ill since you left me as not to have been able to make a beginning if not a progress in the execution of your Commands; but to do any thing without raising a Spirit, (I mean a National Spirit,) with all the energy and much of the conduct of a party Spirit, I hold

---

[1] Admiral Jervis (see above, p. 103) was in command of a fleet off Cadiz.
[2] Johann Amadeus Franz de Paula, Baron Thugut (1736–1818), Austrian Minister of Foreign Affairs.   [3] William Mackinen Fraser (d. 1807).

to be a thing absolutely impossible, and I hold it to be impossible to raise that spirit whilst the minister who ought to excite it and direct it, and to employ it for the purposes of his own existence, as well as of that of his master and his Country, is the very person who oppresses it; and who with double the expence and double the Apparatus of every sort with which our most vigourous Wars were ever carried on is resolved to make no War at all. Our only hope is in a submission to the Enemy by taking up the principles of that Enemy at home, and by submiting to any terms which the directing body of that Enemy abroad shall think fit to prescribe. If they demand Portsmouth as a cautionary town it will be yielded to them; and, as to our Navy, that has already perished with its discipline for ever. I have my thoughts upon a modification without a departure from the terms of our late unhappy submission, but they are of no moment because no attention will be paid to them—What cure for all this? What but in that spirit 'which might create a Soul under the ribs of death'.[1] But to this end it is absolutely necessary that no terms within or without doors should be kept with the French party in our Parliament, who must be treated as public Enemies, else they and the Head of the Republic abroad will infallibly over power all the feeble force of a flying resistance—But can such a Creature as I, undertake this task, when the very ministers, whom I *must by the necessity of the case support*, will the very next day, tho' without any thing reciprocal on the part of their Enemies, will calmly discuss with them the merits of the public measures as if they were members of the same Cabinet differing not in principle but upon some points more or less. Despairing as I do of any thing that can be executed under this prevalence of no spirit, I should not at all despair of the people if they were roused. A Pamphlet has been sent to me called 'Reasons against National despondency'.[2] It is ably written, and with regard to myself personally, it is in one part very flattering[3] but it is all written upon the false principle of decorum

---

[1] See Milton, *Comus*, 561–2.

[2] A pamphlet entitled *Reasons against National Despondency; in Refutation of Mr Erskine's View of the Causes and Consequences of the present War. . .*, London, 1797, was advertised in *The Times* for 28 April.

[3] The anonymous author referred to Burke's efforts at Economical Reform in the second Rockingham administration: '. . . The Reform pointed out by the Nation was undertaken by Mr Burke. He introduced his Bills for the better securing the Independence of Parliament. They were prefaced by a speech which can never be excelled. It is not the fertility of his fancy, the beauty of his language, the force of his illustrations, which excite our wonder; these are the common attributes of uncommon genius. It is his indefatigable research, his laborious attention, his minute examination, his comprehensive views, his cautious progress, that command our astonishment. Mild, gradual but decided in his plan, he reconciles the rights of individuals with the public welfare. He examines the diseases of the constitution with the skill of a statesman, but with the feelings of a father. His system is to watch and follow Nature, not to force her. He probes the wound with gentleness and with caution, but with a fixed eye and firm hand, and does not venture to use the knife until he is assured that the part is

and management with the persons whose Politics it opposes. This is the only tone which I suspect that those who support ministry will bear, because the conduct of ministers makes them look hourly for a change or for a compromise. Yet with all this before me I will endeavour to execute what you desire, tho' as disjoined from the rest of my plan it will lose something of its feeble effect. Another great difficulty there is, which consists in this, that the ministers must overthrow the whole legal establishment of their Army, and that speedily, else nothing can be done agreeably to our plans. I am clearly of Opinion that as we stand at present we are not in a posture any more than a disposition to take the only active measure of defence which remains to us namely, to make an active War in the territory of France. But I wish you would take a real view of our applicable strength, which I am not in a condition to do, and particularly, with regard to what Cavalry could be got together here or in Ireland, after the fatal measure of disbanding several of the Corps of that kind which had been raised. Will you be so good as to furnish me with the details of the killed and wounded in this War, on the Continent, as well as the List, if the Office contains it, of the killed and wounded in the Seven Years War, both on the Continent of Europe, in North America, and in the[1] West Indies, including ours and the Provincial troops at the Havannah. I hope I am not over immersed in details, but I cannot well go on without them. Unfortunately I cannot find that Quiberon Paper,[2] but Nagle and I have hunted for it in vain. God bless you and preserve you to better times.

Mrs Burke always remembers you with affection and gratitude, and I can never think of my miserable health without a proper sensibility to your uncommon solicitude about it. Excepting the difficulty of opening my body, I am otherwise better, and have no bad night since you left us. Adieu, once more God bless you

Yours ever affectionately
EDM BURKE

Bath 26th April 1797

radically unsound. By perseverance, Mr Burke effected a great deal of what he proposed: but he might have done more, if the committees had co-operated with his industry and his zeal. He has left an eternal monument behind him' (p. 11).

[1] MS: the the

[2] In a letter to Burke of 8 February Laurence had written: '. . . the enclosed letter I purposed sending to you two or three days since, I had heard that Lord Spencer and some other good-natured friends had informed Windham of Lord Fitzwilliam's attack on the Quiberon-expedition in the last debate. The explanation which occurred to me, ignorant as I was of the actual words used, I gave from my knowledge of his Lordship's sentiments. I also wrote to him on the subject, and you now will see his answer. In thought, expression, every thing, it is truly worthy of the writer, if my partiality does not deceive me. You will communicate it or not, as you think best, to Windham. The substance of the whole I wish him to know, but there are some phrases which might a little jar upon his fine nerves' (MS Bodleian Library; printed *Burke–Laurence Correspondence*, pp. 111–13). The 'Quiberon Paper' is missing.

To EARL FITZWILLIAM—26 *April* [1797]

Source: Fitzwilliam MSS (Sheffield).
Endorsed (by Fitzwilliam): Burke | april 29th 97.

My dear Lord,

I have no great heart to write in the present State of things. The quick succession of every sort of calamity and disgrace both foreign and domestick has quite overwhelmed my feeble constancy, which, one way or other, has, to this time, kept itself erect. The evil effect of our narrow System of inert and passive defence has already appeard in its operation even on our misapplied means, and the instruments of that false and pusillanimous System. Indeed it is impossible, that a stagnant military force, in times like the present at least, perhaps at any time, should not corrupt and putrifye. The temporary quiet in our marine has been bought at the expence of all future discipline.[1] The concessions are of such a nature, as, I am afraid, take away the possibility of reestablishing it, though *all* the art and management should be used, no part of which, I am persuaded, will be put in practice. A spirit of fear and compromise, if it deserves the name of a spirit, is become universal, or indeed is rather made so. What shall we be under an abject and ignominious peace, if cowardice is the principle of our War. But all is over with the world in which I, and your Lordship at a later period, were born, and in which we wished to die. This is most certain:—and yet I heartily agree with you, that you ought to act in your private Affairs, as if it were to continue for ever. You perform a present Duty—and as to the future it must be committed to the disposal of Providence.

As to the poor friend, so many years known to you only by obligations for which he could make no return—The shadow of him exists. Though the muscular flesh be wasted and indeed almost wholly gone, Some Strength is recoverd and on the whole, the radical malady, (not to be conquerd at my time of Life) excepted, I feel better. Mrs Burke is better of her cold—and we both cordially salute Lady Fitzwilliam. May the God who has made you what you are, preserve to better times.

Ever truly, affectionately and gratefully Yours
EDM BURKE

April 26.1796.

[1] See above, p. 313.

To the PRINCE OF WÜRTTEMBERG—28 *April* 1797

Source: MS Hauptstaatsarchiv, (Stuttgart). Printed Prior (2nd ed.), II, 384–6.
Addressed: His Serene Highness | The Duke of Wirtenburgh.
There are two copies of this letter in the British Museum and one at Sheffield.

Frederick William Charles, Hereditary Prince of Württemberg (1754–1816), later (1806) King of Württemberg, had arrived in England on 11 April. On 18 May he married Charlotte Augusta Matilda (1766–1828), the Princess Royal. An endorsement on the Sheffield copy of this letter asserts that the Prince 'in his Tour through the West of England, previous to His marriage . . . sent a Message by Sir John Hippisley (who accompanied Him in His Tour,) to Mr Burke, at Bath, requesting to be permitted to visit him'.

The author of the Letters, which his Kinsman will have the honour of laying before the Duke of Wirtemburgh[1] would not have presumed to think them in the smallest degree worthy of being so presented, if the extraordinary condescension of his Serene Highness had not made it his Duty to acknowlege his respectful Sense of that condescension by such an Offering to it as alone was in his power.

He would have presented himself personally, according to his S.H.'s gracious permission signified to him thro' Sir John Hippisley,[2] to pay the homage which everyone owes to the rank and virtues of the Duke of Wirtenburgh: But he did not choose to affect his compassion by exhibiting to his Serene Highness the remains of an Object worn out by Age, Grief and infirmity, and condemnd to perpetual retreat.

The author is convinced, that the favourable Sentiments of the Duke of Wirtemburgh with Regard to these Letters are not owing to the Talents of the Writer, but to the Cause, which he has undertaken, however weakly, to defend; and of which his S.H. is the protector by situation and by disposition. This author hopes, that if it should please God, by his all powerful interposition to preserve the Ruins of the civilized world, his S.H. will become[3] a great instrument of that powerful Providence, in its necessary reparation; and that, not only in the Noble Estates which compose his own Patrimony, but in the two Great Empires, in which he has so natural and just an influence,[4] as well as in the third which his S.H. is going to unite in Interest and affection with the other two. In this he will cooperate with the beneficent and enlarged

---

[1] Probably *Two Letters on a Regicide Peace* which Burke had asked Nagle to deliver to the Duke.
[2] Sir John Coxe Hippisley, 1st Baronet (1748–1825), had negotiated the marriage of the Prince to the Princess Royal. He was created a baronet in May 1796 for his services, and the Prince permitted him to use 'his ducal arms, with the motto of the Great Order of Wirtemburgh, "Amicitiæ virtutisque fœdus"' (*Gentleman's Magazine*, 1825, pt I, 643).   [3] MS: be become
[4] One of the Prince's sisters had married the Emperor, another was the wife of the new Czar of Russia.

views of the illustrious house and its virtuous chief, who are on the point of having the happiness of his alliance. To the compleat success of that alliance, publick and domestick, some of the authors latest and most ardent Vows will be directed.

In the great Task allotted to the Sovereigns who shall remain, his S.H. will find it necessary to exercise, in his own Territories, and also to recommend, wherever[1] his influence shall reach, a judicious, well-temperd and manly severity in the support of Law, order, religion and morals; and this will be as expedient for the happiness of the people, as it will be to follow the natural Bent of his own good heart, in procuring by more pleasant modes the good of the Subject, who stands, every where, in need of a firm and vigorous, full as much as of a lenient and healing Government.

With Sentiments of the most profound respect His Serene Highnesses

most faithful
and most obliged humble Servant
EDM BURKE

Bath 28th April
1797

The Prince acknowledged Burke's letter on 6 May, professing himself 'admirateur depuis longtems des Talens de Monsieur Burke' (MS at Sheffield).

To the ABBÉ BARRUEL—1 *May* 1797

Source: Clifford, *Application of Barruel's Memoirs of Jacobinism*, p. ii.

The Abbé Augustin de Barruel (1741–1820), a scholar who had taken refuge in England in 1792, forwarded to Burke the first volume of his *Mémoires pour servir à l'histoire du Jacobinisme*, 4 pt, London, 1797–8, with a brief letter from London ([*ante* 1 May 1797], MS at Northampton, A. XVIII.12) inquiring about Burke's health and referring to their earlier acquaintance.

Sir,

I cannot easily express to you how much I am instructed and delighted by the first Volume of your History of Jacobinism. The whole of the wonderful narrative is supported by documents and proofs with the most juridical regularity and exactness. Your reflexions and reasonings are interspersed with infinite judgement, and in their most proper places, for leading the sentiments of the reader, and preventing the force of plausible objections. The tendency of the whole is admirable in every point of view, political, religious, and, let me make use of the abused

[1] MS: whereever

319

word, philosophical. So far as I can presume to judge of a French style, the language is of the first water. I long impatiently for the second Volume; but the great object of my wishes is, that the work should have a great circulation in France, if by any means it can be compassed; and for that end, I should be glad, upon the scale of a poor individual, to become a liberal subscriber.

I am as yet in a miserable state of health; and if I advance at all, it is very slowly, and with many fallings back.—I forgot to say, that I have known myself, personally, five of your principal conspirators;[1] and I can undertake to say from my own certain knowledge, that so far back as the year 1773,[2] they were busy in the plot you have so well described, and in the manner, and on the principle you have so truly represented.— To this I can speak as a witness. I have the honour to be, &c. &c.

(Signed) ED. BURKE.

May 1, 1797.

Barruel replied on 16 May, expressing his gratitude for Burke's praise (MS at Northampton).

To JOHN GIFFORD—1 May 1797

Source: MS Trinity College, Dublin.
Addressed: John Gifford Esq- | enquire at | T. N. Logman Bookseller | No 7 Walnut Tree Walk | Lambeth.
Postmarked: 10 O'CLOCK|MA.3.|97 F. NOON.
Only the signature of this letter is in Burke's hand. The address originally read 'To be left| T. N. Logman Bookseller| No ⟨3⟩ Paternoster Row'. The bookseller was Thomas Norton Longman (1771–1842).

On 6 January John Gifford (see above, p. 302) published his edition of *A Residence in France during the years 1792, 1793, 1794, and 1795; described in a series of letters from an English lady . . .*, a work by Helen Maria Williams (1762–1827). Gifford dedicated this work to Burke, declaring that it described 'circumstances which more than justify Your own prophetic reflections'.

Sir,

The humanity, which dictated your polite and most flattering attention to me, will I hope excuse my being so late in my acknowledgment of so great an Honour: but I have been in a terrible state both of

[1] Barruel refers to numerous literary men and politicians, mainly French, who in his opinion, had shown hostility to the Christian religion. Of those he names Burke knew at least three: Mirabeau, André Morellet (1727–1819) and Paine; and he possibly knew at least four others—Diderot, Necker, Turgot, and the Duc d'Orléans (Louis-Philippe-Joseph de Bourbon, 1747–93).
[2] When Burke paid a visit to France; see vol. II, 411–25.

Body and mind. For a very long time I seemed to myself and to those about me, every day at the point of Death. I am even now very far from recovered; though I enjoy longer intervals of Ease than formerly. But I am not yet in a condition to write any thing with my own hand; else I should think it could not be better employed than in giving you my part of the thanks due to you by the whole country we belong to for the Zeal, the industry, the energy, the Spirit and the Eloquence which you have displayed in a cause which is not only the cause of that country; but, if any publick Cause was ever so, the Interest of mankind at large in the highest and most important of its Concerns. When I consider the magnitude of that service your kind attention to me ought to be a small part of my consideration. What the Event of your Endeavours will be, it is hard to say—You have done one Man's duty and a good deal more. But I must confess that in a War, and especially in a War like this every thing must depend more on the use of our military and financial Strength, than on the Force of any Reasoning. Unfortunately we see that in proportion to the augmentation of the national Expence all the effect of it in exciting any just apprehensions, on the part of the Enemy, is lessened. A great military Force, the greatest in number and Charge that this country ever maintained, is at best totally useless; and a military power not agitated and ventilated by active operations against an Enemy necessarily corrupts into disaffection and mutiny. That Force, to which ultimately we must trust for the preservation of our lives and liberties may become, if already it has not become, the greatest and nearest source of our danger. Our Ruin is infallible by keeping up all the real charge together with the false image of a War, without the possibility, without the inclination and even without the legal Capacity of employing this force to induce Your Enemy even to afford you the Terms of a decent Capitulation.

I beg Pardon for this Liberty and have the honour to be with a strong sense of personal and publick obligation Sir,

Your most obedient
and humble Servant
EDM BURKE

Bath. 1st May 1797

To LORD LOUGHBOROUGH—1 *May* 1797

Source: Campbell, *Lives of the Chancellors,* VI, 281–2.

Alexander Wedderburn, 1st Baron Loughborough (1733–1805), later (1801) 1st Earl of Rosslyn, the Lord Chancellor, was an old friend of Burke.

Bath, 1st May, 1797.

My dear Lord,

Though not much concerned, nor likely to be long concerned, about any thing on this side the grave, I felt a sincere pleasure on your Lordship's recovery; and do trust and hope, from the energy of your Lordship's character, that you will act your part in a total change of the plan of passive defence, so ruinous in point of charge, and not only so inefficient, but in every point of view so highly dangerous to all things except our enemies abroad and at home. I know it will require the greatest resolution and perseverance to make the necessary change in this unfortunate plan; but if it be not done you are all ruined, and all of us along with you. Pardon this friendly liberty at the time when others take so many liberties that are far from friendly. This, though infinitely of greater importance, is not the subject on which I wish just now to trouble your Lordship. It is relative to a little affair that I mentioned to you about five months ago, and which it is no wonder your serious illness and important occupations have put out of your head. I mean that of two worthy persons that are as nearly as possible at the point of dying from actual famine: the first is that character, not so respectable for his rank and family, which are amongst the highest, as for perfect piety and unbounded charity, the Archbishop of Paris:[1] the other is not inferior to him, in my humble opinion, in virtue and religion, nor in charity neither, according to his more limited means, which, to my knowledge, he particularly extended to distressed English residents at Amiens. The revenue of his bishopric was 2400l. sterling a year, of which he received but 400l. to support himself and his dignity in the Church, and he contributed every penny of the rest in charity. He is now in Germany, in a state of the greatest indigence. His name is Machault,[2] son of Machault formerly Minister of the Marine,[3] and who, I believe, is now living in an extreme old age, and thoroughly pillaged by this glorious revolution. Now I ask nothing but that these

[1] Antoine-Éléonore-Léon LeClerc de Juigné (1728–1811), Archbishop of Paris since 1782.
[2] Louis-Charles Machault (1737–1820) became Bishop of Amiens in 1774. Burke had received three letters from him in 1791 (MSS at Northampton).
[3] Jean-Baptiste Machault, (1701–94), Minister of Marine 1754–7.

two should be each put on such allowance as French bishops here receive, and that it should be a quarter antedated for their present necessities. If your Lordship will permit my friend Dr King, whose hand supplies the infirmity of mine, to manage this affair, he will do it to your Lordship's and Mr Pitt's satisfaction, and with all possible attention to the fallen dignity of the eminent persons to be relieved; and it is for this reason that I wish the affair to be managed by him only.

You will not think a solicitation so worthy of humanity to be unworthy of you. God direct you at this arduous moment. Believe me, my dear Lord, with sincere respect and affection, your friend of thirty-five years' standing, and always your most obedient and obliged humble servant,

EDM. BURKE.

Loughborough replied on 3 May: 'Every Testimony of your Kindness must at all times be most acceptable to me, But It is a pain to me that I cannot confirm any expectation your partiality for me had provided on the appearance of my Recovery. An Effort to discharge some parts of my Duty brought me out as soon as I had the physical power of moving, But for above a week past I have been again confined to my Bed and Chair. My Spirits not only feel the necessary depression from bodily weakness, but lowered as They are from other Causes retard the return of Health'. Loughborough enclosed this letter in one dated 4 May—probably written to Walker King—in which he explained that he was 'not sure whether He [Burke] ought to receive It' but that he was 'incapable of writing in any other Strain'. As regards relief for the bishops, Loughborough thought 'It must be done by private and Individual aid' (MSS at Sheffield).

To RICHARD TROWARD—1 *May* 1797

Source: Windham, *Diary*, pp. 359–60.

Albany Wallis (see above, p. 306), who had made himself responsible for the erection of a monument to David Garrick in Westminster Abbey (see vol. VII, 560–1), had requested Burke to supply an inscription for it. Evidently Burke had done so, but Wallis's legal partner Richard Troward (see above, p. 63), who was also a friend of Burke, in a letter of 27 April reporting on the progress on the monument, incidentally complained to Burke, 'The tablet will not admit of so long an Inscription by more than half and I am disappointed to find Mr Windham did [not] consult with you as to what should be done—what you wrote is about 1250 letters, but the inscription table will hold only 500 or 550 letters . . .' (MS at Sheffield).

Bath: May 1, 1797.

Dear Sir,—If I am at all really recovering, it is very slowly and with many drawbacks. I am glad you are pleased with the figures for the monument of our late friend. I thought Hickey's design admirable, and I should think the execution of the gentleman who has undertaken to finish it equal to the original model.[1] As to the epitaph, which I sketched, it was my design to make it plain, grave, and moral. In general I prefer epitaphs in prose—you may put more into a line, if that is convenient for the marble. It need not be divided into paragraphs; but the place of division may be supplied by one of those large full points in the middle of the line, after the last letter; as we see done in some ancient monuments. I cannot contrive to shorten what I have wrote more than by the few lines that I have marked; and I am sure that my faculties are not capable of anything better than what I have done. As I ought to do, I have done my best. If anything were to be corrected I was in hopes Mr Windham would rather have exercised his own judgment than remitted the affair to mine, which is at present very infirm, and certainly no better than it was when I wrote the inscription.

As to the verses,[2] they appear to me to be very spirited; but they are a copy of verses, and not an epitaph. I am in general an enemy to epitaphs in verse; but when they are used they ought not to exceed ten lines at most, and ought rather to resemble some of the fine serious epigrams of Martial than the style of an elegy, to be distinguished by their fine finishing and polish more than for any stretch of fancy or exuberance of thought. I can do nothing towards the correction of these verses. To write a verse is a matter of great labour; to attempt to correct it is still greater; and I am ill-fitted for labour of the slightest kind. Of all this Mr Wallis, on consulting with Mr Windham, will be the best judge. You may show him this letter; it is entirely submitted to Mr Wallis's discretion, but I could wish it a discretion so advised as I propose.

The erection of this monument does honour to Mr Wallis's friendship,[3] which does not end with the life of its object, but extends to his fame.

I am, with very great regard and esteem, dear Sir,

Your faithful and obliged humble servant,
EDMUND BURKE.

To R. Troward, Esq.

Garrick's monument was unveiled on 12 June (*Annual Register*, 1797, p. 34). It does not have Burke's inscription (printed in Windham's *Diary*, p. 361), but a twelve-line verse epitaph by Samuel Jackson Pratt (1749–1814).

[1] John Hickey (1751–95), a protégé of Burke, had originally been engaged to undertake the monument, but had died before it was erected (see vol. VIII, 115). Henry Webber (1754–1826) completed the work.
[2] Troward enclosed with his letter an alternative inscription (missing) composed by a friend of his. The friend (not identified) was willing to have Troward make alterations in his text or reject it completely.
[3] Wallis had been a close friend of Garrick and was one of his executors.

EDMOND MALONE *to* EDMUND BURKE—2 *May* 1797

Source: Fitzwilliam MSS (Sheffield).
Addressed: To | The Right Honourable | Edmund Burke | Bath.
Postmarked: ⟨CHARING CROSS⟩ MA|2|97|⟨F⟩.

Queen Anne Street, East, May 2, 1797.

My dear Sir,

I have sent by one of the Bath Coaches that goes from Charing Cross, this morning, one of the large-paper Copies of our late excellent friend's Works, directed for you. I suppose the books will readily find their way to you; but lest they should neglect to forward them, thought it best to give you this notice—As you have probably not seen his Journey to the Netherlands, it may perhaps afford you some little amusement.[1]—In my contract with Mr Cadell,[2] (who pays £350 for the Copyright of the Discourses &c) I took care to reserve *eight* Copies; five of them to be applied to the use of his Executors,[3] Lady Inchiquin,[4] and Mr Mason,[5] who has been carried away from us, just as the *book* was about to issue from the press: but I conceive it will be proper to send his set to some one nearly connected with him; and perhaps his oldest friend, Mr Stonehewer,[6] to whom he has left all the papers bequeathed to him by Mr Gray, has the best claim.—The sixth copy is for the King; and will it not be right to deposite *one* in the council chamber of the Royal Academy; and to send the other to the present Emperor of Russia, in return for the patronage and favour shewn to the Author by the late Empress?[7]

I request to know whether you approve of this distribution.—I was most heartily glad to hear that you were even *a trifle* better, and I trust that the worst is now past, and that your amendment will be regular and progressive.

I beg to be very kindly remembered to Mrs Burke, and that you will believe me ever, with the truest respect and attachment, my dear Sir, Your most affectionate

and faithful Servant,

EDMOND MALONE

---

[1] See Malone, *Works of Reynolds*, II, 1–124.
[2] Thomas Cadell (1773–1836) and William Davies (d. 1820) were the printers of Malone's *Works of Reynolds*.
[3] Malone himself, Philip Metcalfe and Burke; see above, p. 308.
[4] Sir Joshua's niece; see above, p. 218.
[5] William Mason (b. 1724), the poet, biographer of Gray and friend of Horace Walpole, had died on 7 April.
[6] Richard Stonehewer (*c.* 1728–1809), friend of Gray and a correspondent of Burke.
[7] There is in the Malone papers a copy of a letter from the Countess of Inchiquin (see above, p. 218) requesting Paul I to accept a copy of the *Works* (MS Malone 41).

To EDMOND MALONE—4 *May* 1797

Source: Victoria and Albert Museum (Forster Collection, MS 48 D 2).
Printed Leslie and Taylor, *Life of Reynolds*, II, 638 n.
In Walker King's hand but signed by Burke.

My dear Sir,

I have received your valuable Present; very valuable indeed from what it contains of your own, as well as of the works of our inestimable Friend. Your Life of him is worthy of the subject, which is to say a great deal.[1] I have read over not only that Life but some part of the Discourses with an unusual sort of pleasure, partly because being faded a little on my memory they have a sort of appearance of novelty, partly by reviving recollections mixed with melancholly and satisfaction. The Flemish Journal I had never seen before—You trace in that every where the Spirit of the Discourses supported by new examples: He is always the same Man, the same philosophical, the same artist-like critick, the same sagacious Observer, with the same minuteness without the smallest degree of trifling. I find but one thing material, which you have omitted in his Life—you state very properly how much he owed to the writings and conversation of Johnson;[2] and nothing shews more the greatness of Sir Joshua's Parts than his taking advantage of both; and making some application of them to his profession, when Johnson neither understood, nor desired to understand any thing of painting, and had no distinct Idea of its nomenclature even in those parts which had got most into use in common Life: But Though Johnson had done very much to enlarge and strengthen his habit of thinking, Sir J. did not owe his first rudiments of Speculation to him. He has always told me, that he owed his first dispositions to generalize—and to view things in the abstract to old Mr Mudge,[3] Prebendary of Exeter and brother to the celebrated mechanick of that name.[4]— I have seen myself Mr Mudge the clergyman at Sir Joshua's house. He was a learned and venerable old man, and as I thought very much conversant in the Platonick Philosophy and very fond of that method of philosophizing. He had been originally a dissenting minister, a description which at that time bred very con-

---

[1] Malone's biographical introduction occupies the first sixty-eight pages of volume one.

[2] Reynolds himself acknowledged this indebtedness. He said of his own *Discourses*: 'Whatever merit they may have must be imputed, in a great measure, to the education which I may be said to have had under Dr Johnson...he qualified my mind to think justly' (*Boswell's Life of Johnson*, ed. G. B. Hill, rev. L. F. Powell, Oxford, 1934–51, III, 369 n.).

[3] The Rev. Zachariah Mudge (1694–1769).

[4] Thomas Mudge (1717–94), appointed King's Watchmaker in 1776, was the son of Zachariah Mudge.

siderable men both among those who adhered to it and those who left it. He had entirely cured himself of the unpleasant narrowness, which in the early part of his Life had distinguished these Gentlemen and was perfectly free from that ten times more dangerous enlargment, which has been since then their general characteristick. Sir J. Reynolds had always a great love for the whole of that Family; and took a great Interest in whatever related to them. His acquaintance with the Mudges ought to be reckoned among the earliest of his literary connexions. If the work should come to a second Edition, I hope you will not omit this very material circumstance in the Institution of a mind like that of our Friend. It was from him that I first got a view of the few, that have been published, of Mr Mudge's sermons[1] and on conversing afterwards with Mr Mudge I found great traces of Sir Joshua Reynold's in him, and, if I may say so, much of the manner of the master.[2] I cannot finish this part of my Letter without thanking you, for the very kind manner in which you are pleased to speak of me;[3] far indeed beyond any thing which I can have a claim to, except from your extraordinary good nature.

There is a matter, which I am now going to mention to you which is so full of delicacy, that I should not dare to touch it except through the confidential hand of our friend Dr King, who has been charitable enough to visit me here and so condescending as to employ himself for me in the manner that you see. You mention the Copy money for which you have agreed with the Bookseller. If I were to consider, that the Life which you have written is entirely your own Work and that the compilation has been made and superintended by your own care in common justice the money is your property: but if you should consider yourself, perhaps too generously, as holding the money in trust for Lady Inchiquin as an executor, permit me to remind you of one circumstance and to entreat you to touch it as delicately as possible to Lady Inchiquin.—When one wishes to pay homage to the memory of departed Eminence in a friend with whose cast of complexion and turn of mind we are acquainted, we ought to do it in the way, in which, if living, we know that he would have desired. I can say with certainty that nothing would have given him more pleasure, than to be assured, that a monument should be

---

[1] Mudge published: *Liberty; a Sermon...*, London, 1731; *The Nature and Extent of Church-Authority. A Sermon...*, London, 1748; *Sermons on Different Subjects*, London, 1739.

[2] In his second edition Malone printed the present letter to this point (I, pp. xxxii–xxxv).

[3] Malone mentions that Reynolds was 'lavish in his encomiums' on Burke's *Reflections* (I, p. lvii), and when referring to Burke's anonymous obituary of Reynolds (printed vol. VII, 75–6), Malone himself says: 'the hand of the great master, and the affectionate friend, is so visible, that it is scarcely necessary to inform the reader that it was written by Mr Burke' (I, p. lxviii).

erected to his memory in St Paul's Church.[1] He had too proper a sense of Reputation to give any such thing in charge to his Representatives. You remember that after his Death it was talked of in his Club[2] and in a manner resolved upon, that a monument should be erected for him, the basis of which should be laid in the subscriptions of the Club. As I was a large legatee[3] I was willing to subscribe £100. Now I do not know how the money arising from his Works can be so well employed, as in further contributing to his fame, in a way connected with the Arts and appropriate to his particular Relish. And if you do not chuse to make your own use of your own money I do not know in what way it can be better applied. I am sensible of the enormous price which the fashionable artists demand for works of this kind. But I know that there are others of less name but of merit, which Sir J. R. would not think contemptible who would execute a very handsome monument for £1500; towards making up which, besides the £350[4] and my £100, Lord and Lady Inchiquin would naturally wish to be very liberal contributors—The Club, his friends and his fame would do the rest—at least I fancy so.[5] All this however I submit to your judgment, without any reservation of a further opinion of my own. You will speak to Mr Metcalfe[6] about it of course.

As to myself in whom you are pleased to take an Interest, my health is so variable that I do not know well what to say upon the subject. When I wish to turn my thoughts abroad I see nothing but what tends to make my retreat even into the feelings of my own illness a sort of consolation. Great means of Power destroyed by mean, pusillanimous and most mistaken measures in the use of them. Every thing menacing from abroad, every thing convulsed within,—the violent convulsions of feeble nerves—As to what has happened in Ireland I expected nothing else from what has been done in that country—There I doubt we do not so much agree about the cause as we must concur in sorrow concerning the melancholly fact of the situation of that country. I shall therefore say no more upon this subject; but most cordially wish for success in all your

[1] Reynolds, who thought that St Paul's looked 'forlorn and desolate', or at least 'destitute of ornaments suited to the magnificence of the fabrick', while Westminster Abbey was 'encumbered and overloaded with ornaments', successfully insisted that Dr Johnson's monument should be placed in St Paul's. Malone, in his second edition of the *Works of Reynolds* (II, 343) expressed the hope that monuments to both Reynolds and Burke would be erected in St Paul's.
[2] The Literary Club, of which Reynolds 'had the merit of being the first proposer'; see *Boswell's Life of Johnson*, I, 477.
[3] Reynolds had left Burke £2000, in addition to cancelling a bond for £2000; see vol. VII, 87.　　　　　　　　　　[4] See the previous letter.
[5] Reynold's monument, by John Flaxman (1755–1826), was erected in St Paul's Cathedral in 1813. Members of the Literary Club agreed to contribute '5 *guineas each* only as being likely to induce members to subscribe' (*Farington Diary*, ed. James Greig *et al*, London, 1922–8, III, 188).
[6] See above, p. 308.

most virtuous and liberal pursuits, as long as the state of the World will permit you to continue them.

I have the honour to be, my dear Sir,
Your most faithful and affectionate
and obliged humble Servant

Bath 4th May. 1797.

ED. BURKE

At some time Burke set down the following 'few hints' on Reynolds's character for Malone's use (Victoria and Albert Museum, Forster Collection, MS 48 D2; printed Leslie and Taylor, *Life of Reynolds*, II, 637–8):

Sir Jos Reynolds.

He was a great generaliser, and was fond of reducing every thing to one System more perhaps than the variety of principles which operate as in[1] the human mind and in every human Work will properly endure. But this disposition to abstractions generalizing and classifica[tions] is the great glory of the human mind, that indeed which most disting[uishe]s man from other animals and is the Scource of every thing that can be called Science. I beleive his early acquaintance with Mr Mudge of Exeter, a very Learnd and thinking man, and much inclined to Philosophise in the Spirit of the Platonists, disposed him to this habit. He certainly by that means Liberalized in an high degree the Theory of his own Art; if he had been more Methodically instituted in the early part of his Life, and if he had possessed more leisure for Study and reflexion he would in my opinion have pursued this method with great success.[2] [He] had a strong turn for humour and well saw the weak sides of things. Was *timid*[3]—enjoyd every Circumstance of his good fortune and had no affectation on that Subject.[4] I do not know a fault or weakness of his that he did not convert into something that bordered[5] on a virtue instead of pushing it to the confines of a Vice.

This paper was endorsed by Malone: 'These Short notes were written by Mr Burke, in consequence of my requesting him to throw his thoughts on paper relative to Sir Joshua Reynolds, while I was employed in drawing up the Account of Sir Joshua which was published in 4to in the latter [part] of April 1797: But Mr Burke being very ill from the beginning of that year, could do no more than put down these few hints, which after his death were transmitted to me. They were not however found till Jany 1798, when a great part of the Life in the 8vo form was worked off. However, I contrived to insert almost the whole of this paper. The observation that "Sir J.R had a strong turn for humour," I had made myself before and had added it to my former account. I adopted however Mr B's expression that "he quickly saw the weak Sides of things"'.

[1] MS: as in in
[2] In his second edition Malone printed the fragment down to this point (I, p. xcviii).
[3] Malone has added a note at this point: 'This the only observation which I have not taken in. It is perfectly true'.
[4] Malone has another note at this point: 'I had said this nearly, in other words'.
[5] MS: boderd

To Earl Fitzwilliam—7 *May* 1797

Source: Fitzwilliam MSS (Sheffield).
Endorsed (by Fitzwilliam): Burke | may 12th 97.

My dearest friend,

Things grow every day, so monstrously out of all form and order of any kind, that I much doubt whether it be in human Wisdom to suggest any *effectual* remedy, or one that so much as bids *fair* in any rational mind for a probable cure. The people in power there and here[1] have carried their System of coercion, Legal and illegal, as far as it will go; and the irritated (I may say the justly irritated) Minority, seeing, that they cannot maintain themselves even in a state suitable to a respectable minority, *in Parliament,* have thrown themselves wholly upon the mixed Mass of disaffection *without doors*; and having taken the whole body of its principles and views, without any selection or discrimination whatever, are not in a situation, if they were so disposed, to support any regular Government. Every support they could give it must be at the expence of all their Credit. Without that they could do nothing: as to the little Blackguard Click that has long domineerd there, (and in Truth even here,) the ill State of their Country, they have always considerd, as a means of perpetuating their power. The Parliament, and in general the people of Landed property, give a blind support to the existing junto, merely because it does exist, without affection or attachment to it, but entirely from their dread of that Jacobinism, which so openly attacks their property, and perhaps their Lives. But, just at this moment, these very fears begin to induce them to take a contrary Course—and finding Government, as it is called, unable to protect either them or itself, they are ready, many, very many of them, to fly for refuge to that very discontented body, the apprehension of which has hitherto made them cling to the Castle. This defection of property to anarchy, I have reason to suspect, indeed to be assured, grows more diffused every hour, especially in the North. Two months ago, a concession, or even a civil temporary refusal to the Catholicks, would have fixed that description, though both fearing and hating the Junto, in the Interests of the Crown and of the two Kingdoms; But now I am satisfied, that, though such a late ungracious and forced concession might possibly do some good, I am far from relying upon it, especially in those parts, such as Ulster, and the Counties next adjoining, and the City of Dublin where the discontents of the Protestants and Catholicks run into one common Channel. All this is the more unhappy for both sides of the Water,

[1] In Ireland and in England.

because all these discontents, without management or disguise, unite in French Jacobinism, and the general Hostility to Ministers resolves itself into their supposed Enmity to the Interests of France. The very moment that Ministry had formed a plan of Fraternization with that Robbery your Lordship expected nothing better than has happened, with regard to all our foreign and all our domestick concerns. Gods will be done. I should send you a Copy of the Petition presented on behalf of the Catholicks, by Lord Kenmare &c[1] but I suppose you have it.

I do not know whether your Lordship has heard, that there is a subscription going on in Dublin, for the Tradesmen unemployd by the late failure in Credit.[2] Might it not be proper, if you get any rents in Ireland, to desire your Steward[3] to put your Lordship down for a subscription? At this moment all attentions of the kind are politick. As to the feeble hand that writes this I dont [have] much to say of it or the body it belongs to, better than that I do not think my Life very immediately threatned tho' I decay very fast. The Mind has some participation with the body in this Case or the body with it. But to the last I am most faithfully and gratefully Yours

EDM BURKE

Bath May 7.1797.

To the BISHOP OF WATERFORD—12 May 1797

Source: Fitzwilliam MSS (Sheffield). Printed *Corr.* (1844), IV, 447–8.
Addressed: The Revd Doctor Hussey | R :C: Bishop of Waterford | Waterford | Via Milford Haven.
Postmarked: BATH.
This letter is corrected by Burke but only the signature is in his hand.

[1] Early in 1797 a group of Catholic peers, Lord Kenmare (Valentine Browne, 5th Viscount Kenmare, 1754–1812), Lord Trimleston (Nicholas Barnewall, 14th Baron Trimleston, 1726–1813) and Lord Fingall (Arthur James Plunkett, 8th Earl of Fingall, 1759–1836), presented a memorial on behalf of the Roman Catholics of Ireland to the Lord Lieutenant. The memorialists dwelt on the loyalty of His Majesty's Catholic subjects and requested complete Catholic emancipation. The Lord Lieutenant transmitted the memorial to the Home Secretary, adding that he considered that 'those persons who are principally concerned in the Petition . . . would be perfectly satisfied with the prayer of that petition being complied with, and that they look neither to alteration in the Representation nor in the Establishment. They have however no influence over ⟨. . .⟩—the active agitators of the Roman Catholic Committee, who look to Power and Authority from this concession which would not be given, unless other changes were to follow it' (*Annual Register*, 1797, p. 151; Camden to Portland, 3 April, Public Record Office, H.O. 100/69, fols 176–182).
[2] At a meeting in the Mansion House, Dublin, on 31 March it was resolved that the 'present calamitous situation of the working manufacturers of this city and its liberties calls for immediate attention and relief'. It was suggested that the exclusive use of Irish manufacturers for the following twelve months would help to alleviate distress and the public were asked to subscribe to a relief fund (*Dublin Journal*, 4 April).
[3] William Wainwright (d. 1813).

My dear friend

My not having heard from you and my Strong suspicion of the uncertainty, not to say the infidelity of the communication between this and Ireland, makes me fearful of your not having my last two long Letters.[1] I am so anxious about you in your present critical position, that I shall not feel perfectly easy until I hear from you. There is another matter upon my mind of the greatest magnitude with regard to your Church in Ireland, and indeed to the welfare of all Churches and to the State there, that I would buy if it were possible, half an hours discourse with you almost at any price, but as this cannot be had, I must take the Opportunity of some safe hand for submitting to you my Sentiments by Letter.[2] Adieu, Pray let me hear every circumstance relative to you both public and private; the more minute you are the better. As to me I am extreamly feeble; but in other respects, thank God, not worse. Pray tell me a little of your mind how far a concession to the Catholics at this time, and done with as good a grace, as our ungracious circumstances will admit, might tend to prevent the spreading of the Spirit of the North in the South of Ireland. Cork is not far from you and a visit there to your worthy Brother Bishop[3] might be of use in helping you to form a judgment on this arduous matter.

> Believe me ever, most truly and Affectionately
> Yours
> EDM BURKE

Bath
   12 May 97

To FRENCH LAURENCE—12 *May* 1797

Source: Fitzwilliam MSS (Northampton). Printed *Burke–Laurence Correspondence*, pp. 204–18.
Although it has minor corrections by Burke, this letter is not in his hand. There is a copy at Sheffield and another in the Osborn Collection.

My dear Laurence

The times are so deplorable that I do not know how to write about them. Indeed, I can hardly bear to think of 'em. In the selection of these mischiefs, these, which have the most recently, oppressed and over-

[1] Hussey wrote to Burke from Waterford on 9 May explaining that he was 'in a distant part of this Diocese' when Burke's 'last kind letter of the 27 april arrived'. He went on to give statistical information concerning priests and communicants in the diocese, which apparently Burke had asked him to supply (MS at Sheffield, printed *Corr.* (1844), IV, 444–6). Burke's letter of 27 April and the other 'long' letter are missing.
[2] Burke wrote to Hussey on 16 and 22 May; see below, pp. 341–6, 357–8.
[3] Dr Moylan; see above, p. 303.

powered rather than exercized the shattered remains of my Understanding, are those of the Navy and those of Ireland. As to the first, I shall say nothing, except this, that you must remember from the moment the true genius of this French revolution began to dawn upon my mind, I comprehended what it would be in its meridian; and that I have often said, that I should dread more from one or two maritime provinces in France, in which the spirit and principles of that Revolution were established, than from the old French monarchy possessed of all that its Ambition ever aspired to. That we should begin to be infected in the first Nidus and hot bed of their infection; The subordinate parts of our military force, and that I should not be surprized at seeing a French Army convoyed by a British Navy to an attack upon this Kingdom. I think you must remember the thing and the Phrase. I trust in God that these mutineers may not as yet have imbrud their hands deeply in blood. If they have, we must expect the worst that can happen. Alas for the mischiefs that are done by the Newspapers and by the embicility of the ministers, who neither refuse or modify any concession, nor execute with promptitude the resolutions they take thro' fear; but are hesitating and backward, even in their measures of retreat and flight. In Truth they know nothing of the maneuvre either in advance or retreat.

The other affair hardly less perplexing, nor much less instantly urging, is that of Ireland. Mr Baldwin[1] was here and he spoke something, though indistinctly and confusedly of a strong desire that he supposed the Duke of Portland to have to be reconciled to my Lord Fitzwilliam. Whether this is meer loose talk such as I have uniformly heard from the day of the fatal rupture is more than I know. My Answer was, that while the cause of this calamitous rupture was yet in its Operation, I had done every thing which A man like me could do, to prevent it, and its[2] effect but that now the question was not, what should reconcile the Duke of Portland to Earl FitzWilliam, but what would reconcile Ireland to England. This was very near the whole of our conversation. You know he does not see very far, nor combine very much. I have had a hint from another quarter not indeed very direct, to know whether it was my Opinion that a concession to the Irish Catholics would quiet that Country. To this I have given no answer, because, at this moment, I am utterly incapable of giving any the least distinct. Three months ago, perhaps even two months ago, I can say with confidence, notwithstanding the hands from which it would be offered, it would have prevented the discontents from running into one

---

[1] William Baldwin; see above, p. 81.   [2] MS: its its

Mass; even if the compliance had been decently evaded, and future hopes held out, I think these mischiefs would not have happened; but instead of this, every measure has been used that could possibly tend to irritation. The rejection of the memorial was abrupt, final, and without any temperament whatsoever.[1] The Speeches in the House of Lords in Ireland were in the same strain;[2] and in the House of Commons, the Ministers put forward a wretched brawler one Duigenan of your profession to attack Mr Fox,[3] tho' they knew, that, as a British Member of Parliament he was by them invulnerable; but their great object was to get him[4] to rail at the whole body of Catholics and Dissenters in Ireland, in the most foul and unmeasured language. This brought on as they might well have expected from Mr Grattan, one [of] the most animated Philippics which he ever yet delivered against their Government and Parliament.[5] It was a speech the best calculated which could be conceived further to inflame the irritation which the Castle Brawlers long harrangue must necessarily ⟨...⟩ have produced. As to Mr Fox, he had all the honour of the day, because the invective against him was stupid, and from A man of no authority or weight whatsoever: and the Panegyrick which was opposed to it was full of eloquence, and from a great name. The Attorney General in wishing the motion withdrawn, as I understand, did by no means discountenance the principle upon which it was made, nor disown the attack which was made in a manner, upon the whole people of Ireland.[6] The Sollicitor General went the full length

[1] See above, p. 331. In March Camden informed Portland that a similar memorial to the one he had transmitted to England had been presented to him and that he had told the Catholic peers presenting it that he 'considered this as a great constitutional Question upon which Parliament had decided [in] 1795 with great temper and with every attention to the subject—as I saw no difference in the Question, I could not give encouragement to its being again agitated, as I thought it could lead to no good end and might be the cause of much discontent and misinterpretation'. In reply Portland conveyed to the Lord Lieutenant the King's approval of his answer (Camden to Portland, 21 March; Portland to Camden, 27 March, Public Record Office, H.O. 100/69, fols 168–168 v; 188–9).

[2] Burke is probably referring to the speeches in support of the Government's policy, delivered in the Irish House of Lords on 4 May by Charles Dillon Lee, 12th Viscount Dillon (1745–1813), and on 13 May by Charles Coote, 1st Earl of Bellamont (1738–1800), and Andrew Thomas Blayney, 11th Baron Blayney (1770–1834).

[3] On 1 May in the Irish House of Commons Patrick Duigenan (c. 1737–1816) proposed 'in a speech of three hours' that Fox's speech of 23 March, when he had proposed the House of Commons should request the King to take into consideration the condition of Ireland, should be read at the bar of the House. At the close of the debate Duigenan's motion was negatived without a division (Irish Parliamentary Register, XVII, 490–515; Dublin Evening Post, 2 May).

[4] Duigenan.

[5] Grattan, having pointed out that Duigenan 'scorned anything that was classical, moderate or refined and preferred as more effectual, the gross and the scandalous', went on to denounce the unconstitutional methods by which the British Government exercised control over Ireland.

[6] Arthur Wolfe (see above, p. 117), the Attorney General, thought the House should take no action in the matter.

of supporting it.[1] Instead of endeavouring to widen the narrow bottom upon which they stand, they make it their Policy to render it every day more narrow. In the Parliament of Great Britain Lord Grenvilles speech turned the loyalty of the Catholics against themselves; he argued from that zeal and loyalty they had manifested, their want of a sense of any grievance.[2] This speech, tho' probably well intended, was the most indiscreet and mischievous of the whole. People do not like to be put into practical dilemmas. If the people are turbulent and riotous, nothing is to be done for them on account of their evil dispositions. If they are obedient, and loyal, nothing is to be done for them, because their being quiet and contented, is a proof that they feel no grievance. I know that this declaration has had its natural effect, and that in several places, the Catholics think themselves called upon to deny the inference made by Ministers from their good conduct. It seems to them a great insult to convert their resolution to support the Kings Government into an approbation of the conduct of those who make it the foundation of their credit, and authority that they are the enemies of their description. I send you two Extract's of Letters for Lord FitzWilliams and your information from intelligent and well informed people in Cork; and one of them from a Gentleman of much consideration and influence in that place.[3] These will let you see the effect of that conduct which tends to unite all descriptions of persons in the South, in the same spirit of discontent and in the same bonds of sedition with those of the North.

So far as I can find no part of the Army in Ireland is yet tainted with the general spirit; but under a general discontent it is impossible it should long continue sound; and even if it did, it is as impossible that such a Country can be ruled by a military Government, even though there were no Enemy, abroad to take advantage of that miserable state of things. Now suffer me to throw down to you my thoughts of what might be expected under the existing circumstances from the meer grant of an Act of Parliament for a total emancipation. This measure I hold to be a fundamental part in any plan for quieting that Country and reconciling it to this; but you are well aware, that this measure, like every other measure of the kind, must depend on the manner in which it is done, the persons who do it, and the skill and judgment with which the whole is conducted. And first, my clear opinion is, that as long as the

[1] John Toler (1745–1831), later (1827) 1st Earl of Norbury, supported the attack on Fox (*Dublin Evening Post*, 2 May).
[2] In the debate of 21 March on Lord Moira's motion respecting the state of Ireland, Grenville had referred to the loyalty displayed by the Catholics when Hoche's expedition was off the Irish coast (*Parliamentary History*, XXXIII, 131).
[3] Two extracts are printed in the *Burke–Laurence Correspondence*, pp. 208–9; MS copies are at Sheffield, F 30f.

present Junto continue to govern Ireland, such a measure, into which they must manifestly appear to be reluctantly driven, never can produce the effects proposed by it; because it is impossible to persuade the people that as long as they govern, they will not have both the power and inclination, totally to frustrate the effect of this new arrangement as they have done that of all the former. Indeed, it will appear astonishing that these men should be kept in the sole monopoly of all power, upon the sole merit of their resistance to the Catholic claims, as inconsistent with the connexion of the two Kingdoms; and yet at the same time to see those claims admitted and the pretended principle of the connexion of the two Countries abandoned, to preserve to the same persons the same monopoly. By this, it would appear, that the Subject is either to be relieved, or not; and the Union of the two Kingdoms abandoned or maintained just as it may answer the purposes of a faction of 3 or 4 individuals.

But if that junto was thrown out to morrow, along with their measure, Government has proceeded in such a manner, and committed so many in violent declarations on this subject that a compleat emancipation would no longer pass with its former facility, and a strong ferment would be excited in the Church party, who, though but few in numbers, have in their hands most of the ultimate and superior property of the Kingdom.

The difficulties appear to me to be great. Certain it is, that if they were removed, the leaders of the Opposition must be taken into their places, and become the objects of confidence to an English Government. They are to a man pledged for some alteration in the constitution of Parliament. If they made no such alteration, they would lose the weight which they have; and which is so necessary to quiet the Country. If, on the other hand, they were to attempt a change upon any of the plans of moderation, which I hear they have adopted, they would be as far from satisfying the demands of the extravagant people whom they mean to comply with, as they would be in preserving the actual constitution, which was in a great part fabricated in 1614.[1] The Second infallible consequence would be that, if a Revolution of this kind (for it would be a Revolution) were accomplished in Ireland, tho' the grounds are a little different yet the principle is so much the same, that it would be impossible long to resist an alteration of the same kind on this side of the Water; and I never have doubted, since I came to the Years of discretion, nor ever can doubt, that such changes in this Kingdom would be preliminary steps to our utter ruin: But if I considered them as

[1] See above, p. 125.

such, at all times, what must they appear to me at a moment like the present.

I see no way of settling these kingdoms but by a great change in the superior Government *here*. If the present Administration is removed, it is manifest to me, that the Duke of Bedford[1] and Lord Guilford,[2] and the D. of Northumberland[3] and Lord Lansdown,[4] all, or most of them, under the direction of Mr Sheridan and Mr Fox, will be the sole option; That if they took in the Duke of Portland, they must take him in, at best, in the state of utter insignificance in which unfortunately he now stands—That they would gladly take in my Lord FitzWilliam, I have no question; but, I am sure, he would have no support, and never would be suffered to play any principal part, as long as he holds the maxims, and is animated by the sentiments for which, as a Statesman, we value him. He certainly would do best in Ireland, but I am very far from being sure that his connexions there would look up to him with the same simple and undivided Affection which they formerly did; and I am equally uncertain whether He would leave behind him A ministry, which, in the Mass, would be better disposed to his support, than those who had formerly betrayed him—Besides, I cannot look without horror, upon his being conjoined, (and possibly found in a new reign in such a conjunction,) with a Ministry, who, have spared no pains to prove their indifference at least, to the local honour and interest of their Country, or to the general liberty of Europe. And, indeed, who have wished to leave no doubt upon any mind that it is their ambition to act in this Country as a subordinate department to the Directory of the French Republic.

I see no ray of hope, but in some sort of Coalition between the heads of the factions who now distract us, formed upon a sense of the public danger. But unfortunately their Animosity towards each other grows with the danger. I confess that if no such coalition is made, and yet that a change should take place, I see in the present ministry and its partizans an Opposition far more formidable in numbers and connexion, than that which we have at present; and that after a while at least their principles and their modes of proceeding will not be found very different from those of the present Opposition.

I must add, since I am opening my mind so much at large, that when I look at the State of the *civil* List in Great Britain, which I have reason to know and feel, to be full 2 years in debt to most of the

[1] Francis Russell, 5th Duke of Bedford (1765–1802).
[2] George Augustus North, 3rd Earl of Guilford (1757–1802).
[3] Hugh Percy, 2nd Duke of Northumberland (1742–1817).
[4] See above, p. 281.

departments,[1] I see no means of carrying on Government upon any thing like a broad bottom even Officially. To say nothing of the necessary accommodation[2] to those expectants who will look, to come forward with advantage, or to retire without marks of disgrace; and both parties have emulously concurred in cutting off, all those extraneous means of accommodation which might supply the deficiency of the civil List resources.

In Ireland things are yet worse. They have seized upon all the means of Government in order to accommodate one family and its dependancies;[3] and they have so squandered away every resource under the pretence of providing a Home defence, that not only is Ireland unable to form a System of comprehension, but England will soon find itself unable to supply that Kingdom with the means of its ordinary existence.

To whatever point of the compass I turn my eyes I see nothing but difficulty and disaster, you will naturally say, why therefore do you reason in a state of despair. I do it that Lord FitzWilliam and yourself may see my melancholly reveries in this deplorable state of things. The very consideration of the difficulties which strike me may suggest to better heads, than mine, the means of overcoming them.

I do not know whether you have seen Hussey's Pastoral Letter.[4] It is written with eloquence and energy, and with, perhaps, too little management towards the unfortunate System which rules in Ireland, at present; but it is the product of a manly mind, strongly impressed with the trust committed to his hands for supporting that religion, in the Administration of which, he holds a very responsible place, and which he considers as in the commencement of a new persecution. It is therefore no wonder that he recommends an adherence to it under all circumstances, which many people animated by a contrary party zeal may not approve: But men must act according to their situation, and for one I am of Opinion that it were better to have a strong party Zeal, provided it is bottomed in our common principles, than any thing resembling infidelity, which last we know, by woeful experience is as capable of religious persecution as any Sectarian spirit can possibly be.

I received your Letter of yesterday.[5] Nothing can equal the precipitation of ministers, in acceding to the demands of the first mutiny. Nothing but want of forsight can be alledged in favour of the formal-

---

[1] Three classes of the Civil List had exceeded their estimates for some years past (*Report from the Committee on Civil List Accounts . . . ordered to be printed 15 March 1802, H.C.* (1801–2), II).
[2] MS: accomodation.
[3] Presumably Burke refers to the political position of the Beresford family (see vol. VIII, 186–7).   [4] See above, pp. 302–4.
[5] MS Bodleian Library; printed *Burke–Laurence Correspondence*, pp. 201–4.

izing delay to effectuate the purposes of the grant which had been extorted from their peers. But this will ever be the case of those who act from no principle but that of fear. The moment that is over they fall into a supine security. I agree with you that no folly ever equalled their attempt to beg off discussion upon this subject. They ought to have known that it could have no other effect than what it had, which was to provoke and inflame the discussion, they so childishly sought to avoid; but the whole is the result of that meanness[1] of Spirit which has brought on all our misfortunes and rendered all our resources fruitless.

Delicacy alone has been the sole cause of my silence to Mr Windham, with relation to the affairs of Ireland;[2] otherwise he is entitled to, and he possesses, my most unreserved confidence. I have therefore no sort of difficulty in wishing him to know my thoughts upon that Subject. They will not be very encouraging to him, because I am greatly afraid that the preposterous method beginning with force, and ending with concession, may defeat the effect of both. If things had been in Their natural course, I should certainly have agreed with him. No concession on the part of Government ought ever to be made without such a demonstration of force as might ensure it against contempt. It will always be a matter of great moment in whose hands the force to be applied in domestic disturbances is placed. Never, no Never, shall I be persuaded, that any force can appear otherwise than as odious, and more odious, than dreaded, When it is known to be under the direction of Lord Car-hampton.[3] I will not enter into all the particulars but among the many mischievous measures lately adopted, his nomination to the Office of Commander in Chief, led to by far the worst consequences. When I am opening my mind to you, I must add, that as long as a shallow hot-headed puppy, proud and presumptuous, and ill behavd like Mr Cooke[4] has the chief or any credit at the Castle, or with ministers here, I can expect no sort of good from any thing that can be done in Parliament. When we talk of giving way to Mr Grattan and the Ponsonby's, I suppose it is meant that they should be taken into the Irish ministry; else, to give them a triumph and, at the same time to leave them in a state of discontent and dissatisfaction, if we consider the interest of

[1] MS: meaness
[2] Laurence had told Burke: 'Windham is getting right about Ireland . . . He wishes to have your opinion; but he is a little afraid to ask it, from his former difference on that point. You may write to me as if I had asked for it myself, and I will communicate with him . . .'. Writing to Mrs Crewe on 30 September 1796, Windham said on the subject of Irish politics: 'Mr B. is wrong, by excess and exaggeration, I dare say; but whether he is so in the main, I should much doubt' (Windham, *Diary*, p. 342).
[3] See above, p. 117.
[4] Edward Cooke (1755–1820). He was Under-Secretary in the Military Department 1789–95, 1795–6, and Under-Secretary in the Civil Department, from 1796 until 1801.

Government as Government is to act against the most obvious dictates of common sense. Adieu, I may truly say, with Addison's Cato 'I am weary of conjectures'.[1]

I will not add with him, 'that this must end them'; But they must soon be ended by the Master of the Drama, to whose Will, pray with me, that we may be all, in all things submissive. Don't forget to send me the report of the House of Commons, and that of the House of Lords, if you can get it;[2] though I do not know why I am anxious about it, because as a Nation our fate seems to be decided, and we perish with all the material means of strength that ever Nation has possessed, by a poverty and imbecility of mind, which has no example I am sure, and could have no excuse, even in the weakest.

> Adieu, adieu,
> yours ever
> E B

Bath 12th May 97

P.S: This, with the extracts of the Letters[3] will be in three Covers.

Nagle told Woodford (in a letter postmarked 13 May) that Burke had written 'a very long Letter' to Laurence 'of 4 sheets, on Irish Affairs, together with two Extracts of Letters from very respectable and intelligent people in Cork—not Sir P: oConor... nothing but extream delicacy prevents Mr Burke from writing to Windham on the Subject of Ireland' (Add. MS 37,843, fols 185–6).

EARL FITZWILLIAM to EDMUND BURKE—15 *May* [1797]

Source: Fitzwilliam MSS (Sheffield).
Endorsed (by Jane Burke): Lord Fitzwilliam | May 15 97.

My dear Burke

We are at length arriv'd in town: nothing, going forward is of a nature to give one any satisfaction: the best circumstance is, that it will now be in my power to do what I have long wish'd for, which is to make you a visit: I hope by the end of this week or the beginning of the next to be able to set out for Bath.

I have seen your letter to Lawrence,[4] and it is a pleasure and great

---

[1] See Addison's *Cato*, V, 1, 20.

[2] Burke is probably referring to the third and principle report of the Secret Committee of the House of Commons appointed to inquire into the total amount of outstanding demands on the Bank of England which was presented to the House of Commons on 21 April, and to the report of the Secret Committee of the House of Lords appointed to inquire into the causes which produced the order of council of 26 February, which was presented to the House on 28 April (*Journals of the House of Commons*, LII, 476; *Parliamentary History*, XXXIII, 441–63; *Journals of the House of Lords*, XLI, 186–262).

[3] See note above, p. 335   [4] The previous letter.

satisfaction to find that, upon a consideration of the great turn of affairs, and of the new aspect of things, my own mind gives much into your way of thinking—the day is now pass'd, and safety is no longer attainable upon the solid ground of preventing the danger: all that is now left, is to put ourselves into such a situation as to wait with the least inconvenience, and with the least risk, events which we cannot foresee: that harbour of safety into which it has pleas'd us not to steer the vessel, chance may toss it into—cherishing this hope, and relying, from necessity, on some fortunate accident happening in our favor, it dispirits me beyond measure, when I look to the state of Ireland: I tremble lest things should be brought to such a pitch, as to preclude even the operations of accident from saving us; and yet they are at present going on in a train, that must end in that desperate state—a report has reach'd me, that Government think of sending Lord Cornwallis over;[1] intending to concede to the Catholicks, but certainly to preserve their own abominable junto and system in every thing else—whatever such a concession would have done time back, single it will do no good now, and carried over by Lord C. it will do infinite mischief—with whatever views the Ministry may send him, the Irish will certainly consider it as a denunciation of a system more military even than hitherto, and not unlikely it will prove the tocsin of instant insurrection—the fatal issue of such an event is too certain.

A report prevails that the K of Prussia is dying[2]—ever affectionately Yours,
                                                            W.F.
London
May 15

To the BISHOP OF WATERFORD—16 *May* 1797

Source: Plowden, *History of Ireland*, II, Appen. pp. 290–2.

At least five pamphlets were published in reply to Hussey's Pastoral, and Pelham told Dr John Thomas Troy (1739–1823), the Catholic Archbishop of Dublin, that the Pastoral 'was very intemperate and inflammatory, little expected from any Catholic pastor ... in these times of public agitation, when every honest man should endeavour to allay the ferment instead of opening old sores'.

[1] There were rumours that Charles Cornwallis, 1st Marquess Cornwallis (1738–1805), would be sent to Ireland as Commander-in-Chief. Writing to Camden on [19] May, Portland expressed his belief that Cornwallis was 'not averse' from going to Ireland as Commander-in-Chief (*The Times*, 17 May; Public Record Office, H.O. 100/69, fol. 268). On 23 May, Camden, writing to Cornwallis, hoped he 'could be prevailed upon to accept the Lord Lieutenancy of this kingdom' (*Correspondence of Charles, First Marquis Cornwallis*, ed. C. Ross, London, 1859, II, 326–7).
[2] Frederick William II died on 16 November after a protracted illness.

Troy assured Pelham that the Pastoral had been published 'without the approbation or knowledge of any of our prelates, and that we all considered it as unseasonable and reprehensible in its tendency'. Pelham concluded the discussion by remarking that 'Hussey is very warm, and has acted without reflection' (Troy to P. J. Plunket, 23 May, quoted in A. Cogan, *The Diocese of Meath, Ancient and Modern*, Dublin, 1862–70, III, 212).

My Dear Friend,

I hope in God this letter will find you in Ireland. From the moment that the government who employed you betrayed you, they determined at the same time to destroy you. They are not a people to stop short in their course. You have come to an open issue with them. On your part what you have done has been perfectly agreeable to your duty as a Catholic bishop and a man of honor and spirit. Whether it is equally agreeable to those rules of circumspect prudence, which ought to have their weight perhaps in an enslaved country, may admit of some question. That many of your people will be ready to condemn you is very probable: it is more than probable that they will give you but a feeble support, however the less you have to rely on others, the more you are to rely upon yourself. There is nothing I wish for more than to have some conversation with you. But if just now you were to come to England, it would be construed into a flight from the attack of Lord [Dillon][1] and Mr [Day],[2] at the same time that you will naturally act in a manner agreeable to the courageous dispositions, which you have from principle, from disinterestedness, and a degree perhaps from mental constitution, you will be careful to preserve that temper, in which the conflict which I fear you will be called to will certainly require. I expect you will be called before Lord D[illon]'s committee.[3] I did not conceive that a man of so little estimation in either kingdom, would have the lead of the House of Lords committed to him, without some purpose, that required that kind of instrument. I therefore am

[1] In the Irish House of Lords on 4 May, Dillon (see above, p. 334) 'in very strong terms commented on an incendiary publication called a pastoral letter to [sic] the titular bishop of Waterford, which tended so much to encourage the evil dispositions of the day'. He called it 'the most inflamatory pamphlet' he had ever read (*Dublin Evening Post*, 6 May, *Dublin Journal*, 6 May).
[2] Robert Day (1746–1841), Chairman of Quarter Sessions, County Dublin 1790–8, Justice of the King's Bench 1798–1818, in *A Charge Delivered to the Grand Jury of the County of Dublin . . . on Tuesday 25 April 1797*, Dublin, 1797, declared that 'even the fidelity of our brave and loyal soldiery is practised upon—that implicit submission to authority which is the mainspring of the military machine, the soldier's first and paramount duty, without which an army becomes a rabble, formidable only to those who pay it—by a minister of peace, bending under the favour of that government whose main pillars he thus, with a boldness beyond all parallel attempts to shake'.
[3] Dillon was a member of the Secret Committee appointed by the Irish House of Lords on 5 May (see below, pp. 351–2). On 13 May he moved an address to the Lord Lieutenant thanking him for the measures he had taken to suppress the traitorous conspiracy described in the reports of the secret committees (*Dublin Journal*, 16 May).

of opinion, that instead of coming direct from W[aterfor]d to England, you ought to go without delay to Dublin. How could they expect that you, a Catholic bishop, should not prefer your own religion to all others? How could they expect, that you should be of any other opinion than mine, in which you know we frequently agreed, 'that if the Catholics were seduced or bullied from the only religion they have or can have, they must fall into indifference or into actual atheism, or its concomitant direct tendency, actual rebellion'. How could they expect, that if you as a Catholic pastor, did not strongly assert the advantages and pre-eminence of your own religion, yet as a good citizen you would endeavour to keep the people attached to the only religion which they can possibly have. How dare they assert it is not the religion of the country, in which more than 100 to 1 in your diocese are of your communion.[1] If they should say, as that buffoon D[uigena]n does, that this is the religion, of the common people,[2] it is only to speak more in its favor, because it is for them that all religion, and eminently the Christian religion is meant for a guide, for a control and for a consolation. These are principles you have always held. To be sure Christ himself has given as a conclusive proof in his answer to John the Baptist of his divine mission, that the gospel was preached to the poor.[3] The other part of the divine answer, if you cannot imitate in miracle you may as you have always done imitate in charity. As to what you said to the soldiers, why should it be wrong in you to say of them exactly what Tertullian has said of the Roman soldiers in his day?[4] You cannot alter the language of the church, and I believe there is no Protestant pastor (and I believe you may appeal to his Grace of Cashel)[5] who should attempt by any rigor inflicted or threatened to bring his people to mass. Who would or could mean any other language than what you have done? The great point for you (as I wrote to you before in my first long letter,[6] because I knew that the castle junto do absolutely deny the fact) is to establish the circumstance either of menace, coercion, or punishment as the case may be. When you have bottomed yourself well upon these

---

[1] Hussey had told Burke in his letter of 9 May that there were by his best calculation 280,000 Catholic communicants in his diocese and not more than 2500 Protestants.

[2] In his speech on 1 May Duigenan declared that 'it was necessary to state that the whole of the Irish beggary falls to the share of the Romanists, and that the wealth of the Irish Protestants is, to that of the Irish Romanists, at least as twenty to one' (*Dublin Journal*, 4 May).   [3] See Matthew, XI. 5.

[4] In *De Coronā Militis* Tertullian laid down that a convert to Christianity if a soldier must either quit the service or 'must in every way demur to doing anything against God, which things are not allowed, no, not on the ground of military service'. He gave as an example, wearing crowns of laurel and myrtle—the laurel and myrtle being sacred to heathen gods—or renewing vows in heathen temples (Tertullian, *Apologetic and Practical Treatises*, translated by C. Dodgson, Oxford, 1842).

[5] Charles Agar (see above, p. 258).   [6] Missing.

facts, you need not be afraid to meet the vindictive[1] Lord D[illon] upon
this ground. I should not be sorry, that the Catholicity of this nobleman's family should be alleged as an excuse for thinking well of your
religion for that whatever respect you have for the present Lord D[illon],
you cannot think better of him than you did of the old lord,[2] who
certainly had been a most zealous Catholic, that if any person of those
families became more enlightened you could have no objection to it,
but you could not think the better of them on account of their conversion, and that you hoped they would not persecute you on principles
which would equally well have justified a persecution of their ancestors
and nearest relations. That you would heartily wish, that every man in
the kingdom had as much zeal for the crown, and as much abhorrence
for jacobinical principles as you have shewn. I revert to it again, you
cannot leave Ireland until you have seen Dublin. There is a direct attack
intended to be made on all your episcopacy. Dr Troy has not fared
better than you, notwithstanding his caution and the sermons he has
published against the taking of oaths.[3] For I have this day a letter from
a most respectable and dignified clergyman of the church of England,[4]
in which he tells me, that the Dublin castle runners in London propagated every where, that this prelate actually had taken the oath of
united Irishmen. If you have not wisdom enough to make common
cause, they will cut you off one by one. If you are called on, my opinion
is, that you ought to recapitulate all the proceedings at Laughlinstown,[5]
and to state that you consider that as the pledge of government, that on
your going to Ireland you would find the same course persevered in.
That let them determine what they will, you are determined to do your
duty. That if you have expressed your apprehensions from the persons
commonly called the *junto*, it is nothing but what you are justified in by
their own repeated declarations of dislike to your whole body, and the
repugnance which they have always publicly expressed against the
repeal of the several persecuting and disqualifying laws. This last is only
a hint in case they should urge you upon the point. I feel as much

---

[1] Plowden, *History of Ireland*: vindical
[2] Henry Dillon, 11th Viscount Dillon (1705–87).
[3] Dr Troy issued in August 1795 a pastoral warning to his flock against taking the
Defenders' oath (*Dublin Evening Post*, 11 August 1795). On 10 March 1797 he published
his *Pastoral Address to the Roman Catholicks of the Archdiocese of Dublin delivered...in
the Chapel of Francis-Street Dublin, on Thursday 16th February MDCCVII the day
appointed for a solemn thanksgiving to Almighty God, for having mercifully preserved this
Kingdom from the late impending horrors of a French invasion.* After making a strong
attack on 'the impious demagogues' of France, Troy warned his flock against engaging
in oath-bound conspiracies. 'To promise on oath', he wrote, 'which may excite or
promote rebellion, the invasion of an enemy, sedition, disturbance of public peace,
injury to any community or any individual in person, property or reputation, is contrary
to justice'.   [4] Not identified. The letter is missing.
[5] See above, p. 168.

concerned in you as if I was in my own person in Ireland, and in your situation, because you know I advised you to accept the D[uk]e of P[ortlan]d's invitation; though I confess (and I am sure you remember) that I trembled at your being committed at such times and with such people:[1] but I thought it an imperious duty, and so did yourself to do every thing in your power to check the growth of jacobinism upon one hand, and oppression, which is its best friend, on the other. I hope you have put down what you intended about the protest you entered into with the D[uk]e of P[ortlan]d's and Mr P[it]t. Adieu. I am with little ceremony, but great truth,

Yours, &c. &c.
E.B.

Bath, 16th May, 1797.

To WALKER KING—16 *May* 1797
Source: MS Osborn Collection.
This letter is not in Burke's hand.

My dear Walker

I send the Receipt[2] as you wish directed as you desire to No 6 Burlington Street Westminster.[3] Let me [know] whether it is come to hand.

Nothing can equal the madness and folly of all the proceedings in England; except the madness and folly of the proceedings in Ireland, which not only equal but far exceed them in every particular of insanity and absurdity. As to their charge of illegal and seditious oaths upon the most timid, passive and inert man, Dr Troy, Catholic Archbishop of Dublin, it is equal to any piece of invention in the whole of their drama. I dare say that on sending to Coghlan[4] you may [buy] his Sermon or pastoral mandate, against such oaths[5]—In the mean time you will be so good as to let me know if possible who they are that have propagated this Story. By their putting forward Lord Dillon in the House of Lords,[6] the lowest, the most lying and every way the most contemptible wretch in Ireland, Peer Or commoner to attack Dr Hussey, and to lead in the secret Committee with the Archbishop of Cashel[7] and Lord Shannon,[8] they certainly intend to raise a new and

---

[1] The official world in Ireland.
[2] This is probably the receipt for the legacy from Lord John Cavendish (see above, pp. 289, 290).
[3] John Heaton, the Duke of Devonshire's agent, lived at 6 Old Burlington Street.
[4] James Peter Coghlan (*c.* 1732–1800), Catholic bookseller, printer and publisher.
[5] Dr Troy's *Pastoral Address* published in March; see the previous letter.
[6] MS: Lord   [7] See above, p. 258.
[8] Richard Boyle, 2nd Earl of Shannon (1728–1807).

formidable persecution of the Roman Catholics; and they will begin by taking the Ecclesiastical preferments of that religion into their own hands and will fill those places with the worst and meanest of their tools: and then you will see nothing but irreligion and confusion throughout the whole Country. In the mean time they are keeping up a standing Army of 70,000 Men to coerce the Country which produces nothing but a stagnation of all business, the utter destruction of the Revenue and public Credit and the Non-payment of Rents. Assure my Lord FitzWilliam, that nothing on Earth could give me greater pleasure than the hopes of seeing him before I die. As to my suggesting any thing I am at my Wits end. Now to turn to the private matter you mention to me.

Inform Mrs Silburn[1] of my constant regard and value for her, and that I should feel great satisfaction in obliging her in any thing which depended upon me; but the School is not mine to dispose of at my pleasure, and I am but a trustee for Government upon the plan which I have myself proposed, which is, only for French boys; only for those under certain descriptions and to the limited number of 60—Mrs Silburn is not aware that I should be guilty of a scandalous breach of my trust if I suffered an English Boy to be introduced into that School. I send to Government a regular return of all the Boys in it, and if I admitted[2] these young persons, it must be in a fraudulent and clandestine manner. Mrs Silburn will therefore consider this as one of the matters that are wholly out of my choice, and indeed, I dont know that she has any loss, for a more unfit school than this for English boys of any denomination I cannot possibly conceive. As to Mrs Edwards[3] I know her full value as a faithful, diligent and attached Servant, but farther than that, she has nothing to do with the School. Mrs Silburn talks of beds. The Boys are already so crowded and incomoded that there is no room for any thing of that kind. I have already refused the solicitations of persons of the first distinction belonging to France to have their children admited as Supernumeraries, tho' they have offered to pay the whole charge.

Will you be so good as to pay the two Guineas as directed in the enclosed Letter[4] taking the necessary receipt. I am my dear Walker

ever Affectionately yours
E B

Bath

16th May 1797

[1] See above, p. 9.   [2] MS: admitted
[3] Mary Edwards (*née* Tomkins; *c.* 1740–1802), the Housekeeper of the Penn school.
[4] Missing.

To WILLIAM WINDHAM—16 *May* 1797

Source: British Museum (Add. MS 37,843, fols 187–90). Printed (dated
10 May) in *Burke–Windham Correspondence*, pp. 244–6.
Addressed: Private | The Right Honble | William Windham | &c &c &c | Park
Street | Westminster | London.
Postmarked: BATH FREE|MA|⟨ ⟩|97|C.
Only the signature and the word 'Private' of the address are in Burke's hand.

Discontent caused by inadequate pay, defective victualling and harsh discipline had been growing for some time in the Navy and on 16 April the men of
the Channel Fleet at Spithead refused to obey orders. When it was promised
that their grievances would be redressed, they returned to duty on 23 April
(see above, p. 313). But the legislation providing for an increase of pay was not
introduced for a fortnight. The men grew suspicious and on 7 May they again
refused to obey orders. The Government quickly took steps to increase the
seamen's pay and the Spithead mutiny finally ended on 15 May. A few days
earlier, on 12 May, mutiny had broken out on the ships stationed at the Nore
(including ships of the North Sea Fleet). The Government took strong measures
and by 15 June the mutiny at the Nore had collapsed also.

My dear Friend

You cannot be very much at a loss for the cause of my not answering
your last Letter[1] before this time, though its kindness well deserved
my most early attention; but grief, shame, indignation, and utter
despair, have so fermented in my mind, as to produce there a disorder,
as strong, as the fermentation which my food undergoes in my miserable
Stomach. What could I give you but one of my Mental eructations?
There is an end of us. The Revolution is accomplished, even before the
Jacobin Peace. It has happened as I long feared it would that the
danger has commenced in the very foundations of our false security.
We have paid near £600,000 A year for the destruction of our Naval
discipline and Naval fidelity for ever:[2] and this unfortunate measure of
buying mutiny and unsubordination in the Navy, has been followed by
a beginning in the Army,[3] which will run through the whole, and as
most certainly it will be the measure on such a peace as they will make,
to keep up a great Military and Naval establishment, the expence will be
enormous. Among the people it will be a perpetual source of discontent;
and in proportion as Troops and Seamen are idle and unemployed, in
that proportion, will be their disposition to every species of insubordina-
tion: But Among all the parts of this fatal measure the Mission of my

---

[1] Windham's letter of 30 April; MS at Sheffield.
[2] The total cost of the concessions made to the mutineers at Spithead was estimated
by Pitt at £536,000 per annum (*Parliamentary History*, XXXIII, 478).
[3] 'The Chancellor of the Exchequer gave notice, that it was his intention, on Monday
next [22 May], to bring forward a proposition for making such allowances to the Army
and Militia as the House should think proper' (*The Times*, 17 May).

Lord Howe[1] has been by far the most mischievous. Had a great Naval Commander been sent down 'bravem pietate et meritis virumquem'[2] to awe the seditious into obedience, it would have been the best thing that could be thought of; but to send the first name in the Navy, and who had been but lately a Cabinet Minister and first Lord of the Admiralty at upwards of 70 years of Age, to hunt amongst mutineers for grievances, to take the Law from (*Joice*) a seditious Clubist of Belfast,[3] and to remove by his orders some of the principal Officers of the Navy, puts an end to all hopes for ever. Such mischief need not to have been attended with so much degradation. There is an amnesty for rebellion, but none for Officers who do their duty. They, and they only, are punished and degraded.[4] The mutineers now choose their own Officers, or have at least a Negative on them, and all officers who go to Sea are apprized of the tenure by which they hold, and must, in future, comport themselves, not as Naval commanders, but as Candidates at an election. All this is the fruit of the snug system of our plan in a Home defence. I see by the Irish Government Newspapers[5] that 8,000 men have been either sent or are sending, to Ireland to support a military Government there under the auspices of that Junto to which both Kingdoms are sacrificed. Do you really beleive, or does any one beleive, that such a military Government can be supported by the joint finances of both Nations. I am sure Ireland can contribute little or nothing towards it. I see they are making a run through the most contemptible wretch on Earth Lord Dillon; and another, not much less so, a Mr Day, at my friend Doctor Hussey,[6] upon account of his Zeal in strengthening his flock according to his principles, against the religious persecution, which, under pretence of military discipline, has been exercized against the Roman Catholic Soldiery. Excuse me if I speak my mind freely. These people have perfidiously quarreled upon this very head, with one of the worthiest, most disinterested, most able and most zealous friends that Government ever had. When the Duke of Portland sent him to Ireland, he declared to His Grace in the fullest manner, that if it was intended that He should go over for the purpose of deluding any of those of his

---

[1] On 11 May Richard Howe, 1st Earl Howe (1726–99), Admiral of the Fleet, paid a visit to the Fleet at Portsmouth during which he listened to the seamen's grievances.

[2] Tum pietate gravem ac meritis si forte virum quem conspexere silent; then, if haply they set eyes on a man honoured for noble character and service, they are silent (see Virgil, *Aeneid*, I, 151).

[3] Valentine Joyce, one of the delegates appointed by the crew of the *Royal George*, was said to be 'a *Tobaconist* of Belfast, in Ireland, shipped on board a Tender, with many others, by the order of Lord Carhampton for his seditious harangues' (*True Briton*, 12 May).

[4] The Admiralty removed from their ships a number of unpopular officers.

[5] e.g. *Freeman's Journal*, 13 May; *Dublin Journal*, 11 May.

[6] See above, p. 342.

own communion, and particularly, the Catholic Military, to whom He was appointed Chaplain General, into an acquiescence under Oppression or persecution, that He never would act that part; and he explained himself in the same manner to Mr Pelham.[1] But I see that the plan is to remove, and if possible to destroy, any of that religion, who will not be their tools in establishing a Jacobin indifference to all religion; and a hatred to the ruling one among the common people who are altogether composed of Catholics, and, who, if they have not that religion, will have no other. It is all over with the Peace and property of that Kingdom. Adieu, my dear friend, and beleive me ever faithfully and affectionately

Yours
EDM BURKE

Bath 16th May 97

There is nothing that gives me so much consolation as that I have opened my mind very fully on Irish Affairs to Mr Dundas, in two conversations which lasted for four hours.[2] I entered into the minutest details concerning Ireland, to make him sensible of the consequences of what was then doing, and I must do him the Justice to say, that He heard me not only with great patience, but with the utmost humanity and kindness, though I very soon found, that neither my laborious remonstrance nor his indulgent hearing produced any effect whatsoever for the purpose I had so much at Heart the peace of Ireland, its consolidation with this Kingdom, and a direction of our common force, against our common Enemy.

FRENCH LAURENCE to EDMUND BURKE—18 *May* 1797

Source: MS Osborn Collection. Printed *Burke–Laurence Correspondence,* pp. 221–7.

May 18th 1797

My dear Sir,

Your letter[3] too just, though so melancholy, I have read both to Lord Fitzwilliam and Mr Windham. I have given a copy to the former and promised one to the latter.

Lord Fitzwilliam, I must inform you in confidence, seems to be more pleased with your opinion that some *coalition* is the only chance of safety, than deterred by the horror which you express of one particular junction. He is very eager that Windham should take his stand on the

---

[1] See above, p. 141.   [2] See vol. VIII, 179.   [3] Of 12 May; see above, pp. 332–40.

affairs of Ireland, and go out, if necessary, on the question of changing the Ministry there.

Windham seems to be impressed with the impossibility of doing any thing through the present men in Ireland. I sent him an extract from the Chancellor's Speech in 1793 against the Catholic Delegates and in support of the Popery Laws of Ireland, in which he stated all of that religious persuasion to be essentially traitors:[1] and Windham owned he was satisfied. He then asked me as to the details of a new arrangement. I professed myself wholly unable to answer, but said I thought that was a subsequent consideration. The first thing was to settle the general principle whether a fundamental change were necessary, and if so, what connexion of men must be received into the Government. Then, it seemed to me the natural and wisest mode of proceeding, to give the new Ministers as fair and full confidence, and make the detail of arrangements in consultation with them. I was particularly asked about a new Chancellor, but that I avoided.

Lord F. was sounded nearly in the same manner by Lord Carlisle.[2] The latter considers Fitzgibbon as a Protegé of his own, he having first appointed him Sollicitor General;[3] but he said that private partialities must now give way to publick safety: the Chancellor must go; but who should succeed him? Would Lord Chief Justice Carleton[4] do; or would they take *an English Chancellor*: Would ⟨Lord F.⟩ recommend Serjeant Adair?[5]

I believe there is a disposition to send the latter, and to get Lord F. if possible to let it be considered as a Job for him. ⟨Adair⟩ came to me the other evening twice in the House of Commons for the first time since I have been a member, sate down by me, and was very gracious. He enquired very affectionately for Lord F. and regretted that he had not seen him since his arrival in Town. His Lordship, however, is as correct

[1] During the debate in the House of Lords on the second reading of the Catholic Relief Bill of 1793 Fitzgibbon in a powerful speech had argued from Irish history that it would be unsafe to grant the Catholics any degree of political power.
[2] Frederick Howard, 5th Earl of Carlisle (1748–1825), had 'been talking with Mr Pitt on the subject of Ireland'. Fitzwilliam seems to have met him on 16 and 17 May and in the course of their conversation Fitzwilliam gathered that 'there would be no difficulty about Removals—the bitter pill is the Admissions—Not any difficulty about measures, unless it be about Parliamentary Reform'. Shortly before meeting Carlisle, Fitzwilliam had heard that 'a Member of the Cabinet' (i.e. Windham) was 'very uneasy about the affairs of Ireland, and consequently very intent upon a change of system'. Fitzwilliam informed Ponsonby about these developments and implied that he hoped Ponsonby would be prepared to take office (Fitzwilliam to W. Ponsonby, 20 May, MS copy at Sheffield, F30f).
[3] Fitzgibbon, who at the outset of his political career was a strong supporter of Carlisle's administration in Ireland 1780–2, never held the office of Solicitor General. He became Attorney General in 1783.
[4] Hugh Carleton (1739–1826), later (21 November) 1st Viscount Carleton, Lord Chief Justice of the Common Pleas 1787–1800.   [5] James Adair; see above, p. 81.

on this subject, as he usually is in all his public sentiments. He answer'd Lord Carlisle, that he lamented the situation to which Ireland had been reduced and which made it necessary in his opinion, contrary to his general wishes and inclinations, to have for that country a government which more immediately belonged to the Country itself: the connexion must in that respect be weakened for the present, to be preserved at all for the future.

Other topics arose. The full admission of the Catholick claims seems to be agreed as of course; and Parliamentary Reform, as it is miscalled. Lord F. had forgot the particulars of G. Ponsonby's former motion,[1] but remembered the aristocratical nature of it. The representation which he gave, seemed to be highly satisfactory, and he understood that it was intended to yield in that point also.

Should that take place, though G. Ponsonby's plan is the least exceptionable which I have seen, though it is most on the original basis of our constitution, being wholly built on the landed interest by throwing in all the freeholders of £10 a year within 4 miles of every Borough; yet as I think it too uniformly aristocratical in the same mode and kind of aristocracy even for me, and above all as it admits the necessity of altering the existing Constitution, I shall consider it, if it really takes place, but as the first breach to let in ruin. Ponsonby has given notice, I see, of his motion next week.[2] It may be useful, if he is not indiscreet in his manner of doing it. It will certainly be negatived, and then the new Government of Ireland would have a year before them at least without being goaded on that subject, and may give their ill success now as a reason, if they please, for not reviving the question hereafter.

Have you seen the Report of the secret committee in Ireland.[3] What

[1] William Brabazon Ponsonby (1744–1806), later (1806) 1st Baron Ponsonby, introduced two reform bills into the Irish House of Commons: the first on 4 May 1794, the second on 15 May 1797. The first provided that every county and the cities of Dublin and Cork should each return three members, and that the boundaries of existing boroughs should be considerably extended. In the extended constituencies all ten-pound freeholders were to be enfranchised. The 1797 bill was more drastic. It provided that each county should be divided into districts each containing six thousand houses and returning two members. All forty-shilling freeholders, holders of leases of a certain annual value, householders possessing a house of a certain value, freemen of cities, and all who had resided for a certain number of years in any city or town following a trade, were to be enfranchised. The first bill was rejected by 142 to 94; the second by 117 to 15 (*Irish Parliamentary Register*, XIV, 62–8; XVII, 530–70). Laurence seems to be confusing the two brothers, William and George Ponsonby (1755–1817)—possibly because George had presented a reform bill on behalf of his brother at the end of the parliamentary session of 1793.

[2] It was reported in *The Times* of 17 May that Ponsonby had in the Irish House of Commons on 11 May given notice that he intended to introduce the subject of parliamentary reform at the beginning of the following week. The defeat of his motion was reported in *The Times* of 22 May.

[3] On 29 April the Lord Lieutenant informed the House of Commons that on 14 April the members of two societies meeting in a house in Belfast had been arrested

a horrible formed system of Jacobinism had been established there! Actual Tribunals, the sentences of which were carried into execution by Assassinations, Taxes levied, troops arrayed and a train of Ordnance provided. They had their emissaries in Scotland where the lower orders, I am told, are exceedingly discontented.

The cause of the Olive-Branch an American Vessel laden with nearly 15000 Muskets and Bayonets and 21 Brass Field-pieces, 4 Pounders, which, it has been suspected, were destined to Ireland, comes on to-morrow in the Admiralty Court.[1] I have just been looking into my Papers, but I cannot prove what we so much suspect. The arms are stated to have been purchased by contract for the militia of Vermont, and to have been to be delivered at New York. The pretended contract was made in July last, and the vessel with the arms was stopped and seized near Scilly in *November last*, just coinciding with the time that Hoche's expedition was almost ready to sail against Ireland.

As to our domestick politicks, I gave you a hint of Lord F's opinion in the beginning of this letter. He wants Pitt and the Grenvilles to go out, and Fox to form a junction with the Duke of Portland, Windham and the rest. Of himself he says nothing. Windham on the other hand wishes Lord F. the Duke of Leeds[2] and others to be united with Fox supposing the necessity of the latter coming into Power; that there may be some check upon him, and that he may have an aristocratical authority to hold forth if he pleases, to some of his Colleagues: but Windham says nothing of the Duke of Portland or himself. I see little chance indeed of safety and less of honour in either of these schemes, and can form no speculation myself for a single instant, to which I can look with a rational hope.

> Clouds and ever during dark
> Surround me.[3]

If you think my dear Sir, of throwing forth your thoughts on any of these subjects to his Lordship or to W. you may do it as before through me. You may, if you will, suppose me to have consulted you upon the details of an Irish Ministry and the two schemes of a new Ministry here,

and their papers sealed. The House of Commons appointed a committee on 1 May which reported on 10 May. A similar message was sent to the House of Lords on 3 May; the House appointed a committee on 5 May which reported on 12 May. The reports of these committees declared that a conspiracy existed to overthrow the laws and constitution, which if successful would end in 'anarchy, confiscation of property and the extermination of its proprietors' together with the separation of Ireland from Great Britain. The report of the House of Commons' committee, which with its bulky appendix was laid before the House on 10 May, was widely published in the press.

[1] See above, p. 175.
[2] Francis Godolphin Osborne, 5th Duke of Leeds (1751–99).
[3] See Milton, *Paradise Lost*, III, 45–6.

though in truth I despair too much to make a serious question about them. I would particularly wish your opinion as to Windham's going out on Irish affairs, if, what I think will hardly be, there should be a determination to grant everything rather than a new Administration there. Your authority would go a great way either with Lord F. or Mr W.

In another cover I shall send you some fragments of a letter from an Irish Barrister of good talents and principles to his brother here. If I get the whole, when Mr Pitt has done with it, I will send it to you.[1]

I have not yet got the two Secret Reports.

Remember me to Mrs Burke. It is a long time since I have heard of your health. In all your long letter not a word upon that, no less interesting subject than all the rest, to my feelings.

What think you of the following description of—I had almost said our Parliament—but I mean of the Roman Senate—by Cicero. 'Quo me dolore affici creditis, cum alios male sentire, alios nihil omnino curare videam, alios parum constanter in susceptâ causâ permanere, sententiamque suam non semper utilitate reipublicae, sed cum spe, tum timore moderari?[2]

Believe me to be
My dear Sir
Ever most gratefully and affectionately Yours
FRENCH LAURENCE

P.S. I will thank you for a copy of Lord Kenmare's petition,[3] which no one here has seen.

To FRENCH LAURENCE—18 *May* [1797]

Source: Burke–Laurence Correspondence, pp. 218–21.
The names in angle brackets are John Wilson Croker's readings (see above, pp. vii–viii).

Bath, 18th May. [1797.]

My dear Laurence,

I send you the copy of the Memorial which you desire; which surely if any one thing rather than another could less deserve the proud and disdainful reception and negative which it met with, it must be that

[1] In the Fitzwilliam MSS at Sheffield (F 30*f*) there is a copy of a letter, dated 7 May, from a lawyer in Dublin, John Schoales (*c.* 1768–1850), a member of the Irish bar, to a friend in London, giving an account of conditions in Ireland.

[2] With what grief do you suppose I am filled, when I see some disaffected, others utterly careless, others with small resolution to abide by the cause they have undertaken, and regulating their opinions not always by the advantage of the State, but now by hope, and now by apprehension; see Cicero, *Philippics*, XIV, vii, 17.

[3] The Catholic petition; see above, p. 331. It was forwarded with the next letter.

paper. I believe you will coincide with me in opinion. I think you read
it to Mr Windham, and that he saw nothing objectionable in it; but, on
the contrary, a degree of moderation much to be commended.—A letter[1]
from Dr W. King gives me to expect to see Lord Fitzwilliam here in
this week or the beginning of next. If he should not then come, I wish
he would not trouble himself in coming at all; as, in my own opinion,
and that of my physician, I am to expect no further good from the
waters here; and he more than doubts, whether his permitting me to use
them upon the credit of the benefit I derived from [them] last year, has
had the support of experience. The fact is, I am just where I was when
you left me; and if there be any difference, it is, that I find myself
weaker, and more emaciated. So, that my purpose is, to point my view
homeward, and to proceed on my journey only as my strength shall give
me leave; and as I think to proceed only as by airings, to take the way by
the Vale of Rodborough, Cheltenham, and Oxford. But on this point
I am not determined. As to my general regimen, and course of physick,
if it pleases God to continue me a little longer here, I can observe
[them] at home; and if I should die, I should certainly die with something more [of] satisfaction there. All this you will communicate in
substance to Lord Fitzwilliam. I shall certainly not set off until Wednesday or Thursday next;[2] and it is likely that I shall be four days, at least, in
going home.

What I have now to say, you cannot directly communicate either to
Windham or to ⟨Lord Fitzwilliam⟩. I am astonished to find ⟨Lord
Fitzwilliam⟩ approving as he does, in a short letter to me,[3] my ideas upon
the subject of a coalition,[4] and yet proposing a plan in direct opposition
to it—namely, the total turning out of this Ministry, and substituting
in its place all the leaders of Opposition. I consider what he says of Mr
Windham and the D. of Portland as no exceptions, because they would
be as insignificant in such an arrangement as they are in the present;
and after all the foul motives assigned by that Opposition, publickly, for
the part they have taken, between you and I, I do not see how, as men of
honour, they can arrange with it; particularly the Duke of Portland, who
is not in the habit of explaining and defending his conduct—and therefore is wholly at the mercy of others in every step of life that he takes.
I am bitterly sorry for it, but he has had his day and he is no more. As
to ⟨Lord Fitzwilliam⟩, I believe they would be very glad to take him in;
but upon whose support is he to depend? whether he is to stay in
cabinet here, or to trust himself to the tempestuous sea of Ireland, as

---

[1] Missing.   [2] 24 or 25 May.   [3] See above, pp. 340–1.
[4] For Burke's ideas on a possible coalition see above, pp. 337–8.

Lord Lieutenant; because for him to advise a system of administration in which he has no part, is so unwise a proceeding, that, most assuredly, for one, I shall never recommend it. Indeed I shall never recommend the Jacobin Ministry he proposes; with principles unretracted, and with propensities unchanged—without either direction or controul. I am astonished at ⟨Lord Carlisle⟩'s impudence in speaking to him at all; but much more of his speaking in favour of that low, intriguing, and perfidious tool ⟨Adair⟩,[1] whose sole recommendation to the great office he holds,[2] and which is much above his merits, was his betraying ⟨Lord Fitzwilliam⟩. At ⟨Adair⟩'s impudence I am not surprised. If I should have the happiness of seeing ⟨Lord Fitzwilliam⟩ when he has himself communicated to me his own ideas, I shall give my opinion upon them fully and freely. What is the reason that among the removals they say nothing of ⟨Foster⟩,[3] who is a more mischievous person even than the Chancellor. Why talk of ⟨Carleton⟩, when Yelverton[4] has[5] upon all accounts the fairest pretension upon a change conducted on ⟨Lord Fitzwilliam⟩'s ideas. But I shall not just now trouble you any more upon this part of the subject. I shall certainly never desire Windham to resign, for the destroying this Administration, without seeing distinctly what other can be made. It would be highly dishonourable for him to quit Administration, merely because it is in difficulties, for the direct purpose of bringing in their enemies. The publick is gone irrecoverably, and there is nothing left to individuals but to fall with decorum.—Mrs Burke is tolerable, and yours as usual. Adieu.

Yours ever,
E.B.

To EARL FITZWILLIAM—21 *May* 1797

Source: Fitzwilliam MSS (Sheffield).
Endorsed (by Fitzwilliam): Burke | may 22.97.
This is the last known letter wholly in Burke's hand.

My dear Lord,

I am deeply penetrated with your goodness in proposing to visit me in this remote place. But as any real recovery is a thing now out of the Question, and as without (at least) any Benefit, I have given a very long Trial to these Waters; and as I daily decline in Flesh and strength, it is

[1] See above, p. 81.
[2] Adair was a King's Serjeant-at-law and Chief Justice of Chester.
[3] John Foster (1740–1828), later (1821) 1st Baron Oriel, Speaker of the Irish House of Commons 1785–1800.
[4] Barry Yelverton, 1st Baron Avonmore (1736–1805), later (1800) 1st Viscount.
[5] *Burke–Laurence Correspondence:* was

thought advisable, whilst the thing is possible, that I should be removed by easy Stages to Beconsfield; there to finish my carreer along with that of the civil and moral World. I see your Lordships situation as one of the most difficult of any, even in these times of difficulty. You are in a terrible dilemma. On one hand it is impossible for you not to be shocked with the monstrous wickedness of the Jacobin Agitators in Ireland, and not to be frighted at the regularity, the order, and the combined movement of which so many persons, low and illiterate in appearance, are capable. On the other hand, little can be done in a display of Horrour at their proceedings, (which howerver it is natural, and in some degree necessary to shew) without affirming the power, and forwarding the designs of those, who trusting in a military power have thought proper to despise all the principles of reason, justice humanity and policy. I do not believe that any serious intention exists of varying the plan of Government either as to persons or things. If there be any change here it will be wrought by abdicating responsible situations in a fright—and instead of cowardly sneaking Statesmen in an English Interest, we shall have French Jacobins without a mask, and without control, paying their Court to sedition at home, and to a ferocious Despotism abroad. But of all this, more at large, when we meet, at Beconsfield; for I should be sorry, that your Lordship should now think of coming hither as I propose to be off before the End of the Week. In the mean time I have only humbly and earnestly to wish that you would not take any advice or listen to any suggestion about either persons or things, except from those, you have reason to believe steady friends to you and your Cause especially in the late trying exigency. Our most respectful, and affection-ate compliments to Lady Fitzwilliam—and believe me ever My very dear Lord

> Your faithful and most obliged
> friend and humble Servant
> EDM BURKE

21.May 1797

To MRS JOHN CREWE—21 May 1797
Source: Corr. (1844), IV, 448–9.

Bath, May 21, 1797.

Dear Mrs Crewe,

We are very much obliged to you for the comfort we have had (the greatest we have had), by your company and correspondence since we came hither.[1] We have now to let you know, that all hopes of any recovery to me, from any thing which art or nature can supply, being totally at an end, and the fullest trial having been given to these waters without any sort of effect, it is thought advisable that I should be taken home, where, if I shall live much longer, I shall see an end of all that is worth living for in this world. We may be some time, perhaps four days, on the way; but that will depend upon my strength. The times, indeed, are deplorable; and the spirit in England appears to be, if at all, not much better than in Ireland; nor is the club at the Crown and Anchor[2] one jot less treasonable than the committee at Belfast;[3] and, what is worse, the names are higher, and members of parliament openly show themselves there; whereas, it does not appear that, in Ireland, any of the principal people are at all connected with the seditious French revolutionists of the lower order. But I cannot look at the disorders there or here without reflecting with sorrow and indignation at the provocations given to disorder of every kind, by what is called the government, in Ireland, and by the treacherous and pusillanimous conduct of government, both here and there, in concealing and positively denying, as you know they did, the existence of these disorders, until they broke out in the dreadful manner we see them. You know that they have, over and over again, represented the people there to be happy and contented under their direction, and now no army is large enough to coerce them. God bless you until we meet.

Yours ever and ever,
EDM. BURKE.

To the BISHOP OF WATERFORD—22 *May* 1797

Source: Fitzwilliam MSS (Sheffield). Printed *Corr.* (1844), IV, 450–2.
Addressed: Revd Doctor Hussey | R:C: Bishop of Waterford | Waterford | Via Milford.
Postmarked: BATH.
Only the signature is in Burke's hand.

My dear friend

I hope you received my last Letter,[4] strongly recommending it to you, of whatever force your calls hither might be, not to quit Ireland, whilst you had reason to apprehend, that any serious accusation against you

---

[1] Mrs Crewe's letters are missing. Early in April she had paid the Burkes a visit in Bath (*Public Advertiser*, 6 April).
[2] On 18 May there had been a meeting at the Crown and Anchor of the supporters of parliamentary reform, including Sir Francis Burdett, 5th Baronet (1770–1844), and Horne Tooke (*The Times*, 19 May).
[3] See above, pp. 351–2.
[4] Of 16 May; see above, pp. 341–5.

should be preferred in any shape[1] whatever: lest your coming hither on your affairs should by your Enemies be construed into a flight; and this, from the nature of the Enemies you have to deal with, could only serve to render them more ferocious, untractable and dangerous. My Opinion [is] that you ought to go to Dublin, and there quietly to wait until they should make some attack upon you. I then hinted Some heads, very short, and scanty indeed, for your[2] defence; but they were such as I had taken principally from your own conversations: and so[3] were intended as nothing more than means to recall them to your memory. If all this affair be blown over what I have said ought to pass for nothing; I would neither shun nor court enquiry; but, in case they should proceed in any judicial or in any parliamentary way after I had made my defence personally, if the parliamentary mode should be pursued, I should insist that before they proceeded to any resolution against me, which should affect me in my reputation, or otherwise, I should be heard by my Counsel; and for that Counsel, I should certainly choose Mr Curran;[4]—the most able Advocate that I know. If they proceeded to indite me or to move an information against me as for a misdeamenour, I would proceed just in the same way and defend myself in the same manner, more shortly but modestly and firmly, in my own person, more at large by the same Counsel: But I trust they will in one thing have prudence and let you alone; contenting themselves with the illiberal abuse they have thrown upon you. When you come to England,[5] you will not find me at Bath. I am to be taken from this place next wednesday that is the day after to morrow, as all hope of a recovery from my original disorder is over, tho' my Life is not immediately threatened. There is not even a remission in the original complaint; so that I shall be better at Home in all probability than any where else: and there, in your way to London, and the more frequently afterwards, the better, I shall be most happy to see you. Mrs Burke presents her most Affectionate Compliments, and beleive me, my dear Sir,

Most truly yours:

EDM BURKE

Bath 22d May
     1797

[1] MS: in any shape in any shape
[2] MS: you
[3] MS: to
[4] John Philpot Curran (see above, p. 122).
[5] Hussey had left for England by 19 May (Troy to P. J. Plunket, 23 May, quoted in A. Cogan, *The Diocese of Meath...*, III, 211–12).

To Mrs William Leadbeater—23 *May* 1797

Source: MS Osborn Collection. Printed (in part) Prior (2nd ed.), II, 394–5.
Addressed: Mrs Leadbeater | Ballytore | Ireland.
Postmarked: BATH   M⟨Y⟩|2⟨4⟩|97.
Only the signature is in Burke's hand. There are three copies of this letter in
the Osborn Collection and one in the Library of the University of California
(Santa Barbara). The MS of the original has been repaired with tape. About
twenty-five words have been written back in another hand.

Mrs William Leadbeater, (Mary *née* Shackleton, 1758–1826) was the daughter
of Burke's old school friend Richard Shackleton (1726–92), and still resided
in Ballitore where Burke had attended school.

My dear Mrs Leadbeater

I feel as I ought to do your constant hereditary kindness to me and
mine. What you have heard of my illness is far from exaggerated.[1] I am
thank God alive and that is all—Hastening to my dissolution I have to
bless Providence that I do not suffer a great deal of pain. I am very glad
to hear that the vexatious dispute which has been raised[2] against you
about the few miserable trees of which, if I do not mistake, I remember
the planting, is likely to be settled to your satisfaction. I have never
heard of any thing so miserable as this attempt upon you.[3]

Mrs Burke has a tolerable share of health in every respect, except much
use of her limbs.

She remembers your mother's most good-natured[4] attentions,[5] as I
am sure I do, with much gratitude. I have ever been an admirer of your
talents and virtues: and shall ever wish most cordially for every thing
which can tend to your credit and satisfaction. I therefore congratulate
you very heartily on the birth of your Son;[6] and pray remember me to
the representative of your family, who, I hope, still keeps up the School[7]
⟨of⟩ which I have so tender a remembrance.

Tho' after so long an absence and so many unpleasant events of
every kind that have distracted my thoughts, I hardly dare to ask for

[1] Mrs Leadbeater's letter on this subject is missing.
[2] The MS has been repaired with tape and the words 'deal of pain...raised' copied
back in another hand.
[3] There is an account of a dispute about felling trees in Mary Shackleton's Diary for
1 and 5 April (MS National Library of Ireland), and in the *Leadbeater Papers*, London,
1862, I, 269.
[4] The words 'She remembers . . . good-natured' have been copied back in another
hand.
[5] Elizabeth, *née* Carleton (1726–1804), the second wife of Richard Shackleton, who
had received Jane and Edmund more than once on visits to Ballitore in the 1760s; see
vol. I, 268.
[6] Richard, born 24 September 1796; he died in 1881.
[7] Abraham Shackleton (1752–1818), Mary Leadbeater's brother. Burke attended
the school when it was run by his grandfather Abraham Shackleton (1696–1771).

any one, not knowing whether they are living or dead lest I should be the means of awakening unpleasant recollections. Beleive me to be with the most respectful and affectionate regard,

My dear Mrs Leadbeater,
Your faithful friend and very humble Servant

Bath 23d May   EDM BURKE
1797

P.S: Pray remember me to Mr Leadbeater.[1] I have been at Bath for these four months to no purpose and am therefore to be removed to my own House at Beaconsfield to morrow to be nearer to a habitation more permanent, humbly and fearfully hoping that my better part may find a better mansion.

Mrs Leadbeater answered this letter on 28 May with 'a heart melted to over-flowing...on receiving the greatest' but she feared 'the last proof' of their friendship. She explained that her mother was declining but she sent Burke as much love as she was capable of sending and hoped he had lived such a life that at the end he would be 'crowned with peace'. Abraham Shackleton added a postscript to the letter (MS at Sheffield; printed in *Corr.* (1844), IV, 454–6).

To RICHARD TROWARD—23 *May* 1797
Source: Windham, *Diary*, p. 364.

Bath: May 23, 1797.

My dear Sir,—I am to quit this place to-morrow, having received no benefit, and expecting no further. As to the epitaph,[2] I cannot, upon my plan, and in order to do full justice to the subject, shorten it very considerably. They who like an impassioned style upon monuments will not be pleased with this, whether it be long or short; but for my part I hate all general expressions of admiration, which may as well be applied to one man as another. I think these things in churches, particularly, ought to have a moral turn, and ought to account why it is fit that an actor should have a place in so solemn a temple, among legislators, heroes, saints, and the ornaments of science, erudition, and genius. I think Garrick well entitled to that place, though I think that others of the same profession were not; and the reason ought to be assigned, as in that epitaph I have assigned it. I could wish that Mr Windham could see this epitaph, together with this, and my last letter to you upon the sub-

---

[1] William Leadbeater (1763–1827), whom Mary Shackleton married in 1791.
[2] For David Garrick; see above, pp. 323–4.

ject.[1] But, to be sure, it is Mr Wallis that must finally determine. For my part, I am the more indifferent about everything of the kind, as I do not think that these memorials, nor the temples that contain them, or any of our frail works, can long continue. If you can't get at Mr Windham (as in the present state I don't wonder that you cannot, for I think he must be nearly heart-broken, as in truth I am), be so good as to hand the papers I speak of to Mr Woodford, who has the last chance of catching a flying moment of his leisure.

> Believe me, my dear Sir,
> Your very faithful and obedient servant,
> EDMUND BURKE.

To R. Troward, Esq.

To ARTHUR YOUNG—23 *May* 1797

Source: Fitzwilliam MSS (Sheffield). Printed *Corr.* (1844), IV, 452–3.
Addressed: Arthur Young Esqr | &c &c &c | Whitehall | London.
Postmarked: BATH   MA|24|97|A.
Only the signature is in Burke's hand.

Burke's old friend Arthur Young (1741–1820) was at this time Secretary to the Board of Agriculture. At the close of 1795 it was announced that Burke intended to publish a letter to Arthur Young on an 'Increase of Day-labourers in Husbandry and other Topics of Rural Concern'. On learning of this the President of the Board of Agriculture (Sir John Sinclair; see above, p. 271) sent Burke some of the Board's publications (see Todd, *Bibliography*, p. 227; vol. VIII, 459).

Dear Sir

I am on the point of leaving Bath, having no further hope of Benefit from these Waters; and as soon as I get home, (if I should live to get home,) if I should find the Papers transmitted me by your Board,[2] I shall send them faithfully to you; tho', to say the truth, I do not think them of very great importance. My constant opinion was, and is, that all matters relative to labour, ought to be left to the conventions of the parties. That the great danger is in Governments intermeddling too much. What I should have taken the liberty of addressing to you, had I had Strength to go through it, would be to illustrate or enforce that principle. I am extreamly sorry that any one in the House of Commons should be found so ignorant and unadvised, as to wish to revive the senseless, barbarous and, in fact, wicked regulations made against the free trade in matter of provision, which the good sense of late Parliaments

[1] Burke's letter of 1 May.
[2] The papers from the Board of Agriculture have not been found.

had removed. I am the more concerned at the measure as I was myself the person who moved the repeal of the absurd code of Statutes, against the most useful of all trades, under the invidious Names of forstalling regrating:[1] But however I[2] console myself on this point by considering that it is not the only breach by which barbarism is entering upon us. It is indeed but a poor consolation and one taken meerly from the balance of misfortunes. You have titles enough of your own, to pass your name to posterity, and I am pleased that you have yet spirit enough to hope that there will be such a thing as a civilized posterity to attend to things of this kind.

I have the honor to be, with very high respect and esteem,

Dear Sir,
Your most obedient and very
humble Servant,

Bath 23d May
1797

EDM BURKE

To CAPTAIN EMPEROR JOHN ALEXANDER WOODFORD— 31 *May* 1797

Source: Copy in Fitzwilliam MSS (Sheffield).
Only the signature is in Burke's hand.

Burke arrived in Beaconsfield 'in a feeble state' on Saturday 27 May (*The Times*, 30 May).

My dear Woodford

Yesterday Lord FitzWilliam rode over to Eton to see his Son, so that I had not as full a conversation with him as I could wish to enable me to answer your Letter.[3]

Lord F: observes, that he is left quite in the dark as to the parties by whom his Opinion is desired. Whether by Mr Windham single; or by the Cabinet entire—or by higher authority.

He is somewhat surprised there should be a serious talk of Judges, and Courts of Justice, when the Irish Government, having first, by seperate Proclamations put divers districts out of the Law, have at last, by one

---

[1] Burke was one of the members appointed in March 1772 to prepare and bring in a bill for remedying the evils occasioned by the laws then in being, relating to badgers, engrossers, forestallers and regrators, which received the Royal Assent in June 1772. When in May 1787 a petition suggesting that the laws against forestalling should be revived was presented to the House of Commons, Burke strongly opposed it, arguing that 'a free commerce was that species of commerce most likely to flourish'. He declared he wished to 'prevent the dry bones of those gibbeted laws from being again clothed with flesh' (*Journals of the House of Commons*, XXXIII, 590, 957; *Parliamentary History*, XXVI, 1167–72).

[2] MS: I however I   [3] Missing.

short sweeping Proclamation of a Commander in Chief, subjected to the arbitrary discretion of a *military* power, the *whole* Kingdom of Ireland;[1] Altho' two of its Provinces[2] are *wholly*, and the far larger *part of the third*,[3] is untouched with sedition or rebellion; or even the appearance of it;— whatever discontents and grudgings may every where exist against those who direct affairs at present.

If an intention should exist of abandoning the scheme of a military Government and of conducting things upon the principles of civil and political prudence, whatever is said of this or that man must be with reference to those principles.

On that supposition he says, that at no time, has he thought of the appointment of a new Chancellor meerly as a judge, not having heard that, in the *common exercise of the functions of his Court*, Lord Clare[4] had caused any dissatisfaction. If ever he thought of the removal of that person, it was as a part, and *only as a part*, of a mischievous System, of which he is indeed a considerable Member; but by no means the worst, the most active, or, at present, the most accredited Member. As Lord F: is of Opinion that every judgment which he ought to form relative to the situation of an individual, must depend entirely not only upon the arrangement which is to be changed, but that also which is to be adopted in its place, and as he has had no communication whatsoever relative to both, or either of those plans, he does not consider himself as in the least authorized to give an Opinion.

With regard to Mr Justice Lawrence,[5] his Lordship does not know him personally. He has heard a good character of him in his profession; but cannot form a judgment of his aptitude to take a leading part as a statesman in a new political arrangement for the satisfaction of Ireland, and for the settling the distracted state of that Kingdom.

This is the result of my conversation with Lord FitzWilliam. These are his sentiments, and given nearly in his words.

What I have to say myself upon the subject of Ireland, I shall speak to you a little more fully, as soon as I have any degree of Strength for the purpose. Assure Windham of my Affectionate attachment and beleive me, my dear Woodford

ever yours

Beaconsfield   EDM BURKE

31st May 97

[1] On 17 May the Irish Government issued a proclamation declaring that there was a traitorous and seditious conspiracy by a number of persons calling themselves United Irishmen, and that orders had been issued to all officers commanding His Majesty's troops to use their utmost force to suppress the same.
[2] Connaught and Munster.   [3] Leinster.
[4] See above, p. 222.   [5] Sir Soulden Lawrence (1751–1814); see the next letter.

To FRENCH LAURENCE—I *June* 1797

Source: *Burke–Laurence Correspondence*, pp. 231–6.
The names in angle brackets are Croker's readings (see above, pp. vii–viii).

Beaconsfield, 1st June 1797.

My dear Laurence,

It is not easy for me to describe to you the state of ⟨Lord Fitzwilliam⟩'s mind. Indeed the condition of all affairs, of Irish affairs in particular, expecially as they relate to him, both as a man and as a statesman, are enough to perplex a very clear understanding, such as in truth his understanding naturally is; but independently of these difficulties, which I feel to press equally upon any judgment of my own, he has those which result from his own passions, from a strong predilection to Mr Fox with regard to this side of the water, and a still stronger with regard to Mr William Ponsonby[1] on the other side. As to Mr Ponsonby, he seems to be guided by nothing but his passions. He is by his natural temper perhaps the most vehemently irritable and habitually irritated of any person whom I have ever heard of—I mean of a man conversant with publick affairs; and he is even yet more hot in deliberation and council than he is in debate.[2] ⟨Lord Fitzwilliam⟩ has not only his predilections, but he is influenced, too much so in my opinion, though very naturally and very excuseably, by a rooted animosity against Mr Pitt, and, indeed what he has not in particular to himself, an incurable suspicion of his sincerity. If his predilections had been returned by any correspondent degree of attachment or confidence on the part of Mr Ponsonby or Mr Grattan, I should not be inclined to blame the confidence which he has in them, because, independently of their conduct (under great provocations, I admit) they are, especially the latter, men of integrity and publick spirit; but they not only do not act in confidence or in concert with ⟨Lord Fitzwilliam⟩ but they are actually engaged in personal connexion and combined in publick arrangements in a manner that would virtually exclude ⟨Lord Fitzwilliam⟩ as much from all influence and direction in publick affairs as Mr Pitt does, or possibly can do. It is plain that Ponsonby has concerted the infernal plan of what he calls Parliamentary Reform,[3] with the Opposition here, and eminently with his son-in-law, Mr Grey, with whom

---

[1] See above, p. 351.
[2] In fact on 2 June Fitzwilliam received a reply from Ponsonby to his letter of 20 May (see above, p. 350) in which, having bitterly criticized the Irish Administration, Ponsonby declared that he considered himself to be 'an Irish Country Gentleman' and was determined not to take office—'While I live I will be my own Master' (Ponsonby to Fitzwilliam, 29 May, MS at Sheffield, F 30*f*). [3] See above, p. 350.

he is connected full as much as by politicks as he is by family ties.[1] ⟨Lord Fitzwilliam⟩ sees this Parliamentary Reform thus pushed in concert by the Opposition in both kingdoms exactly in the same light which you and I do, and yet without regard to the dreadful consequences which he forsees from this measure, and without regard to the total, at least temporary, alienation of those people from his confidence, his connexion, and his principles. I plainly perceive that if he was consulted, he would advise to throw every thing into their hands. If I am asked what I would myself advise in such a case, I should certainly advise the same, but with this temperament and express previous condition, that they renewed their confidence in ⟨Lord Fitzwilliam⟩, whom I hold to be the only person to settle Ireland; and that they give him some assurance as a man, a gentleman, and a friend, that they will be practicable about their schemes of changing the constitution of the House of Commons; and that they will desist from the scheme of an absentee tax, which in its principle goes more to the disconnexion of the two kingdoms than any thing which is proposed by the United Irishmen. As to Mr Grattan's other project, of laying new taxes upon English commodities,[2] and the principle upon which he proposes it,—namely, that England is a foreign and a hostile kingdom and adverse in interest, [it] is, I think, a measure he would hardly persevere in. I think the difficulty of the case is extreme, when you consider the military government established on the one hand, and the wild democratick representation proposed as its cure [on] the other. If ⟨Lord Fitzwilliam⟩ cannot be the Lord Lieutenant, a thing to which he never would consent, and indeed in prudence ought not to do, leaving an adverse Cabinet behind him, and if that adverse Cabinet be, as it is, full as little disposed to trust to him as he is to rely upon it, the only way in which he can be serviceable is in a mediatorial capacity; and this office of a mediator he certainly cannot perform in the temper he is in at present. I have entered into a very great detail with him, perhaps into too great a detail upon all those points, not being quite sure that I should live to converse with him again upon the subject; yet I am afraid that I have poured too much into a mind in itself over anxious and over full. He does not like, nor indeed do I much, the manner in which he seems to be

---

[1] Charles Grey (see above, p. 152). On 26 May he had asked for leave to introduce a reform bill. In 1794 he had married Mary Elizabeth (1776–1861), only daughter of William Ponsonby.

[2] On 22 February in the Irish House of Commons's Committee of Ways and Means Grattan had opposed a salt tax proposed by the Government. He suggested as an alternative, import duties on drapery and malt liquors. 'He meant certainly', he explained, 'to establish a principle by which the nation who admitted our goods of a similar description into their ports should be exempt from any duty here' (*Dublin Evening Post*, 25 February).

indirectly and without the least confidence consulted about a particular member of an arrangement, I mean that of naming your namesake, Judge Lawrence, to be Chancellor of Ireland. It is plain that they mean some change to satisfy the people, but not essentially to alter their system, or to bring in any man whose local weight and authority might counterbalance that of Lord Clare and his faction, or prove a gratification to any description of the people, or to facilitate any general arrangement; and they seem to want a sort of sanction from ⟨Lord Fitzwilliam⟩, with regard to a single member of some system with which he is wholly unacquainted. The thing was first suggested to him by Lord Carlisle,[1] and Woodford in a letter to me[2] made the same suggestion, to be communicated to ⟨Lord Fitzwilliam⟩ as from Mr Windham. He was naturally much against giving any opinion on the subject; for which he gave many good reasons; but he was so hurt at those unconfidential confidences, that he was for some time unwilling that I should communicate his reasons for declining any opinion in my answer to Mr Woodford's communication.[3] However, I persuaded him to let me do it, as I am sure that guarding himself by a prudent suspicion, he ought to be as open to hear, as cautious to determine upon any matter relative to Ireland. This is all with which I have to trouble you at present.

As to the state of my body since my return, I cannot help smiling at the thought of Woodford's seeing it in so gay a point of view; for I am sure if I should live to see you, you will rather think me a man dug out of the grave than as a man going, as I am, into it. I am infinitely weaker than when I left this, and far more emaciated. 'Pallor in ore sedet, macies in corpore toto.'[4] I look like Ovid's envy, but thank God without much envying any one; and certainly not in a condition to be envied, except by those who prognosticate the dreadful evils of every kind which are impending over us. Adieu. Mrs Burke salutes you cordially; and believe me

Ever yours,

E.B.

P.S. I forgot to tell you that I have seen and conversed, though not enough, with Dr Hussey; but this I know, that he has stated facts sufficient to justify almost every thing which might have been considered as indiscreet in his pastoral letter.

[1] See above, p. 350.
[2] The letter is missing.
[3] Burke's letter of 31 May; see above, pp. 362–3.
[4] Pallor o'erspreads her face and her whole body seems to shrivel up; see Ovid, *Metamorphoses*, II, 775.

To EARL FITZWILLIAM—4 *June* 1797

Source: Fitzwilliam MSS (Sheffield).
Endorsed (by Fitzwilliam): Burke | june 5.97.
Only the signature is in Burke's hand.

My dear Lord

I sent you enclosed the Copy of the Letter in which I conveyed your Sentiments through Mr Woodford, to Mr Windham.[1] I am not at all sorry that I have as explicitly stated to them your Lordships sentiments as you delivered them to me; altho' I find that there was no solid foundation for thinking there was any serious design to take your opinion with regard to any settlement in Ireland; or indeed to follow any sound opinion relative to that object.

Mr Windham talks of what Woodford wrote to me[2] as nothing more than a suggestion of his own; and with regard to any authority from which he spoke I beleive it to be nothing more or better; But that the matter itself did not arise in his mind I am sure, for I do not beleive that He has the least connexion with Justice Lawrence, but He must have heard it, tho' I beleive in nothing better than loose conversation from Mr Pitt; and I am the more convinced of this from its conformity with the proposition which you had thro' Lord Carlisle. If I were to form a Judgment Mr Pitt has yet formed no fixed plan, whatever for the Affairs of Ireland. These are things only floating in his thoughts, and varied according to the intelligence which he receives by every Post. On the whole I am convinced that the only thing in which they are settled is a plan of military coercion. I know they flatter themselves, that, what they call Peace, which they hope to obtain by new humiliations will quiet these disturbances but surely they reckon without their Host. Adieu, my dear Lord; This Evening I am weaker than ever; and therefore I am as little able, as desirous, to dilate upon this mellancholly subject. For my short ever,

I am truly yours
EDM BURKE

Beaconsfield
   4th June 1797

[1] See above, pp. 362–3.
[2] In Woodford's (missing) letter, p. 362–3.

To FRENCH LAURENCE—5 *June* 1797

Source: *Burke–Laurence Correspondence*, pp. 236–8.

Beaconsfield, 5th June 1797.

My dear Laurence,

I am satisfied that there is nothing like a fixed intention of making a real change of system in Ireland; but that they vary from day to day as their hopes are more or less sanguine from the Luttrellade.[1] The system of military government is mad in the extreme—merely as a system, but still worse in the mad hands in which it is placed. But my opinion is, that if Windham has not been brought into an absolute relish of this scheme, he has been brought off from any systematical dislike to it. When I object to the scheme of any military government, you do not imagine that I object to the use of the military arm in its proper place and order; but I am sure that so long as this is looked upon as principal, it will become the sole reliance of Government—and that from its apparent facility, every thing whatsoever belonging to real civil policy in the management of a people will be postponed, if not totally set aside. The truth is, the Government of Ireland grows every day more and more difficult; and consequently the incapacity of the jobbers there, every day more and more evident; but as long as they can draw upon England for indefinite aids of men, and sums of money, they will go on with more resolution than ever in their jobbing system. Things must take their course.

As to the state of this kingdom, it does not appear to me to be a great deal better than that of Ireland. Perhaps in some points of view it is worse. To see the Thames itself boldly blocked up by a rebellious British Fleet, is such a thing as in the worst of our dreams we could scarcely have imagined. The lenitive electuary of Mr Pitt's bill[2] is perfectly of the old woman's dispensatory. The only thing which he spoke of, and which has any degree of common sense, is a general association of the whole kingdom to support Government against all disorders, and all enemies foreign and internal;[3] but I doubt whether he has stuff enough in him to carry it into execution. What is all this

[1] Lord Carhampton's military rule. Presumably the name is coined on the analogy of *dragonnade*.

[2] A bill to prevent the seduction of soldiers and sailors from their duty was introduced by Pitt on 2 June.

[3] In his speech on 2 June in which he announced his intention of introducing the bill, Pitt had emphasized the duty of every man 'who felt he was a Briton...to unite in measures of national defence against all the menaces of open foes, or insidious attempts of internal enemies' (*The Times*, 3 June).

coquetting with Sheridan?[1] and what, except shame, do they get by it?
Farewell, and God bless you.

Yours ever,

E.B.

To UNKNOWN BISHOP—6 *June* [1797]

Source: Copy (in Nagle's hand) in Fitzwilliam MSS (Sheffield).
The 6th of June fell on a Monday in 1796 and on a Tuesday in 1797. The
concluding lines of his letter suggest that it was written in 1797.

My dear Friend

I received your Letter with the Notes[2] on your pastoral charge.[3] I wish
they had been more full; but, on that we shall speak when we meet. I
wish the Bearer of this my worthy young Kinsman Richard Bourke[4]
may be able to meet you at Home. I wish him to have the advantage of
being acquainted with you; and his having been a Namesake and a
favourite almost from his Infancy of your late Friend,[5] will be a recommendation to him. He will have a reasonable good Fortune, tho' it is
but the wreck of that which was left to His Father.[6] As to the great scale
of Politics in Ireland I cannot think that they have any idea of a change
in it; at least of any that is substantial and benificial. If I understand the
matter, the great grievance of the Catholics is that they are treated as a
sort of public Enemies; and that persons are supposed to hola their
situations upon the principle of their disposition to treat the great body
of their Countrymen as such Enemies. As long as that principle is held
up it is absolutely impossible that any scheme of equalization in nominal
privilege should ever quiet the Country. It seems to me always as if I had
a vast deal to talk to you upon these subjects. As to Lord FitzWilliam,
my clear opinion [is] that Ireland cannot be settled without him; but this
is what they never will think of: and God knows whether the extravagant
courses taken by our friends in Ireland would leave him master of his

[1] During the debate on the bill Sheridan said that whatever difference in political
opinion might exist in the House they had come to a time when the King had the right
to expect the zealous cooperation of all his subjects. Dundas responded by empha-
sizing that he agreed at least with part of Sheridan's speech. A few days earlier Fox
had referred to the 'incurable itch that he [Sheridan] seems to have of distinguishing
his conduct from that of those with whom he wishes to be supposed united' (Fox to
Lauderdale, [2 June], Add. MS 47,564, fols 13–15).
[2] Missing.
[3] If this letter was addressed to the Bishop of Waterford, this presumably refers to the
pastoral letter which he published in April 1797 (see above, pp. 302–4).
[4] (1777–1855), later (1835) K.C.B.; he was Governor of New South Wales 1831–7,
and a co-editor of Burke's *Correspondence* (1844).
[5] Richard Burke, Jr.
[6] John Bourke (*c.* 1742–95), of Dromsally, County Limerick, and St Anne's,
Dublin.

measures, or these Gentlemen even masters of their own. Every thing is running to some desperate extremity and military Government. Despotism is only to be cured by popular Phrenzy—Adieu. God bless you.

Most truly and cordially yours
for the little time that I remain
E: B.

Beaconsfield
Monday Night
6 June

To EARL FITZWILLIAM—18 *June* 1797

Source: Fitzwilliam MSS (Northampton).
Endorsed (by Fitzwilliam): Mr Burke | june 23.97.
Only the signature is in Burke's hand.

My dear Lord

There was a matter upon my mind when you were here, which, I dont know how it happened, I forgot to mention to your Lordship. I am of Opinion, and I beleive you will not differ from me, that our excellent friend Doctor Hussey is strongly disposed and eminently qualified to be useful to the Diocese which he administers not only in point of religion and morals, but in giving a direction to the industry and pursuits of the Inhabitants. He has had much experience and observation in all parts of Europe. He has a statesman like Head, and yet can descend to very minute parts of local management and Oeconomy. Lismore is in his Diocese; and of course some considerable part of the Duke of Devonshires property. Does your Lordship think it would be amiss to speak with Lord Frederick Cavendish[1] about getting a Letter from the Duke of Devonshire to recommend Doctor Hussey to the particular attention of His Graces principal Agents and managers there. I wish indeed that before He goes over He should be made personally acquainted with the Duke of Devonshire. I think His Grace would like him, from the plainess and directness of his manners and character: and you know that his principles and yours are exactly the same; with a temper, if ever man had it made for manly and rational freedom; and abhorrent of every thing base and servile; and equally removed from the hideous Jacobinism of the Hour, which deranges every thing from the first Nobility of the Kingdom to the meanest Seaman of the Fleet, and leaves us nothing abroad or at Home, on Sea or on Land upon which we can rest with a

[1] See above, p. 209.

moments security. I have said nothing of this to Doctor Hussey, not knowing what the Duke of Devonshire's sentiments might be on the occasion; nor shall I, tho' I expect him here on Tuesday,[1] but will leave the matter entirely to your Lordship. The account you gave me of Lord Frederick Cavendish's health has given me great comfort in the unfortunate State of my own,[2] which remains, and will always remain, the same, till it shall please God to settle the hour of my departure.

The most affectionate regards and grateful Sentiments of the remains of this poor House, are always engaged to Lady FitzWilliam.

I am, my dear Lord, with the most devoted attachment to the last,

Your most affectionate friend,
and obliged humble Servant,
EDM BURKE

Beaconsfield
   18th June 1797

The Duke of Devonshire (William Cavendish, 5th Duke of Devonshire, 1748–1811) wrote to Fitzwilliam on 7 July saying that he would certainly recommend Hussey to his principal agents in Ireland. He added 'I should feel some awkwardness in writing to Mr Burke, (as you propose to me) to desire to see Doctor Hussey, as I should have nothing particular to say to him, if I saw him, but at the same time I cannot possibly have any objection to see him, either in town or by going to Beaconsfield for the purpose, and should be very glad to see Burke again, tho' I am afraid I should see him in a state of health that would give me pain' (MS at Northampton, Box X 515/113).

To the ABBÉ DE LA BINTINAYE—25 June 1797

Source: Fitzwilliam MSS (Northampton).
Addressed: À Monsieur | Monsieur L'Abbé de la | Bintinnai.
Only the signature is in Burke's hand.

My dear Abbé

I give you a thousand thanks for your kind solicitude with regard to my health.[3] I am no stranger to the opinion which many entertain of the efficacy of Fowl and veal broths; but from my experience I know that all such broths disagree with my Stomach more than any thing else; tho' I beleive they have done good to many persons as well as to you; and I have observed that frequent eating in small quantities has always disagreed with me. As to the rest I have no great opinion of any other medicines, or of any other course of diet; being very conscious, that in so

[1] 20 June.
[2] Lord Frederick was almost Burke's age.
[3] If this was expressed in a letter, it is missing.

371

inveterate a complaint as mine, and at my age, that there is no course of medicine, nor of diet, that can be materially serviceable to me. I am not, however the less obliged to you for the kind concern you are pleased to take in my health.

I am my dear Abbé, with the greatest respect
and regard,
Your very obedient Servant
EDMD BURKE

Beaconsfield
25 June 1797

To UNKNOWN FRIEND at Oxford—3 July 1797
Source: MS Osborn Collection.
Canon Murray says that this letter was sold on behalf of Mrs Winston Churchill's Aid to Russia Fund. Only the signature is in Burke's hand.

My dear Sir

I should ill acquit myself to my own sentiments and do as little justice to the sentiments of others if I did not join with them in acknowledging your extraordinary kindness to the friends[1] whom I recommended to you in their tour thro' Oxford. You went beyond my wishes, and even my desires. You received my French Emigrant friends not as poor exiles, but as Princes on their travels. In this you consulted the generosity and nobleness of your own nature; and you have sent these Gentlemen back not only contented but infinitely flattered: and I beleive, very grateful. I am sure I am so. I continue in my intervals from pain excessively weak and reduced.

I have the honour to be, with mine, and Mrs Burke's affectionate regards,

My dear Sir,
Your most faithful and obliged
humble Servant,
EDM BURKE

Beaconsfield
3 July 1797

JANE BURKE to CHARLES JAMES FOX—[ante 9 July 1797]
Source: Prior (2nd ed.), II, 397.

At some time close to Burke's death, Fox made an attempt to arrange a last reconciliatory meeting with him. Prior printed the reply Mrs Burke returned him.

[1] Not identified.

Mrs Burke presents her compliments to Mr Fox, and thanks him for his obliging inquiries. Mrs Burke communicated his letter to Mr Burke, and, by his desire, has to inform Mr Fox that it has cost Mr Burke the most heart-felt pain to obey the stern voice of his duty in rending asunder a long friendship, but that he deemed this sacrifice necessary; that his principles remained the same; and that in whatever of life yet remained to him, he conceives that he must live for others and not for himself. Mr Burke is convinced that the principles which he has endeavoured to maintain are necessary to the welfare and dignity of his country, and that these principles can be enforced only by the general persuasion of his sincerity. For herself, Mrs Burke has again to express her gratitude to Mr Fox for his inquiries.

FRENCH LAURENCE *to* EARL FITZWILLIAM—9 *July* 1797
Source: Fitzwilliam MSS (Northampton), Box 52.

Beaconsfield July 9, 1797

My dear Lord,

Mr Nagle will have given your Lordship a short account of our poor friend's loss.[1] In the overwhelming affliction that surrounds me here, I have but one consolation, that I arrived in time for a last interview. I saw him, I talked with him; I saw him after He had ceased to talk at all; I joined in prayer with his other friends and family around his bed; I was present when the last breath passed so gently that no one can exactly say when he expired. When I first entered his room he seemed much better and stronger than he had been. From some confidential directions which he gave me I know that he considered his dissolution as fast approaching, but not so instant as it proved to be. He talked of public affairs and private with his accustomed interest and vivacity. He asked me if I had read Mr Grattan's address.[2] On being told that I had, he entered into a comment upon it, praising the brilliancy of some of the declarations, but censuring the false taste of the whole, particularly blaming, yet rather lamenting than blaming, more in sorrow than in anger the bad politics of beginning, continuing and ending with what is called parliamentary Reform. I observed to him the new and cruel difficulties which such intemperate declarations throw in your way, when turning to me he said, inform 'Lord Fitzwilliam from me, that it is my dying advice and request to him, steadily to pursue that course in

[1] Burke died shortly after midnight on the morning of 9 July.
[2] Grattan's address to the citizens of Dublin was published in the *Dublin Evening Post* of 1 July, which arrived in England on 5 July.

which he now is. He can take no other, that will not be unworthy of him'. Mrs Burke, I believe, was then in the room. She can bear witness to the solemn injunction, of which I have now acquitted myself. As I remember, this was almost if not quite the last thing which he said on public affairs.

His funeral (he told me,) he had by his will directed to be private;[1] but he explained to me that he did not mean to preclude his friends from those last offices, which might be attended with gratification to them, though with no advantage to him. When the day of the interment will be, I am not certain. I do not mean to fix it till I hear whether Dr W. King can come here to consult upon the subject. In any event, it will not be earlier than *Saturday* next, perhaps not till Monday.[2] Will you my dear Lord, allow me to name your Lordship for one of the Pall-bearers, to shew the last respect to the memory of a man, who while living ever loved you most affectionately and ardently? It may however be right to advertize your Lordship that from some late most kind messages, and from his having borne the pall over poor young Richard, it will be impossible to pass over the Duke of Portland on this melancholy occasion.[3]

Mrs Burke, of whom you and Lady Fitzwilliam will I am sure be most anxious to hear, shews a fortitude truly worthy of the character which we have ever known her to possess. She feels that she has duties to discharge, for the sake of which she thinks herself bound to take every care of life, though in itself it has no longer any pleasure for her. Her behaviour is most unaffectedly heroic.

I shall protract my stay here till Wednesday[4] and then must go to London for a day or two.

Oh! my dear Lord, what an incalculable loss have his family, his friends, and his countrymen suffered in that wonderful man, preeminent no less in virtues than in genius and in Learning! So kind to all connected with him, so partial to those whom he esteemed, ever preferring them in all things to himself; yet so zealous and resolute a champion in the cause of Justice, social order, morals and Religion. The private vanishes before the public calamity. When he fell, these kingdoms, Europe, the whole civilized world, lost the principal prop that remained, and were shaken to their very centers.

> Believe me to be
> My dear Lord
> Ever most gratefully and affectionately Yours
> FRENCH LAURENCE.

[1] See next page.   [2] The funeral was on Saturday 15 July at Beaconsfield.
[3] The pall bearers were: Windham, the Earl of Inchiquin, Earl Fitzwilliam, the Duke of Devonshire, Sir Gilbert Elliot, Henry Addington, the Duke of Portland, Lord Loughborough.   [4] 12 July.

APPENDIX
Burke's Last Will and Testament

Source: MS Public Record Office, Prerogative Court of Canterbury Special Wills (Prob. 1), no. 21.

Burke's will was signed in August 1794, two days after his son's funeral.

If my dear Son and friend had survived me any Will would have been unnecessary: But since it has pleased God to call him to himself before his Father, my Duty calls upon me to make such a disposition of my worldly effects, as seems to my best Judgment most equitable and reasonable—Therefore I Edmund Burke of the Parish of St Jamess Westminster, though suffering under sore and inexpressible affliction, being of sound and disposing mind, and not affected by any bodily infirmity, do make my last Will and Testament in manner following.

First, according to the antient, good, and laudable Custom, of which my heart and understanding recognizes the propriety, I bequeath my Soul to God; hoping for his Mercy thro' the only merits of our Lord and Saviour Jesus Christ. My Body, I desire, if I should die in any place very convenient for its Transport thither (but not otherwise) to be buried in the Church at Beconsfield, near to the Bodies of my dearest Brother,[1] and my dearest Son, in all humility praying, that as we have lived in perfect unity together, we may together have a part in the Resurrection of the Just.

I wish my funeral, to be (without any punctiliousness in that Respect) the same as that of my Brother; and to exceed it as little as possible in point of charge, whether on account of my family, or of any others who would go to a greater Expence; and I desire in the same manner, and with the same qualifications, that no monument, beyond a middle sized Tablet, with a small and simple inscription on the Church wall, or on the Flagstone, be erected. I say this, because I know the partial kindness to me of some of my friends—But I have had, in my Life time, but too much of Noise and compliment.

As to the rest, it is uncertain what I shall leave after the Discharge of my Debts, which when I write this are very great. Be that as it may, my Will concerning my worldly substance is short. As my entirely beloved, faithful, and affectionate Wife did, during the whole time in which I lived most happily with her, take on her the charge and management of my affairs, assisted by her Son whilst God was pleased to lend him to us,

[1] Richard Burke, Sr, died in February 1794.

375

and did conduct them, often in a state of much derangement and embarrassment, with a patience and prudence which probably have no example, and thereby left my Mind free to prosecute my publick Duty, or my Studies, or to indulge in my relaxations, or to cultivate my friends, at my pleasure, so, on my Death, I wish things to continue, as, substantially, they have always been: I therefore, by this my last and only Will, devise, leave, and bequeath to my entirely beloved and incomparable Wife Jane Mary Burke the whole real Estate of which I shall die seized, whether Lands, Rents, or Houses, in absolute Feesimple; as also all my personal Estate, whether Stock, furniture, Plate money, or securities for money, annuities for Lives or years, be the said Estate of what nature, quality, extent, or description it may, to her sole uncontrolled possession and disposal as her property, in any manner which may seem proper to her, to possess, or to dispose of the same; (whether it be real Estate or personal Estate) by her last Will, or otherwise—It being my Intention, that she may have as clear and uncontrolled a Right and Title thereto and therein as I possess myself, as to the use, expenditure Sale, or Devise. I hope these words are sufficient to express the absolute and unconditiond unlimited right of compleat ownership I mean to give to her to the said Lands and Goods; and I trust, that no words of surplusage or ambiguity may vitiate this my clear Intention. There are no persons who have a right, or, I beleive, a disposition to complain of this bequest, which I have duly weighed, and made on a proper consideration of my Duties and the relations in which I stand. I also make my Wife Jane Mary Burke aforesaid my sole Executrix of this my last Will, knowing that she will receive advice and assistance from her and my excellent friends Dr Walker King and Dr Laurence, to whom I recommend her and her concerns; though that perhaps is needless, as they are as much attachd to her as they are to me. I do it only to mark my special confidence in their affection Skill and industry.

I wish that my dear Wife may, as soon after my decease as possible, (which after what has happend she will see with constancy and resignation) make her Will with the advice and assistance of the two persons I have named. But it is my wish also that she will not think herself so bound up by any bequests she may make in the said Will, and which whilst she lives can be only intentions, as not during her Life to use her property with all the Liberty I have given her over it, just as if she had written no Will at all; but in every thing to follow the directions of her own equitable[1] and charitable mind, and her own prudent and measurd understanding.

[1] MS: aquitabe

Having thus committed every thing to her discretion, I recommend, (subject always to that discretion) that if I should not during my Life give or secure to my dear Niece Mary C. Haviland, wife of my worthy friend Captn Haviland,[1] the sum of a thousand pound, or an annuity equivalent to it, that she would bestow upon her that sum of money or that annuity conditiond and limited in such manner as she my Wife aforesaid may think proper, by a devise in her Will or otherwise as she may find most convenient to the situation of her affairs without pressure upon her during her Life. My Wife put me in Mind of this, which I now recommend to her. I certainly some years ago gave my Niece reason to expect it—but I was not able to execute my Intentions.[2] If I do this in my Lifetime, this recommendation goes for nothing.

As to my other friends, relations, and companions thro' Life, and especially to the friends and companions of my Son, who were the dearest of mine, I am not unmindful of what I owe them. If I do not name them all here and mark them with Tokens of my Remembrance, I hope they will not attribute it to unkindness, or to a want of a due Sense of their Merits towards me. My old friend and faithful companion Will Burke knows his place in my heart. I do not mention him as Executor or assistant. I know that he will attend to my Wife—but I chose the two I have mentiond, as from their time of Life, of greater activity. I recommend him to them. In the political world I have made many connexions, and some of them amongst persons of high rank. Their friendship from political became personal to me; and they have shewn it in a manner more than to satisfye the utmost demands that could be made from my Love and sincere attachment to them. They are the worthiest people in the Kingdom. Their intentions are excellent, and I wish them every kind of success—I bequeath my Brother in Law John Nugent, and the friends in my poor Sons List,[3] which is in his Mothers hands, to their protection. As to them and to the rest of my companions, who constantly honourd and cheerd our House, as our Inmates, I have put down their names in a List that my Wife should send them the usual remembrance of little mourning Rings as a token of my Remembrance. In speaking of my friends to whom I owe so many obligations I ought to name specially Lord Fitzwilliam, the Duke of Portland, and the Lord Cavendishes with the D. of Devonshire the worthy head of that Family.

If the intimacy, which I have had with others has been broken off

[1] Captain Thomas Haviland (d. 1795).
[2] Mrs Haviland received a legacy of £5000 from Jane Burke (Prior, 2nd ed., II, 405–6).   [3] Missing.

by a political difference on great Questions concerning the state of things existing and impending, I hope they will forgive whatever of general Human infirmity, or of my own particular infirmity, has enterd into that contention. I heartily entreat their forgiveness. I have nothing further to say.

Signed and seald as my last Will and Testament this 11th day of August 1794 being written all with my own hand.

EDM BURKE

In presence of
    DuPont[1]
    William Webster[2]
    Walker King

On reading over the above Will I have nothing to add or essentially to alter; but one point may want to be perfected and explaind. In leaving my Lands and Hereditaments to my Wife, I find, that I have omitted the words which in Deeds create an Inheritance in Law—Now, tho' I think them hardly necessary in a Will, yet to obviate all Doubts, I explain the matter in a Codicil which is annexed to this.

EDM BURKE

Jany 22. 1797

Only the concluding part of the Codicil is in Burke's hand (see note below) the rest is in the hand of Walker King.

I Edm. Burke of the Parish of Beaconsfield in the County of Bucks, being of sound and disposing Judgment and memory make this my last Will and Testament, in no sort revoking but explaining and confirming a Will made by me and dated the eleventh of August 1794. in which Will I have left devised and bequeathed all my Worldly [effects] of whatever nature and quality the same may be whether Lands, Tenements, houses, freehold or Leasehold Interests, Pensions for Lives or years, Arrears of the same, Legacies or other debts due to me, Plate, household Stuff, books, stock in Cattle and horses, and utensils of farming and all other my good and Chattels to my dear Wife J. M. Burke in as full and perfect manner as the same might be devised, conveyed or transferred to her by any Act or Instrument whatsoever, with such recommendations as in my Will aforesaid are made, and with a wish that in the discharge of my debts the course hitherto pursued may be as nearly as possible observed. Sensible however that in payment of debt no exact rule can be preserved

[1] Pierre-Gaëton Dupont (1762–1817), translator of the *Reflections* into French.
[2] See above, p. 308.

378

the same is therefore left to her discretion, with the advice of our friends whom she will naturally consult—The reason of my making this Will or codicil to my former will, is from my having omitted in devising by that Will my Lands and hereditaments to my Wife aforesaid the full and absolute Property thereof and therein, I have omitted the legal words of Inheritance—Now tho' I think those words however necessary in a deed are not so in a Will, yet to prevent all question, I do hereby devise all my lands, Tenements, and hereditaments, as well as all other property that may be subject to a strict rule of Law in deeds and which would pass if left undevised to my Heirs, I say I do devise the same lands tenements and Hereditaments to my Wife Jane Mary Burke and her heirs for ever in pure absolute and unconditional fee simple.

I have now only to recommend to the kindness of my Lord Chancellor, Lord Loughborough, to His Grace the Duke of Portland, to the most honourable the Marquess of Buckingham, to the Rt Honble Wm Windham and to Dr Lawrence of the Commons[1] and member of Parliament, that they will after my death continue their protection and favour to the Emigrant School at Penn, and will entreat, with a weight on which I dare not presume, the Rt Hon. Wm Pitt to continue the necessary allowances, which he has so generously and charitably provided for those unhappy children of meritorious Parents,—that they will superintend the same, which I wish to be under the more immediate care and direction of Dr King and Dr Lawrence, and that they will be pleased to exert their influence, to place the said young persons in some military Corps, or other service, as may best suit their dispositions and capacities, praying God to bless their endeavours.[2] Signed and seald as a Codicil to my Will or a confirmation and explanation thereof, (agreeably to the Note, which some days ago I put to the End of it)—This 29th January 1797

EDM BURKE

In the presence of
Walker King.
Richd Bourke
Ed Nagle

The Will and Codicil were proved on 26 July 1797 before French Laurence as surrogate.

[1] Doctors' Commons.
[2] The rest of the codicil is in Burke's hand.

PART TWO

ADDITIONAL LETTERS

This concluding portion of the *Correspondence of Edmund Burke* is divided into three sections. The letters printed in Section A are of two sorts. There are 'new letters' which have become available, or come to our editors' attention, too late to appear in their proper chronological places in this edition. There are also letters which have been printed in earlier volumes, either completely or in extract, of which superior versions have now appeared. The letters printed in Section B are those to which no adequate date can be assigned. Section C consists of entries from Autograph Dealers' Catalogues which preserve useful information about letters whose whereabouts we have not discovered.

The editing of the 'new letters' and of the undated letters presents no difficulty. They are annotated in full. The letters which have been printed before in whole or part offer a more difficult problem. Where the full text has already been printed, they already have their explanatory notes: the reader has only to turn to the earlier volumes in which they appeared. They will not, however, have been transcribed according to the principles followed in this edition, and some of them contain serious textual inaccuracies. We have therefore re-transcribed them here, treating spelling, punctuation, capitalization, paragraphing and so on as we would have treated them if the superior version had been accessible in time. Sometimes this has required the adding of textual notes, and even of explanatory notes for words or passages which are now available for the first time.

A. LETTERS WITH FULL OR ADEQUATE DATES

To PATRICK NAGLE—11 *October* 1759

Source: MS New York Public Library.

Printed in vol. 1, 134–6, from the *New Monthly Magazine*.

Dear Sir

My Brother has been before hand with me in almost every thing I could say. My conduct stands in need of as many apologies as his, but I am afraid our apologies might be almost as troublesome as our Neglects. All I can say is, that I have been, I think it is now eleven years, from the county of ⟨Cork⟩ yet my[1] remembrance of my friends there is as fresh as if I had left it yesterday. My Gratitude for their favours, and my Love for their Characters is rather heightened, as the oftner I think of them they must be, and I think of them very often. This I can say with great Truth. Believe me dear Sir, It would be a great pleasure to me to hear as often from you as it is convenient; Do not give yourself any sort of trouble about Franks; I value very little that triffling expence, and I should very little deserve to hear from my friends, if I scrupled to pay a much higher price for that Satisfaction. If I had any thing that you could have pleasure in, to send you from hence, I should be a punctual correspondent; There is nothing here, except what the Newspapers contain that can interest you; but nothing can come from the Blackwater which does not interest me very greatly. Poor Dick is on the point of quitting us; however he has such advantageous Prospects where he is going that I part [from] him with the less regret. One of the first Merchants here has taken him by the hand and enabled him to go off with a very Valuable cargo. He has another advantage and satisfaction in his Expedition; One of our best friends here goes at the same time in one of the first Places in the Island.

Mrs Burke is very sensible of your Goodness, and desires that I should make you her acknowlegements. We equally wish it were in our Power to accept of your kind invitation; and that no greater obstacle intervened to keep us from seeing Ballyduffe, but the distance. We are too good Travellers to be frighted at that. I have made a much longer Journey than the Land Part of it this Summer. However it is not impossible but we may one day have the pleasure of embracing you at your own house.

[1] The MS has been repaired by tape and the words 'think it is...yet my' have been copied back in another hand.

I beg you will Salute for us the good houses of Ballywalter, Ballylegan and Ballynahalisk, et nati natorum, et qui nascuntur ab illis. Our little Boys are very well, but I should think them still better, if they (or the one that is on his legs) were running about the Bawn at Ballyduffe as his father used to do. Farewell My dear Uncle

and believe me your affectionate Kinsman

Wimple Street   and humble Servant
   Cavendish Square   EDM BURKE.
      11th October 1759.

I forgot to say any thing of the irregularity which you may have found in the Papers for some time passed. The summer has made the Town thin of Members of Parliament, so that we were sometimes at a loss, but now we shall be pretty secure on that head,[1] and you shall have your Papers more regularly.

To MRS ELIZABETH MONTAGU—[4 *March* 1763]

Source: MS Bath Public Library.

Printed in vol. I, 163, from Blunt, *Mrs Montagu*, as of [3 March 1763]. The 'Friday' of the original establishes the date as 4 March 1763.

Permit me Madam, to condole with you on the very melancholy account which for the first Time I heard in the Evening paper of last Night. What an heart like yours must feel from such a blow to such a friend I can easily conceive from what you suffer on much lighter occasions. However you have occasion for all your Spirits in order to lighten to my Lord the sense of his great misfortune; and if in these circumstances any thing can be called happiness, it is such to his Lordship to have a friend so capable of sympathising with his sorrows and of releiving them. Be so good to let me know whether I may with propriety send or wait on his Lordship, and how soon. I am really very much concerned; I would not be deficient in an attention which is so much my Duty; on the other hand a violation of propriety on these occasions is of all others the greatest Error.

I am

Madam

Your ever obliged
and obedient Servant

Friday.   ED BURKE

---

[1] The words 'we shall be...regularly' are not entirely legible in the MS and are here printed from the text published in the *New Monthly Magazine*.

To Mrs Elizabeth Montagu—29 *July* [1763]

Source: MS Princeton Library.

Printed in vol. I, 170–3, from Blunt, *Mrs Montagu.*

July 29.

Madam,

I have forborn writing all this time in hopes of some News which might entertain you. But I am resolved to wait for it no longer. I have been for these two months past an insufferable companion to others, in order to qualifye myself to be an agreeable correspondent to you; My whole conversation turned upon nothing but what might lead to intelligence; However I have succeeded so ill, that I fear my eagerness may have frustrated my pursuit; and I fancy people began at length to take me for a Spy; a Character in which (as I receive none of the secret service money), I do not yet chuse to appear. I confess that until this moment I could not call up confidence enough to address a letter to you without the passport of some sort of News; But as I see the Court forsaken, Westminster Hall shut, the Dinners adjourned, the War Kettle[1] coverd with cobwebs; the cheifs of the opposition hanging their Trophies oer their Garden Gates, the ministers employd only in scraping together reversions, and Mr Wilkes only scraping together a Guinea subscription, the whole political campain reduced to a *petite Guerre* of Printers, Devils, and Diablotins, and that the very best of our paltry but furious animosities afforded nothing that was worthy of Mrs Montagu, I have at length sat down to write, because in Duty bound, without the least hope of diverting you or of satisfying myself; for if I were to speak from what I feel of my opinion of Mrs Montagus Genius, of her Virtues, and of my innumerable obligations to her friendship, I should say indeed what would be very sincere and very true but then I should say, what to her would be the most unentertaining thing in the world. So that the only subject upon which I can speak is the only one which it is improper for me to mention. Besides Madam, I observe that Panegyric even when applied to those who deserve it most or like it best is sure never to please above one, and will certainly offend fifty. To say the Truth, Satyr is now so much the safer, and (what is now the only rule of right) the more popular way, that I am resolved to stick to that; especially if I can have the good fortune to get elected for Aylesbury. The old rule was, pictoribus atque poetis, quid libet audendi semper fuit æqua[2] potestas. This shall, for the present at

[1] 'Among North American Indians, a kettle which was set on the fire as part of the ceremony of inaugurating a war' (*Oxford English Dictionary*).   [2] MS: aqua

least, be limited by a little Scholiasts remark in the Margin, 'provided they have privilege of parliament' which is a privilege as extensive as ever the wildest Poet in his wildest reveries could ever figure to himself. In the next Session it is reported, that they will extend this privelege to us all, or take it away from themselves; otherwise there will be no fair play; the report of the former part is however predominant; All our Law de Libellis famosis, is to be changed, and the Pillory is only to be reserved for unsuccessful Flatterers. Having therefore much regard to the Law, more to the Fashion, and most of all to my Ears, I think to try my hand at invective and to sketch out a North Briton which shall equal the Spirit of the celebrated and indeed *Golden Number*. 45. The Subject of it shall be, for we scorn Blanks and dashes,—Mrs Montagu herself. After a few preluding touches upon scotchmen and Excise I intend to observe on the scandalous Neglect of our Board of Treasury, who have sufferd the most valuable staple products of the Kingdom to be carried out without the least opposition. I shall shew that France has of late discoverd that she wants our Wisdom as much in her manufacture of Policy and War, as she[1] does our Wool in her cloths and stuffs; and yet that I could prove our Ministry sufferd to be shipped for Calais in one Vessel and in one day, more Genius, more Learning, more Wit, more Eloquence, more Policy, more Mathematics, more Poetry, more Philosophy and Theology than France could produce in a Century. I shall point out that Mrs Montagu who has long been a clandestine dealer in Goods of this sort, and who had several of them about her own person at the very time was the Capital Smuggler on this occasion, and carried off all the Rest. Whilst I was preparing this wonderful piece, my Lawyer whose opinion I take on all my Libels, and who points out exactly how far the breach of the Law may be seperated from its penalties, informed me that this time my satire was quite stingless. That no *Ne exeat regno* lay for Wit and Genius: That we might freely export the whole Sense of the Kingdom. (I dont mean the sense of the Nation, for thats quite another thing.) He thought this freedom founded upon a very proper principle; That it operated like the Bounty upon the exportation of Corn, which only made it the cheaper and more plentiful at home. This Theory I confess had something specious in it; but as I have been a sort of Dabbler in Theories myself, I was no way surprised to find that on experiment it did not prove worth a farthing; for I cannot discover, that any thing extraordinary has started up to supply the great loss we have had; we do not grow, as bodies sometimes do, a bit the fatter, for all this Bleeding. As the Nation had so great a loss I wanted to

[1] MS: and as she

know whether the revenue had any great Benefit by this extraordinary trade. On examining the Custom house Books I found, you may imagine to my astonishment, a small but heavy parcel marked with a capital M. was charged but at one penny three farthings Duty. The Officer told me that on the Entry he claimed more and would have had twice as much had the point been tried by the Excise Laws; but that he was obliged to try it by a Jury *mis parties*,[1] or as our Lawyers would express it, *de medietate Linguæ*, of six Ladies from this end of the Town and six of Wapping, who unanimously brought in a Verdict by their forewoman that no higher rate than 25 per Cent ad valorem should be laid on such goods so that they valued the whole parcel just at seven pence and no more; and I am informed that if they had summond four fifths of the Ladies of the Kingdom they would not have rated it a penny higher. I had a curiosity to look at the import of this Kind; and the State of the revenue on this Branch was flourishing. It consisted for that day of three parcels of the French academy Manufacture the 1st a Scheme for opening living sculls in order to discover the seat and nature of the Soul. The second was a proposal to dig to the center of the Earth by a confederacy of Princes in order to settle more effectually the Ballance of power; the third was to promote the happiness of mankind and the prosperity of States by extirpating religion and Virtue, and substituting self interest in their place. Thus stood the Trade; and I was obliged to suppress my Libel.

Might I presume to flatter myself with an Idea of hearing how the Spaw has agreed with you? I enquired as long as I could find anybody to inform me? Can you think of London surrounded by Princes and Heroes, whilst the Terrors of Europe are prancing about on Poneys, and whilst you grow familiar with every thing which we admire. Be so good to thank Mr Montagu for his kind remembrance of me before his Departure; and present mine and my Brothers humble and grateful respects to Lord Bath; we are infinitely obliged to him for his generous endeavours though things remain just as they were. Be so good to make my Compliments to Miss Carter and to Dr or Colonel Douglass. Be so kind to forgive me for having wrote so tiresome a Letter. It is the longest I ever wrote in my Life. Believe me Madam with the truest respect and sincerest[2] Gratitude your most obedient and obliged humble

Servant E BURKE

[1] The meaning of this term has not been discovered.
[2] MS: sincrest

To CHARLES LLOYD—1 *October* 1765

Source: MS Sir John Murray.

Printed in vol. I, 214–15, from the *Grenville Papers.*

Dear Sir,

I hope you will do me the Justice to believe that my long delay in answering your Letter did in no respect arise from a disregard to your Character or an indifference to the Success of your desires. A good deal of Business, together with some returns of the same complaint I sufferd under when you saw me, were the real and only causes of a delay, which I confess I cannot entirely excuse, but which you will have the goodness to forgive.

On communicating the Contents of your Letter to Lord Rockingham, his Lordship seemed much surprised to find that you think you have *already* received some marks of his displeasure, as you have used the expression of a fear of *further* marks of it. His Lordship thought you had been sufficiently apprised of the true Cause of your removal from the Office of Receiver of Gibraltar; this change having been in consequence of a general arrangement which his Lordship and his friends apprehended to be required from them by the rules of strict Justice in favour of former sufferers; and by no means from any particular dislike or resentment to you. Many persons sufferd from the Same disposition, whose persons Lord Rockingham valued, and whose situations he sincerely pitied.

As to the expression in my Letter to which you have excepted, I must beg leave to explain myself, and to assure you that it related to the substance of the Question and not at all to your motives in asking it. It was meant to express the impropriety of giving any answer to it, from the obvious consequences which must have resulted from an Answer; and not from the smallest intention of reflecting upon you, for your having desired satisfaction upon a matter, concerning which you must naturally be very anxous.

I am with great Esteem and very real goodwishes
Dear Sir
your most obedient
and most humble Servant
E BURKE.

Q. Ann Street
 Octr 1st 1765.

JANE *and* EDMUND BURKE *to* MRS JULIANA FRENCH—
6 *February* 1766

Source: MS Osborn Collection.
Addressed: To | Mrs French.

Printed in vol. 1, 235–6, from Prior (2nd ed.).

[Jane begins]

I most truly and affectionately wish you my Dear Sister joy on the Change[1] you have made in life. It is a change that I make not the least doubt will insure happiness to you, and to all your friends the pleasure and satisfaction that an union made by you must give them; we are all very happy in being connected with a Man of Mr French's Character, which Mr Ridge has very fully, and very satisfactorily given us. I wish you many years to enjoy that satisfaction and happiness that lies before you; and many years I hope you will live to enjoy it; I can only add my prayrs and hearty wishes that you should, which I do from the bottom of my heart. I leave it to you, and surely I cannot leave it in better hands, to make my love to Mr French. I wish I had it in my power to wish you both joy myself by word of mouth, but I hope before the Summer is over I shall do so, as we think if possible to take a turn to Ireland about that time.

I had wrote thus far, when I got your letter, and it makes us all very happy to hear you are so well, and so much pleased with your present sittuation. Ned is so taken up that he has scarce time to eat, drink, or sleep; he has not been in bed this week untill three or four o Clock in the Morning, and his hurry will not be over, I am afraid, the whole winter; if he can, he will add to this, but if he should not be able so to do; I am sure you will not doubt of his love and affection for you both. Dick is not yet come home, but we expect him every day; nay he may be here before I seal this, and if he is you shall hear of him. Your Nephew is grown very stout, strong and tall, he is at school about four miles from Town, he is now learning lattin and very eager he is at it. He does not forget his Aunt Julian nor her goodness to him. He is to be home Satturday for a Week, which he has got on account of his birth day so that you see what consequence a birth day is to him now.

Mr William Burke desires I would assure you from him how happy he is at every thing that gives you pleasure, and that he sincerely wishes you joy on the present occasion. My Father joyns in the same wish and Mr W. B in love and Compliments to Mr French and you. Believe me

[1] MS: Chang

389

my Dear Sister, no one more truly and affectionately loves you or wishes for every happiness to attend you more, than your

affectionate Sister, and very
humble Servant.
JANE: BURKE

Queen Anne Street
Feby 6th 1766.

[Edmund begins]

My dear Julian, upon my Word, I have only time to say I most heartily wish you and Mr French much joy; and to you both the good-sense and goodnature to make it your endeavour to contribute all you can to one anothers happiness. I wish you both many years enjoyment of it and am with my regards to my Brother my dear Julian

Your most affectionate
E BURKE

To JOHN HELY HUTCHINSON—3 *August* [1767]

Source: Donoughmore MSS.

Printed in vol. I, 318–20, from Hist. MSS Comm. (*Donoughmore MSS*), which omitted some parts of the original. Burke's opening sentence answers Hutchin-son's, which was: 'Are you yet able to make an irish Chancellor?'.

Indeed I am not; nor his Trainbearer. I assure you, my dear Hutchin-son, I have a very sincere desire, in my present humble Situation, to do any thing that may be pleasing to you; I should have the same, if I had as much power as your Partiality could wish me. But I cannot move the Machine, or even grease the wheels. My friends are out of power; and likely to continue so. Lord Rockingham is gone to the Country, without Office and with Dignity. Lord Bristol I could not even know: Lord Townshend I do know too well. His Brother has no regard for me, and I have no confidence in him. Just so matters stand; and I will not make any Parade of my willingness to run your Errands, because it would look like that cheap and common-place way of shewing ones good inclinations, when no service is desired, because no service can be done. I think it very likely, that the Chancellor will be appointed from hence. In the conversations which I hear, it is talked of as a sort of Maxim of Govern-ment. But in the End the accommodation of their own arrangement is the principle they will proceed upon. It was this principle that made

Lord Townshend Lord Lieutenant; at least I cannot conceive any other; and have but a moderate opinion of their Policy even in that. On Lord Chathams decline in health and capacity, Lord Rockingham was wished, with his friends, to accede to the remains of that administration; He tryed to form a plan of strength; but in this attempt he failed, and he was unwilling to form the project of a weak one, or to make a part in such a System. The D. of Grafton and Mr Conway, who seemd at first very sensible of the deficiencies of their own System, took courage from the failure of their Negotiation, and resolve, to all appearance, to hold on that Bute bottom upon which Lord Chatham had left them. As their Garrison is very small, it became absolutely necessary that there should be more harmony amongst them than appeard in the last Session. Townshend is become of more consequence; and if possible, to fix his Levity, they have made his Brother Lord Lieutenant; which I know to have been long his object. Lord Townshend is thought to have a great ascendant over Charles. I imagine this has been their motive; they have wanted agreement within themselves; for I am sure this has given them no strength from without. If they should attempt to enlarge themselves, and to extend their Line of Debate, they will probably attempt to get Sir Fletcher Norton. If they can compass this, the Master of the Rolls will be thrown upon you; and Oh! Earth lye light on him! sure no man ever burthend it so much. I think their attempt on Sir Fletcher very likely; because I know they had a Negotiation with him last Winter. If this should fail, and they think of your side, the consideration of the Offices which you have to resign, would I should think weigh a great deal with Lord Townshend provided he has any man whom he loves enough for the moment to wish a provision for. Adieu my dear Sir; I am in much hurry, having just Slipped from a company who dined with me, or I might say more; if any thing particular should come to my knowlege, you will hear of it. I took the Liberty of recommending a foreign Gentleman of merit to your attention.[1] He goes off tomorrow and will deliver you my Letter, I am with the greatest Truth ever yours

E BURKE

Parsons Green 3d Augst

You may depend on my Secrecy. When I can do no good; I ought to do no mischief.

[1] He has not been identified.

To the MARCHIONESS OF ROCKINGHAM—*22 October* 1767
Source: Ramsden MSS.

Madam,

I presume your Ladyship is not so thoroughly rusticated by your late perfect retirement at Wentworth, and by my Lords absence, as to grow quite indifferent to all sorts of Politicks. I therefore take the Liberty of telling your Ladyship a piece of News, on a matter, which greatly concerns my Lord Rockingham and the party; and about which I have myself been in great anxiety for some days past. I am not sure whether you have heard, that General Conway[1] thought proper to send an Offer of half the pay Office, vacant by Lord Norths new promotion,[2] to Lord Edgcumbe; with the friendly purpose, I imagine, of taking one Peer, about six Commoners, and all confidence and Credit from the Party.[3] This you will allow to be a tolerable Cause for uneasiness. However I have the pleasure of informing your Ladyship, that he took a very manly and becoming resolution on this offer and refused it; but he would have the Offer and the refusal kept as secret as possible.[4] I knew nothing of his final determination until this moment. I am not quite clear, whether a Letter wrote to night would meet Lord Rockingham at Newmarket tomorrow, or I should be glad to relieve him by the earliest intelligence of it. If he should not hear it by another Channel, your Ladyship will have the pleasure of communicating it to him.

After this news, so honourable to Lord Edgcumbe, I must venture to tell one, not quite so reputable to myself, and to a noble person concernd with me. It is that Lord G. Cavendish[5] and I left Newmarket on Tuesday[6] just as the Horses were led out to Run without waiting the Issue of the Race. I think we can never appear there again with much Credit. But what will do as well, my Lord Marquess and the Cavendishes are agreed with me on the Lancaster Business, which was the Cause that took me to Newmarket.[7]

[1] Henry Seymour Conway (1719–95), Secretary of State in the Chatham Administration.
[2] Frederick North, styled Lord North (1732–92), later (1790) 2nd Earl of Guilford, had become Chancellor of the Exchequer.
[3] George Edgcumbe, 3rd Baron Edgcumbe (1720–95), whose dismissal from office in 1766 precipitated the breach between Rockingham and Chatham (see vol. I, 280), had remained on the fringes of the Rockingham party. Edgcumbe controlled six Cornish seats.
[4] Edgcumbe was not, as it turned out, happy in Opposition and went over to the Government in 1770.
[5] Lord George Augustus Cavendish (*c.* 1727–94), M.P. for Derbyshire.
[6] 20 October.
[7] They had agreed that Burke should not contest Lancaster at the next election (see vol. I, 326, 330, 332–3).

May I beg your Ladyship to present my Compliments to Miss Ramsden.[1] I fear I sent the Spilikins[2] in a very awkard manner without any Note intending[3] to return to the house at Grovenor Square to direct them—but I was prevented—and so Thos Hankin[4] has sent them as he could.

Your Ladyship will have a great deal of goodness, if you excuse this extraordinary compound of a Letter consisting of Politicks, Newmarket and Spilikins! I am with the highest respect and esteem

> Madam
> > Your Ladyships
> > > most obedient
> > > > and most humble Servant
> > > > EDM BURKE

Parsons Green Octr 22.1767.

I am afraid I have given improper directions about the Buck for Lancaster. It was to have been there on the 26th of this month or even on the 25th and not before. Directed to Mr Bowes Mayor of Lancaster.[5]

To JAMES BARRY—15 April 1768
Source: MS New York Public Library.

Printed in vol. I, 349–50, from Barry, Works.

Dear Barry,

I am heartily ashamed, for myself and all your friends, that we have so long neglected to write to you. By and by we may make up for our Neglect. At the present I have only to say, that I thank God we are well, that we shall endeavour to make amends for this Neglect, and that you will be so good to continue in Rome until you hear again from some of us.

> My Dear Barry
> > most affectionately yours
> > EDM BURKE

April 15. 1768

[1] Elizabeth Ramsden (d. 1831), Lady Rockingham's half-sister. She married William Weddell (1736–92) in 1771.
[2] Spillikins was a game 'played with a heap of slips or small rods of wood, bone, or the like, the object being to pull off each by means of a hook without disturbing the rest' (Oxford English Dictionary).
[3] MS: intend
[4] Thomas Hankin was a servant at Rockingham's house in Grosvenor Square.
[5] John Bowes (d. c. 1798), was elected Mayor on 22 October.

To GEORGE DEMPSTER—[*ante* 26 *September* 1768]
Source: Blair-Adam MSS.

The following passage is from a (missing) letter of Burke to George Dempster (1732–1818). It concerns the Kinross-shire election of 1768, in which Robert Adam (1728–92), the architect, defeated Major-General John Irwin (*c.* 1728–88). The election resulted in both legal proceedings and a petition to the House of Commons (*The History of Parliament: the House of Commons 1754–1790*, ed. Sir Lewis Namier and John Brooke, London, 1964, I, 486–7). Dempster answered Burke's (missing) letter on 26 September (MS at Sheffield) and quoted from it in a letter of 3 October (Blair-Adam MSS) addressed to John Adam (1721–92), brother of Robert Adam. 'In a Letter I had tother day from Burke', he wrote, 'he writes me relative to Your Affair in the following words':

If the Facts be as they are represented in the Paper you sent me[1] I think I never knew a more extraordinary proceeding. Surely no judicious person will choose with ever so many Advantages of Legal Rigour, to be exhibited before a Public Judicature in the Colours of that narrative well Established. I have long known General Irvine, and with much regard, as a very worthy honest goodnatured man. I am therefore very sorry to find him committed with your friends especially on such ground. Immediately on the receipt of your Letter I went to Town with a view of doing my best to persuade him to the Course you recommend, but I had not the Luck to meet him, when ever I do I certainly will labour that point as much as I possibly can.

In his letter of 3 October Dempster wrote that Burke was 'much connected with Irwine. I would fain hope some good might come from his apprehending the Case so truely and so much according to our Wishes'. James Adam (d. 1794) wrote to Dempster on 17 November that his brother Robert was most grateful for his assistance in obtaining Burke's support (MS at Sheffield, Bk 4*a*).

To THOMAS WHATELY—21 *August* [1769]
Source: Copy British Museum (Add. MS 42,087, fol. 64).

Printed in vol. II, 55–6, from the *Grenville Papers*.

Gregories 21st Augst.

Dear Whately

I hope you have not entirely forgot your Promise of spending a Day here, in your way to or from Mr Grenville's. I wish the Pleasure of seeing you from Motives as independant of Politicks, as the Course of my Life and Thoughts here have been generally removed from all Ideas of

---

[1] The paper is missing.

that kind. This I thought not amiss to say, when I am just going to mention a Particular, that looks a little towards Business; I should be glad to have some Notion of what your friends think ought to be done at Aylesbury, in the Meeting which is advertised for next Month; for my own part, I am wholly for a Petition, and for as strong a one as can consist with Decorum and Propriety; but entirely averse from making it a Farago of wild indigested Matter. In Worcestershire they have confined themselves to one or two Points; I think it would be rather awkward to go to the Meeting, without any distinct Idea of what is to be proposed; and I would just hint to you, that some Gentlemen, and Friends of yours too, on this Side of the Country, seem rather hurt, that no Communication has been made to them; I the rather mention this, because Lord Verney moved the meeting in the Grand Jury, in concurrence with Lord Temple. I am &ca

EDMUND BURKE.

To GARRETT NAGLE—2 *January* 1771

Source: MS Osborn Collection.

Printed in vol. II, 179–81 from the *New Monthly Magazine.*

My Dear Garrett,

I am so heavily in your Debt on account of Correspondence that I must trust more to your good nature, than to any means of payment which I have, for my acquittal. I am now at Beconsfield, in order to enjoy a little leisure in rural amusements and occupations after a sitting of some fatigue, though of no very long duration. I imagine that our business will be full as heavy upon us at our next meeting; in the mean time we are indulged with a recess full as ample as could in reason be expected. We are all thank God well. Mrs Burke perfectly recoverd in every respect but flesh, some of which however she could well enough spare. Little Richard after the holidays goes to Westminster School; so that I beleive we shall all take our leave of the Country, until the approach of Summer. Dick sometimes hears from our Young Seaman at Portsmouth; and Mrs Burke had a letter from Captn Stott yesterday in which he mentions him, as he has always done, in Terms of the highest approbation. The Captain and his wife attend to him with a sort of parental affection. I shall give you what Stott says of him in his own words; 'Nagles things are come down safe, and he thanks you for them. I assure you upon my word, that he is the best and briskest that I have upon my quarter Deck. He will make a fine Officer. Now the Ship is at Spithead he is at his Books'. I think it must give you pleasure to hear of the good opinion which his commander entertains of your Nephew. He has in the same manner endeared himself to his shipmates while he was in the Companies Service. Indeed he seems to be a lad of great good nature and of most excellent principles.

I had Letters from my Uncle at Ballylegan and from Mr Archdeacon of Corke wishing me to undertake the Guardianship of young Therry; I deferred taking my resolution upon the subject until I had consulted Mr Ridge. It was a long time before he gave me an answer; and though he is not quite clear, whether it may not bring me into some difficulties, I will (and so let my Uncle know) accept it, wishing him and Mr Archdeacon to consult Mr Ridge upon the Steps which are proper to be taken.

We have had the most rainy and stormy season that has been known. I have got my Wheat into ground better than some others; that is about four and twenty acres; I proposed having about ten more; but considering the Season this is tolerable. Wheat bears a tolerable price though a good deal fallen. It is 42 Shillings the quarter that is two of your Barrels. Barley 24s Peas very high 27 to 30s the quarter; so that our Bacon will come dear to us this Season. I have put up four hogs. I killed one yesterday, which weighed a little more than 12 Score. Of the other three, one is now near 15 Score, the others about 12. I shall put up seven more for pickled pork; these weigh, when fit to kill near 7 Score a piece. To what weight do you generally feed Bacon Hogs in your part of the Country? Here they generally fat them to about fourteen or fifteen Score. In Berkshire near us they carry them to 25 or thirty score. I am now going into some new Method having contracted with a London Seedsman for early white peas at a Guinea a Barrel. These I shall sow in Drills in February, dunging the Ground for them. They will be off early enough to sow turnips. Thus I shall save a Fallow without, I think, in the least injuring my Ground, and get a good return besides. A crop of such Peas will be nearly as valuable as a crop of wheat; and they do not exhaust the soil; so little, that as far as my experience goes, they are not much inferior to a fallow. I will let you know my success in due time. Remember me most cordially to your family and to all our friends on your Rivers. Beleive me most affectionately yours   EDM BURKE.

Beconsfield 2d Jany 1771.

I heard not long since from my Brother who was thank God, very well. Let me hear from you as soon as you can. Whenever I wrote I forgot to desire you to give a Guinea from ⟨Shane⟩ to his father at Killivullen. For my delay be so good to give him half a Guinea more.

To UNKNOWN—5 *June* [1771]

Source: Lonsdale MSS.
This letter of 'June 5. Wednesday morn' was almost certainly written
in 1771, when 5 June was a Wednesday.

My dear Sir,

I am extremely obliged to you for the honour you intend me. I should
be extremely desirous of so very agreeable an object, in so very agreeable
a way. But the fact unluckily is, that Lord Cholmondely[1] sent me word
last Saturday, that he would come down to my house and dine with me
on Thursday, and as it is absolutely the first time of my seeing him,
though I knew his Grandfather and his relations for several years very
intimately, I cannot by any possibility put off this Engagement; but
must be at home early on Thursday to meet him. This is, you may be
sure, very mortifying to me. But any other day, which will be suitable
to you, and to Sir James,[2] I shall come to Town with great pleasure and
obey your very obliging Commands. I am with the greatest Esteem and
Regard

> Dear Sir,
> Your very faithful
> and obedient humble Servant
> EDM BURKE

June 5. Wednesday morn

To CHASE PRICE—20 *November* 1771

Source: Cecil MSS (PRI/3/9).

In 1767 Sir James Lowther, 5th Baronet (1836–1802), M.P. for Cockermouth,
later (1784) 1st Earl of Lonsdale, had petitioned the Treasury for a grant of the
forest of Inglewood and the Socage of Carlisle Castle, asserting that they had not
been included in William III's grant of the Honor of Penrith to the ancestor of
William Henry Cavendish Bentinck, 3rd Duke of Portland (1738–1809). There
followed a complicated legal battle between Lowther and Portland. On 20 November 1771 the Court of Exchequer non-suited Lowther, holding that the
grant to him of the forest of Inglewood was invalid. Chase Price (*c.* 1731–77),
M.P. for Radnorshire, was an old protégé of Portland.

My dear Price,

A thousand thanks for your early and most agreeable intelligence.
Then the great Knight of the North is defeated in his first Essay of

[1] George James Cholmondeley, 4th Earl of Cholmondeley (1749–1827). In the
previous year he had succeeded his grandfather, George Cholmondeley, 3rd Earl of
Cholmondeley (1703–70), who was Horace Walpole's brother-in-law.
[2] Sir James Lowther; see the next letter.

Arms! He has found the Forest of Inglewood a well fought field; and I trust he will find the Castle of Carlisle impregnable.[1] I wish the Duke of Portland Joy most sincerely on this happy Event. I agree with you that, it is extremely singular, that those who were so sharpsighted with regard to the defects in the grants of others, should look so poorly into the validity of their own. You do not mention, (but I dare say I shall shortly hear) wherein the defect lay.[2] Will they now make out a new Grant to Sir J. Lowther, and turn the Nation upside down to support him in it? It will have a most gracious appearance to the world if they should; and add not a little to the reputation they have gained by their first proceeding. At present I conceive the principal mortification will be to Sir J. Lowther—If the others have sense, they will consider this event, as not only quiet to the D. of Portland, but as an escape to themselves. Once more I thank you for your News, and assure you that I am with very sincere Regard

Dear Chase

most sincerely and affectionately

yours

EDM BURKE

Beconsfield Nov. 20. 1771.

To SERJEANT JOHN GLYNN—14 *March* 1772

Source: Glynn MSS.

This letter to Serjeant John Glynn (1722–79), M.P. for Middlesex, relates to the proceedings between 4 March and 13 March in the House of Commons on the Royal Marriage Bill. The Bill, which made it necessary for members of the royal family to have the consent of the King before they married, had been presented to the House of Lords on 21 February and passed on 3 March. For Burke's views on the Bill see vol. II, 309.

Dear Sir

We are very unlucky in not having your assistance at this very busy moment; but I flatter myself that you are not wholly indifferent to the Event of our proceedings. We have fought the Royal Marriage Bill with various fortunes, but with equal Spirit in all the stages. The first reading past off without observation. We moved to inspect the Lords Journals. The ministry gave us our motion, by which we got the opinion

---

[1] The legal issue was finally settled in Portland's favour in 1777 (see vol. III, 289–90, 327–8).

[2] The Court held that the grant to Lowther of the forest of Inglewood was invalid because the quit-rent was less than a third of the annual value of the property, which was contrary to a statute of Queen Anne (A.S. Turberville, *A History of Welbeck Abbey and its Owners*, London, 1938–9, II, 125–6).

398

of the Judges, and the protest of the Lords in a parliamentary way before us.[1] Previous to the second reading Mr Dowdeswell moved that the proposition in the K's Message, claiming the Prerogative &c was not agreeable to the Law of the Land or warranted by the opinion of the Judges.[2] After a long and good debate, in which, the stress of the Law part of the combat lay between Dunning[3] and Wedderburne,[4] we divided, on the question for the order of the day, 140 to 268. The plan which had been settled by our friends was, to go after this directly into the Committee, without contesting the second reading. This was thought the most advisable Course for many reasons. It had produced no sort of inconvenience in the other house; It was the most advantageous Ground on which we could post ourselves for a close attack on the merits of the Bill; It was that on which we might probably hope to draw to us all those who disliking the Measure were not in general ill disposed to the Ministry. However some Gentlemen in opposition, to whom our being of one opinion is sufficient reason for embracing another, not only chose to oppose the second reading of the Bill, but to attack us as being lukewarm in the Cause, for not following their opinions.[5] This produced a good deal of derangement. Some of our best friends were put into great perplexity by the maneuvres of these Gentlemen; Parties were mixed and confounded; Mr Dowdeswell, myself, and some of our friends divided for the committment, not that a question of that kind could have any great merits; but it was necessary to shew, that a plan settled should not be suddenly alterd without reason, and upon arguments that were neither solid nor friendly. The division for the commitment was 300 to 64. The Ministry seemd to Triumph on the smallness of the minority, and much more upon the causes of it, which were but too apparent. However their Wednesdays Triumph was but of short duration. On Friday[6] we got into the committee, and Mr Dowdeswell moved an

[1] This was on 4 March. The Judges were of opinion that approval by the King of the marriages of his children and grandchildren and of the heir presumptive to the Crown was already necessary, 'but to what other branches of the royal family such care and approbation extend we do not find precisely determined'. The Rockinghamite peers had entered a protest on the passage of the Bill through the House of Lords (*Parliamentary History*, XVII, 387, 391–4).

[2] William Dowdeswell (1721–75), M.P. for Worcestershire, had introduced the following motion on 9 March: 'That it does not appear that the proposition affirmed in his Majesty's Message to this House, viz. "That the right of approving all marriages in the royal family has ever belonged to the kings of this realm as a matter of public concern," is founded in law, or warranted by the opinion of the judges of England' (*ibid*. XVII, 402).

[3] John Dunning (1731–83), M.P. for Calne, later (1782) 1st Baron Ashburton.

[4] Alexander Wedderburn (1733–1805), M.P. for Bishop's Castle, later (1780) 1st Baron Loughborough. He was Solicitor General 1771–8.

[5] This was on 11 March. A list of speakers for and against going into Committee is given in *Parliamentary History*, XVII, 409.

[6] 13 March.

amendment, the effect of which was to leave out the assertion of the obnoxious prerogative. The Speaker[1] opend the debate upon their side, by endeavouring to find a line which would serve to confine the danger-ous Latitude of the description of persons under the name of the Royal family. He admitted the objection in all its force; he denied that a precise line could be drawn; but he said, that a clear principle might be laid down which might serve to guide the Judges in ⟨determining⟩ who were or were not within the description of the act. This principle was, that not proximity in blood, but propinquity to the Crown made persons of the Royal family; that whenever the publick attention attachd itself on any man as the next in succession he became of the Royal family and within the act. You see what sort of a rule of Law this formed. The house receivd it with astonishment, our side with some pleasure; the Ministry with infinite mortification. Not one of the Lawyers of his own side would stand by him; some openly renounced his doctrine. The effect in our favour was prodigious, and it appeard in the division; the numbers, on our side 164 on theirs 200 so that they fell off[2] 68 from the first division we had gained 24. We go on to the first Clause next monday.[3] I wish you a pleasant Circuit. I can hardly attend to what I write—the Room is full; and a great deal of talk about me—Lord Rockingham at whose house we are[4] desires his best compliments. I am with great Truth and regard

Dear Sir

Your obedient and humble Servant

EDM BURKE

March 14.1772.

The Bill was further debated in Committee on 16, 18 and 20 March and was reported on 23 March. It had its third reading and was passed on 24 March. The Opposition did not succeed in obtaining the amendments they desired.

To UNKNOWN—[ante 17 November 1772]

Source: Draft in Glynn MSS.
In Burke's hand but not signed.

This letter was written before the election of the Recorder of London on 17 November 1772. James Eyre (1734–99), who had been Recorder of London, had retired when he was appointed a Baron of the Exchequer. He kissed hands for his new office, and was knighted, on 28 October.

[1] Sir Fletcher Norton (1716–89), M.P. for Guildford, later (1782) 1st Baron Grantley.
[2] MS: of
[3] 16 March.
[4] Rockingham's house was in Grosvenor Square.

Dear Sir,

I deceive myself very much if, whenever I take the Liberty of speaking to you in any matter relative to your publick Conduct I am not chiefly influenced by a very warm regard to your honour and advantage.

The Choice of a Recorder for the City of London is, at this time particularly, possibly at all times, a matter of moment. Mr Glynn I understand is a Candidate for that Office. Besides his Rank at the Bar as Serjeant as far as I am capable of Judging on the merit of a Lawyer, he is a man of very extraordinary Learning both general and professional. He is a man strenuously, and I have reason to think soberly attached to the principles of Liberty. I believe too that he is a man of uncommon good parts and of great Rectitude and Integrity. Indeed there are few Men of whom I entertain a better opinion in all respects; and it is my firm persuasion that he would be an Ornament to the Office of Recorder. He would strenuously support the Rights of his fellow Subjects and of the City; and where these Rights were not concernd would consult their peace and Tranquility. These are my Sentiments of Sergt Glynn. When I think thus of that Gentleman and consider that his very publick spirited Conduct has excluded him from any hope of those professional advantages to which his Learning and Talents otherwise give him so good a Title, it seems very hard that he should also be shut out from those which are in the Gift of the Subjects, and ought to be given as a reward for an attachment to their Liberties.

You will I am sure forgive me for my earnestness in favour of this valuable man. Your support of him will certainly detract nothing from your Weight and Interest in the City, and I would almost add my Wishes to consider your voting for him as an obligation to myself.

I have known nothing of the State of this Business until this day. If you are under an Engagement to another Gentleman You will suppose my application not made. But if any thing should happen to disengage you I really think your support of Mr Glynn would be honourable to you both.

At the Court of Aldermen on 17 November Glynn was elected Recorder of London by a single vote.

To SERJEANT JOHN GLYNN—[31 *October* 1773]

Source: Glynn MSS.

Written before William Dowdeswell left England in October 1774. Burke and Glynn acted together on the proposed Irish Absentee Tax of 1773, and they met, as the next letter shows, on Sunday, 31 October 1773, to discuss it.

Mr Burke presents his Compliments to Mr Sergt Glynn and begs leave to remind him of his obliging engagement to meet Mr Burke at Mr Dowdeswells this morning at ten o'Clock—or as soon after as he conveniently can. Mr Dowdeswell lives in upper Brook Street.

Sunday morn

To SERJEANT JOHN GLYNN—2 November 1773
Source: Glynn MSS.

This letter relates to the opposition to the proposed Irish Absentee Tax of 1773, which was led by Lord Rockingham. Serjeant John Glynn, Recorder of London, was attempting to persuade the Common Council of London to take action. He was not to succeed in this task (see vol. II, 481–4).

Dear Sir,

I take it for granted that you have seen your Brother Member *de jure*,[1] and that you have settled with him the Plan for proceeding in the Common Council. I think the motions were right in the Main. You forgot them at Grovenor Square; but they were sent to you that Night. I forgot to speak to you about them on Sunday morning;[2] but I take it for granted that you received them. If they are not yet moved you will consider yourself at Liberty to make any alteration that you and Mr Wilkes shall think advisable; but it would be against all reason to suffer others to alter them essentially in the Court. I do not see what substantial Objection can be made to doing something. I shall be in Town on Thursday evening[3] and if you have any thing material to communicate you will send it to my house in Westminster.[4] With the most unfeigned Esteem and regard I am

Dear Sir
your most faithful
and obedient humble Servant
EDM BURKE

Beconsfield Nov. 2. 1773.

[1] John Wilkes (1725–97), elected four times M.P. for Middlesex in 1768–9, but declared incapable of taking his seat. Glynn had been elected for Middlesex in a by-election of 1768.
[2] 31 October.
[3] 4 November.
[4] In the Broad Sanctuary.

To LORD HOLLAND—*September* 1774

Source: British Museum (Add. MS 51,451, fol. 161).
Endorsed: Edd Burke | Septembr | Recieved Octo 11th | 1774.

In the General Election of 1774 Burke strongly supported his patron, Ralph Verney, 2nd Earl Verney (1714–91), in his efforts to retain his seat for Buckinghamshire (see vol. III, 32–4). In this letter he appeals for the assistance of Stephen Fox, 2nd Baron Holland (1745–74).

My dear Lord,

You will have the goodness to excuse the Liberty I take of troubling you with a request, which on many accounts I have very much at heart. Lord Temple[1] intends to put up his Nephew[2] for the County of Buckingham in opposition to Lord Verney; and is canvassing with the greatest diligence. Lord Verney would think himself infinitely honourd and obliged for your Lordships Interest and support at the general Election. If there be any Gentleman in our County upon whom your Lordship has an influence, and who is now resident in the County, his attendance in support of Lord Verney at the meeting at Aylesbury Quarter Sessions on the sixth of next Month will be a particular favour. It is then, that[3] Lord Temple will make a push for the nomination of young Mr Grenville. Your Lordship will be so good as to present my best Compliments to Lady Holland,[4] and to beleive me with the highest Esteem and regard

My dear Lord
Your Lordships
most obedient
and humble Servant
EDM BURKE

Beconsfield Septr 1774

To JOSEPH SMITH—19 *November* 1774

Source: MS Osborn Collection.

Joseph Smith (1745–1815) had acted as Burke's host during the Bristol election of 1774. He acknowledged this letter on 29 November (MS at Sheffield).

[1] Richard Grenville Temple, 2nd Earl Temple (1711–79).
[2] George Grenville (1753–1813), later (1779) 3rd Earl Temple and (1784) 1st Marquess of Buckingham. He was elected for Buckinghamshire, but without displacing Lord Verney (see vol. III, 40–2).
[3] MS: that that
[4] Mary, *née* Fitzpatrick (d. 1778).

403

My dear Sir,

I could not sit myself down at home, without remembering those, who have made that home additionally agreeable to me, by the Joy they have diffused over it. While you were contributing, with my other worthy friends, to my honour in publick, Mrs Smith[1] had the goodness to make the happiest, the easiest, and the most comfortable retreat to me and to my Brother[2] that could be imagined. We experienced, that the most flattering attentions, and the most perfect Freedom could be united. Mrs Burke will think herself but too happy to have an opportunity of seeing you and Mrs Smith in her house here to thank you for the goodness you have both shewn to her husband and to her Brother. We may flatter ourselves with that satisfaction as soon as Mrs Smith has given you that Little one, in whom you have permitted me to claim an Interest.[3] We are in your Road. We are but 6 Miles from the Bath Road, taking it from Maidenhead Bridge; and to go by Oxford is but four Miles difference. As to yourself we may possibly see you sooner if your Business leads you to London. Adieu! my dear Sir, Kiss your amiable Children for me. Present mine and my Brothers most sincere regards to Mrs Smith. Mrs Burke hopes to be reckond amongst her friends; and beleive me ever with the truest and most grateful Esteem

> My dear Sir
> your very affectionate
> and obedient humble Servant
> EDM BURKE

Beconsfield Nov. 19.1774.

To JOHN HELY HUTCHINSON—[21] *January* 1775

Source: Donoughmore MSS.
21 January 1775 was a Saturday.

Printed in vol. III, 103–5, from Hist. MSS Comm. (*Donoughmore* MSS), in which the final paragraph, complimentary close and date-line were omitted.

Dear Sir,

I received the printed papers relative to your Conduct as Provost, sent, I flatter myself, by your directions. I am extremely obliged to you for this fresh mark of your friendly and polite attention; tho' perhaps nobody wanted it in this instance less than I did. I hope I do not too

[1] Sally, *née* Pope.
[2] Richard Burke, Sr.
[3] Burke acted as godfather to Edmund Burke Smith (1775–1851), born on 3 March 1775.

easily give Credit to any sort of charge against those who honour me with their friendship. I must have strong proofs indeed, before I condemn them; and as I am not called upon to be their Judge, much less their prosecutour. I do not search for that kind of Evidence with any industry, or listen to it with any pleasure.

You have given Lustre to every situation where you were placed; and I made no doubt, that you would distinguish yourself in that of Provost by very signal services to the University. I consider the Pamphlet I received, not as a vindication of your Conduct, which, I am sure, with me, it did not want, but as the means of enabling me, to enter into the detail of what I had presumed before, in the general Idea, I had formed of your Conduct from my knowlege of your Character.

Indeed, my dear Sir, I never entertaind the least doubt that you would seek and find reputation every where. But when you had chosen academick Ground, I was greatly apprehensive that your Choice would produce, far more Benefit to the Education of youth, than repose and tranquility to your own Mind. It seemd to me impossible, that the animosities and emulations, which must ever attend the great and conspicuous part you have acted in publick Life, should not follow you into your Learned retreat; where they would be more poinantly felt, and would of Course greatly disquiet a man of your tender and exquisite sensibility. None of your friends wished you with more Sincerity every object which could contribute to your real satisfaction. But I could not prevail on myself to wish you Joy of your Choice of this new way of Life. Though highly honourable in itself, I could not consider it as promotion to *you*; and most certainly I could not congratulate you on what I knew must infallibly bring on you, as it has done much anxiety and uneasiness.

I had always thought that this Office is best suited to a man of the Ecclesiastical Gown, and a meer Academick. I am not alterd in my opinion by the present exception—for every Layman and every man of Business is not an Hutchinson. However, since you are in that walk, I sincerely recommend you to proceed in your own great Line of publick service with less anxiety about vulgar Judgments; and do not be ashamed to cultivate, yourself, Philosophy, within those walls where, you are to teach it to others. Æque neglectum pueris, senibusque Nocebit.

Yesterday we had a great Debate in the house of Lords. Lord Chatham made a Motion for recalling the Troops from Boston. It was done without concert with our friends; and Lord Chathams friends say without any concert whatsoever. The Minority was only eighteen, as no measures had been taken for an attendance. The worst circumstance in the debate, was Lord Suffolks declaration, that Ministry had determined against conciliation in the present State of things, and for maintaining the late Acts of Parliament with regard to the Colonies. Perhaps it is some, to us unknown, but certain information, which inspires Ministry with its present confidence, after so many disappointments.

Be so good as to present mine and Mrs Burkes most cordial regards and respects to Mrs Hutchinson[1] and all your family. Beleive, that we are most sincerely interested in all your publick, and all your domestick satisfactions. I am with great Truth

Dear Sir
Your most obedient
and affectionate humble Servant,
EDM BURKE

Westminster Jany 20.1775.
Saturday.

To ROBERT SMITH—6 *April* 1775

Source: MS Society of Merchant Venturers.

Robert Smith (*c.* 1739–1812) was Master of Merchants' Hall, Bristol, from November 1774 to November 1775.

Sir,

This day I received a Letter from you, directed, I apprehend by mistake, to Henry Cruger and Edm Burke Esqrs. The greater part of that Letter applies indeed to both your representatives; The last paragraph can relate only to me.[2] On that subject I have nothing to say, but that if you are, in all respects, satisfied with the Behaviour of the Gentleman whom you mention, I have no Objections to it. If you are pleased, the affair is not deserving of any further Notice on my part— I therefore pass to Business.

---

[1] Christiana, *née* Nickson (1732–88), later (1783) Baroness Donoughmore.
[2] It was in fact not included in the letter sent to Henry Cruger (1739–1827), Burke's colleague. The paragraph read: 'We observe what you say respecting the Collector. We beg leave to remark that, that Gentleman's Conduct as an Officer has been considered by the Merchants in a Light truly honorable to himself, faithfully attentive to the Revenue and much to the convenience and benefit of Commerce, nor do We know that he has in this or any Instance merited the least reflection' (letter of 4 April, entered in the letter-book of the Masters of Merchants' Hall, MS Society of Merchant Venturers). Burke had criticized Daniel Harson (d. 1779), the Collector of Customs, for refusing to allow the importation of Irish provisions while the act to legalize it was being enacted (see vol. III, 132, 141, 143, 144–5).

This day most of the Gentlemen concerned in the Stourbridge Canal, had a meeting in one of our Committee Rooms. They were unanimous in their opinion of the propriety of postponing their Bill to another year. I believe dispassionate men will find little difficulty in admitting the extensive utility of the design. But things have happend which make it advisable to postpone its execution; and rather to delay the Bill for another year than to hazard it, so late in the Session, against an opposition, which is carried on with so much heat and from such a variety of Quarters. I agreed with the Gentlemen originally and principally concerned, in the propriety of their resolution; and by common consent, Sir William Bagot will move tomorrow for putting it off.[1]

I enclose you a printed Bill for securing to Mr Watt an exclusive property in his Fire Engines for a Term of years.[2] This Bill at its first appearance seemd to me very exceptionable. A Mr Blakey[3] petitiond against it, and was to be heard by Counsel on the Bill; but having suddenly withdrawn his petition, the Bill got a step forward, almost unknown to most of the house, and particularly to the Members of the Mine Counties. However on our making a pretty strong representation to those concernd in carrying it on, he has consented to the amendments which you see in Manuscript; which amendments remove most of my Objections. But as others may remain, I wish to have it communicated to such Gentlemen in Bristol as may be affected, and to know their Sentiments as soon as possible.[4]

I have acted on the bringing in the Bill for the Lighthouse on the Smalls agreeably to the Ideas of your petition.[5] I did not oppose the first reading of the Bill. My Objections were conditional and qualified. I think the Clauses you propose very proper;[6] and when the Bill gets into the Committee, which I think will not be until after the Hollidays I hope I shall be able to carry them.[7] The Liverpool Members[8] do not

---

[1] On 24 February a petition had been presented to the House of Commons for the construction of a canal from Stourbridge in Worcestershire to Stourton in Staffordshire, where it would connect with the Staffordshire and Worcestershire Canal. The construction of the canal was opposed by the coal mine owners of the Wolverhampton area, and by other iron and coal mine owners (*Journals of the House of Commons*, XXXV, 148, 211, 215, 231). The Bill was postponed on 7 April, to be revived the following year. Sir William Bagot, 6th Baronet (1728–98), was M.P. for Staffordshire.
[2] A Bill to extend the patent of James Watt (1736–1819) for the sale of his steam engines, 'commonly called Fire Engines' (see vol. III, 240).
[3] William Blakey, the engineer.
[4] The Bill received the Royal Assent on 22 May, without having encountered any formal opposition from Bristol.
[5] The Society of Merchant Venturers had petitioned the House to obtain amendments to a bill to make perpetual the patent of John Phillips to collect tolls from ships passing 'the Smalls'—a group of rocks in St George's Channel (see vol. III, 128–9).
[6] The clauses proposed were outlined in the letter of 4 April.
[7] The Bill was defeated on its third reading on 16 May.
[8] Sir William Meredith, 3rd Baronet (*c.* 1725–90), and Richard Pennant (*c.* 1736–1808).

take up the opposition upon grounds so strong as those you have
mentiond. At least it does not appear at present.[1] I imagine I mentiond
this particular to you in my Last. Lancaster and Glasgow seem the
strongest in the opposition.[2] I am
                                          Sir
                               Your very humble Servant
                                          EDM BURKE
Westminster April 6.1775.

To JAMES SEARLE—[1775]
Source: MS Pennsylvania Historical Society.

James Searle (1733–97) was a Philadelphia merchant. He was in England in
1775.

Mr Burke presents his best compliments to Mr Searle and thanks him
for the Paper which Mr Searle has been so obliging as to communicate
to him.[3]

Wednesday evening.

To the MARCHIONESS OF ROCKINGHAM—4 January [1776]
Source: Ramsden MSS.
The 1775 of Burke's date-line is an obvious error for 1776.

When Admiral Sir Charles Saunders (c. 1713–75) died on 7 December 1775 he
left his electoral interest at Hedon, which he had represented since 1754, to
William Iveson. Rockingham persuaded Iveson to support Lewis Thomas
Watson (1754–1806), eldest son of his relation, Lewis Watson, 1st Baron Sondes
(1728–95), at the by-election. After a contest Watson was elected on 1 January
1776.

Madam

It was with the greatest Satisfaction I received the News which your
Ladyship sent me and for which I beg leave to return my best ac-
knowlegements. It is indeed an Election exceedingly honourable to the
Memory of our deceased friend; and no less so to the Credit of Lord
Rockingham. I was beginning to be a little anxious, about the Event; and

---

[1] Smith had written that the Bill 'is powerfully opposed by the Town of Liverpool
who say their people know the situation of the Smalls so well as always to avoid it'.
Several petitions from Liverpool against the Bill were presented to the House.
[2] A petition from the merchants of Lancaster had been presented on 20 March;
one from the merchants of Glasgow on 3 April.
[3] It has not been identified.

should have written to enquire about it, if your Ladyships goodness had not set my Mind at ease this morning. I hope Lord Sondes is recoverd of his Labour pains, and is as well, as can be expected from one in his Condition. He has got a very fine boy in this borough of Heydon; and all is well. Nothing worse will happen than a little too much Merriment at the Christening. Lord Rockingham who, with less fear, has had something more trouble, is, I hope not so much hurt by his Endeavours, as cheerd by his Success.[1] When his Lordship thinks of Business I shall be at his humble Service, and all here are with the truest respect and regard to him and your Ladyship, as I am,

Madam
Your Ladyships
most obedient and
most obligd humble Servant
EDM BURKE

Beconsfield Thursday. Jan.4.1775.

If your Ladyship sees Miss Pelham,[2] you will offer her my best congratulations on this Event; and though she is a Ministers daughter, on the Triumph obtained over the Treasury.

To the MARCHIONESS OF ROCKINGHAM—
[21 *February* 1776]

Source: Ramsden MSS.
Addressed: To | the Marchs Rockingham.

The main content of this letter is a report of the debate in the House of Commons which began on 20 February 1776 and finished in the early hours of Wednesday, 21 February. The debate was on a motion of Charles James Fox to set up a committee to inquire 'into the causes of the ill success of his Majesty's arms in North America, as also into the causes of the defection of the people of the province of Quebec'.

I am infinitely[3] obliged to your Ladyship for your most acceptable News—and your taking the trouble of giving it to me so much in detail after so late at Night and after so fatiguing a day very much heightens my obligation. I could perceive a vast sollicitude almost general in the house on occasion of Lord Rockinghams illness. It is in such moments

---

[1] The contest had been an expensive one, and Rockingham took no further part in Hedon's electoral affairs.
[2] Frances Pelham (1728–1804), daughter of Henry Pelham and aunt of Lewis Thomas Watson.
[3] MS inffinitely

409

we discover how much he is loved and valued. We were not up until three. The Debate for some time was warm and interesting. Charles Fox opend with great ability and replied in the conclusion with still greater. Lord Ossory[1] seconded. Young Fitzpatrick[2] spoke with great elegance. Another young Speaker, Lord Butes son,[3] who came in for Sir George Macartneys seat,[4] made in a *thundering* tone an *unnecessary* apology for his Modesty and diffidence—and declaring strongly in favour of the most violent measures against America, and against the Enquiry, did the Ministers more service than all their speakers put together. Burgoyne[5] was called up. He fought shy about every thing essential; expressed some faint dislike of Measures; but declared strongly against the enquiry, as it might inflame the fever of Party; I answerd him. On their side spoke Lord Clare,[6] Ellis,[7] Elliot,[8] Wedderburn, Lord North.—Lord G. Germaine[9] said nothing. On our side, besides those I mentioned, Govr Johnston. T. Townshend Young Adam, Col. Barré, Sir Edwd Deering.[10] Ch. Justice Hey[11] made a very long speech; It was intended for them—but it served us—as he effectually exposed the ill effects of the Canada Bill which he defended, and displayed in all its nakedness the unprotected State of the Province. The division was 240 to 104. I am with the greatest sense of my obligations to your Ladyship and with sincere Joy for the good hopes of Lord Rockingham. Ever

Your Ladyships
most obedient
and most humble Servant
EDM BURKE

Wensday morn

[1] John Fitzpatrick, 2nd Earl of Upper Ossory (1745–1818), M.P. for Bedfordshire.
[2] Richard Fitzpatrick (1748–1813), M.P. for Tavistock; Lord Ossory's brother.
[3] Frederick Stuart (1751–1802), M.P. for Ayr burghs, third son of John Stuart, 3rd Earl of Bute (1713–92). His speech is not recorded in the *Parliamentary Register*.
[4] Sir George Macartney (1737–1806), later (19 July 1776) 1st Baron Macartney, Bute's son-in-law, had given up his seat when he became Governor of Grenada.
[5] Major-General John Burgoyne (1723–92), M.P. for Preston.
[6] Robert Nugent, 1st Viscount Clare (1709–88), M.P. for St Mawes, later (21 July 1776) 1st Earl Nugent.
[7] Welbore Ellis (1713–1802), M.P. for Weymouth and Melcombe Regis, later (1794) 1st Baron Mendip.
[8] Sir Gilbert Elliot, 3rd Baronet (1722–77), M.P. for Roxburghshire.
[9] Lord George Germain (1716–85), M.P. for East Grinstead, later (1782) 1st Viscount Sackville.
[10] George Johnstone (1730–87), M.P. for Appleby; Thomas Townshend (1733–1800), M.P. for Whitchurch, later (1783) 1st Baron Sydney; William Adam (1751–1839), M.P. for Gatton; Isaac Barré (1726–1802), M.P. for Calne; Sir Edward Dering, 6th Baronet (1732–98), M.P. for New Romney. Dering, who was usually a Government supporter, is not recorded in the *Parliamentary Register* as a speaker. Burke does not mention the speech of his own colleague, Henry Cruger.
[11] William Hey (c. 1733–97), M.P. for Sandwich, Chief Justice of Quebec.

To CAPTAIN EDWARD THOMPSON—[*circa* 1 *July* 1776]

Source: MS (incomplete) Lille Municipal Library.
MS torn.

Captain Edward Thompson (*c.* 1738–86) of the Royal Navy was the editor of a three-volume edition of the *Works* of Andrew Marvell, of which the publication was advertised on 1 July 1776 (e.g. in the *Public Advertiser*, 1 July 1776).

Mr Burke presents his best compliments and thanks to Captain Thompson for the obliging communication of Marvells Letters with which he has honourd Mr Burke and which he has read. Every thing which concerns so eminent a person and so interesting a period of History must certainly be entertaining; but as these Letters were originally of a publick Nature, and wrote with extraordinary Caution, they are rather less agreeable than if they were private, and containd Marvells free opinion of the

To GARRETT NAGLE—2 *August* 1776

Source: MS Columbia University Library.

Printed in vol. III 283–5, from *New Monthly Magazine*.

My dear Garrett,

I do most heartily wish myself with you. I should wish it, even if I were not put in Mind by this burning weather of the breezy mountains, shady woods, and refreshing Waters of Killarney. We have got a Summer at last; and it is paying off its arrears of heat with compound Interest. Indeed I long sincerely to see you; and if I were not held by various ties, and engaged in various occupations, (though neither very pleasant or important) and if I were as rich, as, I thank God, I am still healthy and active, I should this Summer pay you a visit in your Woodhouse— that is to say, if you would deign to receive so humble a person after all your great and titled Guests. If I see Lord Kenmare I shall certainly thank him for his Civilities to you. I certainly am as much pleased with them as if they were offerd to myself; and indeed a little more. My acquaintance with Lord Winchelsea is very Slight; But I have known Lord Pembroke pretty intimately for some time. We may meet this Summer; and we shall talk you over. I wish you had named me to him.

What you say of Lord Shelburne is more important. I very well remember your application to me some time ago; I remember too that

I mentiond it to Col. Barré. Nothing further came of it; I believe that Agency was not vacant when you wrote. Between ourselves, and I would not have it go farther, there are I believe few who can do less with Lord Shelburne than myself. He had formerly at several times professed much friendship to me; but whenever I came to try the Ground, let the matter have been never so triffling I always found it to fail under me. It is indeed long since he has made even professions. With many eminent qualities, he has some singularities[1] in his Character. He is suspicious and whimsical; and perhaps if I stood better with him than I do, perhaps my recommendation would not have the greatest weight in the world. This I mention as between ourselves. In the mean time if an opportunity occurs I shall do the best I can for you. I hope I am not inattentive to my friends to the best of my power, and let me assure you that I have ever looked upon you as a friend whose ease and welfare I have at heart as much as the Interest of any person whatsoever. But indeed there is little in my power; and if I can serve any person it is by meer accident. I gave assurances to Ned Barret when I thought myself sure of an Object for him. But I was disappointed; and few things have given me more concern. Both he, and Frank Kiernan have informed me of your engagement for the Woods. I trust it will turn out as much for your advantage as you expected.

Poor Ned Nagle, when he came from the Meditterranean and had hopes of relaxing himself for a while on the home Station, was suddenly orderd out. Whither his Ship is gone is not yet certainly known, but the opinion is that she is orderd to cruise off St Helena to secure the East India Ships against the American Privateers. Wat is in London. I saw him some days ago. He is well; and I believe a goodnatured worthy man. The Company has agreed to make him an allowance until he can be regularly employd again. As to Ned Nagle he is perfectly liked by all the Captains he has served under, as a very good Officer. He may probably do good service in some better times, and in a Course of employment which I may like better for him, than any which the present War affords.

My Son is now at home with me at his Vacation. I think you would like him if you were acquainted. Richard the older is in Town. If his Business had prospered you would have been one of the first to hear of it. But we do not trouble our friends except with pleasing News. He has had much wrong done to him; but the thing is not yet desperate. I beleive that the Commissioner who goes out will not have adverse instructions.

[1] MS: singularlities

I have not been punctual in the Newspapers—nor can I undertake it, we are so little regular. But I shall endeavour now you are from home to amuse you a little.

Wat Nagle was punctual about the Money you orderd; I thank you for that and every thing; and am ever with the greatest regard

My dear Garret
Your affectionate Kinsman
&ca &ca
EDM BURKE

Beconsfield. Augst 2.1776.

Mrs Burke desires her Love to you.

To WILLIAM EDEN—12 *August* 1776
Source: MS Morgan Library.

Printed in vol. III, 287, but only as an extract preserved in Murray Papers. The Irish bearer of the letter has not been identified.

Dear Sir,

If there be any foundation for the Facts alledged in the Petition which my Countryman will have the honour to deliver to you, I am sure you will think them deserving your attention. If the poor Man be innocent I do not know that it is worth while to hang him, though he is an Irishman. He certainly is in great danger from the Character of[1] that Country, if not from his guilt; For he has neglected to make any application, even so far from the Scource of power as myself, until this time, at Beconsfield, two o Clock on Monday; and he is sentenced to die on Wednesday. The bearer will give you the particulars, which may be necessary to induce your humanity to make an application for a respite for this unfortunate wretch until further Enquiry can be made about his Case. The Bearer I know is an honest poor man, and believes himself in the innocence of his Compatriot. At any Rate I do not think much harm can be done by delay where there is the least Chance of innocence. Even if that were not quite clear, I must think, that he might be as well employd in cleaning the Thames, on the principles and for the purposes of your Bill, as, on the old Scheme, poisoning the air at Tyburn. You will oblige me by looking into this Case. If there be any Grounds for Mercy, either of total pardon or commutation of Punishment, The thing

[1] MS: if

cannot be in better hands. I beg a thousand pardons for the Trouble and am with the greatest Esteem and regard

Dear Sir
Your most obedient
and humble Servant

Beconsfield Augst 12.1776.   EDM BURKE
    Monday.

As the time presses I recommend this poor Blunderer to your immediate attention.

To the MARCHIONESS OF ROCKINGHAM—
[28 *March* 1777]

Source: Ramsden MSS.

This letter can be dated from John Yorke's answer of 30 March 1777 to Lady Rockingham's letter (see note below). Burke's date-line shows that it was written on Good Friday, which in 1777 fell on 28 March.

This and the following letter relate to the activities in the East India Company, following the news that George Pigot, 1st Baron Pigot (1719–77), Governor of Madras, had been deposed and imprisoned by his Council. Pigot was connected with the Rockingham party. While Lord Rockingham was absent at Newmarket, Lady Rockingham set about gathering support for Pigot for a special ballot of proprietors of East India stock on 31 March.

It is impossible that any thing could be more prudently imagined, or better expressed, than your Ladyships Letter to Mr Yorke.[1] It is what Lord R. must undoubtedly approve. He has a full right to expect thus much, at least, from the house of Yorke, and your Ladyship is perfectly correct with regard to all parties, to Lord R. to Mr Y. and to Lord Pigot. I am sure the Last will be as much wanting to Justice as his worst Enemies, if he is not sensible indeed of the Zeal with which you protect him. I am always with the highest Esteem

Madam
Your Ladyships
most obedient and obligd
humble Servant
EDM BURKE

Friday *good* day and good deeds.

[1] John Yorke (1728–1801), M.P. for Reigate, was a supporter of Government, but had previously been attached to Lord Rockingham and sat for Rockingham's borough of Higham Ferrers from 1753 to 1768. Lady Rockingham's letter to him is missing; his answer, of 30 March, is in the Ramsden MSS.

414

To the MARCHIONESS OF ROCKINGHAM—
2 *April* 1777

Source: Ramsden MSS.

Madam

I am infinitely obliged to your Ladyship for your goodness in communicating to me the very acceptable news of Lord Pigots triumphant success.[1] I am sure if he be worthy of his good fortune he can never forget the ample share your Ladyship had in it. This is one of the few obligations, for which a mans pride must make him grateful. Indeed you exerted yourself most wonderfully. If we all acted in the affairs we have in hand with the same Zeal, industry, and Spirit, nothing could overcome us. I hope we shall improve by your Ladyships example and be animated with your Success. I am ever with the highest respect and regard

> Madam
> > Your Ladyships
> > > most obedient
> > > > and obligd humble Servant
> > > > > EDM BURKE

April 2.1777

To the REV. JAMES BIRT—[*August* 1777]

Source: MS (incomplete) in the Osborn Collection.
Endorsed: E. Burke Aug. 1777.
Dated by the endorsement.

In 1795 Burke described the Rev. James Birt (*c.* 1717–1801) as 'a very dear friend of more than forty years standing' (see vol. VIII, 283). In 1777 Birt was a Canon of Hereford and Vicar of Woolhope and Fownhope.

My dear Birt,

We do not know anyone but you to the Westward, who could think of us so often, as to send the Severn and Wye to our Doors in this thirsty Country. Besides who but you could so obstinately persevere in sending us your presents though we never so much as thank you for them. But you Fishers of men must throw away your good advice on the impenitent,

---

[1] Lady Rockingham had written that a motion in favour of Lord Pigot had been carried at the ballot of proprietors of the East India Company on 31 March by 382 to 140 (letter of 1 April, MS at Sheffield). Later it was decided to recall both Lord Pigot and his Council.

and confer your Benefits on the ungrateful. However, I assure you, if we neither amend by your doctrine, nor acknowlege your favours, we sometimes drink your health, and after think of you as we ought. We have had some excellent Madeira from Bombay of which we have sent[1] you a Taste. (3 doz. per Monmouth Waggon Car. pd.) It is the Wine in which we ⟨...who is gone⟩ to that remote part[2]

To the MARQUESS OF ROCKINGHAM—
[16 December 1777]
Source: Ramsden MSS.

This letter of 'Tuesday night' reports to Lord Rockingham the arrival in London on Monday 15 December 1777 of the official dispatch from General Burgoyne, dated 20 October, giving his account of his surrender at Saratoga. The first news of the surrender had reached London on 2 December (see vol. III, 406).

My dear Lord,

Very unexpected Business has prevented me, or I should have dined with you at Wimbledon today, and told you every thing that is current here with more or less authenticity. Lieut. Cragg[3] who was sent express to Carleton[4] arrived last Night, and brought[5] Burgoines publick Letters to Office as well as his private to Lord Derby.[6] I receiv'd some account of the former from D'Oyley;[7] and of the Latter from the rebound of Almacks[8] where Lord Derby read, before Discretion could interpose, some interesting particulars to the Company of that place. As to the first it confirms in every particular the Boston Gazette; and it will be the ornament of that of London, about four o'Clock tomorrow morning;[9] for, as the Letter is of an extreme length, and is not (if Mr D'oyleys advice be followd) to be curtailed, they cannot get it out of the press before that hour. D'oyley told me fairly, that Burgoine throws the whole upon his positive Orders.[10] In the circumstances, it does not much

[1] MS: have send
[2] Burke is presumably referring to William Burke, who had set out for India in June 1777.
[3] Captain James Henry Craig (1748–1812), knighted in 1797.
[4] General Guy Carleton (1724–1808), later (1786) 1st Baron Dorchester; Governor of Quebec.
[5] MS: brough
[6] Edward Smith Stanley, 12th Earl of Derby (1752–1834), Burgoyne's nephew.
[7] Christopher D'Oyly (c. 1717–95), M.P. for Wareham.
[8] The club which became Brooke's in the following year.
[9] The dispatch was printed in the London Gazette of 13–16 December.
[10] Burgoyne wrote that he had held no council on the decision to pass the Hudson River to force his way to Albany because of 'the peremptory Tenor of my Orders'.

differ from what we have had before. Some of the Gentlemen who are come with these advices (for there are more than one) are high in Commendation of the generosity, honour, and politeness of the Americans. In particular, they say, that when the Allied Army came to lay down their Arms, Genl Gates[1] had removed all his troops quite out of sight, so that no one hostile or insulting Eye was witness of their humiliation. Such a strain of refined Magnanimity has not often appeard in the world. B. in his Letter to Lord Derby which is enormously long, commends the good treatment the Americans gave to him personally, and uses it as a proof of their being thoroughly convincd, that the charges of cruelty made upon him, were without foundation. He says that he is sure that he does not overrate matters, when he affirms that the army to which he surrenderd, was not less than 16000 men; and that he overrates their *Condition* not more than their Numbers when he asserts, that he has not seen an army better provided, better armed, better appointed, and better disciplined; and that we shall do very well, if we can send out in another Campain, Troops, that shall exceed them in all these particulars. No returns of the killed and wounded are come; but Doyley does not know that any more are killed, than what we have already heard of, except Sir Francis Clarke.[2] Burg. was at Albany, and D'oyley said pleasantly and possibly truly enough that the insurers at Lloyds will have a good Scuffle in Westminster Hall upon this Subject. He told me nothing more; but seemd to talk of Ministry as in a state of great distraction. I asked him whether they had sent any one to Franklin,[3] as I had heard reported—he spoke as if they did not know what to do, or which way to *turn* themselves. I said, that I knew none, but to *turn* themselves out. However as all this is Doyleys, it is between ourselves. As to Burgoine, I find his *Style* is not in the least alterd by his misfortunes. It is just as pompous as ever. What is the worst, the *matter* is as pompous as ever; for the *Style* he cannot help; it is his mother Tongue.

I find Ticonderoga is evacuated, and the works &c. blown up. 1600 men are got back from thence to Canada; and with these and other Troops, I understand Carleton considers Canada as safe. There is much talk of an action between Howe[4] and Washington. I am not very apt to Credit reports, when I cannot trace their origin; but I incline to beleive this. It is variously told. The runners speak of a great Victory; 7000 taken, and Washington along with them. But I trust more to the

---

[1] Horatio Gates (*c.* 1729–1806).
[2] Sir Francis Carr Clerke, 7th Baronet (1748–77).
[3] Benjamin Franklin (1706–90), American representative in Paris.
[4] General Sir William Howe (1729–1814), M.P. for Nottingham, later (1799) 5th Viscount Howe.

other, which speaks of the thing as a sort of drawn Battle; in which Washington retreated; but with a much greater loss on Howes side than his own.[1] I find that Strahan[2] the Member of Parliament printer beleives this. I had half an hours conversation with him. He tells me that some News went to the K. last Night; and that he went to bed very melancholy.

I had a long talk with Panchaud[3] of Paris on the State of France and the steps that Court has taken in all these American affairs. On the whole the representation of this able man, is not discouraging. Whatever *may* happen, America most certainly, does not *yet* belong to France. To prevent the possibility of this I think, I more than *think*, *some* Efforts ought to be made. However, the moment this Business, which keeps me in Town is over, I shall not trouble anybody any longer. I shall go to the Country. I shall endeavour, by other thoughts and other occupations to quiet that anxiety which possesses me, from an opinion, possibly an opinion very wild and erroneous, that this is, perhaps that this is the most critical moment for the publick, for the party, and for all those noble Objects to which your Lordship has devoted your Life, that ever did happen; and that the salvation or ruin of this Country may depend on the use that shall be made of *moments*. I think I am not a fanatick—But surely this is no *common* time. I have wrote this over my Chop; and your servant is impatient. Adieu my humble Duty to my Lady and thanks for the Copy[4]—for ever

My dear Lord
Your Lordships most obedient
and humble Servant
EDM BURKE

Westmr Tuesday night.

To [JOHN] DAUBENY—26 *March* 1778

Source: MS Society of Merchant Venturers.

John Daubeny (1751–94), Warden of the Society of Merchant Venturers from November 1777 to November 1778, wrote to Burke a (missing) letter, asking for his help in obtaining the release of Bristol pilots who had been impressed.

[1] This was unfounded rumour. There had been no battle between Howe and Washington since Germantown on 4 October.
[2] William Strahan (1715–85), M.P. for Malmesbury.
[3] Isaac Panchaud (1726–89); see vol. II, 414.
[4] This has not been identified.

House of Commons 7 o'Clock ⟨Pt M.⟩ March 26.
1778.

Sir,

Mr Stephens[1] was not in the House at the time of my receiving your
Letter.[2] But I have lost no time in transmitting it to him with my best
recommendation for an immediate compliance with your desires. I have
the honour to be with great Esteem

Sir
Your most obedient
and humble Servant
EDM BURKE

To [JOHN] DAUBENY—27 *March* 1778

Source: MS Society of Merchant Venturers.

Sir,

I enclose to you the Letter I receivd from Mr Stephens relative to the
Pilots and men employd on our River.[3] As soon as the expected return
arrives I shall not be wanting in any particular which may be necessary
to our immediate relief. I have the honour to be

Sir
Your most obedient
and humble Servant
EDM BURKE

March 27.1778

To SAMUEL SPAN—31 *March* 1778

Source: MS Society of Merchant Venturers.
Addressed: To | Samuel Span Esquire | Master of Merchants | Hall | Bristol.

Samuel Span (d. 1795) was Master of Merchants' Hall, Bristol, from November
1777 to November 1778.

Sir,

I am sorry to inform the Hall that the equitable clause proposed by
them, and moved by me, this day, relative to the lights on the Smalls,

[1] Philip Stephens (1723–1809), M.P. for Sandwich and Secretary to the Admiralty,
later (1795) 1st Baronet.
[2] Missing.
[3] Philip Stephens had written on 26 March (MS Society of Merchant Venturers).

was rejected in the Committee, altho I was not wanting to support it in the best manner I was able.[1] There is a good deal of diference between the power which I have on this subject at present, from that which I possessed on the former Bill. It was then in private hands; It is now in those of the Trinity House, which has many friends and a powerful Admiralty interest. Following as nearly as I can the spiritt of your instructions, I shall oppose the Bill on the report tomorrow; and I am very desirous of your further opinion relative to my conduct in this affair. If you think that your interest is so considerable in opposing this Bill as to ballance the expence of the opposition, I hope you are yet in time to be heard by your Council on a new petition, so to be heard by the House of Commons on the third reading of the Bill;[2] but if they should hurry it on, you[3] are still in time sufficient for a petition to the House of Lords and to be heard by them[4] and you are to send up evidence to support the allegations of your petition but of the propriety and prudence of all this you are to Judge. I do not feel myself perfectly satisfyed of the practicability of the scheme itself so as to produce a durable light-House on the smalls. At the same time I think it right to inform you that so far as things appear to me at present our opposition is not likely to be successful but you are to consider whether it may not be proper for you, (and sometimes it is proper) to continue your opposition tho without any[5] considerable prospect of success.

> I have the honour to be,
> Sir
> Your most obedient and
> Humble Servant
> EDM BURKE

Westmr March 31. 1778

[1] The question of the lighthouse on the Smalls (see above, p. 407) had been taken up by Trinity House. The clause to which Burke refers probably limited the payment of the duty imposed by the Bill to ships which benefited from the lighthouse. The comments of the Hall on the Bill were sent to Burke in a letter of 26 February (letter-book of the Masters of Merchants' Hall, MS Society of Merchant Venturers). The Bill embodying the proposals of Trinity House had been referred to a committee on 23 March.

[2] A petition from Merchants' Hall was presented on 6 April and the Hall was represented by counsel on the third reading on 13 April, but the Bill was passed by a vote of 57 to 21.

[3] MS: your

[4] A petition to the House of Lords was drawn up, identical to that to the House of Commons, but was not presented.

[5] MS: any any

To SAMUEL SPAN—9 *April* 1778

Source: MS Society of Merchant Venturers.
Addressed: Saml Span Esqr.
Endorsed: Mr Burke Apl 9.1778— | read Apl 13.1778.

Printed in vol. III, 426, from Clarke, *Merchant Venturers*, in which the beginning and end are omitted.

Westmr April 9. 1778.

Sir,

I have the honour of transmitting to you the Copy of some resolutions reported from the Committee on the Trade of Ireland. They have been supported by Administration, and by several unconnected and independent Members. It is found absolutely necessary for many obvious reasons to improve the portion of this Empire which is left, so as [to] enable every part to contribute in some degree to the Strength and Welfare of the whole. Our late Misfortunes have taught us the danger and mischief of a restrictive, coercive, and partial policy. The Trade in some degree opend by the inclosed resolutions is necessary, not so much for any benefit thereby derived to Ireland, as to satisfye, and unite the minds of men at this Juncture, by a sense of a common Interest in the common defence. If nothing of this Kind should be done I apprehend very serious consequences from it. Ireland may thereby in some future time come to participate of the Benefits which we derive from the West India Trade. But Ireland being a Country of the same Nature with this can never be beneficial to this Kingdom, but by pursuing several, if not all, of the Objects of Commerce and manufacture which are cultivated here. The world, I apprehend, is large enough for us all; and we are not to conclude, that what is gaind to one part, is lost, of Course, to the other. The prosperity, arising from an enlarged and Liberal System, improves all its objects; and the *participation* of a Trade with flourishing Countries is much better than the *monopoly* of want and penury. These Opinions, I am satisfied, will be relished by the clear understandings of the Merchants of Bristol, who will discern that a great Empire cannot, at this time, be supported upon a narrow and restrictive Scheme, either of Commerce or Government. I have the honour to be with great Esteem and regard

Sir
Your most obedient
and humble Servant
EDM BURKE

To the EARL OF SURREY—10 *May* 1778

Source: MS Arundel Castle Archives.

Charles Howard, styled Earl of Surrey (1746–1815), later (1786) 11th Duke of Norfolk, was one of the leaders of the Roman Catholics. The Catholics were pressing for a relaxation of the penal laws.

Beconsfield Sunday evening
May 10. 1778

My Lord,

I did not receive the Note[1] which you sent to my house in Town until this morning and at this place. It gave me the greatest concern, that I was not in a Situation, which should enable me to receive your Lordships Orders. I am however extremely happy in finding that your Business is got into hands as capable of conducting it to the End which must be desired, by every well wisher to the Cause of Humanity and Justice.[2] I hope they will not aim at any other modifications of the act, than that which relates to the Chancellours power of appointing a maintenance for the Eldest Son.[3] Prejudice will be as much alarmed, in asking for the smallest relaxation of injury, as for the most substantial Benefit. The discussion will be just the same, with regard to the grand point of Debate. Indeed in one point it will be worse; for if it be admitted, that it is necessary to restrain Roman Catholicks, either in the Keeping or acquiring property, the principle of the Law is affirmed, and its policy ascertain'd. Who then can undertake to say, how much or how little restraint is necessary? *Some* restraint is admitted to be proper—Why then depart from what is established? I am sure, by abundant experience, that total repeals, as far as they go, are the easiest of all acts of Parliament, when once people begin to be out of humour with the general Idea on which the old Law has been made. A number of qualifications and exceptions are complex and vexatious things, and there is no End of the discussion of them. Your Lordship perceives, I only speak to the Act of of K. William; which, when it is repeald, will leave the Rom. Catholicks

[1] Missing.

[2] A motion for leave to introduce a Bill to repeal the 'Act for the further preventing the growth of Popery' (11 and 12 Will. III, c. 4) was made on 14 May by Sir George Savile, 8th Baronet (1726–84), M.P. for Yorkshire, and was seconded by John Dunning. The effect of repealing the act of King William would be to enable Catholics to hold and acquire property on the same terms as other subjects, and to take away the threat of forfeiture to Protestant relatives and informers. Savile's Catholic Relief Bill was duly passed into law, receiving the Royal Assent on 3 June. See vol. III, 449, 452.

[3] The form that the Catholic Relief Act of 1778 took was a repeal of 'so much of the said Act' of King William as related to specified matters. The power of the Lord Chancellor to provide a maintenance for the Protestant eldest son of a Catholic out of his father's estate was not mentioned in the Act.

no more Liberty of conscience than they have now; but it takes the power out of the hands of the interested informer; and the interested relation. This entirely cancels[1] however, an whole line of proceeding. It is on the Idea of that distinction, that I drew the Sketch of the preamble,[1] which I made in conformity to your Lordships and Lord Petres wishes[2]—I shewd it to Lord Rockingham, who has the Cause of Liberty civil and religious so sincerely at heart; He approves it very much. I spoke also to Mr Fox before I left Town; He has great ability; and great good wishes for what is right; and he cannot be consulted too soon. I am quite clear, that if the Ministers act their part with fairness, and with any degree of spirit, the Business may be done in this very Session. Whatever is done ought to be *compleat as far as it goes*. A little of unqualified right, is better than a great deal of puzzled and confounded matter; Such matter is fitter to breed uneasiness and litigation than to give any real relief. I have the honour to be with the greatest regard and Esteem

My Lord
Your Lordships
most obedient and humble Servant
EDM BURKE

To SAMUEL SPAN—12 *May* 1778

Source: MS Society of Merchant Venturers.
Addressed: Saml Span Esqr. | Master of Merchants Hall | Bristol.
Postmarked: 14|MA S.C FREE.

Printed in vol. III, 446–7, from the copy in Fitzwilliam MSS (Sheffield).

Sir,

I am honourd with your answer to the Letter which I wrote in explanation of my Conduct on the Commercial Regulations now before the House. You may be assured that nothing could give me a more sincere pleasure than to obey the commands of the Society when I am not morally certain that I should do them a serious injury by my Compliance with their Wishes.

No pains have been omitted to make an amicable adjustment of a Business, whose very principle is the concord of the British dominions.

[1] This does not seem to have been used by the drafters of the Bill.
[2] On 1 May Lord Surrey and Robert Petre, 9th Baron Petre (1742–1801), with Charles Stewart, styled Lord Linton (1744–1827), later (1779) 7th Earl of Traquair, representing the Scottish Catholics, had presented the Address of the Roman Catholic Peers and Commoners to the King (see vol. IV, 45).

The Gentlemen of Ireland who attend to the matter here have been found very moderate and practicable, and have given up some points for the present which in justice ought to have been granted to them.

As to those Members of the British Parliament, whom you speak of as advocates for the Bills, and as interested persons, who have nothing in View but the improvement of their extensive Estates in Ireland; I really do not directly know to whom you allude. Many Members of Parliament have considerable Estates in Ireland; but whether the enlargement of these be their motive for the vote they give, is more than I can tell; nor am I very sollicitous to know, as it [is] much more easy for me, and much more my Business, to judge of the Arguments they use, than the motives on which they act. As to the rest, I take it, that the Interest, which a party has in a Cause, though it disables him to be a Witness, does not at all lessen the favour with which he ought to be heard as an Advocate. The desire of improving ones private fortune, by the general improvement of a Country, I have always considerd rather as praiseworthy than blamable; and in particular I cannot comprehend how the wish of encreasing an Irish fortune, the whole product of which is spent in England, can be objected to by any of the people of this Kingdom. But indeed Sir, the greatest part of the great Majority of last Thursday, have their whole fortunes in Great Britain; for whose sake, primarily, it is, that they wish to remove the injudicious restrictions laid upon Trade by antient acts of Parliament. This last is a fact in which I cannot be mistaken. With regard to my opinions, I may be very wrong in them; but be assured that my Errour arises neither from ill will, or obstinacy, or a want of the highest regard for the Sentiments of those from whom I have the misfortune to differ; and when I take the Liberty of stateing my Notions to you at large, it is not for the sake of entering into any controversy; but solely to acquit myself of any intentional fault. I have the honour to be with great Esteem and regard

Sir

Your most obedient
and humble Servant
EDM BURKE

Westmr May 12. 1778.

To JOHN NOBLE—5 *May* 1779

Source: MS Harvard Library.
Endorsed (in John Noble's hand): London 3 May 1779—
| Edmd Burke | Recd | Ans.

A brief extract was printed in vol. IV, 66 (under date of 3 May 1779) from a
Maggs Catalogue.

My dear Sir,

I have receivd your Letters by express and post;[1] and though my
health is not of the best and my Business more than for several years past,
I lost no time to do for you what I could. I have great good wishes for
Mr Harson[2] on account of his abilities, his original principles, and his
constant attention to Trade, and am totally indifferent to the consideration of any particular friendship to me. I know and value his general
Character and that is enough. I went to the admiralty to prepare the way
in case an ultimate resort should be had to that quarter, though officially
the matter does not belong to them. If Sir Geo. Hay[3] my good friend
had been alive, I should not have had the least difficulty in the Business.
My acquaintance with Sir James Marriot[4] is less; but I have some, and
do not despair of success.

As to the proposal you make about your Vessel I hope you will not
dislike the result of my Negotiations on that Subject. The Lords of the
admiralty will direct the Navy board to hire your Ship if equipped in
the manner you propose, provided you consent to her being commanded
by a Leiutenant in the Navy; and in that Case their Lordships will not
object to your having that reasonable profit on her which is allowed to
other Vessels employd by Government in such services.[5] You are
desired to transmit to Mr Stephens[6] a letter to be laid before the Board
with the Terms, stating as a part of them that the Vessel is not to
commence pay until her arrival on the Station agreeably to your
original proposal. You ought also to mention when she will be ready
to sail.

The other protections I shall set about as soon as possible. I rather
think the Numbers to each Ship greater than I can answer for. You must
send me the Names description and Numbers of the Newfoundlanders,

[1] They are missing.
[2] Daniel Harson, the Collector of Customs at Bristol, whose conduct Burke had
severely criticized in 1775 (see above, p. 406). Harson died on 29 May.
[3] Sir George Hay (1715–78), Judge of the High Court of Admiralty.
[4] Sir James Marriott (*c.* 1730–1803), Hay's successor as Judge of the High Court of
Admiralty.
[5] See vol. IV, 66, 68, 75.
[6] See above, p. 419.

for which you desire protection.¹ My best regards to Mrs Noble.²
Remember me to Champion³ and all friends. Ever yours

EDM BURKE

Wednesday Night.
5th May 1779.

I shall lose as little time as possible on Mr Harsons Business but in
Truth—I am much occupied and fatigued. I think to be able to finish it
tomorrow, if they should not prove refractory.

To JOHN NOBLE—[6 *May* 1779]

Source: MS New York Public Library.

Printed in vol. IV, 68, from Murray Papers. Canon Murray transcribed 'Mr Harson' as 'Mr Hewson'.

My dear Noble,

Mr Marsh was with me this morning and assured me that the omission
of Mr Harson in the Admiralty Warrant was nothing more than a Clerks
mistake and would be instantly set to rights accordingly I gave him the
Papers to be filled up in a proper manner. I am glad to find there was
nothing of malice in the affair. If there was a timely movement was of
use; and it has ended properly. I have put the other matter in Train and
I hope it will succeed.⁴ My last Letter speaks fully of your armed
Vessel, and I hope that matter also will be concluded to your satisfaction.
You must lose no time in making the necessary arrangements. Let me
know too the names and circumstances of the Fishing Ships for which
you want Protections and the Number of men. Mr Protheroes and
Mr Weares I hope will go to them by this Nights post. They shall if I
can help it. I am just going to the House to hear Lord Cornwallis's
examination. Yours always

E BURKE

Thursday.

The commission for examination of prizes is full and there lies the
principal indeed the sole difficulty I shall have.

¹ See vol. IV, 66, 68.　　　　　² Mary (d. 1804).
³ See below, p. 449.　　　　　⁴ MS: suceed.

To GARRETT NAGLE—[*post* 24 *June* 1779]
Source: MS Lord Dunsany.
Printed in vol. IV, 92–5 from the *New Monthly Magazine.*

My dear Garret,

I am come hither for two or three days to enjoy, what, I think, in my whole Life I have never more wanted, a little repose and tranquility. For the present I cannot enjoy it very long; but I am not without hopes, that in less than a fortnight, I may be able to leave Town for the Summer. As I mention leaving Town, I ought to let you know, that I have quitted the Broad Sanctuary, and am returned to Charles Street St James's Square where I formerly lived.

I am much obliged to you for the unprofitable Trouble you have had about my poor concerns. I am sensible that your residence at Killarney for so considerable a part of the year must make it very difficult for you to attend to that Business. I shall certainly make the friendly pains you take for me as light as possible; and therefore shall write by this Nights post, as you wish I should, to Mr Kiernan. I cannot conceive why the Tenants should be so very much behind hand. I know that the markets are not only reasonably good, but extremely high. Butter was last Christmas at Cork considerably above fifty Shillings an hundred; and if Corn was or is cheaper with you than with us it is cheap indeed; but I believe it bears a better price at Cork than it does here. I think it therefore not unreasonable, that they should be compelled to pay; and the sooner the better—for if persons so poor as they are, should be sufferd to run long in arrear nothing will be got from them. If they were straitned by any accident, it were but reasonable I should bear part of the loss; but this I do not conceive to be the Case; and I am satisfied that they have their farms at a moderate price. As to Mr Nagle, his refusing to pay is indeed very extraordinary. I am not without a strong feeling of his Behaviour.

Poor Wat Nagle died of a putrid fever the day before I left Town. I heard nothing of his illness until there were very little hopes of his Life. My Brother went to see him; and stays in Town to take care of his funeral, and whatever may be necessary for the settlement of the triffling effects he may have left. Very triffling I fear they are; and he has two Children at school in Staffordshire probably unpaid for, and certainly without the least provision, or any means of their settlement in the world. He has been for some years wholly out of employment, my Interest in the East India company being gone ever since that body has been brought under the influence of the Ministry. Had he lived, possibly something might have been done for him at a future time; he was really a good natured man, and capable of Business as well as deserving to be employd in it. What to do about his Children I know not. I am sure I am not able to provide for them.

Our worthy friend Mr Purcell called on me a few days ago with Garret of Rinnys Son. They were going to the Camp at Coxheath. Mr Purcell has got him a Commission in the Somersetshire Militia. This is, it is true, only a temporary provision; but if he has anything like ability, and behaves so as to please his Colonel, it may lead to something in the regular Service. Ned Nagle has written to you, though I know not by what means you missed receiving his letter. He was not long out of employment. He is now gone to Newcastle to bring round a Frigate built there for the Kings Service, to which he is appointed Leiutenant. She is called the Syren. If he could have been sent to the West Indies again I am not sure, that Sir Peter Parker would not have found means, in a short time to have given him an higher command. He behaves extremely well, and is reputed to be as good an Officer as any of his standing in the Service. He came a little thin from the West Indies, having been in a bad Ship, and sufferd a good deal of hardship in bringing her home; but the air and amusements of this part of the Country soon recoverd him.

Be so good as to give my best compliments to Lord Kenmare and thanks for his obliging remembrance of me. His favour and kindness to you lays the greatest obligation upon me that he can possibly confer on me.

I am extremely pleased with what you tell me, and indeed what I had before heard of several young Roman Catholicks at Cork. The manner in which they were treated by the association was certainly very improper, but I would not have them to be discouraged by that rude and ill judged conduct of unthinking men; but to persevere in every mark of their good affections to the Government under which they live. Whenever it comes into wise and manly hands they will find the Benefit of it, notwithstanding the shameful surrender that was made of the powers of Government on a late occasion in Scotland; which has indeed inflamed the Spirit of Bigottry, and revived a Temper which I thought had nearly been extinguishd in every part of the world.

Some letters were receivd here, concerning the dispositions shewn by the lower sort of people in Cork during the apprehension of an invasion, as if they were on the point of making an insurrection for the plunder of that City. I suspect that there is not much if any Truth in the

Story. I wish you would inquire and let me know what foundation there was for it. I am ever with the greatest regard

My dear Sir
Your affectionate Kinsman
and humble Servant
EDM BURKE

To UNKNOWN—[post 9 December 1779]

Source: Extract printed in Bisset (1st ed.), p. 327.

Bisset prints this extract after describing the criticism made in Ireland of the failure of the English Opposition to support openly Lord North's resolutions of 9 December 1779 on Irish trade. 'Burke', he stated, 'wrote a letter to his friends in Ireland, in vindication of his own conduct'. Burke certainly resented the Irish criticism and replied to it (see vol. IV, 171, 181).

till the Minister had been driven to some serious attention to the affairs of Ireland, by the measures adopted in that kingdom, his conduct had been extremely dilatory, indecisive, and equivocal: and that the minority were justly incensed at him for having so grossly sacrificed the honour of the nation and the dignity of parliament, as to refuse to afford any substantial relief to the Irish nation, till their own spirited exertions had made every thing that could be done by Great Britain to gratify them appear not an act of choice, but of necessity.

To JOHN ALMON—[1779]

Source: Almon, *Memoirs*, p. 113.

John Almon (1737–1805), the bookseller, printed this letter with an introductory note: 'The following letter related to a political pamphlet, written in the month of April, 1779'. Burke cannot have written his letter in April, since he did not move to Charles Street until June 1779. Almon does not say whether he published the pamphlet: if he did, it cannot be identified.

Sir,

The gentleman who delivers this to you, is a friend to the author of the pamphlet, which accompanies it.[1] As far as I am capable of judging, the subject is handled with a very considerable degree of ability; and though the opinions, toward the latter end, differ a good deal from mine, the public I think may profit by the discussion of them. How far it may

[1] Neither the author of the pamphlet nor his friend has been identified.

429

suit you in the way of trade, you can best judge; or how far the public is or is not satiated with this sort of speculation. On these matters, I ought rather to take your opinion, than to attempt to lead you by any of mine, as the author is wholly unknown to me.

> I am, with great regard,
> > Sir, your most obedient and humble servant,
> > > EDM. BURKE.

Monday Noon,
Charles-street.

To the EARL OF HILLSBOROUGH—12 *July* 1781

Source: MS California University Library (Santa Barbara).

Printed in vol. IV, 356–8, from a copy in the Fitzwilliam MSS (Sheffield).

My Lord

I trust you will have the goodness to excuse the Liberty I take in interfering a second time in favour of the Marattà Agents. The original Neglect of the company; The sending them out of London, when by your Lordships interposition they were at length taken Notice of; and the late rude and abrupt order for their departure; all taken together will hardly furnish in the East the most favourable Idea of our National Character or of our Conduct towards a people who are to be, as hitherto they have been, the main supports of the power and greatness of this Nation.

It is true, that there have been dissensions among these Agents, and that there is something mysterious and unaccountable in the behaviour of one of them. But these Circumstances furnish no reason why they should be treated in a manner unworthy of ourselves, and unbecoming to their Commission, since they are undoubtedly sent by an Ally of this Country, late a sovereign Prince of extensive Dominions, and by whose grant the Company are possessd of Territories of very great Value.

Mr Rouse and I called upon them, and found, that the Parsi, Manuar Restangi, had been at the India house some days ago. The Chairman told them that they should receive their dispatches *seald*; He refused to communicate the contents; or to give any answer whatsoever to the propositions which had been verbally made. This Treatment threw the Agent, who was there with his Son, into some heat, in which he used some expressions, not the most measured. The directors put them out of the Room, after telling them, (with little Dignity in my opinion) that they were eating the Companies bread; and, that if they did not depart in a few days, their allowance would be stopped.

In the present State of the Maratta War, I do not believe it would be prudent in the directors to write anything very definite. But the same indefinite answer which is given in writing may be given verbally; and the less significant it is, the less inconvenience in the communication. To give to men in their Situation a sealed Letter, without any sort of verbal answer, is a great, and I conceive a very needless insult: and as to the measure of driving them away before they can receive any civility from individuals, such as might give them kind wishes towards the Country, it is hardly prudent, to say no worse of it. Permit me to add, that as these persons are come to the King, though his Majesty may decline very properly to give them any answer through his Ministers, yet the same propriety may make your Lordship think, that everything ought to be done to impress them with an Idea of the National Hospitality, and to send them away in good humour. They ought certainly to be clad new, and in an handsome manner; and, according to the usage of the East, to be sent off with presents. Triffles would serve, and I am sure, I could point out such, as would be perfectly grateful to them, and send them off in good humour, at an Expence of not more than an hundred and fifty pounds, or some such Triffle.   It is as nothing to the Company, whether we consider them as rich or poor.

Your Lordship, so far as you are concerned, have done everything for them, both personally and by your influence; It is because I consider them as under your particular protection that I take this Liberty. I hope your Lordship will not think this to be meant as a complaint against the directors, or any of them. It is only an hint, which your Lordships prudence and benevolence will know how to improve, so as to use means to persuade the Chairs into a little more soft and Liberal management. I beg leave to inform your Lordship, that Mr Verelst and Mr Rouse are not only of my opinion but that it is much at their desire that I write.

I have the honour to be with the greatest respect and Esteem

My Lord
Your Lordships
most obedient
and humble Servant
EDM BURKE

Charles Street July 12. 1781

431

To UNKNOWN—[*post* 14 *April* 1782]

Source: MS Wilmarth S. Lewis.

The reference to 'the Duke of Portlands Government' shows that this letter was written while the Duke of Portland was Lord Lieutenant of Ireland during the second Rockingham Administration. Portland arrived in Dublin on 14 April 1782. The letter was presumably written before the death of Lord Rockingham on 1 July 1782.

Dear Sir,

I should be most sincerely concernd if this affair should not end to your satisfaction, and to the Ease and honour of the Duke of Portlands Government. But I can interfere no further. My affection both for my Native and my adopted Country lead me to wish for Settlement. But by what I hear every hour of the State of that Country, a little parliamentary arrangement whether Right or wrong, is totally swallowd up in concerns of a more arduous Nature. I have the honour to be with the most sincere regard

Dear Sir
Your most faithful
and obedient humble Servant
EDM BURKE

To ANDREW STUART—[23 *June* 1782]

Source: National Library of Scotland (MS 8256, fol. 130).
Burke is replying to a letter from Andrew Stuart of Sunday, 23 June 1782 (copy in National Library of Scotland, MS 8256, fol. 127).

Andrew Stuart (1725–1801), M.P. for Lanarkshire, an Edinburgh lawyer chiefly famous for his participation in the Douglas Case, devoted much time to defending his brother Colonel James Stuart (d. 1793), who had been responsible at the behest of the Madras Council for the arrest of Lord Pigot (see above, p. 414). He sent Burke the book in which he had collected his letters in his brother's defence.

Mr Burke presents his best compliments and thanks to Mr Stuart for the honour he has done him by sending him his Book.[1] Mr Burke believes that it is the same that Mr B. had read before relative to the unfortunate Transactions at Madrass in 1776. upon which, on the whole, Mr Burke must (very reluctantly he sincerely assures Mr Stuart) entertain the same opinion he expressed in Parliament at the first

[1] *Letters to the Directors of the East-India Company, and The Right Hon. Lord Amherst.*

432

account receivd in Europe of that Business.[1] In all other respects, no man has an higher value for the services and abilities of Col. Stuart than Mr Burke, nor a stronger Sense of his sufferings in the Cause of the Company in its Military affairs,[2] as well as of the Wise and humane part he has taken relative to the Poligars.[3]

Sunday two o'Clock.

To the DUKE OF PORTLAND—[19 *March* 1783]

Source: MS Osborn Collection.
Endorsed (by Portland): Mr Burke.

The dating of this letter presents great difficulties. It must relate to some stage in the lengthy political negotiations which led up to the formation of the Fox–North Coalition Government on 1 April 1783. The only specific clue as to the date of the letter is the reference to Mrs Siddons. The Duke of Portland attended her benefit on 18 March (*Public Advertiser*, 19 March). If this is the occasion on which Mrs Siddons used the phrase which Burke quotes, then Burke is writing on 19 March, presumably before the meeting between the Duke and the King which took place on that day (see vol. v, 75).

My dear Lord,

The Circumstances are indeed untoward; But the Step you take, I fear, inevitable. The consequences never can oppress honour and virtue. When people enter with little Hope there cannot be much disappointment. The great point is to use your moments well; and, as Mrs Siddons told us last Night, you have the Work of years to do in Moments.[4] Adieu. God bless you and bring you well through it. O! it is a fearful undertaking. Most sincerely and gratefully

ever Your Graces &ca
EDM BURKE

To SIR PETER BURRELL—8 *January* 1788

Source: MS Northumberland County Record Office.

Sir Peter Burrell, 2nd Baronet (1754–1820), later (1796) 1st Baron Gwydir, was Deputy Lord Great Chamberlain. He was responsible for the issue of tickets for the Hastings Impeachment, which began on 13 February 1788.

[1] Burke had spoken in the House on 22 May 1777 (*Parliamentary History*, XIX, 284–6).   [2] Stuart had lost a leg at the Battle of Pollilore on 27 August 1781.
[3] A poligar was a subordinate chief in South India.
[4] Sarah Siddons, *née* Kemble (1755–1831), had returned to the London stage, for the first time since 1776, in October 1782. At her benefit on 18 March, she played Zara in Congreve's *The Mourning Bride*. The phrase which Burke quotes is not taken from the play, but Mrs Siddons seems to have spoken on her own account from the stage (*Public Advertiser*, 19 March).

Dear Sir

As I know perfectly well how much you must be incumberd with sollicitation at this time the first favour I beg of you, before I speak to you of my further object, is, that you will not give yourself the trouble of answering this with your own hand. For the rest what I have to request is, a few Tickets for the Trial in Westminster Hall. I am utterly ignorant, whether in my Character of Manager I am intitled to any; or in my other Character of Privy Counsellour. But whether I am or not, I had much rather owe this convenience to my family to your kindness than to any right. I have the honour to be with the greatest respect

Dear Sir
Your most obedient
and faithful humble Servant
EDM BURKE

Tuesday Jany 8. 1788.

I am obliged to go down to the Committee,[1] which does Business during the recess, or I should wait on you myself.

Burrell summarized his reply at the end of the letter: 'Answered That no Manager or Privy Counsellor had a right to tickets. But that I should be happy to be of any use to Mr Burke during the Trial of Warren Hastings Esqr. PB D.G.C.'.

To STEPHEN THURSTON ADEY—[29] *June* 1788

Source: Sotheby Catalogue, 19 July 1965, no. 839.

Only an extract from this letter to Burke's banker, Stephen Thurston Adey (d. 1801), is known. The letter from which it is taken was described in the catalogue as 'A.L.S., 1 1/2 pp., 4to, Beconsfield, Sunday 28 June 1788, to Adey, sympathising with him on his financial losses'. 29 June 1788 was a Sunday.

I was in hopes that these violent Commercial Storms[2] would not have reached the family of a friend in whose welfare we took a deeper Interest than in that of any commercial house in the world....

To WILLIAM WYNDHAM GRENVILLE—[30 *April* 1789]

Source: Fortescue MSS.

This letter of 'Thursday morn.' can be dated from its reference to Burke's 'Trial on the Charge of Mr Hastings and his Agents'. This took place on Thursday, 30 April 1789 (see vol. v, 465–6).

Burke's remark in his opening speech on the Presents Article that Hastings had murdered Nandakumar 'by the hands of Sir Elijah Impey' (see vol. v, 465–

---

[1] Of Managers.   [2] It is not clear to what Burke is referring.

6) had provoked a petition from Hastings. On 27 April, when the House had agreed to receive the petition, Major John Scott (1747–1819), M.P. for West Looe, announced that he would bring the matter before the House on 30 April, and Pitt had suggested that the Impeachment proceedings should be put off from 30 April to 1 May. William Wyndham Grenville (1759–1834), later (1790) 1st Baron Grenville, was at that time Speaker of the House of Commons.

Sir,

I have received with some surprise a Message from our Committee Clerk,[1] that we should prepare ourselves this day for the Trial, and that you would take the Chair at half an hour after ten.

I left the house on Tuesday Evening[2] with a full assurance that this Business of the Trial could not come on until Friday, if then; and that arrangements would be made with the Lord Chancellour[3] for adjourning to that day—tomorrow. In a conversation which I had the honour of holding with Mr Pitt I understood that he had not then decided whether the Trial was to come on this week.

I am, for my own part, always in some sort of readiness to proceed; but I am really apprehensive that the Sollicitor[4] and those Gentlemen who assist me during my speech with all the passages to which I have occasion to read and refer to, having conceived very differently of the day, will not be in any sort of forwardness. I believe, that the Gentlemen of the Committee have no Idea that the Trial would stand for this day, it being appointed for my Trial on the Charge of Mr Hastings and his Agents—and accordingly the Short hand writer[5] has been sent to, and Gentlemen who choose to attend the Criminal Enquiry against me, are to peruse the Notes, and to examine him upon the Subject.

You will excuse the Trouble I take the Liberty of giving you; as perhaps the meeting may be only formal, and for the purpose of adjournment—I shall take it as a very great favour, if you will be pleased, in a Line, to inform me of the real situation of things. In truth, from my opinion, that Friday was the Business day I am myself up an hour later than otherwise I should have been.

I have the honour to be with great respect

Sir

Your most obedient

and humble Servant

Thursday morn.   EDM BURKE

Our Council[6] have no Notice and certainly will not attend at the time.

---

[1] John White was clerk to the Committee of Managers of the Impeachment.
[2] 28 April.   [3] Edward Thurlow, 1st Baron Thurlow (1731–1806).
[4] Richard Troward (d. 1815).   [5] Joseph Gurney (1744–1815).
[6] The Committee had chosen five counsel (see vol. v, 324).

When the House met, the Impeachment was postponed, and it was decided that the petition of Hastings should be discussed the following day (see vol. v, 465–9).

To WILLIAM WYNDHAM GRENVILLE—*8 June* 1789

Source: Fortescue MSS.

William Wyndham Grenville was M.P. for Buckinghamshire. His appointment as Home Secretary made it necessary for him to seek re-election.

Sir

I am honourd with your Letter[1] relative to your Reelection, at which, I do not hear, that you are likely to meet with any opposition.[2]

I am perfectly sensible of your politeness and attention in making an application to one of so poor an Interest as I possess in the County. I must always be concernd when the situation of political connections prevents me from shewing my personal respect to you.

I beg leave to congratulate you on your new Office. I have the honour to be with Sentiments of the highest respect

Sir

Your most obedient
and humble Servant
EDM BURKE

Gerard Street
June 8 . 1789.

To JOHN KING—*1 May* 1791

Source: Sotheby Catalogue, 23 February 1959, no. 341.

A collection of letters from Burke to John King (1759–1830) was sold at Sotheby's on 23 February 1959. The catalogue prints the following extract from one of these letters, supplying the date but no further details. The subject of the extract is the manifesto dated 23 April 1791, of Armand-Marc, Comte de Montmorin de Saint-Hérem (1745–92), the French Minister for Foreign Affairs (*Ancien Moniteur*, VIII, 213).

I write to you relatively to this French Business, which comes at last in such a shape, that I do not think it in the power of the ministers to be wholly silent upon it . . . They have the impudence, formally and thro' their Ministers, to read a Lecture of Politicks morals and legislation, to his Majesty and to all the crowned heads in Europe . . . one could not

[1] Missing.
[2] Grenville was re-elected on 19 June without opposition.

believe, that anything like it could be conceived in the most distempered imagination before it was brought forth in their Manifesto. The absurdity of those Fanaticks does not render their attempts the less dangerous: perhaps it only makes them the more so . . .

To HENRY DUNDAS—23 [*September*] 1791
Source: MS Osborn Collection.

A brief extract from this letter was printed from a *Sotheby Catalogue* in vol. VI, 409. The letter forms part of the extensive correspondence relating to the mission of Richard Burke, Jr, to Coblenz. Burke had met Dundas on 20 September to protest against the British Government's alleged refusal (as reported by Richard) to allow the Emperor Leopold II to remove troops from the Austrian Netherlands, which it was believed prevented the Emperor from joining Frederick William II, King of Prussia, in an invasion of France. Dundas denied that the Government had imposed any such restriction on the Emperor, and, after further inquiry, confirmed this denial in a letter of 22 September (MS at Northampton). This is Burke's answer to that letter. For the full story see vol. VI, 381–2, 387, 400–1, 403–4, 404–5, 405–8, 409–15.

Dear Sir,

I give you many thanks for your Letter which I received this morning; Though I do not know whether the Substance of it ought to give me more pain or pleasure; for I agree with my Son that it is more likely that our Court would set to rights a mistake than the Emperour should correct an Evil inclination.[1] As you wished I copied from my Sons Letter, the account of the manner in which the answer here was understood at Pilnitz, and the effect it produced on the princes, and the unhappy body of Gentlemen, who, without a Crime, are obliged to fly their Country.[2] You seemd rather to wish that I should write to Lord Grenville the substance of my whole conversation with you, containing the Hints I wished to submit to Ministry in this exigence—But upon much reflexion, I rather thought it better to postpone it, until I knew, whether the suggestion of my Ideas was most likely to be thought a forward intrusion, or a well meant Effort of anxious Zeal to a proper Cause. I told Lord G. that I should proceed or not as he should encourage me. It is not but that, in this critical moment, I am infinitely sensible to the value of time;

[1] Richard had written to Dundas on 10 September that the alleged restriction on the Emperor ought not to have caused any uneasiness 'nor would it have done so, if it had not happen'd that the great engine employed to obstruct the success of this cause has been the diffusion of suspicions in every court relative to the intentions of G. Britain' (MS London School of Economics Library).
[2] i.e. Burke copied the passage from the letter which Richard wrote to him on 10 September when he himself wrote to Lord Grenville on 21 September (see vol. VI, 405–7). Lord Grenville had become Foreign Secretary in 1791.

but there is nothing got by an attempt to force upon any person more than he is willing to hear.[1]

I have had from Lord Fitzwilliam a most satisfactory Letter on the subject of my appeal.[2] I hear that the D. of Portland, intends to express himself to me fully;[3] and that for that purpose he means to read over again all I have written on the subject—not he says that he is in the least likely to alter the opinion he had of my first publication when he put it into the hands of his two Sons.[4] I am glad of this; and if you take any Step in this Business, I think you will not be likely to suffer much by their opposition. In Truth what I write, or what they think if it, signifye very little, as long as this horrible mischief, menacing to the whole world, exists in France. As to the Emperor perhaps he is betrayd by himself. I *am sure* one of his ministers, both I *believe*, do not wish to defeat the French System.[5] The discourse I had with Bintinaye[6] since I saw you, concurring with my own Observations on De Mercys conversation, leave me in no sort of Doubt of the present indisposition of that Minister to do any thing right, or of the causes of his strange conduct.[7] But a decisive word from the K. of P.[8] would oblige the Emperor to lose no time in exerting himself.

> I am with sincere respect and Regard
> > Dear Sir
> > > Your faithful
> > > > and obedient humble Servant
> > > > > EDM BURKE

Beconsfield Friday 23. 1791

[1] See the end of Burke's letter to Grenville of 21 September (vol. VI, 408).
[2] For Fitzwilliam's letter in praise of the *Appeal from the New to the Old Whigs* see vol. VI, 401–2.
[3] Portland did not write to Burke about the *Appeal*. For his views on it see vol. VI, 369, 418.
[4] Burke is here referring to Portland's approval of the *Reflections*, expressed in a letter to French Laurence of 29 August (see vol. VI, 161). Portland had four sons: William Henry Cavendish Bentinck (1768–1854), styled Marquess of Titchfield, M.P. for Buckinghamshire; Lord William Henry Cavendish Bentinck (see below, p. 450); Lord William Charles Cavendish Bentinck (1780–1826); Lord Frederick Cavendish Bentinck (1781–1828). Probably the Duke meant his two younger sons.
[5] Wenzel Anton, Prince von Kaunitz-Rietberg (1711–94), and Johann Philip, Graf von Cobenzl (1741–1810), were the Emperor's two principal ministers. Burke may, however, have meant Prince Kaunitz and Florimond-Claude, Comte de Mercy-Argenteau (1727–94).
[6] Agathon-Marie-René de La Bintinaye (b. 1758), called the Chevalier de La Bintinaye. He had just come to England as agent for the French Princes.
[7] For Burke's report on his conversation with the Comte de Mercy see vol. VI, 367–8.   [8] The King of Prussia.

To JOHN KING—2 *November* 1791

Source: MS Professor Frederick W. Hilles.

John King was at this time close to Lord Grenville, who had become Foreign Secretary in 1791. Burke had written a letter to Catherine II, Empress of Russia, which he wished Lord Grenville to see. This is his covering letter to King (see vol. VI, 440–1, 441–5, 446–8).

My dear John,

I believe I told you, that I thought myself obliged, (or [at] least justified in doing so) to thank the Empress of Russia, for the civil things she said of me and my Book on French affairs.[1] The subject naturally led to more; and I thought I might take that opportunity of throwing out some thoughts pretty freely, (though under the Vehicle of compliment) for her consideration. She is accessible enough, through that medium. You see how the Emperour has acted.[2] Words cannot express the folly and perfidy of his proceeding: But he is in her hands; and if she acts with firmness in support of the Step she has taken, she will bring him to do as she pleases. This is a *Crisis*. Ambassadors will be sent, out of the very worst their Pandemonium affords; who will be Spies and agents for their Fanatical System. *One Period* is past; *another*, more humiliating to Sovereigns and more dangerous, commences. It is at the hinges of affairs, that the Steps taken decide on every thing. The foreign System will now settle domestick politicks. Though I do not ask leave to send this Letter, yet I rather wish you to shew it to Lord Grenville, and he may, if he thinks proper, communicate it to the King. No Minister is responsible for me, or for any thing I do; I cheerfully take every thing at my own risque. However, if I am absolutely forbid, I will not send it. Adieu my dear friend. God bless you.

ever yours
EDM BURKE

Beconsfield Novr 2. 1791.

To JOSEPH HILL—20 *June* [1792]

Source: MS New York Public Library.

This letter was described in *Myers Catalogue*, 343 (1945), no. 69, as '1 p., 4to, June 20. to I. Hill, arranging a meeting'. It is probably one of a series of letters (see vol. VII, 153–7) relating to the financial arrangements for the forthcoming marriage of Mary Palmer (1751–1820), Sir Joshua Reynolds's niece, to Murrough O'Brien, 5th Earl of Inchiquin (1726–1808), later (1800) 1st Marquess of Thomond. Joseph Hill (*c.* 1720–1811) was Lord Inchiquin's legal adviser.

[1] See vol. VI, 442.   [2] See vol. VI, 446.

Dear Sir,

I am just going out. I shall see Mr Metcalfe[1] as soon as I can—and will do every thing in my power to facilitate and expedite the Business.

I have the honour to be
very sincerely Yours
June 20.   EDM BURKE

To JOSEPH HICKEY, JR.—29 *July* 1793

Source: MS Osborn Collection.
Addressed: Joseph Hickey Esqr Junr | Jermyn Street | London.
Franked: Free | Edm Burke | Beconsfield July twenty ninth | 1793.
Postmarked: BEACONS|FIELD   FREE|JY|30|93|P.

Joseph Hickey, Jr (1745–1827) was the son of Burke's old friend and legal adviser Joseph Hickey (*c.* 1714–94).

My dear Sir,

I do not blame you for it; for the thing is universal. You use many reasons to persuade me, that what you want from the Chancellour[2] is good for you, and that you ought to have had it; but you have not said a word to make out to me, how I can contrive to obtain more influence on him than I possess; or how I can give him a better Memory about what he intends to do. He was not three days in Office[3] when an application was made to him in your favour; and all that you State, and more, was stated to him; and he expressed with great distinctness, and great Kindness, his disposition to give you the Office. It seems he has since filled the Commission without thinking of you.[4] Had I known any thing of the filling of that Commission, I should have again applied at the time. But I knew, and indeed could know, nothing of the matter. You were more likely to have intelligence of things of that Nature than I can possibly have. You know, that the Chancellour is Strongly possessed of my desire and earnest wish that you may be served. Therefore Sollicit him yourself, and you may use my Name freely *for this Object*; because he gave it originally at my recommendation; and cannot forget, that it was again

[1] Philip Metcalfe (1733–1818), M.P. for Plympton Erle. Metcalfe, Burke, and Edmond Malone (see below, p. 455) were Reynolds's executors.
[2] Lord Loughborough.
[3] Loughborough received the Seal on 28 January.
[4] Probably Hickey wished to become a Bankruptcy Commissioner—as he ultimately did. There is a letter from Loughborough to Burke, dated only 'Wednesday', which reads: 'Your moderation is equal to Your Influence and both are Irresistible; By the aid of an able Secretary I have found out an immediate Vacancy without any breach of all the Rules I have stated to you and Mr Hickey is appointed' (MS Osborn Collection).

strongly urged to him: It is not that I decline any trouble: But, to succeed, you must watch the times, and sollicit your own affairs. I am with very sincere regard

                    My dear Sir
                         Your most faithful
                              and obedient humble Servant
                                   EDM BURKE

Beconsfield Monday.

To JOHN KING—29 October 1793

Source: Sotheby Catalogue, 23 February 1959, no. 341.
The catalogue supplies the date of this letter, but gives no further details.

Captain Emperor John Alexander Woodford was interested in obtaining the governorship of New South Wales (see vol. VII, 463).

I have again had some talk with my worthy and excellent friend Captn Woodford about his views with regard to the Government of Botany Bay. I find him seriously set upon it . . . I confess, if I were young myself, I should like this Employment. To turn what is dangerous to society to its advantage is a great, and if it is managed with ability, an honourable Task . . .

To the REV. DAVID HUGHES—25 November [1793]

Source: Copy in British Museum (Add. MS 37,843, fol. 216).

Burke had first come into contact with the Rev. Dr David Hughes (*c.* 1754–1817) in October 1792 (see vol. VII, 269–71). The 'Affair which I would fain forget for ever' is almost certainly the attack made upon Burke by William Markham (1719–1807), Archbishop of York, on 25 May 1793 (see vol. VII, 369–70). After the death of Richard Burke, Jr, who was Markham's godson, in August 1794, the Archbishop and Burke are said to have joined in 'a kindly interchange of letters' (Sir C. R. Markham, *A Memoir of Archbishop Markham,* Oxford, 1906, p. 65). It seems probable therefore that this letter was written in 1793.

My dear Sir,

   I understand, that the corrupt Voice of Indian Calumny is again busy in traducing me, and that, by round about ways, it has again found it's Way to Oxford. I have long since heard of this miserable work, and long since I have despised it, as I do now—Oxford is a Seminary, eminently for the Church; secondarily for the State; I should be truly sorry, that it should be disgraced by that foulest of all possible corruptions, Indian Influence. I hope such a Corruption is far from general— If it is, the coming Generation is undone. If They do not teach better Lessons, I hope the House of Commons will at least continue to give sound Instruction.

As to what you say of the A[rchbisho]p of Y[ork']s introducing me to Lord R.,[1] there is not a single Syllable of Truth in it—I am little concerned about the Matter, except as it is a Fact—If He had, which He did not, Lord R., if He were alive, would have gratefully acknowledged it, as a great Obligation to him. I certainly lived for several years in the early Part of my Life, in much Friendship with his Grace—He would then have served me, if He could, I have no Doubt of it; except by civil and kind Conversation it did not lie in his Way—I would have done the Same to him—He has no Doubt of that—But if his Grace had introduced me to an hundred Lords, and I had lain under a thousand Obligations to him, what Reason, in common Sense, does that furnish to him, for degrading *himself*, and the Place He sits in, by scurrilous Invectives and foul-mouthed Language against me, for doing my Duty in Obedience to the Commands of the House of Commons? If any Provocation could make him pardon *himself* for such Things, what Provocation could I give him? What have I ever done or said, to hurt him in his Fame, in his Fortune, or in the Objects of his just Ambition? Surely his Friends (if such They are) had best hold their Tongue on this Business, and not compel me to speak on an Affair which I would fain forget for ever—I am my dear Sir ever faithfully yours &c

EDM BURKE

Novr 25.
   The Revd Dr Hughes
       Jes. Coll.

To JOHN KING—8 *February* 1795

Source: MS Osborn Collection.

An extract from this letter was printed in vol. VIII, 142 from a *Maggs Catalogue*. On the basis of the entry in the catalogue the letter was assumed to have been written to Walker King. The full text shows that it was almost certainly written to John King, Under-Secretary of State to the Duke of Portland in the Home Department.

[1] Lord Rockingham.

My dear King—

I send you the Paper I spoke of in my Note.[1] I have wrote *at* Lord Fitzwilliam about the matter.[2] I know he will find abundance of people to persuade him, that it is better to have it hushed up: But this is great imprudence, both with regard to Government, and to the unfortunate people who are thus treated.

I find, that De Curt,[3] of whom the D. of Portland spoke to me, is named agent to the superiour Council, that is the supreme Court of Justice in Martinico. Du Pont[4] told me, you were so good as *to suggest*[5] *an employment of the same kind* for him with regard to St Domingo. I think the employment of the utmost necessity on account of the appeals.[6] I dont know so fit a man for it as Dupont who is a Lawyer that knows their Language and ours and their Law, with a very tolerable notion of the English Law. Your Opinion of his Talents and his integrity agrees with mine; and you know how much I wish every thing he wishes. As to the mode of putting this Business in a proper Train, you can best judge of it, as you can best help in it. Mrs Burke salutes Mrs King[7] as I do. At a leisure moment present my affectionate respects to the Duke of Portland. Yours ever most truly

EDM BURKE

Feb. 8. 1795

To HENRY DUNDAS—[*circa* 5 *March* 1795]

Source: MS Osborn Collection.
For the date of this letter see vol. VIII, 177.

An extract from this letter was printed in vol. VIII, 177 from a *Dobell Catalogue.*

My dear Sir,

I have had Letters by this post from Ireland.[8] There is some Guard and reserve in them, with regard to the Post office, which is a Channel

---

[1] Burke's note is missing. The paper is presumably 'The Case of James Hyland' (see vol. VIII, 145, n. 3). For James Hyland see vol. VIII, 124.

[2] Presumably Burke refers to his letter to the Rev. Thomas Hussey (1741–1803) of 4 February (see vol. VIII, 136–40). Burke wrote to Fitzwilliam himself on 10 February (see vol. VIII, 144–8).

[3] Louis, Chevalier de Curt (b. 1722); see vol. VIII, 142.

[4] Pierre-Gaëton Dupont (1762–1817), who had translated Burke's *Reflections* into French.

[5] King has attached a note at this point: 'I suggested that if the Council appointed him it might probably be attended to by the Duke of P. as in the case of De Curt'.

[6] To the Privy Council.

[7] Harriot Margaret, *née* Moss (*c.* 1768–1841).

[8] Presumably letters of [27 February] and 28 February from the Rev. Thomas Hussey; see vol. VIII, 162–3, 163–4.

in the opinion of most (and most certainly in my opinion) much vitiated by its connexion with certain Cabals. I find, if my correspondent is right, that the Business, on which I spoke to you is decided, and Lord F. absolutely recalled. This I ought to have known, in order to save you a deal of most fruitless Trouble. The Letters are in the same desponding Style. None from Grattan.[1] I forgot in the vast hurry of Business to Let you know, that Lord Moira talked of saying something on it in the house of Lords[2]—and I begged him first to shew you his Letters. I am ever with most sincere Respect

and regard My Dear Sir
ever Yours
EDM BURKE

A Deputation from the Catholicks is I believe now on its way hither.[3]

B. UNDATED LETTERS

To THOMAS BARNARD—n.d.

Source: Crawford MSS.

Thomas Barnard (1728–1826) was Dean of Derry from 2 June 1769 to 20 February 1780, when he became Bishop of Killaloe.

Undoubtedly that line cannot be in Juvenal or Persius. I know not where it is. I seem to have often heard it and think with you it is in Martial—but I know nothing for certain about it. It is not impossible that it may be the line of some modern Latin Writer. I was under the Razor or I would have sent my Verdict of *ignoramus* before. I am very truly and with much Esteem and regard Mr Deans most Obedient

E B.

To the REV. JOHN BOWDEN—n.d.

Source: MS Professor William B. Todd.
Addressed: To | The Revd Mr Bowden.

This letter was written between 1761 and 1764, while Burke was acting as secretary to William Gerard Hamilton (1729–96), Chief Secretary to the Lord

[1] Grattan wrote on 11 March a letter which Burke received and answered on 20 March (see vol. VIII, 185, 205).
[2] Francis Rawdon-Hastings, 2nd Earl of Moira (1754–1826), later (1817) 1st Marquess of Hastings, does not appear to have spoken in the House of Lords on Irish affairs until he supported Lord Fitzwilliam on 8 May (see vol. VIII, 238).
[3] See vol. VIII, 163.

Lieutenant of Ireland. The Irish House of Commons sat during this period from 22 October 1761 to 30 April 1762 and from 11 October 1763 to 12 May 1764. The Rev. John Bowden (*c.* 1732–76) became curate of St Bride's in Dublin in 1764. For his association with Burke see vols I, 195; III, 274–5; VII, 104.

Dear Bowden

People expect a grand debate to day and that the house will be extremely full; I am not quite sure whether I can be there at least not in time to secure a place in the Gallery and there will be danger that the body of the house will be cleard. I have a friend[1] who is exceedingly desirous to be there, but is a stranger in the Kingdom, if you will be so kind to take charge of him and to go early enough to secure a place I shall be much obliged to you: if you will breakfast with Mrs Burke at ten you will meet him at my Lodging for I go myself a little way into the Country this morning.

Yours sincerely
E Burke.

To [Dr Richard Brocklesby]—n.d.

Source: Sotheby Catalogue, 21 June 1881, no. 17; *Maggs Catalogue,* 365 (spring 1918), no. 118.

The letter from which two extracts are here printed presents several problems. It is not easy to be sure to whom it was addressed, and its date is uncertain. In the *Maggs Catalogue* it is described as 'A lengthy A.L.S. to his friend, Dr French Laurence. 3 pp., folio. Beaconsfield, 13th April, 1792'. The letter was almost certainly not addressed to French Laurence (1757–1809). In Hist. MSS Comm. (*Morrison* MSS) it is summarized as follows: 'Declaring himself in health, for which he has reason to bless God and thank the physician to whom the letter is addressed, the writer speaks highly of the animosities he has roused by recent expressions of sincere opinion. Laughing at a pamphleteer who declares him to have lost the friendship of the Duke of Portland and Lord Fitzwilliam, Burke reports that those noblemen show him more personal kindness than ever' (p. 485). The likely recipient of the letter is Dr Richard Brocklesby (1722–97). The substance of the letter itself does not fit easily into Burke's correspondence in 1792, though he was at Beaconsfield on 13 April. It is the kind of letter which Burke might well have written following the quarrel with Fox and the publication of the *Appeal from the New to the Old Whigs* in August 1791 (see vol. VI, 291, 330–1, 335–6), but until the original of the letter becomes available it is impossible to be certain of the date. The first extract is from the *Sotheby Catalogue:*

They are not to be persuaded that Mr Fox and other gentlemen who do not favour me with their good opinions, vary as much from my sentiments (which are their own) as I *apprehend,* and as they *profess* to do; or if there really exists such a diversity, that it is not likely to be

---

[4] Not identified.

followed with such effects as I dread from the propagation of the principles and politics which they encourage, I heartily wish, without being able to change my opinions, that these my excellent friends may be found in the right.

The second extract is from the *Maggs Catalogue* and is introduced as follows: 'A most voluminous letter of great interest. After referring to some pamphlet attacks on himself, and his rupture with Fox over his (Burke's) hostility to the French Revolution, he at great length discusses and defends his political opinions':

I have not lost one friend. I have only been put into the situation in which men make discoveries. I have found out, that all those were not my friends who formerly appeared to be such. I am undeceived; and that is the whole of the matter . . . If anyone, in whose judgment I had confidence, was to say, that I might be betterd, in knowledge or in morals, by a perusal of the writings of these Gentlemen, I should read them. But as I do not hear from you, or anyone else, that much is to be learned from them, I do not like to spend my money in the purchase, or my time in the reading, of Books, upon the sole merit of their personal Malignity to myself . . .

My principles upon any publick matter are of no great importance: for, there is an end of my political exertions. Whatever they are, they are sufficiently declared. Whether they are allowed to be Whigg principles, or not, is a very small part of my concern. I think them exactly such as the sober, honourable, and intelligent in that party, have always professed. I think, I have shewn, beyond a possibility of debate, that they are exactly the same. But if any person or any number of persons, choose to think otherwise, and conceive that they[1] are contrary to the Doctrines of their Whigg party,—be it so. I am certain, that they are principles of which no reasonable man or good citizen need be ashamed of. If they are Tory principles, I shall always wish to be thought a Tory, If the contrary of[2] these principles be Whigg principles, I beg, that you, my Dear Friend will never consider me as belonging to that description: For I look upon them to be wicked and absurd in the highest degree; and that wherever they shall become the ruling maxims, they must produce exactly the same Effects, which they do, in the miserable, depraved, and contemptible Nation in which they now predominate. So far for the Whiggs, who do not consider me as a Whigg. Whilst they retain their present unhappy notions I should be mortified indeed, if I were thought, directly or indirectly, to belong, to such a faction . . .

[1] *Maggs Catalogue:* that if they
[2] *Maggs Catalogue:* contrary, if

That perpetual wheel of the Republick, which must carry with it all those who act, and would act wisely and virtuously,[1] in the State, is perfectly true. It was, in part, applicable to Cicero, as a compleat defence of his conduct. In part it was not; for many of the turns of that wheel were given, or accelerated by himself and on considerations relative to his own ambition.

To Sir Thomas Charles Bunbury—n.d.

Source: Hist. MSS Comm. (*Bunbury* MSS), p. 240 b.

The Historical Manuscripts Commission found three letters of Burke in the papers of Sir Thomas Charles Bunbury, 6th Baronet (1740–1821). The letters are summarized as follows:

> 'Three letters by E. Burke; in the first he condemns our treatment of America; in the second he treats of the connexion of Ireland and England; in the third he treats of Reform in Parliament.'

To Lord John Cavendish—n.d.

Source: Draft in Fitzwilliam MSS (Sheffield). Printed *Corr.* (1844), IV, 527–31.
Endorsed: To | Lord J. Cavendish.

It is impossible to assign this letter to any year. The probability is that the draft was written after Lord John Cavendish's defeat in 1784 and before the quarrel between Burke and Fox in 1791. There is no evidence that it was completed.

My Lord,

I address my thoughts upon a Subject which has long engaged my Mind and deeply affected it, to your Lordship; because I know you. I am sure that if I have conceivd an Esteem for your Character it is not because I have seen it at a distance, have seen you placed after long meditation in a single chosen light with spikes between you and the Crowd;[2] enlarged by the deceptions of Art above the human form, and painted out for Theatrical shew and Vulgar admiration. I have walked all round you and have seen you at all hours and in all humours. And I who have brought my Mind so exclusively to veneration for the[3] divine perfections, that I have no admiration left for those of men beyond my understanding of them; am yet very willing to recognize and honour Virtue so far as I am able [to] comprehend it. I should be ashamed to look for it in Statues and on Shelves and to neglect it in Life. But if I see

---

[1] *Maggs Catalogue:* virtuosly
[2] A common feature of eighteenth-century theatres, to protect the actors against rioters in the audience.   [3] MS: the the

the same great qualities in John or Charles[1] I trust that I am disposed to give them as much Credit, and to love them full as well, as when I read of them in a Cato or a Timoleon. The heart is pinched up and contracted by the very studies which ought to have enlarged it, if we keep all our praise for the Triumphant and Glorified Virtues and all ones uneasy suspicions, and doubts, and criticisms and exceptions for the companions of our Warfare. A mind that is temperd as it ought, or aims to come to the Temper it ought to have, will measure out its just proportion of Confidence and Esteem for a Man of invariable rectitude of Principle, steadiness in friendship, moderation in Temper, and a perfect freedom from all Ambition duplicity, and revenge, though they see[2] the owners of these inestimable qualities in the Tavern and on the Pavement, as well as in the Senate, or with what appears more decency than solemnity even there; He will put his confidence in them though they should appear in a figure not lofty nor much imposing. Though his address should at first be cold dry and reserved and without any thing at all of advance or Courtship in it. Far from taking away his value every thing makes simple virtue accessible and familiar and companionable makes its use more frequent, and its reality a great deal less doubtful. Neither I[3] apprehend is the value of great qualities[4] taken away by the defects or errors that are most nearly related to them. And men of moderation will sometimes [be] defective in vigour. A simplicity and a Want of Ambition does something detract from the Splendour of great qualities. Minds[5] (and these are the best minds) which are more fearful of reproach than passionate[6] for glory, will want that extemporaneous promptitude and that decisive stroke which is often so absolutely necessary in great Affairs. And I have often thought that it is one of the main advantages in the social endeavours of publick men acting by joint principle, consent and council, that they produce opposite Virtues and faults whilst they honestly ⟨stick together⟩ and bear one anothers Burthens as men and Christians ought and temper one another, and make an excellent Whole out of defective parts.[7] It is fit that our social condition should be our best. The knowledge of the world will operate differently[8] according to our Temper. Almost every body in the sanguine season of youth, looks for more perfection in the world than he is likely to find. But a good

---

[1] Lord John or Charles Fox.   [2] MS: they see they see
[3] MS: I Neither I   [4] MS: great qualities is
[5] MS: A Minds   [6] MS: passionate passionate
[7] In the margin at this point Burke has written: 'The Individual is to be sure the less perfect for this; and those who love to whine over human infirmity rather than to releive it will think it a subject of great lamentation; Yet many a thing which single is mischievous, in arrangement is useful. Let this man [act] with another, and his very defect will be of service. You know my opinions upon insulated morality and politicks'.
[8] MS: different

temperd man, that is to say a man of a wise constitution, will be pleased to find[1] the Beneficial effects of human faults whereas the other grows peevish at finding what he will as certainly find the ill consequence attending the most undoubted Virtues. I believe we shall do every thing something the better for putting ourselves in as good a humour as possible when we set about it.

EDMUND *and* WILLIAM BURKE *to* RICHARD CHAMPION—n.d.

Source: Fitzwilliam MSS (Northampton), A.1.7.

This letter to Richard Champion (1743–91) was written after the Bristol election of 1774 and before Burke left his London house in Broad Sanctuary in June 1779. From the formal references to 'Mr Burke' and 'Mr B' it was probably written at a fairly early stage in the association between Champion and the Burkes—in 1775 or 1776.

[Edmund begins]

My dear Champion,

I heartily long to see you. Mr Burke I believe you will find in Town. Me you will find here, or you will bring to Town as best suits your conveniency. I long to see you, and am ever with the greatest regard and affection

My dear friend

ever yours faithfully

Sunday.   E BURKE

Mrs Burke has been a good deal out of order—but is now much better again adieu. You had better go and lie at my house in the Sanctuary.

[William begins]

My dear dear Champion This instant friday, I discover this Letter—whether I find it among Mr Bs Letters or from those of my own pocket, I dont know, nor even whether a Letter of so late date, I cant decide, but I am vexed sadly—Mr B is himself in town, and it will not ease my vexation by communicating it to him, tho it cannot be of consequence neither, for if you are come to town you naturally go to the Brd Sanct—but yet it vexes me not a little—my dear friend God bless you, I hope and trust Mrs Champion[2] and the little folks are all well, God preserve you.

[1] In the margin at this point Burke has written: 'in the midst of his disappointment to find that if the ⟨Virtues⟩ of men are below his wish and calculation, their faults.'
[2] Judith, *née* Lloyd (d. 1790).

To CAPTAIN WILLIAM CUPPAGE—n.d.

Source: Fitzwilliam MSS (Northampton), A.XIV.38.

This letter must have been written before 1794 since it mentions both Richard Burkes. It was probably written after Lord William Henry Cavendish Bentinck (1774–1839) joined the army on 27 January 1791 at the age of sixteen. Although it is not certain what 'great loss' Captain William Cuppage (1759–1832) had suffered, it seems likely that the Mrs Cuppage of Coleraine, who died on 16 June 1792 (*Dublin Chronicle*, 5 July 1792) was Cuppage's mother (*née* Kirkpatrick); his father, the Rev. Burke Cuppage, had been Rector of Coleraine. The watermark of the paper on which Burke's letter is written occurs in the Burke MSS in 1792. The date of the letter is therefore probably June or July 1792.

Wednesday

My dear Cuppage—

Mrs Burke receivd your Letter[1] this morning. We are sorry for our disappointments in seeing you; but much more for the Cause of it. We sympathise with you most cordially on your great loss. We think too well of your heart not to know how much you must feel it; but we think also too well of your Courage, not to be very sure you will bear that, and every other disposition of Providence as you ought to do. Your self condemnation is natural to those, who are anxious about the Duties of Life, and think, that tho' much has been performed, something is left undone—and this adds to affliction where no amends for little neglects ever can be made. I had a Letter[2] from Lord William Bentinck today to excuse himself from your joint engagement. My dear Cuppage—ever Most truly and affectionately, yours

EDM BURKE

Our Richards are both in Town.

To [JAMES DODSLEY]—n.d.

Source: Sotheby Catalogue, 2 July 1962, no. 225.

Only an extract from this letter, presumably addressed to James Dodsley (1724–97), is known. The letter is described in the catalogue as 'A.L.S., 1/2 page, 4to, Bd Sancty. Friday morn, [*c.* 1770], [to Dodsley], asking him to send'

my *Observations on Mr Grenville's State of the Nation* and the *Causes of the discontents*.

---

[1] Missing.   [2] Missing.

To PHILIP FRANCIS—n.d.

Source: Extract printed in Parkes and Merivale, *Memoirs of Francis*, II, 257.

Parkes and Merivale date this extract 'apparently 1788'. It would appear however to have been written earlier, since by 1788 Fox would have known Philip Francis (1740–1818), later (1806) K.C.B., very well. Fox called upon Francis on 8 August 1784 'to request Conference, Connexion, and Intimacy—opened his thoughts about moving for the recall of Hastings, and then for impeaching him' (India Office Library, MS EUR.D.20, p. 57).

It was with unmixed pleasure that I heard Mr Fox the other day do justice to my friend, by owning the information he had, and the wisdom he might have gained, had he had such a flapper at his elbow in his most high and palmy days. 'I have sucked many brains in my time (he said), and seldom found more to reward me. Few men say so much in so few words.' 'Aye, sir,' I replied, '*multum in parvo*: his style has no gummy flesh about it.' But I must not enlarge; for I am so much yours, and have so much of yours, that your triumphs puff me up as with a sense of personal merit. Still I may allow myself the more satisfaction in finding that Mr Fox acknowledges your value; as I know he has earwigs about him, who buz in his ears all the pitiful calumnies that a Hastings or a B. and Co.[1] have deluged the town with since your return from India;[2] and I feared the fatal facility of his temper, which yields to proximity rather than be at the trouble of examining and detecting.

To DAVID GARRICK—n.d.

Source: MS copy at Sheffield. Printed Prior (5th ed.), pp. 113–14.

The original of this letter to David Garrick (1717–79) evidently had no date. Prior, who owned it, supplied a date of August 1769 (5th ed., pp. 113–14). The copy at Sheffield is dated 'June 1769'. The copy, however, preserves on the back the address: 'To | David Garrick Esqre | Adelphi'. Garrick did not move to the Adelphi until 1772. The meaning of Burke's date line is obscure. Parliamentary sessions began on Tuesdays or Thursdays. The only relevant occasion on which it might be held that the session began on a Wednesday was in 1774, when the House met on Tuesday, 29 November, solely for the election of a Speaker, and the session proper began the following day. The 'finishing stroke' to which Burke refers might be either the final establishment of his right to sit for Bristol, or the completion of the separation between Britain and her American colonies.

[1] Richard Barwell (1741–1804) and Company.
[2] Francis had arrived in England in October 1781.

June 1769

Dear Garrick,

I send you a *Rosa sera*[1] a *late* Turtle—an entertainment at least as good for the Palate, as the other for the Nose. Your true Epicureans are of opinion, you Know, that it contains in itself all Kinds of flesh, fish, and fowl. It is therefore a dish fit for one who can represent all the solidity of flesh, the volatility of fowl, and the oddity of fish. As this entertainment can be found no longer any where but at your Table, or at those Tables to which you give conviviality and chearfulness, let the Type and shadow of the Master grace his board. A little *pepper* he can add himself. The *wine* likewise he will supply—I do not Know whether he still retains any friend who can finish the dressing of his Turtle by a gentle squeeze of the Lemon. Our best regards to Madam[2]

ever Dear Garrick
Most faithfully your obedient Servant
EDM. BURKE.

Westmr Tuesday—one
day before the meeting
of the Session that gives
the finishing stroke.

To MRS DAVID GARRICK—n.d.

Source: MS Osborn Collection.

This note is associated with a number of letters written to Mrs Garrick about the time of her husband's death. Burke came to London from the Court Martial of Admiral Keppel at Portsmouth to attend Garrick's funeral, which took place on 1 February 1779 (see vol. IV, 42). This would be the kind of note he might have left at the door, when calling on Mrs Garrick.

Mr Burke to pay his very respectful and very affectionate Compliments to Mrs Garrick.

To SERJEANT JOHN GLYNN—n.d.

Source: Glynn MSS.
Addressed: To | The Recorder of London.

This letter was written after Glynn was elected to the Recordership of London on 17 November 1772 and before Burke left Broad Sanctuary in June 1779.

[1] A late rose; see Horace, *Odes*, I, XXXVIII, 3-4.
[2] Eva Maria, *née* Veigel (1724–1822).

Mr Burke is always very much concerned when he cannot have the honour of meeting the Recorder especially at this interesting time. He will endeavour to avail himself of Mr Recorders first leisure moment. He does not mean to give him the trouble to come to this part of the Town; but if Mr Recorder will inform him of the time he can best spare Mr Burke will pay his Compliments to him at Red Lyon Square.

Broad sanctuary Friday morn.

To MRS WILLIAM HAVILAND—n.d.
Source: Extract printed in Prior (2nd ed.), II, 422.

It is impossible to feel certain of the date of this letter. The military careers of General William Haviland (1718–84) and of his son Thomas Haviland (d. 1795) make it unlikely that they were at Penn together during the American War. Moreover Burke's friendship with Mrs Haviland—Salusbury, *née* Aston (c. 1730–1807)—appears to have been a late development. The most probable date for this letter is therefore late December 1783 or early January 1784.

In order that I may turn over a new leaf with you, in wishing you, and all with you, in *General*, and in *particular*, a thousand and one happy years—when may every one of them, and even the odd one, be as pleasant, but a little more real than the Thousand and One Arabian Entertainments! This we all cordially wish. Mrs Balfour[1] is well, to all appearance, of all rheumatism. May you all be well of all complaints. God bless you. Your's ever, my dear Madam, Sirs, young and middle aged—for self, wife, and son, &c.

EDMUND BURKE.

EDMUND *and* JANE BURKE *to* MRS WILLIAM HAVILAND—n.d.
Source: Prior (2nd ed.) II, 310.

Prior assigned this letter to the late summer or early autumn of 1795. Burke, however, is promising to 'write to you from Bath'. He went to Bath in late July 1796 (see above, p. 61).

My dear Madam,

We think this *too much* at any time; *now*, we will not take it; on your return we will think of it; we do not refuse but postpone it, for as I

---

[1] Mary, *née* Aston (c. 1730–89), widow of William Charles Townley Balfour. She was Mrs Haviland's twin sister.

know pretty nearly how two things stand,[1] we do not at this time want it; when we do, I assure you solemnly and sincerely we will call for it. We shall write to you from Bath.

> I am ever to you and our dear Nabby,[2]
> Your most faithful and affectionate friend,
> JANE BURKE AND
> E. BURKE.

Sunday.

To MRS WILLIAM HAVILAND—n.d.

Source: MS Osborn Collection. Printed Prior (2nd ed.), II, 310–11.
Addressed: Mrs Haviland.

Prior states that this letter was written 'some months' after the previous letter. It would therefore appear to have been written after Burke's return from Bath in September 1796 (see above p. 84).

My dear Madam

Mrs Burke and I have just heard, thro' their usual kind attentions of the arrival of our worthy Physicians of Bath,[3] at the metropolis of this district. A thousand thanks to you and to them, there and here. Most unfortunately to me I am obliged to be in London tomorrow—But if you and they will suffer Mrs Burke to represent me, you will dine here with these Gentlemen, tomorrow Sunday. And if the continuance of the good weather should tempt them to remain in this pleasant Country—I shall please God be back on Tuesday evening, and shall have the satisfaction of engaging you and them for that day also. All the Ladies here kiss yours and Mrs Astons hand. They must not talk of kissing the Gentlemen no not the younger Mr Fitzherbert,[4] though I know they long for it. Ever Yours

                                              EDM BURKE

Saturday.

To WALKER KING—n.d.

Source: MS Harvard Library.

This letter of 'Tuesday evening' was written after the marriage of Walker King on 21 August 1794. It may possibly be the letter of 'last Night' which Burke

---

[1] Obscure. Perhaps Burke is referring to the finances of the Penn school.
[2] Presumably Miss Abigail Aston (*c.* 1734–1814), Mrs Haviland's sister.
[3] Presumably Dr Caleb Hillier Parry (1755–1822) was one of the physicians.
[4] Not identified. Possibly the son of Samuel Fitzherbert (d. 1826), who had married Mrs Haviland's daughter.

mentioned when he wrote to King on 21 December 1796 (see above, p. 191). 20 December 1796 was a Tuesday. Burke had then recently returned to Beaconsfield from London, where he appears to have seen the Lord Chancellor (see above, pp. 179–80).

My dearest Walker,

I came hither, without pressing you, as I meant to do at my departure, to see the Chancellour[1] as early as possible, and by all means before you leave Town, to thank him[2] for his obliging expressions to me on the Object of your pursuit. You can take that opportunity of pressing the necessity of an early application which may prevent the preoccupation of the Ground by other Pretenders. Get Angelo[3] also to call upon him to thank him in the same manner and to supplicate his good Offices for putting his Pension on the civil List. His claim is strongest indeed on the Prince, who has treated him thus unworthily; but in reality, he is an old servant of the whole Royal Family[4]—Our love to Mrs King[5]—I have been off and on; but on the whole, I thank God, a little better and am light and easy. Mrs Burke and all here salute Mrs King and you most cordially and wish you every happiness.

Tuesday evening.

To WALKER KING—n.d.

Source: Sotheby Catalogue, 29 March 1926, no. 228.
Only an extract from this letter is known. The letter from which it is taken is described as 'A.L.S. "E.B." 1 1/2 pp. 8vo. to Walker'.

I daresay that the Lady Abbess[6] has already repented of her getting rid of the House, go and console her afterwards come and cheer me.

To EDMOND MALONE—n.d.

Source: MS Osborn Collection.

This letter, dated only 'Thursday', almost certainly relates to the decision of Lord and Lady Inchiquin to sell the pictures bequeathed them by Sir Joshua Reynolds (see above, p. 439). Burke, Philip Metcalfe (see above, p. 440) and Edmond Malone (1741–1812) were Reynold's executors. The pictures were finally sold in 1795.

[1] Lord Loughborough.   [2] MS: thank you
[3] Domenico Angelo Malevolti Tremamondo (1716–1802).
[4] Angelo had been fencing master to the Prince of Wales and to other members of the Royal Family. He does not appear to have obtained a pension on the Civil List.
[5] Sarah, *née* Dawson (*c.* 1772–1822).
[6] Not identified.

My dear Sir,

I can do nothing against folly and madness. They are going to throw away their fine Collection of Pictures, the Bulk of their fortune. I send you the Letter signed[1] and am ever

My dear Sir
Your most faithful
and obedient humble Servant

Thursday.   EDM BURKE

To MRS ELIZABETH MONTAGU—10 *February* n.y.

Source: MS Professor Frederick W. Hilles.

Mrs Elizabeth Montagu (1720–1800) was a friend of long standing of Burke. They first became acquainted in the 1750s. This letter presumably belongs to the 1770s or 1780s, because of its reference to the two Richards.

Dear Madam

Saturday being a day of leisure, it is with the greatest satisfaction we find, that your kindness has made it something more than a day of rest to us; It will be an old sabbath in serenity and repose and a modern festival, in cheerfulness and conversation; and indeed what few old Sabbaths or modern festivals have had, no small improvement on the part of the Guests old and young. This we promise ourselves by no uncertain anticipation. Mrs Burke and my Son are in Town. My Brother is not. We had not before heard of your having been ill but trust we shall find no remains of your Complaint on Saturday. I have the honour to be with the most real respect and sincere regard

Dear Madam
Your most faithful
and obligd humble Servant

10. Feb.   EDM BURKE

To [CAPTAIN JOHN WILLETT PAYNE]—n.d.

Source: MS Osborn Collection.

This letter almost certainly relates to the Regency crisis of 1788–9, or its immediate aftermath. It reads like an answer to a letter of 'Saturday' from Captain John Willett Payne (1752–1803), M.P. for Huntingdon, a close friend of George, Prince of Wales. That letter reads: 'The Prince has desir'd to beg

[1] It has not been identified.

the favour of seeing you tomorrow at 12 o'Clock. I have just heard the message you left, which, if it requires seeing you before that time I will contrive to wait upon you this evening' (MS at Sheffield). There was a meeting at Carlton House on Sunday, 31 May 1789, attended by Burke, Sir Gilbert Elliot, and Richard Brinsley Sheridan (1751–1816), M.P. for Stafford. The purpose of the meeting was to discuss a letter from the King to William, Duke of Clarence (1765–1837), afterwards William IV (Minto, *Life of Elliot*, I, 320).

My dear Sir,

Every purpose that I could wish will be answerd by the time which his Royal Highness has condescended to appoint. I rather think, if there should be no Objection, that Sir Gilbert Elliot[1] should attend along with me— and I will send to him accordingly. I am ever most truly yours

EDM BURKE

To the MARCHIONESS OF ROCKINGHAM—n.d.

Source: Ramsden MSS.

The following letter clearly replies to a (missing) invitation to visit the Rockinghams on Lord Rockingham's birthday. Lord Rockingham had been born on 13 May 1730, but after the change in the calendar celebrated his birthday on 24 May. The watermark of the paper on which Burke's letter is written (W. Quelch) occurs in the Burke MSS in 1778. Burke was therefore probably writing on Saturday, 23 May 1778.

I hope that one part of your Ladyships description will prove very true, and that the birth day to which your Ladyship has the goodness to invite me, may be *hereafter*, that of a very *old* man. I am sure that it is the birth day of the man, on whose Birth this Country has the most reason, (I was going to say) to *rejoice*; but certainly to *console* itself—for reason for rejoicing, I fear nobody can give to this Country. I shall certainly consider no engagement on a day that so much supersedes all other attentions. I am ever ever, with the most zealous wishes for many returns of so good a day, and with the most real Attachment

Madam
Your Ladyships
most obedient
and obligd humble Servant
EDM BURKE

Saturday night.

[1] 4th Baronet (1751–1814), M.P. for Berwick-upon-Tweed, later (1797) 1st Baron Minto.

To RICHARD SHACKLETON—n.d.

Source: MS New York Public Library. Printed *Leadbeater Papers*, I, 134.
There is a copy of this letter in the Osborn Collection.

Richard Shackleton (1726–92) was a regular visitor to the annual London meeting of the Society of Friends.

My dear Shackleton,

We shall wait for nine tomorrow with impatience; and shall be happy to see your *whole* Self without any distinction of parts. The snuff I have presented. Mrs Burke wishes heartily to see the presenter. Yours ever

EDM BURKE

To RICHARD STONEHEWER—n.d.

Source: Public Record Office (C 106/193, Pt I).
Addressed: To | R. Stonehewer Esqr.
Dr Thomas Moffatt was in England in late 1765 and part of 1766.

Richard Stonehewer (*c.* 1728–1809) was Under-Secretary of State for the Northern Department during the first Rockingham Administration.

Dear Sir,

The bearer Doctor Moffat is a very ingenious, learned and worthy Gentleman, though he had his house pulled down and was burned in Effigy, in Rhode Island.[1] With us he has been a little better received. He goes to sollicit you in favour of his fellow sufferer Martin Howard.[2] How can I excuse the trouble I have so repeatedly given you in this affair, but beleive me I am very sensible of your kindness, and set a proper value on your friendship. I am Dear Sir

most sincerely yours

E BURKE

Grosvenor Square[3]
Friday morn

[1] Dr Thomas Moffatt (d. 1787), a physician of Newport, Rhode Island, was one of the leaders of conservative opinion in that colony. His house had been sacked on 28 August 1765 in the riots occasioned by the Stamp Act, and he had come to London. He became Collector of Customs at New London, Connecticut.
[2] Martin Howard, Jr (d. 1781), a leader of conservative opinion in Rhode Island, had suffered, like Moffatt, in the riots. He became Chief Justice of North Carolina.
[3] Burke is presumably writing from Lord Rockingham's house.

To UNKNOWN—n.d.

Source: MS Osborn Collection.

This letter refers to one of the reports of the Select Committee on Indian affairs (see vol. IV, 352), of which General Richard Smith (1734–1803), M.P. for Wendover, was chairman. The reports were issued between 8 May 1781 and 20 November 1783.

My dear Sir,

I just arrived at the Moment of your departure. I am infinitely pleased with the Spirit with which you enter into this Business, and augur much good from it. I shall be happy to see you if possible at eight tomorrow which will give us three hours good. For at eleven I must attend General Smith to prepare the report to be presented, tomorrow.[1] Adieu. I am ever yours

EDM BURKE

Sunday Night

To UNKNOWN—n.d.

Source: MS Morgan Library.

This letter was written during one of the two periods in which Burke was Paymaster—that is during either the second Rockingham Administration or the Fox-North Coalition. Burke speaks of dining at Trinity House on Monday. Anniversary dinners at Trinity House were held on 27 May 1782 and 16 June 1783 (information supplied by Trinity House).

My dear Sir,

I shall be much obliged to you if you should not find it very in-convenient to call upon me this morning, as soon as you please. But, if that should not suit you I shall wait upon you; as a very respectable person, a friend of mine[2] wishes the honour of being introduced to you. Make the thing the most convenient to yourself. I am

My dear Sir
Your most faithful
and affectionate humble Servant
EDM BURKE

Pay Office Saturday morning.

[1] No report was in fact presented on Monday: 'tomorrow' here presumably means Tuesday. Five reports were presented on Tuesdays.
[2] Not identified.

Very unluckily on Monday I was engaged at a publick dinner with the Trinity house, and these things one cannot get off. If you should remain on Tuesday you would make us most happy in favoring us with your Company that day. I really forgot my engagement when I asked you.

To UNKNOWN—n.d.

Source: Myers Catalogue, 331 (1940), no. 42; *Michelmore Catalogue*, 15 (1929), no. 16.

Only an extract from this letter is known. The letter from which it is taken is described in the *Myers Catalogue* as 'I p., 4to, Saturday, no date'. The *Michelmore Catalogue* supplies about thirty words which are omitted in the *Myers Catalogue*. There were a number of occasions when Burke, Fox and Sir Gilbert Elliot worked together—for example the preparation of the East India Bills in 1783 and of the various documents relating to the Regency crisis of 1788–9. It does not seem possible to identify the precise event to which the extract relates.

My dear Sir, As the part you wish me to send you is that which had this morning been essentially altered, the sending it to you could only tend to mislead you and to give you double work. If you could only call upon me with the paper noted by Mr Fox,[1] we may work together in the parts in which our ideas have met and on the modifications suggested by Sir Gilbert Elliot.

To UNKNOWN—n.d.

Source: Incomplete draft in Fitzwilliam MSS (Sheffield).

The paper on which this draft is written has a watermark which occurs in the Burke MSS in 1793, 1794, and 1795. On 31 July 1793 John Wilde (*c.* 1764–1840), an Edinburgh advocate, had written to Burke to thank him for having praised his book (MS at Sheffield). Wilde's book was *An Address to the lately-formed Society of the Friends of the People* in which he described himself as a Rockingham Whig and lauded Burke. It had been published on 25 June (*Caledonian Mercury*, 24 June). It seems probable that this incomplete draft was the basis of the letter which Burke had sent to Wilde.

Sir,

I am much ashamed to find myself so late in my acknowlegements to you for the honour you have done me in sending me your very able and instructive performance, in my opinion, the best which has appeard in the controversies concerning the Theory of Government, to which this unfortunate French revolution, and its still more unfortunate principles have given rise. I hope you will excuse this apparent neglect

[1] *Myers Catalogue:* Mr Fore,

of no trivial Duty. But the truth is, I have been so much, so variously, and sometimes so very unpleasantly, though necessarily occupied, that I have not been able to indulge myself so much as I could wish in reading. Until within a few days, your Book, lay with others of various, but all very inferiour merit, unopend on my Table. Within these few days I have read it though not yet with all the attention it deserves. I have

To UNKNOWN—n.d.

Source: Draft in Fitzwilliam MSS (Sheffield).

The watermark of the paper on which this draft is written occurs in the Burke MSS in 1793 and 1794. The poem to which Burke refers has not been identified.

Dear Sir

I give you many thanks for your fine stanzas. This production of your relaxation and entertainment is so well finishd, that it would do Credit to the serious Labour of those who have cultivated Poetry as the sole means of their reputation. If the Poetry be, as it is, elegant and feeling, its religious turn gives it a double value; at all times this circumstance would have enhanced the value of your piece. These are times that make such moral writings precious. After the Testimonies you have received mine can be of little satisfaction to you further than as your goodnature may make you wish to give pleasure to every body.

To UNKNOWN—n.d.

Source: MS Professor and Mrs Charles G. K. Warner.

My dear Sir,

The attempts upon you, in consequence of your Zeal and faithful attachment to your Cause and your principles are worthy only of those who use them. I cannot flatter myself with having any ability to serve you in the present emergency; You are I understand supported by the strength and choice of the Bar; or I should have cheerfully offerd the assistance (very poor assistance indeed) of this family. At present I am happy that you are in no need of it. I do most sincerely wish you well out of this unpleasant affair brought upon you by your Virtues and the malice of your Enemies. I am my dear Sir

most faithfully and sincerely Yours

Saturday.   EDM BURKE

To UNKNOWN—n.d.

Source: MS National Library of Ireland.

Dear Sir

I am much obliged to you for your kind attention. I should be sorry to give you unnecessary trouble; and hope I may see the plan some other time. It may appear perhaps not so justifiable in me to obtrude my opinion on a Matter so much out of my way. But I do seriously recommend it to those who have power in this Business, that they will not suffer a publick Garden which is a matter of health, satisfaction, and ornament, to be destroyd. We do not abound with such things in this City in a degree in the least adequate to the Magnitude of the place. You who have so much Elegance of mind, as well as publick spirit, will interpose I trust to prevent the publick from being robbed of this convenient Elegance and accommodation. By the way, what should attach your Architect so much to his plan of making a street, that he could not change it to a design of more Unity and Grandeur. I am dear Sir

Your most obedient
and humble Servant
EDM BURKE

To UNKNOWN—n.d.

Source: Incomplete draft Fitzwilliam MSS (Northampton), A.XXI.17.

Sir

It is now I believe ten or twelve years ago since I have had the satisfaction of conversing with you. This however was misfortune on my part not ⟨choice⟩. I have however entertained high respect to your Talents, and in common with many others I have profited of your Labours and your publick Spirit. You are now under the frowns of authority or menaced with them, and there are circumstances, in which, a man, such as you must be guilty of Crimes black and enormous indeed, if they did not make it a Duty of honour and Gratitude to take a particular Interest in you. You will be pleased therefore to[1] indulge me in my desire of renewing the honour of the acquaintance[2] I had formerly with you and,

---

[1] Burke has crossed out 'to' by mistake.
[2] MS: acquaintance acquaintance

C. LETTERS MENTIONED IN AUTOGRAPH DEALERS' CATALOGUES

This list of letters which have been sold by autograph dealers is restricted to items about which the catalogues provide useful information—the date of the letter, or the recipient of it, or an indication of the contents. Where the entry in a catalogue has already been reproduced in full in a note, a simple cross-reference is given. For the convenience of scholars all surviving extracts from letters of Mrs Burke, Richard Burke, Sr, Richard Burke, Jr, and William Burke are included. The papers of Canon Murray contain a few items derived from dealers catalogues which have not been traced to their source; his notes are also included in this list.

A. LETTERS WITH DATES

To UNKNOWN—*January* 1764
Source: Amateur d'autographes, II, 203.

Described as 'L.a.s.; janv. 1764, 3p. in 4.—28 fr. (No 212, Esterhazy, 1857.)'.

To UNKNOWN—2 *May* 1772
Source: Sotheby Catalogue, 27 November 1890, no. 53.
Described as 'A.L.S. 1 p. 4to, May 2, 1772'.

To JOHN BOURKE—27 *October* 1773
Source: Sotheby Catalogue, 15 July 1892, no. 410.
Described as 'A.L.S. 1p. 4to, 27 Oct. 1773'. See vol. II, 473.

PHILIP FRANCIS *to* EDMUND BURKE—27 *October* 1773
Source: Sotheby Catalogue, 27 November 1897, no. 57.

Described as 'Draft in his autograph, signed, of a letter to Burke, Oct. 27, 1773'. With an extract as follows: 'Only that I observe the shortness of this Life, and think it bad Policy to Postpone my Pleasures. I should tell you that tomorrow sennight will suit me exactly as well as Friday next. I shall give notice to our friend, and, if I hear nothing to the contrary, shall expect to have the Pleasure of seeing you on Thursday the 4th of next month. If I do not mistake, the day [the anniversary of the Revolution of 1688] deserves Celebration'. See vol. II, 473.

To WILLIAM PONSONBY, 2nd Earl of Bessborough—10 *May* 1774.

Source: Maggs Catalogue, 262 (December 1910), no. 425.

Described as 'A.L.S. to Lord Bessborough; 1 1/2 pp., 4to, "Westminster, May 10, 1774"' and summarized as follows: 'Regarding a letter of Introduction from Lord Bessborough for a friend of Burke's'.

To JOSEPH SMITH—1775

Source: Sotheby Catalogue, 14 December 1931, no. 675.

Described as: 'A.L.S. 1 1/2 pp. 4to, 1775, to Joseph Smith of Bristol'.

To UNKNOWN—[*June*] 1776

Source: American Book Prices Current, XIII (1907), 611.

Described as: 'A.L.S., 2 pp., 4to. 1776. Introducing a nephew of Sir Joshua Reynolds'. The nephew was the Rev. Joseph Palmer (see vol. III, 274–6).

To UNKNOWN—15 *July* 1776

Source: American Book Prices Current, XII (1906), 696.

Described as 'A.L.S., 2 pages, 4to. July 15, 1776, to a friend in Dublin'.

To JOHN NOBLE—*March* 1777

Source: Maggs Catalogue, 362 (Christmas 1917), no. 2497.

Described as '3 pp., 4to. March 1777. Summarised as follows: 'A lengthy letter of North American interest, dealing with the claims of the British merchants in respect of the damage done to the British ships by the American men-of-war under Paul Jones and others in the American service. Burke adversely criticizes Lord Sandwich and other members of the Government'.

To CHARLES BARROW—11 *September* 1780

Source: Bruton, Knowles Catalogue, 15 December 1904, no. 345.

Described as: 'A.L.S. 1 p. 4to., dated Bristol, Sep. 11th 1780. Refers to his declining to contest Bristol, and expresses his sympathy with Sir Charles Barrow on having to fight a contest at Gloucester'. See vol. IV, 281.

To CHARLES BARROW—14 *September* 1780

Source: Bruton, Knowles Catalogue, 15 December 1904, no. 344.

Described as: 'A.L.S. 1 p. 4to., dated Bristol, Sept. 14th, 1780. Warmly congratulating Sir Charles Barrow on his unopposed return as M.P. for Gloucester'. See vol. IV, 281.

To CHARLES JENKINSON—25 *October* 1780

Source: Sotheby Catalogue, 29 July 1912, no. 228.

Described as: 'Short A.L.S. 3rd person, to the same [Jenkinson], respecting an appointment, Oct. 25, 1780, with address and fine seal'. See vol. IV, 320 n. I.

To SIR GILBERT ELLIOT—[7 *March* 1782]

See vol. IV, 420.

To UNKNOWN LORD—22 *March* 1782

Source: American Book Prices Current, LIX (1952–3), 588.

Described as: 'A.L.S, 22 Mar 1782. 1 1/2 pp., 4to. To "My Dear Lord". Political letter, on court matters, etc.'.

RICHARD BURKE, SR, *to* T. L. O'BEIRNE—6 *September* 1783.

Source: Sotheby Catalogue, 18 December 1905, no. 155.

Described as: 'A.L.S. 1 p. 4to, Weymouth, 6 Sept 1783, to Rev. Mr O'Beine [*sic*], mentions C. J. Fox, etc.'.

RICHARD BURKE, JR, *to the* DUKE OF PORTLAND—23 *November* 1783

Source: Thorpe Catalogue (1840), no. 155.

Described as 'Autograph Letter to the Duke of Portland, communicating to his Grace a Conversation that Lord Thurlow would probably accept Office under his Grace's Administration, &c.' and dated 'Lincoln's Inn, 23d Nov. 1783'.

RICHARD BURKE, SR, *to* GEORGE LEONARD STAUNTON—
17 *February* 1785.

Source: Henkels Catalogue, 1473 (31 January 1933), no. 182; *Sotheby Catalogue,* 5 July 1900, no. 132.

Described in the *Henkels Catalogue* as 'A.L.S. 2pp. 4to' and in the *Sotheby Catalogue* as 'dated Feb. 17, 1785'. The latter catalogue provides the following extract from the letter: 'Lord Macartney was yesterday nominated and elected Governor-General of Bengal.'

To MICHAEL BOURKE—1785

Source: Christie Catalogue, 23 July 1856, no. 904.

No details given.

To UNKNOWN—1785

Source: Sotheby Catalogue, 3 May 1889, no. 183.

Described as 'A.L. 3rd per. 1p. 4to, 1785'.

RICHARD BURKE, [JR] *to* UNKNOWN—1785

Source: Sotheby Catalogue, 13 December 1886, no. 246.

Described as: 'A.L.S. 2pp. 4to, 1785'.

RICHARD BURKE, [SR] *to* SIR CHARLES BARROW—10 *September* 1787

Source: Bruton, Knowles Catalogue, 15 December 1904, no. 343.

No description given.

To SIR WILLIAM HAMILTON—29 *December* 1787

Source: American Book Prices Current, VI (1900), 516.

Described as 'A.L.S., 3 pages, 4to. Beaconsfield, Dec. 29, 1787, to Sir William Hamilton'.

To UNKNOWN—7 *May* 1788

Source: American Book Prices Current, XXXIX (1933), 569.

Described as: 'A.L.S., 4to. [London,] May 7, 1788. Personal letter'.

To UNKNOWN—10 *August* 1788

Source: Sotheby Catalogue, 26 November 1945, no. 424.

Described with a letter of 8 September 1794 (see below) as 'on Political affairs' and with that letter as '4pp. 4to'.

JOHN HELY HUTCHINSON *to* EDMUND BURKE—13 *December* 1790

See vol. VI, 192.

RICHARD BURKE, JR *to* UNKNOWN—13 *January* 1791

Source: Sotheby Catalogue, 18 December 1905, no. 155.

Described as: 'A.L.S. 1 p.4to., Beaconsfield, Jan. 13, 1791'. Murray Papers summarize it as 'Concerning an appointment'.

To UNKNOWN LORD—17 *February* 1791

See vol. VI, 226.

SIR HERCULES LANGRISHE *to* EDMUND BURKE—10 *December* 1791

Source: Sotheby Catalogue, 23 February 1959, no. 344.

Described as: 'A.L.S. 7 1/2 pp. 4to, Dublin, 10 December, 1791, to Edmund Burke, discussing in detail the position of the Roman Catholics in Ireland.'

To [JOSEPH] HILL—*April* 1792

Source: Sotheby Catalogue, 8 February 1901, no. 18.

Described as 'A.L., 3rd Person, to Mr Hill, April, 1792, making an appointment'. See vol. VII, 153 n. 4.

RICHARD BURKE, JR *to* JOHN KING—1 *August* 1792

Source: Sotheby Catalogue, 23 February 1959, no. 341.

Described with a letter of 4 August 1793 as '13 pp. folio and 4to' and summarized with that letter as 'discussing the Irish Question at length'.

To MRS CREWE—24 *August* 1792

See vol. VII, 182 n. 4.

To UNKNOWN—2 *June* 1793

See vol. VII, 358 n. 3.

RICHARD BURKE, SR *to* EVAN NEPEAN—7 *December* 1793

Source: Maggs Catalogue, 326 (May–June 1914), no. 1325.

Described as: 'A.L.S. to Evan Nepeau [*sic*]. 1 page, 4to. Beaconsfield, 7th Dec., 1793'. Summarized as: 'Concerning a prisoner in the Newgate of Bristol'. The catalogue attributes the letter to Richard Burke, Jr.

RICHARD BURKE, JR *to* HENRY DUNDAS—1793

Source: Sotheby Catalogue, 26 April 1926, no. 89.

Described as: 'two A.L.S., one 7 pp. folio, Beaconsfield, 1793, dealing with Ireland; and two others'.

To OLIVER DOLPHIN—30 *January* 1794

See vol. VII. 494.

To UNKNOWN—30 *June* 1794

Source: American Book Prices Current, 1 (1895), 346.

Described as 'A.L.S., 4to, 2 pages, June 30, 1794, with address'.

30-2

To Walker King—*August* 1794

Source: Parke–Bernet Catalogue, 1270 (8 October 1951), no. 93.

Described as: 'Autograph note signed, 1 p., 4to, five lines, dated August 1794, presenting a book to his "dear friend Dr Walker King".'

To Unknown—8 *September* 1794

Source: Sotheby Catalogue, 26 November 1945, no. 424.

Described with a letter of 10 August 1788 (see above) as 'on Political affairs' and with that letter as '4 pp. 4to'.

William Burke *to* Colonel [Alexander] Ross—1794

Source: Sotheby Catalogue, 18 December 1905, no. 155.

Described as: 'A.L.S. and L.S. 1794–5, to Col. Ross, mentions the Marquis of Cornwallis, Edmund Burke, etc.'.

To Unknown—18 *January* 1795

Source: Sotheby Catalogue, 2 December 1913, no. 211.

Described as 'A.L.S. 4 pp. 4to, Beaconsfield, January 18, 1795, on Political matters'.

To Unknown—2 *June* 1795

Source: Murray Papers.

Murray summarized the contents of this letter as follows: 'Burke has much to say on the position of Roman Catholics in Ireland'.

To Albany Wallis—1795

Source: Sotheby Catalogue, 5 August 1851, no. 33.

Described as 'two Letters to Albany Wallis, on the Epitaph and Monument erected to D. Garrick. 1795'. For one of these letters, dated 15 January 1795, see vol. VIII, 115.

William Burke *to* Colonel [Alexander] Ross—1795

For description see the letter to Colonel Ross of 1794 above.

To Stephen Thurston Adey—1 *May* 1796

Source: The Collector, 646 (February 1946), no. J210.

Described as: 'A.L.S., 1 p., 4to, Beconsfield, May 1, 1796. To Mr Adey. Requesting him to honor a draft drawn on his house'.

To UNKNOWN—9 *November* 1796

Source: *American Book Prices Current*, XIII (1907), 611.

Described as: 'A.L.S., 2 pp., 4to. Nov. 9, 1796'.

To M. LEWIS—1796

Source: *Sotheby Catalogue*, 10 July 1848, no. 127.

No description given.

To MRS HENRY WILLIAM BUNBURY—2 *February* 1797

See above, p. 235.

JANE BURKE *to* THOMAS VENABLES—23 *April* [1797]

Source: *Maggs Catalogue*, 352 (Christmas 1916), no. 1783.

Described as: 'A.L.S. to Thomas Venables, of Chester. 2 1/4 pp., 4to. Bath, 23rd April, 1897 [*sic*]. Concerning her husband's kinsman William Burke, supposed author of the "*Letters of Junius*" whom they had befriended and given a home at Beaconsfield; also as to the state of her husband's health; he died the same year.' An extract from the letter is given: 'The trouble you have so often . . . taken about our poor friend, ought to be a reason with us, not to add to that trouble, but instead of this consideration having that effect, it imboldens me to throw still more upon your shoulders for indeed your goodness to that poor friend, and us, has kept him out of a prison, and if your kindness is not continually exerted for us, we shall not be able to keep him where he is, which is the only place of safety for him . . . he thanks Mr Burke for his kind letter, though I told him Mr Burke was here, and so ill that he could not write a single note . . . Mr Burke has for the last three weeks been gaining ground in every way. We shall stay here while the waters continue to agree with him. Mr Burke joyns in love and thanks to you and Mrs Venables for all your goodness to us, on this melancholy occasion and all others.'

JANE BURKE *to* THOMAS VENABLES—*June* 1797

Source: *Puttick and Simpson Catalogue*, 11 July 1900, no. 15.

Described with the preceding letter of 23 April 1797 as '4 pp. 4to'.

To DR CALEB HILLIER PARRY—[1797]

See above, p. 235.

B. UNDATED LETTERS TO KNOWN ADDRESSEES

To MISS ABIGAIL ASTON—n.d.

Source: Sotheby Catalogue, 18 January 1877, no. 32.

Described as: 'A. Note S. To Mrs Aston. 1 page 8vo. Saturday morn.'.

To [JOHN] BOURKE—n.d.

Source: Sotheby Catalogue, 2 March 1905, no. 407.

Described as: 'A.L.S. 1/2 p. 4to, to Mr Bourke, in reference to him paying Burke a visit'.

To THEOBALD BOURKE—n.d.

Source: Henkels Catalogue, 1473 (31 January 1933), no. 182.

Described as: 'A.L.S. 4to N.P., N.D. To Theob. Bourke, with address.'

To ROBERT DODSLEY—n.d.

Source: Evans Catalogue, 13 February 1833, no. 325; *Sotheby Catalogue*, 12 May 1851, nos 92, 93, 98.

At least four letters of Burke to Robert Dodsley of which the originals are missing have been sold at auction. The *Evans Catalogue* advertised 'Various letters and notes addressed to Dodsley [by Burke], and a receipt for editing the Annual Register of 1763 [now in the Morgan Library]'. The *Sotheby Catalogue* lists four letters, without giving any details.

To DAVID GARRICK—n.d.

Source: Sotheby Catalogue, 20 July 1887, no. 135.

Described as: 'A.L.S. 4 pp. 4to. to Garrick'.

WILLIAM BURKE *to* DAVID GARRICK—n.d.

Source: Sotheby Catalogue, 12 May 1851, no. 92.

No description given.

To WALKER KING—n.d.

Source: Sotheby Catalogue, 3 December 1888, no. 295.

Described as: 'A.L.S. 1 p. 4to, n.d. to Dr King.'

To WALKER KING—n.d.

Source: Sotheby Catalogue, 13 May 1901, no 361.

Described as: 'A.L.S. 1 1/2 pp. 4to., n.d. to "dear King" on business and other matters'.

To WALKER KING—n.d.

Source: Sotheby Catalogues, 27 November 1913, no. 59; 10 March 1920, no. 41.

Described as: 'A.L.S. 1 1/2 pp. 4to (no year), to Dr Walter [*sic*] King, respecting the French Clergy; A.L.S. (initials), 1 1/2 pp. 8vo, respecting a sermon on the alliance between Church and State; and two incomplete A.L. of Burke; others of Mrs Burke, wife of Edmund Burke, Lord Loughborough, Lady Rockingham, etc.'. The two incomplete letters are described in the second catalogue as '1 1/4 pp. 4to' and '2 1/2 pp. 4to'.

To EDMOND MALONE—n.d.

Source: Thorpe Catalogue (1833), no. 114.

Summarized as: 'Letter to Malone returning thanks for his invitation, but regrets that previous and unavoidable engagements prevent his dining with such an agreeable party of friends: has received the poem, which he will read instantly, &c.'.

The MARCHIONESS OF ROCKINGHAM *to* EDMUND BURKE—n.d.

Source: Sotheby Catalogue, 30 January 1918, no. 380.

Described as 'A.L.S. 1 p. 4to (no date), to Edmund Burke'.

To GEORGE LEONARD STAUNTON—n.d.

Source: Sotheby Catalogue, 15 May 1939, no. 181.

Described as 'A.L.S., Charles St., Monday morn. one page 4to, to Sir G. L. Staunton'.

C.   UNDATED LETTERS TO UNKNOWN CORRESPONDENTS

To UNKNOWN—n.d.

Source: American Book Prices Current, LXI (1954–5), 556.

Described as: 'A.L.S. [n.d.] 1 p., 4to. Urging action in a matter before the House of Lords'.

To UNKNOWN—n.d.

Source: Edwards Catalogue, 451 (October 1923), no. 48.

Described as: 'A.L.S., 1 p., 8vo., no date, expressing pleasure at receiving certain guests at a Farmer's dinner.'

To UNKNOWN—n.d.

Source: Inventaire des autographes, II, 343.

Described as: 'L.A.S. à un libraire de Londres, 1 p. in-4. Il le prie de lui envoyer un exemplaire de l'*Analyse de la Beauté* de Hogarth'.

To UNKNOWN—n.d.

Source: *Sotheby Catalogue*, 22 December, 1896, no. 318.

Described as: 'A.L.S. 1 p. 4to, n.d. mentions a Poem by Crabbe, short Note signed at bottom of Letter of T.L. O'Beirne'.

To UNKNOWN—n.d.

Source: *Sotheby Catalogue*, 8 November 1899, no. 259.

Described as: 'A.L.S. 1 p. 4to, n.d. asking for pass tickets'.

To UNKNOWN—n.d.

Source: *Sotheby Catalogue*, 15 April 1918, no. 1318.

Described as: 'A.L.S. 1/2 p. 4to, Wednesday, six o'clock (no year); Doc. S. 1 p. folio, February 29th, 1796. Petition from the inn-keepers of Beaconsfield, begging for relief in the matter of the number of men and horses quartered upon them. Burke has written at the top "I have reason to believe the underwritten to contain a very fair representation of hardship."'

RICHARD BURKE, SR *to* UNKNOWN—n.d.

Source: *Sotheby Catalogue*, 15 April 1899, no. 109.

Described as: 'A.L. 3rd person, 1 p. 4to, in reference to obtaining seats for Mrs Francis at the Warren Hastings trial.'

INDEX

A list of persons mentioned in the letters and notes of this volume. No distinction is made between mentions in letters and in notes, or between a name mentioned once or more than once on a page. Indented sub-headings after a name (e.g. 'from Edmund Burke, 47–8', 'to Edmund Burke, 94–6', after 'Laurence, French') refer to letters to or from that person.

A comprehensive index, including subject-entries, will be found in the final volume of the *Correspondence*.

481